PENGUIN MODERN CLASSICS

The Letters of Nancy Mitford and Evelyn Waugh

Evelyn Waugh was born in Hampstead in 1903, second son of Arthur Waugh, publisher and literary critic, and brother of Alec Waugh, the popular novelist. He was educated at Lancing and Hertford College, Oxford, where he read Modern History. In 1928 he published his first work, a life of Dante Gabriel Rossetti, and his first novel, *Decline and Fall*, which was soon followed by *Vile Bodies* (1930), *Black Mischief* (1932), *A Handful of Dust* (1934) and *Scoop* (1938). Waugh travelled extensively and also wrote several travel books, as well as a biography of Edmund Campion and Ronald Knox. Other famous works include his *Sword of Honour* trilogy, and *Brideshead Revisited* (1945).

Nancy Mitford (1904–1973) was born in London, the eldest child of the second Baron Redesdale. Her childhood in a large remote country house with her five sisters and one brother is recounted in the early chapters of *The Pursuit of Love* (1945), which according to the author, is largely autobiographical. Apart from being taught to ride and speak French, Nancy Mitford always claimed she never received a proper education. She started writing before her marriage in 1932 in order 'to relieve the boredom of the intervals between the recreations established by the social convention of her world' and had written four novels before the success of *The Pursuit of Love* in 1945.

Charlotte Mosley has edited *Love From Nancy: the Letters of Nancy Mitford* and a collection of Nancy Mitford's journalism, *A Talent to Annoy*. She has worked as a publisher and journalist and lives in Paris.

The Letters of Nancy Mitford and Evelyn Waugh

EDITED BY
CHARLOTTE MOSLEY

PENGUIN BOOKS

PENGUIN CLASSICS

Published by the Penguin Group
Penguin Books Ltd, 80 Strand, London WC2R ORL, England
Penguin Group (USA), Inc., 375 Hudson Street, New York, New York 10014, USA
Penguin Group (Canada), 90 Eglinton Avenue East, Suite 700, Toronto, Ontario, Canada M4P 2Y3
(a division of Pearson Penguin Canada Inc.)
Penguin Ireland, 25 St Stephen's Green, Dublin 2, Ireland (a division of Penguin Books Ltd)
Penguin Group (Australia), 250 Camberwell Road, Camberwell, Victoria 3124, Australia
(a division of Pearson Australia Group Pty Ltd)
Penguin Books India Pvt Ltd, 11 Community Centre, Panchsheel Park, New Delhi – 110 017, India
Penguin Group (NZ), 67 Apollo Drive, Rosedale, North Shore 0632, New Zealand
(a division of Pearson New Zealand Ltd)
Penguin Books (South Africa) (Pty) Ltd, 24 Sturdee Avenue, Rosebank,
Johannesburg 2196, South Africa

Penguin Books Ltd, Registered Offices: 80 Strand, London WC2R ORL, England

www.penguin.com

First published by Hodder & Stoughton 1996
Published in Penguin Classics 2010
006

Printed in Great Britain by Clays Ltd, St Ives plc

A CIP catalogue record for this book is available from the British Library

978-0-141-19392-2

www.greenpenguin.co.uk

Contents

Acknowledgements

I should like to thank the Duchess of Devonshire and Auberon Waugh for making available to me the letters reproduced in this book, and for their help in elucidating many puzzles. I am deeply indebted to Lady Mosley for her patience and unfailing powers of recall.

Helen Marchant at Chatsworth and Sally Brown of the Department of Manuscripts at the British Library gave much valuable time and assistance. Anne-Pauline de Castries's unfalteringly accurate transcribing has been inestimable. Jane Birkett helped with the painstaking task of checking the manuscript letters against the typescript.

I am very grateful to the following people for suggestions and help: Sir Valentine Abdy, John Armbruster, Alan Bell, Theodora Brinckman, Mollie Buchanan, Artemis Cooper, Romaine Dennistoun, Desmond Guinness, Lady Selina Hastings, Lady Dorothy Heber-Percy, Lady Anne Hill, Sebastian Faulks, Patrick Leigh Fermor, Virginia Fraser, Geordie Greig, James Lees-Milne, Sir Charles Marling, Marilyn McCully, Bernard Minoret, Stuart Preston, Sir Tatton Sykes and Hugo Vickers.

Mark Amory's editing of *The Letters of Evelyn Waugh* (1980) has served as a model and inspiration throughout. The following books have also been useful sources of reference: *Mr Wu & Mrs Stitch: The Letters of Evelyn Waugh & Diana Cooper* (1991) edited by Artemis Cooper; *The Diaries of Evelyn Waugh* (1976) edited by Michael Davie; *Nancy Mitford: A Biography* (1985) and *Evelyn Waugh: A Biography* (1994) by Selina Hastings and *Evelyn Waugh: No Abiding City 1939–1966* (1992) by Martin Stannard.

Most of Evelyn's articles that are referred to in this volume have

viii Preface

been reprinted in *The Essays, Articles and Reviews of Evelyn Waugh* (1983) edited by Donat Gallagher. Nancy's journalism has been collected in *A Talent to Annoy* (1986, n.e. 1996) edited by Charlotte Mosley.

List of Illustrations

The illustrations are from private collections, unless otherwise stated.

Evelyn, August 1934
Laura Waugh, 1940s
Evelyn and Randolph Churchill
Nancy, *c.*1948
Peter Rodd and John Sutro, 1933
Peter Rodd during the war
Gaston Palewski (*Bibliothèque Nationale*)
Rue Monsieur by Vivien Hislop
The hallway at 7 rue Monsieur
Lady Mosley, 1940s
The Duchess of Devonshire, 1950s
Harold Acton, 1933, by Thomas Handforth
Christopher Sykes
Stuart Preston, July 1943 (*Courtesy of Didier Girard*)
Evelyn with family and household, 1948
Piers Court
Lady Diana Cooper, 1958 (*Douglas Glass, © J. C. C. Glass*)
The Vicomtesse de Noailles and Duff Cooper, early 1950s
Nancy and John Julius Cooper at Château St Firmin, 1950s
Sir Maurice Bowra, 1952 (*Douglas Glass, © J. C. C. Glass*)
Cyril Connolly, 1953 (*Douglas Glass, © J. C. C. Glass*)
David Herbert, Nancy and Prince Pio, Majorca, 1954
Manuscript letter Nancy to Evelyn, 19 February 1953 (*British Library*)
Cecil Beaton's cover for *Madame de Pompadour*, 1954
Raymond Mortimer, 1953 (*Douglas Glass, © J. C. C. Glass*)

Graham Greene, 1953 (*Douglas Glass, © J. C. C. Glass*)
Lady Pamela Berry by Vivienne (*Camera Press*)
Clarissa Churchill, 1952 (*Camera Press*)
Ann Fleming (*Camera Press*)
Evelyn, 1951 (*Douglas Glass, © J. C. C. Glass*)
Manuscript letter Nancy to Evelyn, 25 September 1952 (*British Library*)
Combe Florey, 1960s
Manuscript letter Evelyn to Nancy, 19 May 1959 (*Chatsworth*)
Jessica Mitford, 1960
Nancy and Diana Mosley, Inchkenneth, May 1963
Nancy and Jessica Mitford, 1962
Manuscript letter Nancy to Evelyn, 4 March 1966 (*British Library*)
Evelyn, June 1960 (© *BBC*)
Manuscript letter Evelyn to Nancy, Shrove Tuesday 1965 (*Chatsworth*)

Chronology

DATE	EVELYN WAUGH	NANCY MITFORD
1903	Born on 28 October	
1904		Born on 28 November
1926	Journalist on *Daily Express*	
1928	*Rossetti: His Life and Works* Marries Evelyn Gardner *Decline and Fall*	
1929		Writes for *Vogue* and *Harper's Bazaar*
1930	Divorce *Vile Bodies* *Labels: A Mediterranean Journal* Converts to Roman Catholicism	Contributes to *The Lady*
1931	*Remote People*	*Highland Fling*
1932	*Black Mischief*	*Christmas Pudding*
1933	Meets Laura Herbert	Marries Peter Rodd Moves to Strand-on-the-Green
1934	*Ninety-Two Days* *A Handful of Dust*	
1935	*Edmund Campion*	*Wigs on the Green*
1936	*Waugh in Abyssinia* *My Lovely's Little Outing and Other Sad Stories*	Moves to Blomfield Road

Year		
1937	Marries Laura Herbert	
	Moves to Piers Court	
1938	*Scoop*	*The Ladies of Alderley*
1939	*Robbery Under Law: The Mexican Object-Lesson*	*The Stanleys of Alderley*
	Joins Royal Marines	War work at St Mary's Hospital, London
1940	Transfers to Commandos	*Pigeon Pie*
		Runs canteen for interned French soldiers
1941	At Battle of Crete	Looks after East End families
1942	*Put Out More Flags*	Assistant at Heywood Hill bookshop
	Work Suspended	Meets Gaston Palewski
1943	Resigns from Commandos	
1944	In Yugoslavia with Military Mission	
1945	*Brideshead Revisited*	*The Pursuit of Love*
1946	*When the Going Was Good*	Moves to Paris
1947	*Scott-King's Modern Europe*	Leases 7 rue Monsieur
1948	*The Loved One*	
1949		*Love in a Cold Climate*
		Weekly article for *Sunday Times*
1950	*Helena*	Translates *The Little Hut*
		Translates *La Princesse de Clèves*
1951		*The Blessing*
1952	*The Holy Places*	
	Men at Arms	
1953	*Love Among the Ruins*	
1954		*Madame de Pompadour*
1955	*Officers and Gentlemen*	'The English Aristocracy': U and Non-U
1956	Moves to Combe Florey	*Noblesse Oblige*
1957	*The Ordeal of Gilbert Pinfold*	*Voltaire in Love*
		Divorce
1959	*The Life of Ronald Knox*	
1960	*A Tourist in Africa*	*Don't Tell Alfred*
1961	*Unconditional Surrender*	
1962		*The Water Beetle*
1963	*Basil Seal Rides Again*	
1964	*A Little Learning*	
1966	Dies on 10 April	*The Sun King*
1967		Moves to Versailles
1968		Onset of Hodgkin's disease
1970		*Frederick the Great*
1973		Dies on 30 June

Editor's Note

The correspondence between Evelyn Waugh and Nancy Mitford comprises just over five hundred letters, some two hundred from Evelyn and three hundred from Nancy. Except for a letter congratulating Nancy on her engagement in 1933, no letters exist until the last two years of the war when Evelyn was stationed abroad and Nancy was working at Heywood Hill's bookshop in London. After Nancy's move to Paris in 1946, they began to correspond regularly and continued to do so until Evelyn's death in 1966.

There are remarkably few gaps in the correspondence. Missing letters from Nancy date mostly from the war, when circumstances made it difficult for Evelyn to keep track of papers. Among Evelyn's lost letters are those he wrote to Nancy when she was away from home and unable to stash them into the envelopes which she kept for the purpose. Occasionally she forwarded his letters to friends who never returned them, and once Evelyn asked her to burn a particularly unkind letter about a mutual friend. At least three letters from Evelyn that were made available to his biographer Christopher Sykes have since disappeared.

Some of the letters reproduced here have already appeared in *The Letters of Evelyn Waugh* (1980) and *Love From Nancy: The Letters of Nancy Mitford* (1993). In this volume, their full correspondence has been brought together for the first time; eighty per cent of Nancy's letters and forty per cent of Evelyn's are previously unpublished. I have not included Evelyn's earliest letter to Nancy, because it would necessitate thirteen footnotes in as many lines of text to explain people who do not reappear in the correspondence. Two of Evelyn's postcards and two wartime letters have also been omitted for the same reason. Out of Nancy's letters, two which dealt with travelling plans have not been included. About a dozen potentially libellous references have been removed from the correspondence as a whole, but many of the passages that were cut in *The Letters of Evelyn Waugh*, for reasons of libel or to avoid repetition, have been reinstated here. The editor's excisions are shown by three ellipses in square brackets: [. . .].

Nancy was punctilious about dating her letters which has made the dating of Evelyn's, who often omitted the year and sometimes the whole date, easier to establish. The speed of the post at the time is impressive: a letter sent by Nancy from Paris was often on Evelyn's breakfast table in Gloucestershire the following morning.

Nancy was a poor speller and Evelyn, who prided himself on being a good grammarian, was not infallible. Their spelling has been corrected and apostrophes added for consistency. Proper names of places, people, books, plays and films have been regularised but capital letters have not been added where there were none in the original. Alterations to the punctuation have been kept to a minimum and made only where necessary to the sense.

In his autobiography, *A Little Learning*, Evelyn wrote of his father: 'He had no itch to get to the truth of a story, frankly preferring its most picturesque form.' This was a preference shared equally by both Evelyn and Nancy. Their letters were written to amuse, distract or tease and should be read for entertainment, *not* as the unvarnished truth.

Charlotte Mosley
Paris, 1996

Preface

Both Nancy Mitford and Evelyn Waugh had the gift of writing letters as though they were talking to each other. Reading their correspondence is like overhearing a conversation between two quick-witted, provocative, very funny friends, who know the same people, read the same books, laugh at the same jokes and often share the same prejudices. It is rare for such a long correspondence to be so readable throughout – a testimony to the pleasure they both derived from it.

Evelyn enjoyed the company of women and had other regular female correspondents, including Ann Fleming and Diana Cooper who were the kind of clever, stylish *femmes du monde* he admired. His letters to Ann Fleming are enlivened by a brittle display of elevated social gossip, whilst those to Diana Cooper are written in a rather self-consciously juvenile manner, based on an ancient infatuation. But Nancy was a *femme de lettres* as well, who earned her living as a writer, and this common ground of literary activity leavens their exchange of letters. Nancy was a prolific letter writer and more than eight thousand of her letters have survived. She corresponded with other literary figures, such as Raymond Mortimer and Heywood Hill, but none inspired her to the same heights of sustained levity and wit as Evelyn.

Their friendship was primarily a literary one; although they were deeply fond of each other, they were never romantically involved. Both were reticent about expressing their deeper emotions and they rarely discussed the intimate details of their lives. Concealing their feelings behind a barrage of banter, they found it easier to conduct a friendship on paper rather than in person. When they did meet,

Evelyn's bad temper and Nancy's sharp tongue – qualities which
enhance their correspondence – often led to quarrels. Nancy was an
optimist, more successful at disguising her unhappiness and keeping
up a cheerful front than Evelyn, who became increasingly misanthropic
with age. They were well matched in their love of teasing; Evelyn
could be a merciless bully and Nancy was one of the few people who
not only stood up to, but actually enjoyed his goading. They disapproved of each other's politics: Nancy called herself a 'milk and
water Socialist', which Evelyn liked to pretend meant she was a dangerous Communist undermining the very foundations of society. Evelyn
was a born reactionary who regarded it as his duty to oppose the
encroachment of the modern world in any form.

They shared a nostalgia for a passing way of life which depended
on a small group of people, aristocratic by birth and mentality. Evelyn
had discovered this world at Madresfield Court, Worcestershire, seat
of the Earls Beauchamp. In 1931, when the 7th Lord Beauchamp
was implicated in a homosexual scandal and driven into exile by his
brother-in-law, his children were left the run of the house. Evelyn
befriended the two eldest Lygon sons at Oxford and became a confidant of Lady Mary and Lady Dorothy Lygon in the early 1930s.
The atmosphere he found at Madresfield exemplified the tradition of
continuity and discriminating taste that he so admired, and which he
subsequently idealised in *Brideshead Revisited*. Nancy found her romantic
ideal at Fontaines-les-Nonnes, a château near Paris belonging to the
Comtesse Costa de Beauregard, where nothing seemed to have
changed for the last hundred years. She spent many weeks at Fontaines
in the 1950s and early 60s, and it inspired the Château de Bellandargues in her novel *The Blessing*. Much of what can be seen as Nancy's
snobbery and Evelyn's infatuation with the aristocracy arose from their
respect and yearning for the permanency and self-assurance symbol-
ised by these stately surroundings.

Nancy and Evelyn met in the summer of 1928. At twenty-four, he
had just married Evelyn Gardner, a close friend of Nancy, and had
begun to establish a literary reputation with his biography of Rossetti.
Nancy, a year younger than Evelyn, was living out a prolonged adolescence. Tired of the frivolity of the London season and the round of
country-house parties, she longed to be independent of her strict
parents and was seeking ways to earn a living. In June 1929, the
Waughs invited Nancy to lodge in the spare room of their small flat
in Canonbury Square, Islington, to keep She-Evelyn company while
He-Evelyn went to the country to write. In his absence, his wife fell
in love with John Heygate, a news editor at the BBC, and after a
brief attempt at reconciliation, the Waughs' marriage broke up. His
wife's desertion was a terrible blow to Evelyn's pride, leaving him
humiliated and deeply unhappy. Nancy was shocked by her friend's

infidelity and never saw She-Evelyn again. In He-Evelyn, however, she had found a lifelong friend.

Evelyn was born in 1903, son of the managing director of the publishers Chapman & Hall and a parson's daughter. He was educated at Lancing and Hertford College, Oxford, where little work and huge quantities of drink earned him a third-class degree and a large overdraft. Like many clever, penniless men of his generation, he took a job as schoolmaster in a boys' preparatory school. Two years of teaching provided the raw material for *Decline and Fall*, which enjoyed a critical, if not a commercial, success. His second novel, *Vile Bodies*, published in January 1930, was a best-seller and made Evelyn a celebrity; he was soon taken up by the fast, smart set whose goings-on he had caricatured in the novel. Realising the importance for a young author of keeping his name in the public eye, he deliberately set out to cultivate friendships in both the literary and aristocratic worlds.

Nancy moved in much the same circles. She was the eldest of Lord and Lady Redesdale's six beautiful daughters, three of whom, by their extreme political convictions, brought notoriety to the name 'Mitford' during the 1930s. Diana, the Redesdales' third daughter, married in 1936 the leader of the British Union of Fascists, Sir Oswald Mosley. Their fourth daughter, Unity, was a fanatical admirer of Hitler. Jessica, the fifth sister, joined the Communist Party and married another member. The Mitfords grew up mainly in the country and were privately educated by a succession of governesses. Nancy resented this lack of formal schooling, blaming it for her perceived literary shortcomings (it later proved a handy defence against Evelyn's criticisms of her prose style and grammar). Even before they met, she and Evelyn had many friends in common, particularly among his Oxford contemporaries. Through her family connections and seasons as a debutante Nancy was introduced into the society that had adopted Evelyn as a young literary lion. For four years after the break-up of Evelyn's marriage, they saw each other often: at literary cocktail parties with the Sitwells, Cyril Connolly, Harold Acton, Robert Byron and John Betjeman; at the theatre with Cecil Beaton and Nancy Cunard; or at house parties with Viscount Weymouth, Frank Pakenham and Randolph Churchill.

During this period Evelyn encouraged Nancy to write, and assumed the role of her literary mentor. She began to contribute articles to *Vogue* and *The Lady* on fashionable topics such as shooting parties and society weddings. Adopting the point of view of a caustic outsider, commenting on the world of which she was a part, she displayed the same tone of playful, mocking irony as Evelyn. In 1931 she published her first novel, *Highland Fling* which, like *Vile Bodies*, was set in the frantic world of the Bright Young Things. It enjoyed a modest success and was followed over a period of nine years by *Christmas Pudding*, *Wigs*

on the Green and *Pigeon Pie*. These four pre-war novels were immature
forerunners of Nancy's four glorious post-war novels in which the
experience of falling in love transformed her slight, romantic comedies
into comic masterpieces. Evelyn was a fierce critic who took the art
of writing seriously. Nancy did not. Although she always sought his
opinion and sometimes followed his advice, she realised that she could
not live up to his exacting literary standards. Evelyn pretended to care
what Nancy thought of his books but his letters make it clear that he
did not take her very seriously as a critic.

In 1928 Nancy fell in love with Hamish St Clair-Erskine, an under-
graduate in his first year at New College, Oxford. Evelyn noted in his
diary on 18 June 1930 that he had had tea at the Ritz with Nancy:
'She was worried because Hamish had told her on Sunday evening
that he didn't think he would ever feel up to sleeping with a woman.
I explained to her a lot about sexual shyness in men.' No amount of
explaining could make up for the fact that Hamish, a homosexual,
was an entirely unsuitable man for Nancy to fall for. With characteristic
loyalty and unwillingness to face the truth, Nancy clung to Hamish
for five years until his behaviour made it no longer possible even for
her to ignore the evidence. On the rebound, she was soon engaged
to Peter Rodd, always known as 'Prod', and they were married in
December 1933.

Peter was the second son of Lord Rennell, a diplomat and Ambassador to Italy 1908–19. In Peter's favour, it has to be said that he was
clever, good-looking and not deliberately unkind, but these qualities
were eclipsed by his pedantry which was oddly combined with utter
irresponsibility. When he and Nancy got engaged, Lord Rennell used
his influence to find Peter work in a bank. But he was incapable of
holding down a job and it lasted only a few months. In an article he
contributed to *Horizon* during the war, 'The Psychology of Refugees',
Peter Rodd could have been giving a description of himself: feck-
lessness and loss of initiative, depravity and lawlessness, difficulty in
reconciling fantasy with reality, the inability to accept routine and a
tendency to cheat or defy authority. Evelyn, who had known Peter at
Oxford and had considered him one of the most precocious boys
of his generation, heartily disliked and disapproved of him. Nancy's
marriage meant that Evelyn saw little of her over the next decade.

In September 1930, Evelyn was received into the Roman Catholic
Church. This he regarded as the most important event of his life
and, thereafter, spiritual beliefs became central to his existence. His
approach to religion was unemotional and doctrinaire; he regarded it
as a bulwark against the anarchy and despair that threatened his inner
world, and a defence against the disintegrating values of the world
outside. The seriousness of his beliefs was not something that Nancy,
who did not think deeply about God, could share. It irked her that

his faith failed to make Evelyn happy, nor did it seem to make him any nicer. She teased him about being dogmatic and once – perhaps the only time in the whole correspondence – succeeded in making him really angry by daring to venture an opinion on the excommunication of a Jesuit priest.

For seven years after his divorce in 1930, Evelyn lived a restless and unsettled life, moving between his parents' house, London clubs, country pubs and the houses of friends. He took on many journalistic assignments and travelled abroad almost every year, to Abyssinia for Haile Selassie's coronation, to Zanzibar, East Africa, British Guiana, Brazil, Morocco and Jerusalem. This period produced several travel books as well as the brilliant comedies *Black Mischief* and *A Handful of Dust*. In 1933 he fell in love with seventeen-year-old Laura Herbert, a shy, pretty, Catholic convert. After a long courtship during which he managed to obtain the annulment of his first marriage, they were married in 1937 and settled at Piers Court, a handsome Georgian manor in Gloucestershire. During the two years leading to the outbreak of war, Evelyn finished *Scoop*, produced a volume of short stories and wrote a biography of Edmund Campion. The first of his six children was born and although money was always short, he began to lead the well-regulated life of a country gentleman, planning his garden and embellishing his house.

Nancy's marriage limped through the years leading up to the war. She tried to make ends meet with her novels and journalism, and she edited two volumes of letters: *The Ladies of Alderley* (1938) and *The Stanleys of Alderley* (1939). She remained loyal about Peter in front of friends, making light of his profligacy and infidelities, but she was not happy. Two miscarriages, which threw doubt on her ability to have a family, added to her misery. By the time war was declared, her marriage was over in all but form.

Part I

1944–1946

NANCY SPENT the war in London, at first in the small house that she and Peter rented in Blomfield Road, Maida Vale, and later, when bombs began falling on Paddington Station, at the mews of her parents' house in Rutland Gate, Kensington. The first two war years were miserable ones. Her family was coping with the attempted suicide of one sister, Unity, whose admiration for Hitler had driven her to shoot herself in the head when war was declared. Another sister, Diana, had been arrested with her husband, Sir Oswald Mosley, under Regulation 18B, which made provision for the internment of 'persons whose detention appears to the Secretary of State to be expedient in the interests of the public safety or defence of the realm'. Nancy found work as a volunteer at St Mary's First Aid Post, she looked after families of evacuees and helped in a canteen for French soldiers in west London. It was an exhausting and dispiriting time. Peter was abroad with a refugee organisation and on his occasional visits to London preferred to stay at his club rather than see her. Desperately short of money, lonely and unhappy, Nancy embarked on a brief affair with a Free French officer which resulted in an ectopic pregnancy. An emergency operation saved her life but left her unable to have children, a sorrow she characteristically made light of.

In 1942 she took a job much more to her liking at Heywood Hill's bookshop in Mayfair where she worked as an assistant until 1945. Since its opening in 1936, the shop had attracted customers from society and the intelligentsia, amongst whom Nancy numbered many friends. Her work involved packing and sorting books but left plenty of time for gossip. According to Heywood Hill's wife, Lady Anne Hill, who also worked in the shop, Nancy brought in many customers, 'though there was also a minority whom she frightened, and who fled, not daring to return'.

In September 1942, when she was thirty-seven, Nancy met Gaston

Palewski, a Free French colonel who was General de Gaulle's *directeur de cabinet* in London. Although not at all handsome, he was cultivated, witty, adored women and had the irresistible charm of an enthusiast. His effect on Nancy was similar to that which Fabrice, the short, stocky, very dark Frenchman in *The Pursuit of Love*, has on the heroine of the novel: 'Linda was feeling, what she had never so far felt for any man, an overwhelming physical attraction. It made her quite giddy, it terrified her.' Nancy's love affair with 'the Colonel', as she always called Gaston, lasted until May the following year when he left to join de Gaulle in Algiers. For Gaston, Nancy had represented little more than a delightful flirtation; she made him laugh, flattered him with her adoration and amused him with stories of her unusual family. But for Nancy, Gaston had become the very centre of her existence.

The war proved a bitter disillusionment to Evelyn, and an even greater blow to his self-esteem than the failure of his first marriage. In September 1939, he let Piers Court to a group of Dominican nuns and settled Laura, who was expecting her second child, with her mother at Pixton Park in Somerset. He applied for a job at the Ministry of Information but was turned down and it was not until the end of December that he finally obtained a commission in the Royal Marines. Evelyn was eager to fight but spent most of 1940 on training courses in different parts of the country where forced marches, physical discomfort and the frustration of waiting around were not at all to his taste. He soon gained a reputation for impatience, insolence and an inability to get on with other ranks. His company took part in the abortive raid to seize Dakar in September 1940, which left Evelyn feeling that bloodshed had been avoided 'at the cost of honour'. Then, by a complicated manoeuvre which involved his transfer to the Royal Horse Guards, he managed to get seconded to Colonel Robert Laycock's Special Air Service 8 Commando, and in May the following year saw action during the Battle of Crete. The collapse of the British Army in the face of advancing German paratroopers and the scramble to evacuate the island appalled him. Where he had expected to find discipline and courage he found only confusion and cowardliness.

Evelyn spent the next two years in Britain, a period of futility and frustration. Colonel Laycock informed him that he was 'so unpopular as to be unemployable' and his superior officers vied not to be saddled with him. When 8 Commando sailed for Italy in June 1943, Evelyn was left behind. He took the unusual step of applying for leave to write, and between January and May 1944 completed *Brideshead Revisited*. In June he joined the 2nd SAS, but it soon became clear that he was not welcome and that there was nothing for him to do. A telegram from Randolph Churchill inviting him to join Brigadier Fitzroy Maclean's Military Mission in Yugoslavia rescued him from idleness and ignominy. He flew to Croatia in July and stayed until early December, when he left for Dubrovnik to act as liaison officer between the British military and Tito's Partisans. In September 1945 he was demobilised and returned to Piers Court with Laura and a family that now consisted of three girls and a boy.

Nancy and Evelyn renewed their friendship in 1942 and 1943, when his routine included a visit to Heywood Hill. They may have corresponded fitfully during the war – Nancy kept Evelyn supplied with books from the shop – but there are no letters of hers before 1944, and only two of his. Their regular correspondence begins in 1945, a turning-point in both their lives. With the success of *Brideshead Revisited*, Evelyn retired to Piers Court and gradually turned his back on the world. His periodic forays to London and abroad only confirmed him in his growing antipathy to post-war England. *The Pursuit of Love*, published in December 1945, established Nancy as a best-selling author. It gave her the financial independence to go to France, ostensibly to buy French books for Heywood Hill but in reality to be near the Colonel. She spent two months in Paris in the autumn of 1945, and returned in April 1946, determined never to live in England again.

[May 1944]   Pixton Park[1]
                                        Dulverton
                                         [Somerset]

Darling Nancy

We are so delighted that you will be godmother. The child[2] is being christened on Sunday. It has red hair and a placid disposition & is to be called Harriet after an ancestor of Laura's[3] who was painfully pro American and also after H. Wilson.[4]

I found T Eliot Elliot Eliott Elliott's poems here so that is OK. Thank you very much for kind efforts. I still want F Brown's Omnibus[5] very much if it is procurable. Returning Chagford[6] Monday.

One US officer murdered another in the Chagford Mermaid last week.

Re rewriting magnum opus madly. It is lapsing into verse whenever it is not carefully watched.

    Best love
        Evelyn

[1] Evelyn's mother-in-law's house bore a close resemblance to Boot Magna Hall in *Scoop* (1938).
[2] Harriet Mary, born on 13 May 1944. Evelyn's youngest daughter became a novelist and critic. Married the art critic Richard Dorment in 1985. Nancy's duties as a godmother had been outlined in a previous letter: 'We do not look to you so much for spiritual instruction as for knowledge of the world, savoir faire, joie de vivre and things of that kind.' (EW to NM, 18 May 1944).
[3] Laura Herbert (1916–73). Married Evelyn as his second wife in 1937. See Biographical Notes.
[4] Harriette Wilson (1786–1846). Regency courtesan who left a frank account of her adventures in *Memoirs of Harriette Wilson, Written by Herself* (1825).
[5] G. K. Chesterton's stories of a Roman Catholic priest turned detective.
[6] Evelyn had been granted leave at the beginning of the year to work on *Brideshead Revisited: The Sacred and Profane Memories of Captain Charles Ryder* (1945). He retired to the Easton Court Hotel at Chagford, Devon, an establishment expressly run to suit the needs of writers.

9 September [1944]   Force 399
                                         CMF
                                       [Topusko
                                       Croatia]

Dearest Nancy

Randolph[1] & I got back to our headquarters after a prolonged luxury tour & found an accumulation of mail which gave me an afternoon of exquisite delight. Thank you so very much for writing so often. All your letters have arrived safely and are worth a guinea a piece to me so please go on spending sixpences & charge them to Heywood Hill as out of pocket expenses in keeping customers' good will. The books of course haven't arrived yet but I await them with the keenest expectation.

I found hundreds of chums & near chums in Rome. My illness there was excruciatingly painful[2] & my convalescence retarded by heat

& lack of light. N. Birch[3] spoke of you with particular love. Randolph
speaks of you often with something stronger. I had a curious encounter
in Corsica where I was stopped in the street by a young, spruce French
officer who said did I understand French and if so might he speak to
me on a subject of extreme delicacy. I presumed it was money or
buggery he wanted but no quite the reverse. He wanted advice as to
English etiquette. He wished to send a souvenir to an English lady of
good position and unimpeachable honour who had shown him much
hospitality. He wanted to send her his photograph. Could he do so
with propriety & inscribe it 'with love'. I told him yes. He pressed the
matter: did this not presume carnal knowledge? I told him no. He
then said that he had put the question in this form because of his
great distress & proceeded to pour out the story of his married life in
Tunis. He had been a prisoner of war. He returned to find his wife
more tepid in her affection and a photograph from a British officer
inscribed as he had described. Was this not evidence of adultery? I
told him no, but perhaps with less inward conviction. He showed me
a photograph of her. I remarked how pretty she was. Yes, yes, that is
what makes it so terrible. And then as a culmination: You understand
I am an officer too. It is not as though I were a private soldier.

Freddy B.[4] hasn't come & I think won't come now. Instead Bloggs
Baldwin[5] is with us which is very nice. I wish I could write more fully
but everything I want to say is a kind of military secret.

But please go on writing to me.

Best love
Evelyn

Capt. E. Waugh R[oyal] H[orse] G[uards]

[1] Randolph Churchill (1911–68). Journalist and author. Conservative MP 1940–45. Obstreper-
ous only son of Winston Churchill who had recruited Evelyn to join him on Brigadier Fitzroy
Maclean's Military Mission in Yugoslavia. Randolph was a cousin of Nancy; she deplored his
arrogance and rudeness but found his charm hard to resist. Married to Hon. Pamela Digby
1939–46 and to June Osborne 1948–61.
[2] While recovering from injuries incurred in a plane crash, Evelyn developed a large boil on
his neck and spent ten days in hospital.
[3] Nigel Birch (1906–81). Economist and politician who served on the General Staff in Italy
during the war. Created Lord Rhyl in 1970.
[4] 2nd Earl of Birkenhead (1907–75). Joined the Military Mission at Topusko in October 1944.
He has described this period vividly in *Evelyn Waugh and His World* edited by David Pryce-Jones,
including the incident in which Evelyn appeared in a white duffle-coat during a German attack
and countered Randolph's furious orders to take it off with: 'I'll tell you what I think of your
repulsive manners when the bombardment is over.' (Weidenfeld & Nicolson, 1973), p. 151.
[5] 3rd Earl Baldwin (1904–76). Son of the Prime Minister and a friend of Evelyn's youth.

17 October [1944]   'M' Military Mission
                                                     C.M.F.
                                                     [Topusko]
Darling Nancy

[. . .] Freddy turned up the other evening unannounced and as
unexpected as though the question of his coming had never been
discussed. We had despaired of him. He looked like a ghost after a
fortnight's dysentery in Bari. It is a great joy having him not only for
his own sour & meaty company but as a relief from perpetual watch
with your cousin Randolph whose boisterous good nature, after five
weeks solitary confinement with him, has begun to exhaust me. Better
the late colonel toll gating[1] than Randolph's pep talks.

Bullet in the Ballet[2] is O.K. Will you please collect & send to Pixton
a set of Max Beerbohm's[3] early editions, also *Trivia*, also *More Trivia*;[4]
will you get R. Knox's[5] *New Testament* and send them. Mine was burned
in my great accident.

A very sad thing has just happened. I had settled down to a luxurious
day's solitude – Freddy & Randolph having driven off to the forests.
I had a box of cigars, six new books (thanks to you), a deep sorrow
(thanks to Debo)[6] – all the makings of profound self indulgence. F &
R have just returned, their expedition postponed. Damn.

Mr Gatfield of Chapman & Hall has just kicked the bucket. Why
don't you go in for publishing? You would be supremely good at it.
I read a very serious letter from you in *The Times* newspaper. Couldn't
see the joke anywhere.[7]

Maimie[8] tells me the frogs tried to shave Mrs Corrigan[9] as a collabor-
ationist & had a rude shock.

Do keep writing. Charge the 6d's to my account. I quite realize
that with the late colonel at your elbow there is no money left for
stamps.

You cannot conceive (or perhaps you can after Spain) of the hideous-
ness of the communist women – straggled bobbed hair, cigarette in
the mouth, pimply legs, men's boots, pistol & hand grenade on the
belt, square bottoms in battle dress – and the exquisite grace and
dignity of their peasant sisters.

We have a pig that lives for nothing but pleasure. It digs mud baths
for itself and chases the chickens round the yard laughing openly.

Love
     Evelyn

---

[1] Hon. Peter Rodd (1904–68), (Prod). Second son of the diplomat Lord Rennell. Married to
Nancy 1933–57. He had been made a temporary colonel during the war and acquired the
nickname of 'Old Toll-Gater' because of his habit of holding forth, at great length, on the
intricacies of the toll-gate system in Great Britain. See Biographical Notes.
[2] Caryl Brahms and S. J. Simon, *Bullet in the Ballet* (1937). A detective novel.
[3] Max Beerbohm (1872–1956). Essayist, critic and caricaturist, regarded by Evelyn as a master

of English prose. He completed one novel, *Zuleika Dobson* (1911), and published several collections of essays including *The Works of Max Beerbohm* (1896), *More* (1899) and *Yet Again* (1909). Knighted in 1939.
[4] Commonplace books by Logan Pearsall Smith, published in 1902 and 1922 respectively.
[5] Monsignor Ronald Knox (1888-1957). Writer and theologian. Ordained as an Anglican clergyman in 1912, he converted to Catholicism in 1917. Chaplain to Roman Catholic undergraduates at Oxford 1926-39. Evelyn befriended him in 1934 and wrote his official biography, published in 1959.
[6] Hon. Deborah Mitford (1920-), (Debo). Nancy's youngest sister for whom Evelyn felt an unreciprocated love. In 1941 she married Lord Andrew Cavendish who succeeded as 11th Duke of Devonshire in 1950. See Biographical Notes.
[7] Nancy had written about the distribution of British books on the Continent (16 September 1944).
[8] Lady Mary Lygon (1910-82), (Maimie). Third daughter of 7th Earl Beauchamp, and Evelyn's closest confidante before the war. Married to Prince Vsevolode Joannovich of Russia 1939-56.
[9] Laura Whitlock (1879-1948). American-born London hostess, married to steel magnate James Corrigan in 1915. She spent the first two years of the war in Paris and received the Legion of Honour from Marshal Pétain for her donations to the Vichy government. She was quite bald and wore a wig.

12 November [1944]   37 M Mission
                                                                  C.M.F.
                                                                  [Topusko]

Darling Nancy

So they have changed our address again. I wish the change was more than words & numbers but Randolph & Freddy & I are still immovable and practically incommunicado.

In the hope of keeping him quiet for a few hours Freddy & I have bet Randolph £20 that he cannot read the whole Bible in a fortnight. It would have been worth it at the price. Unhappily it has not had the result we hoped. He has never read any of it before and is hideously excited; keeps reading quotations aloud 'I say I bet you didn't know this came in the Bible "bring down my grey hairs in sorrow to the grave"' or merely slapping his side & chortling 'God, isn't God a shit!'

The Semi-attached Couple[1] arrived safely & was a joy to me. The first half better than anything by J. Austen. What are her books on India like?

I say, V 2?[2] Curzon Street must be hell. Our hearts bleed for you.

How odd of C Connolly[3] to have been taken in by Maugham's[4] mysticism. I want to write a sad story of a man who gave up drink and hated all his chums. It is me.

One of our servants got drunk the other night & as he was brandishing a loaded revolver about I put him under arrest and we all forgot about it next morning. Then the communist commissar came to call & said the sentence had not been promulgated yet; they would like to consult Randolph before carrying it out to see if it corresponded to British military custom. They were going to shoot him. We got him reprieved and the man forgot all his marxism and said with tears and an american accent 'Jesus Christ bless youse guys'.

Freddy has taken to talking mock Serbo-croat to himself in the earth closet. I thought there were two Jugo-slavs in there together having an altercation. Then I saw the door open & out walked Freddy. Very disturbing.

We ate Randolph's goose – there was not enough on it to make a meal for four after its cruel treatment.

> Best love
> Evelyn

Will you be very kind & deal with my Xmas presents to my god children – Elwes,[5] Guinness[6] (I say how funny about Lord Moyne[7]) Hollis.[8] Latter's address is John Hollis, Claveys Farm, Mells, Frome, Somerset. Handsome improving volumes.

You ought by the time this comes to have received *Brideshead Revisited*.[9] Please tell me what everyone says behind my back.

Oh then there is Angie's child. I have forgotten its name but Miss Laycock, care Maj. Gen. R. E. Laycock,[10] 1a Richmond Terrace, S.W.1. will find it. Will you send it a handsomely bound Bible or Prayer Book (Protestant) or *Pilgrim's Progress* or something to show affection to its parents.

Just remembered the name EMMA LAYCOCK.[11]

[1] By Hon. Emily Eden (1860).
[2] The first German rocket bomb had landed in Britain in July.
[3] Cyril Connolly (1903–74), (Smartyboots, Boots, Bootikins, Bonny Boots). The critic and author spent the war editing the monthly arts magazine *Horizon*. See Biographical Notes.
[4] W. Somerset Maugham (1874–1965). The hero of his novel *The Razor's Edge* (1944) visits an Indian ashram to study Vedanta, the philosophy of attaining enlightenment through knowledge.
[5] Dominick Elwes (1931–75). Son of the painter Simon Elwes and Hon. Gloria Rodd, Nancy's sister-in-law. Married Tessa Kennedy in 1958.
[6] Jonathan Guinness (1930–). Eldest son of Nancy's sister Diana and her first husband Bryan, newly inherited as Lord Moyne. His other godfather was Randolph Churchill.
[7] Walter Guinness (1880–1944). Created 1st Baron Moyne in 1932. He was assassinated in Cairo on 6 November 1944 by the Jewish Stern Gang.
[8] John Hollis (1931–). Son of Evelyn's Oxford contemporary and lifelong friend Christopher Hollis.
[9] Evelyn sent advance copies of the novel to his friends; it was not published until May 1945.
[10] Robert Laycock (1907–68). Household Brigade officer who was promoted to Major-General and knighted by the end of the war. Evelyn's commanding officer until 1943, when he was appointed Chief of Combined Operations. Married Angela Dudley Ward in 1935.
[11] Emma Laycock (1943–). Married Richard Temple in 1964.

12 December 1944   12 Blomfield Road
                                                      London W9

Darling Evelyn

I've just found this old crumpled air letter, & as I'm in bed & bored with Fred Emney[1] I take up my pen.

I'm sending you a book called *Love on the Supertax*.[2] A very droll idea which you, or even I, would have made much funnier I think, but which has moments of making one laugh out loud & that is something to be grateful for.

Heywood Hill[3] has engaged an old Jew called Jutro[4] to be my boss – the idea is he should know all about old books & lure a lot of other old Jewtros in to buy them. So I am biding my time. If I can keep him like Caliban in the cellar & get him up to do my work when I feel like a brisk walk round the Park, well & good. But if he is going to join in the cocktail party atmosphere I so carefully foster, I shall leave & write a book. Oh how I long to, in any case, but £ s d rears its ugly head – I write so slowly & my books always come out at moments of crisis & flop (my last 2 never covered their advances & as you know that is not encouraging. And one was a loss to C & H[5]).

The Xmas rush is complicated this year by the fact that there are no other presents to be given but books. Today two quite separate people came in & asked me to think of a book for the Duke of Beaufort 'he *never* reads you know'. If somebody could write a book for people who never read they would make a fortune.

Do come back soon, you are greatly missed in Curzon St.

I find that all the people who ran away to America, after they have been back a fortnight & heard one V2 fall 20 miles away, go on as if they had lived all through the air raids, it is faintly irritating.

I wonder what you think of the behaviour of your co-religionist Mary Dunn.[6] David[7] says 'The curse of the Cecils is upon her'. I wouldn't care to be cursed by such a pious & socially important family would you? Robin[8] came in today to buy *Grave*.[9] I thought he looked self conscious. What do you think of *Grave* I ache to know.

Much love
    NR

---

[1] Fred Emney (1900–80). Fat music-hall actor who had a weekly programme on the BBC Home Service.
[2] By Marghanita Laski (1944).
[3] Heywood Hill (1906–86), (Dearest, Corporal). Founded a bookshop in Curzon Street, Mayfair, in 1936 which he ran until his retirement in 1966. Married Lady Anne Gathorne-Hardy in 1938.
[4] In fact it was the non-Jewish Handasyde (Handy, Handycrafts) Buchanan (1906–84) who was hired. He joined Heywood Hill in 1945, became a partner in 1953 and retired in 1976. Married Mollie Friese-Greene in 1949.
[5] Chapman & Hall, of which Evelyn was a director, published two volumes of letters edited by Nancy: *The Ladies of Alderley* (1938) and *The Stanleys of Alderley* (1939).
[6] Lady Mary St Clair-Erskine (1912–93). Married to Sir Philip Dunn 1933–44, to Robin Campbell 1946–58, to Charles McCabe 1962–9, and again to Sir Philip Dunn in 1969. Lady Mary had two daughters by Sir Philip but no son.
[7] Lord David Cecil (1902–86). Biographer and scholar. Professor of English Literature at Oxford 1948–69. Author of a life of Lord Melbourne (2 vols., 1939, 1954).
[8] Robin Campbell (1912–85). Officer in No. 8 Commando with Evelyn who declared him 'improved out of all knowledge by military training and a very companionable man'. Director

of the Arts Council 1969–78. Married to Hon. Mary Ormsby Gore 1936–46, to Lady Mary
Dunn 1946–58 and to Susan Benson in 1959.
[9] Cyril Connolly, *The Unquiet Grave* (1944). A book of nostalgic and melancholic reflections
published under the pseudonym 'Palinurus'.

25 December 1944   37 Military Mission
                                                    CMF
                                                    [Dubrovnik]

Darling Nancy

Your letter (written on the 12th) was my only Christmas mail – my
only mail for some time – and very nice too.

The Curse of the Cecils – goodness. Is it something like haemophilia
they can only give each other or is it like the common cold something
they can give us? Come to think of it I think that M. Bowra[1] must
have had that curse for many years; the war cured it, hence his sudden
frightful fertility.

I have escaped from your cousin Randolph and am now on my
own in the Pearl of the Adriatic, which looks a little less pearlish with
all the renaissance façades daubed with communist slogans in red
paint. I have spent a solitary Christmas which next to having Laura's
company or the few friends I can count on the toes of one foot, is just
as I like it. I dined alone sitting opposite a looking glass & reflecting
sadly that the years instead of transforming me into a personable man
of middle age, have made me into a very ugly youth.

Well last Christmas I dined with Maimie & Vsevolode and M and I
O'Brien[2] and some howling cads. It is better than that. But two years
ago I was with D. Weymouth[3] & first met Debo. It is a great thing not
to be with my children at Pixton at this season. So I met Taffy Rodd[4] at
that social centre Bari just out of Athens with alarming tales I have since
learned to be untrue. And a Capt Elwes[5] called on me today. It is interesting that H. Hill has engaged a Jew named Sutro[6] to watch the till. I
knew him well at the University. You will find he fits in beautifully to the
Sergeant Preston[7] life in Curzon Street. It is very good news that you
may take up the pen again. Please give the results to Chapman & Hall.
They love losing money & I will get you a substantial over advance. One
thing about your letter saddens me. It does not say 'Thank you for your
beautiful Xmas present of *Brideshead Revisited*. It is a beautiful work'. Is it
too bad to mention or has V-2 blown it up? You should have got it by
now, and though I know it will shock you in parts on account of its piety,
there are a few architectural bits you might like.

I wonder what *Grave* is. Perhaps a book on its way to me? The last
I had was an attempt to whitewash Bryan Guinness[8] called *Belchamber*[9]
which I enjoyed enormously. I lent it to Randolph who was so much
moved that he said he could never commit adultery again – at any
rate not with the same innocent delight.

I wish I could write to you fully & freely about my military life which is full of fun. It may not be long now before I come home; I am reluctant to leave a wine growing country for V2. I may linger in Italy which is full of chums. My work will soon be over here I think.

Is London appreciably improved since the Americans went away? Has Sergeant Preston made the supreme sacrifice yet?

It is very sad if V2 has blown up my magnum opus because it might work a moral change in M. Dunn. It might have been written for her.

I see a man every day called Major Hamilton-Hall. Twice, yesterday and today, I called him Heywood Hill. He is a worm anyway.

It is extraordinary what a people's army we have now. I went to a cocktail party of officers and there was not one who was not purely proletarian. It does not make them any more sympathetic to the partisans though.

The partisans are celebrating Xmas by firing off all their ammunition under my window. My nerves are not as steady as they were before my harrowing life with R. S. Churchill.

A very nice skier named Peter Lunn[10] claims close friendship with Dekka.[11] True? Do you remember the M.P. who tried to seduce Romilly in Madrid?[12] He is here too.

> Love and kisses
> Evelyn

[1] Maurice Bowra (1898–1971). Classicist, critic and legendary Warden of Wadham College, Oxford, 1938–70. He had published nothing for six years, then produced three books in the space of two years: *The Heritage of Symbolism* (1943), *A Book of Russian Verse* (1943) and *Sophoclean Tragedy* (1944). Knighted in 1951.

[2] Murrough O'Brien (1910–2000). Major in the Irish Guards. Married to Irene Richards 1942–51.

[3] Hon. Daphne Vivian (1904–97). Biographer of Emerald and Nancy Cunard (1968), Iris Tree (1974), and Gladys, Duchess of Marlborough (1978). Married to Viscount Weymouth (later 6th Marquess of Bath) 1927–53 and to Xan Fielding 1953–78.

[4] Hon. Gustaf (Taffy) Rodd (1905–74). Nancy's brother-in-law. Married to Yvonne Marling 1932–48 and to Rosemary Calvert 1948–66.

[5] Jeremy Elwes (1921–99). Nephew of Simon Elwes. Married Clare Beveridge in 1955.

[6] John Sutro (1904–85). Celebrated mimic and close friend of both Evelyn and Nancy. Founder of *The Cherwell* and the notorious Railway Club at Oxford. Produced films such as Michael Powell's *The 49th Parallel* (1941) and Carol Reed's *The Way Ahead* (1944). Married Gillian Hammond in 1940.

[7] Stuart Preston (1915–2005), (Serge). American art historian. Art critic for the *New York Times* 1949–65, author of books on Vuillard and Titian. Served as a sergeant in the US Army in London during the war, where he enjoyed a great social success.

[8] Hon. Bryan Guinness (1905–92). Poet and novelist. Succeeded as 2nd Baron Moyne in 1944. Married to Nancy's sister Diana in 1929, divorced in 1934 when Diana fell in love with Sir Oswald Mosley. In 1936 he married Elisabeth Nelson.

[9] Howard Sturgis, *Belchamber* (1904). Novel in which an adulterous wife is responsible for the break-up of her marriage.

[10] Peter Lunn (1914–). Captain of the British Olympic ski team in 1936.

[11] Hon. Jessica Mitford (1917–96), (Decca). Author and journalist. In 1936 Nancy's younger sister eloped with her cousin Esmond Romilly who was fighting in the Spanish Civil War and they married the following year. He was killed in action four years later. In 1943 she joined the Communist Party and married Robert Treuhaft, an American civil rights lawyer.

¹² An unnamed Conservative MP on a delegation to report on the Civil War made amorous advances to Esmond Romilly. Romilly threatened him with public exposure unless he agreed to support the Republican cause. Both parties kept their side of the bargain.

22 December 1944   12 Blomfield Road, W9

Darling Evelyn

Brideshead has come, *beautiful* in orig. boards, a triumph of book production. And a great English classic in my humble opinion. Oh how I shld like to chat about it – there are one or 2 things I long to know. Are you, or not, on Lady Marchmain's side? I couldn't make out. I suppose Charles ends by being more in love than ever before with Cordelia – so true to life being in love with a whole family (it has happened in mine tho' not lately). *Oh* Johnjohn & Caroline & that awful wife are simply perfect. Sebastian reminded me of Henry Weymouth¹ & a little of Andrew Cav:² I'm so glad you're nice about Brian³ this time too. One dreadful error. Diamond clips were only invented about 1930, you wore a diamond *arrow* in your cloche. It's the only one, which I call good – the only one I spotted at least. I think Charles might have had a little more glamour – I can't explain why but he seemed to me a tiny bit dim & that is the *only* criticism I have to make because I am literally dazzled with admiration. I must read it again as I *had* to skip sometimes to get on with the story & I read it all night till one with increasing eye strain & very tired. (Xmas rush.) I told Osbert⁴ today how wonderful it is & he said I am jealous of all writers except Evelyn whom I regard as being on our side.

Mr Trumper⁵ died this week. He cut off Driberg's⁶ ear & died. The shop (Trumpers) shut for a day & Mollie⁷ & I wished it had been Dearest so that we could shut for a day too. It's like hounds not meeting, isn't it, a new point of etiquette to me.

I must tell about Alan Lennox-Boyd.⁸ Well he went to get his annual injection against colds, got a whopper & went to the House where he was on a committee. He felt queer, rather in a coma, when he heard a man opposite him say to the Chairman 'I think I must be going mad because Alan L. B. seems to have swollen in the last few minutes to twice his usual size.' 'My God' said the chairman 'he has.' And he had. And the dr had given him elephantiasis by mistake.

Well, it took 2 ambulances to get him away & he now lies on 4 beds with his trunk hanging out of the window. Let nobody say that war time London lacks fantasy. Gerald⁹ has wired that I am to let him know if Chips¹⁰ turns into any sort of animal as that would be worth coming up for.

Love from
NR

[1] Viscount Weymouth (1905–92). Very good-looking contemporary of Evelyn at Oxford. Succeeded as 6th Marquess of Bath in 1946. He was one of the first to realise the tourist potential of a stately home and opened his house, Longleat, to the public in 1946. Married to Hon. Daphne Vivian 1927–53 and to Virginia Parsons in 1953.
[2] Lord Andrew Cavendish (1920–2004). Second son of 10th Duke of Devonshire. Succeeded to the title in 1950. Married Nancy's youngest sister, Hon. Deborah Mitford, in 1941.
[3] Brian Howard (1905–58). Gifted and flamboyant Anglo-American homosexual who reached a pinnacle of success at Eton and Oxford. Evelyn mocked him as the affected Ambrose Silk in *Put Out More Flags* (1942) and drew on his physical appearance and characteristics for Anthony Blanche, the 'aesthete *par excellence*', in *Brideshead Revisited*.
[4] Osbert Sitwell (1892–1969). Champion of the artistic avant-garde and prolific author of poetry, fiction and autobiography. He wrote a letter of congratulation to Evelyn but in private told his friends that he found *Brideshead* unspeakably vulgar. Succeeded his father in the baronetcy, 1943.
[5] George F. Trumper, gentleman's hairdresser in Curzon Street.
[6] Tom Driberg (1905–76). Gossip columnist, Labour MP and flagrant homosexual. Discovered by Mass Observation to be one of the five most influential opinion-makers after the war. Created Baron Bradwell in 1975.
[7] Mollie Friese-Greene (1909–2005), (Freezers). Joined Heywood Hill bookshop in 1943 where she did the accounts until 1973. Married Handasyde Buchanan in 1949.
[8] Alan Lennox-Boyd (1904–83). Huge Conservative MP for mid Bedford. Parliamentary Secretary to several ministries, including the Ministry of Food 1939–40. Created 1st Viscount Boyd of Merton in 1960. Married Lady Patricia Guinness in 1938.
[9] 14th Baron Berners (1883–1950). Composer, artist and writer. Author of several novels and two volumes of autobiography. In 1937 he printed for private circulation *The Girls of Radcliff Hall*, a *roman-à-clef* in which he appeared as the headmistress of a girls' school; his pupils were thinly disguised portraits of Cecil Beaton, Oliver Messel, Peter Watson and Robert Heber-Percy.
[10] Henry (Chips) Channon (1897–1958). American-born MP and diarist whose ability and ambition helped him make a rapid rise in English society. Married to Lady Honor Guinness 1933–45. Knighted in 1957.

7 January 1945   37 Military Mission.
                                                  [Dubrovnik]

Dearest Nancy,

Yes I know what you mean; he *is* dim, but then he is telling the story and it is not his story. It is all right for Benvenuto Cellini to be undim but he is telling his own story and no one else's. I think the crucial question is: does Julia's love for him seem real or is he so dim that it falls flat; if the latter the book fails plainly. He was a bad painter. Well he was as bad at painting as Osbert is at writing; for Christ's sake don't repeat the comparison to *anyone*.

Lady Marchmain, no I am not on her side; but God is, who suffers fools gladly; and the book is about God. Does that answer it?

Bad about the clip. Too late for the first edition & there are no second editions these days.[1] I knew I should have submitted it to you for criticism. The definitive (ha ha) edition is substantially different from the first so if you really feel disposed to reread it, as you say, wait a month or two for that.

A lovely parcel of books from you. Connolly's *Grave*. What he writes about Christianity is such twaddle – real twaddle – no sense or interest – that it shakes me. And he seems ashamed of the pleasant part of himself – as a soft, sceptical old good liver. I am shocked by the *Grave*. But I have read only five or six pages. My father was a better classical scholar than Connolly but he did not trot out his recondite quotations in at all that way. I think Connolly has lived too much with communist young ladies. He *must* spend more time in White's.

So today is the Orthodox Christmas and I was asked to tea by the military at 3 pm. One never knows what one will get in this country. Today we were seated at tables, without a greeting from our hosts, and given (a) green chartreuse (b) tea and ham sandwiches (c) cakes and cherry brandy & cigarettes (d) two patriotic speeches. Then it seemed reasonable to think the party was over, but no, in came cold mutton & red wine. It is unsettling at my age.

50 copies of *Brideshead Revisited* went out, 40 of them to close friends of yours. Do please keep your ear to the ground & report what they say. For the first time since 1928, I am eager about a book.

Love
    Evelyn

[1] The diamond clip in Julia's hat was changed to an arrow in later editions.

17 January [1945]   [Dubrovnik]

Darling Nancy,

I take it very kindly indeed that you and Raymond Mortimer[1] should have been to the trouble to help correct Great English Classic. When I came to read it I was appalled at the mistakes I found, and I only see one in five. Thank you both with all my heart. I am delighted to hear that Raymond M. likes G.E.C. I remember years ago when I put on the wrapper of *Decline & Fall* 'Mr. R. Mortimer says "extraordinarily clever & amusing" ' and C & H printed it 'extremely clever' and I was furious saying, rightly, that there was all the difference in the world between the extraordinary & the extreme.

I am sitting for my bust to a Mr Paravicini whom I found starving and have fed up to his former great powers. He is responsible for all the most preposterous of the monuments of the Karageorgevitch dynasty. The bust in grey mud grows more formidable daily & will soon be petrified. Short of getting myself stuffed – and not very far short of it – I do not know how I could better perpetuate myself. It will not I think be one of those works of sculpture defined by Eddy[2] as 'dangerous to touch for fear they snapped one's fingers like a mouse trap'. It is like a protestant Bishop of 1870. I am astounded at the dexterity of the old boy. I have always thought it very clever to paint bad pictures but bad sculpture is ten times more exacting. If I can get the object back to England I will have a terra-cotta replica cast & present it to

Heywood Hills (as Sligger's[3] father did to the Hammam Baths) in remembrance of happy hours spent there.[4]

It is agony to be so far from Curzon Street with *The Unquiet Grave* in my mind. Lacking you to talk to I have covered my copy with annotations in red ink.[5] I am quite fascinated by it. There was a large blank in my acquaintance with Cyril which must I suppose have been a deformative period in his life. He wrote in a book that he could no longer be polite to young men with bowler hats & umbrellas. As I then thought of myself as young, sometimes wore a bowler in London & always carried an umbrella, I thought that let me out. When I next met him he was the genial host of Bedford Square and the enviable possessor of Lys.[6] In between he had shed Jean[7] & espadrilles & lemurs and, I rather believe, some other mistress too. Now he is White's bar chum & literary successor of E. Gosse. What a surprise then is his book! First, how Irish. I have made the note in my copy: 'An Irishman's eschatology. The English Gallows; the judgement of Father O'Flynn; the U.S.A.; Hell, a dark place peopled densely with ancestral enemies.' Cyril is poor paddy escaped from the tyranny of the bog priest, dazzled by the jolly splendours of Tammany Hall, quite at a loss what to do with his freedom. Then Eton & Balliol with best & worst results – worst the middle article dissertations on Chamfort etc. But the exquisite poetic laments then creep in again & again. Then there are frightful, inexplicable lapses into the woman novelist's causerie and Joad[8] at the microphone. This feature I can't explain except as the product of the oojah board.

I have no Angst & I don't believe you have. Has Prod?

How could you let Mrs Friese-Greene send me such a revolting book as *The Creative Centuries*?[9]

The god-sons are *disgusted* with their dictionaries of quotations.

I think I want to return to England before it gets hot in the Adriatic. Can you find out for me whether my enemy Ferguson still commands at the Cavalry Barracks, Windsor? If he has shot himself, as seemed probable, I will come home quick.

Do repeat any more you hear about G.E.C.'s reception. Good & bad.

Perhaps Gerald Berners has Angst.

Has Sergeant Preston Angst? I never thought about it or indeed heard of it before. Now I look at everyone with no other curiosity.

Best love
    Evelyn

[1] Raymond Mortimer (1895–1980). Literary and art critic who, after Evelyn, was Nancy's foremost literary mentor. Literary editor of the *New Statesman* 1935–47, chief book reviewer on the *Sunday Times* from 1948 until his death. After their first meeting in 1928 Evelyn described him as 'a disappointment' and 'a second-rate young man'. He nicknamed him the 'Wild Beast', probably because he was quite the opposite.

[2] Hon. Edward Sackville-West (1901–65). Novelist, literary critic and biographer of De Quincey. Succeeded as 5th Baron Sackville in 1962.

[3] F. F. Urquhart (1868–1934). Influential Dean of Balliol 1916–33. His father, a fervent supporter of the Turks, installed a Turkish bath in Jermyn Street.

[4] The bust eventually reached England and stood on a sideboard at Piers Court. After Evelyn's death, Laura had it copied in plaster and terracotta.

[5] Twenty-six years later, Cyril Connolly caught sight of Evelyn's copy of *The Unquiet Grave* in an American library and was bitterly hurt by his contemptuous marginalia.

[6] Lys Dunlap (1917–88). Business manager at *Horizon* and a girlfriend of Cyril Connolly. She took Connolly's name by deed poll but, because of complications arising from his divorce, they were never married. Married to Ian Lubbock 1938–44 and to Sigmund Koch in 1956.

[7] Jean Bakewell (1910–50). Married to Cyril Connolly 1930–45.

[8] Dr C. E. M. Joad (1891–1953). Author and philosopher who appeared regularly on the BBC programme *The Brains Trust*. In 1942 Evelyn had been invited on the panel with Joad, whom he described as 'goatlike, libidinous, garrulous'.

[9] H. J. Randall, *The Creative Centuries: A Study in Historical Development* (1944).

17 January 1945   12 Blomfield Road, W9

Dearest Evelyn

I have a great deal to say – 2 air letters (1/-, agony) if necessary & the whole evening before me. So long as my pen behaves (it has been more of a fountain than a pen lately) & so long as V[2] leaves me alone (& all London *prays* for it to get me as I am the only person who doesn't mind it, so it's an ill wind) we are all set for an immense tome.

I am answering your letter about *Brideshead*. I quite see how the person who tells is dim but then would Julia *and* her brother *and* her sister all be in love with him if he was? Well love is like that & one never can tell. What I can't understand is about God. Now I believe in God & I talk to him a very great deal & often tell him jokes but the God I believe in simply *hates* fools more than anything & he also likes people to be happy & people who love each other to live together – so long as nobody else's life is upset (& then he's not sure). Now I see that I am absolutely un religious. I also see this because what is a red rag to a bull to several people about your book is the *subtle clever* Catholic propaganda & I hardly noticed there was any which shows I am immune from it.

Now about what people think:

Raymond: Great English classic.

Cyril: Brilliant where the narrative is straightforward. Doesn't care for the 'purple passages' i.e. death bed of Lord M. Thinks you go too much to White's. But found it impossible to put down (no wonder).

Osbert: Jealous, doesn't like talking about it. 'I'm devoted to Evelyn – are you?'

Maurice [Bowra]: Showing off to Cyril about how you don't always hit the right word or some nonsense but obviously much impressed & thinks the Oxford part perfect.

SW7 (European royal quarter): Heaven, darling.
Diane Abdy:[1] Like me & Raymond, no fault to find.
Lady Chetwode:[2] Terribly dangerous propaganda. Brilliant.
General View: It is the Lygon family. Too much Catholic stuff.

I am writing a book,[3] also in the 1st person. (Only now has it occurred to me everybody will say what a copy cat – never mind that won't hurt you only me.) It's about my family, a very different cup of tea, not grand & far madder. Did I begin it before reading *B.head* or after – I can't remember. I've done about 10,000 words & asked Dearest for a 3 month holiday to write it which I believe I shall get. I'm awfully excited my fingers itch for a pen.

[1] Lady Diana Bridgeman (1907–67). Married to Sir Robert Abdy 1930–62.
[2] Hester Alice Stapleton-Cotton (1871–1946). Mother of Penelope Betjeman. Married Sir Philip (later Field Marshal) Chetwode in 1899.
[3] Nancy had started work on *The Pursuit of Love* (1945). It was Evelyn who came up with the title, having found '*Linda*', Nancy's suggestion, too boring.

4 February [1945]   [Dubrovnik]

Darling Nancy,

Well those were two splendid letters. What a bob's worth – theology, belles lettres, biography – the whole of Everyman library. First, *Belles-lettres*. How delighted I am to hear you are writing a Great English Classic too. What a subject! Tell your publisher at once or there will not be paper for months after it is written. The first person singular is a most treacherous form of narration, I found. It is so fatally easy in some ways, one can go on and on almost effortlessly & then one comes up against something which 'I' cannot possibly say, which must be said. I believe you will manage it more skilfully than I did. I pant for the proofs.

Theology. There is no doubt that God does like dunces repugnant as it is. I think it is like the lower classes – everyone loves the simple gaffer until he starts telling us what he heard on *The Brains Trust* the evening before. We are all *very* lower class to God and our cleverness & second-hand scholarship bore him hideously.

I don't like your defence of Windsor and Mrs. S. It is certainly true that people often feel qualms of conscience about illicit love only when they are beginning to get bored; also that self restraint usually takes the form of not falling in love, rather than falling & then having a dramatic renunciation. But it must be nonsense to say people never give up sleeping together for 'abstract' principles. Anyhow why 'abstract'? Is the crown of England or the love of God abstract? Of course with Julia Flyte the fact that the war was coming and she saw her life coming to an end anyhow, made a difference.

Biography or *Medicine*. Croatia is thrilled about Lennox-Boyd's

elephantiasis. Army signals busy supplying Randolph with clinical
details. I think it may have some connection with Guinness's Zoo
advertising.[1] Now Simon.[2] I can't make out from your description –
stark, is the word – whether he was blown up by V2 or struck down
in his prime like Lord Randolph.[3] If you put it in a book no one
would think it at all 'convincing'. Heaven help us when you atheists
get full control as in Germany and go round the sick rooms murdering
the sick & infirm. I should be an early victim. My blood pressure is
giving me trouble again.

Drama. Diane [Abdy] writes to me that her life is 're-orientated'.
What does she mean?

Criticism. It is interesting how all the English think my G.E.C. Rom-
ish propaganda. You never hear them speak of Henry Yorke[4] as writing
atheist propaganda. Penelope Betjeman[5] has written me a long letter
treating the story purely as a controversial tract. Katharine Asquith[6]
on the other hand writes 'When will you stop writing novels and try
your hand at a *book*?' Pansy Lamb[7] says I give an entirely false view
of debutante life in the early 20s. It is heaven for me hearing all these
criticisms.

Autobiography. My life continues very easy, comfortable, irresponsible,
safe. I know the stones of Ragusa well & can tell just what is genuine
Italian & what is Slav imitation. Most of my day is spent dealing with
pathetic people of confused nationality seeking to escape the horrors
of liberation.

I was called on by a man who looked just like Prof. Joad who
introduced himself 'I am the poet Kosov'. He gave me the English
translation of a play of his called, literally, 'Passion's Furnace'. The
dramatis personae are:

Peter Nebogin . . . about 40 years old
Idan . . . a young man, 27 years old
A young girl aged 14.
Four Men in crimson attire
Eight Men in handsome attire
A Woman who abuses her husband
An old woman in national costume who abuses Idan
Young Women & Men in Roman costume.

Act I. Night. Gaslight. On the table lies a paper and pencil. On
the smaller table a bottle of absinthe and several small glasses.

Mr Kosov stayed to luncheon & left very tipsy quoting Rimbaud
in German.

We had a sad little festival yesterday when the partisans made the
people observe St. Blaise's Day with all its ceremonies – no tourists,
no peasants in from the villages, the inhabitants too weak from hunger
to stand & too scared of the secret police to sneeze. Why cannot you
send Prod here to help civilian relief.[8] He would be very welcome to

yours truly. Bless him you never mention him now. The Savile Club
I suppose.

Thank you very much for *Love on the Supertax* which arrived today.
I haven't opened it yet but look forward to doing so.

> All love
> Evelyn

[1] An advertisement showed an elephant delicately removing with the end of its trunk a glass of Guinness from its keeper's hand.

[2] Simon Elwes (1902–75). Portrait and landscape painter. A severe attack of thrombosis had recently deprived him of the use of his right side. Married Hon. Gloria Rodd, Nancy's sister-in-law, in 1926.

[3] Winston Churchill's father died aged 46.

[4] Henry Yorke (1905–73). Novelist who wrote under the pseudonym Henry Green. Evelyn greatly admired his early novels *Living* (1929) and *Party Going* (1939) but his admiration waned with Green's later books. Married Hon. Adelaide (Dig) Biddulph in 1929.

[5] Hon. Penelope Chetwode (1910–86). Writer, traveller and expert horsewoman. Encouraged by Evelyn, she converted to Roman Catholicism in 1948. Married John Betjeman in 1933.

[6] Katharine Horner (1885–1976). Widow of Raymond Asquith, eldest son of the Prime Minister, who was killed in the First World War. Converted to Roman Catholicism in 1924. Her deep faith and love of literature made Evelyn respectful of her judgement. In her letter thanking him for sending *Brideshead Revisited*, she wrote: 'I suppose I'm too old for novels really tho anything you write commands my attention and admiration.'

[7] Lady Pansy Pakenham (1904–99). Married the painter Henry Lamb in 1928.

[8] Peter Rodd was working for UNRRA, the United Nations Relief and Rehabilitation Administration

25 September 1945   Piers Court
                                                           Stinchcombe
                                                           Glos.

Darling Nancy

So I am back in my own home & don't give a fig for your Paris.
Not that I do not suffer. The planners have diverted the village water
supply so I spend most of the day carrying buckets of water from the
well to the lulus. The house is shabby & lacking many essential bits
such as door keys. The garden is a bombed-site jungle. But there is a
fair amount of wine in the cellar & heaps of books I forget having
bought.

I went to London for one night for Philip Dunne's[1] wedding –
the old number eight commando gang in force and champagne in
cascades.

What I am really writing for is to keep a promise to your cousin
Randolph. He is as you know now correspondent for an American
series of newspapers. He wants what he (& other people) calls 'contacts'.
He has seen some of your well-known letters & wants some for himself.
He will pay two guineas a week for a weekly letter. I don't know if
you would do this. I pass on the offer as he made it. Your name would
not appear, your own words would not be quoted. He just wants

gossip about Paris. What he writes only appears in U.S.A. No shame, no effort. If you like, write now your first letter to White's.

I am sorry you have not been able to rewrite the unsatisfactory section of your book in time for the first edition. Start rewriting it *now* for the Penguins. It is the difference (one of 1000 differences) between a real writer & a journalist that she cares to go on improving after the reviews are out & her friends have read it & there is nothing whatever to be gained by the extra work.[2] There is a very good theme in the Spanish refugees camp and it was vicious to falsify the facts to make them flat. The contrast of Linda with her manorial soup and port benefactions and her communist husband with his zeal to re-equip the militant workers for the class struggle in Mexico could be excellent. It would give point to her bewilderment that the Spanish gentry did nothing to help. You could make a dramatic climax in the sailing of the evacuation ship with the communists taking off the distressed families in order to pack it with international thugs.

To revert to Randolph. He does not want you to reveal the state secrets of Fabrice[3] nor yet to say what Millicent Duchess of Sutherland is doing to her villa. Well you know what the boy will want.

The planners are making further cuts in paper imports.

Love from
  Evelyn

[1] Philip Dunne (1904–65). Royal Horse Guards 1928–33. Conservative MP 1935–7. Member of No. 8 Commando with Evelyn. Married Audrey Rubin on 18 September.
[2] In his diary Evelyn noted: 'Nancy has written a novel full of exquisite detail of Mitford family life, but planless and flat and hasty in patches.' *The Diaries of Evelyn Waugh* edited by Michael Davie (Weidenfeld & Nicolson, 1976), p. 633.
[3] Gaston Palewski (1901–84), (Fabrice, Colonel, Col). The love of Nancy's life was the inspiration for all her post-war fictional heroes, as well as being an influence on her portrayal of historical personages, from Voltaire to Louis XIV. He made his first appearance as Fabrice, duc de Sauveterre, in *The Pursuit of Love*. See Biographical Notes.

29 September 1945   20 rue Bonaparte
                                                     Paris VI
Darling Evelyn

I couldn't write to Randolph for £2 what I write to you for nothing. I don't believe it would work. I'm writing articles for French papers like mad & getting £10 for 500 words (thank heaven for paper shortage) which you must say not bad. You would roar – any subject from feminism to LITERATURE & as I know the eye of no mocking buddy will ever fall upon them I race ahead with perfect serenity.

I found this empty flat & moved in a fortnight ago. Today, like R. Crusoe, going to the kitchen to hot up a pannikin of washing water, I found an EGG which certainly hadn't been there before. I awaited the next development with some trepidation & presently in came a fat bald little Frenchman & said he lives here too & do I mind? No, so long as he doesn't turn me out, & indeed I haven't seen him since & suspect he just lays his head here & that's all. But next week a Swiss lady returns from her holiday who seems to be the terror of the whole neighbourhood & then I feel I may have to go. Fabrice says shall he have her stopped at the frontier but I thought that was going too far all the same! Oh how I don't want to leave this happy life, the lovely food, the always champagne even for luncheon & all the fun & gaiety.

Did Mr (or General?) Dunne marry the lady who loved him so long or some rich monster with one tiny foot?

I can't begin again on Linda so I am a journalist. Besides I meant Xian to be like that even if Communism isn't. Fabrice made *many* of the same criticisms as you but he seems gratified that the book is dedicated to him on the whole tho' he rather dreads the Communists here getting on to it (fatal name of Mitford). They have got a tremendous anti-Fabrice campaign going on at present & all their papers are nothing but caricatures of him – some very funny. He thinks if they get in they'll pop him straight into prison.

I've bought a lot of nice books, & sold a lot too for the shop. But nobody in London takes the slightest interest in my activities, Dearest doesn't answer my letters & Mollie just says it makes more work for her – I see her point vividly but it's all rather discouraging I must say. What I've done in fact is to establish a branch of H.H. here wh will take up to any amount of books from us @ 30% more than we pay for them which must be quite a cop, specially as the ones they want happen to be ones it's quite easy to get. Among the books I've bought is a history of RHG with very pretty coloured plates – never seen it before.

I had a wonderful description from a French friend of Smarty-boots meeting Valéry.[1] The French don't think SB knows the language at all & they said they could see it was dreadful torture to him to be in the same room with the master & not be able to understand one word he said. SB turned first one ear then the other but all in vain.[2]

You see – Hamilton[3] advertises Linda as one long scream. I knew it. But Fabrice says he thinks in many ways it's more serious than your book but perhaps that's just sucking up. He's greatly tickled by the portrait of himself but says it makes an unlifelike figure as Fr dukes are not at all like that – he then introduced me to one to show & indeed he could hardly have been more like the late Hartington[4] & less like Fabrice. Still – fiction.

Somebody asked F what he thinks about the atom bomb to which he replied 'Comme amateur de porcelaine –'

I'm glad you're back in your house except I suppose one will never see you now.

I'll try Randolph & see what happens but feel doubtful really.

Love from
    NR

P.S. Just been to the kitchen for my pannikin – shockingly late – find a note saying do have some coffee or an egg & anything you like.

Well you must call that kind – I haven't had any breakfast for a month as have no ration card.

Fabrice not awfully pleased at hearing a male voice when he rang up – not too easy to explain with M[ale]V[oice] in the next room either! Bedroom farce situation develops apace.

I've written to Randolph, don't know if it's what he wants, we can but see. Social gossip not my strong point specially not here where I see nobody.

[1] The French poet Paul Valéry (1871–1945) was interviewed by Cyril Connolly for a special issue of *Horizon* devoted to French literature.
[2] Connolly put his problem rather differently: 'How can one communicate to a small mocking figure across a tea-table the glory of the wake which the passage of the great vessel of his work has left for over twenty years across the ocean of European thought?' *Horizon*, November 1945.
[3] James Hamilton (1900–88), (Hamish, Jamie). In 1940 he published *Pigeon Pie*, Nancy's unsuccessful fourth novel, which she later described as 'an early and unimportant casualty of the real war which was then beginning'. His faith in Nancy's talent was rewarded by the huge success of *The Pursuit of Love* and he remained her friend and publisher until her death. Married Jean Forbes-Robertson in 1928 and Countess Yvonne Pallavicino in 1940.
[4] Marquess of Hartington (1917–44). Eldest son of 10th Duke of Devonshire. Married shortly before his death in action to Kathleen (Kick) Kennedy, President Kennedy's sister.

14 November 1945   G. Heywood Hill Ltd.
                                          17 Curzon Street
                                          London W1

Darling Evelyn

I am an exaggerated journey-dreader but I so long to see you, if you could bear to have me, that I would even face standing.

Advantages (as a guest) cheerfulness, willingness (make own bed etc) KEEN to please. Disadvantages can't cook at all (but can peel potatoes), a sort of gramophone record which rings out wild bells all day in praise of life in France (this can be checked by really determined yawning).

Oh do let me come. When you've finished with les villes universitaires[1] could I come one Sat & could I possibly stay till the Monday morning business rush is over as that is the dreadful thing about trains – but then I know how one longs for people to *leave* on Mon: morning. If I came very late on Sat you might be able to bear it. I hope Harriet is there I want to begin on her.

BUSINESS

We have heard of that pretty N York Henry James set, green & gold you know the one, £25 to us. Crafty[2] threw the report away but I fished it out because it is such a pretty thing & you might like it for £30 wh: you could have it for. Anyway worth telling you.

Say a date then & tell the train & I'll be there. I DIE for you.

Love
    NR

---

[1] Evelyn had been lecturing to Catholic graduates at Oxford, Cambridge and London University.
[2] Handasyde Buchanan.

22 November 1945   12 Blomfield Road, W9

Darling Evelyn

The enclosed letter from Decca might amuse you – specially the last bit.

I shall be there, Sat 15th, by the 4.25, & am longing for it.

Poor Smarting Smarty came to see me & said he hadn't meant to read the review[1] but that wicked Raymond told him it was most flattering & led him on. I said it paid him out for his imitation of Ld Marchmain's death bed upon which he struck an attitude of innocence & said he never had.

His description of the final Bluefeet[2] parting beats everything – when I leave Prod I shall *not* confide in Smarty. He says in the end it was all so mixed up with who should have the electric boiler that sentiment & feeling seemed no longer to exist. He is very cross because now Mrs Hugefeet will be very poor & Smarty foresees lodgers, & worse.

You see Fabrice got the better of the Communists, I told you he would. And you'll see he'll be on top now for years. Clever old thing.

The rough notes for my book come out on the 12th Dec I am very excited I must say. Old John [Sutro], now a magnate, says would it make a film? Would it? Hardly I think. I *must* get rich so as to live in France.

Well, see you 15th if not before.

Love
    NR

Business

Freezers cried without any prompting from me when she heard she had to order more *God & the Atom*.[3]

Godsons. Oh Lord. Jonathan is easy – by the way *Ox Bk Quotes*: was his favourite present last year. I'll try & think.

[1] Evelyn's savage review of *The Unquiet Grave* in the *Tablet*, 10 November 1945.
[2] Janetta Woolley (1922–). Worked on *Horizon* during the war and shared a house in Sussex Place with Cyril Connolly after the break-up of her relationship with Kenneth Sinclair Loutit. Married to Robert Kee 1948–50, to Derek Jackson 1951–6 and to Jaime Parladé in 1971. Evelyn nicknamed her 'Bluefeet' after seeing her barefoot on a visit to Sussex Place.
[3] A pamphlet by Ronald Knox in 1945, in which he tried to accommodate the atom bomb within the religious scheme of the universe.

26 December 1945   Compton Place[1]
                                                   Eastbourne
                                                   Sussex
Dearest Evelyn
     [. . .] Randolph has written an absolutely hateful article against Fabrice in a French communist paper[2] – how I wish none of my friends could hold a pen. Uncle Matthew[3] has been here, deep in my book. He says he once read a book that ended badly & hasn't ever been the same since – it was called *Tess of the d'Urbervilles*.[4] This is news to all of us & very interesting news too.
     By the way will you tell Laura I've never had such a wonderful luncheon-in-the-train as she gave me that day. She is kind.
     I hope Harriet had a nice Xmas. Here it has been heavenly.

     With love from
          Nancy

[1] Nancy was spending Christmas with her sister Deborah.
[2] Randolph Churchill had written in *Libération* that Palewski was 'probably the most hated man in France'.
[3] 2nd Baron Redesdale (1878–1958), (Farve). Nancy's father was the model for the inimitable Uncle Matthew in her novels.
[4] Thomas Hardy's novel was read aloud to Lord Redesdale by his wife soon after they married. When he began to cry at the book's ending, she comforted him with: 'Oh darling, it's only a story.' 'What?' he stormed. 'Do you mean the damned sewer *invented* it?'

4 January [1946]   12 Blomfield Road, W9
Darling Evelyn
     I'm in quarantine for scarlet fever – Gladys[1] was removed sobbing to hospital after having been looked after by me until a hospital could be found to take her. It is perfect bliss until I get it, when my fate will be unthinkable (fever hospital in *their* nightdress, for one month & no visitors). But I haven't got it, I never catch things, & as Davey[2] always says 'you are such a strong woman, Nancy'.
     So here I am all alone reading *Guermantes*[3] & quite absolutely happy. (It is Eddy's copy – marked & most revealing!)
     Fabrice rang up & kind people are giving luncheon parties to discuss the book[4] & the Windsors[5] have given it to everyone for Xmas. Rather low brow circles I fear but still!
     Thank you so much for the *Tablet*. I left it at the shop & haven't

been able to go back for it – the one day I was there I was overwhelmed with work. The franc situation has set certain problems but benefits me in the long run of course.

Oh *Guermantes*. What is the point of writing books at all. The curious thing is it must have some kind of rhythm because it went on & on in my head long after I was asleep, no sense but a sort of thump thump like a band.

Peter is back which is bliss except that I hardly see him. He was full of this thing about the Jews that Morgan was sacked for saying[6] was telling me all about it just before it came out on the wireless. He says it's perfectly true every word – & you know how pro-Semitic Peter is. He is also wildly anti-Tito, but says most of the Yugos seem to like & want him but he is simply Hitler. Nothing like foreign travel for widening one's views – eh?

What a clever man he is (Prod I mean) & so *good*. The late Colonel.

I've just got a letter from Davey imploring me to hang sheets soaked in Jeyes over every door – he lives in the days when whole families of parsons were wiped out by scarlet fever.

I enclose a letter from Jonathan [Guinness] who appears to think you live with me. How awful for an intelligent boy to have Bryan for a father. I like the crack about improving literature however!

I hear Prod stirring like a hibernating animal in the spring so must go & see to his breakfast.

Best love
    NR

[1] Nancy's maid.
[2] Edward Sackville-West was the model for the hypochondriacal, health-obsessed David Warbeck in Nancy's novels.
[3] Marcel Proust, *Le Côté de Guermantes* (1920).
[4] *The Pursuit of Love* sold 200,000 in the first twelve months after publication.
[5] The Duke and Duchess of Windsor returned to Paris in autumn 1946, after spending the war in the Bahamas where the Duke had been Governor.
[6] General Sir F. E. Morgan, chief of UNRRA operations in Germany, had been called on to resign after declaring at a press conference that a secret organisation existed to further an exodus of Jews from Europe. He was eventually dismissed six months later after alleging that UNRRA was being used as a cover for Soviet agents.

5 January 1946   Piers Court
                                                  Stinchcombe

Darling Nancy

Death is not certain; blindness & baldness are. Still it will save you from seeing Picasso & wigs are easier on girls than chaps.

Please, before your sight fails, order Mrs F Greene to send you the *Tablet* and read my opening chapter of the life of the Empress Helena.[1] I want your opinion on it.

This Prod-worship is not healthy. Clever perhaps – good no. You must get a nun to nurse you through your fever. She will explain what goodness is.

I am very jealous of R. Mortimer and Debo. It was unfeeling of you to tell her he was like a wild beast. She was clearly very much over excited before his visit. I hope it was a bitter disappointment.

Picasso is the head of the counter-hons.[2] I went to his disgusting exhibition to make sure. Klee rather old-maidish & sweet in a finicky way. It is a pity you do not read *The Times* Newspaper it has been full of tremendous art balls lately. I have had a great fan mail about Picasso – all from Surrey.[3]

Miss Hunter Dunn[4] is a real person, her sister is engaged to be married to a Major this morning.

With your resistance weakened by so many dinners at the Dorchester the fever may prove fatal.

My two eldest children are here and a great bore. The elder[5] alternates between strict theology & utter silences; the boy[6] lives for pleasure and is thought a great wit by his contemporaries. I have tried him drunk & I have tried him sober . . .

How nice to be able to read Proust in his own lingo. I tried in Scottish[7] and couldn't get on at all. Take *Henrietta Temple* (Disraeli) to the lazar house.

I have just got to work again on *Helena* – now the Cinema company from whom I have been happily drawing money all these years suddenly demand my services. It is a great nuisance.

Yesterday I went to an excruciating Pantomime at Bristol. I asked Maria Teresa how she had enjoyed it. 'All except the jokes, papa.'

In a moment of Christmas sentiment I wrote to the nuns who had this house during the war to say I would let them off paying the damages & losses (assessed at £214 by the agents). The Mother Superior wrote to say that she was 'glad our little difficulty was forgotten'.

Our nursery maid at Pixton has fallen ill so Laura goes off next week leaving me alone here.

A chap I know was lately possessed by the devil and has written a very interesting account of the experience.

I saw Bowra drunk in White's with Smarty. Smarty never comes in now except on Saturdays when one is allowed a guest to luncheon.

The first thing Maria Teresa asked for on her arrival from her middle class convent was a 'serviette-ring'.

Counter Hon Quennell[8] behaved well about *Love* in his *Daily Mail*, I was glad to see. I look for other reviews but don't see them. Your cousin Ed[9] thought the communist part particularly good.

Try not to die. It is the strong ones who go under easiest.

Love
    Evelyn

Death to Picasso the head of the Counter Hons.

[1] The first three chapters of *Helena* (1950), a novel about the mother of Constantine the Great, were published in edited form in the *Tablet*, 22 December 1945.
[2] The Hons (derived from Nancy's younger sisters' private language in which 'Hon' meant 'Hen') were the Radlett children's secret society in *The Pursuit of Love*. Anyone not a friend of the Hons was a Counter-Hon.
[3] Evelyn had written to *The Times* attacking an exhibition of Picasso and Matisse at the Victoria and Albert Museum.
[4] Joan Hunter-Dunn was a doctor's daughter from Aldershot who ran the canteen at the Ministry of Information during the war. John Betjeman admired her strapping good looks and jolly nature and immortalised her as the heroine of 'A Subaltern's Love Song'.
[5] Maria Teresa Waugh (1938–). Lawyer. Married John D'Arms in 1961.
[6] Auberon Waugh (1939–2001). Columnist, reviewer and novelist. His autobiography *Will This Do?* (1991) gives a stark view of Evelyn as a father. Married Lady Teresa Onslow in 1961.
[7] *A la Recherche du temps perdu* was first translated into English by the Scotsman C. K. Scott Moncrieff.
[8] Peter Quennell (1905–93). Man of letters. Editor of the *Cornhill Magazine* 1944–51 and of *History Today* 1951–79. One of Evelyn's *bêtes noires* and the frequent butt of his malicious humour. He had given Evelyn's *Rossetti: His Life and Works* (1928) an unfavourable review and this may have been the beginning of hostilities. Knighted in 1992.
[9] 6th Baron Stanley of Alderley (1907–71). Rich, good-looking, heavy-drinking and much-married cousin of Nancy.

7 January [1946]   12 Blomfield Road, W9

Darling Evelyn

I wish I knew why one ever goes out in the world. I have been completely happy – blissful, knowing I couldn't, reading *Guermantes*, being Mrs Every Listener. Yet my quarantine is over today & I'm going out every night this week. It can't be as an insurance against old age because old & deaf & infirm one will long more than ever for one's own fireside I suppose. Habit. Perhaps really I would die of boredom if I had much more than a week alone. The worst of it is one can't (unless very rich & can entertain oneself) do it a little – it must be all the time or not at all.

Don't be depressed about your children. Childhood is a hateful age – no trailing clouds of glory – & children are generally either prigs or gangsters & always dull & generally ugly. There is a young woman who lives next door here with 3 & I pity her from morning to night (& she pities me,[1] so all is well really). I mind less & less not having any except I do think when they are puppies, from 1 to 4 they are rather heaven. 4–20 is unbearable.

There was a good review in the *Spectator* saying (rather gratuitously I thought) this is not great literature or great wit but otherwise all right.[2] And H.H. are printing another 5000 making 20 in all so Mr Popkin[3] will have something to work on. Vic Cunard[4] met Mrs P who said 'I turn Mr Popkin out like a little lord'. Oh how sweet.

I have been doing housework it makes me cry with fatigue & when

I review my work it has just been making my bed & washing up
breakfast after which (it takes the entire morning) I sleep until dinner
time. What *can* this mean & how can people DO whole houses? I
don't understand a word of it. Did you see Raymond's remarks about
(HON) Picasso? It seemed right to me. I went scattering gems at the
V & A & thought them more wonderful than those I saw in Paris,
more wonderful than I had been led to suppose they were – but the
Matisse very shoddy I must admit. I wish you weren't on the other
side & don't really understand it quite. The crowd very boring & self
conscious I thought.

Wild beast Mortimer went down very well with all at Compton
Place & enjoyed his evening. Hamish[5] is here for a week in such a
nice mood.

If *ever* there was a saintly character it is Prod & I bet you'll see him
nestling away in heaven from a distance long before you get there
yourself.

Love from
Nancy

[1] Nancy had undergone a hysterectomy during the war which left her unable to have children.
[2] The review of *The Pursuit of Love* concluded: 'But it has more truth, more sincerity and more
laughter than a year's output of novels in the bogus significant style.' *Spectator*, 4 January 1946.
[3] Percy Popkin (d.1960). Nancy and Evelyn's tax adviser.
[4] Victor Cunard (1898–1960). A close friend and correspondent of Nancy, who settled in
Venice for most of his life.
[5] Hon. James Alexander (Hamish) St Clair-Erskine (1909–73). Capricious homosexual to whom
Nancy was unofficially engaged for four years; their unsatisfactory relationship ended just
before her engagement to Peter Rodd. He contributed to the character of Albert Memorial
Gates in Nancy's first novel *Highland Fling* (1931) and appeared as the affected and precocious
Bobby Bobbin in *Christmas Pudding* (1932).

17 January 1946   12 Blomfield Road, W9

Just had a letter beginning 'I've only twice before written to an Author
– once to a very old American[1] who wrote a book about a white mule
& the other was to Evelyn Waugh about *Put Out More Flags* but I never
posted that one –'

Randolph has just telephoned, very governessy 'please make a note
of my new number'. I forgot until I'd accepted to go & see him that
I'm not on speakers with him because of his behaviour to Fabrice –
but it's no good not being on speakers with R'dolph because many
have tried it before & not succeeded.

I must now confess that the *Tablet* got lost – *entirely* my fault, it was
given to me, but I simply must have mislaid it. But I can read it in a
day or 2 as Gerald will lend me his/Penelope [Betjeman]'s copy. *Don't*
be cross, it was the s. fever day & I was disrupted.

Xopher[2] tells me the Bloomsbury Home Guard are gunning for me

– he says Smarty's friends think my book utterly indecent on acc/ of not being about cabmen's shelters & Hons' Cupboard makes them vomit & they are all the more annoyed because they think it's quite well written.

I've just had this month's Smarty's Own Mag[3] & of course the great joke is one does write better than all of them (not SB himself) because even when they quite *want* to be understood they can't be. As Tonks[4] used to say 'Why don't they stick to cooking?'

Diana[5] has been in her flat & somebody has written shit & things on the door & D said 'Of course they think the busy little housewife will clean it off, but really darling I *can't* be bothered.'

Fabrice has invited Debo & Andrew for a week in Paris, they are thrilled & so is he, & will no doubt give them a wonderful time.

In spite of your counter-honish thoughts I never got the fever you see.

Picasso is a Hon – I've now got 3 lovely books about him in the shop so I gloat all day.

There was a cocktail Party at the Tower of London – Violet T[6] said to me 'When I got to the Traitor's Gate I heard 2 well-known voices & it was Emerald[7] & Daisy[8] –' If you don't know Violet you should, you would appreciate her.

Prod is off to Spain he hopes for the revolution – I might go with him as far as Perpignan, I hear it's very gay, & the hotel we used to stay in is now the Roussillon Ladies Socialist Club – made for me!

I am warmly & happily in bed & can't switch on the wireless until after Northern Music Hall is over which is why you are getting this screed.

Goodness Proust is smutty – I'd forgotten. I wonder if the Scotchman really puts it all in?

Love
NR

P.S. Xopher is writing about Robert[9] – have you any letters?

[1] William Carlos Williams (1883–1963). Poet, novelist and short story writer.
[2] Christopher Sykes (1907–86). Novelist, journalist and biographer. In 1975 he published a biography of Evelyn, dedicated to the memory of Nancy. Married to Camilla Russell, daughter of Russell Pasha, Chief of the Cairo Police, in 1936.
[3] *Horizon*.
[4] Professor Henry Tonks (1862–1937). Head of the Slade School of Fine Art where Nancy studied briefly in 1927.
[5] Hon. Diana Mitford (1910–2003), (Honks). Nancy's younger sister. Maried 1929–34 to Bryan Guinness and in 1936 to Sir Oswald Mosley, founder of the British Union of Fascists. See Biographical Notes.
[6] Violet Keppel (1894–1972). Novelist better known for her scandalous affair with Vita Sackville-West than for her literary output. Married Denys Trefusis in 1919.
[7] Maud Burke (1872–1948). Lavish hostess, social lioniser and patron of the arts. Married

Sir Bache Cunard, the shipping millionaire, in 1895 and, after his death in 1925, decided to change her name to Emerald.

[8] Marguerite (Daisy) Decazes (1890–1962). Daughter of a French duke, and heiress to the Singer sewing-machine fortune; she was reputed to cross herself for luck whenever she passed a shop with the Singer sign. Married to Prince de Broglie 1910–18 and to Hon. Reginald Fellowes in 1919. Her daughters Emmeline and Jacqueline de Broglie were accused of collaboration during the Occupation.

[9] Robert Byron (1905–41). Byzantinist, travel writer and journalist. Author of *The Road to Oxiana* (1937). Evelyn and Byron were contemporaries at Oxford, where they were both members of the Hypocrites Club (motto: 'water is best'); they later fell out over Byron's anti-Catholicism. He was dearly loved by Nancy who wrote many years after his death in action that she missed him most of all her friends. *Four Studies in Loyalty* (1946) by Christopher Sykes included an essay on Robert Byron.

28 January [1946]   Piers Court
                                                  Stinchcombe
Dear Nancy,

My little trip to London passed in a sort of mist. Did I ever come to visit you again after my first sober afternoon. If so, I presume I owe you flowers. I left a trail of stunted & frightfully expensive hyacinths behind me. On the last evening I dimly remember a dinner party of cosmopolitan ladies where I think I must have been conspicuous. Were you there? I awoke with blood on my hands but found to my intense relief that it was my own. I sometimes think I am getting too old for this kind of thing.

I have just read an essay by a jew which explains the Mitford sobriety and other very peculiar manifestations of the family. You all live on a single plane. There is a lucid diagram of a flight of stairs to explain this. It is called *Yogi & Commissar II*[1] I believe this jew is a chum of S. Boots Esq & all the little Bootses.

Business. I have got a working edition of Gibbon so only want 4to now. Are you a newsagent? If so please send me *Horizon*, *Polemic*, *Contact*, and all the Boots & counter Boots journals regularly. Please send E. M. Forster's lecture[2] reviewed by Desmond[3] yesterday.

Please send the two Penguin pamphlets about counterhon painters reviewed yesterday too.[4] (*Sunday Times*)

Please get me sets of *Cambridge Ancient Modern* & *Mediaeval History*. Also *Oxford Books English* & *Victorian Verse*.

Also Eliz. Bowen's[5] book when published. End of Business.

I was asked to tea by Andrew to meet Debo but had the decency to refuse. She would have thought me a wilder beast than Mortimer.

I was sent a tiny box of completely unsmokable cigars on which I had to pay a prodigious fine by whom do you think? Sergeant P[reston].

My great new friend B. H. Bennett[6] has turned absolutely beastly to me.

Sykes seems the main source of the tale that the Bootses hate your charming book. I heard it several times but in each case traced it back to Sykes. It is generally said in White's that your dedication to the Polish fascist is a blind & that the real Fabrice is someone named Roy.[7] I gave no opinion on this but nodded sagely.

I go today for two nights to my beloved Asquiths at Mells where ᴼˢˢᵉ˲ᵈ is not mentioned. I am taking my unhappy little boy to his first boarding school. He is going in a high state of pleasurable excitement poor beast. I think he lives on one plane like the Mitfords.

Can you politely ask any of your jewish friends whether they know the sources of the Wandering Jew legend? *Encyclopaedia Brit.* is very weak on the subject. I am introducing him (B. Howard again) into the Helena book & would like to get the full facts.

I say is this all right; I am bringing out a book of extracts from my travel books & dedicating it to all the people the original books were dedicated to. One was Diana Mosley. Will she mind or be quite pleased? Should I ask her? I can't just say Diana because there is a second Diana (Cooper)[8] so I have to put Mosley & that means I have to put Bryan Moyne. It is a point of delicacy but perhaps I am scrupulous.[9]

I am having a very interesting correspondence with Mrs Betjeman about horses & sex. Half of it gets confiscated in the post by the socialists.

Death to Picasso. I had ¼ of wild beast Mortimer's article sent me by a press agency. What these wild beasts can't realise is that Picasso is old and has been at his dirty work for decades, so it is no use their saying 'You cannot appreciate this glorious genius because he is New and you are too crusted to receive new impressions.' The pure clear witness against him grows with the years. You are all either dupes or traitors. You are a traitor.

Love from
    Evelyn

[1] Arthur Koestler, *The Yogi and the Commissar* (1945).

[2] E. M. Forster, 'The Development of English Prose between 1918 and 1939'.

[3] Desmond MacCarthy (1877–1952). Influential literary journalist and regular reviewer for the *Sunday Times* 1928–52. Married Mary (Molly) Warre-Cornish in 1906. Knighted in 1951.

[4] *Edward Burra* by John Rothenstein and *Victor Pasmore* by Clive Bell, in the Penguin Modern Painters series, were reviewed by John Russell.

[5] Elizabeth Bowen (1899–1973). A collection of short stories, *Selected Stories*, was published later in the year. Her story 'Gone Away' was published in the *Listener*, 3 January 1946, but did not appear in book form until 1965.

[6] Basil Bennett (1894–1966). Camp commandant to No. 8 Commando. After the war he became chairman of the Hyde Park Hotel where Evelyn often stayed on visits to London.

[7] Roy André Deplats-Pilter (1904–45). A Free French officer with whom Nancy had a brief affair during the war which resulted in her ectopic pregnancy.

[8] Lady Diana Manners (1892–1986), (Honks). The greatest beauty of her generation had been a friend of Evelyn since the 1930s. Married Alfred Duff Cooper in 1919. See Biographical Notes.

[9] *When the Going Was Good* (1946) was dedicated to Bryan Moyne, Diana Mosley, Diana Cooper, Perry and Kitty Brownlow and the memory of Hazel Lavery.

29 January 1946   12 Blomfield Road, W9

Darling Evelyn

We can't supply mags – yr other esteemed orders are noted. The
dry rot is being dealt with, i.e. two men have erected a tent inside the
shop from beneath the folds of which they emerge every few minutes
with thousands of £'s worth of penicillin. Too easy. Mollie sits in front
of the tent looking like Helen of Troy while Handy sulks in the front
of the shop & I burst my sides laughing. Did you know Pat Russell?[1]
She has written complaining that in Austria she was raped by a Cossack
& got syphilis. This is hard cheese as she is a Liz. I wrote & told her
about Dora Morris & the American major to cheer her up. Allies are
like that.

White's *have* got the wrong end of the stick, as people always have
when they begin on other people's private lives. Sucks to them as
St Helena would say – (I've read it).

No you were stone cold (in every sense of the word) sober when I
saw you, in a driving coat. Beastly the way you never looked in again
but then *I* am not an Asquith.

Sutro may film my book[2] he has got an actress called Miss Gray
who wants to be Linda. He told me this as though it were such a
dazzling piece of news that I didn't like to say I'd never heard of her.
I've had a letter from Eton, praising the book & ending up 'your fans
at Eton eagerly await you', so I foresee some nice Woodley[3] life.

Cocktail party at Oxford on Sat – all the dear old faces, it was very
nice. I had 48 hours (crowded) of glorious life with Gerald at Faringdon, every single meal out. St Helena Betjeman in characteristic form.
Everybody very sorry for the poor old fathers who run the *Tablet* &
don't know smut when they see it[4] – awful of you, it is thought, to
trade on their saintly innocence like this. However when somebody
in the congregation finally opens their eyes no doubt they will have
you walled up & serve you right – only I hope *I* don't get locked into
the church that night by mistake.

What's happened to New College New Forest New Friend?[5] This
is dreadful news, he is my gossip as you may remember.

Prod is off to Spain in a month when I hope to go to Paris – that
is if I can get my domestic affairs settled first. Fabrice rang up in floods
of giggles, most reassuring. He has gone to live with General Molinier
who is a glamorous air force general. In the war Fabrice (then in
Eritrea) heard that Corniglion-Molinier had been killed flying, so he
advanced to the French radio & delivered a funeral oration beginning
'Adieu Corniglion, toi qui comme un lion volais dans le ciel, n'es plus
qu'un petit tas de cendres dans le désert – mais de ce petit tas de
cendres, comme le phénix etc etc'[6] which was listened to with some
amusement by Corniglion-Molinier in a Cairo hotel bedroom where
he had happened to turn on the wireless.

Davey has sent me some vitamin C isn't he a love –
Do tell some more about us being on a single plane?

[1] Lady Patricia Blackwood (1902–83). Married to Henry Russell 1926–37.
[2] *The Pursuit of Love* was never filmed but has been adapted for television.
[3] A Mitford word describing a young admirer, from John van Druten's play *Young Woodley* (1928) about a boy falling in love with his housemaster's wife.
[4] Evelyn had invented sexual fantasies connected with riding for the heroine of *Helena*.
[5] Basil Bennett; he and Nancy were both godparents to Harriet Waugh.
[6] 'Adieu Corniglion, you who were flying like a lion in the skies are now but a small heap of ashes in the desert – but from that heap of ashes, like a phoenix ... etc etc.'

1 February [1946]   Piers Court
                                                 Stinchcombe

Darling Nancy,

Commerce

Can you get an original issue of Badminton Library *Football* for my god-son John Hollis & send it with my compliments to Stonyhurst College, Blackburn, Lancs.

Drama

I have not seen Miss Gray perform but I once saw her in an hotel & thought her *very* pretty. But Miss Fontaine is the one for Linda or failing that a Miss Todd who greatly overexcited me yesterday afternoon at the Dursley Cinema.

Education

It is neither less nor more reprehensible for a young pagan girl to have her first love-reveries about horses than about film-actors, but it is aesthetically more interesting.

Autobiography

I took my poor little boy to school & left him there looking a midget in a new blazer and cap.

I bought six Ionic columns to cheer an old man whom I had upset by deriding his second-hand sculpture. Would you like them for your shop? or for your garden?

Laura is still away involved in nursery troubles at Pixton but I hope to have her tomorrow.

Anthropology

Just wait till your book comes out in America. They are hell. Yesterday I had a letter from *Life* saying that they proposed to publish a series of photographic illustrations to my novels. Would I please supply a list of originals from which the characters were copied & induce them to pose. 'Contemporary costume essential.' Come to think of it it might be rather fun to have a séance & materialize Elizabeth Ponsonby & David Greene & Basil Murray & Lois Sturt & Napier Alington & William Acton and all.[1] They, the Americans not these dead chums, will write you letters even when they have not read your book saying

how much you will be interested in the reviews in their local paper
and they don't get around to reading much themselves but do you
like Emerson.

One thing, it is all over in a month & then they go to someone
new.

Medical

I am down to my last dozen bottles of claret. Can your Free (Ha
Ha) French help?

Deportment

You don't give advice about Diana dedication in your letter.

Polite Interest

Was Prod one of the communists shot trying to land in Spain?

Love from
    Evelyn

---

[1] Friends and acquaintances of Evelyn who formed part of a group labelled by the popular
press as the 'Bright Young Things'. They were notorious for their wild parties and extravagant
behaviour and contributed to aspects of characters in *Vile Bodies* (1930).

3 February 1946   12 Blomfield Road, W9

Darling Evelyn

I think *my* characters would rejoice if *Life* did that to me – Ld
Merlin[1] has already telephoned to ask if he can be himself in the film.

Oh the BALL last night was such heavenly fun. Chips said to
Emerald 'This is what we have been fighting for' (we?) as he surveyed
the scene to which clever old Emerald replied 'Why dear, are they all
Poles?'

I'm trying to answer your letter.

Claret. Is *Brideshead* being published in French if so you will have
some francs which you can spend on wine.

Deportment. Don't know, can't say. Why not Bryan & Diana then
nobody will think it's Cooper. Why not write & ask Diana – Crowood,
Ramsbury is the address.

Peter Q[uennell] last night, gazing at a very pretty débutante 'Isn't
it nice, we can see her darling little eyebrows going up & down & her
darling little mouth opening & shutting without having to listen to the
dreadful rubbish that's coming out of it –'

Prod never gets shot, it's one of the nice things about him.

The columns sound heaven they also sound heavy – where are
they? (I'm answering like mad, do admit.)

All this talk about film stars & horses is a red herring – smut is
smut & you have filled the *Tablet* with it & us Protestants are tickled
to death about it.

Is *Brideshead* going to be filmed & do you know anything about the business side of all that?

I hear you've sold half a million copies – Osbert is pretty furious.

Sykes has chap: & v: about Smarty & my book. He has a witness called Grisewood. I think it may be true as I saw SB the other day & he never said 'My *dear* your book is too *too* divine' nor indeed did he mention it at all.

I think of letting this house & going to Paris for a few months, life here is really too difficult & depressing & I long for the darling Frogs. A Frog woman publisher has been over here in a huge yellow soufflé (hat) & she gave me great nostalgia for all that bubbling & cheerfulness & endless endless flattery which goes on ceaselessly there.

They never seem to want to take one down a peg like English people do, & they *seem*, which is all that matters, to love one so much. Angels.

Are you coming back soon to smash up a few brandy glasses?

Love from
      NR

[1] Gerald Berners appeared as the cultivated, exquisite squire of Merlinford in *The Pursuit of Love*.

4 February 1946   Piers Court
                                                       Stinchcombe
Dearest Nancy,

Since sending you a post-card today I purchased the *New Statesman*. I thought 'Reed's' review of your book egregiously silly both in praise & blame.[1] I love all the Mitford childhood, as you know, but to single out the buffoon father while totally ignoring the unique children's underground movement is brutish. He calls your one false character[2] 'a brilliant sketch'. You know better than I how wrong he is about Fabrice. The review irritated me greatly. I wonder who it is who writes it. Plainly a homosexual; perhaps a Lesbian?

I looked at other pages of the paper & was astounded that you take it in. I read Eddy [Sackville-West] describing the use of the word 'brothel' on the wireless as 'a refreshing experience' which 'spoke eloquently of the intelligence, sanity and good feeling of ordinary people'. I read 'Nothing can stop big Powers bullying their small neighbours if they wish to do so'. Last time I had the paper in the house it was boiling to attack Germany & Italy for no other reason. I read the wild beast saying that Mr Sutherland's painting 'rivals butterflies' wings' in 'delicacy'.[3]

The only thing that made any sense in the paper was a grovelling apology to a soldier they had insulted, but that had been dictated, presumably, by some intelligent solicitor.

How can you read it? It explains all that modern trash that encumbers your shop.

Evelyn

[1] The poet Henry Reed (1914–86) described *The Pursuit of Love* as 'rewardingly funny in places' but that this was 'the least, and indeed the most, one can say of it'. *New Statesman*, 2 February 1946.
[2] The Communist Christian Talbot, whose character was partly based on Peter Rodd.
[3] In a review of *Approach to Painting* by Thomas Bodkin, Raymond Mortimer wrote that the texture of Graham Sutherland's pictures 'frequently rivals butterflies' wings in the delicacy of their mottlings'. *New Statesman*, 2 February 1946.

5 February [1946]   Piers Court
                                                      Stinchcombe
Darling Nancy

I seem to write to you twice a day.

£2000 is the least you should take, £5000 the most you can hope for for film rights. It will be a lump sum, not royalties. If you were not a socialist I should advise you to have it paid in two instalments on Apr. 6th 1947 and 1948 so that it does not all go to the State, but of course, that is what you like.

Whose ball? Why was I not asked? Why was Quennell asked? He should not be allowed to see, let alone meet, still less criticise a debutante.

Ever since I bought that terrible socialist paper I have been haunted by the image of Eddy sitting night after night beside his loud-speaker with strained face, waiting for the word 'brothel'. At last his vigil is rewarded and his faith in the decency of common humanity is restored. I know him so little. It does not at all square with Uncle Davey. I re-read his essay on Mr Sutherland last night & studied the 'butterfly plumage' of the penguin reproductions.[1]

You are all stark mad in London.

E

Commerce: No books have come tho several I ordered are modern trash.

[1] Edward Sackville-West contributed a monograph on Graham Sutherland for the Penguin series on modern painters, published in 1943.

10 February 1946   12 Blomfield Road, W9

I've ordered myself a day in bed as I feel very overtired so everybody is being inflicted with letters – Gerald, the Colonel, Debo & you. Debo has pneumonia in Derbyshire so write to her – Churchdale Hall, Bakewell. Prod is away, he has left me a gun wh fires 9 times, at full cock, wh I find infinitely reassuring. He showed me how to use it, with the barrel waving about between my heart & my tummy till I became quite fidgety.

I hope you didn't mind the shop sending you that huge Gibbon on approval – we only had it on approval ourselves & I didn't think you'd be back for a while.

Yesterday I went to tea with Miss Ivy Compton Burnett.[1] There were 2 cultured young men with double names & as we walked away together they said she had told them a terrifying French lady was coming. Me. Was I pleased? Yes.

I met S. Boots. He said to me the book is well written but the people are too rich. He told Jane Watson[2] he was horrified by the snobbishness of it. She says he complained that I am very unkind – she said 'But Nancy is so *kind* underneath' & S. replied 'But so *unkind* on top' & that Baroness Budberg[3] who was there said '& she only likes well dressed people'.

Needless to add that I am perfectly enchanted to have been such a topic – Jane says they went on for an hour.

We are dining on Tues to meet the Ds of Kent. I've offered Prod 2/6 not to embarrass me, as I used to do with my sisters when my young men were coming to stay but I fear Prod is less venal & I dread his views on monarchy being aired. I wriggled like an eel to get out of taking him, in vain – he even put off some Armenian reds in order to come. I positively dread it, will give a report later in the week.

Best love from
NR

[1] Ivy Compton Burnett (1884–1969). Novelist whose highly condensed and abstract writing was greatly admired by Evelyn.
[2] Wife of Francis Watson (1907–92), the assistant keeper and later director of the Wallace Collection 1938–74.
[3] Maria (Moura) Kakrevskaïa (1892–1974). Author and translator. Daughter of a Russian senate official, mistress of Sir Robert Bruce Lockhart, Maxim Gorky and H. G. Wells. Married to Ivan Alexandrovitch von Benckendorff 1911–17 and to Baron Budberg in 1922.

21 February 1946
G. Heywood Hill Ltd.
10 Curzon Street
W1

Darling Evelyn

You know how Eddie Devonshire[1] persecutes me by saying 1st he is Uncle Matthew, & 2nd Linda is Debo & how dare I give him an immoral d in law. Well, the Macmillan girl went to stay with the old Duch of Dev:[2] lent her *Brideshead* smelt burning rushed downstairs found D of D *trying* (viz library at Alexandria) to burn *B.head* & saying 'how *dare* he write about my family like this.' So it must be a family mania to think all books are about them.

Have you heard about the Mouse @ Bay?[3] Some other women were saying how the virility of men is in relation to the size of their noses & the M @ B jumped out of her chair & said 'It is quite untrue, Cyril has a *very* small nose.' Also about Brownell[4] being raped by Heygate[5] & telling somebody how dreadful it had been & how he has S[yphilis] & G[onorrhoea] & ending up '& the worst of it is he doesn't seem to realize what Cyril stands for'. Perhaps you knew all this how dull for you if so, but if not, rather enjoyable.

Are you coming to London soon? I've got a lot to tell you – a long story about Prod & the Duchess of Kent.[6]

Love
    NR

[1] 10th Duke of Devonshire (1895–1950).
[2] Wife of the 9th Duke; her daughter Lady Dorothy married Harold Macmillan in 1920.
[3] Lys Lubbock.
[4] Sonia Brownell (1918–80). Disciple of Cyril Connolly at *Horizon* and the inspiration for Julia in George Orwell's *Nineteen Eighty-Four* (1949). Married the dying Orwell in 1949.
[5] Sir John Heygate (1903–76). Writer who ran off with Evelyn's first wife to whom he was married 1930–36. Evelyn characterised him as the worthless John Beaver in *A Handful of Dust* (1934).
[6] 'Got away in time to catch Nancy as her shop was closing and take her to tea at the Ritz. She was full of funny stories about Prod and the Duchess of Kent, Cyril, Dowager Duchess of Devonshire and *Brideshead*.' *Diaries of Evelyn Waugh*, p. 643.

13 April 1946   Hôtel de Bourgogne
                                                  7 rue de Bourgogne
                                                  Paris VII
Darling Evelyn
You were hell to go like that, everybody is furious, it was such fun with you here. Marie-Louise[1] does a wonderful turn on yr appearance at her house. 'He came in & just sat down & told us about Nuremberg & there we were, *at Nuremberg* – c'était génial.'[2] Everybody fearfully jealous of her for having got you there & the ones who omitted to go that day tearing out their hair! You can't think what a lion you are, such fearful waste.

I had my luncheon party & unlike most repeats it was great fun. Maurice [Bowra], Marie-Louise, Paz Subercaseaux,[3] the Col & a friend of the Col's called Prince de Chimay whom he utterly adores but who to everybody else seems utterly pointless. You know how nearly everyone has these pointless friends. When the Colonel came in & saw a bottle of champagne on the table he simply roared & said Vive la Littérature. He keeps saying me being rich is like something in a book. (I shan't be for long, I have committed some fearful follies.)

Last night I dined with Maurice at La Pérouse, a fearful tum-stretcher lasting from 7.30–11. Goodness I felt well this morning, overeating does *suit* me. And I'm glad to say there is a really wonderful bistro in this street where one can get an excellent blow out a bit cheaper. It's kept by one of those terrific French pansies. Maurice says he's certain he's got 6 children.

The Colonel is in his own flat – I wish you could see it you would be impressed. *The beauty!*

If ever you come back you must stay in this pub, it is ideal. I've never been in an hotel before where you can spend a whole afternoon without a sinking feeling of gloom – this is like being in one's own house & so pretty.

Dined at the Embassy on Thurs: Stephen Spender[4] – I suppose you hate him. He told me an awfully funny story about when Cyril was living with Jean & Diana Witherby[5] & caught them both out having affairs with other people & said to Steve, almost in tears, 'It *is* hard, here have I been absolutely faithful to 2 women for a year, they've *both* been unfaithful to me.'

Your friend Kaltenbrunner[6] seems to have had a bit of ragging I'm glad to see.

I've ordered a ball dress so please give a ball.

Why don't you come here when Laura has the baby instead of London? Oh DO.

Much love
Nancy

[1] Marie-Louise Valentin (1890–1977). Lively hostess who held a literary and artistic salon from the beginning of the First World War until shortly before her death. Married to the playwright Jacques Bousquet.
[2] 'It was brilliant.' Evelyn spent two days at Nuremberg observing the war crimes trials. Of his visit to Marie-Louise Bousquet he recorded in his diary: 'I was a fish out of water. They were all very flattering. Mostly buggers.' *Diaries of Evelyn Waugh*, p. 647.
[3] Paz Subercaseaux; a well-educated, cultivated Chilean who lived in London.
[4] Stephen Spender (1909–95). Poet, playwright and critic. Associate editor of *Horizon* 1939–41, co-editor of *Encounter* 1953–66. Evelyn deplored his left-wing politics, considered him a mediocre poet and lost no opportunity of attacking him. Knighted in 1983.
[5] Diana Witherby (1915–). Poet who worked for a time at *Horizon*.
[6] Ernst Kaltenbrunner (1903–46). Nazi Chief of Secret Police who was tried at Nuremberg and executed on 16 October 1946.

Maundy Thursday   Piers Court
[18 April] 1946   Stinchcombe

Darling Nancy

Paris was heaven but goodness it was exhausting. It so much overexcites me nowadays to meet new people that I cannot sleep after it. I should be neither genial nor génial after a second Thursday at Mme Bousquet's. I shall lie awake thinking of the adventuress who pouched the forks. As for the Colonel, he is never out of thoughts – the Beauty.

I should like very much to know more of Quennell. At five a.m. on my last morning he had a seizure brought on by sexual excess. Did he die of it?

I delivered the ribbon at Corporal Hill's & had a civil letter of thanks from Mrs Friese-Green. With Debo I was less successful. I went to her slum & found her door surrounded by unemptied dustbins, dead flowers & empty bottles; all windows shut; a telephone ringing unanswered upstairs – plainly the scene of a sex-murder so I went away, wrote to her (to the scene of the outrage) saying the hat[1] was at White's to be called for, but have heard nothing since.

The customs-men were most obliging. I had a big cargo by the time I left – millinery, champagne, cheese, scent, toys, etc. They said: 'Let's call it a fiver.'

I have put myself on a Belsen diet for Holy Week & feel alternately faint & furious.

All my children are here for the holidays – merry, affectionate, madly boring – except Harriet who has such an aversion to me that she screams when she catches sight of me a hundred yards away.

My garden is not at all like Sir Leicester Kroesig's[2] at the moment. Laura has bought a minute tractor, like a doll's pram, and has ploughed every available rood up to the windows in order to grow kale & mangolds. I run behind collecting bulbs in full flower as she turns them up. I have been elected chairman of the Parish Council. I have also been to a cocktail party where the smart hunting set were segregated from the dowdy village worthies in two rooms. Laura & I were put in the dowdy room in spite of the fantasies in her hair.

Love from
    Evelyn

[1] Evelyn had bought a hat for the Marchioness of Hartington which he tried on himself in the shop to see if it would suit.
[2] 'A lady water-colourist's heaven, herbaceous borders, rockeries and water-gardens were carried to a perfection of vulgarity, and flaunted a riot of huge and hideous flowers, each individual bloom appearing twice as large, three times as brilliant as it ought to have been and if possible of a different colour from that which nature intended.' *The Pursuit of Love* (Hamish Hamilton, 1945), p. 92.

Easter Day [21 April 1946]	Hôtel de Bourgogne, VII

Darling Evelyn

Peter Q didn't leave his bones here – I saw him long after you had left arm in arm with a sexy-looking English blonde in the Rue de Rivoli. Such a nice man.

Yes I'm glad you loved my darling Colonel – he adored you & Maurice, but doesn't approve of Maurice being a don. I've always thought it strange, myself. As for Marie-Louise she had a coup de foudre for Maurice & can talk of nothing else. I went to her jour on Thursday again but it was very homosexual, the guest of the day being a little Argentine monkey called Lopez[1] who keeps all the Paris buggers in the luxury to which they are accustomed & who has returned from running away in the war with a wife. She, poor thing, has chummed up in a big way with the wife of Étienne de Beaumont (Palamède).[2]

So Little Baby Randolph is arriving here. At luncheon today a Comtesse de Contades described, con spirito as they say in Victorian novels, how L.B.R. fell upon her after a dinner chez les Windsor. There was a look of scepticism on some faces, but not on mine. L.B.R. has sent on my home work – please have 4 articles ready for me – one on how the poor live, one on the collections, one on boîtes de nuit[3] & one on hostesses. It is a shame how I have to slave away while he no doubt will pass his time between boîtes de nuit & falling upon hostesses.

Laura must have been reading the papers, & what's more believing them. She must also be an optimist if she thinks she will get you to eat mangel wurzels – even washed down with champagne. Give her my love & give Harriet a hug if you can get near her. I've got her such a fascinating toy, at least I think it is. I do think it's waste for you all to live among worthies & wurzels instead of glittering away in Paris, with birds in your hair. I deplore it.

As for me, what am I to do. I never never want to go home again, & yet even Linda won't keep me here indefinitely & the Colonel hasn't got a cent & is living on old tins people have sent him from America – 'Ma chère, j'en ai assez du high grade'.[4] Isn't life difficult. At present, with Blomfield Road running full blast I certainly ought *not* to be here – & yet it's rather a drastic step to get rid of that.

Did you see the Spaniards demonstrated outside the Fr: Embassy 'Liberate Pétoit'.[5] The French all think it a terrifically good joke as indeed it is.

Have you read *Gigi* by Colette? I don't know if you like her books but feel they are made for you.

I spent today with 2 English 1 Pole 3 French 1 Russian & 1 Swede – at Violet Trefusis' house. Not for you, really.

Much love
    NR

[1] Arturo Lopez-Wilshaw (1900–62). Immensely rich and generous Chilean. Married his cousin Patricia Lopez de Huici.
[2] Comte Etienne de Beaumont (1883–1956). Patron of the arts and giver of legendary fancy-dress balls. Although a friend of Proust, he was not the model for Baron (Palamède) de Charlus in *A la Recherche* but appears as the hero of Raymond Radiguet's *Le Bal du comte d'Orgel* (1924). Married Edith de Taisne de Raymonval in 1907.
[3] Nightclubs.

[4] 'My dear, I've had enough of the high grade.' Palewski's American friends used to send him tins of high-grade pork to augment his rations.

[5] Dr Marcel Pétiot was sentenced to death for the murder of 27 people during the Occupation. He lured them to his house by promising safe conduct out of France, injected them with cyanide, dissolved their bodies in quicklime and burnt the remains in his stove.

6 June 1946   Hôtel de Bourgogne, VII

Dearest Evelyn

You owe me a letter – fiend! However I am seized with insomnia so I will overlook the fact.

The reason I am thus seized is that I went to a ball at Princess de Bourbon-Parme's, duly binged up as one is before balls with champagne, black coffee & so on. Well we hadn't been there 2 minutes before the Colonel said we couldn't stay on acc/ of the great cohorts of collaborators by whom we were surrounded, & firmly dumped me home. I perceive that I have made enemies for life of Pss Radziwill[1] who took me & Pss B-P because there was only one entrance over which they were both hovering.

I know you are rather pro-collaborators anyway & probably think the Col was being babyish. Anyway here I am wide-awake for hours. [. . .]

You wouldn't come back for a week? You could eat, drink, see Diana, see me – John Sutro – Harold[2] – not see Bébé[3] – Marie-Louise – see the Col. Evelyn *do*.

Randolph

Sexual instinct now canalized by young blonde called Mrs Harrison[4] greatly to the relief of several French comtesses I could name. Has taken said Mrs H. on honeymoon trip to Italy – back in a fortnight when you could see him too. You would very much have enjoyed a description he gave me of what happens to him if he goes to sleep in the afternoon. Wakes up sweating, wet through, retching, giddy – etc. He is awfully nice here, like everybody, though rather given to post-night-club telephoning.

I've been translating a film from French into Eng: for John,[5] which has enabled me to stay on greatly to my joy. Not very difficult as it was nothing but 'See, here come 2 officers' but very long – I didn't realize films were so long. I've sold mine to him all against your advice for £1000 & 5%. We shall see.

I long to live here but what would Prod live on? Isn't one's life complicated. But I can't stay here for ever & keep Blomfield at full blast & Prod installed with unrestricted use of telephone. Even Linda can't pay for that. I wish I could see my way ahead – of course there is the path of duty – but so thorny.

The people who are translating my book have just done A. A. Milne.

Evelyn now *do* come.

Love from
    NR

P.S. More wide awake than ever.
P.P.S. There is a nice man here (awfully nice to me) called Moans. Do you admit one might as well be called Groans? It's his Xian name, he's a Swede.[6]

---

[1] Princess Dolores (Dolly) Radziwill (1886–1966). She became one of Nancy's closest friends in Paris. Married to Mogens Tvede in 1932.
[2] Harold Acton (1904–94). Novelist, poet and historian. Contemporary of Evelyn at Oxford where he was the leading aesthete. Lived in Peking during the 1930s and after the war settled at his family home, La Pietra, near Florence. A lifelong friend of Nancy, he wrote her first biography: *Nancy Mitford: A Memoir* (1975).
[3] Christian (Bébé) Bérard (1902–49). Painter, stage designer, fashion and book illustrator. 'Pink and pudgy with melodramatic eyes, clad in soft velveteens and so strongly scented that you smelled his approach before seeing him, he suggested a bearded lady at the fair.' Harold Acton, *More Memoirs of an Aesthete* (Methuen, 1970), p. 159.
[4] Colette Thomas, ex-wife of the actor Rex Harrison.
[5] John Sutro had asked Nancy to translate the script for Turgenev's 'Torrents of Spring'. The film was never made.
[6] Mogens Tvede (1897–1977). In fact, a Dane. Architect and painter married to Princess Dolly Radziwill in 1932.

---

8 June [1946]   Piers Court
                                                       Stinchcombe

Darling Nancy

I am off to Spain[1] next week so will you please ask Prod & Picasso & Huxley[2] and all your bolshie chums to postpone their invasion until the second week in July when it will be all clear.

I suppose you will not come back to this country. You are very wise. The food gets drearier & drearier. Today the Government are staging the most extraordinary masquerade. Mr Attlee & Mr Chuter Ede[2] (they and no others of the Cabinet) are driving round London in a carriage borrowed from the King, representing themselves to the lower classes as the men who won the war. It seems an odd choice even for Mr Attlee as he could have found two or three colleagues who were at least doing some kind of work however mischievous. But no Attlee & Ede it is. Behind them follow a ramshackle troop of Brazilians, Mexicans, Egyptians (Egyptians!) Naafi waitresses etc. All the builders of the country have been taken away from building houses in order to erect grandstands & triumphal arches for this exhibition of vanity.

The Stinchcombe Parish Council under my chairmanship voted that no celebrations were to be held here.

I have been reading your Stanley letters again with intense delight. I think they should come out again soon. If you would like it I will

mention it at Chapman & Hall's. I rather favour an omnibus. Would
you be ready to write a new introduction. The last was topical and
subversive.

I long to hear about your American public. Are you greatly troubled
by admirers.

Do you want any money? I owe you I don't know how much for
Debo's hat. Shall I tell that tricky looking frog who publishes for me,
to make some cash over to you? Would you like all my francs? I don't
think there are many of them but you are welcome to what there are.
It must be a great expense keeping the colonel.

I went to Oxford for their Eights Weeks Debate & stayed with
Maurice in complete comfort. I should have thought my Union speech
a great success if I had not heard the previous speakers & seen the
audience falling off their benches with laughter at the most banal
jokes. Then they rolled about for me too but it was not so gratifying
as if I had been the only speaker & not known how easy technicians
are to amuse. They all treated me with great respect & tenderness as
a ghost from *Sinister Street*.[4] I liked *that* very much.

If Spender or Quennell do not blow me up I return from Spain in
July & set up at Hyde Park Hotel.

I went to London once to get my hair cut & hurried home aghast
at all I saw. I looked into your shop. There was a woman like an
elementary school teacher in your chair. Handycrafts tried to make
me pay 12 guineas for a book I had lately bought for 7/6. He has
quite lost his reason about prices. Nothing under a tenner & most of
his battered works £25 or £50.

Graham Greene[5] has gone to live in Kenya.

I have written a treatise on wine – very bad – for Vsevolode.
Maimie's nasty little dog was kidnapped & held to ransom. She paid
up.

Laura has bought another cow & two pigs.

It never stops raining.

Do you know a very nice war hero called Bill Deakin?[6]

Can you get rubber corsets in Paris, Laura asks. It is very important
to have them after having a baby. If they are procurable do send her
a pair by the next chap coming over. I will try in Salamanca but I
do not speak *any* Spanish so shopping will be difficult. Also my memory
is that Spanish shops are never open.

Your god daughter is wilfully backward & will not speak though
her face is alive with malevolent intelligence.

I think of you with compassion every Thursday at 6 p.m.[7] & with
envy all the rest of the week.

    Best love
      Evelyn

[1] To attend a conference in honour of Francisco de Vitoria, the 16th-century Dominican theologian and writer on international law. This tedious and uncomfortable visit inspired Evelyn's novella *Scott-King's Modern Europe* (1947).
[2] Julian Huxley (1887–1975). Zoologist and philosopher. First director-general of UNESCO in 1946. Knighted in 1958. Nancy had worked with his wife Juliette during the war in a canteen for interned French soldiers.
[3] Clement Attlee (1883–1967), Prime Minister 1945–51, and James Chuter Ede (1882–1965), Home Secretary 1945–51, were taking part in Victory Day Parade.
[4] By Compton Mackenzie (1913–14).
[5] Graham Greene (1904–91). Evelyn was at Oxford with the novelist but they became friends only later when conversion to Roman Catholicism and admiration for each other's books brought them close. Greene's best-known works of the 1940s include the novels *The Power and the Glory* (1940), *The Heart of the Matter* (1948) and the screenplay for *The Third Man* (1950).
[6] F. W. D. Deakin (1913–2005). Historian and literary assistant to Winston Churchill; led the first British Military Mission to Yugoslavia in May 1943. Warden of St Antony's College, Oxford, 1950–68. Knighted in 1975.
[7] When Marie-Louise Bousquet held her salon.

11 [June] 1946   Piers Court
                                                        Stinchcombe

Darling Nancy

Our letters crossed. [. . .]

If it is Mona Harrison Williams[1] Randolph has eloped with, that is old stuff.

Collaborationists my foot. Does it not occur to you, poor innocent, that that continental colonel went back to the aristocratic ball & that while you lay sleepless with your fountain pen, he was in the arms of some well born gestapo moll?

Father D'Arcy[2] has written a rival treatise to yours on love. It is very much harder to understand.

I have guests coming for the night and am thrown into agitation by it & keep trotting up to their room to see if it is still all right.

God I wish I had some neighbours I could bear to speak to. There must be plenty in this populous countryside but they never come our way.

Love from
    Evelyn

[1] Mona Travis Strader (1897–1983). Elegant American beauty. After two marriages to wealthy American businessmen, she acquired a fortune by marrying Harrison Williams, one of the richest men in America, and then a title by marrying Count Edward von Bismarck. In 1971 she settled for an Italian doctor, Umberto de Martini.
[2] Father Martin D'Arcy (1888–1976). Worldly Jesuit priest who instructed Evelyn on his conversion to Roman Catholicism in 1930. Master of Campion Hall, Oxford, 1932–45. In 1945 he published *The Mind and Heart of Love: A Study in Eros and Agape*.

7 August [1946]   Hyde Park Hotel
                                              Knightsbridge
                                              London, SW1

Darling Nancy

My last day in London & goodness I am pleased. Without you at
Heywood Hill's my days have been empty. It is six weeks now I have
been sitting about in hotels & clubs bored bored bored.

Last week was made hideous by the arrival of a Hungarian countess
who pretended to be a French poet.[1] An egocentric maniac with the
eyes of a witch. All the ladies fell at her feet to be hobbled over. I
understood it in tender creatures like Diana [Cooper] & Miss Capel[2]
but when I found stout old hearts like Venetia's[3] & Daphne [Wey-
mouth]'s bleeding, dripping oozing, I felt sick to the stomach. She is
the Spirit of France. How I hate the French. They are sending us
Camembert cheese made of UNRRA dried milk. It turns to chalk &
moss instead of melting. Also they are deliberately destroying all the
Rhine vineyards. They have even stopped doing the one thing they
are good at – making wine – and mix it all up in milk churns & send
it to us labelled 'Burgundy' & 'Claret', quite simply. Down with the
beastly French. At least you have had the better taste to choose a
Pole. [. . .]

I have given a series of champagne parties hoping to make some
nice new friends – old cronies turned up with gratifying regularity but
no one new.

Debo has disappeared from my life & heart.

I sent you my second barrel at Smarty boots.[4] I think I shook
out a few feathers. His stock is *very* low even in the Dorchester
Hotel.

Randy has been roaring round insulting Lords Kemsley, Camrose
& Rothermere.[5]

I am rather keen on Miss Capel.

I went to a circus entirely run by half-witted boys. Such a good
idea. They get on far better with the animals than sane people &
tumble about as clowns with great seriousness.

Is the Heath case[6] reported in France. It has been a very clever
move by the socialist government to take the housewife's mind off her
troubles. Just as the French (Bah!) did with Landru[7] at the time of the
massacre at Smyrna. Strachey[8] & Co got two loyal socialist girls &
carved them up in the most imaginative way & are trying an airman
who is the dead spit of Beverley Nichols[9] for murder. No one now
mentions bread rationing or Palestine.

Very sad & shocking about Diane.[10]

Maimie was burgled last night & lost 48 bottles of Pol Roger, 6
whiskey and a gold cigarette case.

I went with Harry[11] to the Marx brothers. He fell fast asleep as he sat down & snored until we had to go. He said he found the film disappointing.

Not legible?

Best love
Evelyn

[1] Louise (Lulu) de Vilmorin (1906–69). Minor poet and novelist, but great seductress. Her many lovers included Duff Cooper and André Malraux. Married to Henry Leigh Hunt 1925–37 and to Count Palffy 1938–43.
[2] June Capel (1920–2006). Married to the pianist Franz Osborn in 1948, widowed in 1954; courted by Cecil Beaton and married in 1966 to Jeremy Hutchinson (later Baron Hutchinson of Lullington).
[3] Hon. Venetia Stanley (1887–1948). Confidante of the Prime Minister H. H. Asquith. Married Hon. Edwin Montagu in 1915.
[4] 'Palinurus in Never-Never Land Or, The Horizon Blue-Print of Chaos', *Tablet*, 27 July 1946. Evelyn's withering response to an article in the June issue of *Horizon* in which Cyril Connolly had set out his ground plans for a 'civilized' community.
[5] Proprietors of the *Sunday Times*, *Daily Telegraph* and *Daily Mail*, respectively.
[6] The trial of Neville Heath, a former pilot, accused of the murder of two women. He was found guilty and executed on 16 September 1946.
[7] Serial killer executed in 1922 for murdering eleven people whose bodies he disposed of in his kitchen stove.
[8] John Strachey (1901–63). Unpopular Minister of Food at a time when rationing was still in force.
[9] Beverley Nichols (1898–1983). Composer, playwright and journalist. Author of *Down the Garden Path* (1932) and *Thatched Roof* (1933). 'A mercenary, hypochondriacal, flibbertigibbet who doesn't take in one of six words addressed to him – but civil to old ladies.' *Diaries of Evelyn Waugh*, p. 566.
[10] Lady Diana Abdy had been caught smuggling her jewellery from France into England.
[11] Lord Stavordale (1905–64). Brother officer with Evelyn in No. 8 Commando. Married Helen Ward in 1931. Succeeded as 7th Earl of Ilchester in 1959.

9 August 1946   Hotel de Bourgogne, VII

Darling Evelyn

Oh how glad I am you feel like this about Lulu – I can't sit in a room with her she makes me so nervous. And vicious – why she even shocked Romie[1] with her suggestions for a happy evening once. She is much more like a middle European than a French woman & the proof is that before, & some say during, the war she lived for preference in Berlin.

I will tell you now about the French, after 4 months of study I have come to certain conclusions. The French upper classes are very dull indeed or else very vicious. I don't see one person I should like to be great friends with. The dull ones are worse than Pont St & the vicious ones think such as me a standoffish prig. In any case none of them count in the life of the country they are a sort of side line. But the middle class intellectuals are absolutely delightful & have no equivalent that I can see in England. I mean all the people on the fringes of literature, booksellers, translators, publishers & so on – I don't know

any of the important writers – but I have great friends now among
the ones I describe & absolutely *love* their company & have the greatest
regard for them as human beings. Then servants, shop people etc etc
are far nicer to one than in England, so friendly & anxious to please,
& say hullo if you see them in the street as though it was a village. In
fact all those relationships are more like those of the English countryside when I was a child & before it became full of deck chairs. A
waitress from a restaurant I go to stopped me in the street & said 'you
never come now – & where is the fat gentleman (Randy)'. Imagine in
London –! Another thing. English servants, if you lie on your bed all
day reading a book, or just lying, give great furious sniffs & clearly
regard you as a disgusting rotter. The French, even the maids in an
hotel, regard reading & thinking as highly honourable occupations.

I know now I couldn't bear to live anywhere else. The country
bores me you see, & London is a factory more than a town, & so so
ugly & I live a great deal by my eyes. Also I like to be warm. But
there's no doubt I shall find that friends like you & Gerald [Berners]
are irreplaceable, for the reasons I have mentioned. So you must
sometimes come & stay – it's not as though one had retired to the
South Pole.

I adored your renewed Boots-bait. Mr Cockburn,[2] who is in this
hotel, is also delighted as he says it all spurs on idle old Boots to be
keener on the Party.

Are you a Garth addict?[3] (*Daily Mirror*) If so tell me as I've found
Garth in French & will send, it's utter bliss.

Have you read *La Princesse de Clèves*?[4] She might take the taste of
Lulu out of your mouth. [. . .]

[incomplete]

[1] Rosemary (Romie) Hope-Vere (1907–90). Friend from Nancy's youth. Married to John
Drury-Lowe 1930–32, to Quintin Gilbey 1933–42 and to Sir Roderic Brinckman in 1943.
[2] Claud Cockburn (1904–81). Author and journalist. Founder and editor of the Communist
paper *The Week*, 1933–46; contributor to *Private Eye* 1963–81. A cousin of Evelyn.
[3] Strip-cartoon hero.
[4] By Mme de La Fayette (1678). Translated by Nancy in 1950. 'I like fact better than fiction
and I like almost anything that makes me laugh. But my favourite book falls into neither of
these categories: it is *La Princesse de Clèves*.' *The Times*, 20 November 1961.

14 August [1946]   Piers Court
                                                     Stinchcombe

Darling Nancy

It is heavenly of you to ask me to stay but alas! I cannot accept. I
have come home to the responsibilities of family life, am teaching my
ignorant & slothful son English history & am writing the history of
Saccone & Speed wine merchants which requires constant trips to
London & in fact can't get away. How I wish I could.

I am also buying another house – a large, early Victorian building surrounded by 160 acres of woods in the Blackdown Hills near Taunton, and selling this little house which I love dearly but which is becoming suburban & cramped. I shall be entirely ruined by the transaction as it will cost about £2000 in carpets alone; it is full of miles of deal passages & staircases. I shall also have to get tons of mahogany & acres of oil paintings. So I shall have to write a great number of books in the next six months. There is a fine stretch of heather for Laura to plough up. The whole project is stark crazy. [. . .]

What precisely did Baroness Palffy propose to Mrs Drury-Lowe, and when? If you cannot write it in English or Latin pray do so in French & I will rush to Cassell's dictionary.

The French, historically & artistically, have been the destroyers of Europe for 200 years. The only thing they are fit for is to grow wine & that they seem to have stopped doing. They produce saints. But it is a measure of French civilization that for 150 years or more the only great French men & women have been found in convents.

I have just read in a painful translation Aragon's *Aurélien*[1] with great enjoyment.

Quennell seems to me to qualify completely as 'a middle class intellectual on the fringes of literature' so does Lady Colefax[2] & Corporal H. Hill. Why do you say we have none in England? If that is what you want, come home & face the regime you worked so arduously to establish. Also if you want to be stopped in the street by impertinent enquiries from waitresses I am sure you could find plenty of that in the new housing estates. One of the few remaining good qualities about the English is their respect for privacy but that is going fast. All you need do is wear flannel trousers & a turban and you will find yourself with a host of chatty bores.

Damn the French. I bet my cousin Claud is up to no good. He is the product of a high minded sceptic as a father. I was led to believe the Hotel de Bourgogne was a nest of Gaullists.

Think of those two skinny creatures Quennell & his moll, *slapping one another all night* as I am told they do. Gruesome.

Tell me your opinion of Miss Capel.

20,000 is a very good sale in U.S.A. considering that you would not rewrite the middle section of your book as Conscience directed.

I was enormously gratified to hear that the only comment Baroness Palffy would make on me was 'intimidant'.

Liz[3] has become a scold & will become a shrew soon. I have a horrible feeling that Quennell is waiting for her round the corner.

Did I tell you the very alarming fact that H. Acton has written his memoirs. It is like the Honble Freddie Threepwood.[4] When I asked him what he had said about me he answered: 'Well, my dear, it is

mainly directed against Connolly.' That man knows far too much about
my extreme youth.[5]

    Best love
        Evelyn

[1] By Louis Aragon (1945).
[2] Sibyl Halsey (1874–1950). Active society hostess who married Sir Arthur Colefax in 1901.
Co-founder of the decorating firm Colefax and Fowler.
[3] Lady Elizabeth Paget (1916–80). Married Raimund von Hofmannsthal in 1939.
[4] Lord Emsworth's goofy younger son in P. G. Wodehouse's novels; the memoirs, however,
were written by Lord Emsworth's brother, the Hon. Galahad Threepwood.
[5] '[Evelyn] pretended to dread the appearance of my *Memoirs* . . . Evidently he anticipated
some shaft of malice, though he was the last person I should have wished to offend. When
the book appeared he wrote me a characteristically generous letter and our friendship remained
unshaken until his death.' Acton, *More Memoirs of an Aesthete*, p. 226.

18 August 1946   Le Mé Chaplin[1]
                                                        Jouy en Josas
                                                        S et O

Darling Evelyn
    You *are* good to write when you have so much work on hand.
    Question time first.
    1. Countess Palffy. Romie was taken by Hamish [Erskine] to stay
with her in Austria. After dinner the girls went off to Lulu's bed-room
to have a hair brush talk & maybe a little more as Romie at that time
was a roaring Liz. Presently in comes Palffy, says 'this is just what I
like, 2 pretty women. Get into bed girls, & we'll have a ménage à
trois.' Romie had never heard of such a thing, was utterly appalled
& flew to Hamish's room saying we must leave at once, now, I can't
stay here another moment.
    Hamish crossly told her not to be so middle class, but she insisted
on spending the night on the sofa in his room & on leaving before
breakfast the next day.
    You might use this for Saint Helena – the saint with a horse & a
mule or something.
    2. Miss Capel. I scarcely know her but am disposed to like her.
From the fact that she is a friend of Debo & Andrew I assume she is
rather dull, but I may be quite wrong?
    3. Harold's autobiography. I do know that Osbert took Harold for
a walk in Florence & said 'You know, Harold, Evelyn is very fond of
you & I'm afraid he won't like what you've said about him.' But then,
my dear Evelyn, think what many have endured uncomplainingly
from you, & not least darling Harold himself. I don't think you have
much of a come-back there. *Think* of your inhumanity to poor Boots
who is *very* fond of *you*.
    4. Your cousin Claud is supposed to be at the Peace Conference

but actually he sits all day in his room typing. It reminds me how Peter used to say When Nancy is editing letters she sits out in the garden with a pad on her knee, writing very fast. *Utterly* untrue –!

Middle class people on the fringes – Hill & Colefax. Agreed, but they are not fascinating, they don't give one heavenly long meals & then sit till 4 in the morning talking about a literature which they really know & love, & they don't *love* ONE & give cries of joy when they see one or say what a pretty hat one has got. In short *I like* the human race, & I long to be liked back, & here I am liked back. See –?

An uncle of mine I saw yesterday has a friend who knew one of Heath's victims (was she called Marjorie?) Anyway he told my uncle 'oh yes, poor old Marge, she always did enjoy a good hiding –'

Still I suppose there are hidings *and* hidings so to speak. Diana [Mosley] says 'shall we be 2 of the not-so-young women who fight their way into the court room.'

Think of the papers next day!

Your godson is coming to stay with me for the Christmas holidays. I can have Harriet can't I when older.

I wish I had a pretty writing like yours, your letters are a pleasure to see though sometimes a puzzle – I always decipher them in the end.

I've seen a lot of your Diana [Cooper] lately. She invites me by fits & starts, but she is always my heroine & I love & admire her beyond words.

Stop damning the French, they are all the things you like & you know it.

Love from
   NR

P.S. [. . .] Do you know about the Abbé Bremond?[2] He was my Colonel's godfather & the Col always has a photograph of him by his bed, & (as you know the Col is a great hero worshipper) he seems to be on the same level as Lyautey[3] & Gen de G.[4]

[1] Nancy was staying with Alvilde Chaplin at her house outside Paris.
[2] Henri Bremond (1865–1933). Author of *Histoire littéraire du sentiment religieux en France* (1916–32).
[3] Marshal Lyautey (1854–1934). Palewski acted as his political adviser 1924–5.
[4] Charles de Gaulle (1890–1970). He had resigned as President on 20 January 1946 and remained out of office until June 1958.

21 August 1946   Le Mé Chaplin

Darling Evelyn

Don't dream of answering – I know too well the burden of one extra word. I've been alone 2 days (so good for me) & have thought of things to say.

First – will you sometime explain about saints. You say the French are the lowest of the low – they do however produce saints. Can it be that you really think a saint is about on the same level of humanity as those idiot girls who materialize poltergeists? You'll give me an answer I can't understand, as you did about Sebastian's mother, no doubt. *I* revere saints –

You should read Brogan's latest book[1] if only for the essay – far far too short – on Proust. But I think you'd enjoy many of them, by no means all. It's a pity he hasn't your style, or you haven't his ideas – that to me would be perfection. The Colonel brought 2 of Oriane (Mme Greffulhe)'s[2] nephews to dinner last night – skilled workmen out of a job exactly describes them,[3] specially the Noailles one. I told them this comment of Brogan's but it didn't go down very well.

I sent 'Never-Never' (it was a wrench but I know it by heart) to Jonathan as Diana tells me all Eton boys live for *Horizon*. Just as you say about soldiers no doubt.[4]

I wish you were here. The food is utterly delicious, all cooked in butter, & *such* meat that has never seen a frigidaire, I'd forgotten the taste. I go for huge walks, see beautiful dream houses to buy & have seldom been more contented. Only I must write another book, to support life, & can't think of one. Trollope's *Autobiography* is too much to bear – how *could* he write all those hours every day?

Of course the French send us poor stuff – for one thing we won't pay for the better & then they are convinced we *like* it. As we accept it & seem enchanted I don't see what's to contradict the idea? In *no* sphere does a buyer who insists on cheap & nasty get anything else. Admit.

I hear Portia Lady Stanley[5] has been nabbed getting black market money & is to appear at Bow St – also that there is to be a round-up of everybody who has written cheques abroad. Bow St will have a delightfully Ritz bar aspect that day, won't it.

I repeat about not answering – the question about saints can wait, I know I shan't understand what you mean when you have told me. But if you revere saints, which you clearly don't, one wld expect you to revere the country which produces them. By the way, what saints? I can only think of the Little Flower beneath the Foot –[6]

Much love
NR

What is your new boy[7] called? New boy is just about right – it is a school now isn't it –
Mrs Chichester[8] & Lady Dashwood[9] are descending, goodbye to all reading (I *promise* they wouldn't have been allowed to if you'd come).

[1] Denis Brogan, *French Personalities and Problems* (1946).
[2] Elisabeth de Caraman-Chimay (1860–1952). Beautiful Parisian hostess who was one of the

models for both the Duchesse and the Princesse de Guermantes in Proust's novel. Married Comte Henri Greffulhe in 1878.

[3] Brogan compared the Duc de Guermantes to 'a skilled workman unable to practise his trade', as he helped a *roturier* on with his coat 'with a skill intended by heredity and training to be used on a royal shirt'.

[4] Evelyn had written that *Horizon* 'came to represent to countless soldiers the world of culture which they had left'.

[5] Hon. Sybil Cadogan (1893–1969). Married Lord Stanley (son of the Earl of Derby) in 1917. She was fined £2,500 for contravening currency regulations.

[6] Saint Teresa of Lisieux.

[7] James Waugh (1946–). Evelyn's fifth child was born on 30 June.

[8] Pamela Peel (1900–62). Married to Charles Chichester 1924–8 and to John Wrench in 1934.

[9] Helen Eaton (1899–1989). Married Sir John Dashwood in 1922.

26 August [1946]   Piers Court
                                                                   Stinchcombe

Darling Nancy

Of course I revere saints. I mentioned them not as a further cause of complaint but as the one good thing about the frogs. But the saints, you see, are the opposite of modern French culture & they find it almost impossible to lead normal lives with their fellow countrymen, they have to go into convents or be missionaries. The French are absolutely splendid missionaries.

They are not 'low' in the way Hindus & Egyptians & most Americans are. They are an ingenious & discriminating people who have deliberately chosen the evil way. It comes out in everything they have done for centuries. One typical manifestation is their giving up everything that is meant by Chivalry – which was originally their invention. But of course when they are touched by Grace they are all the nobler for the qualities that make them so very vile in their corruption.

Saints are people who have a peculiar intimacy with God and as a result give evidence of sublime virtues and usually of miraculous powers. You can never understand them unless you start with God, then go to man as his creation – a special order of being with unique limitations, opportunities & obligations. Saints are simply men & women who have fulfilled their natural obligation which is to approach God. It is in that that all mankind has a different nature from the rest of the animal kingdom.

There is no such thing as a 'religious temperament' or a 'religious type'. Saints are as different from one another as it is possible for humans to be. St Thomas More, Bernadette, John of the Cross, etc. all wildly different. But some nations, probably in providence because of their greater spiritual dangers, tend to produce more saints than others. U.S.A. have not produced one except an Italian-born immigrant. France hundreds, of all types. It is to make up for the Zolas & Gambettas & Martys[1] & Picassos. By the way a league has been formed 'to counteract the evil influence of French painting'. Headquarters suitably at Kelmscott Manor.[2] I have joined you bet. It is called 'Rhodian'. Why? [. . .]

———

I have just come back from a week-end at Pamela Berry's.[3] Very luxurious. Betjeman[4] came over & read poetry. Most enjoyable. I went to call on Peter Fleming[5] who lives next door. Too extraordinary. He is very rich and has built himself the most hideous little Golders Green villa. He farms 2000 acres & never has an egg or a pat of butter & lives on rations from the local Cooperative Stores. He dresses in khaki shorts & military shirt. His wife has had to leave the stage because they have no cook.

The Betjemans both put on Jaeger combinations on the 1st of September & keep them on for all purposes until the 2nd week of May. A horse sleeps in the kitchen.

———

What is a Mé. Can't find it in Cassell's dictionary.

———

Pam has May, Bryan & Diana's old parlour maid, who was seduced & had a baby, did you know?

———

Daisy F[ellowes] is said to have taught Gerald B[erners] to take cocaine.

———

Deauville is full of stranded chums who can't cash a cheque to get home. [. . .]

———

The price of the vile French wine they send us is 3 times what good wine was in 1939. We all *hate* it. The Camembert cheeses, are all made of chalk & never ripen do what one will to them. No one here thinks them delicious but they are one better than Woolton-Strachey's 'Processed'.

———

There is a better Brogan than yours. Colm.[6] A brother?

———

        Love from
        Evelyn

[1] The anti-Catholic writer Emile Zola (1840–1902), the Republican politician Léon Gambetta (1838–82) and the Communist leader André Marty (1896–1956).
[2] Oxfordshire house where the artist William Morris lived from 1871 until his death in 1896.
[3] Lady Pamela Smith (1914–82). She and her husband, Hon. Michael Berry (created Lord Hartwell 1968), had a country house at Kidmore End near Reading. See Biographical Notes.
[4] John Betjeman (1906–84). His fourth volume of poetry, *New Bats in Old Belfries*, had been published the previous December. Married to Hon. Penelope Chetwode 1933. Knighted in 1969. Poet Laureate 1972.

[5] Peter Fleming (1907–71). Writer and traveller. Married the actress Celia Johnson in 1935. After the war he settled down to the life of a country squire at Merrimoles, the house he had built at Nettlebed in Oxfordshire. His grandfather made a fortune in the City but, owing to a muddle over his will, Fleming inherited nothing and lived off the money he earned as a writer.

[6] Colm Brogan (1902–77). Journalist and teacher. Younger brother of Sir Denis Brogan. Editor of *Round the World*, a magazine of current events, 1945–6. His publications include *Who Are the People?* (1943) and *The Nature of Education* (1962).

16 October [1946]   Piers Court
                                                            Stinchcombe

Darling Nancy

It was indeed a bitter disappointment to us both to learn that we shall not see you. My only consolation is that my water supply failed last night so that your visit would not have been comfortable.

I must beg you with all earnestness if we are to continue friends, never use the word 'progressive' in writing to me. It upsets me more than 'note paper' upset your fastidious father. It makes me sick and agitated for hours to read it. Please please never again.

There was so much I wanted to talk about & was keeping for your visit. Now 'progressive' has dried up all my sympathy. I could have spoken with feeling about Debo's future love life.

I do not know your friend R. Mortimer. I understand he is like a wild beast but I don't think we can object to having our novels labelled historical. After all they are very literally dated.

I foresee great professional difficulties for you. You have used your two great plots – Farve & Fabrice. You have set yourself up in a style of life which only continuous success can support. You have isolated yourself among cosmopolitan riff-raff from the sufferings of your fellow countrymen. What will you write about unless you make yourself a historical writer of the 20s? You might perhaps start a genre of *San-Michele–Elizabeth-and-her G. Garden*[1] about exile in Paris. But you must drop that dirty word 'progressive' if you are to do that. How I wish you were back in Curzon Street. No one's departure has left such a yawning (literally) hole in London as yours.

I am anxious to emigrate, Laura to remain & face the century of the common man. She is younger, braver & less imaginative than I. If only they would start blowing the place up with their atoms.

My lecture at Bristol was hell – to graduates of the University on book collecting. A Catholic assembly. I accepted as an act of piety. The secretary said he would call for me at 6.45 and drive me there. Would you not have supposed that such an invitation included some sort of meal? I met him with a keen appetite from having dug all day. 'What time is our meeting?' '7.30. Plenty of time.' So I lectured & a lot of Catholic ladies came & shook my hand trembling with hunger. Then he drove me back, arriving here at 10.30 with not so much as a bun or a cup of coffee. He was a perfectly civil, cultured young man. It is just that those who have grown up since 1939 have lost all idea of hospitality.

When you get back to Paris do write me a full account of all you have seen in England. Boots?

I go to Eton at John Julius's[2] insistence to lecture to the Literary Society. Perhaps I shall see Jonathan [Guinness]. What is the news from him.

Did you hear any complaints of my behaviour at Debo's ball?

How delighted the people in the Dorchester must have been to have that revolting cook & those insolent waiters on strike. Hyde Park remained loyal.

I am writing a dreary short story about Spain.[3]

Harriet had been shown her tea-pot for the first time in preparation for your coming & was overjoyed with it. Played with it continually. Now it has been taken away again & put in a drawer in tissue paper until your next visit. It is a comfort to think she will never be too old to enjoy it.

Is it not odd how Poppy[4] goes to *all* funerals?

I am tempted to come to Paris after Christmas. Is it easy? Can one just go to Victoria & get in a train? I think I shall go to California in February. I am bored here by lack of company. If only country neighbours would talk like Jane Austen's characters about gossip & hobbies. Instead they all want to know about Molotov & de Gaulle.

What has become of Prod?

Do write me a long informative letter. I know you can't do it in London but from Paris yes?

Love
    Evelyn

[1] *The Story of San Michele* (1930) by Axel Munthe, a Swede who settled in Capri, and *Elizabeth and her German Garden* (1898) by Elizabeth von Arnim, who was born in Australia, brought up in England and married to a German.
[2] John Julius Cooper (1929–). Writer and broadcaster. Only son of Duff and Lady Diana Cooper. Later 2nd Viscount Norwich.
[3] *Scott-King's Modern Europe.*
[4] Poppy Baring (1901–79). Married to the wine merchant Peter Thursby in 1928.

21 October 1946   Hôtel de Bourgogne, VII
                                   after 26th: 20 rue Bonaparte
                                   Paris VI
Darling Evelyn

I don't understand about progressive, it's a word I never use (I thought) & indeed it took me ½ an hour of poring over your letter to make out what this dreadful word might be. Because reading your letters with me is a sort of water beetle performance & if I ever stopped to think of how I do it I should sink. Well progressive sunk me for quite a while.

Oh good oh good I see you are coming here again, that is good news.

You would have enjoyed *Lakmé*,[1] an opera, which I went to last night. It's all about the British Raj in India & there is a character called l'Honorable Mrs Tenterdon who sings in an English accent.

Yes it is dreadful how I've now got a taste for money & *specially spending* it which is worse (I mean if I was merely a miser it wouldn't matter so much). Also *you* see what nobody else seems to that having used up Farve & Fabrice I am utterly done for – all the rations have gone into one cake. Now what? A life of somebody perhaps, but would I have the application – not living here I'm afraid. Well, when I am ruined I could go to the island & do some solid work, but then I should come back here & find all situations altered for the worse.[2] Yes it is a puzzle. But I can go on like this for another 2 years & by then the atom may be at work, who knows?

No complaints of your behaviour at Debo's ball. I went to get a trinket for Harriet & got myself a pearl necklace instead which she can have when 18. Was that mean? So I sent her a book as a token instead. I thought I might as well benefit while I'm fairly pretty still & that she'll like it better than the kind which would be suitable for a child & which she would hardly ever wear really, in the country.

In London I saw nobody except Raymond M. because the 4 days I was there were taken up with relations, old nannies & so on – you know.

I hope you'll see Jonathan at Eton, but anyway you'll see him here if you come in the Christmas hols as he's coming for the whole of them – I long for it.

Prod is off to Abyssinia for 6 months at £130 a week, to make a documentary film for Rank, clever little fellow.

Do give Harriet her tea pot for good, it was only meant to be a toy.

Diana C is away which is sad. Ran Antrim[3] is in love with Lulu [de Vilmorin] poor him. 'It's so romantic' he kept saying 'she grows wheat'. I forbore to point out that all my relations grow wheat, the ones that don't grow oats at least, & nobody thinks it at all romantic.

Today I bought a hat a suit 2 pairs of shoes & a bag I am tired but happy. In fact I am so happy that I long for every hour to become 2 & every day to last for ever.

The French are in fits about le petit ménage Windsor who left saying France is on the verge of communism & they must put their jewels in a safe place.

Adelaide[4] & Bridget[5] arrive next week, B to stay with me, also

Dearest. I utterly long for your visit – Maurice I believe is coming
again too.

    Much love
       NR

[1] By Léo Delibes (1883).
[2] Palewski's incessant womanising made Nancy reluctant ever to leave Paris.
[3] 13th Earl of Antrim (1911–77). Chairman of the National Trust 1965–77. Married to Angela
Sykes in 1934.
[4] Hon. Adelaide Stanley (1906–81). Sister of Edward Stanley and a girlfriend of Peter Rodd
for many years. Married Hon. Maurice Lubbock in 1926.
[5] Lady Bridget Parsons (1907–72). Beautiful daughter of the 5th Earl of Rosse.

24 October [1946]   Piers Court
                                                     Stinchcombe
Darling Nancy,
    It was charming of you to send Harriet the Walter Crane. She was
allowed a few minutes fascinated glimpse of it before it disappeared
into my library. She may be allowed to look at it again on Christmas
day – also the tea pot. At present she has two oyster shells which she
bangs together in the stable yard for hours at a time in apparent
contentment.
    You used the accursed word 'prog' in connexion with Farve. The
fact that you forget it convicts you of using it naturally. It is like the
beasts who still write to *The Times* newspaper 'In these enlightened
days . . .' Can I say nothing to convey to you the contempt & loathing
with which we English regard absentees like you and Prod who stir
up class war and then bolt from the consequences of your frivolity
and vice? I think of abjuring the realm & becoming Irish. Do you
know anything of Gormanston Castle Co. Meath now for sale? Seat
of Lord G., 20 miles from Dublin, near the sea. It is advertised as
having 'Ballroom unfinished' which might be exquisitely romantic. I
am going over to see it soon & perhaps buy it.
    It is really too disgusting about Ran – a man I love & respect.
Daphne [Weymouth] rocks about crooning 'Her mother was called
Melanie'. Does Bridget know Lulu? I should think *that* acid might
expose the base metal.
    Your literary future is insoluble I think. You see even the most
bookish & meditative minds, like A. Huxley's,[1] decay in exile. He
never wrote a good novel after *Antic Hay*. You are so topical and on
the spot & so radically English that you must feed on a fresh English
diet. As an English observer thinking foreigners absurd you might be
able to write about them. As a cosmopolitan you are lost. But I am
relieved & delighted to hear that you can support yourself & Fabrice
for another 2 years. I imagined he had swiped the whole kitty already.

As you say in 2 years anything may happen. You may well return to us like the Bolter[2] babbling the jargon of the 30s. 'Progressive. Antisocial. Fascist. Workers. Dear Mr Gollancz.[3] Munich. Picasso.' You will be very welcome.

I think an insuperable difficulty of your writing a book about the French is the conversational language. Do you write idiomatic English and so make the characters English despite yourself or translate Gallicisms literally with scattered italic phrases? Henry James did the latter. So did the Parisian diarist in the *Bystander* in the 20s. I simply don't believe it is possible.

Next week I am 43. I have minded no birthday since my thirtieth. Now I strain forward to senility.

I think you have a possible theme for another historical novel in the Strand-on-the-Green world of Basil[4] & Ankaret[5] & Sieps[6] etc. but I do not think it would be popular at the moment. Avoid at all costs 'Britain can take it' and memories of how matey you were with the lower classes at the warden's post.

I have two shots in my locker left. My war novel and my autobiography. I suppose they will see me out.

I go to the Cinema 4 times a week. I suppose I have seen more bad films than any living man in the last six months. I forget them like dreams the moment I leave the building.

Patrick Balfour[7] is coming to stay to Laura's horror.

My love to Bridget & my regards to Mrs Lubbock.

Love from
    Evelyn

[1] Aldous Huxley (1894–1963). The novelist lived in Italy and France during the 1920s and 30s, before moving to California in 1937. *Those Barren Leaves* (1925), *Point Counter Point* (1928), *Brave New World* (1932) and *Eyeless in Gaza* (1936) were all published after *Antic Hay* (1923).

[2] A character in *The Pursuit of Love* based on Lady Idina Sackville (1893–1955), who was married to Euan Wallace 1913–19, to Charles Gordon 1919–23, to 22nd Earl of Erroll 1923–30, to Donald Haldeman 1930–38 and to Vincent Soltau 1939–46.

[3] Victor Gollancz (1893–1967). Publisher and writer. Founded the Left Book Club in 1936 to combat Fascism and Nazism.

[4] Basil Murray (1902–37). Rebellious son of Gilbert Murray, Regius Professor of Greek at Oxford. Journalist and author of a biography of Lloyd George whose secretary he was. Evelyn described him as 'satanic' and drew on him for the character of Basil Seal. Married Pauline Newton in 1927.

[5] Lady Ankaret Howard (1900–45). A first cousin of Basil Murray, who married William Jackson in 1927. They owned Rose Cottage at Strand-on-the-Green, Chiswick, where Nancy lived for three years after her marriage.

[6] Eric Siepmann; political journalist and a crony of Peter Rodd.

[7] Hon. Patrick Balfour (1904–76). Contemporary of Evelyn at Oxford. Journalist and author. His job as gossip columnist for the *Sunday Dispatch* and the *Daily Sketch* before the war inspired the character of the Earl of Balcairn in *Vile Bodies*. Succeeded as 3rd Baron Kinross in 1939.

31 October 1946   20 rue Bonaparte, VI

Darling Evelyn

All that you say is true, specially about the difficulties of dialogue.
But if you think Lulu isn't providing me with ideas of great value think
again. Only of course I should have to wait until the Duffs[1] have either
gone or have died or have quarrelled with the daughter of Madame.
The other shot in *my* locker is my book called The Ambassadress
which can be written when my ma in law[2] has kicked the bucket.

You may like to hear that one of Lulu's brothers turned up at
Philippe de Rothschild's when Peter was there, to sell some vine shoots,
& was given his luncheon in the servants' hall. You may also like to
hear that when I was young I once sat next to an old Frenchman at
dinner who said 'Always remember, my dear young lady, that *all*
Lesseps & *all* Vilmorins are DULL'. Lulu told Ran that she is 34 –
this has given *me* ideas.

Of course Bridget utterly dies to meet her but she is having the
cancer carved out of her lung as usual & seems not to be around.

You don't understand about Fabrice – he is penniless but proud &
won't allow me to pay for anything so that when we dine together I
dine alone at a restaurant & he eats what he calls Le high grade out
of some awful tin at home. It is a great great bore I can tell you, &
not what I am accustomed to from gentlemen, as you know. But
cheaper in the end, of course.

Next month I am 42 (Many happy returns by the way). I don't
care, I am settled in life now, & anyway for a woman 30 is the rubicond
(or rubicon? Pity not to be educated, & it comes out more in writing
than in speaking when one can slur things over a bit).

I live in a girls' school here. Bridget, Adelaide, Ad's daughter, Billa
Harrod[3] all come & eat & sit & we go for walks in a crocodile. I like
it, but they I think rather long to be taken to Montmartre by glamorous
gentlemen.

Prod is here until Sunday, he is a wonderful courier, provider of
theatre tickets & so on. Off to Abyssinia next month.

How awful for Laura about hateful Kinross – I *feel* for her.

Much love from
    Nancy

The girls' school *is* expensive, not poor Fabrice.

[1] Alfred Duff Cooper (1890–1954). Conservative politician who resigned from the Cabinet over
the Munich agreement. Ambassador to Paris 1944–7. Married Lady Diana Manners in 1919.
Created Viscount Norwich in 1952. Famous for his philandering and violent fits of temper
('veiners'), he and Evelyn usually quarrelled whenever they met.
[2] Lilias Guthrie (1846–1951). Married in 1894 to 1st Baron Rennell who was Ambassador to
Italy 1908–19. Nancy drew on her mother-in-law's character for the 'relentlessly rude' and
'rampantly vulgar' Lady Montdore in *Love in a Cold Climate* (1949).
[3] Wilhelmine (Billa) Cresswell (1911–2005). Married the economist Roy Harrod in 1938.

26 November 1946   20 rue Bonaparte, VI

Dearest Evelyn

I hope Miss Harriet will shortly receive a muff, from me. May she please be allowed to wear it, as it is intended to keep her hands warm, delicate & white, & *not* to be stuffed away in a drawer.

I am in great despair – I *can't write a line.* I try & try, make beginnings which get no way at all & simply nothing happens. Isn't it awful – meanwhile the thousands on which I foresee I shall have, in the end, to pay 19/6 in the £ (because this thing about being abroad is most tricky unless you lived there before the war) are flying out of the window in a truly hateful way. And oh oh I missed the big prize in the lottery (8,000,000 fr:) by one figure last week, you must say almost unbearable.

Maurice came, he *was* nice. He gave the Colonel & me a truly wonderful blow out at the grandest & prettiest of all the restaurants here (it was shut when you were here last) called the Véfour.

Fancy, I've been reading a book by Mr Maugham & it says Mr Waugh despises people who write in the 1st person.[1] Do, or did you?

What did you think of Xopher on Robert [Byron] – I enjoyed it but it didn't make the Colonel like Robert so then I felt it can't be quite right all the same. He thought R sounded violent & silly. I don't know, can't say, I loved Robert too much to read it objectively I daresay. Wonder what Mrs Byron thinks. [. . .]

Everybody here says Queen Mary stole the Windsor jewels[2] – is that the view at home?

When do you come? Soon I hope – perhaps when Jonathan is here that would be very nice.

I've made a great new friend called Madame Auric[3] you wouldn't like her. She has painted, & sold me, a truly wonderful picture of the Colonel it makes my life.

Much love & come soon
   Nancy

[1] In *Cakes and Ale* (1930) Somerset Maugham quotes Evelyn on the 'contemptible practice' of first-person narration.
[2] Pieces of the Duchess of Windsor's jewellery were stolen while she was on a visit to England; there was a rumour that uncut heirloom emeralds originally belonging to Queen Alexandra were among the gems taken.
[3] Nora Auric (d.1982). Society portraitist. Married the composer Georges Auric in 1930.

27 November [1946]   Piers Court
                                                        Stinchcombe

Darling Nancy

I expect you have been very busy electioneering for the communists & transshipping Jewish terrorists to Palestine. I hope you are gratified by your successes.

I go to Ireland next week to inspect a castle where I hope to immure myself and family. Before that I have to go under the surgeon's knife for a painful, costly & indelicate operation. I cannot say the word, can I write it, well – piles. That is to be my January. For February & March I go to Hollywood if the American civil war has not cut all communications. Then I hope to my castle. Have I told you about it? Well I will when I have seen it. Rats leaving sinkers or birds of delicate plumage migrating to a more genial climate – however you care to look at it.

Since I last wrote I have been on for me an adventurous round. First to Oxford to wait on H. E. Cardinal Griffin[1] who is a Truman–Attlee–common-man. I dined sumptuously with Bowra the famous stakhanovite (?) scholar.[2] Then to the Betjemans in a house which smelled like a village shop – oil, cheese, bacon, washing but the fare was not as frugal as Dorchester Hotel. Harness literally everywhere. Books to make Handy blink and seize a pencil & start writing £100 in each. Nasty talk about protestant clergymen. Then to Eton where at John Julius' insistence I lectured to some bright civil boys. I met a dull master who worked in College. He said 'Guinness has turned the corner'.[3] Jonathan came to my lecture but I failed to recognize him so sent him a sovereign. The housemaster's wife with whom I stayed very pretty with purple finger nails. Then to London where it was just White's & Hyde Park Hotel. Pansy Lamb came to dinner – thin old half-starved clever shy. A beast called Rayner Heppenstall[4] tried to make me go a round of Europe to broadcast a message of Xmas goodwill. Me of all people. I said £300, he said £50 so there the matter ended. I wonder whom they will send.

Here I have entertained Patrick Balfour, very bland & plump & bureaucratic, zealously coming to terms with the socialist state. Also Frank & Elizabeth Pakenham.[5] I think he is seeing a glimmering of the disaster ahead which he has worked so hard to bring about. S Boots Connolly has fled the country. Some say from his debts. I see he has hired a woman to attack me in his absence.[6]

I let your god daughter see your tea pot once more. It is in fragments. She is becoming a droll little girl. My son told his headmaster's wife that it was no good writing to me as I had left his mother & 'lived purely in Africa now'.

Christopher Sykes has written an exquisite life of his great-uncle[7] and a lot of balls about the late Robert Byron.[8]

I was offered £50 for 50 words by a yank magazine on my favourite quotation. If I go to Ireland money will once more recover some value. I have written a very very long short story about my trip to Spain.

Who is the Mr Rodd who has bought Buckland Abbey?

How I dread Christmas. The operating theatre & nursing home will come as a welcome treat after it.

Do you see Picasso every day?

Yorke has written a book called *Back*. In the middle he inserts a long & irrelevant & inelegant translation from the French.[9] Very mad. He & Dig frequent the night club where Heath met poor old Marge.[10]

Best love from
Evelyn

[1] Cardinal Griffin (1899–1956). Appointed Archbishop of Westminster in 1943.
[2] Maurice Bowra had published four books in three years.
[3] One of Jonathan Guinness's school reports at this time recorded that he was 'already an incurable oddity and in danger of becoming a museum piece'.
[4] Rayner Heppenstall (1911–81). Novelist, critic, criminal historian, and feature writer for the BBC.
[5] Hon. Frank Pakenham (1905–2001). Labour politician. Parliamentary Under-Secretary of State 1946–7. Succeeded as 7th Earl of Longford in 1961. Married the author Elizabeth Harman (1906–2003) in 1931.
[6] The December issue of *Horizon* carried a critical review by Rose Macaulay of Evelyn's books.
[7] *Four Studies in Loyalty* included a chapter on Sykes's great-uncle who squandered his fortune entertaining the Prince of Wales (Edward VII).
[8] 'Your essay on Robert is utterly misleading. He couldn't write and his ideas about art were as ludicrous as his politics. He was a modern version of Roger Fry, without Fry's occasional instinct for a good painting. Besides your essay was squeamish. You said nothing about his perpetual buggery.' Letter from EW quoted in Christopher Sykes, *Evelyn Waugh* (Collins, 1975), p. 303.
[9] Henry Green's novel includes an extract from the *Souvenirs de la Marquise de Créquy* (1710–1803).
[10] The murderer Neville Heath met one of his victims, Margery Gardner, at the Panama Club.

12 December [1946]   Piers Court
                                                          Stinchcombe

Darling Nancy

Just home to find Harriet rejoicing in her muff. It is the most delicious & imaginative present. She is completely fascinated by it & I have allowed her its unrestricted enjoyment. Goodness she needs it, too, this weather. Thank you so very much. You are a perfect Godmother.

The Irish trip was enjoyable but unsuccessful. Gormanston Castle was vast & grim & haunted & I had decided to buy it when just in time the announcement appeared that Mr Butlin has purchased a site within a mile of it for a Holiday Camp. Well you would have thought that an added attraction with your love of the mob but not so me so I was able to cancel the sale just in time.

It is very hard cheese for the widowed Lady G. who has remarried an epileptic and lives in frightful poverty. Her one hope of life was to sell her castle and now no one will buy it.

We are looking for other houses.

Have you heard that Duff is selling his son into slavery to the Bolshevists?[1]

I had hoped to have an Xmas present for you – one of a dozen copies of a rehashed travel book[2] which I have had printed on hand-made paper. But of course they aren't ready & won't be for months. So I can only send love.

Sykes is having a great success with his life of Robert. I am delighted.

Love from
    Evelyn

[1] Duff Cooper was trying to organise a visit to Moscow for John Julius who was studying Russian.
[2] *When the Going Was Good* (1946).

16 December 1946   20 rue Bonaparte, VI

Darling Evelyn

So glad she liked the muff, it's such fun getting things for a little girl, nearly all my relations of that age are boys except Emma[1] who has too many adorers & doesn't even glance at a present if you give her one.

I feel very worried about your operation – the only thing is I believe it is always a guaranteed cure for ever. I've never had piles, understand they are past a joke – not that I ever regard physical pain as a joke myself.

Stephen Tennant[2] is here, he makes my life. You know you're not allowed to take jewels out of England, so as he can't be parted from his he went to the Board of Trade & asked what to do, so they put them under a B of T seal, in a parcel, & he brought them like that, but 'not a tiny *trinket* for the train'. The Colonel is perfectly fascinated by him – at the same time likes him. You really can't help it, there's something very sweet about him.

The French hatred of UNESCO is very funny! I expect you don't know what it is, well a lot of Americans headed by Prof: [Julian] Huxley have come here to educate the French. The first thing they want to do is to shut the museums – of course a roar as of a wounded bull has gone up – you know how the French love their musées. What can be the idea? These hateful beasts live like millionaires on the Black Market in well heated rooms & wish to take their only pleasure from people who can do neither. In return they recite poems by Steve Spender to music on the wireless, cold comfort indeed. I feel you will be on my side over all this.

Are you coming? Oh *please* do. Diana Cooper is now so dazzled by Lulu that she has no time for anybody else, & when people go there at 6 they are shown straight into Lulu's bedroom where Ran [Antrim] lies weeping across the foot of her bed. Couldn't you do a little debunking? Nobody else could. (Don't repeat all this it is for your private ear – you know how much I love & revere Diana.)

Sorry about Gormanston. Even I couldn't stand Butlin quite so near though of course I'm glad to know that it exists. I thought Lady G was a young wife who, supposing her husband to have died in the war, married again & had some trouble when he returned in explaining away the pram in the hall & the Teddy Bear on the sofa. Is this all what Romie [Brinckman] calls a pigment of my imagination? I showed the photograph to my mother[3] who has been here & she said 'Suitable for religious bodies – *very* suitable then for Mr Waugh.' My mother dined with the Colonel, picked all the truffles out of her omelette & left them. The Col delighted – '*Most* people pick out the truffles & leave the rest, very patrician of her.'

Have a Happy Xmas, love to Laura & you from
Nancy

[1] Lady Emma Cavendish (1943–). Nancy's niece. Chairman of National Trust Gardens Advisory Panel since 1985. Married Hon. Toby Tennant in 1963.
[2] Hon. Stephen Tennant (1906–87). Irresistibly charming and androgynously beautiful homosexual who inspired the character of Cedric Hampton in *Love in a Cold Climate*.
[3] Sydney Bowles (1880–1963), (Muv). Married in 1904 the Hon. David Mitford, who succeeded as 2nd Baron Redesdale in 1916.

Part II
1947–1949

AT THE end of 1947, after eighteen months of living in hotel rooms and borrowed flats in Paris, Nancy found a permanent home of her own in a rented apartment on the ground-floor of a handsome eighteenth-century house in the rue Monsieur. Gaston Palewski had not encouraged her move to Paris and kept her at arm's length when she arrived, making it quite clear that he was not in love with her and had no intention of being faithful. Nevertheless, Nancy nurtured the hope that she was an essential part of his life and organised her days around the short moments he would spare her. Her husband Peter was an intermittent visitor, appearing when he had nowhere else to go or was in need of money.

Despite the unsatisfactory nature of her relationship with the Colonel, Nancy was far from unhappy; *Love in a Cold Climate* was another best-seller and she was able for the first time in her life to indulge her love of expensive clothes and pretty objects of art. She enjoyed entertaining and made a wide circle of friends that included intellectuals and artists as well as members of the old French nobility and café society. The British Embassy under Duff and Diana Cooper formed the hub of her social life. When Duff was replaced by Sir Oliver Harvey at the end of 1947, the Coopers moved to the Château St Firmin in Chantilly where Nancy soon became an habituée.

Evelyn's experiences as a soldier were to provide him with material for some of his best writing: the *Sword of Honour* trilogy, which he completed between 1952 and 1961. But war also destroyed the values and way of life that he held dear. He was only forty-two at the end of the war but thereafter began to adopt the stance of an old man. Like Mr Pinfold, the hero of his novel, 'his strongest tastes were negative' and he abhorred everything that had happened in his lifetime.

In the light of his distaste for the modern world, his liking for America was unexpected; but his books sold well there and brought in substantial royalties. He also knew that showing enthusiasm for the country was an unfailingly successful way of teasing Nancy, whose anti-Americanism was irrationally violent. Evelyn and Laura spent the first three months of 1947 in America as guests of MGM who had bought the rights to *Brideshead Revisited*. The film project foundered but a visit to Forest Lawn cemetery in Los Angeles inspired *The Loved One*, his brilliant satire of Californian burial customs. Evelyn was delighted with its favourable reception, which helped to make up for the tepid reviews of his novella *Scott-King's Modern Europe*.

Nancy's infatuation with France and all things French grated on Evelyn, as did her protestations of complete happiness. Her enjoyment of life pointed up his own discontent and he was shrewd enough to see through to the hollow at the heart of her relationship with Palewski. After the fiasco of his visit to Paris in May 1949, Nancy was left feeling 'like the morning after an air-raid'. She had asked him to lunch with a Dominican priest, Père Couturier, whose trendy views on religion and admiration of Picasso enraged him. The following day she accompanied him to St Firmin where he quarrelled with Duff over dinner and was rude and tactless to Diana Cooper the next morning. Nancy wrote to her sister Diana: 'I weathered the storm with my weak character, giving way in everything.' It was easier to stand up to Evelyn on paper; she retreated behind the shelter of their correspondence and fired her shots at him by letter. They did not meet again until the following year.

19 January 1947   Piers Court
                                                          Stinchcombe
Darling Nancy

You are the most wonderful god mother – something out of a
pantomime. I came back from three weeks shame & pain in hospital
to find Harriet clutching her delicious purse and cautiously exhibiting
it with cries of 'Mine. Mine'.

I will pass over the last three weeks in silence. I sail for U.S.A. at
the end of this week.

Your young man sent me an Xmas card. Look how he addressed
it.

I hear on very good authority that the Cinema rights of *Pursuit of
Love* were sold in Hollywood last month for 35,000 dollars. Of course
Sutro is legally entitled to do this but if he makes £7,000 profit out
of an old and needy chum I shall think the worse of him. Please assure
me that he has given you some bonus anyway.

   Love
       Evelyn

Next address Hotel Bel Air, Hollywood, California, U.S.A.

23 January 1947   20 rue Bonaparte, VI

Darling Evelyn

Hateful of you to go to America & not here. Well you are horrid
about the Colonel's Xmas card such a pretty one too. The addressing
like that is because my dear Col can't write so M. Blum's secretary
came to address his cards for him & she rang me up & I spelt it all
out on the telephone, but unfortunately I *can't* learn the alphabet in
French so got it all wrong no doubt.

If Sutro did that I shall be surprised – do find out for certain. I
think the poor old boy has had dreadful business worries, & I know
he was in a nursing home with a nervous breakdown. But you know
(I've just done the sum) he gave me £3000, so he only makes about
double & having been in trade myself I don't call that very wicked.
Probably he'd done a lot of work on it already, casting & so on.

I am dreadfully bothered because I can't write any more, I've never
been so lacking in all ideas. It's a nuisance, not because of money,
but because I'm beginning to feel bored with nothing to do & not
fond enough (never have been really) of social life for that to become
a whole time job.

I had Jonathan & Ann Murray[1] (Basil's daughter) here for the whole
Xmas hols – I so adored that, that when I am old & penniless I intend
to keep a hostel for the young here, don't you think it's a good idea

& will you send me yours? Jonathan is a charming boy, I hardly really knew him before & as for Ann, she is a saint. How can she be, with those forebears? What a mystery it all is.

There is an interior decorator here called Geffroy[2] whom everybody has suddenly begun to hate very much. Last night at a dinner party we played a guessing game, & one of those twittering bird-like little Princesses went out & we chose Hitler. What sort of furniture? Table de Nuit avec un pot.[3] What sort of vehicle? Train blindé.[4] Flower? Nettle. Finally, What historical personage? Attila. 'Geffroy' she guessed, triumphantly, & simply wouldn't believe it when we said no. It has made me happy for ever – the others didn't think it a *bit* odd.

Your translator came to see me. When I couldn't cope with shy-making[5] he lost interest. I took a great dislike to him (not only wounded pride).

Do write from Hollywood if you can.

All love
NR

P.S. Prod is on his way back, having finished his film 'For whom the gate tolls'. He admits himself it is a tollgate to end all TGs, the commentary is delivered by himself!

[1] Ann Murray (1928–). Married to John Powell-Jones in 1949 and to Janus Paludan in 1969.
[2] Georges Geffroy (1905–71). Fashionable decorator who helped design Duff Cooper's library at the Paris Embassy.
[3] Bedside table with a chamber-pot.
[4] Armoured train.
[5] Rendered as 'intimidant' by Louis Chantemèle, French translator of *Vile Bodies*.

14 February 1947   20 rue Bonaparte, VI

Darling Evelyn

I wrote to old John & said if you've really sold *P of L* for huge sums *do* give me a little more I do so love money. No answer. He told my agent it's not true, but I wonder. Anyway he's had a bad time lately & been cheated right & left himself so I don't bear much of a grudge.

I sat next at luncheon to an old Marquis of the old school & he said did I know Emily Brontë because he had so enjoyed her book (just translated) on the vie de château in England. So I said I knew her well & all her sisters (delicate, unfortunately) & that her father was at school with mine. I thought it better not to mention poor Branwell. So you see we lady novelists have our admirers, even here.

There is a great deal of talk in French circles about an English widow, riche à millions, who has settled here & wants to make un beau mariage. Me. Picture my delight. I now see why my staircase at

Xmas time was one huge queue of French princes with boxes of chocs
– do admit it's a joke.

Somebody said you are going to live in S. Africa – you are *not* to
take Miss Harriet to S. Africa – give her to me you've got heaps of
others. Did I tell you Mrs Hammersley[1] who saw Laura on a retreat
said she & her sister are like tiger cubs – a very good description I
thought. I hope Harriet also has that look, it is fascinating.

Jonathan wrote a b & b letter in which he said 'You *are* lucky to
be middle aged.' I agree.

Diana took her youngest child[2] to luncheon at the Hyde Park grill
& said 'Just go out & see if the car has come.' He came back saying
I can't go out, there is a guard on the door (Commissionaire).

Really the modern world! Might amuse your gt new friend.

Do write & tell what you are up to.

Love from
Nancy

[1] Violet Williams-Freeman (1877–1964). A great friend of the whole Mitford family and an
important correspondent of Nancy. Married Arthur Hammersley in 1902.
[2] Max Mosley (1940–). President of the Fédération Internationale de l'Automobile since 1992.

30 April 1947   Hôtel Madison
                                                       Bd St Germain
                                                       Paris VI

Darling Evelyn

I'm delighted to see that you are back in Europe again[1] – oh how
I long to hear all before you've forgotten it.

I was supposed to be going home tomorrow for a month to write
dialogue for a film[2] – but the lawyer here said if I did that I would
pay taxes for the whole year, so now I have laid it at the feet of darling
Mr Popkin & am *hoping* & *hoping* he'll say no & that I can stay here.
I went home in March & nearly died of gloom – then I went to Spain
with Prod. Seville is like a dream, have you ever been there? But I
really hate travelling & am quite happy here – though I'm in rather
a do because I *cannot* start another book. I got a beautiful idea for one
& wrote a promising 1st chapter & then suddenly realized it's exactly
the same story as *P of Love*, which clearly will not do. Oh dear.

Wherever I look I see *Retour à Brideshead*, they must have printed a
huge edition. Shall you come out again soon – I expect not as you've
been away so long.

My hatred for Americans has now overflowed its banks – the town
is full of them hanging in front of shop windows & saying Why in
Wisconsin you can get that for 30 cents. An awful old brute called
Mrs Snow,[3] editress of *Harper's*, made me go to all the dress collections

with her & I wrote a really very funny article which she turned down
as not high class enough so I suppose my wounded vanity has turned
me against them still further –

Prod has stayed on in Spain with all my travellers cheques so I'm
starving in a garret like *La Vie de Bohème*[4] – really my life.

How is Harriet – & all the family. You must be pleased to be back.

I hear Légionnaire Smarty boots is here – I die for him but evidently
he doesn't die for me – too low brow.

I would snap my fingers at the high brows if I could write another
best seller, but as it is I am racked with inferiority feelings. So long
as Mr P. saves me from Ealing Studios –

It's no use writing to me here as even if I don't go home I shall
leave this hotel as soon as Prod comes to get me out of pawn. The
book shop will know as soon as I have an address. Oh if I could only
find a flat & settle down for good.

  Much love from
    Nancy

A lady called Mme Drilhole has had a hole drilled in her by her
adopted son, the papers call him *ce triste individu*.
I adored your article – saw it quite by chance.

[1] Evelyn's article 'Why Hollywood is a Term of Disparagement' had appeared in the morning's
Daily Telegraph.
[2] *Kind Hearts and Coronets* (1949). The Ealing comedy, starring Alec Guinness and Dennis Price,
about a genteel murderer who sets out to kill the eight relations who stand between him and
the family title and fortune.
[3] Carmel White (1888–1961). Dublin-born fashion editor of *Harper's Bazaar* 1932–58, said to
have coined the term 'New Look' for Christian Dior's first collection. Married George Snow
in 1925.
[4] Henry Murger, *Scènes de la vie de Bohème* (1848), the theme of Puccini's opera.

4 May 1947   Madison Hotel, VI

Darling Evelyn

Just got your long letter for which many thanks. Also news of you
from Momo[1] with whom I lunched & S. Boots whom I met accompanied by Mrs Boots when walking through the Louvre on my way
home.

As I think of 0 but the Loved Ones I tried them out on Momo –
absolutely no response & I much suspect that your novel[2] will not go
down with the American public. It will with me however.

Prod has appeared with a 34 lb ham which is making me popular
in this meatless town. He thinks he can fix it (flying in the face of
Popkin) for me to go home & do the film after all. Oh I don't want
to, shan't be any good at it, & long to stay here. Why does one ever
leave Paris when it may so soon be blown up – every minute away

seems dead waste to me. Yes isn't the food in Spain awful – as for the wine it is Guinness & water. But I enjoyed the masses of fruit, also the sherry.

I hear Randy is upon us (in every sense of the word). Yes this lecture is well known to me & to various French ladies of my acquaintance. It is varied by 'you think things are only important when they go on for years, but a short relationship can be just *as* important'.

Boots says you bullied him. Lys is fleeing home on account of Intrator,[3] but Boots can stay a bit – business. Perhaps he agrees with Mr Bevin[4] that taking yr wife to Paris is like taking a ham sandwich to a banquet. Poor wives.

I'll let you know if I go home oh how I hope not.

Love from
NR

[1] Maud (Momo) Kahn (d.1960). Daughter of Otto Kahn, the wealthy American financier. Married General Sir John Marriott in 1920.
[2] Evelyn had started work on *The Loved One: An Anglo-American Tragedy* (1948).
[3] Max Intrator, a notorious crook who operated in the South of France, had been helping British nationals contravene currency restrictions by illegally cashing their cheques abroad.
[4] Ernest Bevin (1881–1951). General Secretary of the Transport and General Workers' Union 1921–40. Foreign Secretary 1945–51.

14 May 1947   Hotel Madison, VI

Darling Evelyn

In floods & floods of tears, & in order to earn about what Prod spends & loses in a week (disloyal but true) I'm going back on Sunday. I shall be with Mark[1] at Kew, 51 Kew Green, Surrey. It is to work at the Ealing Studios, writing dialogue for a film called *Kind Hearts & Coronets*. Smarty will say more than ever I'm a snob – he gave me a great talking to about the snobbishness of my book – I hadn't realised. It's note paper that did it – if I'd known I'd have laid all that on much much thicker, to tease. Another complaint was that everybody was rich. My great trouble is I never read modern novels except yours where everybody is always *lovely and rich* – but are the people in other novels always poor nowadays? How boring.

What do you think? Lulu has got me a job which brings me in a steady sum *in francs* & gets me a permanent carte d'identité so that I can never be sent away or hauled back by the English. I make no comment.

Have you seen a film called *Brief Encounter*?[2] I went last night. It is both dreary & unrealistic, unlike our books.

I must see you. I think I shall be *tremendously* busy, since the Lulu job will be going on at the same time, but you I must see. Not Momo however. I dined with her & Randolph & the Col & Randolph turned on the Colonel with such venomous hatred & bawled such filthy insults at him – I could hardly believe what I was hearing. I've now got, what I haven't had for years, an ENEMY, & have ranged myself on the side of the hottest Randolph haters. Couldn't even enjoy my excellent dinner, my food being drenched in spit & sweat which flowed in a steady stream from my delightful cousin.

    Best love from
       Nancy

[1] Mark Ogilvie-Grant (1905–69). An old friend of Nancy's and a contemporary of Evelyn at Oxford.
[2] Directed by David Lean, based on *Still Life*, a play by Noël Coward, it starred Celia Johnson and Trevor Howard.

[May 1947]   [Piers Court
                                                Stinchcombe]
Darling Nancy
    It is shocking that you have taken employment under Lulu rather than enjoy the social conditions you have striven so hard to create in your own country. You were full of patriotic claptrap when it meant the destruction of Italy & Central Europe. Now that it means paying taxes in order to establish your egalitarian world, you prefer to write advertisements for poppy seeds or whatever it is that earns you French nationality. You cannot conceive how much I despise you.
    I long to see you however. But I don't come to London any more. B. Bennett like all jaggers[1] turned on his master so that I no longer care to patronize the Hyde Park Hotel & all other hotels are full of industrial crooks going to exhibitions. Will you not spare a few nights to come here? Surely the seedsmen & the film studio neither work at Whitsun. You know the disadvantages of coming here but it would be a great treat to us if you could bear it.
    Hatty has become the despair of all. Would you like to take her to Paris with you? She won't eat. Well I can't blame & won't let either of two quite pretty nursery maids touch her which is less excusable. She yells. In her rare moments of self-command she is extremely droll. Do adopt her.
    Sykes has been here for Sunday. Camilla was sick. His son Mark is being expelled from school. We too have a ham. Nothing else. Bet you can't read this. The trouble is that I bought this *WRITING* paper in Hollywood & ink runs on it so I have to use a kind of stylo.
    It is all Yorke's fault. No one wrote about the poor before him. Greek thought defined tragedy as dealing with people of the highest rank only. In Shakespeare the low born are always buffoons. Connolly thinks I spoke of Lys when I spoke of Loutit. It is all too difficult.

If Auberon Herbert[2] marries Elizabeth Cavendish[3] will my love for Debo be incestuous?

I hear ghastly accounts of Antrim.

This paper is called 'Greylawn Baronial Letter Sheets'. How does Connolly like that?

I have lost all interest in book-collecting.

Love to Mark.

Love. Come soon
        Evelyn

---

[1] A term coined in the 1920s by Evelyn and the Lygon sisters to describe a devoted and undemanding friend; taken from the name of a spinster who lived at Madresfield Court and who embodied these useful qualities.

[2] Auberon Herbert (1922-74). Evelyn's brother-in-law. Joined the Polish forces during the war after being rejected on medical grounds by those of his own country. He never married.

[3] Lady Elizabeth Cavendish (1926-). Daughter of 10th Duke of Devonshire and thus sister-in-law of Deborah. She never married but was John Betjeman's close companion from 1951.

22 May 1947   71 Kew Green
                                                     Kew
                                                     Surrey

Darling Evelyn

All right, don't tease about being unpatriotic, I count England & France as the same. Quite as bad to live in Ireland & I hope you become engulfed in Butlin's jolly days with loud speakers shouting cheery slogans in your ear for ever.

Your writing paper is far prettier than mine I am jealous.

Yes I'll have Hatty as soon as I am established with the cours [lessons] etc necessary to her development. I shall bring her up to be *very* ladylike & French, the kind of person so full of sensibility that she shudders at the idea of leaving the house, except in a car & with her *own*, *trusted* chauffeur. You know.

Connolly is very touchy about Bluefeet I noticed that in Paris. Love I expect. Lys was sent home so that Connolly could entertain intellectuals on her £75.

Can I come & see you when I've found out what the Studio expects of every man. So far they've paid me £75 & said come back next Tuesday. Quite nice if I didn't want to be in Paris. They have an earl in the film & he is called alternately Earl, Your Grace & Your Worship & I think it looks too snobbish if I begin telling them. Isn't it a problem? His wedding invitation runs: You are invited to the wedding of the 18th Earl Gascoigne to The Hon Miss E. Pickering. What *can* I do?

Come to London. But I must go to you on acc/ of seeing Hat (not Bruno).[1]

Dined with Mrs Kahn & Momo last night, rather by mistake. I rather love Momo though I must say.

Love from
  NR

[1] In 1930 Bryan and Diana Guinness organised a spoof exhibition of paintings by Brian Howard and John Banting which they pretended were the work of an unknown German genius, Bruno Hat. Tom Mitford impersonated the artist and Evelyn wrote a preface to the catalogue. The hoax took in no one but received huge publicity.

Thursday in Whitsun Week
[29 May] 1947

Darling Nancy
    What exquisite presents you do find for your godchild. The *WRITING* paper and *ONvelopes* have been shown to Hattie causing her to chuckle with pleasure, & then locked away for a few years until she can write & thank you herself. Everything you send her should form her taste & help to make her such a desirable girl as you describe.
    At present she refuses her food and yells when handled by the nursery maid.
    I expect that your work at the studio will take many months.
    Did I tell you I have practically decided on my Irish house – a large prosaic Early Victorian baronial mansion in flat hunting country near Dublin and Ld Fitzwilliam. The romantic castle was condemned by the architect I sent to vet it, as moribund.
    I do not think that all my teasing has brought home your beastliness to you. Do you not realize you are the most hated woman in England & the reason is not that you have run to France but that you voted socialist. Beast. What is more you made a secret socialist cell of your shop in Curzon Street introducing Handycraft who is red too – *next door to Trumper's.*
    Come soon

Love
  E

28 July 1947   20 rue Bonaparte, VI

Darling Evelyn
    What an excitement for me[1] – I've never had a book dedicated to me though darling Robert once said he was going to but when I looked, all excited, it was Emerald.[2] I *was* disappointed I remember.
    I spent yesterday evening with Jeannie Connolly – need I say it was the Serge [Preston] that arranged it, & then when she arrived at the

rendezvous she had never met the Serge before & didn't know his name. I was greatly mystified & haven't yet cleared the thing up – you must confess it's odd –? He's bringing me together with E Bowen[3] tomorrow so you see my social life looks up when he is here. If you came over he would introduce us – I wish you would.

It is so hot that my butter here is running like the butter you have with asparagus, a thing I've never seen before – in a north kitchen too. I *love* it (the heat) but most people are getting rather testy I note. It's been over 95 for a week, & a good deal over today I guess.

Lulu is my employer now & I see her neither as heroine nor villainess but a jolly intelligent woman who finds quality in what I do. I translate away happily all day, it is perfect work for one who enjoys writing English as I do but who is lacking in creative talent.

I've finished French Letters & am now doing French Race Horses – very soothing. Meanwhile I'm reading all E F Benson's Lucia books which I've found here – oh the bliss. Oh by the way, thoroughly overtired – how I shrieked.

This paper keeps being blown away by a hot dry wind & without being thoroughly overtired I am sleepy so good night.

Love
    NR

I met your brother in law, he referred to my god daughter as Mad Hatty I was furious.

[1] Evelyn dedicated *The Loved One* to Nancy.
[2] *First Russia then Tibet* (1933) by Robert Byron was dedicated to Lady Cunard.
[3] Elizabeth Bowen made frequent visits to Paris to see her lover Charles Ritchie, Counsellor at the Canadian Embassy 1947–50.

6 August [1947]   Piers Court
                                                   Stinchcombe
Dearest Nancy

I am so very sorry to have put you to trouble over the book for Diana. I idiotically misread your last letter. You spoke of Debo & Diana in one paragraph as being in Paris and I took it to mean your Diana. Please forgive me & send the silly volume at your leisure by anyone travelling. It is only a long-overdue edition-de-luxe of that travel book dedicated to her. All the chic has gone out of it by the printers' six months delay & it can well wait till doomsday now.

I went to London for Daphne [Weymouth]'s ball which I enjoyed enormously. All old chums making hay and a few pimply & pouting juniors standing about disconsolately. Maureen[1] gave Randolph a ter-rific box on the ear. Instead of striking back like a man he tried to pacify her. They stood in the centre of the ball room sweating &

arguing for three minutes and then – another more terrific box. I said to her: 'I am all for Randolph being struck but why particularly do you strike him now.' She: 'He never wrote me a letter of condolence when Ava was killed.' So now I keep rather clear of widows. Kick [Hartington] has had the most god awful posthumous portrait made of her Loved One. I saw Debo at the ball & took up a great deal of her time. She was in fine looks but lacking in elegance. The same dress she wore at her own party last year and all her friends look like recently demobilized G.I.s. Should not a girl with her beauty wit and high position make a bit more of herself?

Diana Cooper was in London last week – sane and sweet. I met her quite unexpectedly at dinner at Lady Rothermere's's[2] & enjoyed it very much. I spent the week-end at Pam Berry's and was never so sumptuously fed or delicately flattered. Maurice Bowra was there. He greatly lacks frankness, I thought, and I believe all his pretensions to understand foreign poetry an imposture. Lady Pamela seems much occupied with thoughts of sex. Then I went to the Betjemans for a night. Penelope just off for a camping holiday in a nearby field. Soon I go for a little jaunt to Scandinavia. You see I am getting about a bit.

Lady Colefax catechised me about your financial stability. I was unable to satisfy but hinted at the worst.

Hatty is indeed eccentric but far from insane.

Love from
    Evelyn

Can you give me any details of June Capel's engagement (marriage?)? Do you prefer 'Mitford' or 'Rodd' in dedication? The former suggests the sister of the pen biter.[3]

---

[1] Maureen Guinness (1907–98). Married the 5th Marquess of Dufferin and Ava in 1930; he was killed in action in 1945.
[2] Ann Charteris (1913–81). Social and political hostess who became a close friend of Evelyn in the 1950s. Their correspondence has been published in *The Letters of Ann Fleming* (1985) edited by Mark Amory. Married to 3rd Baron O'Neill 1932–44, to 2nd Viscount Rothermere 1945–52 and to Ian Fleming, creator of James Bond, in 1952.
[3] Probably Unity Mitford (1914–48), (Bobo), the Redesdales' fourth daughter, who was an object of hatred in Britain before the war because of her admiration for Hitler and Nazism.

12 August 1947   20 rue Bonaparte, VI

Dearest Evelyn
    Perhaps Mitford, yes I think so. I often & often wish I'd started writing *after* I was married like Mrs Humphry Ward,[1] but as I didn't –
    Delighted to hear that Randolph is now an open Aunt Sally, just wait till I get in my whack – specially now I know he's a turn the other cheeker. I heard about Daphne's party from 2 enemies of yours,

Cecil[2] & Ali[3] whom I met dining with some people called Cooper (who could have introduced them?) but they omitted these tough details & contented themselves with the news that Letty[4] looks like a great grandmother & that all the debs are hideous. I am appalled by Debo's clothes every time I see her – she used to be really elegant as a girl what can it be?

I found all I had to do with Diana's book at the Post Office since it only had to be re-addressed, was throw it into a basket, which I did. So the fuss was about nothing!

Miss Capel. Started her career with a long & fruitless (no issue) affair with Anthony Chaplin[5] a very fascinating man who now lives here. Last winter became engaged to a bald Jewish dwarf called Osborn – some think in the hopes A.C. would then marry her. This was the occasion of a letter from E Sitwell[6] to a mutual friend saying, 'The Capels are a family of whom it is impossible to think highly – I hope the girl realizes that Franz has 300 years of civilization behind him IN HAMBURG.' Two days before the marriage she chucked him. His friends all very angry, specially because he had already given up his flat & moved with 2 grand pianos into hers – an embarrassing position, they say, in view of the housing shortage. I think that's all I know. I don't like her, but he is like something from another & far more terrible world.

Next day

Hardly were these words about Randy out of my pen than a noise like an old rusty bicycle going up a hill announced that he was 'on the line'. So of course I went to see him & now the Colonel has begun to talk about cocks crowing & so forth & gone crossly away for a week. Oh dear. I can't but rather love Randolph, can't imagine why.

Must get on with my work – oh how I *long* for · *The Loved One* – when?

Love from
     NR

[1] Mary Augusta Arnold (1851–1920). Under her married name, novelist and founder of the Women's Anti-Suffrage League.

[2] Cecil Beaton (1904–80). Evelyn's bullying of the photographer, which began at their Hampstead prep school, created a lifelong animosity between the two men; he is ridiculed as David Lennox, the society photographer, in *Decline and Fall* (1928). Nancy loved Beaton's company and admired his work. Knighted in 1972.

[3] Alastair Forbes (1918–2005). Prolix American-born journalist whom Nancy liked but Evelyn dismissed as a 'fuddy-duddy'.

[4] Lady Lettice Lygon (1906–73). The eldest Lygon daughter. Married to Sir Richard Cotterell 1930–58.

[5] Viscount Chaplin (1906–81). Married to Alvilde Bridges 1933–50 and to Hon. Rosemary Lyttelton in 1951.

[6] Edith Sitwell (1887–1964). In 1947 she published *The Shadow of Cain*, a book of odes in the grand manner. Dame of the British Empire 1954.

Darling Evelyn

May I ask your help – it's about my next novel.[1] I've got a story
for it & the story is roughly this: Ld & Lady Mondor, infinitely grand
& rich, he an ex Viceroy, absolutely top Englishman, she a vulgarian
not unlike my ma in law. They have one daughter Leopoldina no
heir. This is not much of a sorrow to them as they love their daughter
so much, but they do rather imagine that she will marry, if not the
Prince of Wales, then some terrific Duke. Rather disturbed when she
reaches the age of 23 unmarried. (She is beautiful but dumb.) Lord
Mondor has a sister married to a Mr X who is a great deal at their
house & fetches & carries for Lady M & probably is her lover as well.
Lady Patricia X very delicate, stays at home a good deal. She dies.
Picture the situation when, a week after the funeral, Leopoldina
announces that she is going to marry X (allowed by law since 19–?).

She does so & is extremely happy, though persecuted in every
possible way by her mother (I may say the mother is the central
character in the book). Then Lady Mondor dies. Leopoldina prostrated
with grief takes a wild hatred for her husband, X. X is an odious
character but he suffers. He suffers intensely & after a bit he has a
stroke. (Must bring in Simon [Elwes]'s stroke.) Leopoldina does not
behave nicely – she wishes he were dead & says so. He dies & she
settles down to an extremely conventional country life, beloved by all
her neighbours (not sure of the end, hope I shall get ideas as I go).

Now I need the impact of the Radlett family upon the Mondors –
contrast between Aunt Sadie & Lady M, the 2 (neighbouring) house-
holds & the Radlett children's comments on the whole affair. Lady
M sends Leopoldina there hoping she will be talked out of the engagement. I've got over them not having met in the *P of L* by the Mondors
being in India – Leopoldina is younger than Linda & Linda has been
married a year or 2 when all this happens. What I want to ask you
is can Fanny tell the story again? I find it *so much* the easiest formula,
but I know people did object & said I cheated by Fanny describing
things she didn't see. Do be kind & advise me. I'll be back in Paris
next week, 20 rue Bonaparte VI will find me. If Fanny doesn't tell it
I think it will be a struggle to write it because of how much to leave
out – for instance I would rather leave it a mystery how far things
had gone by the death of the aunt, & whether in fact X was Lady
M's lover or only a tame poodle. Leopoldina's character, a mystery
to her friends in many ways, is explained by her extreme but hidden
sexiness which exists under an exterior of the utmost conventionality.
Lord & Lady Mondor are going to be excellent characters I hope –
he, grand & noble & taking everybody in, but *silly*, she tough vulgar
snobbish dreadful &, like her daughter, very sexy. I'm in a great do

about it because of not knowing quite how to tackle it, but I've got a great many of the situations in my head & ought soon to begin.

I'm here with Prod – oh it is a funny place. No rules of any kind – result, a great boom going on in a tiny mediaeval village – every form of contraband for sale in every cottage & 1 Andorran in 3 is said to have a motor car. Prod busy egging them on to send a wedding present to Princess E. We leave tomorrow, motoring slowly back to Paris.

I do apologise for bothering you, but you are always so kind. The fact is I've begun to be appalled by the difficulties of technique, a thing which has hitherto never worried me at all –

Best love
    Nancy

[1] *Love in a Cold Climate.*

[September 1947]   Piers Court
                                           Stinchcombe

Darling Nancy

An insoluble problem because of course one always wants to say how one would write the book oneself, not how the chum should.

I am sure you should stick to first person. It suits you perfectly, but the advantage of f.p. is the eye witness account. Can the f.p. you have chosen see enough for herself? Only you can answer that. My fear would be a series of conversations in which other characters come to consult her about their problems so that the readers get the action second hand. Is there no observer nearer the centre of things?

Marriage to deceased aunt's husband has always been legal I think. In fact I'm sure.

I am sorry not to be more helpful but at this stage of the story it is an unquickened embryo & the best gynaecologist can do no more than advise temperate habits.

I met a well dressed yank called Paston, Paton, Patton, Patterne?[1] who spoke of you with love.

Connolly and I are bosom friends. I dined twice with him last week.

Eddy Grant[2] kicked the bucket. You heard of course Harry & Nell's tragedy?[3] He is much set down by it.

No doubt you also heard of Ed [Stanley]'s Duff-Gordon[4] escape from drowning?

Will you miss your compatriots passing through or be glad.

Socialist spies read our letters abroad now so forgive me for saying FUCK THE SOCIALISTS.

Love from
    Evelyn

¹ William (Bill) Patten (1909–60). Financial and economic attaché at the Paris Embassy 1944–54. Married Susan Mary Jay in 1939.
² Edward Grant (1892–1947). Married to Evelyn's sister-in-law, Bridget Herbert, in 1935.
³ Lord and Lady Stavordale's thirteen-year-old son Giles had died following an accident with an airgun.
⁴ A reference to Sir Cosmo Duff-Gordon's escape from the *Titanic* in a half-empty lifeboat; there were allegations that he had refused to allow other survivors to be taken on board.

20 October 1947   Hôtel Jacob d'Angleterre
                                         rue Jacob
                                         Paris VI

Darling Evelyn

Many thanks indeed for the customs (necrological).[1] Goodness! More chic in death than ever before. Won't they look awful at the Judgement – *I* think skeletons are far more chic don't you.

Struggling with the book – it's very bad I fear. First made Fanny tell – after 10,000 words saw it wouldn't do & started again but it's very dull & doesn't come to life – I wonder if it's worth going on with. I *do* go on, in spite of a rather hopeless feeling that it's all no good.

It cheers up a bit when the old characters appear, but they're not the point. Oh the horror of it, what can I do?

I've been lent a lovely flat for the winter by Audrey Bouverie[2] whom I hardly know, a great stroke of luck. I do think hotels are depressing but can't pretend that's the reason for not being able to write, much as I should like to think it.

Will you sometime tell me Harriet's age? I simply haven't an idea (between about 2 & 5) & sometimes see things she might like & don't feel certain they wouldn't be too babyish.

Laura's sister[3] fell in a graceful faint at the Embassy the other day – it was just like a stage one.

What a good paper the *Tablet* is I always enjoy it when I see it. Rather biased of course, compared to *NS & N*.

Prod has had an almighty smash in Florence – his car a total loss, but he is quite unhurt. So thankful I wasn't there it sounds terrifying.

Do come soon (know you won't).

Love
    NR

¹ Evelyn had sent Nancy a copy of his article 'Half in Love With Easeful Death: An Examination of Californian Burial Customs', *Tablet*, 18 October 1947.
² Audrey James (1902–68). Sister of Edward James. Married to Hon. Peter Pleydell-Bouverie 1938–46.
³ Gabriel Herbert (1911–87). Married Alexander Dru in 1943.

23 October [1947]   Piers Court
                                                     Stinchcombe

Darling Nancy

It is very kind of you to think of Harriet. I cannot tell you her precise age but I can describe her condition. She walks & speaks volubly but unintelligibly. A manic-depressive with marked theatrical tendencies, highly popular with other children, hated by servants. Extremely droll. I think the most interesting of my children. Your tea pot was a joy to her. It was repeatedly broken & mended until finally ground to powder. The writing paper not note ha ha still awaits her adolescence. The muff is a winter joy shortly to appear from moth ball.

I expect you are jubilant that the socialists have succeeded in evicting Duff & Diana.[1] The chief pleasure here is in Harold Nicolson's disappointment.[2] He joined the Labour Party six months ago in expectation of the appointment not knowing that Harvey[3] had done so unobtrusively four years earlier.

I think it a very good sign that you find the writing of your new book painful. It is when it runs easily off the pen that one grows apprehensive.

So I was invited to Ealing the other day to write a monologue for a film. It is the film you wrote.[4] They have scrapped everything written up till now & wouldn't show me your contribution which they said was concerned with a bull fight. Bull fight my goodness. I couldn't see why they wanted to film that story at all, particularly as Charlie Chaplin has lately done brilliantly with a similar theme.

I believe you should go to Hollywood. It is not a thing I would advise many chums but I honestly believe you would enjoy it.

Do you still draw profit from Corporal Hill? I loyally spend vast sums there. Mollie [Friese-Greene] looked very ill-conditioned & I remembered what you told me of her beauty treatments.

Happy civil war.

Love
        Evelyn

[1] As a former Conservative minister, Duff Cooper had been unsure of his Ambassadorship since the Labour victory of 1945. Despite Lady Diana's cultivation of a friendship with the Foreign Secretary, Ernest Bevin, Cooper lost his post.
[2] Harold Nicolson (1886–1968). Journalist and biographer. Joined the Labour Party in February 1947 in the hopes of furthering his chances of a peerage. Knighted – eventually – in 1952. Married Hon. Victoria (Vita) Sackville-West in 1913.
[3] Sir Oliver Harvey (1893–1968). Ambassador to Paris 1948–54. Married Maud Williams-Wynn in 1920. Created 1st baron Harvey of Tasburgh in 1954.
[4] *Kind Hearts and Coronets*.

11 December 1947   19 quai Malaquais
                                                    Paris VI
                                                    After 20th inst: at
                                                    7 rue Monsieur, VII

Darling Evelyn

I sent some little utter horrors over for Harriet's stocking – not for
your inspection but the kind of things children like. They will sit at
the Corporal's shop for you to fetch – or tell the Corp: to send.

My news is I've at least got a permanent flat – 18 months at least.
Oh the heaven of not having to move again.

Diana's ball[1] was sad, rather. She is quite out of spirits & so are
her lovers, who are all Paris. The Harveys are what Debo calls the
utter ghastly drear personified & we all proudly say we shan't write
our names in *their* book (as if they'd notice). But Lady H. is said to
like intellectuals so ONE is done for anyway.

Prod appeared in a vast air cooled caravan, he is off to Timbuctoo.
I hope it really exists & is not a mere figure of speech.

I see your brother in law quite often he seems very right wing.
Aren't you coming ever again?

I've had a very funny idea for a tease on Ch Morgan.[2] Somebody
left a book by him here called *The Judge's Story* & it's about an awful
old upright English judge who talks in a ghastly affected way & says
thankee kindly & is keen on Hellenism & Humanism & sometimes
disappears to write his great book called The Athenian. Well I thought
of putting him lock stock & barrel, by name, in *my* book, only when
he disappears it is really to do feelthy things to little girls under the
age of consent. Do admit it would annoy.

A poor young man it seems has been sacked from the Air Force (le
RAF ne veut plus de lui il est trop sentimental)[3] for fucking a Wren.
The French say it's the first time they ever heard of an Englishman
being normal & he should have been given a prize.

Hamish [Erskine] is here, he is planning to start a Travellers Club
in Rome, but he counts on my brother in law Taffy to help & Taffy
is being cut off because of adultery. The truth is he's a very evil man
but nobody ever believes me when I say so.

Do you ever see Diana [Mosley]? She lives in London now. A
long letter from Harold – his book is to be called *Memoirs of an
Aesthete*.

Happy Christmas, happy New Year &

   love from
      Nancy

[1] The Coopers' farewell ball at the Paris Embassy.
[2] Charles Morgan (1894–1958). Novelist and dramatist whose reputation in France has always
stood higher than in Britain.
[3] 'The RAF want nothing more to do with him, he is too sentimental.' The young man in

question, William Cavendish-Bentinck (1925–66), whose father later became the Duke of Portland, was court-martialled and cashiered.

15 December [1947]   Piers Court
                                                          Stinchcombe

Darling Nancy

How very kind of you to remember Harriet. I never go to London so I will ask the corporal to send her your presents. She will be delighted. She is a pretty, droll girl.

The airman you speak of is half-American; Dutch on his father's side. (The family owes its prominence to the unnatural affections of William III.) So I do not think that the English services lose their reputation for sodomy by his action. Anyway I never count the R.A.F. as English.

You must have been having a busy time sabotaging trains. Do not repine at the set-back to the Party. Big things will happen in Palestine where the American jews have made it possible for the Red Army to reach its goal in the Mediterranean.

The story proudly dedicated to you appears in *Horizon* in February & later as an illustrated book.[1] I have found a draughtsman who takes down pictures like dictation. It will be a very pretty little book I think.

I was not asked to Coopers' Waterloo Ball.

I never go anywhere or see anyone. London is infested by Quennell and Alastair Forbes. I do not repine. It seems to me I am keeping my sanity (if that is a good thing) while everyone else is losing, has lost, his. Also my health & shall live to a great age & see the Restoration.

I long to see your novel. Your projected joke has this weakness that practically none of your admirers read C. Morgan. It is living with Frogs has made you think him important.

Do you mean that Hamish or Taffy is a very evil man?

Osbert has become a Trades Union boss & Lord Kemsley has given him £1000 free of tax.[2]

I think I sent you this Spanish yarn when it came out in a magazine but here it is again with my love for Christmas.

Debo has vanished from my life.

Mrs Betjeman says Desmond Guinness[3] is charming. She is becoming a Catholic. Lady Pakenham is my great new friend.

I am now a Doctor of Letters of Loyola University, Baltimore – not an illustrious seat of learning.

Love from
        Evelyn

[1] The issue of *Horizon* containing *The Loved One* sold out overnight; the novel appeared in book form in November 1948 with illustrations by Stuart Boyle.

[2] Osbert Sitwell had been awarded a newly instituted *Sunday Times* book prize of £1000 and a gold medal for the first two volumes of his autobiography.
[3] Desmond Guinness (1931–). Bryan and Diana Guinness's second son. President of the Irish Georgian Society 1958–91. Author of books on Georgian architecture.

22 December 1947   7 rue Monsieur
                                                          Paris VII

Darling Evelyn

I love *Scott-King* more than ever – thank you so much for him. The fact is one reads things more easily when in book form than in high brow mags don't you agree.

I don't know why you think I'm a Communist (must clear this up in your mind). I don't like Communism, I am a Socialist & weakening on that (the others seem to be such fearful duds), but I've never been a Communist & am less than ever now that I see how cowardly they are, fearful cissies, the mere sight of a policeman & off they scoot. I despise them. I've even had to cut myself off from the old country in a most definite manner by refusing to renew my subscription to the *N.S. & N.* on account of their utterly babyish attitude to Continental politics.

Oh my novel has STUCK. I am in despair I can't get on with it – yet there is too much that's not bad to scrap it altogether, besides I *must* make some more lovely money. This new flat of mine seems perfect in every way for working – charming servant, absolute quiet like the country, but the story won't go – can't think what's to happen next. I've done 20 000 words & am in a misery.

I'm awfully excited for *The Loved One*. I thought once more in life I was to be done out of a dédicace as Pam Smith told me the Americans had warned you that if you publish it you'll be for ever undone there. I might have guessed you'd P & be D'd, knowing you.

The Waterloo ball was somehow not cheerful. Le désespoir [despair] de Diana made itself felt, & one's own désespoir, goodness knows. Oh the gloom of the Harveys – parlour games & charades mark my words. Lady H is said to be fond of art. Thank heavens in Feb the Coopers return.[1]

You must one day see this flat it is so pretty & untouched I should say for 60 years. The first evening I gathered up 25 lace mats & put away the objects that sat on them, mostly from the Far East. The furniture which then emerged from beneath this welter of Buddhism, from behind gilt screens & Spanish shawls, is of museum quality – such beauty you can't imagine. I've got a garden, a charming servant & constant hot water, so you see – bliss. If my story could get written I should be in happiness, but it's got on my nerves. Perhaps a visit to England would be the thing.

Did you take on the Ealing film? The silliness of the story – unless they consented to treat it as a pure farce, but that they wouldn't do, in my day at least. They've got psychology on the brain poor dears.

Prod has gone off to Timbuctoo in a huge white air cooled ambulance having left behind, by mistake, a great case of medicine against prickly heat so useful to me & he I suppose is prickling like mad isn't it awful. He'll be away until March.

I mean Taffy is evil. Hamish [Erskine] is here with his lady-love, they go everywhere together like a newly engaged couple & are spending Xmas with Lulu.

Don't hate Ali Forbes – you wouldn't if you knew him. I'm sure London is hell – if I go home in Jan can I go to you for a night or does it mean standing in a cattle truck? I had some fiendish experiences last time.

All love & to Laura & Harriet
Nancy

I heard of you in Denmark[2] from a Danish friend – how you do get about though never here –

[1] Flouting the convention that a retiring head of mission should not return to the country of his former posting until at least a year after his departure, Duff and Lady Diana Cooper went back to France and settled at the Château St Firmin in Chantilly.
[2] Evelyn had made a tour of Scandinavia in the late summer for the *Daily Telegraph*.

26 December [1947]   [Piers Court
                                                       Stinchcombe]

Darling Nancy

Your presents to Harriet were a prodigious success. I found it very bitter to part with the book & not incorporate it in my own library. She had never seen a 'snow-storm' before & it is a delight to her. So were the delicious trinkets. Thank you very much indeed for your imaginative generosity.

Betjeman delivered a Christmas Message on the wireless. First he said that as a little boy he had been a coward & a liar. Then he said he was sure all his listeners had been the same. Then he said that he had been convinced of the truth of the Incarnation the other day by hearing a choir boy sing 'Once in Royal David's City' in King's College Chapel.

All the reviews of *Scott-King*, instead of being about the book, have been about me saying that I am ill-tempered and self-infatuated.

I wrote in a letter to my great new friend Connolly that I sadly missed you in London as I heard no gossip now & would he tell me some. He wrote to say he did not regard the sufferings of his fellow men as the subject for humour.

The only Christmas presents I have received are the exquisite pen from you and some wine from Basil Bennett. I love you both. What a pity you & he never married.

All my most valued books have been eaten by tiny spiders.

Would you say I was a very ill-tempered & self-infatuated man? It hurts.

[Patrick] Balfour is back homeless, penniless, without employment, living at Chagford & trying to write a book – precisely as he was 15 years ago.

Best love from
Evelyn

31 December 1947   7 rue Monsieur, VII

Darling Evelyn

The reviewers are jealous poor things it is a great compliment. A Frenchwoman said to me yesterday how lucky you are in England the way there is no jealousy between artists & writers – I don't know what she meant I'm sure.

Do you remember that girl who stole the spoons? She is now a rich & respected member of the English colony here & she said to me yesterday 'I hear Evelyn Waugh told Duff I stole his spoons.' I think myself, though I rather like her, that she is an almighty liar, she has told everybody here that she was the love of Richard Hillary's[1] life (you wouldn't know who that was but I do, as an ex-bookseller). Well I wonder –

The great excitement here has been the elopement, as a result of Diana's ball, of Laura Dudley[2] & a little man called Cock de something[3] who looks like a guinea pig. The English line on this is 'she couldn't have stayed with Eric, he is so jealous' & the French 'mais, le pauvre, il aime sa femme, ce n'est pas un crime'.[4]

Hamish is here in full flood of first love for Nora Auric, a Russian Jewish Communist who looks like Oliver Messel[5] dressed up. It seems (she tells everybody) that since the war, (since the cradle I guess) he hasn't been able to DO anything & then, 5 minutes before her aeroplane was due to leave Venice, at 8 AM he made it. Train fever of course, I quickly said – it always has that effect on me. Anyway a great fire of love was lit by this & it's flaming merrily away. Like all English people he is gratified to notice the improvement it makes in his health – just like Mollie you see & I've often noticed it's the first thing they think of.

My book has begun to *go*, isn't it wonderful when they do that. Of course it's simply a question of working whatever one may tell oneself.

I went to the Midnight Mass with the Col & Cora Caetani[6] & never have I seen anything as beautiful as she looked, in a black satin long dress sweeping up & down the aisle, curtseying, dipping into H. water crossing herself & all. She is like a wonderful classic statue that has been dripped on for hundreds of years. The audience looked at nothing else.

Now you can't say there's no gossip in this letter & soon you'll see me in the flesh, I go home either next week or end of month.

I rather dreaded you seeing the snow storm – not up to our childhood ones but all I could get. I'm trying to find a child's umbrella for her, to bring when I come.

> All v. best love
> NR

Happy 1948.

[1] Richard Hillary (1919–43). Battle of Britain pilot who was shot down and badly wounded; he was later killed in action. His autobiography *The Last Enemy* (1942) was a wartime best-seller.
[2] Laura Charteris (1915–90). Married to Viscount Long 1933–42, to 3rd Earl of Dudley 1943–54, to Michael Canfield 1960–9 and, in 1972 shortly before his death, to 10th Duke of Marlborough.
[3] Gerry Koch de Gorreynd, an old acquaintance of Lady Dudley, had proposed to her over lunch at Maxim's. Their affair lasted until the spring when the Dudleys were reconciled.
[4] 'But the poor man loves his wife and that is not a crime.'
[5] Oliver Messel (1904–78). Dark and very good-looking stage designer.
[6] Cora Antinori (1896–1974). Florentine who worked for the decorator Jansen. Married Prince Michelangelo Caetani in 1920.

[February 1948]   [Piers Court
                                                  Stinchcombe]
Darling Nancy

I hasten to send you an advance copy of *The Loved One*. The dedication is invisible but in the book it has a page to itself and a terra cotta urn.

I am afraid I have boasted about it so much that it will seem very flat. Do try & laugh a little. It is dedicated to you as the hardest hearted well no toughest is the word girl I know.

Cyril has had an apoplectic seizure & gone to take the waters. The bare footed partisans have got his dining room.

Hamish is entertaining on a large scale – not me.

What a wretched little letter this is. But I want you to read *Loved One* at once & tell me how you take it. It will land me in prison & penury I am warned.

> Love
> E

9 February 1948   7 rue Monsieur, VII

Darling Evelyn

The *heaven* of *The Loved One* oh you are kind to dedicate it to me, thank you thank you for it. I've been utterly shrieking ever since it arrived, luckily was lunching alone. I must say I couldn't quite do it & the foie de veau together (just coincided with the massaging) but combined it happily with a banana, & am now in despair at having finished it. Can't wait to give it to the Colonel.

I had too much of a rush after I saw you to be very enjoyable & was only in London 3 days. I dined with Smarty & thought him sad, but perhaps I bored him. I went to Gerald [Berners] & he only longed to get rid of me, I could see I bored *him*.

I was glad to be back – now my English money is blocked so I can never come back again anyway, rather a comfort. Our evening I enjoyed very much & I was pleased to see Mark [Ogilvie-Grant] unchanged but everybody else seemed depressed & rather cross. Not Diana. Debo I missed.

Your godson Jonathan is at Strasbourg learning German & French & starving on what the Govt gives him. So I told the Colonel & the Colonel told the Mayor & the Mayor rang up to say that l'honorable has now been invited to meals at many bonnes maisons Strasbour-geoises. I can't wait to hear what it's like – lucky boy the tuck will be something to dream of.

Awful about Smarty being so poor. I thought the dirty little note book would have brought in thousands, it seemed such a seller. Wilbur K Lutit – you are such a fool Evelyn. Oh dear I was so *fond* of Sir Francis ('Scottie' Wilson too).[1] Can't wait to read it again. Did you like Smarty's introduction – well it was mostly written by you anyway.[2]

I thought he apologized a little too much for allowing a treat for once.

I go pegging on at my book but without much conviction.

Did you read the Ruskin one?[3] I felt so much on his side, such rot to talk of martyrdom, when there must be millions of women whose husbands hardly ever go to bed with them which after all comes to the same thing as never, for practical purposes.

I do so hope you'll come here before very long – I can offer you my bed dining room & a gentil accueil.[4]

Much love
    Nancy

Dined with a young American last night & told him your book was to be called *The Loved One*. 'What a beautiful name' he said. Poor him.

[1] Wilbur Kenneth Lutit and Sir Francis Hinsley are characters in *The Loved One*. Scottie Wilson was a naïve painter, promoted by *Horizon*, whom Evelyn mocked in the novel.

[2] Cyril Connolly's 'Comment' introducing *The Loved One* drew heavily on a letter from Evelyn. (See *The Letters of Evelyn Waugh* edited by Mark Amory, Weidenfeld & Nicolson, 1980, p. 265).
[3] Sir W. M. James, *The Order of Release: The Story of J. Ruskin, Effie Gray and J. E. Millais* (1947).
[4] Warm welcome.

11 February 1948   7 rue Monsieur, VII

Darling Evelyn

Yesterday I got a *Loved One* sent by Smarty today yours, with love & disapproval. Well love is the thing – *toast*! *Books* Mrs K!

Well the pictures are wonderful though I was shocked by *dear* Sir Francis having a monocle when we are expressly told he didn't & what about the wreath? Dennis is to the life & never has Nancy Mitford looked so pretty. My mother will be appalled & think it bad luck (the urn) but so long as the urn contains me & not *my* loved one I don't mind a bit.

I'm in bed with a horrid sort of 'flu terrific back ache & no temperature so nobody believes I am ill. 'Ah! Madame n'a pas de fièvre?'[1] I had a very bad night during which Brian Howard got mixed up with Mr Joyboy.

Awful about Smarty's stroke. I saw Osbert in the shop & he said I put Cyril very high on the list of those who will have strokes – later at luncheon Lysey [Lubbock] disclosed that Cyril had had one in a train & I never had such winks as Osbert gave me. But as a lover of Smarty I feel sad about him, I thought he seemed wretched the night I dined alone with him.

I wonder if you'll get thousands of furious letters about *The Loved One* – is it coming out in America?

The Colonel says it's wonderful how you have brought out the best in American civilization.

A letter from Jonathan saying 'I've bought 20 Swiss francs from a Communist', so I see he is holding his own in the modern world all right.

The paper is covered with yellow spots so I must stop.

Love from
        NR

P.S. You needn't have wondered whether I would laugh – in spite of Cyril's preface forbidding me to I *bellowed* for an hour & a half gasping for breath.

[1] 'Ah! So you've no temperature, Madame?'

2 March 1948   7 rue Monsieur, VII

Darling Evelyn

The enclosed (don't return it) for your eye alone will make you
laugh – it is from my darling Norwegian maid, you may remember
her, Sigrid. She is married & does part time work to eke out, & I
knew she wasn't very happy in her place so recommended her to
Smarty. I *dote* on them being normal people[1] – shows what an early
training by a Mitford can do for you.

I read *Loved One* every day. My favourite joke is 'They do when
they go to the can'. (So true.) My 2nd favourite is 'what you said
first'.

What's the good of me getting on with Cedric when the Russians
will be here[2] long before I've spent *Pursuit* money. Unable to be angry
with them I am quite simply frightened – I wake up in the night
sometimes in a cold sweat. Thank goodness for having no children, I
can take a pill & say goodbye, but what about my friend the Countess
Costa[3] with 2 darling little black beetle babies of 2 & 4? By the way
she had these kids in an American clinic which she says was exactly
like W. Glades, & she says there is one mistake – you speak of speciality
& it should be specialty.

I had a parcel from Alice[4] yesterday called Xmas Spesh & it contained dates, cranberry sauce, nuts, pastry mix & chopped olives. I
cried. I cry easily now, on account of the Russians coming so anything
like parcels becomes twice as important.

Your godson Jonathan has been with me – is probably still with
me as he's gone off to catch a train which I suspect he's determined
to miss. He's at Strasbourg & likes it. A funny vague boy but I like
him very much, though the vagueness makes him rather a tiring guest
in some ways.

As I wrote the word *some*, back he came, having duly missed the
train & drunk all the wine I gave him, for his dinner, on the station
platform (5.30 p.m.).

I had a letter from Sibyl [Colefax] illegible as usual until one came
to the words please send me a blue veil with chenille spots which a
child learning could read. So now we know.

Oh dear, I'm in a state. But you should see the states of all my
friends here – bags packed & sandwiches cut.

    Best love
        NR

---

[1] Sigrid Edward's letter about her new employer, Cyril Connolly, has not survived.
[2] The Communist *coup d'état* in Czechoslovakia had intensified fear of a Soviet invasion of
France.
[3] Elizabeth (Doodie) Millar (1908–95). Married to Count Amedée Costa de Beauregard in
1940.
[4] Alice Astor (1902–56). Rich, beautiful and generous American. Married to Prince Serge

Obolensky, to Raimund von Hofmannsthal, to Philip Harding and to Hon. David Pleydell-Bouverie.

6 March [1948]   Piers Court
                                                          Stinchcombe

Darling Nancy,

That is a remarkably obtuse letter from the Norwegian. We must get her alone & ply her with snaps schnapps? and questions. Nor do I think it proper for her to refer to her former mistress in those terms. She has made a very bad impression on me.

Did I tell you of Boots's stroke? Not I think paralysis in the full Elwes sense but a definite seizure. His doctor sent him to Tring[1] where he was strapped to his bed for three weeks & treated with enemas & synthetic orange juice. He lost 21 lbs. Well that is a lot for a shortish man. I think it will be the end of him.

Loved One is being well received in intellectual circles. They think my heart is in the right place after all. I'll show them.

I am afraid that when you fall into communist hands you must expect very little gratitude for all your services to the Party. When they were attempting their first coup in Spain, with precisely the same plan as they have employed everywhere since, you applauded ardently. You introduced an entirely false figure into your well known novel simply to suck up to them. But you will get no thanks & no reward.

I am so weary about having been consistently right in all my political predictions for ten years. It is so boring seeing it all happen for the second time after one has gone through it in imagination. For you & Duff & Randolph life must be all one lovely surprise after another.

I am reading Proust for the first time – in English of course – and am surprised to find him a mental defective. No one warned me of that. He has absolutely no sense of time. He can't remember anyone's age. In the same summer as Gilberte gives him a marble & Françoise takes him to the public lavatory in the Champs Elysées, Bloch takes him to a brothel. And as for the jokes – the boredom of Bloch and Cottard.

Osbert Sitwell 3rd volume[2] is out in US. I am reading it. He treads gingerly about Lady Ida's criminal career.[3] Did you know that the Sitwells only trace their descent through a female line. The real name of the family is Hurt. They took the name Sitwell quite lately – about 1800. He avoids this very neatly saying that the lands of Eckington were held by Cytwells in the tenth century & then jumping to Sir Sitwell Sitwell first bart né Hurt. There are precious few Englishmen who could not assume a mediaeval name if they chose to pick about in their pedigree.

Whenever he writes about Ginger[4] he is splendid but there are some awful drab panegyrics of Edwardian hostesses.

How Jewish was Proust? I mean like Sutro & Jessel[5] or like Brian
Howard? Did his parents go to synagogue? If he was a real Jew it
would surely be quite impossible for him to know the haute-
bourgeoisie, though he might meet the looser aristocracy?

Patrick Balfour is going to propose marriage to Diana Campbell-
Gray,[6] then to Coote,[7] then he can't think to whom. He does want a
wife so badly. He has been staying here & has been very nice. He has
£300 in the world & two suitcases of ill-fitting clothes and no prospects.
He is very much nicer in adversity. Well most of his life has been that.
He is trying to write a novel about Angela.[8] It won't be any good.

Henry Yorke is having an affaire with Jennifer Fry.[9]

David Erskine[10] has rewarded (ha ha) the long pursuit of Miss Kelly
by marrying her.

You must have poor Jonathan converted to Catholicism. The only
hope for him.

Best love from
    Evelyn

[1] A fashionable health farm.
[2] *Great Morning* (1948), Osbert Sitwell's third volume of autobiography.
[3] Osbert's spendthrift mother had been entrapped into borrowing money fraudulently and was
sentenced to three months' imprisonment.
[4] Osbert's father, Sir George Sitwell (1860–1943).
[5] Edward Jessel (1904–90). Married to Lady Helen Vane-Tempest-Stewart 1935–60. Succeeded
as 2nd Baron in 1950.
[6] Diana Cavendish (1909–92). Married to Robert Boothby 1935–7, to Ian Douglas-Campbell-
Gray 1942–6, and to Viscount Gage in 1971.
[7] Lady Dorothy Lygon (1912–2001), (Coote). The youngest of the Lygon sisters. She evokes her
early friendship with Evelyn in an affectionate essay, 'Madresfield and Brideshead', in *Evelyn
Waugh and His World*, ed. D. Pryce-Jones. Served in the WAAF during the war; married Robert
Heber-Percy in 1985.
[8] Angela Culme-Seymour (1912–). Married to John Spencer-Churchill 1934–8, to 3rd Baron
Kinross 1938–42, to Comte René Guillet de Chatellus in 1948 and to Mehmet Ali Bulent
Rauf in 1977.
[9] Jennifer Fry (1916–95). A niece of Evelyn's first wife. Married to Robert Heber-Percy 1942–
7 and to Alan Ross 1949–85.
[10] Hon. David St Clair Erskine (1917–85). Hamish's younger brother. Married to Antonia Kelly
1948–59.

13 March 1948   7 rue Monsieur, VII

Darling Evelyn

I am sad to think of *you* reading Proust in English – there is *not one
joke* in all the 16 of S. Moncrieff's volumes. In French one laughs from
the stomach, as when reading you. I don't remember what you say
about time. I am an inattentive reader I fear. The later books are
more enjoyable, & I began on *Albertine*, but you must have read the
earlier ones to get the best out of them. But I see you are against.

Proust's mother was a Jewess – Proust I believe to be a French name. Haas (the original of Swann) is supposed to have been the only Jew really to have been accepted into French society – member of the Société d'Encouragement & so forth. Proust himself knew a few aristocrats, as you suggest, Prince E[dmond] de Polignac, Robert de Montesquiou of course (Charlus) & such. (Pss de P. told me he wanted to dedicate his book to the memory of her husband but, at the mere idea, 'la moutarde m'est montée au nez'[1] & she got her solicitor to warn him not to.) But I don't think he was generally accepted in society. I'll ask the Colonel. The haute bourgeoisie would have been easier as his father was a very well known clever doctor.

I went today to luncheon with my one really Faubourg friend, a saint called Mme Costa de Beauregard.[2] Seven courses and three Dukes. Not like Fabrice. She said 'how is Gaston?' I said 'he wants you to ask him to meet *bishops*.' She said 'I will ask him to meet the modern St François Xavier.' Not at all the same I fear.

Oh do arrange yourself as the frogs say to read French. I thought you *did*, anyway.

Politics. I agree with every word you say, only I humbly submit that communism is a high human ideal. I shall never formulate another political opinion, I am not clever enough.

I saw Diana [Cooper] all & every day for a week – now Lulu is back, silence de glace. Such a bore, I so love her company. Also 2 dinners I was invited to I have been put off in favour of Lulu, the hosts saying sadly that they know I will understand they can't make an enemy of Lulu she is too dangerous. I wish I were dangerous. *Do* come, I so long for you to see my blissful flat. But I know you won't. Instead I get Helen Dashwood.

I should think Miss Fry & Henry very well suited both so sexy. Are you for?

My book is stuck for ever. The Russians the Spring the hats the clothes & a succession of English friends & above all the telephone – I can't, I give up.

Much love
NR

[1] 'I lost my temper.'
[2] Jeanne Aubry-Vitet; married to Comte Carl Costa de Beauregard. A contemporary of Nancy's mother and a half-sister of Violet Hammersley. Nancy depicted her as Mme de Valhubert in *The Blessing* (1951).

2 April 1948   7 rue Monsieur, VII

Darling Evelyn

I've been thinking a lot about Mr Joyboy (M. Joie-Garçon) since the Duchesse de Vendôme's death.

Well, warm weather you know & they show no signs of burying her. Meanwhile the whole of the 7ème, so smart we are here, floats about in crêpe veils looking as if there were a war on.

I've got a young Woodley called young Godley,[1] he wears his pyjamas all day because easier for going to bed. I only know this because they hang down below his trousers & I rather rudely asked. He is v. clever, double 1st at Oxford, & also has a spark of intelligence. He plays the oboe all all day. His dad is called Kilbracken I thought the Colonel would die when I told him & this Kilbracken used to kiss Diana your Diana when she was 12 lucky him.

Do come. You must be getting tired of the Ritz – I mean a little change would do you good. Besides you would like the atmosphere – today I heard one old count say to another old count about a third old count 'Mais mon cher *très* à gauche, il est Orléaniste!'[2] I asked these old fellows about Proust. Only ¼ Jewish, they said, but looked a full Jew. Not much received in society but a tremendous questioner & when he met society people asked & asked & asked & no detail too small to be gone into. Have you gone on reading or given up?

I see Diana a great deal, much more than before as she is at a loose end, lonely even perhaps. Lulu is courting a painter called Jean Hugo[3] in the South.

I am worried about my book, can't write it. Counted the telephone calls this morning, 10 before 11. What am I to do, & it could be *so* good, better than the other by far.

I hope you are all well & Harriet.

I had a letter from Diana, my Diana, saying she had met your brother in law. 'He seems to be off his old head. He says Evelyn *loves* him, this I can scarce believe.'[4] I gather he was a bit drunk.

Best love do write
    NR

Another thing my old count said, speaking of Dsse de V, 'Well, she must be in heaven *by now*' as though she'd caught the 4.45.

[1] Hon. Wynne Godley (1926–). Economist and former professional oboist. Younger son of 2nd Baron Kilbracken.
[2] 'But my dear, *very* to the left, he's an Orleanist.' The 'left-wing' branch of the French monarchists considered the descendants of Philippe Egalité the rightful pretenders to the throne.
[3] Jean Hugo (1894–1984). Great-grandson of Victor Hugo.
[4] When Evelyn heard that Auberon Herbert had said that he loved him, he wrote a furious letter to Diana Mosley, saying: 'He knows quite well I don't love him and he had no business to tell you that I did.' (Lady Mosley in conversation with the editor)

7 April [1948]   St James's Club
                                                        Piccadilly, W.1.

Darling Nancy

I have taken refuge here from White's which has become uninhabitable since the budget – all the men who to my certain knowledge have
not £100 in the world yelling themselves hoarse (and I think sincerely
believing) that they are ruined and the dozen or so really rich men smoking quietly in corners having made themselves registered companies in
Costa Rica years ago. The people who really are ruined are the heiresses
for Sir Stafford[1] has made it a dead loss (literally out-of-pocket) to have
a wife with more than £2000 a year in trust funds.

I had a long week-end in Somerset. First at the Baths – frightfully
noisy & drunken, Daphne keeping me up till 3.30 every night, and
the children riding bicycles round the house with loud cries from 6.30.
No sleep. Jazz all day. Henry at meals reading the most disgusting
pages of Malinowski's *Sexual Life of Savages* (and goodness they are
disgusting) aloud to his 18 year old daughter and 16 year old son. All
Longleat park like Surrey – the woods cut, second growth scrub, tank
tracks & decaying Nissen huts. Then a great change to Mells[2] – all
Pre-Raphaelite paintings & the X-word puzzle with Ronnie Knox.

I visited Olivia Greene[3] – stark mad. She broke her arm writing a letter.

I heard that the Filth-Marine, as Ran calls Palffy,[4] has behaved
badly to Diana.

Mrs J Sutro is giving a subscription ball for Diana & Mme Massigli.[5]
Proust would have some difficult conundrums about that. I persevere
with Proust & still think him insane. Of course I miss all the nuances
of language but the structure must be sane & that is raving. Eg. 'I' is
represented as a chronic invalid of exquisite diffidence etc etc. Then
suddenly in order to illustrate Albertine's slang he says:– 'For example
talking about the seconds I had chosen for a duel I was engaged in . . .'

I go out shopping after a luncheon a bit tight & buy such peculiar
things – 3 tie pins, a ½ ton marble 2nd Empire Clock, a solid silver
1830 candelabrum as tall as myself, a pearl grey bowler, six pounds
of church candles – they keep appearing in my bed-room in the most
disconcerting way. Perhaps it is not drink but insanity.

Randolph is back, exactly 3 times as fat as before.

Mrs Loutit has a new look: silk stockings, high heeled shoes, diamond
clips everywhere. I dined with Boots last evening in his subterranean
dining room superb grub as usual.

I call Handy Handy & he calls me Evelyn now. It is very nice. I
had to write & ask him to.

      Best love
         Evelyn

[1] Sir Stafford Cripps (1889–1952). Chancellor of the Exchequer 1947–51. Married Isobel Swithinbank, an Eno's Fruit Salts heiress, in 1911.
[2] The Manor House at Mells, near Bath in Somerset, where Katharine Asquith lived.
[3] Olivia Plunket Greene (1907–55). Evelyn's first love. Heavy drinking had driven her to depression and religious mania.
[4] Louise de Vilmorin.
[5] Odette Massigli; Swiss-born wife of René Massigli, French Ambassador to London 1944–55.

24 April 1948   7 rue Monsieur, VII

Darling Evelyn

The great excitement of the week has been the death of Pierre Colle,[1] aged 38, of overeating. He *literally* burst. I leave it to you to do what you think best about telling Smarty. Well, when the horrid details became known which of course they did in a moment (oh the telephoning) all Paris went on to a diet of oranges & Vichy & the restaurants were in such a fit about it that the manager of the Méditerranée actually offered me a cocktail free, which of course I refused. Then somebody – the restaurateurs perhaps, had the bright idea of putting it about that it *wasn't only eating*, that he'd had a child at the age of 15 & furthermore that he'd been *too much in aeroplanes lately* – So with sighs of relief we've all fallen upon our food again –! I gather even Whispering Glades wouldn't have made much of a job of him & in fact they hurried him underground the very next day.

Now much news à part cela – I haven't seen Diana since Sutro's party & now she's gone back for the King's – she came this morning at 9.30 with armfuls of tulips (my & Louis XIV's favourite flowers) but dashed off to the station, no time to chat. The heroine of my book gets more like her every page, I suppose it is unavoidable. The book is going very slowly but not badly. I see *Vile Bodies* in French in all the bookshops.

Your shopping sounds just like the Colonel – perhaps it's a thing which overtakes a chap like the change for us. ('I've got a little touch of the change' a charwoman once said to me.) Anyway last week he bought a marble statue of an Austrian Archduke which it took 8 men to carry upstairs & a huge screen, so that one can hardly get into his room now. He then got a picture said to be by the brother of Hubert Robert & another which may have come from the studio of Poussin. Though he stands by all this junk when I teased I think, like you, he is faintly puzzled & not *quite* sure –

Momo [Marriott] has been here, spreading alarm & despondency which she learnt in America ('darling an unknown force of armed men is moving in Italy' she said last night on the telephone. 'Momo –! moving in which direction?' but she was rather vague after that) but very affectionate. I love her she is one of my post-war loves.

Do come over oh do.

My Diana simply adored her luncheon with you, it is a treat to her to see old chums – & surely a treat for them.

I hear Gerald [Berners] has left it in his will that he is to be stuffed & kept in the hall at Faringdon. I think *The Loved One* will have done a great deal of harm in these little ways.

Best love, I *expect* you to come.
    NR

[1] Pierre Colle (1909–48). A Parisian art dealer, agent for several important Surrealist painters and for Christian Bérard. Married to Carmen Corcuera.

29 April 1948   7 rue Monsieur, VII

Darling Evelyn

Thank you for the party[1] – oh bliss. I must say I think it sounds great fun – but still I agree with you the idea of making people pay gives one *the utter creeps, I couldn't.*

Pierre Colle was a hateful art dealer. Aged 38 looked 68. Smarty will know.

Yes I should have thought Smarty was more the kind that gets murdered – which I feel about myself though of course I'm glad too for the murderers' sakes. (It's all part of being left wing & trying to leave the world a better place, you wouldn't understand. Very difficult sometimes I confess.)

I hear the result of *The Loved One* is no American undertaker will look at an English corpse now (revenge) & they are all piling up on rubbish heaps.

Harold's book[2] makes you shriek if read very slowly in his voice. But it's like a translation, he doesn't really know English. Hateful Mollie hasn't sent me Osbert's yet. Oh I say, a letter from my solicitor saying H. Hill made a profit of £6000 last year, of which I'm supposed to get ⅓, & is offering to pay me £150, & nothing for the year before. This is not to be repeated, but you see how right you were. However my Mr Rutherford is calling a meeting & will take the stick to them I hope.

My book is getting on faster. When in type may I send it to you – such an awful thing to ask – but there is nobody here I can read it to & who could help me, as Gerald did with the other. There literally isn't one joke in the whole book so far so I shouldn't think it will have much success. However it's about the aristocracy all right.

I don't remember much about Jack Donaldson,[3] he was a friend of Tom's[4] & his wife learnt farming from Mary Dunn. Oh yes – Peckham Health Centre.

I hear Bob Boothby[5] is on *The Brains Trust* as a light weight & heavy

weight Joad has been sacked for swindling the railways.[6] What about
Bob & the good Czech gold? Oh the bliss of England one really ought
to live there. Joad wrote all about it in the *Continental D. Mail*, rather
a puzzle for French readers I should fancy.

Best love – very dull letter I know but it's really a thank you letter
for the Party.

NR

Just off to see Diana.

[1] Evelyn's missing letter may have included the invitation to Gillian Sutro's subscription ball
for Diana Cooper and Odette Massigli. In a letter to Diana Cooper, he wrote: 'To one earnest
student of the social scene that seems a particularly odd invitation in all ways.' *Mr Wu & Mrs
Stitch* edited by Artemis Cooper (Hodder & Stoughton, 1991), p. 102.
[2] Harold Acton's first volume of autobiography, *Memoirs of an Aesthete*, had just been published.
[3] John Donaldson (1907–98). Farmer and Labour Party supporter. Pioneer of the first Health
Centre in Peckham. Created life peer in 1967. Married in 1935 Frances Lonsdale, author of
Portrait of a Country Neighbour (1967), a memoir of Evelyn. In 1947 the Donaldsons went to farm
in Gloucestershire, where they were near neighbours of the Waughs.
[4] Thomas Mitford (1909–45). Nancy's only brother. Good-looking, intelligent and musical, he
relished an argument and as a child would pay his sisters a shilling an hour to argue. Practised
at the Bar before joining the Rifle Brigade in 1939. He died of wounds in Burma in the last
days of the war.
[5] Robert Boothby (1900–86). Conservative Unionist MP 1924–58. His career as Parliamentary
Secretary to the Minister of Food came to an end in 1941 when he failed to declare a personal
financial interest when debating Czech gold in the House of Commons. Created life peer in
1958.
[6] Dr Joad had been found guilty of trying to evade payment for his ticket on a train journey.

21 May 1948   7 rue Monsieur, VII

Darling Evelyn
    Excellent about it arriving on her birthday which I have never
known & never *can* remember birthdays – how does one unless a
birthday book. *Masturbation.*[1] I used to masturbate whenever I thought
about Lady Jane Grey, so of course I thought about her continually
& even executed a fine water colour of her on the scaffold, which my
mother still has, framed, & in which Lady Jane & her ladies in waiting
all wear watches hanging from enamel bows as my mother did at the
time. This sublimation of sex might be recommended to Harriet,
except that I don't think it changed anything & I still get quite excited
when I think of Lady Jane (less & less often though as the years roll
on).
    Diana has invited me to go & finish my book at Chantilly. I shan't
hurry it at all – Jamie Hamilton has lost all his paper in the Bristol
fire, & Winston I hear has taken 60 miles of cloth binding for his
mémoires, so it can't matter when it appears, & now I have got a
story for once in my life I don't want to skimp it.
    Your friend Baroness Blixen[2] is here, too much sunk in Nordic

gloom for me. (So typical that my one Danish friend here should be called Moans [Tvede].) I really can't stand people who never giggle at all. (Moans doesn't either but he loves me.)

The Hell of the Harveys & their awful behaviour to the Duffs is such that in my book when (what Debo calls) the Utter Ghastly Drear, Boy Dougdale, marries the blissful heroine it is 'I, Oliver Harvey, take thee Leopoldina'.

Do come, Evelyn. S. Boots is coming, & he has a double here, so much so that when a friend of mine said 'You are Cyril Connolly aren't you?' he replied 'No, his double.' So I'm giving a party for them – think you should be there. (Or do you think it will hurt their feelings if I do?)

Much love
    NR

[1] Evelyn's letter to Nancy which provoked this discussion has not survived.
[2] Karen Blixen (1885–1962). Danish author who wrote mainly in English under the pseudonym Isak Dinesen. Best-known for *Seven Gothic Tales* (1934) and *Out of Africa* (1937). Evelyn had met her on his Scandinavian tour.

21 July 1948   Château de St Firmin
                                                Vineuil
                                                Oise

Darling Evelyn

Honks[1] Cooper & I are jolly sad you aren't here – what *is* nettle rash? I write my book all day in the stables & at meal times there are large & cheerful parties so you see it is ideal. I'm getting on like mad with the book seldom less than 2000 words a day does that impress you?

Your post card made me shriek, what does it mean?[2]

A glorious mad girl was here yesterday called Lady Lambton[3] (she is my heroine, I can't have enough of her) & she came to my room to do her hair & said, seeing your post card from Mr E. W. 'now I *am* impressed'. She began to talk about my books & then said 'but this is very dull for you because you must have read them yourself –' So perspicacious of her when I rarely read anything else.

There is another pen pusher here called Lady Jones[4] do you know her? A sort of fearfully nice gym mistress. She did Smarty's cure at Tring, NOT for you & me.

When does your nettle rash finish? Oh *do* come.

Dearest bought Ld Baldwin's library of 4000 books & paid for it all with the sale of one book – pas si bête?[5] How can anybody be so idiotic as to sell their library to a bookseller? I would be gloating if I ever got a D out of Dearest.

My book starts badly but picks up – I must re-do the start. Not so easy. But this time I've resolved no skimping, & refuse to give H. Hamilton a date. Do you remember your cruel words about having read the rough notes for *The Pursuit*.

Powder the rash & bring it.

Love from
    NR

Blissful blissful Honks Cooper.

Debo cries every time she thinks of the Queen because of her great beauty & great cleverness & the fact that she wins by hundreds at racing demon – I'm just the same about H.C.

Lady Lambton lost a valuable jewel somewhere in the countryside & only said 'Well I got it yesterday so now I'm back where I was the day before yesterday so it doesn't matter a *bit*.' Do you know her?

[1] Nickname originally given to Diana Mosley by her sister Deborah; it was adopted by Evelyn for Diana Cooper.
[2] Evelyn had sent an extract from an article which quoted a 'cruel contemporary' as saying: 'One can find Evelyn's biography in the dedications to his books, each displaying a further step in his social progress.' *Time*, 12 July 1948.
[3] Belinda Blew-Jones (1922–2003). Married Viscount Lambton in 1942.
[4] Enid Bagnold (1889–1981). Novelist and playwright. Married Sir Roderick Jones in 1920. The film of her novel *National Velvet* (1935), starring Elizabeth Taylor, was a huge box-office hit immediately after the war.
[5] He's no fool.

[July 1948]   [Piers Court
                                                  Stinchcombe?]
Dearest Nancy

2000 words a day is very good going. I do congratulate & envy you.

Nettle-rash is awful. It comes from eating zoned fish. It is just as tho you had been rolling in nettles. It usually lasts a few hours. Mine has lasted over a fortnight & the doctor is so eager to show his appreciation of 'paying patients' (patient is not the right word for me) that he injects me with expensive & dangerous drugs that leave me stupefied and morose.

Did you like my great friends the Asquiths.

Lady Lambton was a Miss Jones but no relation to pen pusher. I used to despise p.p. until I went to the Church of the Recessional, Forest Lawn (Whispering Glades) and found that she was queen of the place with a special shrine in the reliquarium. So now I respect her but don't like her.

The extract I sent re dedication was from a long article in an American paper (*Time*) saying how beastly I am – sound in principle no doubt but bang wrong in all facts, like all American journalism. It said that my dedications were not, as I had thought, signs of love for chums, but proclamations of rungs in the social ladder successfully ascended. I must say it gives a very odd order of precedence. Mrs Woodruff[1] (*Scott-King*) is very pleased to be six ahead of Honks. Perry Brownlow[2] is very angry at being four down on Randolph.[3]

So a boring neighbour said would I get a 'celebrity' to judge the beauty competition for the village fête. Not so easy because those who are madly famous in London Paris & New York are unheard of in Stinchcombe. I mean they have heard of Mr Churchill & the Duke of Beaufort and I suppose a number of cricketers whom I haven't heard of, but Sergeant Preston would mean nothing to them. I couldn't think who to ask so I got Osbert Lancaster[4] whom I don't particularly cherish because I thought anyway his name is in the *Daily Express* every day. But no one had heard of him and it poured with rain & I took to my bed & poor Laura was left with O.L. for a week-end. Goodness how sad.

The american article said I had a butler with 'impeccable trousers'. On the man-bites-dog theory of news that is most significant. Do most butlers have peccant trousers – no fly buttons, hole in the seat, one leg shorter than the other – or did they expect him to wear a kilt?

Children are beginning to flock back to the house. Harriet has suddenly become much more agreeable than when you saw her.

The order of precedence again: Honks Mosley bottom but two, well I suppose for a divorced jail bird that is fair but poor Bryan, a brewing peer, should surely be above Father D'Arcy. I think Bowra must have told them this story.

All love to Honks
Evelyn

[1] Hon. Marie (Mia) Acton (1905–94). Married to Douglas Woodruff, Catholic journalist and scholar, editor of the *Tablet* 1936–67.
[2] 6th Baron Brownlow (1899–1978). Lord-in-Waiting to Edward VIII at the time of the abdication.
[3] The chronological order of dedications in Evelyn's books to this date was as follows:

Rossetti	Evelyn Gardner
Decline and Fall	Harold Acton
Vile Bodies	Bryan and Diana Guinness
Labels: A Mediterranean Journal	Bryan and Diana Guinness
Remote People	Hazel Lavery
Black Mischief	Mary and Dorothy Lygon
Ninety-Two Days	Diana Cooper
Edmund Campion	Martin D'Arcy
Waugh in Abyssinia	Kitty and Perry [Brownlow]
Scoop	Laura
Work Suspended	Alexander Woollcott
Put Out More Flags	Randolph Churchill
Brideshead Revisited	Laura
Scott-King's Modern Europe	Mia Woodruff
The Loved One	Nancy Mitford

[4] Osbert Lancaster (1908–86). Cartoonist on the *Daily Express* for 40 years. Knighted in 1975.

1 August 1948   Château de St Firmin
                                                Vineuil

Darling Evelyn

As far as I can see (your ref: *Time* Magazine) your end has been in
your beginning with the daughters of second barons of great obscurity.

I am discouraged with my book. It happens in 1930–1 & I had
made the financial crisis & K. Alfonso's abdication 1929.[1] So the house
party says rise above that nobody will notice, but the trouble is me
having noticed. Bother. Apart from that it is *glittering* do promise you'll
read it & tell me what you think I don't want to skimp it this time.

The Derbys[2] are here. Low horse power & no great effort to please.
Diana says to me out loud come on let's get away from these bores.

Lady Jones reveres me, perhaps because of *The Loved One* I now see,
as she is evidently a funeral snob. She cheers my clothes, laughs at
my jokes & reads my books so of course I am for. Apart from that I
see your point.

I am selling out of Dearest & Co. Just like you said he would he
has hotted me. Now I have £3000 to invest I do wish I was a clever
little business woman but as I'm not & I do so *long* for a diamond
brooch I can't help wondering if it wouldn't be a good idea –

Do you ever feel worried about the young? Apart from the dull
Derbys we have had the Cranbornes[3] here [. . .], then of course darling
Lady Lambton is raving mad, Wynne Godley dying of T.B.; never
mind there must be some clever serious sober sane ones about. John
Julius for one. I always think Debo's friends are hell I must say.

I leave here for a small pub in Touraine on Sat: reckon to do
another month of hard work there I shall miss the utter heaven of
Honks. She is off for a hol with Liz [von Hofmannsthal].

You might write. Rue Mr will forward – you know how one *longs*
for letters when quite alone. I rather look forward to it though – too
many people in Paris.

    Best love, love to Laura
       NR

Emerald has left ⅓ to Diana [Cooper] ⅓ to Berty [Abdy] & Nancy
Cunard did you know?[4]

[1] King Alfonso XIII of Spain abandoned the throne and fled his country in 1931.
[2] 18th Earl of Derby (1918–94). Married to Lady Isobel Milles-Lade in 1948.
[3] Viscount Cranborne (1916–2003). Succeeded as 6th Marquess of Salisbury in 1972. Married
Marjorie Wyndham-Quin in 1945.
[4] Emerald Cunard's estate amounted to little more than debts.

10 August [1948]   Piers Court
                                              Stinchcombe
Dearest Nancy

Why not spend your salvaged capital in starting a bookshop in
Paris? It would make the place very much more attractive to your
friends. Take a little shop near the Travellers Club & fill it with light
literature in the English language and fine French picture books & sit
there six hours a day. Do.

I have had a terrible affliction, still not entirely cured, of continuous
nettle-rash. Perhaps I told you. My doctor can only advise change of
air but it is so much effort to move a mile nowadays that one has to
be in bouncing health before thinking of it. Perhaps I shall crawl to
New York in the autumn.

I have all five children & two Eddie Grant orphans and my mother
in the house. It is not big enough. We all went to the cinema which
Harriet greatly enjoyed. She is very much occupied in her mind with
demonology.

Who should turn up the other day in a big motorcar but Randolph
& who should get out with him but his divorced wife wearing heels
nine inches high like something in *London Life* & trailing yellow skirts.
I said 'Are you reconciled?' 'No no just a little trip.'

I do not think poor Pam Berry has long to live. F. E. Smith grew
up in poverty because his father died at 40; *he* died at 50; so did his
brother; Eleanor at 41[1]; Freddie has the mark of death on him. Pam
won't last five years. She is trying to make the best of it.

I am laying out a dank little garden of cobble stones & evergreens.

Sir Alfred D Cooper, the zionist free-mason, writes such balls in
the *Daily Mail* that I am having to go back to the *Express*.

Oh dear this is a dreary little letter but I am leading a dreary little
life at the moment.

    Best love
        Evelyn

[1] F. E. Smith, 1st Earl of Birkenhead, died in 1930, aged 58. His father died at the age of 43;
his two brothers died in 1924, aged 48 and 53. His daughter, Eleanor, died in 1945, aged 43.

28 September 1948   7 rue Monsieur, VII
Darling Evelyn

I hear you say I can't have Diversion[1] & it would have been *so*
perfect.

When do you go to USA – I do so need your help. The MS goes
over on Friday with Moll [Friese-Greene] who will give it to the typist
who seems to think it will take a fortnight or so & I come over with
Debo on the 18th Oct. I do wish you'd come here for the 11th Oct

Debo's visit, rather like the Royal visit to me I must say & almost as alarming since all my friends are so much too old & so much too clever.

Oh dear, the book. I know you'll say you enjoyed the rough notes, it is so discouraging to an author, & H Hamilton is ravening for it. But, *maître*, I shall try & follow your teaching.

I heard about you & the Charles club so you see one gets the news in the end. I shrieked.

I see I'm going to miss the book now it's done – I've never taken so long before – one year & 22 days. Oh I do hope it's good.

What a dull letter I'm so sorry but I've been shut up all this time & seen nobody except my colonel who is on a horrid diet of no wine or coffee & is very low he says he has no incentive. But he was really ill so he is faithfully doing it.

Best love oh do come for THE VISIT. You ought really to come & see Jouvet in Molière's *Dom Juan*, a profoundly fascinating play & extraordinary performance.

    NR

[1] A suggested title for *Love in a Cold Climate*.

[4 October 1948]

Darling Nancy

So my friend Graham Greene whose books you won't read was sitting in a New York hotel feeling quite well when he felt very wet & sticky in the lap & hurried to the lavatory & found that his penis was pouring with blood. So he fainted & was taken to a hospital and the doctors said 'It may be caused by five diseases two of which are not immediately fatal, the others are.' Then they chloroformed him & he woke up two days later & they said: 'Well, we can't find anything wrong at all. What have you been up to? Too much womanizing?' 'No, not for weeks since I left my home in England.' 'Ah' they said '*That's* it.' What a terrible warning. No wonder his books are sad.

I don't go to USA before the end of the month. Date not fixed. Why shouldn't I take your book with me in the steamship & post it back at once from New York – it would only take five days longer than Stinchcombe–Paris & it would be an ideal time to give it the attention it deserves. I long to read it.

I say you & Pam Berry have got crushes on each other. She won't talk of anything else.

No I can't, won't, come to Paris. Connolly says he prefers France to England because no one is interested in religion there. Well that is all I am interested in really. And you know Debo & I don't hit it off.

My love for her is purely physical & unreciprocated and every meeting is a deep disappointment.

Mr Popkin seems to me to be collaborating with the Government. I have had to give him a pep talk. I do not know Ld. Beaverbrook very well but I know Randolph's imitations of him so I did that & Popkin was scared stiff & promised immediate new behaviour.

I went to such an extraordinary house[1] on Wednesday. A side of life I never saw before – very rich, Cambridge, Jewish, socialist, highbrow, scientific, farming. There were Picassos on sliding panels & when you pushed them back plate glass & a stable with a stallion looking at one. No servants. Lovely Carolean silver unpolished. Gourmet wines & cigars. The house a series of wood bungalows, more bathrooms than bedrooms. The hostess at six saying 'I say shall we have dinner tonight as Evelyn's here. Usually we only have Shredded Wheat. I'll see what there is.' Goes to tiny kitchenette & comes back. 'Well there's grouse, partridges, ham, a leg of mutton and half a cold goose' (literally) 'What does anyone want?' Then a children's nannie dining with us called 'Twinkle' dressed with tremendous starched frills & celluloid collars etc and everyone talking to her about lesbianism & masturbation. House telephone so that generally people don't bother to meet but just telephone from room to room. It made quite a change from Stinkers.

Here is a funny picture of my patriarchal home circle.

Best love
      E

[1] Evelyn stayed at Thriplow Farm with Henry Walston (1912–91) and his beautiful American wife Catherine Crompton (1916–78). When she converted to Catholicism in 1946, Catherine Walston wrote to Graham Greene asking him to be her godfather. Greene accepted and subsequently embarked on a passionate love affair with his godchild that lasted until the 1960s.

6 October 1948   7 rue Monsieur, VII

Darling Evelyn

But are the Americans interested in religion? I dare say Cyril's set here isn't but I could put you in touch with hundreds who are, *much more easily* than I can fix Debo in the racing world which is what she asks. Also you are interested in food, also two of your greatest friends live here, none of which makes it understandable why you prefer America (further away, too). Disloyal.

You could hand or post the typescript to my US agent, only then I wouldn't have a chance to make any alterations. You could do so if it seemed all right to you (I mean post it straight to the agent).

How awful about Graham Greene no wonder I can't read his books. Disgusting!!

Oh the photograph it has made me completely happy for ever –
very good of Laura who generally comes out so badly. You look a
regular Uncle Matthew, I must say.

I plan to go to England about the 20th to see about the book, do
hope you won't have left by then.

If you lived here you wouldn't dare have that photograph taken
because having such millions of servants would be a signe extérieur
de la richesse[1] & you'd be taxed accordingly. They even count window
boxes & grand pianos.

I am so glad you beat up Popkin, my friend Mrs Chaplin[2] did it
the other day with wonderful results. As I am too weak kneed myself
I'm delighted when others do it he *must* be kept on our side.

Dined with my Woodley[3] last night. His stepmother went into the
garden, blew ½ her head off with a shot gun (brains on all the shrubs)
lay all night in pouring rain & was fully conscious – rather spry in
fact, when found in the morning – ready for breakfast was the implica-
tion. She died 6 weeks later. Puts one off suicide – well I've never
been tempted by shot guns in any case. The Woodley refers to it as
'the incident' oh how funny boys are – is yours?

So I greatly hope to see you quite soon.

V. best love
   NR

Would the Nuncio be interested in religion? I could get you introduced
to him he is my Colonel's great friend. Old Countess Costa who is
never there for meals because praying in Church must be interested
too. She is 80 & confesses every day & when somebody asked the
priest what she could find to confess he said it was always 'j'ai été
odieuse avec les invités'.[4]

[1] Outward and visible sign of wealth. The photograph showed Evelyn and his family surrounded
by ten members of his household.
[2] Alvilde Bridges (1909–94). Expert on gardens and garden design. Married to Viscount Chaplin
1933–50 and to James Lees-Milne in 1951.
[3] Wynne Godley.
[4] 'I have been vile to the guests.'

[postmarked 8 October 1948]   Piers Court
[postcard]   Stinchcombe

Yanks are madly interested in religion. Frogs are behaving (& have
behaved since 1789) very improperly in a number of ways & it is
wicked to encourage them in their conceit. Besides Americans speak
English far better than I speak French. I shan't sail before 30th, perhaps
not till 6th, perhaps not at all, so we *must* meet. Do come here when
I am in a good temper. I am full of ungovernable rages in London.

Longing to read novel. Of course my advice will involve you in at least six months gruelling work. Cooper lives for pleasure.

E

18 October 1948   7 rue Monsieur, VII

Darling Evelyn

I've taken the liberty to tell my typist to post you a copy (*uncorrected, you must bear in mind*) of Diversion to Piers Court, which she will do about next Thursday. Can you really be bothered to wade through it – I'm taking you at your word you see. A scream from H. Hamilton that he has kept all his paper for it to be his important Spring book & must have it *now* NOW *NOW*. So the sooner I begin on my 6 months' hard work the better.

I come over next Thursday don't know where I shall be, I leave it to Diana [Mosley].

She will be at 21 Chapel St, Slo 3395. I rather expect I shall go to her in the country on Friday unless she is sending me to my mum at H. Wycombe. I intend to correct one copy of the book all that weekend. Then perhaps the following week I could go to you or see you in London?

Oh dear I feel nervous.

Debo's visit a wild success. Lulu laid her hand on Andrew's forehead (high spot).

Very tired, very nervous, prepared to be rendered suicidal by you!!

All love
NR

24 October 1948

Dearest Nancy

Six months hard I am afraid without remission for good conduct. The manuscript was a delight to read, full of wit & fun & fantasy. Whole passages (eg. Cedric's arrival & first evening) might be used verbatim in a book. The theme is original & promising. There is not a boring sentence (except p. 274).[1] But it isn't a book at all yet. No more 40 hour week. Blood, sweat & tears. That is to say if you want to produce a work of art. There is a work of art there, lurking in a hole, occasionally visible by the tip of its whiskers.

The Radletts of course steal the scene again. Jassy & Victoria are intoxicating & real, so real that every other character pales beside them except Cedric who, deplorably, is made to talk in places in exactly their idiom. This is a trick you must look out for. I can just accept Polly speaking exactly like Linda – but Cedric is a Parisian pansy. Oliver Messel doesn't talk like Debo.

Your great failure is 'Boy' who is too important to be left, as he is, a mere collection of attributes. Most of the minor characters are flops. Mrs Corbett begins as though you meant her to be a sort of Jean Norton–Freda Ward[2] but almost at once becomes Erskine–Ogilvie-Grant. She would be greatly strengthened by some of Freda's prudery & shyness. Mrs Cozens is just two or three different people. You start her as a North Oxford don's wife, suddenly enrich & ennoble her and turn her into a hunting girl. There have been rich & sporting dons' homes but not in Banbury Road. They have little manors in the Bicester country (eg. Holland Hibberts & John Buchans).

I don't believe that in a pompous house (not Grace Curzon's[3] anyway) a newly arrived, shy girl would be greeted by gibes about her mother's adultery. I know less of French manners but it is inconceivable to me that Fabrice would talk to a jeune fille as you make him.

Davey was a good foil to Uncle Matthew but he loses point beside Cedric & Boy.

The punctuation is pitiable but it never becomes unintelligible so I just shouldn't try. It is clearly not your subject – like theology.

The narrative doesn't begin until Chapter III and is just developing an intricate & highly enjoyable climax when the siren goes & down tools.

I should mention that (granted the awful failure of Boy to come to life at all) you handle the Polly–Boy relationship admirably everywhere.

Now the book must be saved. So start again. Have no explanations; assume your reader knows *Pursuit of Love*, and plunge him straight into Alconleigh with the Lecturer's first lascivious visit. Then follow him to Montdore and show him as the jagger. Then if you like pack them off to Delhi and start again at your Chapter III. From then on all you have to do is watch the characters & make them speak & behave consistently. Then at the end of Part II Chapter VIII you can get really to work on the serious architectural achievement. It is a Henry James theme, told in a lighter way. Think how James would have developed the final chapters & then write them in your own delicious manner & we shall have a memorable book.

Well I suppose you will hate me now for the rest of our lives.

MS follows by separate post.

Best love
    Evelyn

I was sorry I couldn't dine with Pam [Berry] on Wednesday. That was before I read your notes. Perhaps now it is lucky.

---

[1] A description of Lady Patricia Douglas's dull country house.
[2] Jean Kinloch (1898–1945) married Richard Norton (later 6th Baron Grantley) in 1919 and was

mistress for many years of Lord Beaverbrook. Winifred (Freda) Birkin (1894–1983), daughter of
a lace manufacturer, was mistress of the Prince of Wales in the 1920s; married to William
Dudley Ward MP 1913–31 and to the Marquis Pedro (Bobby) de Casa Maury in 1937.
³ Grace Hinds (1877–1958). Widow of Alfred Duggan, married in 1917 1st Marquess Curzon,
Viceroy of India 1899–1905 and Foreign Secretary 1919–24.

28 October 1948   21 Chapel Street
                                                        London SW1

Dearest Evelyn
    You are *really kind* to have taken so much trouble. I agree with
nearly all you say – I've always known that Boy was too sketchy, &
that the beginning is clumsy. I have re-written the *whole thing* once
already you know. What I wonder is whether I can (am capable of)
doing better. You speak of Henry James but he was a *man* of intellect,
you must remember that I am an *uneducated woman* (viz punctuation)
& that I have done my best & worked hard already. What you say
about the minor characters I don't agree with. Your complaint is that
they are not photographs of existing people, but one must be allowed
to invent people if one is a novelist. I took the trouble to write to a
don's wife about Norma & she said quite possible.
    Oh dear. You see I'm afraid that what you really criticize are my
own inherent limitations. Luckily you also find something to admire,
that is one comfort. But I do feel quite sure that I am incapable of
writing the book you want me to – I can't do more really than skate
over surfaces, for one thing I am rather insensitive as you know, &
for another *not* very *clever*.
    I will have a go at Cedric's talk & do some revising on the lines
that you suggest.

    In haste *much love*
        NR

30 October 1948   Old Mill Cottage
                                                        High Wycombe

Dearest Evelyn
    I've just seen the typescript oh you *have* been so kind – I screamed
with laughter at some of your comments. Oh dear, Gerald has made
me alter such a lot & now you, there'll be but little left of me. As for
re writing I've left it to Jamie Hamilton to decide – given him the
MS & your letter. Diana & Gerald are against – Handy however,
who has read it in handywriting, is gloomy beyond words 'Very patchy'
but rather doubts I think whether there is much to be done.
    Awful about Kurt.¹ I don't know why everything you write doesn't
come out in a pathetic flicker in my books. I've got the memory of a

mouse & never read anybody except you. Is it Kurt's character or the actual name? Diana will know. Yes of course she'd have a maid, I'm providing one.

Could Cedric not pick up a few expressions from Radletts via Fanny? The fast set always talked unsuitably in front of ONE that's why one's Mum was so anti them. Think of Daphne [Bath] rather than Freda. My Colonel knows 'A Thousand Ages in Thy Sight' & Fabrice has been at Oxford. *You* don't know how chaps talk to young girls alone because you've never been a young girl alone with a chap – *I have*. A very pompous gratin [upper-crust] Comtesse I know always called her lover her fiancé – it's true she has since gone mad but she was the bluest of the blue blood & sister in law to a Duc (like me). It was your Church drove her mad which I can't understand – like punctuation.

Jamie has got a punctuator for me so that's all right.

'Why kennels when she's not a dog' is my favourite joke of all. You are just like Eddy 'Funny? Not funny.' I must be allowed it.

Randolph's girl has chucked him. I promised not to say but by the time you get this the news (the electric message) will have come to you.

Oh dear. I suppose girls who don't write books, like Susan Mary,[2] can get away with being quite bright.

Pam Berry said can you tell me anything about some people called Spearman[3] who have painted their door blue? I really couldn't start, but somebody who was there said Oh yes he's a picture dealer so I left it at that.

Fond love & many many thanks for taking so much trouble from the bottom of my heart.

NR

---

[1] Nancy had used the name Kurt for Cedric Hampton's 'hideous, drunken, brutal' German boyfriend in *Love in a Cold Climate*. She changed it to Klugg after Evelyn pointed out that it was the name of Sebastian Flyte's delinquent German boyfriend in *Brideshead Revisited*.
[2] Susan Mary Jay (1918–2004). Married to William Patten, attaché at the American Embassy in Paris, 1939–60. In 1961 she married the journalist Joseph Alsop.
[3] Alexander Spearman (1901–82). Conservative MP for Scarborough and Whitby 1941–66. Married to Diana Doyle 1928–51 and to Diana Ward in 1951. Knighted in 1956.

25 November 1948   7 rue Monsieur, VII

Darling Evelyn

Blissful *Loved One* oh how pretty it is *many* thanks indeed. Just back from London & found it awaiting me – it's my favourite thing in the world, having that dedicated to me.

Randolph came, with wife.[1] She is a beauty. I thought her rather cross but that may be shyness – *he* radiant, subdued, thin, charming, loving, aux petits soins.[2] I believe it may succeed.

Handy, who was rather spiky I thought, told of a *very* young man saying to him 'How sad that Evelyn Waugh isn't likely to write another book.' 'But why not?' 'Oh well, so old –'

Handy rubbed it well in how this applies to us all.

Randolph very gloomy on the future of writers & says that as soon as people can have television they will give up reading books. 'Why do they read? To pass the time. Well, soon they'll have a better way of passing it –' How simply horrid. Do have your children taught to read, all the same, to make a little market for us –

Belcher[3] is Bliss. I suppose you don't get him now you have become an American, I daresay you have more & better scandals of your own, but to us musty old Europeans he seems all right.

Cyril is here. I like to see him, but unfortunately he forms part of a joyeuse bande de noctambules & I can't stick the rest of the bande – a sort of bogus Gauguin with one leg called Campbell,[4] Mary Dunn, Joan Rayner[5] etc etc *all very dirty*, some disfigured by a taxi accident & covered in dried blood – you know, just what ONE doesn't care for.

Best love, happy Mother's Day or whatever it is they call Xmas over there.

NR

[1] Randolph Churchill married June Osborne in June 1948.
[2] Attentive.
[3] John Belcher (1905–64). Labour MP for Yorkshire. He resigned as Secretary to the Board of Trade after being accused of using his influence in return for gifts; these included a bunch of bananas, a bottle of whisky and a new suit. His wife was accused of accepting sausages and a handbag.
[4] Robin Campbell had lost a leg during the war. He once enraged Churchill by telling him how well the Germans had treated him when he was a prisoner of war. Churchill retorted: 'It is a pity they did not take off your head as well as your leg.'
[5] Hon. Joan Eyres Monsell (1912–2003). Photographer. Married to John Rayner 1939–47 and to Patrick Leigh Fermor in 1968.

[November 1948]   New York

Darling Nancy

I think you would wish to hear about Sir O Sitwell. Well he has grown his hair (so carefully kept by Trumper) so that he looks like Einstein. He and Edith (& Mr Horner)[1] are having one hell of a time. Every magazine has six pages of pictures of them headed 'The Fabulous Sitwells'. They have hired the Philharmonic Orchestra which in this town is something very big indeed to play while they recite poetry. Goodness how they are enjoying it. I said 'Is Sachie[2] joining you?' 'Alas. Sachie is High Sheriff of His County and therefore unable to leave the United Kingdom.'

Maureen is here (also Maurice[3] but that is another story) with her bridegroom. They dined with me last night in a fashionable restaurant. The bridegroom wore Wellington boots and a dinner jacket ornamented with gold Grenadier buttons.

I am trying to persuade Sergeant Preston to enter a Trappist monastery. I think he will be happier there.

The shops sell an instrument called the 'Beau Alarm' which emits a noise like an air raid siren. It is for girls subjected to passionate & unwelcome advances.

I have made 2 great new friends & many enemies.

Your last novel very popular here among upper classes.

Millicent Fenwick has written a book of Etiquette – 650 pages and not a dull sentence. Would you like a copy for Xmas?

A lady called Miss Case[4] is in love with me – unreciprocated.

Terrible rumours of Randolph's honeymoon spread by Tanis.[5]

I meet bad native pansies who all claim to be your close friends.

Love from
Evelyn

[1] David Horner (1901–84). Osbert Sitwell's companion for many years.
[2] Sacheverell Sitwell (1897–1988). The youngest of the literary trio had just published *Selected Poems*, an anthology of his best work to date. Married to Georgia Doble in 1925.
[3] Maurice Bowra was lecturing at Harvard.
[4] Margaret Case (1891–1971). Society editor for *Vogue* who was acting as Evelyn's social secretary in New York.
[5] Tanis Guinness (1908–93). Married to Hon. Drogo Montagu 1931–5, to Howard Dietz, the American librettist, 1937–58, and to Edward (Teddy) Phillips.

21 December 1948   7 rue Monsieur, VII

Darling Evelyn

So are you reciting out of *The Loved One* to the accompaniment of lures?*

Are you a little bit gel-gel [jealous] of the Sitwells? Serve you right for going there at all. Your letter was v. tantalizing. First I can't bear you going *there* & never coming *here* it is quite intolerable. Second you touch on subjects in a far more skimpy & unsatisfactory way than I do in that first class novel you were so horrid about 'Maurice is here but that's another story'. Who is Maureen's bridegroom? Maureen Dufferin? Has she *married* – how sinister.

You are *not* to drive my Serge into a monastery. I need him.

I've been reading about Cardinal Manning – goodness!

That lady you met called Susan Mary Patten had a baby. So yesterday Dolly Radziwill rang me up & said 'I've just been lunching with SM & we saw the baby – it is a *real little Noailles*.' Later I saw the Col, who had also lunched there, & he said 'We saw the baby – it is the *image of Duff.'* I was rather bored by them, as I'm sure S-M is very virtuous, so I said 'Well but Duff is the image of all babies.'

I've made great friends with Noël Coward[1] he is bliss. He is acting here in French & the frogs love it, are you a little bit gel-gel?

Kurt was called Willie in the beginning & when I re wrote I thought Kurt would exactly suit. It shows the way one's poor old feather brain works. And I still don't remember him in *V. Bodies*. I've sent for a copy.

I made my will on account of the traffic here & I've left you all the letters I've kept. Mostly your own. Your daughter Harriet might edit them – the Lady of the Rue Monsieur.

Little Momo is here, she is taking her General to Monte Carlo. That man is becoming a figure of opéra bouffe – on ira chez Maxim's –!

The Colonel made a speech in English in the H of Commons & it was (by all accounts) a *wow*. He had a heavenly time in London & even met the Queen.

Have you read a book called *The Americans*[2] by Gorer?

Do write a proper interesting letter as soon as you get this.

Happy Christmas, if you believe in it I'm not sure R.C.s do –?

Love
    NR

* Old Danish trumpets connected with burial customs.

[1] Noël Coward (1899–1973). The playwright was acting in *Present Laughter* which had been adapted into French by André Roussin. The play was a flop in Paris and closed on 26 December after a short run.
[2] Geoffrey Gorer, *The Americans: A Study in National Character* (1948).

[postmarked 2 January 1949]   Piers Court
[postcard]   Stinchcombe

'Kurt' was in *Brideshead* not *Vilers*. Maureen has married a very pretty, very young man named 'Kelpie' Buchanan.[1] I met Jonjon Marriott. Very cold & hungry (me not J.M.) after New York. Returning there in three weeks. I gave Edith Sitwell a pocket air-raid siren & she lets it off when people ask her whether free verse is more truly poetic than rhymed. Very conflicting reports of Randolph's honeymoon. Your note on envelope unintelligible. What 'Elizabeth book' did I offer you? Gel gel indeed. I spend all my ingenuity & agility (not much) in avoiding photographers.

[1] The Marchioness of Dufferin and Ava was married to Major Harry (Kelpie) Buchanan 1948–54.

4 January 1949   7 rue Monsieur, VII

Darling Evelyn

I see you write your letters in a trance. You distinctly said *V. Bodies* – I was very much puzzled – I remember the German in *Brideshead* of course only not his name being Kurt. Then a large proportion of your last letter was taken up with saying that an American lady had written a book of several million words but not a dull one about Q Eliz & would I like it? Never mind.

I heard that Maurice finds American food so horrible that he has food parcels sent from Oxford. Now Isaiah[1] is off to steal some of his thunder. Interesting about Kelpie. KELPIE!!!!

Oh do tell what Jonjon is like. I was with Momo when she was rung up from NY, very discreetly left & afterwards I heard it was you. What a tease.

Malcolm[2] says the only reason the Americans are interested in Osbert is that he is the cousin of Lady Iris.[3] I think *he* really *is* a little bit gell-gell.

I am having a lovely life – only sad that heavenly 1948 is over – except for Bobo's[4] death which I *minded* one of the happiest years I ever had.

On Thurs: I go to a fancy dress ball heavily veiled in crêpe as the Empress Frederick, taking the line that I am too old to dress up as anybody pretty, a tease for all the others who are *all* 70, & all deadly serious about their dresses.

Lulu has been to Vienna, she says everybody there is young. Wouldn't like that much.

Do you ever feel you want to write a play? I long to very much, it's since my great new friendship with N. Coward.

I live here next door to a Cardinal. There is a curious thumping noise which drives me rather mad, when I asked Marie what it could be she replied, reverently 'C'est Monseigneur à côté.'[5] Can you explain?

Honks Cooper is ill with flu so I go twice a day with a pannikin of soup. Always nice to have those one loves at one's mercy like that.

We now receive the day's *Times* at 7 A.M. does this not encourage you to come & live here? Oh Evelyn how *could* you go back to America it's the great mystery of my life. Frankly tell – isn't it simply hateful?

There is a play[6] here about Diana & her 2 sons (Honks Guinness I mean) with a French Uncle Matthew as the father. It is gradually borne in on this poor man that one son is 'une tante intégrale',[7] & the other is kept by a Polish countess with money earned from other lovers. It's really the funniest play I ever saw. The Honks character is all on the side of the boys & there is a wonderful scene when the normal one comes to her, fearfully worried, & says 'Ça va mal pour Lo-lo, Robert l'a plaqué, et avec une femme'[8] & she takes off, beside herself, to where 'Lo-lo sanglotte comme une bête'.[9] I've never laughed so much at any play, but all the French pederasts & drogués of my acquaintance are bitterly shocked by it!!

Silence de glace from my American publisher so perhaps he feels like you about the book. Jamie on the other hand is happily printing away. Oh dear. It's not that I don't wish it were better, but only that I *know I* couldn't do any more to it & if I worked for 6 more years it wouldn't be any different.

> Much love, happy 1949, love to Laura & Harriet
> Nancy

[1] Isaiah Berlin (1909–97). The Russian-born Oxford don and historian of ideas had taken up a visiting lecturership at Harvard. Knighted in 1957.
[2] Malcolm Bullock (1890–1966). Sharp-tongued, mischief-making and gossip-loving Conservative MP 1923–53. Knighted in 1954.
[3] Lady Iris Mountbatten (1920–82). A great-granddaughter of Queen Victoria.
[4] At the outbreak of war, Nancy's sister Unity had tried to shoot herself but the bullet lodged in her brain leaving her an invalid. In May 1948 the passage of the wound became infected and she died of meningitis.
[5] 'It is Monsignor next door.'
[6] *Les Oeufs de l'autruche* (1950), a comedy by André Roussin.
[7] 'A raging queen.'
[8] 'Things are going badly for Lo-lo, Robert has jilted him, and for a woman too.'
[9] 'Lo-lo is crying his heart out.'

10 January [1949]   Piers Court
                                                     Stinchcombe

Darling Nancy

Your letter of 4th Jan to hand. I notice it was posted at Marlborough, Wilts. The socialist underground has slipped up.

The undull book was about Etiquette not Elizabeth. I will send you a copy from New York where I go in ten days to earn dollars for my unhappy country instead of spending them on traitors.

Gel-gel be bugbuggered. No sane man could envy Sir Osbert his ostentatious progress through USA. Nor do the Americans respect him for it. Perhaps I told you that I asked his publisher whether there had been any increase in his sales as the result of all the ballyhoo. 'Yes, 18 copies.' The point is that at last Sir Osbert has found the life that he has groped after all his life, just as you have. So you are both quite happy in your base ways. I suppose you two are the only inhabitants of the Globe (except perhaps the Mountbatten stalking-horse)[1] who can say 'Heavenly 1948'. What an odd idea of heaven. Of course in my country we cannot enjoy the elegant clothes & meals & masquerades which fill your days but Diana has chosen these things also & certainly she is not happy.

I met an expatriate in New York who may be known to you – Anne Fremantle?[2] She too gave her youth to the socialist cause and at once

left the sinking ship when her ends were accomplished. But her literary
skill is not as gravely impaired by the change – perhaps because she
genuinely repented and became a Catholic at the same time. But she
would not say: 'Heavenly 1948' of, I suppose, the blackest year in the
world's history since 1793.

But I am forgetting that Coué[3] was a Frenchman not, as one might
have thought, an American.

The sounds you hear next door are probably His Eminence doing
penance for the frightful sins of yourself & Picasso and that woman
Diana took up.[4]

I never go to the theatre now but I believe that there is a great
scarcity of tolerable comedies. I have no doubt that given an agreeable
collaborator (the just word) you will make a great success of your new
career.

Laura is well but hard-driven by the cares of farm & nursery. She
is seldom seen heavily veiled in crepe as the Empress Frederick. Harriet
is entirely enchanted with the mother of pearl egg which I left in
White's & gave her last week. Both send their love.

Mosley, I read, is selling up.[5]

If you can find Père A. Gardeil's *La Structure de l'âme et l'expérience
mystique* it would be a *great* kindness to send a copy to Thomas Merton,[6]
Gethsemani, Kentucky, USA to whom I promised one & have been
unable to keep my promise. I will send you in exchange his *Elected
Silence* which I am editing (Merton's not Gardeil's).

I pray God you may get a glimpse of Heaven in 1949.

Evelyn

[1] Pandit Nehru (1889–1964). Indian Premier after Independence. He had a close, romantic
relationship with Lady Mountbatten.
[2] Anne Marie Huth-Jackson (1909–2002). Journalist and author. Married Hon. Christopher Fremantle in 1930. Her books include *The Papal Encyclicals in their Historical Context* (1956) and *The
Protestant Mystics* (1964).
[3] Emile Coué (1857–1926). Psychotherapist who studied the influence of auto-suggestion on
health and whose method of cure was to repeat: 'Every day, in every way, I am getting better
and better.'
[4] Louise de Vilmorin.
[5] Sir Oswald and Lady Mosley did not move to France until 1951.
[6] Thomas Merton (1915–68). An American Trappist monk who had written to Evelyn for
advice on his autobiography *Elected Silence* (1949).

11 January 1949   7 rue Monsieur, VII

Darling Evelyn

Don't be so cross & don't tease me about not having children, it
was God's idea, not mine. Do you really think it's more wrong to live
in one place than another or wrong to go to fancy dress parties? I
don't live here for food wine & elegant clothes but because I love the

people. Like Napoleon I wish to be buried parmi ce peuple que j'ai si bien aimé,[1] & one of my Xmas presents this year was a grave in the Père Lachaise, so I shall be.

Don't be angry with me for being happy, you must know as well as I do that happiness doesn't depend on exterior or political events & that the findings of UNO or fresh demands for peace in Nanking are not enough to damp one's spirits for more than the 5 minutes it takes to read them of a morning. I live among good & happy people & my days are *unclouded* from morning to night. You ought to be pleased, you are supposed to be fond of me.

I too earn dollars for the old land, & send them home like a good child to its mother, though not as many as you or this great genius who writes so much better than me, Miss Mrs or Lady Fremantle. (Alas it wouldn't be difficult to write better than me, but I don't like the tone in which it was said.)

Cedric is not being well received in your new country. *The Woman's Home Journal*[2] says he is revolting & that neither they nor any other American mag will touch him.

I'll try & get your book but if out of print it may not be possible, for there is no machinery here as in London for getting O.P. books, a fact which is the bane of my life. Does yr friend really live at Gethsemani, Kentucky? Well.

I am translating the *Princesse de Clèves*,[3] have you ever read it? I do love translating it is the pure pleasure of writing without the misery of inventing.

I am reading Pascal, *Lettres provinciales*. Very strict, isn't he.

There. Honks Cooper rang up & I read her your letter, not the bits about her & Lulu. She says I have much to put up with.

I suppose you think I'm a whore & my immortal soul is in danger. About once a week, for a few minutes it worries me that you should think so. That I can understand though, what seems so unlike you is this Harold Nicolson attitude of disapproval because I live among the flesh pots. (Did you see his article '*we* prefer our *nice little ration books*'.)

I must go out into the brilliant sunshine.

Love from
    Nancy

I went to the ball in black tights & a black beard hoping at last to have a success with the chaps. But they thought I was Edward James[4] & *fled*.

[1] Amongst this people I have loved so well.
[2] *The Ladies Home Journal*, Philadelphia.
[3] Nancy's translation of Mme de La Fayette's novel was published in 1950 by Euphorion Books, a company set up by the Mosleys.
[4] Edward James (1907–84). Immensely rich patron of Surrealist art, described by Dali as a 'humming-bird poet'. Creator of Monkton, a Lutyens house that he transformed into a Surrealist

fantasy in the 1930s, and of a Surrealist palace in the Mexican jungle which remained unfinished
at his death. Married to the actress Tilly Losch 1931–4.

17 January [1949]   Piers Court
                                                     Stinchcombe
Dearest Nancy

Of course I am cross with you for being happy. It is entirely indecent.
And of course I am appalled at the blasphemy of writing 'Heavenly
1948'. I assume you wrote it with the intent to be odious.

It would be just tolerable if you had always set up as a porcelain
marquise advising the starving to eat more cake. But you were always
lecturing us about how much you loved human kind and now with
human misery & degradation everywhere at its blackest you talk like
a debutante after her first party. It is not that I think your soul in
danger but that I doubt if you have a soul at all.

Perhaps Napoleon is not the happiest model to take in your devotion
to the French. Think of these things when you reach your St Helena.

I did not know about your being a whore. In fact I thought whoring
had been stopped in Paris.

Well I am just off to the hideous round of the Middle West, lecturing
to American Catholics who may yet preserve the good things which
the French abandoned. But I don't want to be buried among them.

Yes, I am fond of you. Very fond. That is why I write to you in
this fashion. Honks long ago gave up the attempt to keep my love.

A Canadian named Dunsmore wrote me a slightly lubricious fan-
letter in which he says *The Loved One* formed 'one of the many delightful
bonds that *more or less* platonically unite myself' (Dunsmore) 'and young
Nancy'. My italics.

Tell your chums they must now read the *Month*[1] instead of *Horizon*.

Deep love
     Evelyn

[1] A Jesuit periodical to which Evelyn contributed for little or no payment.

28 January 1949   7 rue Monsieur, VII

Darling Evelyn

Oh joy – Sir Alfred D[uff] C[ooper] agrees that *1948 was a heavenly
year* & you couldn't call him a débutante could you? (This correspondence must now cease. Ed.)

I liked your fan-letter which referred to links with me – young I
liked very much. Do you get many letters from Americans – I had a
few, all about mantelpieces etc. Idiots.

12 Feb Somehow I couldn't get on with this letter well really busyness. I'm translating *La Princesse de Clèves* in the hopes of showing the English (not you) what French society is like because that's exactly what it is like to this day. But it's taking me an age, perhaps I'm too fussy to make a translator. Diana M did the *Duchesse de Langeais*[1] in ¼ the time. So the enclosed cutting made me think of you, the Egerton set as you see is forging ahead.

Pam Berry is here, the bliss of her. We went last night to a lovely play about 2 hunchbacks in love 'Ils chantent Fauré, bosse contre bosse'[2] which everybody but me thinks bad taste but I shriek & so did Pam. (Sir Alfred is nettement choqué[3] by it). Now I'm off for the week end to Chantilly – Lady Di is in London having her face lifted in some R.C. joint, according to the *Evening S*. Utterly untrue & indeed what is there to lift? One wouldn't know where to begin. But the horrid old nuns have behaved with the treachery that all English people expect of papists & given away her whereabouts & of course the rest followed. What comes of adhering to a foreign potentate.

Lady Di is a worry. She's not happy here because she neither likes nor understands nor tries to understand the French. Then when she is unhappy she is violently so. But is it only that? I wish I knew. The great mystery to me is why she, so profoundly British to her backbone, ever thought she would like living here. Sir A. on the other hand is blissful.

I said to Pam 'any messages for me?' 'Only one. Nigel Birch told me to say he has cut you out of his will.' Wasn't it horrid.

I believe it is highly heretical of you to say that I have no soul – even abortions have souls. Just look it up somewhere – Pascal would not admit it but perhaps new laws on soullessness have been passed since his day.

    Much love
        NR

[1] By Honoré de Balzac (1834). Diana Mosley's translation was published by Euphorion Books in 1949.
[2] 'They sing Fauré, hump to hump.' The farce was *Ardèle ou la Marguerite* (1949) by Jean Anouilh.
[3] Thoroughly shocked.

2 April [1949]   Piers Court
                                                     Stinchcombe
Darling Nancy
    Just home. I must say I've seen enough of USA to last me fifty years. It is very degrading to be constantly in the company of people you have to 'make allowances for'.
    Momo telephoned Nin[1] daily from the *Queen Elizabeth* to say what

bliss it was to have the comforts of a cabin after Mrs Otto Kahn's house in Sutton Place.[2]

Randolph told Lady Huggins, wife of Governor of Jamaica, that she was 'an outstandingly common woman in a place where common women abounded' so he was deported from the island to Palm Beach where he & his bride at first attracted salacious crowds & then dispelled them in horror by the fury of their public embraces. At night they cleared the hotel by the fury of their bickering well bickering is not the word struggles to the death & flying furniture.

Please please get me a box of liver pills named BOLDINE or BOLDINI HOUDÉ and send it by hand of first chum crossing. John de Forest[3] gave me some. They are excellent & procurable only in your country.

Laura is the best dressed woman in Dursley & I am the fattest man in White's since our tour.

The paragraph about Honks's face lifting horrified me.

I want to forget about USA so I won't write anything down because that fixes it in the memory. This is really a cadging letter for liver pills.

Love from
Evelyn

[1] Margaret (Nin) Kahn (1902–95). Momo Marriott's sister, married to John Barry Ryan.
[2] A house in New York legendary for its opulence, belonging to Momo Marriott and Nin Ryan's mother.
[3] John de Forest (1907–97). Later Count de Bendern. Amateur golf champion in 1932. Private Secretary to Duff Cooper 1946–7. Married to Lady Patricia Douglas 1938–50.

6 April 1949   7 rue Monsieur, VII

Darling Evelyn

I am glad you're back, not that it brings you much nearer to *me* or may you come Honks-wards? I will faithfully get your pills but I must tell you that Momo, the greatest living expert, I guess, on liver, says Carter's Little L-Ps are unbeatable & so I've often heard from others. On the other hand the French all have trouble with the foie so County, as Debo calls him, may be right.

I went to England & must say I had a whizz of a time, everybody quite angelic.

I had the fascinating experience of being the first fare of a cabby. 'Mount St – now let me see – no don't tell me.' When I had paid him he was at once picked up by another woman & as he drove off he shouted to me 'This is TERRIFYING' in what Diana calls ONE's voice. I guess he was an air vice marshal.

I saw a great deal of blissful Pam Berry. She is expecting the Ran-
dolphs to stay – nice for her won't it be, judging by what you say.

How is Harriet? I have a new love, a little French boy aged 5 –
perhaps she would like to marry him? A co-religionist.

Am I allowed to think that 1949 is a blissful year or not? I'm just
asking before I commit myself.

Honks C is away until end of the month, in Spain. She asked
hundreds of English people to Chantilly, lent it to Dolly Radziwill &
fled. How like her.

Much love from
    NR

[postmarked 11 April 1949]   [7 rue Monsieur, VII]
[postcard]

Your pillules have gone off with La Vicomtesse de Rothermere, at
least I hope so.

I rose at crack of dawn & took them to her hotel *hoping* thus to get
into your good graces again rather pathetic really.

I hear you are conducting a retreat can I come next time. When
it's over do pay a visit here.

Love
    NR

Show this pretty lady[1] to Harriet.

[1] Nancy's postcard was of a sculpture of the goddess Diana, attributed to Jean Goujon.

12 April [1949]   Piers Court
                                                     Stinchcombe
Darling Nancy

You are kind about the liver pills. I will try & get them from Warwick
House[1] without being crossed by the Quennell–Forbes axis. Perhaps
if my liver gets better I shall feel forgiving to you for your vile &
frivolous panglossisme. Now I am in deep misanthropy. I can't bear
anyone else being alive at all & when a man goes past the window
with a barrow or a child shuts a door upstairs I fall into an extremity
of rage. As for the daily papers ... L'enfer c'est les autres[2] I think
your favourite sage says.

One cause for sorrow is that I am bound in honour to write a long
article for *Life* magazine whose money I have been spending like a
drunken sailor, on the state of the Catholic Church in America, and

there is nothing to say except that americans are louts & that Catholic Americans are just a little better than panglossist americans.

So tomorrow I go to Downside taking Frank Pakenham for flaggers no I mean flagers. I have given up cigars & secular reading for Holy Week so I must not read this letter after it is finished so I expect it will have some pretty odd spelling. I gave up wine too but felt so faint at 8 pm last night that I had to mitigate.

My daughter Teresa (age 11) has come back from school with a glowing report by her French mistress, 2nd in class with 82% marks. I asked her to name in French any six objects in the dining-room. After distressed thought she got five, four of them with wrong genders. I know of another girl who came back from another school with a special medal for swimming – a thing like the Garter with a great sash. Her parents put her in the pool and she sank like a stone.

My Gothic fernery, under construction at great expense, is a fiasco. It looks like Lancing College War Memorial 1914–18. So I am making a serpentine walk with a serpent's head & eye but you have to go up in a balloon to see it.

I may come to Paris soon for a day or two because I think it might comfort & humanize me a little to see some French paintings – not of course the filthy moderns nor Manet nor Monet nor worst of all Sisley but Fragonard. I had forgotten how cheering he is until I saw the Mellon collection in Washington. Also what do you know about the Jansenist painters you know the Port Royal group Phil Bubbly etc? And are there many in the Louvre & if not there, where? I saw a lovely reproduction in a shop in Sweden of a nun by candle light with a discipline. Very erotic. Not by Bubbly but by one of his chums.

Is it quite easy to get rooms in a high-class hotel nowadays? Not where you stayed. But I could stay at the Travellers couldn't I. Who has taken Dmitri's[3] place? I have quite a few dollars and I think some francs too. I might come in the beginning of May. Will you be there?

When I say 'where you stayed' I mean where Honks & I picked you up years ago was it the Grand some name like that.

Did I tell you I met Preston père in New York? Spats, noisy, I thought a little tipsy. Sergeant very lonely & disregarded by all.

I no longer want to buy any old books. Sad for Handy.

That was a *very* pretty postcard of Honks you sent me. It made me want more to go to Paris. Is it true I don't have to stand in a queue in Knightsbridge any more to get a visa?

Love from
　　　Evelyn

---

[1] Where Lady Rothermere lived.
[2] 'Hell is other people', from Jean-Paul Sartre's play *Huis clos* (1944).
[3] Prince Dmitri Romanov (1901–80). Son of Grand Duke Alexander and his wife, a sister of Tsar Nicholas II. He was manager of the Travellers Club in Paris.

14 April 1949   7 rue Monsieur, VII

Darling Evelyn

Oh do come. Oh dear I have never heard of Phil Bubbly perhaps the Colonel has. Fragonard I have heard of. There is an exhibition of French painting in progress with 5 lovely Fragonards – he is my favourite painter, the pink bottoms I think are what one can't resist. Then you must be here over a Friday because on that day alone the 18th-Cent French furniture is shown at the Louvre. Then I will take you, where no English ever seem to go, to the French sculpture, Honks & co, which is incredibly beautiful.

Accommodation may be difficult. We are informed that three million tourists are upon us, the Ritz *say* they have no room until 10th Oct but I expect if you wrote with your famous name they couldn't resist you. Travellers might be the best bet. The new Dmitri is a nice sad ex husband of Lady Idina [Sackville] this & that called Charles Gordon, but I believe Dmitri is still the real runner. If all failed I would offer my bed-dining room where nobody, even Prod, is allowed to stay but it is not very comfortable, rather dreary & you share it with my hen (adored pet), at least she doesn't actually sleep there but wanders in & out.

Honks C wrote to me once saying I arrive on Monday with 6 moron hons so I said to Duff who is Honks bringing & he said nobody & I said yes 6 moron hons so he got into quite a stew but it turned out to be moran hens, a new kind that lay chocolate eggs so she hopefully thinks the gardener's wife won't dare to pinch them any more. The only trouble is they hardly ever do lay so it all comes to the same in the end. Still we were let off the hons that time, Honks's hons are occasionally geese. I intend no disloyalty but expect you know what I mean.

Anyway I suppose this is secular reading & you won't be able to read it for ages. Holy Week here makes our courtyard very restless because you have to call 'cordon' to get the door opened & all the French go off to Church at 7 but not in a bunch unfortunately so from about 6.30 onwards it is cordon cordon in varying degrees of shrillness according to how late they are & no sleep for poor heretics. Usually this only occurs about twice a week though there are 2 daily 7 o'clockers. How can they? Well I suppose I would get up at 7 if it was the only chance of seeing the Colonel. But why is God such an early bird? I am thinking out loud, don't expect an answer.

Then I have to go away for Easter so that Marie[1] can be never off her knees those days. Never mind.

The most beautiful picture Fragonard ever painted is in the Banque de France. I will see what can be done about a permit. I saw it in an exhibition last year, but also in the B de F is the salon doré, one of the most beautiful rooms I believe in the world & I long to see that.

Momo is here I do love her. Also Cecil [Beaton] & hundreds of lesser fry.

So come in May. No visa required but book your ticket in good time.

Love from
   Nancy

Don't be sad.

Pangloss indeed. Well neither Momo nor Barbara Murray[2] have ever heard of him so you can safely tell the *Life*-ers that they are, but try & be a little more careful of MY susceptibilities in future, please.

[1] Marie Renard, Nancy's cook and housekeeper.
[2] American-born wife of 18th Earl of Moray.

[April 1949]   Piers Court
                                                               Stinchcombe
Darling Nancy,

Bubbly was a silly joke. I meant P de Champaigne.[1] I must come to Paris for a day or two but I won't invade your flat. It was heavenly of you to offer it. I go to London next week & will make enquiries about Travellers, Ritz etc.

E. Sackville-West has made pansy-high-brow-journalistic history with the phrase 'I seem to feel'. Surely the height of diffidence. First the statement. Then the qualification 'I think'; then the qualification 'I feel'. And now 'I seem to feel'.

I should think it will be 1st week of May, if I can get tickets & a room.

Harriet has overcome her auto-erotic troubles and is really rather a gay & engaging little girl.

Are you having a good influence on young Pam Berry? I suspect not. I have my eye on her for the Church. Lay off.

Dominick Elwes retailed in appalling detail the story of Prod's novel. It was about people protecting themselves with mutton fat against an invisible ray which caused panic. I seem to feel that it will be a very juvenile work.[2]

I go to horrible London for a few days next week & will write you the gossip.

Ann must be eating my pills.

Love from
   Evelyn

[1] Philippe de Champaigne (1602–74). Several of his paintings are in the Louvre, including his masterpiece *Portrait of a Man* (1650).
[2] Peter Rodd never published a novel.

23 May 1949   7 rue Monsieur, VII

Darling Evelyn

Your letter! I shall *have* to frame it. Only I do wish you had enjoyed yourself, & have been thinking ever since that I ought to have produced some of the characters here, old gaffers of the village, for you to note, or even, say, the two chattering young Princes I had lunching today for the Beauty.[1] It was very silly of me I should have gone bravely ahead & done it. Then everybody I see exclaims 'but of course he ought to have met le Père Whatnotoski – or Mgr Dupont – or Brother So & so' & I feel dashed. I may say I got dreadful stick from my Colonel for not being sufficiently respectful to the one I did produce.[2] I said did you notice Evelyn hating him? & he said no why did he? & I said Picasso but he didn't understand. People who live here & regard Picasso as the great ornament of their town can't quite understand though of course I do from my background of Farve & the Army & Navy Stores.

I terribly wish you had enjoyed yourself because I did so *adore* the Visit & long for you to come again & now I see you won't.

I went to the wedding & thankful I am that I did it was extraordinary. Two hideous little brides[3] (not authorized bigamy as you might suppose, 2 sisters marrying 2 young men) one delighted, couldn't get there quick enough, the other cross & dragging. Talk about the pageantry of the RC church – no Here Comes the Bride no King of Love my Shepherd Is & of course no assistance to beauty in the way of tulle & orange blossom, plain little white satin nuns. Put me in my place, I didn't know ONE soul, whereas at Bébé [Bérard]'s funeral I knew everybody in the whole of that vast St Sulpice – anyway by sight.

The Beauty is one, or will be. Too much puppy fat. Fancy, her mother is leaving her with me for a week when she goes home isn't that a treat – the dress can't be made in less than 12 days you see. Such a darling you never saw – I am very much excited to show her the sights. I hardly dared ask but Pauline seemed all for it.

I've been rather worried about what you said about me being so unbusinesslike. It is only too true. What I want is an homme d'affaires who would arrange the whole thing for me, including saying how much I ought to spend every year & so on, like a husband. But where to find such an angel? If you ever think of anybody *do* say.

Much love & love to Laura
    Nancy

Do you think Time may gild the whole thing & make you want to come back?

[2] Pierre (Père) Couturier (1897–1954), ('Father Dressmaker'). Dominican priest, pioneer of the modern liturgical arts movement, who studied art before being ordained in 1930. He was a friend and admirer of Picasso and had eulogised the artist at a luncheon given by Nancy. 'He and Evelyn then engaged, with the help of Nancy who was sitting between them, in a battle of wits in which the Dominican, versed in the arts of apologetics, triumphed easily. The party ended on a note of awkward good humour.' Sykes, *Evelyn Waugh*, p. 333.
[3] Jacqueline and Marthe de Voguë married Comtes Pozzo di Borgo and de Luppé respectively.

31 May 1949   7 rue Monsieur, VII

May I keep the pictures?[1] I screamed aloud – I must say the 4 figures of Dr Huxley is the funniest thing I ever saw & surely quite devoid of talent, must be meant to be funny? (Picasso is not like that you know.) When one *thinks* of the smart little women in air raid shelters – if people had arrived draped in towels I'm sure they would have been lynched.

Your letter to the Père [Couturier] hasn't gone yet because the Col is away – he returns today – & I don't know the address.

Did I tell you about my Beauty of 18 who is staying here? She leaves today saying she *must* come & live in Paris *always*. You never saw such a heavenly girl, so good & so beautiful, the daughter, quite incredible as it seems, of Basil Murray! She has been a magnet for other little creatures who run in & out of the flat all day using my telephone & trying on my clothes – I have very much enjoyed the whole thing. On Sat Desmond Guinness arrives with his mistress called Felicity[2] so of course I can't wait.

Much love
NR

[1] Probably of works by Henry Moore. An exhibition of his sculpture and drawings, including the 1940–41 drawings of sleepers in air-raid shelters, had just opened at the Manchester City Art Gallery.
[2] Felicity Brown (1928–). Artist. Married Colin Millward in 1953.

2 June [1949]   Piers Court
                                                 Stinchcombe

Darling Nancy

Mrs Piper[1] is famous as the Myfanwy of Betjeman's erotic poetry. She is, in appearance, a mixture of Edith Sitwell & Leslie Jowitt,[2] very stout & almost bald.

Have you heard of Sir A. Cooper's very curious conduct. In revenge for our imagined slight on Honks he has vowed to turn my man Sykes[3] & myself out of White's. The method he has chosen is to put Quennell up for the club, abetted by your revolting kinsman Ed [Stanley]. White's, needless to say, are outraged that he should use the club as an instrument of private spite; they particularly resent the fact that two expatriates should conspire to stop the only earth where those of us who are weathering the storms of our unhappy country, can take refuge from the hounds of modernity. It will end, I hope, with the expulsion of Cooper & Stanley. Meanwhile Quennell shows no reluctance to being used as a directed weapon of destruction.

Really, you and your Beauty.

Connolly comes for Whitsun, not bringing Lys.

The architectural effects in my garden are ruining it & me.

I wrote a deeply touching letter to Honks. No answer.

Love from
    Evelyn

The Master of the Air Raid shelter is deeply revered by Picasso lovers in this country. You must send Père Couturier an 'amusing' crucifixion by him.

[1] Myfanwy Evans (1911–97). A swimming blue at Oxford, founder and editor of the arts magazine *Axis*, and librettist for Benjamin Britten's operas *The Turn of the Screw* (1954), *Owen Wingrave* (1971) and *Death in Venice* (1973). Married the painter John Piper in 1935. Evelyn had sat next to her at dinner the previous month and made 'neither head nor tail of her'.
[2] Leslie McIntyre (d.1970). Married in 1913 William Jowitt (created 1st Earl in 1951), Lord Chancellor 1945–51. She was portrayed by Boris Anrep in his mosaic floor *Various Movements in the Day of a Lady of Fashion* (1922) in the Birmingham Museum, and as Thalia, muse of comedy, in the mosaic on the stairs of the National Gallery.
[3] Christopher Sykes had accompanied Evelyn on his visit to Paris. He had not been able to afford the cost of the journey, so in return for making all the travelling arrangements Evelyn paid his expenses.

5 June 1949   7 rue Monsieur, VII

Darling Evelyn

I am horrified by Sir Alf's action but I doubt if it is on account of your alleged inhumanity to Honks as he has been giggling away about it for many a long moon. 3 for 1, well worth it, has been the line. I think he thought Cyril would go too. Pure babyishness because as we know he really loves you all. He said to me as we drove down the other day for the Princess Margaret Reception that you had written Honks a most terribly nice letter & I laid it on again about how it was all a misunderstanding.

The worst of the Coopers is they don't count sight seeing as a factor of human life, their genuine amazement when one comes in having been to the musée at Chantilly is proof of that. With some of the world's greatest treasures under their nose they have been there exactly once – I greatly doubt if they have ever been to the Louvre & they don't even know the names of the lesser museums here.

Desmond Guinness is here. The lives of the very young are a carica-

ture of *Vile Bodies* I think you have much to answer for. He has been
living with the daughter of a Roman Catholic Yorkshire writer called
A. J. Brown[1] (the Col knows about his books, so typical – they are of the
Rambler school). But 'she wants to marry a millionaire so she is engaged
to an Indian'. I said to Desmond what are your plans for the future?
'Well I would *like* to be a great lover of famous women, but if I can't I
will be an interior decorator.' I think I can tell him straight away which
it will have to be. Bryan now has 8 repeat 8 children did you realize?[2]

Two of Duff's mistresses are now living with 2 of Diana's nephews
& the rest are clubbing together to give a party for Diana 'to whom
we owe so much'. It is all rather odd I must say.

Tell what happens about White's please.

Of course as you know I think it very *naughty and silly* of you to take
this line about Peter Q, but if it is really a revenge for what you are
supposed to have done at Chantilly I *can't* say it's quite right of Fred.

The Colonel knew Mrs Piper too – he is much more English than
I am now, as Violet [Trefusis] always says old Colonel Mitford & La
Palewska.

Love & to your Man Sykes
        NR

And thank your Man for his sweet nice letter.
I didn't steam open yours to Fr Dressmaker which is proof of my
wonderful nature, Freddy & Honks were dying to.

[1] Alfred John Brown (1904–69). Author of *Moorland Tramping in West Yorkshire* (1931), *Tramping
in Yorkshire: North and East* (1932) and *Striding Through Yorkshire* (1938).
[2] Lord Moyne eventually had eleven children.

2 June 1949   7 rue Monsieur, VII

Yes of course, milord himself.[1] Must needs tweak the nose & tear the
coat of a plain clothes head cop, a peeler. Seized by 6 other bobbies
& held down while head cop took running kicks at him until both
were worn out. Then bundled off to prison & beaten up a bit more.
Asked his profession 'membre de parlement' 'Ah! Labour partee?'
more tremendous wallops at that. However in the end he & head cop
went off arm in arm & Ed bought him a new coat & they are now
as one. You never saw anything like what he looked like next day the
dear old thing.

Colonel very puzzled by O.P. after the Fr's [Couturier's] name –
what does it mean? Upper classes here cross with the Fr because he
has forced Jean Hugo to marry Cyril's ex mistress Loretta Hope
Nicholson[2] as a result of which Tony Gandarillas[3] may have to marry
the Duchesse de Gramont. I can't explain it would take too long.

Diana met him & said what about you & he said he does worry so dreadfully about little things like Picasso & Liberté Egalité Fraternité!

The Royal Pigmy[4] came to Chantilly, just Duff & Diana & me wasn't it bliss for her.

Love from
NR

[1] Lord Stanley had inadvertently joined a street demonstration in Paris during which he was clubbed and arrested.
[2] Lauretta Hope-Nicholson (1919–2008). Married Jean Hugo in 1948.
[3] Don Antonio de Gandarillas (d.1970). Chilean diplomat who had been in love with the Duchess de Gramont in the 1930s.
[4] Princess Margaret.

8 June [1949]   Piers Court
                                                        Stinchcombe

Darling Nancy

How very odd that the all-knowing colonel does not know the correct form of address of a Dominican Friar. O.P. of course stands for Ordinis Praedicatorum. You are plainly curious about that letter. I was not renewing the attack on Picasso but soliciting help in getting a copy of that book by a French Dominican which I promised an American Trappist and about which I once wrote to you.

Smarty Boots has just left, having spent the week-end in torpor. Needless to say he rushed to the Candidates' Book at White's & put his name on Quennell's page. The election will be interesting. Numbers of cuckolds, fearing accusations of jealousy, having subscribed. What a preposterous ass Sir Alfred is. He must know that no one except Ed VII has ever resigned from White's, except Eddie Grant who did so as a love-offering on the day of his marriage to Laura's sister, Bridget. He rejoined as soon as he was back from the honeymoon. I can well understand that the author of *David*[1] is embarrassed in the presence of professional writers. He will now have four instead of three. But it is generally held that his employers at the *Daily Mail* obliged him to do what he has done.

Whenever Cyril woke up it was to tell me of his enduring loyalty to, & dependence on, Lys.

It is a pity that ces messieurs les agents did not make away with Stanley. They would have averted the great Quennell scandal.

Why, pray, did you tell the Porto Finese that I was due there in Mosley's yacht? My children spent many hours scanning the horizon for a sail.

Love from
Evelyn

[1] A life of the Old Testament figure King David by Duff Cooper, published in 1943.

9 June 1949   7 rue Monsieur, VII

Darling Evelyn

Having met her (you know how people one hasn't seen are the purest shadows) I feel some compunction about having written to you about Miss Brown. *Please* don't get bell, book, candle & the Inquisition to do their worst to her, & please forget what I said. She is such a little darling, so young pretty touching & in love I nearly cried every time I looked at her. Very Catholic, clearly eaten with a sense of Sin. I said to the Col now come off it, admit you've never heard of A J Brown & he replied sadly I was once on a P & O whose only literature was the works of A.J.B. – there was I, twixt sea & sky & nothing to read except *Rambles in Yorkshire Rambles in Gloucestershire Rambles* – Oh shut up Colonel.

Our Archbishop died so Marie & the concierge hurried off to see him & I said to Marie well did he have a lovely red hat? 'I really don't know je n'aime pas beaucoup voir des morts et quant à Madame Brard, Dieu sait pourquoi elle est venue, elle n'est vraiment pas pieuse.'[1] So the whole outing remains a mystery.

I saw Momo, *very* sad. She knows Fr Dior & doesn't like him either. She has also taken against *everybody* here saying they are all pourri [degenerate] – very affected I got quite cross, feeling with Mme du Deffand que ce n'est que le premier pas qui compte[2] & that step after all has been taken both by Momo & by me & it's really not for us to sit at the Ritz glooming away about the sins of our neighbours.

What is all this about me & Porto Fino? I don't spread every rumour that arises on this continent you know & that is a particularly unlikely one.

Good (about Cyril & Lys). I love Lys & she has grown bald in his service it would be a horrid shame if he turned her off now.

Prod is here. He has invented a quiz which goes like this: Sir Albert Duff Cooper is: Minister to Peru, Second Sea Lord, Gladys Cooper's husband, manufacturer of Oxford marmalade, author of David Blaise, etc etc. Funny I thought. Edward [Stanley] has enlarged upon it, done various members of the Travellers & is now involved in 3 libel cases.

Hamish Hamilton wants me to write a short account of my life for publicity. Alas I have sat in front of a blank page for an hour, to which you really owe this letter. I literally cannot think of one thing to say.

        Love from
        Nancy

P.S. I am slightly in love with Momo's general, did he mind about Randolph – please answer.[3]

[1] 'I don't much like seeing the dead and as for Madame Brard, I can't think why she came, she is not a bit devout.'
[2] The 18th-century hostess's most famous witticism: 'It is the first step that counts,' she quipped, when someone mentioned the martyrdom of St Denis who walked to Paris carrying his own head.
[3] Momo Marriott and Randolph Churchill had an affair in Cairo during the war.

12 July 1949   Chez la Princesse Radziwill
                                                Campagne Pastré
                                                Montredon, Pointe Rouge
                                                Marseille

Darling Evelyn

I was delighted to get your letter. I am here on holiday (holiday from what? as my Nanny used to say) in perfect happiness – boiling heat charming friends & exactly nothing to do except decide at what hour to go down to the rocks & swim. Colonel has been here & may come back, & the Mosleys are expected, as at Portofino, on their yacht. I've got my *Princesse de Clèves* with me to give that nice feeling of I really ought to do some work but think I'll go to sleep instead, also the house contains a set of Sainte Beuve, Randolph's friend, who is really an intensely fascinating 19th cent literary digest.

I saw excellent reviews of *Kind Hearts*. I doubt if anything of mine remains because the man who finally took it on very rightly scrapped everything & started again. They wanted me to write dialogue for the impossible characters & situations already invented by other people which of course ended in failure. I adore I shot an arrow,[1] but o to do with me.

I'm sure the Queen is *awful*, everything I hear confirms this impression. Probably you can't not be if you are a Queen, excellent reason for getting rid of them as they have here. The awfulness of Marie Antoinette surpasses imagination until you know something about her – dying bravely is not enough & anyway most people do as we learnt in the late war.

I think it's rather silly for two people who hate each other as much as the Sykeses do to go & live in the country together[2]. May it not end in murder?

Yes I had a card from Mrs Hulton[3] sent to Blomfield Rd. I was very much surprised.

Shall I leave you my skull? You would have to boil it down a bit. But I want my depouilles mortelles[4] to repose at the Père Lachaise, as you know, & it would be rather sinister to have my head cut off first, I think I won't. If you had been going to drink out of it, like the late Ld Byron, perhaps but a mere garden ornament –!

I saw in a paper here that everybody was wrapped in furs at the B. Pal garden party so I presume your drought is over.

I think the Père Cad-Couturier *is* rather awful. He has made poor Jean Hugo marry his mistress & has chased the charming Mlle de Miribelle into a Trappist monastery where she can never speak again & now he hasn't answered your letter which the faithful Colonel swears he forwarded. This is the last time I bring Dominicans into your life, when you & your man come back I shall concentrate on pretty ladies & gallant gentlemen.

How will I earn my living when England falls into what you prophesy? But I think those poor much abused Americans are under the impression that they can't allow it to happen, you know, & will have to go on bolstering in spite of no thanks & nothing but kicks.

This place is so fascinating that I must do one boring picture post card sentence. It's between a white mountain & the blue sea, & the property which is large, is irrigated with thousands of tiny rushing streams so that the grass is greener than England & full of Spring flowers & they take 3 loads of hay every year. Then there are huge pine woods & lakes. You do *see*?

Much love
    NR

You can write here as if I've gone, which I doubt, they will forward. Shan't be in Paris for an age.

[1] As he takes aim at the hot-air balloon carrying his elderly female relation, the hero of the film parodies Longfellow: 'I shot an arrow in the air, / She fell to earth in Berkeley Square'.
[2] Christopher and Camilla Sykes had moved to Dorset.
[3] Princess Nika Yourievitch; married to Edward Hulton, the press magnate, in 1941.
[4] Mortal remains.

13 July [1949]   Piers Court
                                                   Stinchcombe
Darling Nancy
    Love in a Cold Climate has arrived to temper the heat wave with frigid absence of inscription. Well I suppose you could hardly have had all the presentation copies shipped to France & back.

I have re read the first half already & look forward to a very happy afternoon with the second half. It is all very much better than I remembered it. I was quite wrong in advising, as I think I did, that you should scrap the first two chapters. They are very well written. Indeed all the descriptive & narrative passages are *very* good. Conversations poor. Page 28 is hell.[1] But I was wrong in thinking that publication would blight your career. The book will be a great success and is appearing at just the right time when everyone longs for something light.

I can't tell yet whether I shall enjoy the end which I thought so inefficient before. I think I shall.

I have bought two beautiful pictures. Otherwise nothing to say except congratulations on the book & your good sense in not being put off by my ill considered criticism.

But *all* the fashionable talk is awful.

Oh page 28.

Love
    Evelyn

[1] On which the Bolter's adultery is discussed in 'eggy-peggy' language.

[postmarked 15 July 1949]   Piers Court
[postcard]   Stinchcombe

I have finished the book. The last half is not as good as the first but there is more construction than I remembered. The climax is very bad. So is the unnecessary scene of Lady Montdore dining in North Oxford, but her transformation is plausible and excellently written & Cedric is genuinely funny all through. Of course whenever the Radletts appear, all is splendidly well. They are *génial* [inspired].[1]

E

20 July 1949   Montredon

Darling Evelyn

I wrote you a long letter (& *so* witty, as Johnny Stanley[1] used to say when his letters from India went astray) when I just arrived & I think I see from your post card that you never got it.

I didn't mean you to wade all through the book again poor you, I suppose sending out copies to friends is one of the habits I have got into since living here – the French send to everybody they have ever met, it is considered rude not to, & the dédicace must take up at least half a page & bring in the word amitié at least once. I got one the other day 'dans l'espoir d'une amitié'[2] which how *you* would *hate* & what a faint hope that would be –

Not much news. I am very happy as I always am in very hot weather. I follow the Tour de France (bicycle race) with passionate interest. Nobody else does here except Dolly's chauffeur so we get into a corner & pick over the details & he took me to see the coureurs [racers] when they passed Marseille. But it's not so amusing as last year when poor Bobet, the hope of France, suddenly developed a boil where it hurts (& specially hurts a bicyclist) & then, after the supplice des montagnes Bobet a vomi comme une bête toute la nuit after which you will be surprised to hear that son moral s'est effondré[3] & he gave up & the race was won by the Italian Bartali. This year there has never been much doubt that Bartali will win & Lucien (the chauffeur) says 'faut pas être chauvin, faut s'incliner devant cet homme-là'.[4] But I am terribly chauvin I must confess, & had pinned all hopes on Faulteichtover the Frenchman, when *he* got a boil where it hurts & after terrible sufferings, which we all shared for days, he also was obliged to abandon the race. These boils seem to be an occupational disease!

I've just finished Osbert's book[5] which is very pretentious isn't it – arrogant even. I can't make up my mind about it. The *Tatler* bits seem to me rather terrible & the bits about Henry Moat & co perfection, and, just as you think I am good about the children & I cling to Lady Montdore he probably only likes what he wrote about Lady Aberconway. Perhaps one should always cut out what one likes best oneself. How difficult it is to write & in the end what is the aim? I wish I knew. (I think it is very largely the physical pleasure of pen on paper.) I've finished my *Princesse de Clèves* & am lost in admiration of my own translation, & now for the preface. Alas, Mme de La Fayette was such a dreary old bitch in real life I can't get up the faintest interest in her.

Much love & do write if you ever have a minute.
        NR

I leave here for a few days next week but letters will wait for me.

[1] Hon. John Stanley (1837–1878). ADC to Lord Canning during the Indian Mutiny. His letters home are included in *The Stanleys of Alderley*.
[2] 'In the hopes of a friendship.'
[3] And then, after the torment of the mountains Bobet was as sick as a dog all night after which, you will be surprised to hear, his morale collapsed.
[4] 'One mustn't be chauvinistic, you have to hand it to the man.'
[5] *Laughter in the Next Room* (1949), Osbert Sitwell's fourth volume of autobiography.

28 July [1949]   Piers Court
                                                      Stinchcombe
Darling Nancy

Something very odd is happening to the posts. I wrote you a long & rather loving letter when your book first came and a short & less loving card a day or two later. My L and RLL has been stolen. How rude & ungrateful I must seem. Well you all think me that in France I know.

I hope your hostess is not a Jugoslav woman I met in New York.

Holidays are upon us. Oh the Hellikins! I went on Saturday to the Oratory School to give away the prizes. Sixty years ago it was the leading Catholic public school & everyone like Lords FitzAlan & Rank-eillour were there. Now there are 34 boys in a little Queen Anne house smaller than this. All because of the disastrous appointment of an Anglo-Catholic parson, convert & sex-maniac, as headmaster some years ago. Now they have a charming headmaster and all is well but it is Lilliputian. The headmaster's speech '. . . The School platoon has been training at so and so . . . last term we had 98% successes in all examinations, five higher certificates, three entrances into Cambridge, two into Oxford etc . . .' And when it came to the prize winners they all had names like Palewski & Radziwill & Couturier.

Then I went to stay with your great new friend Pam [Berry] but she was very weary from dancing all night & I only had glimpses of her. We went to call on Barbara Rothschild[1] who has married a gentile of forbidding appearance named Warner, not your old admirer,[2] worse. And there were communists there called Day Lewis[3] (very pretty) and Rosamond Lehmann[4] (not bad looking) and we drank boiling champagne & were bitten by flies.

With enormous goodness of heart I am taking my little boy to the seaside in the Vendée, to a place Pam recommends which sounds quite awful. She wants me there to obtain control of my fortune & she has got it. What is the Vendée like. I remember they behaved well in the Revolution. I imagine it all pine & heather & sand like Surrey, is it?

Osbert's book is queer isn't it. It is extraordinary that a man of his humour can write like that of Lord Wimborne and the general strike & Picasso and G. Stein.

Just got my bill from the garden contractors who had laid down a yard or two of gravel and put up a pillar. A cool thou. Impossible to earn because super tax is always a pace ahead. So I am ruined.

All last week we had the 65 year old *Country Life* photographer staying & pottering round with a camera. His aim in art is to make every room look uninhabited & uninhabitable.

I do hope my warm letter about your book turns up. If not I will write it all again.

Love from
    Evelyn

[1] Barbara Hutchinson (1911–89). Married to 3rd Baron Rothschild 1933–46, to the novelist Rex Warner in 1949 and to the painter Nicholas Ghika in 1961.
[2] Fred Warner (1918–95). An acquaintance of Nancy. Ambassador to Japan 1972–5, member of the European Parliament 1979–84. Knighted in 1972. Married Simone de Ferranti in 1971.
[3] Cecil Day-Lewis (1904–72). Poet Laureate 1968. Joined the Communist Party in 1936 in which he was politically active before the war.
[4] Rosamond Lehmann (1901–90). Writer whose novels include *Dusty Answer* (1927) and *The*

Ballad and the Source (1944). Married to the painter Wogan Philipps (later Lord Milford) 1928–
44. Her decade-long affair with Day-Lewis was drawing to an end.

30 July 1949   Montredon

Darling Evelyn

I got the long & rather loving letter after I had answered your
postcard & while I was on the Mosleys' yacht from which I have just
returned. I'm joining them again later.

I'm awfully glad it (book) seemed better. Of course you know it is
very mysterious about books & who likes what in them. Now 2 or 3
people have said they liked the Don's wife best of all the characters
& specially mentioned the dinner party for praise – others that they
can't *bear* the children & so on. I believe most in you because you are
cher maître to me but even so one must write as one can.

The American reviews are so terrible I have given up reading them
– never again will I pay for 'clippings'. No message or meaning – adds
up to just nothing is their parrot cry. I wouldn't mind a bit except
about the dollars adding up to just nothing! Only if I got reviews like
that in England I'd never try another novel again.

No my darling hostess is not a Yugoslav. Née Radziwill, mariée en
premières noces Radziwill, mariée en secondes noces Radziwill, mariée
en troisièmes noces Tvede but rather naturally goes on being Radziwill.
I love her beyond words.

I don't know if this story will make you cross but it made me so shriek
with laughter I think I must tell you. Diana & Tom [Mosley] went to Spain
where of course they had the whizz of a time with special bull fights, official
dinners & so on – & a minister to take them round. This minister of course
very R.C. & said to Diana 'Do you know the famous writer Waugh?' 'Oh
yes he's a great friend' then added brightly '*He's* a Roman Catholic you
know.' 'Oh – but only just for a joke?'

Do admit –!

He didn't speak much English – Diana asked him what the tiny
cages in the bird shops are for & he replied 'It is a little gaol for a
small insect who rubs its jambe [leg] against its aile [wing].'

Yes I didn't think much of Warner, they came to Paris for their
honeymoon before being married (modern fashion).

Don't know much about the Vendée, I hate that coast, myself.

Yes (Osbert's book) the general strike chapter made one simply
blush for him & I can't really swallow Lady Aberconway. But much
of it is wonderful I think.

Very hot – even I say so – & everybody isn't loving it as much as
I do, & even my brain is slightly giving way.

Much love from
    Nancy

P.S. I sent for the Stanley letters for Dolly – how *beautifully* produced they are, I had quite forgotten.

18 August [1949]   Grand Hotel
                                                             La Baule

Darling Nancy

It has been a great pleasure to read your English reviews. I haven't seen the American but I expect they are as foolish as possible. You see Americans have discovered about homosexuality from a book called *Kinsey Report* (unreadable) & they take it very seriously. All popular plays in New York are about buggers but they all commit suicide. The idea of a happy pansy is inconceivable to them.

I am in a town of ineffable horror. You might have warned me. There is a strip of sand, a row of hotels and sand-dunes & pines at the back. This is the worst of the many hotels. I came here with my boy Auberon in an aeroplane on Monday to join your great new friend Pamela. I came to the hotel and was told she was too ill to see me & that there was no room for me in the hotel. I assumed adultery but investigations seem to prove that there was no politician or journalist concealed in her room. The rooms are too small for one. Mine has a 'bathroom' – a sandy trough behind a curtain, a broken bidet & no lulu which is all one really needs. The public lulus are balkan.

I found three disconsolate, shifty urchins[1] under the care of a nannie who knew no French at all & had no money. They had no bathing cabin because that would have cost another ten francs or so. There was a kind of children's beach club with sporting apparatus but they had not been allowed to join that because of expense (Pamela has been buying spurious works of art in Paris). They were half starved, no breakfasts no puddings or sweets or anything 'extra'. They soon fell sick of malnutrition, one with asthma & one with the itch. Their mother remained incommunicada but I learned from a house-maid that she has eruptions on the face (venereal? inherited?) So I dispensed huge sums to relieve the Berries' distress & got a room in the hotel to succour them. The hotel is on the main street down which motor bicycles drive all day & night tooting. No sleep. My day is, wake at five & lie with the noise of traffic getting louder & louder dreading the time I must go the public w.c. Emerge retching & nausea persists all day. From 8 until 12 I sit in a dingy, sandy hall watching the pensionnaires parade in & out in immodest bathing clothes, with bleached hair and blistered navels. Bathe at 12 for five minutes. Water so shallow one has to walk a mile to swim. The deep water full of jelly fish & speed boats. Wait until 1.30 for the Berry family to appear for luncheon. Talk to nannie & provide lemon squash for children.

After luncheon drive Berries in hired car to places of interest recommended by corrupt concierge. These places are either (a) gift-shops, open or (b) chateaux, shut. Return for opening of the roulette room at the Casino. Lose 10,000 francs. The only happy moment is seeing the last counter disappear. I make it a rule not to go until I have lost 10,000. Sometimes it takes *hours* and the rooms are like one of those Smith[2] drawings of air-raid shelters. Dine with Nanny. Back to the Casino & lose another 10,000. Bed. Lie listening to the traffic getting slightly quieter until 5. Doze.

Your great new friend made a brief appearance yesterday to borrow 30,000 and tell me to look out for Prod & Ed who are expected hourly. If Prod comes I shall send him tollgating with Nannie & have some satisfaction. As to Stanley, since his dastardly behaviour about Quennell, he is my abomination. One of your reviewers said you 'spring from' Stanley of Alderley. So do I, a mile.

Well I said I was cured of going abroad after the Sykes expedition. The cure is now complete. Never again Never Never Never Never Never Never. NEVER.

My boy behaves beautifully & is very happy. The more I see of other people's children the less I dislike my own.

Did I tell you about Harriet who came the other day in great excitement to say that the kitchen garden was full of 'white things with horns'. 'Cows?' 'No, smaller than cows.' I thought there must be some visitation of goats & rushed out. It was full of cabbage butterflies. 'You must have seen butterflies before Harriet.' 'Not with horns.' Very odd.

Now it is time to go & lose another 10,000.

Love
      Evelyn

[1] Adrian, Nicholas and Harriet Berry who were twelve, seven and four respectively.
[2] Percy Smith (1882–1948). Painter and etcher.

24 August 1949   Montredon

Darling Evelyn

I really feel *sad* that you had such a hateful time – alas nobody consulted me, or as far as I can see any of us semi frogs, any of whom would have told you that Brittany in the season is hell & La Baule is Eastbourne only worse. When finally you & Pam said you were going all seemed to have been arranged & by then it would probably have been too late to get in anywhere else. Of course the whole of the coast is crowded at this time of year & I feel that people like us who don't *go* to work would do better to have their holidays in June – & then the children can't. It is a problem. The only nice thing to do is take a house & be out of the crowd. This part of the world is perfection, I think, not smart, people go to Marseille for business not for bathing, the sea rather cold & you swim off rocks, & then you have the whole of beautiful Provence to go motoring in. I seriously think of buying a house down here if I could find one near the sea, though the social Colonel thinks I ought to be further along towards Cannes! He comes here for a few days & then Windsors beckon & he hurries off again. We both go back to Paris on Monday next.

The spitefulness of the American reviews is on the grounds that I write about lords – some even complain that the book is dedicated to one,[1] & all aver that you cannot make good literature out of such a subject! Furthermore they all say it is unreadable & I don't think they even got as far as Cedric. Reviews arrive by hundreds every day & the headline is generally UNREADABLE.

'Miss Mitford's book is a slow moving vehicle hardly enlivened by the oh-so-smart-English-type-humor. There is nothing brilliant in the way of characterization & the unceasing effort to be clever can pall after a time. Pick it up later at a book sale if you like reading about the English nobility – I don't.'

You see?

Just received the 50,000 which I will cherish for you.[2] I do so hope it means you will come again when your wounds have healed – didn't you enjoy Paris at all? Oh bother, all Père Couturier's fault. Then I shall never see you again if you don't because I am never going back to England, I hate it too much. (Not England but the travelling & tiredness.) The tiresome thing is you are one of the few English people *made* to like & appreciate the French. Oh dear it all got off on the wrong foot, how boring.

The Colonel paid a long visit to Picasso & came back more impressed than ever. I read this out to him & he said no, more happy & elated than ever. He is horrified at the récit from Pam of her purchases, saying she ought never to have bought all those things without him & he can't guarantee that they are genuine – except the Oudry which is a terribly nice picture don't you think? He says now they are perfectly genuine but he would like to know whether Pam got the pedigree of the Boudin which came from a gallery he doesn't know much about.

I really can't get on with this letter, he keeps reading out loud, singing, asking what I've written & contradicting it. Ha! A man has just arrived to take him, on behalf of the municipality to see a building they are putting up by Le Corbusier, so peace & silence reign. It seems an American at Cannes said to him 'I hear you arrange controversial luncheons in Paris.' '?' 'Evelyn Waugh & Fr Couturier.' 'Nothing to do with me & how do you know?' 'Everybody knows in America.'

Poor Col, it was *entirely* my idea! And not at all meant to be controversial!

Much love, write to Mr Street[3]
    NR

[1] *Love in a Cold Climate* was dedicated to Lord Berners.
[2] Evelyn entrusted Nancy with his French royalties and drew on this nest-egg whenever he
visited Paris.
[3] Rue Monsieur.

29 August [1949]   Piers Court
                                                        Stinchcombe
Darling Nancy,

It was heaven to get home, to walk into White's and find Sykes &
Dunne & Stavordale all drunk & eating grouse, and to hear a member
of committee say that Quennell had 'not a hope in Hell' of election.
But Stinkers was depressing, full of daughters & nieces & sleepy wasps
and flies and the new buildings in the garden hidden in a jungle of
weed & I have been in a melancholy all the week. Stung by a wasp
the day before yesterday & swelled like a bolster.

Best news of the week Eddy West's reception into the Church[1]. No
surprise to me. I knew he was under instruction and I can never
understand why everyone is not a Catholic, but I feel deep joy all the
same.

Pam behaved a little better towards the end of our holiday and very
well indeed finally by taking my boy Auberon off for ten days cruise
in the Camrose yacht. I am still being told by the way, on your
authority, that I am cruising with the Mosleys.

I am very sorry the Americans dislike your book on such frivolous
grounds, particularly as it looks as though soon one American reader
will be worth ten Europeans. I constantly hear of English invalids who
delight in it and the socialists are pleased that you do not suggest any
virtue in your marble halls.

Was it Prod & Ed who started the fires in the Landes?[2] I suppose
so.

The article I went to America to write is coming out shortly in *Life*.[3]
For the last week I have had thousand word cables daily from each
member of the editorial board severally & collectively expressing their
deep appreciation of a distinguished and notable piece of quality journalism etc etc. As my unhappy servants have to take all these testimonials
down on the telephone they have long faces. It is a tremendously
boring article anyway. That is what they like you see.

Why not have Toulon as your market-town? I remember liking it
very much indeed years ago. But of course, the Party will insist on
your being nearer Headquarters in Marseille. Up the Red Maquis.

Come to think of it that is probably why the Americans are being so beastly. You have been denounced for Unamerican Activities.

Why not live in Monte Carlo? Very nice.

I daresay Pam's objets d'art are not really spurious. I should not be able to tell. I just said they were on account of being in a bad temper at having to pay for them. Pam is quite awful with her children, much worse than me or Uncle Matthew or even Decca.

Audrey Dunne's brother blew out his brains in St James's Park on the day she was being eviscerated in the London Clinic. Only *Love in C.C.* cheered her up.

Mrs R. Churchill is said to be treating him slightly more kindly. He is abject.

Best love
    E

[1] Edward Sackville-West's conversion, provoked by reading George Orwell's novel *Nineteen Eighty-Four*, was a surprise to many of his friends.
[2] Forest fires had been raging in south-western France for several weeks.
[3] 'The American Epoch in the Catholic Church', *Life*, 19 September 1949.

31 August 1949   7 rue Monsieur, VII

Darling Evelyn

England in September – what you say does so bring it back to me, the long stuffy boring days & the wasps. And the biting flies. At home there used to be one called the piano fly because it lived in the piano from which it made sorties to inflict agonizing poisonous bites. Then the trees all go black & it becomes damp in the garden after tea. Oh I hope I need never live there again.

You would have enjoyed Marie's description of a visit here from Prod during my absence. 'Monsieur portait une barbe.' 'Quelle horreur!' 'En effet, cela n'avantageait pas Monsieur.'[1] It seems he arrived at 9 AM, slept all day, tried to force open a drawer where I keep a few pound notes & ambled off at nightfall without a word. Marie thinks him awfully eccentric.

I have just lunched with Philip Jordan[2] who has won my heart by passing a note to my neighbour saying have you ever noticed what a wonderful colour Nancy's eyes are.[3] Well you do *see* – especially as I've always felt inferior for not having blue lakes like my sisters. Do you know him? Blissikins.

Fancy Eddy. Surely a good thing.

You've got it wrong about Marseille which is a *tremendous* Gaullist stronghold. The Colonel treated like a king with motors at his disposition whenever he wants one etc & people coming on the chance of a word with him. The Mayor & Corporation all Gaullists & the General came while I was there & had the whizz of a reception.

I don't mind a bit about the Americans liking or not my book &
don't even mind about dollars – all I do mind is having to feel grateful
to the brutes because I really deeply hate them but am forced to feel
grateful & it is beastly. You should see them in the Ritz here as I did
this morning – all dressed in beach clothes with gold shoes. I wonder
if the Russians are really worse – they smell worse I expect. I *hate all*
barbarians why can't they leave us in peace? There was one in the
train making a scene because no tea for dinner – then why not stay
in Boston?

Mary Dunn bought a post card of a Picasso to send to you – I
would like to dissociate myself from this action. Who is Audrey Dunne?

Oh yes, the cables. I got one asking me to do a pen picture of Pss
Margaret for 350 dollars & it went over the page twice. They could
have saved their breath to blow their porridge. I shall hurry to buy
Life Magazine.

   All love
      NR

Trying to screw myself up to do some work (preface to *Psse de C*).
Hence this long letter – any excuse – do you know the feeling?
I've been summoned home to see Korda[4] – trying not to go but if I
do I shall hope for a glimpse of you.
What about this mag: advertised in *Horizon* with a story by you?

[1] 'Mr Rodd had a beard.' 'How awful.' 'Indeed, it didn't improve him.'
[2] Philip Jordan (1902–51). Journalist and novelist.
[3] Nancy's eyes were green.
[4] Alexander Korda (1893–1956). Hungarian-born producer and director whose films include
The Scarlet Pimpernel (1935), *Lady Hamilton* (1941) and *The Third Man* (1949). Knighted in 1942.

15 September 1949   7 rue Monsieur, VII

Darling Evelyn

You were a brute to send me that mag when you know how much
I hate reading sad stories.[1] I hated it.

I had a very funny time with my Dad – he has completely changed
in character & now lives for pleasure, specially cocktail parties, & has
sold his cows because they interfere with the cocktail parties. He gave
one for me & I'm bound to say I would have preferred an hour in a
cow shed – you can imagine the neighbours on that moor 'Mr & Mrs
Wright, our clergyman, Mr Slingsby from the camp, Mr & Mrs Oakes
who keep the Percy (local Ritz)' etc.

All said to be thrilled for the Paris fashions.

I said to him 'Korda has bought all those houses in Piccadilly next
to Apsley House.'

'No! You don't mean it? Jack Cawdor[2] has?'

He said 'I was showing some blasted woman round the garden – I thought it was Lady Northbourne' – long pause – 'Well, it *was* Lady Northbourne.' Isn't he bliss.

I did enjoy seeing you, wish it had been for longer. Do come when Pam does. Neither Col nor I have the moral courage to go & tell the dealer about the Oudry coming back, isn't it awful.

Mollie [Friese-Greene] very thrilled that you are giving them a wedding present.

I'm *appalled* at the idea of starting work again & don't see how I can unless I cut off the telephone.

Much love (& haste, this is to un thank for the *Month*).
       NR

I hear Prod lost his & Ed's traveller's cheques at Baule & Ed knocked him down – also that he has a wonderful new toll gate about tides – high tide at Spitzbergen = low tide at Dieppe & so on. Die for it don't you?

[1] The August issue of the *Month* carried Evelyn's short story 'Compassion' about a British officer's attempt to rescue a party of Jews from a refugee camp run by Yugoslav Partisans.
[2] 5th Earl Cawdor (1900–70).

21 September 1949   7 rue Monsieur, VII

Darling Evelyn

Having been brought up to believe (not by Uncle Matthew) that qui n'a pas l'esprit de son age en a tous les défauts[1] I am appalled to find that in this week's *Horizon* there is not one single article I can understand. It's not a question of 'I don't quite see what you're getting at' I simply *do not understand it*, it's like a foreign language.[2] (Except for one fragment which is too sad to read – yes & why is everything always sad fragments now? You might say of modern books sadly fragmented instead of well documented.) What does it mean – ought I to commit suicide? I don't dare ask Cyril he is so touchy & he might think I imply a reproach.

I've just done my preface to the *Princesse de Clèves*, 5000 words, long for me & am engaged on the bibliography & notes.

Haven't answered the telephone or seen anybody except Col since I got back – all very well & *I love* it only it's dull for the poor Colonel who complains I never have any news to tell him. If you wrote to me I could read it out to him – he is reading all your early works lent by Prince Bibesco.[3]

   Yours etc
       Worried

[1] 'He who shares not the spirit of his age has all its defects.' A misquotation of Voltaire's maxim: 'He who shares not the spirit of his age knows it in all its unhappiness.'
[2] Articles in the September 1949 issue of *Horizon* included: 'The Literature of Extreme Situations' by Albert Votaw, 'A Fragment of Life Story' by Denton Welch, 'On the Analysis of Moral Judgements' by A. J. Ayer and 'San Sebastian' by Ryunosuke Akatugawa.
[3] Prince Antoine Bibesco (1878–1951). Shrewd Romanian diplomat and close friend of Proust. Married Elizabeth Asquith, daughter of the Prime Minister H. H. Asquith, in 1919.

[September 1949]

Darling Nancy

It is interesting that you are troubled by *Horizon*. I have just had a similar experience with this week's *New Yorker*. Not one joke I could make head or tail of. Most disconcerting.

Have you heard about your nephew Dominick [Elwes]? Ran away from Downside (most reprehensible in a big boy) stayed in an hotel in London and had all his meals on tick at the Hungarian Restaurant for three or four days, was caught and sent to Switzerland to a Buchmanite[1] hostel, fled the hostel, stole a car, was chased by Swiss police. When brought to trial the judge turned out to be a Buchmanite & promptly acquitted him. This so much impressed the wretched boy with Buchmanite justice that he now adheres to that horrible sect.

The Prod–Ed Odyssey is legend now in London. It is generally felt that it was very wrong of Prod to play *Boule* with Ed's money. If it had been chemin-de-fer it would have been quite honourable. I met John Marling[2] walking dead lame & asked what had happened. He simply said: 'Ed's yacht.'

Boots's boule de suif what was her name? Sonia something is engaged to marry the dying Orwell and is leaving *Horizon* so there will not be many more numbers to puzzle us.

Randolph's wife is very pregnant and there is still only one room in the house because Randolph moves the walls about like a scene-shifter – literally.

Handy has the itch.

Oh dear that won't interest the Colonel much, will it? I wish I could think of something. Would he like to know that Prince Doria[3] has a bungalow without servants at Birchington and greatly prefers it to his palaces. I lunched with him & he said the trouble in Rome was that there were no boxes provided for used bus tickets so his pockets were always full of them. That ought to amuse Col.

Are you richer or poorer through Cripps devaluing the pound? I am richer but Cripps just takes it all away again so what's the good.

The French Dominicans (Couturier's order) are causing great anxiety to English papists by their collaboration with socialists Buchmanites and a blasphemous travesty of the Life of Christ they propose to make a film of.[4] Their English agents for this film are guess who Lord Halifax,[5] Sir S. Cripps[6] and Irene Ravensdale.[7] They are also warmly supported by the Zionists who think the film will promote dollar tourism to Jerusalem.

I feel very poor suddenly. Do you feel rich & poor by turns. It is all the fault of Popkins.

Love
  E

[1] Frank Buchman (1878–1961). Founder of 'Moral Re-Armament', a movement launched in 1938 based on Christian principles of absolute honesty and purity. Nancy's sister-in-law, Mary Rodd, was a keen adherent of its tenets.
[2] Sir John Marling (1910–77). In 17th/21st Lancers during the war; he and Evelyn were fellow members of White's.
[3] Prince Filippo Doria-Pamphili (1899–1958). Mayor of Rome after the Italian liberation. In 1921 he married Gesine Mary Dykes, who had nursed him during the First World War.
[4] Georges de la Grandière, producer of the successful film of St Vincent de Paul, *Monsieur Vincent*, wanted to make a life of Christ called *The Divine Tragedy*. The project was scuttled by lack of funds and violent disagreements over which version of the Scriptures should be used.
[5] 1st Earl of Halifax (1881–1959). Statesman. His role in the project was negligible.
[6] As Chancellor of the Exchequer, Sir Stafford Cripps's permission had to be sought before any funds could be transferred abroad.
[7] Lady Irene Curzon (1896–1966). Eldest daughter of Lord Curzon. Succeeded her father as 2nd Baroness Ravensdale in 1925 and was created a life peeress under the same title in 1958. The leading force behind the project, she felt it her urgent duty 'to get Christ on the films' and had a nervous breakdown when she failed.

26 September 1949   7 rue Monsieur, VII

Darling Evelyn

Your letter – blissipots. Debo is here so I've got this nice new word, she is living in a suite with Mr Tom[1] the lover of Princess Margaret & they are called the sinners on account of living in, & oh the rush. I'm worn out but they leave tomorrow. Mosleys are here too.

I am dreadfully fussed about work – I feel I shan't be able to do the Korda thing[2] & that will let down everybody including nice Mr Peters.[3] But perhaps it will be all right. Everything I've written so far has been facetious & awful, but perhaps the start is always like that? I seem to remember it is. Now all these visitors so dead stop. Then I've been offered another tempting little job I long to do, about 3 weeks work, but it seems too much out of the 6 months Korda is allowing me. I'm dreadfully over tired on account of sister life. Taking them to my dressmaker tomorrow – a friend of Debo's called Lady Sykes[4] has told her there is nothing under £500 so she is rather impressed. So far she has bought a collar for her dog like a man's evening collar & a machine for blowing bubbles. Have you heard her imitation of the Newbury mummers, I really thought I'd die.

All your stories are perfect for Col thank you thank you. He's away. He's very fed up with Fr Couturier who has a full page studio portrait by Dorothy Wilding in *Vogue* & whom he found screaming with laughter with Lulu & several lesbians in the local smart antique shop here.

I said to the Col 'I don't have to become a Catholic because je suis en règle avec le bon Dieu'[5] & the Col said how do you know? *Isn't* he disloyal. I do know, too.

I lunched with a lot of intellectual frogs today & it was one of those delicious endless meals with everybody shouting about Diderot which I so greatly enjoy. Then they all began shouting about you & I had to tell them that you don't love France to which they said but he doesn't love anything & I said yes he does he loves *me*. But I could see they merely thought I was boasting. They say France is on the verge of a great flowering like that of the 18th century – oh good.

I don't like that Dominick he seems to me a Prod raté [failed] – but then *I* don't like his parents – you I believe do. Though I deplore having no children I feel rather glad I haven't any with Guthrie blood – it doesn't work out very well though one never knows what a sobering admixture of Mitford wouldn't have done.

I long & long & *long* to live quietly in Provence & write books about people like Mme de La Fayette & not always to feel over-done. But it's the Colonel that stops me.

This letter is too long you'll never have got here. Oh I must tell about an American advert: of a book on the back of a cutting I've got. It's a picture of a gentleman in pince nez nearly life size & it's called *The Man of Nazareth as His Contemporaries Saw Him*.[6] I'm so delighted about Atomgrad[7] & only hope they cop it soon.

Fondest love
     NR

[1] Tom Egerton (1918–98). An old family friend of Deborah and Andrew
[2] Nancy had undertaken to produce a film treatment around the idea of a boy who does his best to keep his divorced parents apart. Her script was refused but she developed the story into a novel, *The Blessing*, which was subsequently bought by MGM and made into a film.
[3] Augustus Detlof Peters (1892–1973). Founder of the literary agency A. D. Peters; he represented both Nancy and Evelyn.
[4] Virginia Gilliat (1916–70). Married Sir Richard Sykes in 1942.
[5] 'I'm all square with God.'
[6] By H. E. Fosdick (1949).
[7] The USSR had carried out their first atomic bomb test.

10 October 1949   Piers Court
                                                            Stinchcombe
Darling Nancy

You can imagine the joy your present has given me. How I wish it were twice the size with all the lovely pictures given a page apiece.[1]

It will be the solace of many dark days ahead. It is lucky I don't know French as I fear the written matter would be very offensive to me. From a sentence or two here & there which I managed to construe it seemed plainly to be the work of Père Couturier.

I went to London for a week and hated every minute of it. I saw Cooper walking hand in hand with Palffy.[2] I saw the inside of *Horizon* office full of horrible pictures collected by Watson[3] & Lys & Miss Brownell working away with a dictionary translating some rot from the French. That paper is to end soon. Everyone I met complained bitterly about the injustice of having to earn a living & the peculiar beastliness of his own profession – Cyril about editing, John Sutro about films. I dined with John de Bendern and he was sick three times during dinner. Your publisher H. Hamilton has got into White's. That augurs ill for the Quennell election. It should be a club for gamblers, lords & heroes.

Handy is absolutely covered with sores.

I went to a dinner given by the *Daily Express* and there was an editor dead lame so I said what happened and he said 'it was my own fault I was foolish enough to go to the first night of a play'. It appears that now the Cinema companies take half the stalls & send actresses whom they want to make famous. Then they inform a circle of adolescents of both sexes who turn up five hundred strong break into the theatre & mob the actresses not reverently asking for autographs but fiercely tearing out lumps of their hair and cutting pieces out of their clothes (literally). This editor got caught in a stampede, knocked down, trampled on & left with a dislocated knee and ankle. Old first-nighters like Eddie Marsh[4] don't dare go near a theatre now. Well it is all part of the century of the common man to make any kind of prominence entirely odious. Think what happened to Harewood.[5] Thank God the People aren't interested in letters. But they, letters I mean not alas the People, are coming to an end anyway. Cyril was offered 1500 dollars to write an article about 'Young writers in Britain swing right' and his mouth watered but he couldn't find one writer under 35 right left or swinging.

We have a 'prison without bars' next door to us. 73 escapes in the last eighteen months. The other day an air force officer walked out into a cottage & bludgeoned three inhabitants, one hovering now as they say between life and death. There are 17 murderers there including the licentious steward who pushed the girl out of her port-hole. All are convicted of crimes of violence. The countryside is terrorised and today indignant to learn that last week-end they performed *Rope*[6] with an all murderer cast.

Nice Jack McDougall[7] my publisher is publishing no books at all next year. I said why don't you reprint the Stanley letters and he said I long to but the travellers won't let me.

Love in a Cold Climate has become a phrase. I mean when people want to be witty they say I've caught a cold in a cold climate and everyone understands.

I haven't said half enough about L'Art officiel, it is a joy.

Randolph has contrived a breach between me & your great new friend Pam.

Best love from
Evelyn

[1] Nancy had sent a copy of *Le Point* (April 1949), which carried an article by Francis Jourdain: 'L'Art officiel de Jules Grévy à Albert Lebrun'. It was illustrated with turn-of-the-century paintings of scantily-clothed women in mildly suggestive poses.'
[2] Louise de Vilmorin.
[3] Peter Watson (1908–56). Inherited £2m. at the age of 22. Patron of the arts, collector and connoisseur who financed *Horizon* and was its art director 1939–50. One of the co-founders of the Institute of Contemporary Art.
[4] Sir Edward Marsh (1872–1953). Private Secretary to Winston Churchill 1917–22. Patron of young writers and painters, whose chief interest was the theatre.
[5] 7th Earl of Harewood (1923–). Grandson of George V, imprisoned as a *prominente* in Colditz during the war together with other prisoners with illustrious connections. Director of Royal Opera House, Covent Garden, 1951–3 and 1969–72.
[6] A play by Patrick Hamilton about two young men who commit murder because they claim to be 'superior' persons with the right to kill 'inferior' ones. Filmed by Hitchcock in 1948.
[7] John McDougall (1903–76). Joined Chapman & Hall in 1946 and remained Evelyn's lifelong friend.

14 October 1949   7 rue Monsieur, VII

Darling Evelyn

Oh I know, one longs for them to be given a large page each, it's the only drawback. My favourites are the flood with the poor wet lions (& why haven't the people got anything on – you'd think they would have rushed for their macks) & La Tamise. Couturier's preface is *terrible*, facetious when one longs for information – where all these glories are to be found etc, & takes up valuable pages which might have been devoted to more pictures. Still we mustn't complain. Oh I'm very fond of the salute to the old hero, too, & the lady with the alleged rabbit. I was very much afraid the customs would bag it for being feelthy but perhaps the magic word *Officiel* did its work.

I saw about that first night. You know England is getting past a joke, I thought it more terrible than ever when I was there the other day – everybody so unkind. For instance I went to stay with my uncle & had to take a station bus from Oxford to Burford. When we got there I saw my uncle sitting in his motor & said oh please stop. 'Oh we don't stop there any more' & took me on about ¼ of a mile, with all my luggage. Now here that simply *couldn't happen* you know, so much so that when these things overtake me at home I am so surprised that I almost begin to cry. Have the English always loved teasing people – I can't help feeling it must be latent in the character or it wouldn't have come out so strongly & all over the country. Now the French have a mania for seeing people pleased & happy & that leads to a different annoyance. You say can you do this & they can't *bear* to see your face fall so they always say yes & then it isn't always done. But as for not stopping a bus for you – as I say it *couldn't* happen. Never mind.

I must say I do think it's funny about *Rope*. Have you read *Swinburne*[1] by my great friend Humph Hare? I knew of course in a vague way that he practised (or favoured) le vice anglais but had no idea to what extent – the Whippingham papers & so on – so it has been one long happy shriek for me. How Heywood must die to get his hands on Lord Houghton's library, do you think the Roxburgh have got it?

Faithful Honks Cooper came galloping round because as I don't answer the telephone she supposed I must be dead. She says John Julius, at New College, has to live in a pre-fab hut worse than anything in the Navy. You'd think Oxford would hold out against that wouldn't you?

Oh don't quarrel with Pam. I must say her letter telling about it is the funniest I've ever had, I get asked out to meals to read it out loud – really you are *awful* but one can see how she's loved every minute of it. She has a côté Whippingham hasn't she?

Fancy W H Smith here has got a photograph of me in the window & 9 copies of my book. Unheard of. You can imagine if I am thrilled.

Much love from
    NR

Have there ever been any writers under 35 except you?

[1] Humphrey Hare, *Swinburne: A Biographical Approach* (1949).

6 November 1949   7 rue Monsieur, VII

Darling Evelyn

All my friends have forgotten me & the only letters I get now are from chub fuddlers saying that you can't fuddle chub in Feb (long since pointed out with cold fury by Uncle Matthew himself) & one from a Mr Chub asking to be put in touch with a fuddler.[1] Also one from Mr Berenson[2] asking where I have seen The Gamesters by Caravaggio, a picture he says he has long wanted to trace. Answer: I invented it (!) But you, Pam etc never write now, it is so sad for me. I saw your man Sykes & he held out great hopes of an approaching visit oh *do*, I promise you needn't see Fr Dressmaker.

In spite of the badness of Laffont's translations you are regarded by many people here as the greatest (after Malraux[3] or level with Malraux) living novelist, do be gratified.

Do tell what you think of Mr Fitzroy Maclean's book,[4] I have been living in it (lent by Momo).

I have translated a lovely play called *La Petite Hutte*[5] did I tell you. I so adored doing it & now think only of writing a play but I suppose ONE never could alas.

There are some lovely new rooms open in the Louvre, also I've found a bearded lecturer who manages to get inside the houses of lucky beggars (literally) who inhabit the great mouldering palaces of the Marais. It is a mixed treat to see unrestored Louis XIV ceilings partially hidden by washing & so on, but I go on going & when I am rich I shall live in one.

My American publisher has invited me to go there, everything paid. I said I am too old – true.

Hateful Evelyn do write. I live for the blue envelopes.

Love

NR

[1] In *Love in a Cold Climate*, the annual chub-fuddling event was the high point of Uncle Matthew's season.

[2] Bernard Berenson (1865–1959). Lithuanian-born American art historian; leading authority on Renaissance painting.

[3] André Malraux (1901–76). Left-wing intellectual and novelist; author of largely autobiographical novels such as *Les Conquérants* (1928) and *La Condition humaine* (1933). Minister of Cultural Affairs under de Gaulle 1959–69.

[4] Fitzroy Maclean, *Eastern Approaches* (1949). An account of his pre-war travels through Russia and of the British Military Mission in Yugoslavia during the war.

[5] Boulevard comedy by André Roussin (1947) which ran successfully in Paris for three years before transferring to London as *The Little Hut*.

9 November [1949]   Piers Court
                                                     Stinchcombe

Darling Nancy.

Well why I have not written is that I have just passed the most distressing fortnight of my life since I left the Royal Marines and I did not want to harrow your feelings but I long for a sympathetic ear and you have asked for it though goodness knows how you dare when you say you cannot read modern depressing books. This is a chapter from a very depressing modern book. Ready? Teeth gritted? Right.

Well when I came back from USA I made a pious resolution that for a year I would do everything I was asked to do by Catholic bodies. (I don't mean the late Lord Tredegar.)[1] Luckily I had built up a strong wall of immunity over the years by constant curt refusals. Now it has begun to leak out and I give ghastly lectures to ghastly audiences almost once a week. It culminated in a tour of the Northern Centres of Learning – Edinburgh, St Andrews, Dundee, Aberdeen etc etc. Just when I was setting out, shaking with misery, I got an SOS from Baby

Jungman[2] to come to Mereworth where Peter Beatty[3] was in despair. I went. His melancholy had already quite closed in all round him & would have been impenetrable to the Curé d'Ars[4] (ask Col. if he knows who that was). He had asked a party about as comforting as a cage of parrots – Freda & Bobby [Casa-Maury], Boofy[5] & Fiona, Baby & Zita.[6] We chattered away & Peter wandered in and out of the room hardly aware of us. Pouring rain all the time & pretentious rather nasty food. Two days later as you probably know Peter killed himself. In White's he is talked of as a kind of Captain Oates: 'Good old Peter, game to the last. He did not want to be a burden to others so he took the best way out.' In fact, of course, he was stark mad. The world is full of radiantly happy blind men. I was very fond of him in an odd way & the thing upsets me doubly as showing the huge chasms that separate one from one's friends in all essential things.

I didn't hear of his death until I opened the newspaper in the train on Wednesday.

The tour was torture. Hours & hours in dirty, unheated trains. Staying in hotels where trams always ran under the windows. Modernistic decorations. Revolting food at unsuitable times. The actual lectures were merely a bore, it was the times in between. Being greeted by bevies of poverty-stricken adolescents who once they had said 'Pleased to meet you' lapsed into silence with every sign of displeasure. Hideous, dead industrial towns. Idiotic questions after the lecture, either from Catholics 'How do you account for the element of unpleasantness in Mr Graham Greene's work?', or heathen students of literature 'What Hungarian novelists influenced you most, Mr Waugh, in writing *Decline & Fall*?'

Nine lectures in nine days. Returned to London worn out and aged to find everyone talking about Peter's death in the way I have described and Angie [Laycock] saying to a friend 'I really don't want to meet Evelyn at the moment. He's sure to say something beastly about Peter.'

Home, now, thank God, and at work again on *Helena* which is to be my MASTERPIECE. No one will like it at all.

Were you wise to reject American invitation? You would hate it, of course, but you are so tough. They would only want you to sit 12 hours a day in bookshop windows smiling at the customers and you did that during the bombardment of London most bravely. You would find much material for your new life as dramatist.

Next week I give a great party for Clare Luce[7] and after that I give a 'literary weekend', three discourses & organized discussion, at a Convent in Surrey for Catholic writers & librarians. The only person I know is coming is Mrs Chichester. What a life of suffering.

Baby's boy[8] has gone to my son's prep school. I wrote & told him to look after him. He writes: 'It is hard to be nice to Cuthbertson. He is most disagreeable. Very weak and all the boys & masters hate him.'

I have written a tremendous homily on the nature of the English gentleman who always protects the weak & unpopular. Can't say I ever noticed it much myself.

>   Love from
>   Evelyn

[1] 2nd Viscount Tredegar (1893–1949). A fervent Roman Catholic.
[2] Teresa (Baby) Jungman (1907–). Pretty and vivacious daughter of the Dutch painter Nico Jungman. Evelyn had fallen in love with her after the breakdown of his first marriage and proposed in 1933. His passion was not reciprocated but they remained close friends. Married Graham Cuthbertson in 1940.
[3] Hon. Peter Beatty (1910–49). Younger son of Admiral of the Fleet, Earl Beatty. His sight had been gradually deteriorating and he was almost completely blind.
[4] Jean-Baptiste Marie Vianney (1786–1859). Priest whose simple and austere preaching made his parish a place of pilgrimage in his own lifetime. Canonised in 1925.
[5] Hon. Arthur Gore (1910–83). Succeeded as 8th Earl of Arran in 1958. Successful columnist and eccentric peer who introduced the Sexual Offences Bill and the Badger Protection Bill in the House of Lords. Married Fiona Colquhoun in 1937.
[6] Zita Jungman (1903–2006). Teresa's older sister. Described by Cecil Beaton as 'quite marvellously lovely – great squirrel's eyes, fair hair & nice soft throaty voice'. Sacheverell Sitwell wrote love poems to her beauty. Married to Arthur James 1929–32.
[7] Clare Boothe (1903–87). Playwright, author of *The Women* (1936) and *Margin for Error* (1939). Married Henry Luce, founder and editor of *Time*, *Life* and *Fortune* magazines, in 1935. Ambassadress to Italy 1953–7.
[8] Richard Cuthbertson (1941–65).

12 November 1949   7 rue Monsieur, VII

Darling Evelyn

It does all sound horrible. It is the life the Colonel leads (through political ambition) quite 3 days a week. But in his case he is generally put up comfortably by sympathisers & then, beautiful France! There is nearly always some wonderful musée to visit, a Rubens in a private house or a prehistoric cave.

Even so it is tiring & often depressing. Now his mother whom he so adores is perhaps dying so we are having a sad time.

I should find blindness insupportable – I take in everything through my eyes, can't be read to, could never learn to dictate – unless God came to the rescue but as you say he generally does, or so it seems. Mme du Deffand was very miserable & she was very much like oneself, you see there are such endless hours of boredom. Perhaps it would be all right in the bosom of a large & cheerful family, but if you live alone like Peter Beatty, & have no intellectual interests I suppose it would drive you mad as it did him. Oh how sad.

My exuberant friend Peter de Polnay[1] whom I rather love now, but it is like loving a terribly naughty puppy of some large & uncontrolled breed, has written I think a most brilliant book on Edward Fitzgerald. I really think never has a figure from the past been made so lifelike to me, & goodness knows some are more real than one's own friends.

Secker & W are to publish it, I do wish you'd read it & say what you think.

He (P de P) evidently *lives* in what he is writing – now it is a life of the Pretender. The other day I said to him Peter do tell me was there ever any chance of the 45 succeeding at which he looked conspiratorially round the room & whispered 'Between you & me, Nancy, NOT MUCH.'

A literary party last night, a great deal of talk about you. I made a hit, telling every detail of your luncheon with Claudel[2] it was the success of the evening. Two of the guests had been staying with Henriques[3] at *Bee*bury & H very wisely refused to allow them to see you.

The correspondence between Claudel & Gide[4] is in the press goodness I long for it. Claudel tried to get out of having it published by saying Gide's letters were lost in the Tokyo earthquake, but clever old Gide had kept copies –!!!!!

I'm rather sad about my *Princesse de Clèves*, having just received a copy of the *Duchesse de Langeais* from the publishers – such awful type one really can't read it. Never mind. My film story going rather well.

I can see Honks Cooper thinks it's one's duty to commit suicide under certain circumstances, I even find myself speculating on the best way to do it should the need arise, when with her. She was awfully scornful of poor Venetia[5] for not doing it & made it quite clear what *she* expects of one.

I'll send this now, though really I have more to say. When are you coming? Would your vow make you come if Père Couturier & Picasso & Lulu asked you?

All love
NR

[1] Peter de Polnay (1906–84). Hungarian-born author whose many books include *Into an Old Room: The Paradox of Edward Fitzgerald* (1950) and *Death of a Legend: The True Story of Bonnie Prince Charlie* (1952).
[2] Evelyn had met the writer Paul Claudel (1868–1955) on his visit to Paris in May. After lunch, Claudel showed Evelyn a book of press photographs in which famous people, either by mistake or design, were made to look ridiculous. According to Evelyn, a particularly grotesque photograph had made him roar with laughter, upon which Claudel left the room. The photograph was of Claudel himself.
[3] Robert Henriques (1905–67). Author, farmer, and neighbour of Evelyn. His books include *No Arms No Armour* (1939) and *Through the Valley* (1950).
[4] Letters between André Gide (1869–1951), Protestant writer turned anti-Christian agnostic, and Paul Claudel, a convert to Roman Catholicism.
[5] Venetia Montagu had died of cancer the previous year.

16 November [1949]   Piers Court
                                                      Stinchcombe
Darling Nancy

Tell that flower of the boulevardes Sir A. D. Cooper that in the latest P. G. Wodehouse book[1] when Gussie Fink-Nottle is arrested for bathing in the fountain in Trafalgar Square he gives the name 'Alfred Duff Cooper'.

This is most significant as (a) showing Cooper's fame. Till now Wodehouse characters in these circumstances always call themselves 'Lenin' or 'Aristotle' (b) showing the Master's great ignorance of Cooper's habits. Nothing is more likely than that he would be found wallowing in evening dress at 5 in the morning.

I forgot to say that during the tour of the Northern Centres of Learning I was tormented with tooth-ache and had to visit horrible socialist provincial dentists.

My *Helena* is a great masterpiece. How it will flop.

I wonder if you still correspond with E. Sackville-West. Tomorrow I am having him to dine with the cream of English Catholicism. I shall be interested to hear how he reports on it.

After Pam Chichester's literary retreat I take the chair & speak to Catholic Guild of Artists & Craftsmen. Oh God.

The Midland Gardeners I complained to you about are hard at work doing worse & worse all round the house.

Love from
        Evelyn

Re Suicide. Has it ever occurred to you that bastards are much more inclined to it than those born in wedlock. It has just occurred to me. I can think of so many cases. They know they shouldn't be in the world at all.

[1] *The Mating Season.*

20 November 1949   7 rue Monsieur, VII

Darling Evelyn

The boulevardier is well aware of his luck & goes round boasting of it & we are all gell-gell. I haven't read the book yet but how I long for it I shall borrow boulevardier's copy.

Prod is here & has upset me very much by saying (A) Korda has no intention of using my script & (B) Ian Fleming only asked me to write a Paris letter for *ST* as a joke & has no intention of using that either[1]. It is very discouraging. I do so hate writing as you know & really have worked hard on the film & it really will be good, but I now feel quite disinclined to go on with it.

I wonder if I told you of my long talk with the D of Windsor – the thing is I've been away for 5 days & don't remember if I wrote to you before going. I went to Tanis [Guinness] who has a Surrey stock-broker's house in Normandy, pretty in its way, & we played bridge with gramophone full blast all day till 2 every morning. I won 16,000 francs so it suited me, also it reminded me of what life in England is like, which I had almost forgotten.

I don't correspond regularly with Ed – I wrote when he became a Catholic saying it must be like having a lovely new love affair & he didn't answer, perhaps he thought it an unsuitable simile but it's what I imagine it would be like & I can't think of anything nicer.

The Col just back from another lecture tour saying pâté de foie gras is all right but not at *every* meal –!! But he saw 2 Goyas & a mediaeval Virgin & that cheered him up. The provincial museums here are wonderful you know. He went to La Baule & said *next time you go there* (!!) he must introduce you to all the queer Roman Catholics who live at Guérande & are to your religion he says what the Scotch are to ours. Did you go to Nantes? He can talk of nothing but the musée there.

I've got 400 000 [francs] advance for my 2 books from the respectable old house of Stock, so am very delighted. Laffont wanted them but I wouldn't as they have behaved so badly to various acquaintances & I so hated the translation of *The Loved One*.

I expect you love St Helena because you know nobody else will, like me & *La Princesse de Clèves*. Are you dying for the Gide–Claudel letters – they are very outspoken, the ones I have read.

Been reading a short life of Lady Dilke by Sir Chas[2] – don't love her quite as much as when I thought she was more like ONE. Alas, a reformer & a suffragette I thought she hated Marie Antoinette as I do for bringing all that German taste here but no it is on brioche grounds I fear. But what is remarkable, she was the friend, correspondent & admirer, pupil really, of Ruskin – I think it extraordinary that she should have become the supreme authority on 18 Cent French decoration, don't you?

I am in correspondence with her niece aged 83 who is thrilled that I should be such a fan. Lady D died the month I was born. Hundreds of her letters are in the Bibliothèque Nationale, perfect French, & yet she never seems to have lived here for long. How annoying!

Much love
NR

[1] Ian Fleming's suggestion that Nancy should write for the *Sunday Times* was a serious one. Her first article, 'The Pursuit of Paris', appeared on 11 December 1949 and she contributed a regular column over the next four years.
[2] Memoir of Emilia Frances Strong (1840–1904), the Victorian expert on French art, by her widower, Sir Charles Wentworth Dilke.

5 December [1949]   Piers Court
                                                           Stinchcombe

Darling Nancy,

I was delighted to read that 'the most brilliant of the younger writers'
has joined the staff of the *Sunday Times*. You should have said 'youngest
writers'. We are much younger than Max Beerbohm or E. M. Forster.
There are none younger than us.

I have been an invalid for a week recuperating from a brief visit to
London. I get so painfully drunk whenever I go there (Champagne,
the shortest road out of Welfaria) and nowadays it is not a matter of
a headache and an aspirin but of complete collapse, with some clear
indications of incipient lunacy. I think I am jolly near being mad &
need very careful treatment if I am to survive another decade without
the strait straight? jacket.

My great party for Mrs Luce was very expensive & I think a good
time was had by most. Eddy chucked.

Then I conducted a meeting of the Catholic Guild of Arts & Crafts
where I won their confidence by abuse of Picasso & then lost it with
abuse of Catholic Arts & Crafts. I find it most encouraging that everywhere everyone is seeing through Picasso – even old jaggers like R.
Mortimer.

Then I had an excruciating week-end in a convent in Surrey conducting a 'Catholic Booklovers' Week-End'. The nuns were very attentive with little packets of chocolate and glasses of milk covered with muslin
veils weighted with beads do you know what I mean. When I said I never
drank milk they quite understood & pursued me from breakfast to bed
with a bottle of Burgundy and a medicine glass. The sort of questions
were, of course, 'Why does Mr Greene have such a nasty mind?' and 'Is
it not the duty of the artist to consider the average reader?' Can you
wonder that the mere breath of White's intoxicates?

The backwash of my American jaunt laps all round me. This Sunday
a middle-west publisher (middle west is the agricultural part of USA)
who was flabbergasted at the proximity of Laura's little farm. 'What
is hay for?' literally he asked, and 'But where is it pasteurized?' in the
dairy. He had a patent nylon shirt which he washed in his bath.

Well I suppose you will have to make a Paris home for the Berry
boys (Kemsley) and that will be worse than anything.

I am afraid there may be truth in what Prod tells you of Korda. I
believe the English (ha ha) films are in dissolution. But you can trust
Peters to save something from the wreck.

Mrs Churchill is greatly improved in temper by maternity.[1] Pam
Mrs Churchill is said to be contemplating union with Lord Beatty.
Lady Beatty is said to ditto with a sex obsessed Eden.

I was too drunk in London to get my hair cut. It is so long it tickles.
I can't face going back. What am I to do?

Another White's–VIII Commando suicide last week. Toby Milbanke.[2]

Tommy Rosslyn[3] was living at the convent where I gave my lectures and spoke in a rambling but deeply affectionate way of you. I think she is under the impression that you married me.

I scrapped the library grate last summer & introduced handsome fire dogs. Now it smokes so much that my eyes are dim & bloodshot all day. Is it possible to get spectacles in Paris? And do you think my French is up to explaining to an oculist that I am losing my sight? Je ne veux pas devenir aveugle m. le docteur. Voulez vous me vendre des lunettes.[4] How is that? One can't get spectacles here unless one is a Trades Unionist.

Everyone who came to the Luce banquet sent Laura a Collins[5] except Luce. Don't you think that odd?

I have deeply enjoyed R. G. Hardy's *Recollections of L. P. Smith*.[6] Have you got it yet? Both of them older than us. Will your Paris articles be about millinery or politics? I long for them.

Love from
    Evelyn

[1] Randolph and June Churchill's daughter, Arabella, was born on 31 October 1949.
[2] Sir Ralph (Toby) Milbanke (1907–49).
[3] Vera Mary (Tommy) Bailey (d.1975). Married 5th Earl of Rosslyn as his third wife in 1908. She was the mother of Hamish St Clair Erskine, Nancy's first love.
[4] Doctor, I do not want to go blind. Can you sell me some spectacles?
[5] A thank-you letter. Derived from the fulsome 'bread-and-butter' letter addressed to Mr Bennet by the Reverend William Collins in *Pride and Prejudice*.
[6] Robert Gathorne-Hardy, *Recollections of Logan Pearsall Smith: The Story of a Friendship* (1949).

7 December 1949   7 rue Monsieur, VII

Darling Evelyn

You are horrid. You know quite well *I* didn't say I was the m b of the y ws – I was appalled by the whole thing, specially as the article is deadly beyond belief (Prod says unreadable) & I'd hoped to creep in on the woman's page unnoticed. Never mind I've found a lovely picture for it as I know you will admit – I have to provide my own ill*eo*stration what Cecil [Beaton] calls, it is part of the horror. Now don't let's hear any more about it please. I *must* earn money when I can – I shall never inherit any as far as I know, haven't got any except what I make, & extreme old age looms all too near. Then I shall so want a little fire & perhaps a pair of steel-rimmed specs & a molar or 2 do admit. I think of o else. It (the article) won't do anybody any harm, it can't be worse or more boring than the existing woman's page (which is all about welfare in Scandinavia if you want to know, ask Laura if it's not true) & if unreadable nobody is obliged to read it.

Do come & get some specs oh do. Prod gets his here chez les frères Lissac. Prod is a worry to me. If I were an ordinary wife I should be wheeling him up & down the Invalides in a bath chair with a white stick to show he is blind. He can hardly totter now, or see anything & he has a duodenal ulcer. He sits all day editing his poems & waiting for the end & making me cry with the récit of my sins towards him. He speaks so low now that the other evening I was twice obliged to ask whether we had just had a long speech or a long silence. I have to wear my frownies[1] all day I'm so put out by the whole thing. Last night he went round the brothels with Duff I am thankful to say, hope it cheered him up.

Fancy the Canadian reviews of *LCC* are coming in now & they are thrilled about Cedric being Canadian they can't get over the bliss of it. I'm so surprised, thought they'd be X.

Mr Binkie Beaumont[2] is said to be pleased with my adaptation of *La Petite Hutte* so you may yet see that funniest of all plays in London. Prod on the other hand read my *Princesse de Clèves* & said it is the most gruesome sort of translationese he has ever seen. This has cast me into despair because I thought it so good & so much in a way like the original. Too much, evidently. Oh alas. I see that translating is one of the most difficult of all literary exercises, I mean translating a classic. The *Hutte* was lovely because I put my own words to Roussin's heavenly situations.

Who are these Berry boys you threaten me with? Don't tell me the Kemsleys have children?

Diana [Cooper] said 'can't do it, I've got to take Graham Greene's mistress to the station' or words to that effect. Has he one? Did you know? I was riveted.

I've sold my books here to Stock, an old-fashioned firm, very nice people, £400. Not bad? And got it what's more. Now we are having terrible trouble with translators oh the difficulty. Luckily I am allowed to supervise.

I wonder if Prod would be happier if he were a Catholic, do have a go at him Evelyn be like Claudel with Gide.

Best love don't tease me any more & don't read the *S Times* (useless request).

NR

Who is a man called Eldridge something? He says he met you in a train & you said 'I know you' & never spoke again except to say 'a better class of passenger gets out at Kemble than at Stroud'.

---

[1] Sticky tape applied to the face to ward off wrinkles.
[2] Hugh (Binkie) Beaumont (1908–73). Theatrical manager and director of H. M. Tennent Ltd, he dominated the West End theatre for 40 years.

12 December [1949]   Piers Court
                                                      Stinchcombe

Dearest Nancy,

How very kind of you to remember Harriet's Christmas. The book is not exactly to my taste, nor perhaps to Father Dressmaker's, but I have no doubt it will be supremely delightful to the little girl. I have had some difficulty in getting it out of Laura's hands before she wore it out with overwork.

I thought your *Sunday Times* article excellent – positive, funny, enterprising – all that the *Sunday Times* isn't. Also an entirely new & personal sort of journalism. If you can keep it up you will become what is called a 'pioneer'. We read it aloud at the week-end and all applauded rapturously.

I must warn you of Berries. In England we have, besides the old-established wine merchant, two families of Berry springing from the noble houses of Camrose & Kemsley. The former are sallow, thin, uncertain of themselves and mostly marry Smiths (see Birkenhead, E. of). They are more or less tolerable. The latter, on the other hand, are absolutely revolting – fat, loud, like all the comic bounders of *Punch* 1910. It is these to whom you are enslaved by your new employment.

Eldred Curwen is a very old gentleman who looks rather young. It was a shock to see him in the train because I had heard harrowing accounts of his death at the hands of the Gestapo. He lives very cleverly on very little money the life of a play boy.

Angie Laycock was here yesterday. She wore as evening dress a check lumber-jack's shirt attached to a voluminous flannel skirt which looked when she sat down like a great travelling rug tucked round her. Is this the fashion? Is it what the north Oxford ladies thought so unsuitable in *Cold Climate*? If so I am all for N.O. ladies. I hate woolly stuffs on female flesh, puts my teeth on edge. Must be silk. Am I hopelessly out of date?

Frost has set in hard and I have £200 worth of garden plants unplanted. A wretched business.

Do you know it now costs £1 a yard to put in a hedge – plants almost invisible?

I was too obtuse to understand in your letter (a) have you Prod living in your pretty house? (b) is he losing his sight or merely drinking to excess? (c) what does he do for money? (d) will he die this year? Widows weeds will greatly become you. (e) Are there or are there not brothels in Paris?*

Oh the horror of Christmas a-coming.

All love
    Evelyn

* Subject for your next *S.T.* letter.

14 December 1949   7 rue Monsieur, VII

Darling Evelyn

I'm so delighted you liked the article – I was intensely doubtful about it & rather cross with them because they said I was replacing Mary Delane,[1] whom any child could do better than, & then stuck me in that grand place while M.D. droned on quite as usual about utility furniture. I must say one thing about you, if you say you think a thing is all right one can believe you.

Very sleepy – up too late with a singing admiral – & when I opened enclosed I thought it must be your Xmas card to me so as it's not it can be mine to you.

I never know how well you read French – I suspect perfectly. There is a first class novel called *Week-end à Zuydcoote*,[2] about Dunkirk. Except yours I've never read such good dialogue, quite outstanding – would you like me to send it? I think perhaps it is difficult to read as our Minister here (only just come) who must know French even if rusty said he didn't understand a great deal of it. I guess it won't be translated, there are some very violent scenes. Awfully funny about the English.

Brothels. Well if there aren't any where do Prod & Duff go when Prod gets back at 7 am saying Duff was on all fours barking like a dog. Oh yes, brothels all right.

Prod has left now, but he seems to have moved in here again. I suppose he is poor. The worst of it is I can't work when he is here – I'm sure it's very silly but I can't. He has no respect for work & wanders in & out chatting. I do think he's awfully unwell & awfully blind & halt & so on but of course we are all old now.

I've found out more about Eldred. He lived in the S of France during the war & when he had run out of money the French cashed his cheques because English people are supposed always to pay in the end & he hasn't & his name is mud. Not very nice.

I can't see why I should be teased by these horrid Berrys I can leave their mag the day I want to.

Have you noticed that all babies now are supposed to be Duff's? Caroline's,[3] Susan Mary [Patten]'s, Pat de Bendern's. It's so old fashioned.

No there's no excuse for lumber jacking evening dress now – you can get heavenly velvet quite as warm, besides houses are heated again now.

Have you seen Honks Cooper's advertisement for a lady gardener (I suppose not as she hasn't received any obscene letters yet). One answer said 'I turned an Indian jungle into a most beautiful garden'.

The Mosleys are here, in a whirl of traitors. I suspect they are up to no good.

Best love from
    NR

¹ Mary Delane contributed a regular column to the *Sunday Times* called 'Women and Life', on such subjects as 'Frocks of Today' and 'Hats Are Small But Worn At Any Angle'.
² Winner of the 1950 Prix Goncourt, by Robert Merle (1949). Nancy wrote of it: 'M. Merle's manner is not unlike that of Mr Evelyn Waugh and his characters are more touching, but he has the same gift of hitting the nail exactly and invariably on the head.' *Sunday Times*, 8 January 1950.
³ Lady Caroline Paget (1913–76). Married Sir Michael Duff in 1949.

20 December [1949]

Darling Nancy

So I went to my club where men of influence & discrimination congregate and all were full of praise of your *Sunday Times* article – Birch, Birkenhead, Churchill, Hartington, Head etc. Sunday came & I thought now for a treat, ran for the *Sunday Times* – no treat. Why not?

It is sweet of you to offer me an Xmas present but I don't read modern French at all. I can just stumble through Bossuet but everything after Tocqueville stumps me. I want to send you Gathorne-Hardy's *Logan Pearsall Smith* – a harassing account of the humiliations of a legacy hunter. Have you got it? Can you still easily read English? It is an enchanting book and I was impressed to learn that in old age Pearsall Smith indulged in sending indecent anonymous letters to his acquaintances.

I met Pam Berry white as a sheet and crazy as a March Hare but we kissed & more or less made it up.

Is it true that John Julius Cooper has become a crashing bore? He was such a nice adolescent (tho a beastly child).

Well, a happy pagan festival of the Tree to you.

I read *P of Love* again the other evening. Do you know I always thought that when Linda said 'Surrey' with contempt it was a contemptuous form of 'Sorry' about the move. Now I see it was the county. I think my misapprehension better.

I stayed in Surrey chez Basil Bennett the other day. It is very ugly but not as ugly as Berks in the Bracknell area where too many of my chums seem to live now. In fact physically it wasn't very ugly at all – hills & beech woods and it is full of Pre Raphaelite associations – Millais painting Ophelia's pool at Ewell.¹ Bracknell is the bottom. Do you know Dotty Head² has a house there and every Monday morning a furniture van comes & takes her pictures & objets d'art ha ha up to Westminster & back again on Saturday? *Literally*.

Say if you'd like a food parcel. We killed a pig.

Have you arranged to sell your *excellent* Paris letters in USA? You must be more businesslike with Prod on the pay roll. Why did you fix your articles for *Sunday Times* without Peters?

Death to Honks.
    E

[1] John Everett Millais painted the background for *Ophelia* (1851–2) on the Hogsmill River in Surrey. The model posed in a bath, kept warm by lamps underneath.
[2] Lady Dorothea (Dot) Ashley-Cooper (1907–87). Talented amateur painter. Married in 1935 to Antony Head who was MP for Carshalton Division of Surrey 1945–60.

22 December 1949   7 rue Monsieur, VII

Darling Evelyn

Happy Xmas – mine will be at Chantilly where a huge party will foregather on Xmas day itself I rather dread it. The Colonel's mother is dying & he is in great despair, I don't feel very cheerful.

I dined with the Windsors. She has an erotic picture by Boucher in her bedroom of 2 Lesbians at work. I said 'oh what's that' wondering what she would say. 'Well it seems there was some old god called Neptune who could change himself into anything he liked – once he was a swan you know – & this woman liked other women so he changed himself into one.' I did love the idea of Neptune clanking out of the sea covered with coquillages – maddening for Jupiter. I do hate that Duchess – but I love him. He said 'Did you read the life of my father by John Gore?[1] It was terribly dull.'

N: 'Well why did they give it to him?'

'Shall I tell you why? Because he's CHEAP. My family always do everything on the CHEAP you know.'

He's rather like Alf Beit,[2] knows hundred of facts. Somebody mentioned the duc de Berry 'Murdered in 1824'[3] he said at once.

'Not very nice what that boy wrote about my grandfather & Xopher Sykes[4] – who are these Sykeses, do you know them?'

'Well,' I said, 'there was Sir Tatton –'

'Tatton. Yorkshire name. Shall I tell you how I know that? I was in the Navy with Commander Bower[5] & his second name is Tatton. That was in 1909. I've worn the King's uniform for 40 years off & on.'

I don't know why I arranged the *S Times* articles without Peters, I was mesmerized by handsome Mr Fleming. Anyway as I haven't a contract or been paid anything it may not be too late & I've written to ask. Oh Prod. I feel in despair about him, he's got such expensive tastes.

V best love
   NR

[1] John Gore, *King George V: A Personal Memoir* (1941).
[2] Sir Alfred Beit (1903–94). South African industrialist. Married Nancy's first cousin Clementine Mitford in 1939.
[3] In fact, assassinated in 1820.
[4] In *Four Studies in Loyalty* Christopher Sykes described how his namesake, a great-uncle, was ruined by entertaining the Prince of Wales. His servility was such that when the future Edward VII poured brandy down his neck, he said meekly: 'As your Royal Highness pleases.'

[5] Robert Tatton Bower (1894–1975). Unionist MP for Cleveland 1935–45.

30 December 1949   Piers Court
                                                    Stinchcombe

Darling Nancy

Back from Chantilly? Cooper writes in the *Daily Mail* this morning that he 'prays' for peace. Do you see him at it? To what hideous Masonic Mumbojumbo was he kneeling?

I am most interested in Mrs Simpson's *Neptune*. Did Boucher paint many Lesbians? During a period of the war I used to keep pinned up in my tent a very bad reproduction of a very beautiful picture. Two girls, one dark and importunate, the other coy & fair. Dark one leaning forward & upward to kiss blonde & trying to draw robe from breast. Background sylvan. I can't remember if it was square or oval. But I loved the picture & always hoped to find the original. Can that be Mrs Simpson's.

I suppose you will write to me and say: 'Lovely, lovely 1949.'

I have just caught my son ending his Christmas letters 'wishing you the compliments of the season'.

Did you see Lane Norcott's very fresh tribute to you?[1]

It is quite warm. We all have colds. I am planting great quantities of bamboo & pampas-grass and having the interior of the house heavily grained.

Poor Prod. Poor you.

Love
    E

[1] Maurice Lane Norcott, the humorist, had written: 'A shy kiss under the mistletoe for Miss Nancy Mitford, author of Mr Lane Norcott's Wittiest Book of the Year (Women's Division). To her splendid Uncle Matthew's list of hated words (notepaper, mirror, handbag, perfume) may she soon add "reticule", "juvenile delinquent", "beverage", "fixation", "dentifrice", "starlet", "lingerie", "usherette" and "lounge suit".' *Daily Mail*, 24 December 1949.

30 December 1949   [7 rue Monsieur, VII]

Darling Evelyn

Am I allowed to say I was happy in 1949? Now I must have a long talk with you about Bob G-H's book. First of all I admire it tremendously – so wonderfully well written & so deeply horrible. The reviews I saw, which complained rather whiningly of bad taste, hadn't prepared me at all for the impact which I'm bound to say was stunning. Did it seem to you that he always hated Logan from the very beginning & that what the book describes is the progression of a hatred, not love turning to hate, I never saw any sign of love. The so called halcyon days were nothing but a hornet's nest, one sting after another, & the journey to Tenerife quite as awful in its own way as the one to Iceland. Do you agree? Now *can* you quite believe in the noble bovine botanist? I can't. Gathorne-Hardys are a bande d'assassins one & all why should there be an exception? *I* think he was always pretty bitchy to Logan & jolly well deserved to be cut off – on his own showing I mean, I don't know anything more about it.

I seem to have written tactlessly & not made my meaning clear to Mr Peters whose answer is you are under no obligation don't give it another thought. I long for him to do it – will try again. I wonder what you'll think of the next article – your letter did so cheer me up specially as Prod wrote everyone in London thinks it's hell.

The next is less woman's pagey & better I hope. A description of the Rothschild books – you don't feel inclined to come over & see them? I staggered away dazzled after 1½ hr of peering into cases. Do you agree with me that manuscripts are wonderful & incunabula very very ugly, inaccurately printed & horrible altogether & that printed books are not really desirable until the 17th century? (What *would* the D of Devonshire's librarian say if he could hear me?) You know of all the heavenly things to collect books really are the only possible ones if you're not rich.

Tomorrow a Radziwill ball. I've got a new dress. Dine at *the* dîner élégant, & yet faintly dread it.

Mind you write about Logan while I'm still deeply involved. I've now embarked on his mother the Quakeress[1] but don't know if I can quite swallow her.

Love from
     Nancy

Then who is Mr Russell[2] who inherited all? Camilla [Sykes]'s brother? Do tell everything you know.

[1] Hannah Whitall Smith (1832–1911). Evangelist author of several pious books including the best-selling *The Christian's Secret of a Happy Life* (1896). A selection of her letters, edited by her son Logan, was published in 1949 as *A Religious Rebel*.
[2] John Russell (1919–2008). Art critic of the *Sunday Times* 1949–74, critic for the *New York Times* since 1974. The last of Logan Pearsall Smith's protégés, he inherited the bulk of his estate and published a memoir of his benefactor in 1950.

Part III

1950–1952

EVELYN AND Nancy exchanged over 130 letters during the first three years of the decade, more than in any other equivalent period. Their correspondence had become a necessity for both of them.

In spite of her extravagant Francophilia and her growing dislike of England, Nancy missed old friends. Evelyn could be relied on to supply the hottest gossip and discuss the latest books, as well to give sound advice on her own writing. Her career was flourishing: *The Blessing* was published to poor reviews but sold well, a regular column in the *Sunday Times* introduced her to a new public, and her adaptation of *The Little Hut* was a West End hit that brought in a generous income. These were welcome distractions from her sadness over the Colonel, whose official duties and various love affairs were making him more elusive than ever. She dreaded leaving him to his own devices in Paris, but when Marie, her housekeeper, took her summer holiday, Nancy was obliged to go away too; she established a pattern of spending the months of July and August in the South of France or Italy with friends.

Evelyn entered the middle years of the century in a mood of deep pessimism. He had been overspending recklessly since the war and was now in serious financial difficulties; a deal with Penguin Books saved him from complete ruin, but money worries continued to dog him. Heavy drinking and the drugs he took for insomnia were undermining his health; his stamina was beginning to desert him and he oscillated between elation and despair. He expressed indifference to the mixed reception of *Men at Arms*, the first volume of his war trilogy, but was bitterly disappointed by the failure of his historical novel *Helena* which had taken five years to write and which he considered his best book. Critics ignored *Helena*'s spiritual theme and brayed for more of the ferocious comedy that Evelyn had accustomed them to. His disappointment spilled over into hostility towards his friends, who began to avoid his company and fear for his sanity. Nancy was one of the few who remained close. From a safe distance she tried to cajole him out of his gloom and admonished him for his worst displays of intolerance.

4 January 1950   Piers Court
                                                        Stinchcombe
Dearest Nancy

I am so glad you enjoyed the Pearsall Smith book. I reviewed it
hurriedly & briefly for one of the little magazines no one reads[1] & was
so grateful for having enjoyed it that I just said so & nothing more
but there was *much* more to be said. I barely know the protagonists
but I seem to understand it all.

Smith, I am sure, wanted a Boswell. He felt he was unique & that
he was wasting his genius on little private jokes and had left a perfect
but minute portrait of himself in *Trivia*. He wanted someone to say
about him all the things he couldn't decently say about himself. He
was always trying to train Boswells – Connolly, Sergeant Preston etc.
– but he started much too late. Hardy was his chief protégé but what
a disappointment. He is quite unaware of his own deterioration from
the pretty young aesthete Smith picked up in the bookshop to the
middle-aged plasterer's mate (mot juste) of 1944.

The only way modern books are readable is by reading them
between the lines. I see so many unconscious & conscious dishonesties
in the book which is two books put together – the Boswell and an
apologia for his treatment of the final heir. I don't know anything
except what the book suggests, but I suppose Hardy threatened an
action to prove Smith insane when he disinherited him. I can just
hear the solicitor's voice: 'We have two points to prove Mr Hardy.
First that Mr Smith definitely promised to leave you the capital sum
of your allowance, and that you had amply earned this sum by professional help. Secondly that Mr Smith was definitely insane in Iceland
not merely delirious.' Hardy rubs this in all too fiercely.

You must have noticed often in life as I have that however great-
souled & delicate-mannered people are, financial obligations between
social equals are almost always disastrous. Money runs through the
book. Smith was comfortably off but not rich at all. He was alarmed
by the rich and he expected the poor to be alarmed by him. He was,
of course, a bully & a tease but I suspect Hardy was a bitch & sponge.
I am sure he was always digging small sums out of the old boy.

The most moving part, I thought, was the last 50 pages when Hardy
seems to have convinced himself that it was all in the cause of sacred
friendship that he 'refused to quarrel' with the old man. Really, of
course, he felt, 'I can't at the last moment, let him have an excuse to
cut me out of the will.' A man of honour would have said: 'You beastly
old American cad how dare you talk to me like that. Stick your bloody
dollars up your huge arse!' Instead he sends him trout & offers to lend
his savings as a plasterer.

Anyway what a delightful story.

The Russell is not, I think, related to the great Whig House, he writes very correct little reviews for one of the Sunday papers. The fashionable view rather well expressed. Sycophantish about O. Sitwell, D. MacCarthy etc.

It was a painful shock to find old Smith being imposed on by Trevor-Roper.[2] I hope he gave that blackguard expectations of a legacy.

> Best love from
> Evelyn

Xmas at Chantilly?

---

[1] *New English Review*, January 1950. The editor was Christopher Sykes.
[2] Hugh Trevor-Roper (1914–2003). Historian whom Evelyn disliked for what he considered his anti-Catholicism. His publications include *Archbishop Laud* (1940) and *The Last Days of Hitler* (1947). Created life peer in 1979. Logan Pearsall Smith had written of Trevor-Roper: 'I had a visit this week from the author of that excellent life of Laud ... He loves letters, and what pleased me, he loves my writing, and knows a great deal of *Trivia* by heart ... A charming erudite young man.' *Recollections of Logan Pearsall Smith* (Constable, 1949), p. 174.

7 January 1950   7 rue Monsieur, VII

Darling Evelyn

Well I draw a veil over Xmas at Chantilly, having blotted my copy book by inviting my really impossible friend M. de Polnay for the day. There was a huge party, 26 for luncheon 26 after (& whisky flowing) & I wrongly thought he would be intimidated by all these *excellences* & high class writers & Dukes & things but no. He got drunker than anything I ever saw & Duff was X though is it for Duff to be X about drunkenness? (I enclose a photograph & you are not to say you have seen it as it's really very disloyal of me to send it – loyal to you however.) Well then I was intensely embarrassed so retired to my bedroom with 3 others & played bridge. Honks was X, everybody was X, & I don't think they've forgiven me & indeed I see the point. When I scolded M. de P. after, all he said was 'I didn't break a *thing*' in tones of genuine surprise.

Thank you for your letter about Smith I agree with every word. Mr Hardy reminds me in one way so much of Prod, that is, whereas in human disagreements & quarrels it is fair to assume that it's 6 of one & ½ doz of the other, he & Prod both always insist that they were 100% in the right. Prod now lays *all* his failure in life like an enormous baby at my door, & though I must obviously have some responsibility for it, I refuse to admit the whole. Smith certainly succeeded in teaching G.H. to write – to his own undoing poor old man.

Now you must read Queensberry's *Wilde & Douglas*[1] – another stunning account of a relationship & curiously enough the best of all the many books on Wilde *I* think. After prison he reminds me so much of poor Bobo when she got back from Germany – in so many little ways. Oh dear how sad. And Q. *so much* like my father. I was riveted by it.

Lovely party last night for the fête des rois, a ball at Marie-Laure de Noailles'[2] at which all the guests wore crowns. It was too pretty – in her beautiful house like a museum. The 3rd party in a week, too much for me.

I have translated (adapted really) a very funny play called *La Petite Hutte* for Mr Binkie Beaumont & he is pleased. I'm so excited, wouldn't it be fun to have a play put on. The author who is a great love doesn't know any English at all so I've got away with all my own jokes & dialogue & just kept his situations which are heaven. I now long to write a play myself.

Dull letter I fear – do write, I live for yours.

All love & to Laura
    NR

When you write do send name & address of press cutting agency. I really ought to join one – I did but think it must have expired.

[1] Francis A. K. Douglas, Marquess of Queensberry, *Oscar Wilde and the Black Douglas* (1949).
[2] Marie-Laure Bischoffsheim (1902–70). Poet, novelist and fashionable Parisian hostess. Patron of the Surrealists. Married Vicomte Charles de Noailles in 1923.

11 [January] 1950   Piers Court
                                                     Stinchcombe

Darling Nancy

Woolgar & Roberts, 3 Dorset Buildings, E.C.4. That is the place for press cuttings. It is a great expense having them and for every one that is interesting fifty are unendurably boring and five are painful, but Popkins will charge it against income tax.

Thank you thank you thank you for the picture of Duff. I will take it to White's when I next visit that nest of vipers. I was there yesterday between the Circus & *Peter Pan* and whom should I see but poor Prod. Nothing you told me prepared me for the truth. He has locomotor ataxia and a waistcoat made of an old rug. How you have brought him down. He was such a bright pretty boy. If it were not for his socialism I should have great compassion for him. I thought people like you & he believed in putting the decrepit into gas chambers.

I greatly enjoyed your second article in *Sunday Times*. It has greatly excited the wine lovers. Is the Vigneau '04 not too old? I would dearly like to buy some. Do you know how much one can bring to England without a licence? An excellent feature of your articles is the French. What the English like are phrases of which they easily understand the literal meaning, if possible with words that look like English words, and have quaintness & drollness. That is just what you give them. I mean for instance the warm hampers for the wine. Give us plenty of such phrases, please.

My new Holy Year opens with the prospect of financial ruin. For some time I have been aware that I seemed to be in easier circumstances than most of my friends & accounted for it with saws like 'solvency is a matter of temperament' and by thinking of all the nuns who are praying for me, bringing me in pounds when I give them shillings, and so on.

Well last week I said to Laura 'are you sure you aren't overdrawn at the bank?' 'No, I don't think so. I'm sure they'd tell me, if I were.' 'Well do ask.' So she did and, my dear, she had an overdraft of £6,420 which had been quietly mounting up for years. There is no possible way to pay it off, as her capital is in trust and for me to earn that much more, I should have to earn about 150,000 and we cannot possibly spend less although for three years we have been spending 2,000 more than our income (and that 2000 tax free too). Well it's a sad prospect isn't it. I shall have to go to prison but that is hell nowadays with wireless & lectures & psychiatry. Oh for the Marshalsea.[1]

Please answer my enquiry about Mrs Simpson's *Neptune*.

I do so hate this warm wet winter. We all have colds.

Love
    E

[1] Debtors' prison in Southwark, abolished in 1849 but memorable because of its description in Dickens' *Little Dorrit*.

13 January 1950   7 rue Monsieur, VII

Darling Evelyn

Well the Lesbians. Not yours. No *robe* anywhere in sight, just a lovely huge fair fat lady lying on top of another & various cupids hovering about. Much more like Fragonard than Boucher I thought. Very beautiful, I was gel-gel.

No I am not a Nazi & don't believe in doing away with unhappy people – in fact now that I am happy myself I don't believe in suicide any more. Oh dear, Prod. Yes all you say is true, but can it be my fault? I feel it must be partly, though last time he was here he said that for the last 12 years he has considered himself as married to Adelaide [Lubbock] which seemed to let me out & was a great relief to me.

I think you ought to read the correspondence of Claudel & Gide. It is easy, classical French & full of things that would interest you &

Evelyn in Spitzbergen, August 1934

Left: Evelyn in Croatia with Randolph Churchill, 'whose boisterous good nature, after five weeks solitary confinement with him, has begun to exhaust me' (17 October 1944)

Laura Waugh, 1940s

Nancy, *c.* 1948.

Below left: Peter Rodd (*left*) at his wedding to Nancy, 1933, with John Sutro, his best man

Below: Peter Rodd during the war

Gaston Palewski, 'The Colonel'

Below: Rue Monsieur by Vivien Hislop

Below right: The hallway at 7 rue Monsieur

Lady Mosley, 1940s

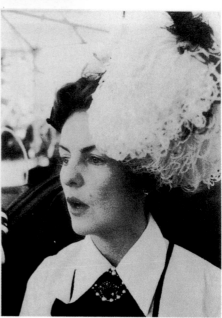

The Duchess of Devonshire, 1950s. EW to NM: 'She was in fine looks but lacking in elegance . . . Should not a girl with her beauty wit and high position make a bit more of herself?' (6 August 1947)

Drawing of Harold Acton,
1933, by Thomas
Handforth, an American
with whom Acton shared
a house in Peking

Below left: Christopher
Sykes, Evelyn's first
biographer

Below: Stuart Preston,
July 1943, the American
Sergeant who was a
celebrated figure in
wartime London and the
model for 'Loot'

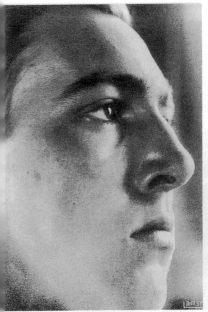

Piers Court, Gloucestershire. EW to NM: 'Just got my bill from the garden contractors who have laid down a yard or two of gravel and put up a pillar. A cool thou. Impossible to earn because super tax is always a pace ahead. So I am ruined' (28 July 1949)

Evelyn with his family and household, 1948. NM to EW: 'If you lived here you wouldn't dare have that photograph taken because having such millions of servants would be a signe extérieur de la richesse & you'd be taxed accordingly' (6 October 1948)

Lady Diana Cooper, 1958. NM to EW: 'She is always my heroine & I love & admire her beyond words' (18 August 1946)

Below left: The Vicomtesse de Noailles and Duff Cooper at Grasse, early 1950s. NM to EW: 'Marie-Laure is ¼ Jewish & the rest of her very grand indeed, she descends from Petrarch & the Marquis de Sade' (10 January 1963)

Below: Nancy and John Julius Cooper at Château St Firmin, Chantilly, 1950s

Sir Maurice Bowra, 1952, shortly after his elevation to a knighthood. EW to NM: 'It is really very odd as he has done nothing to deserve it except be head of the worst College at Oxford and publish a few books no one has ever read' (6 January 1951)

Cyril Connolly, 1953. EW to NM: 'Cyril is poor paddy escaped from the tyranny of the bog priest, dazzled by the jolly splendours of Tammany Hall, quite at a loss what to do with his freedom' (17 January 1945)

is an account really of Claudel's 24 years struggle for the soul of Gide. They haven't spared their punches, either of them.

How awful about the overdraft. I expect you are having the sort of financial crisis Farve used to have periodically which generally resulted in giving up one Sunday paper & bronco instead of bromo. But to arrive at that the grown ups used to be closeted for hours with & without hommes d'affaires. If it's any consolation to you it never made a pin of difference, though the worry seemed to be appalling at the time & went on being appalling for months.

About the French words in my article – I'm glad you approve. What you say was just what I'd figured out. My fan mail very funny. 18 people have sent labels to show that Philippe R[othschild] has labelled his bottles like that for 20 years, one writes to ask which year Mary Russell Mitford was born & another 'sweet of you to say the parties break up for the Mass – in my hotel I was kept awake *all night* without any break at all'. Must I answer them? I *can't*.

Can't you import wine through Berry Bros? How do people lay down cellars nowadays? I think one is allowed 12 bottles in one's luggage (tho I don't know why I think it) but they make you pay on every drop. I sometimes bring brandy for Handy.

Here is the catalogue in case you'd like to have it – I've got two copies. The stuff does seem cheap to me.

The weather here is like a gentle March, heavenly I think, but you know how much I hate the cold.

All love
   NR

P.S. M. Dior is going to Rome to see the Pope. Holy Year is thus brought home to us all.

19 January 1950   7 rue Monsieur, VII

Darling Evelyn

You are *not* repeat *not* to show the photograph of Sir Alf to anybody at all – it was most disloyal of me to send it & I've regretted doing so ever since.

Do try & be noble, like Claudel. Oh the letters, I've lived in them – I think you could read them all right, it is a simple, classical French, & it seems to me that for a Roman Catholic they are indispensable. The day when Claudel, from one short passage in *Les Caves du Vatican*, realizes that Gide is a pederast he writes a letter which made my blood run cold, I can't think how Gide could have read it. Instead of cher ami he starts 'au nom du ciel, Gide –'

Before this the correspondence was loving & they were wonderful to each other, such admiration of the other's works & such mutual help (Gide correcting Claudel's proofs when he was in Japan etc). Claudel of course wanted to convert Gide & very nearly succeeded & his letters on the duty of Catholics are tremendous – he says it is *everybody's plain* duty to be a saint. He is so great that he dwarfs the fascinating Gide I must say completely, though there is nothing petty about Gide, no taking offence (even when C. writes behind his back to his wife). When the storm has broken Claudel begs Gide to see a charming priest who lives at Clichy – Francis Jammes[1] begs him to see another at Passy (do try my dentist) & Gide does so, but notes in his journal 'it will take more than these priests to turn me into a père de famille'.

Poor Mme Gide. He says he loves her more than life itself but can't go to bed with her. But she is no Jane Carlyle – they are all so *noble* in this story. Can you tell me what Claudel was converted from? Gide says Claudel overpowers me – he has more money more health more genius more faith & more children than I –

Claudel says: 'Il y a une police nécessaire contre les empoisonneurs.' They haven't met since 1926.

Did you see Honks Cooper's advert for a lady gardener? Well, after a hundred letters, one saying I turned an Indian jungle into a glorious English garden with sweet peas, she has chosen one. I can't but feel it will end in tears, but we shall see.

The *Sunday Times* like my piece & would like it more often, but I've refused. It wouldn't be so good & would stop me writing anything else. I've told the publishers to send you my *Princesse de Clèves* it is supposed to be out next month – I'd be very glad to know what you feel about it. Prod says it's the most awful translationese he ever read – very hard to avoid in a classic where every meaning *must* be reproduced. After that I've been thinking a great deal about language & came upon a Penguin Conrad. Well in a way he writes in translationese – it's not like the writing of an English person is it & that's what gives it such freshness & colour I believe. I've begged the 2 people who are translating my books to re-write wherever they feel like it, specially the dialogue, & you can do that when the author is alive & consenting, but *I* can't do it to poor Mme de La Fayette, clearly. Claudel has some very interesting things to say about translating English & French but I didn't understand it all because I don't know the terms of grammar – I literally don't know what subjunctive for instance means. Is it too late to learn? If not is there some easy book that would tell me? Oh *can* I be bothered? The horror of not having been educated when young.

Please excuse this long letter. Korda is still sitting on my story (to the consternation of Mr Peters, I seem to have committed an arch folly in sending it) so I've no work at present. Claudel–Gide make everything else seem such small beer that I can't settle down to a nice book –!

All love
    Nancy

[1] Francis Jammes (1868–1938). Catholic poet and novelist. Author of *Les Géorgiques chrétiennes* (1912) and *Le Livre de saint Joseph* (1933).

[January 1950]   Piers Court
                                                  Stinchcombe
Darling Nancy

The harm if harm there is has been done. I sent the snapshot of Cooper to Connolly *not* saying it was from you so no embarrassment can result and really it is from the public prints so no secret is revealed so I don't think it matters a button really does it? Only I'm sorry if you do mind.

Gas chambers were not a Nazi invention. All 'Progressives' like Lord Ponsonby[1] believed in them and called it Euthanasia and had a Society all the Fabians belonged to simply to build gas chambers and that is what Health Centres are for besides castrating men and sterilizing women and giving french letters to children. Didn't you know? So take Prod by the hand & lead him to Peckham where the Donaldsons will deal with him in a jiffy.

So a lady in Middlesbrough said 'I see you dedicated a book to Nancy Mitford. Do you really know her?' 'Well, I know one side of her.' 'I do admire her writing so.' 'So do I. I have just been rereading all her books.' '*Books!* D'you mean to say she writes *books* too? She must be clever. I thought she was only on the *Sunday Times*.'

Everyone is so bored with the General Election. The newspapers have to offer huge cash prizes to get people to write and say that they will vote. The only person excited about it is Maimie who put herself at the disposal of the Central Office and was directed to canvass St Pancras where she claims to have converted 32 proletarian women and heard that the public library is used for orgies after closing time. The only amusing contest is Randolph v. Foot[2] in Devonport. It is nice for the boy to have an opponent just as beastly as himself in just the same way. It is the first time. Up till now he has always stood against decent old buffers.

I woke up in the middle of last night & started worrying about Ed Stanley's brother.[3] Have you ever met him? What is he like?

G. Orwell is dead and Mrs Orwell presumably a rich widow. Will Cyril marry her? He is said to be consorting with a dingy demimondaine called Miss Skelton.[4]

Since our recent terrible financial crash I have saved hundreds of pounds in not buying things.

I think P. Popkin is a snake. At least he is helpful to the poor but as soon as one earns more than he does himself envy steps in and he lets one down. Also he lets one overpay and then pretends to be frightfully clever in bringing back some of the money that ought never to have left the pocket. I am obsessed by poverty at the moment. But not so much as multi-millionaire Graham Greene, the socialist, who I gather has been sniffing round Chantilly.

Poor Patrick has written a novel in praise of Angela.[5] Quite good about her but the rest *Forsyte Saga*.

Love
    E

[1] Arthur Ponsonby (1871–1946). Labour MP. Created Baron in 1930.
[2] Michael Foot (1913–). Labour politician and writer. He held the Devonport seat by a majority of 3,483.
[3] Hon. Lyulph Henry Stanley (1915–71). BBC Home Service announcer 1944–7, Information Officer at the United Nations 1948.
[4] Barbara (Baby) Skelton (1916–96). Beautiful wayward daughter of a Gaiety Girl. Author of two volumes of candid autobiography, *Tears Before Bedtime* (1987) and *Weep No More* (1989). Married to Cyril Connolly 1950–54, to Connolly's publisher George Weidenfeld 1956–61 and to Nancy's former brother-in-law, the millionaire physicist Professor Derek Jackson 1966–7.
[5] Patrick Balfour in *Ruthless Innocent* (1950) based the main character on his ex-wife.

28 January 1950   7 rue Monsieur, VII

Darling Evelyn
    I don't so much mind Cyril having it as Duff is always undeservedly vicious about *him* & says apoplectically anyway Noël Coward is a far better writer than Connolly. I say, what's Cyril living on? Everybody here is very much exercised by this question.

I'm sorry to have to state that you are right about John Julius he has become a crasher. I said have you called on Billa [Harrod] yet? Well you know, what with the French society & the Russian society & theatricals & madrigals I really haven't time for anything. He is like a terribly nice curate – isn't it funny. A re-action from Lulu & co perhaps.

Do read my terrible friend de Polnay's book called *Into an Old Room*, & persevere with it if put off during the first pages, I think it so very good & moving.

I adore the lady who regards me as a real journalist. As the *Sunday Times* is my new toy praise for that outweighs anything on the subject of books, so I was really thrilled. They asked if I would do it more often but I can't, it would mean padding if I did & be far less careful work.

The great excitement here has been over an Austrian Archduke marrying a Ligne because – hold everything – the Lignes are *not mediatized*!!!!!! Horrors!!! As the Col says this will make things awfully difficult in the 2 roomed New York flat where they are going to live.

Diana M is bringing out a little book of questions (parlour game) for next Xmas called Are you a Hon?[1] and I say one of them should be Which would you rather be, an English Bart or a Mediatized German Prince? Another, Would you rather have written *The Loved One* or *Sparkenbroke*?[2] I think it will be bliss.

Oh poor Mr Peters is having such an awful time with me – if you see him do say I am quite aware of it & really will try to be nicer. It's partly I'm so frightened of him the most ghastly things seem to happen like sending back a contract without signing it. I really thought I'd *die*, it flashed into the letter box *as* I remembered –!

I saw Mr Graham Greene & his mistress & I *was* surprised, having pictured her scruffy Bloomsbury, to see a Ritz vision in dark mink. They are kept from one by Lady Honks.

Yes the gardeneress, Miss Fahy pronounced FEY, arrives shortly. I think Honks' plan is for her to be deeply in love 'Oh Lady Diana let *me* see to that' & eventually to run everything there with passionate efficiency. Time will show. Meanwhile Chantilly is rather like Buck: Pal: under the boy Jones, I'm bound to say.

All love
    NR

[1] It was never published. The idea was inspired by a little book called *All About Everybody* which Diana bought in the 1930s. It consisted of such questions as: 'What is your besetting sin?', 'Do you consider yourself good-looking?' and 'What would you rather have, love or money?' Over the years friends and family had filled it in, including Brian Howard, Pavel Tchelitchew, Gerald Berners and Edward James.
[2] By Charles Morgan (1936). A long, introspective novel about art, love and death.

[postmarked 8 February 1950]   Piers Court
[postcard]   Stinchcombe

Another *very* good article in *Sunday Times*. It is your métier. You may well become one of the historic foreign correspondents. I hope Peters is distributing your articles through all the press of the world.

So you are coming to enjoy the second & bloodier triumph of the Common Man. Yes, Laura & I will be at the Savoy.[1] If you have nothing to do dine with us first, but I expect you will be dining with a galaxy of common men chez Pam – Trevor-Roper Quennell Forbes and so on & so forth ad nauseam.

Shall pass through Paris on way to & from Rome after Easter.

E

[1] For an election party given by Lord Camrose. Labour was re-elected with a reduced majority.

9 February 1950   7 rue Monsieur, VII

Darling Evelyn

If I really may dine with you & Laura before the party it would make the whole difference to my evening. How lovely. And how lovely that you are coming here – to buy your capes for Holy Year I suppose, Dior has wonderful ones & I don't mean the Père Couturier though maybe he has a line all his own.

Desmond Guinness & his beautiful mistress Miss Brown have just lunched here. Penniless, they tour Europe in luxury – when asked *how* by the various pompous French I invited to meet them (Desmond only likes princes) I suggested what seemed to me obvious, upon which a deeply shocked silence fell. No wonder the French aristocracy are fading away – if you are too snobbish to work you can't afford these bourgeois prejudices.

If Harriet were 2 years older I'd say bring her & leave her here while in Rome – but perhaps 6 is rather little. What does Laura say? I'd take her to the *Bossu*[1] every evening. I'll take you if you'd like it anyway.

Please read the Claudel Gide letters before I see you I must pick it over with a Catholic & the Col is too busy & then pederasty is not a subject he can be serious on.

I thought the Conservatives (uncommon men like Chips) were going to win. But I suppose it doesn't make a pin of difference who does, with the Russians so nearly here anyway.

Well – I *long* for the party now, I felt nervous about it before.

I'm staying Hyde Park from 20th.

Love from
        Nancy

Thank you *SO* much for your kind words re article – it's a pure pleasure to me, writing it, very different from the slavery of a novel.

[1] *Le Bossu* (1888), a comic opera by Charles Grisart, taken from a famous cloak-and-dagger novel by Paul Féval.

12 February 1950   Piers Court
                                                Stinchcombe

Darling Nancy

That will be very nice. Laura & I will be at Hyde Park Hotel for the night of 23rd. I have no dinner party but if you would like to bring a gentleman please do. You will find whatever dinner I provide uneatable after Paris so I shall not try to impress you as I tried so unsuccessfully with Mrs Luce.

I have written to Col Franks DSO[1] to tell him as he might not have known being a simple fighting man that Mrs Rodd is really the great Miss Mitford. If you are ill treated call for this Col Franks. Well you have a way with Cols, have you not?

G. Greene & Mrs Walston have just left. They are queer fishes. I do not know what the connexion is between them. I would not swear carnal, though G.G. plainly likes it to be thought so. Mrs W. is good at heart I think but she has lived in a terrible under world of Jews & socialists & Americans and Cambridge dons and is not really house trained. G.G. thinks of nothing but *nothing* but money, in very small sums. It is odd. He must be about the richest man we know. I don't mean he is ambitious for more, just that it frets him to spend it like poor Lord Moyne, junior.

Ann Rothermere is giving a rival party on 23rd. Who can they ask? Everyone interested in power will be away in the constituencies.

Oh yes the socialists are quite safe.

It is sweet of you to think of entertaining Harriet. She is far too backward. A merry, likeable creature they say but infantile. I don't mind a bit. When I think of precocity I think of the sad ends of Prod & W. Acton[2] the most precocious boys of my generation.

I am not at all clear in my mind what you imputed to Guinness & Brown, thereby shocking the princes.

Love

E

---

[1] Brian Franks (d.1982). Served in the Commandos and SAS; after the war he became managing director of the Hyde Park Hotel.
[2] William Acton (1906–45). Talented, artistic younger brother of Harold Acton. A fall from an upstairs window at Christ Church and a habit of mixing ether with his drinks undermined his health; he died shortly after his 39th birthday.

2 March [1950]   Piers Court
                                                   Stinchcombe

Darling Nancy

Thinking it over I have decided that the Camrose party was the most gruesome I have ever been to in a long life of gruesome parties.

But Ann's was enjoyable next day.

It was very sad not seeing you & very foolish of me to make you dine at Warwick House. I had foreseen a nice long chat at the Savoy. How wrong how wrong.

Did you know that *MRS* Connolly (Lys) was the one to run off with the Orwell millions & that the O.M.s are about twenty five pounds in all?[1] Very interesting.

I arrive in Paris by Golden Arrow April 11th & go on by Rome Express later that evening. It would be heaven if you would dine with

me on my way through. I shall be travelling without my man Sykes.
I hope I get through all right.

I found Middy O'Neill[2] a great bore.

I went to Mells. Ronnie Knox has given up X word puzzles for
Lent. It only took him five minutes anyway. I have given up cigars &
wine. Nothing to look forward to now in the day. But Sundays are
jolly. I wait till it strikes 12 Sat night with cigar & brandy bottle ready.

Fine conversation piece seen at Ann's party at Dorchester – Lords
Dudley, Rosebery, Sherwood and in the centre of them holding court,
Connolly.

I saw poor Randolph for a minute. 'I tell you what the trouble at
Devonport was, old boy. There just weren't enough conservatives.'

I do hope you got the candle sticks safely to Paris & that the Col.
was pleased.

Love from
E

[1] George Orwell's widow, Sonia, inherited his estate which passed to his adopted son on her
death.
[2] Hon. Mary (Middy) O'Neill (1905–91). A childhood friend of Nancy. Married Derick
Gascoigne in 1934.

9 March [1950]   Piers Court
                                                           Stinchcombe
Darling Nancy

Bathe the legs – not yours, the hen's[1] – in warm water & dry
thoroughly. Then anoint with a compound of vaseline & paraffin in
equal parts. Repeat daily until scales disappear. Another school says:
'kill & boil'.

It is very kind of you to ask me to dinner on April 11th. I look
forward to it greatly. Is it 'a few young men' or 'a jew young man'
who wants to meet me? If the latter could he not have a cocktail with
me at the Gare du Nord?

Another good article.[2] Of course the thing about England *now* – *always*
a little bit but *now* particularly – is that there simply is no 'mode' in anything. There is the general, well grounded assumption that anything new
is inferior to the old & that's that. There is also no 'monde'. Who should
be leading it? Debo? You see it makes no sense. But that is all the less
reason why Mrs Gascoigne should be such a beastly bore. She is not
missing anything by staying in the country. Some of the most exquisitely
entertaining men I have ever known – eg. Conrad Russell[3] – led lives of
complete retirement. Boredom is something in people not anything from
outside. Look at Juliet[4] who all her life has been surrounded by the most
amusing people and remains a crasher. No there was no excuse for Mrs
Gascoigne's beastliness.

I have now written the last word of *Helena* and am quite out of work. I would rather like to write a guide book to Gloucester like E. M. Forster's *Alexandria*.

Stick to Mr Peters come what may. Of course Mr Beaumont prefers to deal with a soft lady. Mr Peters will do & say all the things behind your back that you could not bring yourself to do & say and you needn't know and you will greatly profit *and* be more respected by such as Beaumont.

You know the Goller cure for obesity? You take different coloured pills according to what part of the body you wish to make smaller. Antony Head[5] has been found to be taking breast-pills. I am going to do it for face, neck & stomach and so expect something rather elegant, perhaps unrecognizable, on the 11th.

Honks & Cooper are here honking the French President. You would think they could see him at home without coming abroad for the spectacle.

Love
    E

[1] Nancy's cook had bought a hen with a view to boiling it, but when it laid an egg on the kitchen table its life was spared and it became a pet.
[2] 'Paris à la Mode', *Sunday Times*, 5 March 1950.
[3] Conrad Russell (1878–1947). Youngest son of Lord Arthur Russell. After the First World War he devoted himself to farming, first in Sussex and then in Somerset.
[4] Lady Juliet Lowther (1881–1965). Married to Sir Robert Duff 1903–14 and to Major Keith Trevor 1919–26; thereafter resumed her former name of Duff.
[5] Anthony Head (1906–83). Secretary of State for War 1951–6. Created Viscount Head in 1960. Married Lady Dorothea Ashley-Cooper in 1935.

3 April 1950   Piers Court
                                                 Stinchcombe
Darling Nancy

The *Princesse de Clèves* arrived this morning. It will be a great Easter treat to read it when Holy Week is over. In fact I will read it in the Golden Arrow on Tuesday & ask you to write in it '. . . without whose profound scholarship & unerring taste . . .'

First question: why 'The Princesse'? Surely 'The Princess' or 'La Princesse'. Second question: why did you allow Ph. Jullian[1] to draw so horrible a cover? I will have more questions by Tuesday evening. But thanks awfully for sending me a copy.

I look forward to my holiday with a keenness that can only presage deep disappointment. It is the first treat since the Sykes–Cooper disaster. I attribute the tragedy of that week to my own terrible drunkenness on the first day. That shall not occur again.

I am so thin that I shiver like a dachshund all day long so I shall find the furnace-salon at Rue Monsieur very comforting.

I re-read *Brideshead Revisited* the other day and was appalled. All that those nasty critics said was bang right. But the plot seemed to me excellent. So my summer's task will be to rewrite it entirely.[2] I expect you are busy rewriting *Pursuit* and *Climate*.

Why no more delicious titbits in *Sunday Times*?

Very good new book by Antonia White named *The Lost Traveller*.

Just off to Downside for a monkish retreat.

> Love from
> Evelyn

[1] Philippe Jullian (1920–77). French painter and book illustrator in the rococo style, he was also a novelist and biographer whose *D'Annunzio* (1971) was dedicated to Nancy.
[2] A revised edition was published in 1960 in which Evelyn made 'many small additions and some substantial cuts'.

5 [April] 1950   7 rue Monsieur, VII

Darling Evelyn

I can see you're going to be captious & dreadful – all right.

After many a sleepless night I decided to keep the names & titles in French, except for non French characters like Alba. It may be a bad idea, but the other way round presents difficulties too – how can one translate Dauphin or Vidame? It's really a matter of taste as far as I can see & while in history I am all for *Lewis* XVI & so on in such a delicate little piece of fiction as the *Princesse* I think the other is more suitable & prettier.

What I do suspect is that the English is clumsy & not good. The difficulty of translating a classic seems to me to be that it's one's duty to give the full meaning, with all the nuances of every sentence. Then it becomes unreadable. Then one fidgets about to make it so. Never will I take on such a thing again & I only did it because I so love the book. But I am pleased with the preface.

Haven't seen it yet so can't say what I think of Jullian's cover. Heywood is pleased with it however. Jullian is a friend of mine & I asked for him to do it – he loves the book & generally does very elegant little drawings. Never mind.

Now I shall be at the Arrow but if you miss me come here. Prod always misses me when he comes to meet me but I suspect it's because he's ½ an hour late. I'm told the crowds are awful now so won't come on to the platform but will stay by the engine. Find out for certain what time the train is at G[are] de Lyons.

I long for it.

> Much love
> NR

Maurice [Bowra] is here, eating away, it reminds me of those years ago when you both came. But he leaves tomorrow.

15 April [1950]   British Embassy
                                                    Rome

Darling Nancy

I can't tell you how much I enjoyed my little visit to you. It was just the kind of entertainment one longs for in the middle of a lonely journey. Blissikins is the mot juste I think.

The reason we were wrong about the Rome Express is that it doesn't exist till May 1st. My train was a rapide and God it was slow stopping at every station except two between Modena & Rome. And a very austere functional diner. All the same I enjoyed the journey & I have greatly enjoyed the last few days here. I have seen mostly English people but that is quite a treat living the life I do.

I am intriguing to get a private chapel at Stinkers behind the back of the Bishop of Clifton who hates private chapels as undemocratic and not contemporary. After seeing a lot of Princes & Cardinals I found the man who really decides such things is a plain Padre Costa, a Brazilian living in the suburbs. I went to him & he received me with great geniality until he learned my name was not Vaughan as he supposed & that I was not a bastard grandson of Cardinal Vaughan. All seemed lost until I found he came from Manaos and by an extraordinary piece of Prodlike scholarship I happened to know that Manaos was the first town in the American continent to have a tramway. After that all was sunny again & I think I may succeed in my pious ambition.

This is a hideous house full of Nazi decorations but with a fine garden. It was the Villa Volkonsky of which Hare[1] says 'permesso to view may be obtained from your banker'. I have fallen in love with a cousin of Laura's called Cécile Howard[2] (French).

Victor Mallet[3] keeps saying 'Let us give a party for Evelyn' and Peggy looks steel & flint at him. No party. I must say they behave rather unsociably. Today we drove out to a luncheon party with a nice old Duke and immediately after luncheon Victor assembled a fishing rod & went off to try & catch trout by himself (no fish) and Peggy set off alone for a two hour walk up a precipice. I sat next to Cécile again & that was heaven. Your Colonel's chum Coussel (?)[4] was at the party. I said 'I saw Col' (in French) he answered in French and I didn't understand a word but I think he was very much *for* Col.

Prod is said to be here by Angela whom he evicted from Via Giulia, but our paths have not crossed yet.

Well this letter is really a Collins for lovely reception. I will write more Gossip soon.

By the way a Viper of Milan has made away with most of my fortune so if Boots has not had all my franc hoard try & save enough for me to take you out to dinner on my way home.

Love
    E

[1] Augustus Hare (1834–1903). Author of anecdotal guides to Italy.
[2] Cécile Geoffroy-Dechaume; married in 1936 to Hon. Edmund (Mondi) Howard, second secretary in Rome 1947–51.
[3] Sir Victor Mallet (1893–1969). Ambassador to Italy 1947–53. Married Christiana Jean (Peggy) Andreae in 1925.
[4] Baron Geoffroy de Courcel (1912–92). Chef de Cabinet under General de Gaulle in 1940, Counsellor in Rome in the 1950s, Ambassador to London 1962–7.

20 April 1950   7 rue Monsieur, VII

Darling Evelyn

Awful about the viper because of course I gave poor Bootikins all – I mean having just lost 50 millions as he had I could hardly have done otherwise. Can I beat up Mrs Bradley[1] for you – or Peters? I shall *die* of disappointment if you don't stay a jew days & so will the jew friends. But if you haven't got a jew francs coming to you somebody must have blundered, or worse, as your books sell like mad here.

I've struggled with your grammar & note that I am the Corelli[2] of the modern world & it fascinates me but I can't see how to use it. But you will tell. Meanwhile Raymond says he can teach grammar & if I put him up in the Continental with a suite on the Tuileries gardens he will teach me in return, so I'm considering it. The odd thing about the grammar is I can see at once why all *its* examples are wrong, so why don't I see when it's me? Bother.

Who is Cécile? I only knew one & she was burnt to death. And who is Angela? Never mind. You are *not* to be disloyal with Prod about the *Princesse* by the way – he thinks it's awful too. There was a review by Harold N. saying I write like Roedean[3] – just when I so wish I'd been there & learnt grammar. It is all very sad, & shows how one mustn't have literary ambitions if one is ONE but must be contented with being Marie Corelli. The joke is there's an article in next month's *Table Ronde*[4] which I've seen the proofs of, saying I write wonderful English & am England's gift to France so I've got away with something.

I asked my darling publisher to come & meet bootikins & he couldn't & wrote saying 'j'ai rêvé toute la nuit de Connolly – un jeune homme aux yeux noirs et le regard chaud'.[5]

Not bad? Boots has gone off with Miss Skeleton, both, apparently, in a very cross mood.

Col loves & adores Courcel, too.

Now do come back – tell me what I can do about francs for you.

Fond love
   NR

Such a joke, Boots's 50 millions were won by a very poor old lady in the next street to me.

[1] Mrs W. A. Bradley; Evelyn's literary agent in Paris.
[2] Marie Corelli (1855–1924). Popular author of far-fetched romantic melodramas.
[3] In a generally favourable review, Harold Nicolson wrote: 'She catches and reflects the tone of the original; but there are moments when fatigue overcomes her and she relapses from the style of the rue de Vaugirard into the style of Roedean.' *Observer*, 16 April 1950.
[4] 'A la poursuite de l'amour et de la satire avec Nancy Mitford' by Bernard Minoret, *Table Ronde*, May 1950.
[5] 'I dreamt of Connolly all night – a young man with black eyes and a burning look.'

26 April [1950]   Pensione Villa Natalia
                                                  Via Bolognese 106
                                                  Firenze
Darling Nancy

Let us begin with a little grammar: *Princess de Clèves* (Mitford's version). Preface. p. 1., para 1. 'Allowances have been made for her both by her contemporaries and ever since.' Here you have put two linguistically dissimilar forms into close association. Perhaps it is not absolutely wrong grammatically but it is barbarously inelegant. You must either say: 'both in her own time and ever since' or 'both by her contemporaries and by posterity'.

See?

More next time.

I have come back to Florence after an enchanting festa at Portofino.[1] Say what you like for your snooty frogs, the wops are top nation for simple fun & prettiness. It really was lovely & gay & holy all at the same time. I found my poor mother-in-law in circumstances of dire distress in her large 1880 unfurnished villa, with no hot water & no fire wood and nothing to eat except baskets of ornamental vegetables which her contadini bring her in lieu of rent. Laura's sister, Gabriel (barmy) had come, also penniless, in the hope of curing her arthritis in the sun. It was frightfully cold all the time & wet most of the time. Johnny Churchill's[2] awful frescoes are all that survived the German occupation. They thought they were Giottos and reverently covered them with six layers of canvas & tarpaulin & ply wood while they were wrecking the rest of the charming Victorian interiors. (Laura's grandfather had all the materials for building shipped out from England.)

I met a lively young lady[3] who said she knew you – granddaughter of William Nicholson, married to a sort of war correspondent.

She had Osbert Lancaster staying with her. Well say what you will I don't mind him a bit, in fact rather like him.

Victor Mallet came for the festa. All the English colony at Portofino inhabit the tops of separate conical hills, unapproachable except on foot up flights of iris bordered steps – real mountains in most cases. Poor Victor promised to have tea with each severally on the single day of his visit thinking he could whizz from one to the other in a motor car spending ten minutes with each. Well he found his mistake all right.

Harold [Acton] lives a life of great severity. His parents will not permit his going out when they have guests or his staying at home when they are alone, so half his time is spent being polite to aged American marquesas and half eating in poky restaurants. He is not allowed in his father's car and lives three miles out of town. He will treat me like an aged American marquesa, bows me in & out of doors, holds umbrellas over my head & pays me extravagant compliments. But he knows everything about ART.

We went to see B. Berenson, like Trotsky, in a house which after Harold's is a miserable hole. La Pietra really is very fine. Much more than I ever expected.

I went to see the Master Sir Max Beerbohm at Rapallo. Fatuous Lady B would talk but it was blissikins just to be in a room with him.

Tomorrow I go to Montegufoni.[4] Then with Harold to Verona.

The franc situation is not desperate. I can have a day or two in Paris. I think it will be about May 13th. What I'll do is to telegraph you the day of my arrival, make straight for Travellers hoping to find a note there telling me where you have found for me to sleep. I wouldn't really mind sleeping at Travellers. But could you get someone to explain to Mr Gordon (if that is his name) that I have a week's membership deferred from the time I was there with Sykes & bought a fortnight's membership. Otherwise one has to be put up & recorded all over again, I think, & pay another whacking big subscription.

Angela was Lady Antrim of course. Cécile has passed out of my heart. It was burning passion at the time. Easy come, easy go.

I daresay I'll have something to report at Montegufoni.

Such thinness as you may have observed on my passage through Paris has gone. I am back to normal. Tho wop food is *not* what one needs really. Nor the wine.

It might be a good plan if you happen to have any dealings with Laffont or Bradley just to ask if there are any francs for me as it is madness to spend dollars if one hasn't got to.

Did I tell you Chips took P. Coats[5] to the Vatican to have their union blessed by the Pope?

Love

E

On the day before the festa the Archeprete of Portofino went round
the town with a paste pot & stuck up everywhere posters saying quite
simply 'Arch-Priest, we love thee'.

[1] Laura Waugh's grandfather, the 4th Earl of Carnarvon, built a large villa at Portofino
overlooking the sea. It was known as 'Altachiara', a translation of 'Highclere', the Carnarvons'
seat in Berkshire.
[2] John Spencer-Churchill (1909–92). Painter and author, whom Evelyn described as a 'bald
crazy mural decorator'. *Letters of Evelyn Waugh*, p. 80.
[3] Jenny Nicholson (1919–64). Journalist. Daughter of the poet Robert Graves. Married in 1945
to Alexander Clifford, war correspondent for the *Daily Mail*, and later to Patrick Crosse of
Reuters.
[4] The Sitwells' vast medieval castle in Tuscany.
[5] Peter Coats (1910–90). Known as 'Petticoats', he was an intimate friend of Chips Channon
from 1939.

19 May [1950]   Piers Court
                                                       Stinchcombe
Darling Nancy
    Grammar. 'Mediatize'. I have investigated. This was definitely a step
down not a step up. Princes were the *immediate* vassals of the Emperor.
Then in the 19th century their property was annexed by superior
princes eg. Electors and they became only mediate vassals of Emperor
and immediate vassals of other princes. But process of mediatization
acknowledged that they had once been sovereign princes & explicitly
gave them royal rank.
    'Protagonist.' Besides your chum who looks like a Maltese pimp,
what is his name, [Raymond] Mortimer, others have written to me
about this word.[1]
    It is an English word meaning 'leading actor'. Some dramas, most
Greek dramas but not for example Aeschylus, have only one leading
actor. Such as *Hamlet*. But other plays eg. *Macbeth* 2 protagonists *Julius
Caesar* 3 protagonists. If you only allow one protagonist you have to
use 'deutagonist' and 'tritagonist' which are not English words at all.
So balls to the Maltese pimp.

————

Collins. How kind you were to me in Paris. Thank you, thank you.
I need not have fussed about train. It goes at 12.30 after 14th
May.

————

I await *E. S[ackville] West* with great anxiety & have killed all
the livestock on the place so that he may have fresh meat twice a
day.

————

Laura is not as well as I could wish, but not so ill as to make me
anxious.

————

Harriet is very pretty & engaging.
————

Love from
   Evelyn

[1] Evelyn had used the word in the plural in a review of *The Lost Traveller* by Antonia White, *Tablet*, 22 April 1950.

22 May 1950   7 rue Monsieur, VII

Darling Evelyn
   I enjoyed your visit terrifically though of course the responsibility
harrowed me & so did the fact that for some reason Xopher [Sykes]
got a very much better lunchyon (as Col calls it) here than you did &
of course shovelled it in without noticing what loovely stoof it was.
The food here is really outside my control on account of Marie being
a saint.
   A letter from my Dad, to whom I wrote saying if you don't hear
from me as often as you ought to it's because I have such a mass of
writing. He says yes *don't* people write a lot of meaningless letters I
can't think how they can afford it I can only imagine they must steal
stamps from their servants. Quite a new idea to me.
   I see why mediatized is grand. It is far grander to come down in the
world than to go up (nouveau riche, nouvelle noblesse etc) isn't it.
   Who is Emily Post please? The *NS & N* says I am the modern she.
   Are you *loving Nothing*?[1] I am. But R Macaulay[2] is miserably bad.
   I didn't tell you – when I apologized to Dolly R for my country
clothes she said 'mais chérie, il n'y a qu'une chose détestable, c'est
une demie-toilette' (meaning a quick change without a bath) 'et on
peut être décoiffée, mais pas mal coiffée.' Isn't she bliss. So all was
well.
   I shan't be able to write for an age which is why I seize my pen at
once. Tomorrow 40 intellectuals here to meet the H[amish] Hamiltons
– then Peter Brook[3] & Robert Morley[4] to talk about the play, then
Debo & Mr Peters together, oh my *life*.
   Are you noticing the perfect style & syntax of this letter?
   I had a long talk with Col, who *loves* you by the way, about the
people you hate. He says you only like first class people. Well it's not
enough, that's all, though possibly flattering to ONE to think it.
   I have been asked, with several Cedrics, to a dinner for Sumner
Welles.[5] Momo & Susan Mary Patten can *hardly* bear it – so *unsuitable*
they keep wailing & echoes of the wails have come back to me, greatly
to my delight. I do love doing serious ladies in the eye.
   Well dearest goodbye.

Love to Laura – hope she's better, do say.

Love
    NR

[1] Henry Green, *Nothing* (1950).
[2] Rose Macaulay, *The World My Wilderness* (1950). A novel.
[3] Peter Brook (1925–). The most original theatre director of his generation was just 25 and the *enfant terrible* of the British stage.
[4] Robert Morley (1908–92). Took the part of the cuckolded husband in *The Little Hut*.
[5] Sumner Welles (1892–1961). American Under-Secretary of State 1937–43.

25 May [1950]   Piers Court
                                                 Stinchcombe

Darling Nancy

Emily Post is not a very gratifying comparison. She was the great American authority on etiquette and a very bad authority too.

I am having great trouble about protagonists. Not only the wild beast of Bloomsbury but people as far West as Harley Street write me abusive letters on the subject and Eddy Sackville-West who knows no Greek supports them.

His visit was a heavy responsibility. I gave him fresh meat at every meal but he took a great number of pills. Were they in order to ameliorate the cooking or reinforce the vitamins? He drinks only whisky in tiny quantities and I generally count on large bumpers of goodish wine dulling my guests' consciousness of their discomforts. Also he dislikes cross-word puzzles and Ronnie Knox made us do them all the evening in a special way devised by himself to make them more difficult. He (Eddy) looked very elegant, & except for pimples, pretty. He has a dear little dinner jacket with a velvet collar & tiny black suede shoes. I took him for a breathless hot walk and he seemed to enjoy the countryside but he moaned pitifully with the pain of my picture books. He got up at dawn and sat in his overcoat in the drawing room before the fire was lit. Oh dear I don't think he can have enjoyed himself at all. I do like him so. Attempts to make a joke of his tendencies fell very flat. I am afraid Ronnie who thinks only of the Grenfells & Shaw Stewarts thought him rather cissy.

And now I am in great embarrassment because there are some very stiff local grandees called Guise who have lived quite lost on the banks of the Severn since about 1150 and their daughter is to marry a Catholic (a Fraser to make things worse)[1] so Ronnie wanted her asked so I did so though I hardly know them and they are very haughty about it. Oh dear. She is coming any minute.

Laura is much better, leading a nice lazy life warm in bed in freezing room where I sit most of the day.

Tomorrow I go to stay with Maud Russell.[2] I asked Eddy whom I should find and he said Peter Quennell for certain.

I read that all the French police are on strike. That must be a comfort for all.

I have been invited to spend a Cultural Week at The Hague. Would that be funny or horrible? I've never been there and the only Dutch I know are the Jungman sisters and Henry Yorke's pa. He's rather cultural in a gruesome way but not Jungmans.

Bogey Harris[3] is dead.

Donaldsons went all the way to London for Anthony Mildmay's[4] funeral and their names were omitted from *The Times* list so they are much more socialistic.

I have asked Mr Peters to see that middle-class man with the muffler in Paris.

My garden really looks rather well.

I hope the middle class man's motor car got cured.

Ronnie is sitting saying his rosary over the fire. Is that a good sign? I fear not.

> Love from
> E

Love to Debo – a faint fragrance of dead romance.
H. Hamilton indeed. Why do I dislike him? I don't know him at all & he has done me no injury, but I wish him boiled in oil.

[1] Philippa Guise, daughter of Sir Anselm Guise, married Alastair Fraser on 1 July 1950.
[2] Maud Nelke (1892–1982). Widow of Gilbert Russell, a brother of Conrad Russell. She entertained writers and artists at Mottisfont Abbey, her home in Hampshire.
[3] Henry Harris (d.1950). A well-known figure in late Victorian and Edwardian society. Collector of early Italian majolica. Trustee of the National Gallery 1934–41.
[4] 2nd Baron Mildmay (1909–50). Amateur National Hunt jockey who died in a swimming accident off the Devon coast.

27 May 1950   7 rue Monsieur, VII

Darling Evelyn

I found protagonist*S* in *Arts*, that intensely highbrow weekly here, so I believe you. The French are nothing if not fussy over these things.

You wouldn't write a Boswellian account of Dr Acton in the Western Apennines I suppose – posterity would bless you & your contemporaries praise your name. Oh DO.

You won't regret it if you swap over to Stock from horrible Laffont & you need never see green scarf again.

I'm taking Mr Peters to a literary tea on Monday where he will find several publishers I think. My party for the Hamiltons was great fun, I adored it. Thirty publishers booksellers writers etc. Hamilton was wonderful I thought, took such a lot of trouble, learnt all their names beforehand & appeared to be in raptures of happiness for 3 long hours (they all came at 6 & left at 9 I was pulverized with exhaustion). I cannot imagine why you hate him. He is *good*, a good character & good at his work. You've never heard of him playing somebody a dirty or even slightly dirty trick, & he sees the point of people like poor old Polnay whom everybody flees from but me, puts up with him for 2 whole hours of his visit here & is loyal enough not even to hint PHEW at the end of it. The only person here he can't stick is Duff. I don't know why I'm going on like this, I shan't change anything. He asked me if I could throw any light on the reasons for your animosity & I said no, beyond a general loathing of the human race. He asked me if I had any control over Randolph or Christopher [Sykes] so I suppose you've turned those loyal old wolfhounds on him. Very silly & babyish.

I loved your description of the old bombed house (Ed) it brought so vividly back to me those months I spent at W. Wycombe with him during the war. The tiny black suede shoes, the shivering, in a cape it used to be then with heavy silver buckles, before breakfast, the array of pills before his plate. Well, all described in *The Pursuit* really, though not so vividly – your well known knack of one tap on the nail & in it goes, whereas the rest of us hammer & pound for hours. I'm glad you love him, *so* do I. I feel sure he enjoyed himself terribly.

How *more* than odd you liking Maud Russell. Je ne vous suis pas sur ce terrain-là.[1] But I guess the grub is good. Can't get out of bed for matching bit of paper. I don't feel well & shan't until it's warmer. Everything aches & I feel old – I've cancelled all plans & huddle at home cooking my article which is very bad this time I fear.

Best love
    NR

Col says 'The Virgin in French Art' (an exhibition here) is an artistic event of the 1st importance. I haven't been yet – too crowded. *What* a pity you missed it.
Mrs Bradley came to my party, very sub-acid.
Well all my fans here have written off for the works of E Post saying you can't have enough of a good thing – Loyal?

[1] I don't agree with you on that count.

28 May [1950]   Piers Court
                                                       Stinchcombe

Darling Nancy
    Try & get hold of *New Yorker* for May 13th. It has a gruesome & fascinating description of Mr Ernest Hemingway.[1]
    A sad final incident to Eddy's visit. He had an elaborate train

journey to Blandford so I sent him all the way to Bath in the village taxi in the hope that it would mitigate his austerities. The taxi-man got him there in nice time, then sat back & lit a pipe to refresh himself. Suddenly he saw a figure like frightened ghost dash from the station lugging two suitcases & a medicine-chest, look round wildly, fail to recognize him, leap into another taxi & drive away. There are two stations in Bath & he had been taken to the wrong one. I said at Mottisfont 'he ate nothing'. 'He simply gorges *here*.'

It was the craving for social life took me to Mottisfont. Well it was all dishevelled war widows playing Conasta (?) One of these widows was Diana Campbell-Gray. I asked her if she remembered the French tutor. Yes, indeed, & described him accurately. But he was not then called M. Bay but another quite different much longer word beginning with B. So I suppose he is M.B. like Mme X.

I think nothing of *Nothing*. I began it with the highest expectations & please try & believe me, no tinge of jealousy, and was sharply disappointed. Some lovely lyric flashes, some very funny characters Liz, Penelope the sainted darling, but the idiom rang false everywhere. That idiot paper *New Statesman* of course got the exact opposite of the truth. What Henry never did for a moment was to define his characters' social position. Sometimes they spoke 'Mrs Chichesterese',[2] sometimes Air Force, sometimes sheer Gloucester peasant – 'Leave me be': 'Why-ever for.' He has just lost his ear through spending so much time with low-class women. All the characters are frightfully common but not consistent in their sort of commonness. Don't you agree. 'I'll take a sherry.' 'Phone me' all the joke-charade vulgarities. Well Etonians of 45 don't talk like that. He might have made a nice contrast with the young, who some of them do, I believe, but not the young men I saw at Mottisfont – Mark Bonham Carter,[3] Nigel Nicolson[4] etc. They couldn't make out the slang of their generation (in this novel I speak of) but were quite willing to suppose that we talk like John Pomfret & Liz. I daresay Henry never could write dialogue at all & has been bluffing all the time. I mean, we have all said 'how wonderfully Henry has caught real proletarian speech' while all the time it was just as false as his 'Knightsbridge' characters. And anyway what is a Knightsbridge character? I don't regard it as having ever been a defined class, unless he means the royal tarts in the Trevor–Montpelier area. But Maimie wouldn't say 'Let's give a "do" ' for a party. Perhaps Sibell[5] might since she moved into Midland industrial circles. I believe that's it. He has got his poor mind all jangled up by Birmingham business chums & Miss Glass. Well it's a rotten book, but I'm glad the Americans are lapping it up.

He stole from me the idea of a character having his leg off bit by bit & then dying. I used it about a little boy in my first book, who was shot at the school sports.

Do read the article on Hemingway. If you can't get it, I'll send it grudgingly.

Love from
Evelyn

[1] A famous profile by Lillian Ross, in which she described two days spent in the company of the heavy-drinking author while he talked non-stop about war, guns and champagne. (Reprinted by Penguin Books in 1962.)
[2] Pamela Chichester spoke in a genteel manner.
[3] Hon. Mark Bonham Carter (1922–94). Liberal MP 1958–9. Director of William Collins 1955–8. Chairman of the Race Relations Board 1966–71, Vice-chairman of BBC 1975–81. Created life peer in 1986.
[4] Nigel Nicolson (1917–2004). Author. Conservative MP 1952–9. Son of Sir Harold Nicolson and Hon. Vita Sackville-West.
[4] Lady Sibell Lygon (1907–2005). Second daughter of 7th Earl Beauchamp. A keen horsewoman married to Michael Rowley, a fighter pilot, 1939–52.

9 June 1950   7 rue Monsieur, VII

Darling Evelyn

A day with nothing to do, almost too wonderful. So in theory I can write some letters, go & see the Virgins & put on no stockings but in 5 minutes I expect the telephone will ring & I shall find myself a lady in waiting again to some English friend, be it only Diana Coo.

Also I'm having a TIME with the journalists, because my book is coming out next week & they launch books here with much more of a splash than we do at home – articles in all the papers even the yellow press, a party of 150 critics etc at the publisher's & so on. So I've had never less than 2 long interviews a day all this week which is very tiring as one has to defend oneself tooth & nail against serious intellectual young men shooting off questions like schoolmasters. I never can remember, can you, how one's books were conceived etc etc. What has done me a great deal of good here is the *Psse de Clèves*. The French, less conscious than you of collective nouns, admire the translation & very much admire the preface, which is going to be published in French, & it pleases them that I took the trouble to do it. So that was not, all the same, quite in vain.

About Eddy. He's *always* like that – the word querulous was invented for him. A friend of his said the other day (Jim L. Milne,[1] also an R.C.) that Ed will never feel really at home in R.C. company & that may be very true. I'm perfectly certain that Laura's condition wouldn't affect him a scrap.

Do you know anything about making oneself into a company for reasons of tax? Prod was muttering away about it & of course I didn't understand one word.

The Col's clock has arrived at his house clean & going & he loves it so much he sleeps a new way round so that he can look at it. Really it *is* a beauty. What a dull letter – all about ONE do forgive & write soon.

Love
    NR

P.S. Quite forgotten that I haven't yet *taken* (as Mrs Hammersley wld say) Henry's book. Well I thought the unreality of the dialogue must be intentional, meant to produce a sort of dream like effect – art as opposed to photography. Nobody could make it as unnatural as that by accident surely? 'The good ring is most suitable.' Yes I also saw more than a touch of Britten-Jones & co which surprised me – is he friends with all of them? I suppose the lady with the great eyes is Jennifer [Fry]. Phone etc must be a concession to the critics we would all do well to make.

Did you read Rose Macaulay? Really TOO bad I felt ashamed for her – once such a favourite of mine. Perhaps it shows that one mustn't let 10 years go by without writing a novel.

Peter de Polnay's beautiful young wife is riddled with cancer & must die. He writes in terrible despair. Oh poor people.

re love
    NR

P.S. Prod says if people say only one protagonist allowed, it simply means they don't know the classics.

[1] James Lee-Milne (1908–97). Diarist, biographer and architectural historian. Converted to Roman Catholicism in 1934. Married Alvilde Chaplin in 1951.

18 June 1950   7 rue Monsieur, VII

Darling Evelyn

Thanks so much for the *Month*.[1] I'd sent for one from Heywood which I'll pass on to some frog. *Helena* seems wonderful & I long for it. I hope you thought it big of P Quennell to dole out all that praise but I expect you were sick. How dull, what Mauriac[2] says about Claudel & Gide hardly worth translating.

I've got Jonathan Guinness here – he is like a pregnant lady. Gets up at 12.30 – back in bed with his boots on the moment he has swallowed his luncheon &, in short, flops from bed to day bed & from day bed to sofa until lights out at 9.30 – unless I drag him to some play. He is very nice, I am fond of him, but more than ¾ dead. I suppose it's a symptom of the decline of the B. E.

I've had *such* a week with my book coming out – interviews every day, an afternoon at Stock signing the book for the critics (they send out 400 free copies, to anybody you have ever heard of in the literary

world, & all signed) a morning at Bouffemont the famous girls' school
to be photographed with 'les girls du finishing' telling them, presumably, about love. I asked the principal if her girls have happy lives on
the whole to which she replied that one already had 7 husbands.
Anyway the girls had bought 40 copies of *A la Poursuite de l'amour* so it
was good for trade!

My play[3] opens 24 July in the country – Brighton they think, &
mid or end of Aug: in London. They want me for 10 days at the
beginning so I suppose I shall stay on in England until the 1st night
in London, going to Muv Farve & so on. Must shut up here at least
a month. I utterly dread it, the cold & wet & gloom & being away
from my own bed all that time. Never mind. I'm being nicely boiled
up now so can't really complain. Today huge garden party for the
book, given by Stock. Refused to allow Maurois[4] to be asked, rightly
I think – otherwise it's everybody you've ever heard of. I do wonder
who'll come.

This letter very disjointed I see, too much telephoning while I write.

Best love
     NR

[1] Extracts from *Helena* appeared in the three Summer 1950 issues of the *Month*.
[2] François Mauriac (1885–1970). Fervent Roman Catholic writer whose novels explored the
murky recesses of the human psyche. In an open letter in the June issue of the *Month* he
branded the Gide–Claudel correspondence as 'pathetic' and publication of the letters as
'evidence of a disintegrating society'.
[3] *The Little Hut*.
[4] André Maurois (1885–1967). Writer who, in spite of his Jewish origins, was pro-Vichy at the
beginning of the war. Made his reputation with *Les Silences du Colonel Bramble* (1918) and *Les
Discours du Docteur O'Grady* (1922) and went on to write biographies, novels and popular histories.

[postmarked 19 July 1950]   7 rue Monsieur, VII
[postcard]

Is it true you have a new son? If so fond love & congrats: to Laura
& you. Har*old* told me he is here the dear old thing.

I leave for the cold climate very sad & low & feeling like Marie
Stuart (Edinburgh you see) on Sat. Do come to my play in London
end of Aug: *Do* write to me Caledonian Hotel Edin:

3 August [1950]   Piers Court
                                             Stinchcombe
Darling Nancy
     Yes it is true that Laura has a son. She is very well & the baby is said
to be satisfactory. It is named Michael Septimus.[1] I am not counting in
your other god-child to make this my seventh. We have one who died

in infancy. How much is a 'quiverful'? Seven I think, or was it nine?

I hope you enjoyed Edinburgh. Betjeman, the silly ass, says without qualification that it is the most beautiful city in Europe. It has some handsome aspects. The Caledonian Hotel used to be excellent but I went there lecturing the other day & found that the State Railways have painted all the beautiful mahogany doors apple-green. Beasts.

Was your obscene play well received?

I am rather back in love with Debo. She gave a party on the river and wore false eye lashes made of sort of lulu brush bristles stuck on crooked, and I must say my old heart melted.

How I hate the English summer, well any summer for that matter. Weeds everywhere & children & insomnia. Randolph is off to Korea lucky him.

I had a brief London season & enjoyed it in the evenings when there were parties but oh the length of the days sitting in White's or Hyde Park Hotel. Momo gave a really lovely ball. Everyone went round saying 'What d'you suppose it's costing her?' Vulgar yes no. I mean of them to ask not of her to spend it. Well she built a great palace for it. I made Boots hire a tail coat and the first thing he saw when he arrived were Henry Bath and the Duke of Marlborough both in dinner jackets so next night he went to Ann Rothermere's in a dinner jacket tho it had 'White tie' rather rudely written on the card. He looked horrible too because his dinner jacket was covered in soup & lipstick. Then I saw him going to the country dressed for St Tropez 1926. That was horrible too.

So there was a great dinner for Fr D'Arcy. Eddy came & how he complained of the placement.

I opened *Life* magazine & what should I see but a full page portrait of Friar Couturier followed by pictures of a disgusting church he has built. Oh for an atom bomb.

I read with interest how the politest people in the world treated the Italian cyclists.

Why no articles in *Sunday Times*? I look every week and am always disappointed.

Laura and I go to New York in Oct. Do come too then.

Debo calls Ran [Antrim] the lavatory chain because he is always flushing.[2]

Not kind.

Love from
    Evelyn

---

[1] Evelyn's youngest child was born on 9 July.
[2] Evelyn had crossed out this sentence.

9 August 1950   Redesdale Cottage
                                                     Otterburn
                                                     Northumberland

Darling Evelyn

I'm in bed with no writing paper so you must lump this.

Here with my dad, in a tiny cottage stuffed with old masters between which hang oil paintings by a local lesbian of my dad's Staffordshire terriers. It's on a beautiful moor, the cottage, an oasis from these huge industrial towns whose station hotels are now my home. I leave for Newcastle this afternoon alas. Well you know what it's like from your lectures, but I shall have had a solid month of it, except for 3 days here. I am letting off steam in a *Sunday Times* article on 'Britain'.[1]

In fact I've rather enjoyed it all, in spite of the discomfort. I've re written great hunks of the play, to the instructions of clever Mr Brook, & it's very amusing to see the rehearsals & then see how the new bits go with an audience. The actors! I never knew such people. Any good line is '*my* good line' or '*my* laugh' & the rest are 'that's a very flat line of *yours* darling' (to me).

Shall I see you in London? I'll be there from 20th – about 1st Sept, staying with Mark O.G. at Kew. 10 Curzon are supposed to be forwarding my letters, though I *never* get any.

Travelling as Mitford not Rodd I find I am quite famous – people even come to hotel bedrooms for signatures & bring my books to the stage door (greatly to the rage of the actors).

The leading lady[2] who is a beauty not unlike Camilla [Sykes] keeps a husband, the image of Smartyboots, in her bedroom. They have breakfast at 12.30 & luncheon at 4, in bed, in duffel coats, every window sealed. I had to go & see her so I know.

I feel very dépaysée, & my wireless talks English not French which I should have foreseen but hadn't – Haven't seen a single French sporting paper so I've missed the end of the Tour & don't even know who won. They want me to go to America with the play in Oct: but once bitten twice shy – Rex Harrison,[3] of whom they speak in bated breath, comes to see it on Sat with a view to acting in it over there.

Best love, do write
     NR

The pictures in the Edin: & Glasgow galleries can only be described as *smashing* – have you seen them?

[1] 'So now I know what it must feel like to be a foreigner in Britain. My impression is that the hotels are good, that the art galleries are full of treasures, and furthermore run with great taste, energy and discrimination, and that the food, though not good, is not as bad as people suppose. The railways are truly terrible, however, and so is the climate. During the whole month of August I have worn nothing but last winter's clothes, and I think there has hardly been a sunny day.' 'Britain Revisited', *Sunday Times*, 27 August 1950.

[2] Joan Tetzel, an American actress, played the wife, Robert Morley the cuckolded husband, and David Tomlinson the disgruntled lover. The sets were by Oliver Messel.
[3] Rex Harrison (1908–90). He did not act in *The Little Hut*, but directed another of André Roussin's comedies, *Nina*, in 1955.

[August 1950]   Royal Station Hotel
                                                 Newcastle-on-Tyne 1

Darling Evelyn

I wish you hadn't missed my last *Sunday Times* article about the Tour. It so happens I didn't see it myself so don't know if they printed what I said about you[1] but I know the biking part went in because my fan mail is VAST & all about that.

I shall never leave France again if I can help it I am too miserable here. But I have seen some beautiful things – today a house called Seaton Delaval, as good, in its tiny way, as anything anywhere. A ruin, of course. Then from Leeds I shall be able to see Haworth,[2] I've always wanted to. My room here has neither bath nor telephone & the basin gurgles. Alas alas. I'm doing a *Sunday Times* on all this – quite good so far I think.

Do come to the play – no you hate them don't you? Besides there is your nonconformist conscience.

You wouldn't come to the 1st night with Laura? I'll send tickets if so – oh *do*. Let me know to 10 Curzon fairly soon.

Best love
      NR

[1] They did not.
[2] The West Yorkshire town where the Brontë family lived.

16 August 1950   The Queens Hotel
                                                 Leeds

Darling Evelyn

How tedious of me – it's Lyric Theatre 23rd Aug: Could you wire me here – everybody I know is badgering for tickets aren't people peculiar. Perhaps they think I dispose of the entire theatre. Oh *do* come it would *make* my evening.

Terrible press here – poor Miss Mit in trouble again.

Talent Wasted say the headlines meaning the actors' talent how horrid. Packed house however.

Fond love
      NR

25 September 1950   7 rue Monsieur, VII

Darling Evelyn

It's an age since I heard from you. The *Sunday Times* asked me to do a 'short but astringent' caption to your photograph in Portrait Gallery however I said no. I wonder who they'll get 'must be somebody who knows him well'.

Would you like to hear about Smartyboots only keep it a secret please. Well the smart old creature sent his mistress off to join Farouk[1] & lived for quite a while in affluence here on what she managed to put up her knickers at the casino & remit. Then he got £40 out of the *Daily Mail*, saying he must have a manicure & so on & then would see Farouk with a view to identifying the unidentified blonde. When he arrived at Biarritz however Farouk refused an interview but lent him the blonde for his birthday. Meanwhile blonde, as well as her gambling money, was given £100 a day but only on condition she spent it during the day, so she bought bales of stuff, crates of sugar & so on which have all been sent in the Egyptian bag to Sussex Place. Now this all excited Boots to a frenzy & he rushed her off to the consul (on his birthday) to marry her, but the consul didn't believe him when he said he was a widower, why? & wouldn't marry them. Then Farouk gave her a jewel said to be worth £1000 & sent them both packing. Oh & I forgot to say he would have interviewed Boots if B had consented to be flown to Cairo to see the Prime Minister first, but Boots seeing himself probably ham-strung in the Bosphorus, very wisely refused.

This is the main outline of this interesting tale, there are countless little details as you may imagine which my aching arm refuses to write. But you'll get it out of Boots if you try, he loves telling. I had it all like a lovely serial story day by day like Rip Kirby[2] oh *did* I enjoy it.

I got some lovely letters while I was in England saying go back to the Paris brothels where you belong etc etc so you see the poor French shut their brothels & nobody even knows about it. I see the Pope scolded them about their plays but really American plays are much worse. Do tell him.

Tomorrow I dine with the Windsors & on Tues I go & stay with an old Catholic Royalist super gratin[3] friend in her lovely lovely house so after all that I'll write again only you must reply. Perhaps a letter from you was amongst those abstracted & lost by Prod when he passed through Paris & I was away. He does more harm than a bomb.

Best love
NR

---

[1] King Farouk of Egypt (1920–65). Barbara Skelton has described her affair with the King in her autobiography.
[2] *Daily Mail* comic-strip detective story.
[3] Very upper-crust.

27 September [1950]   Piers Court
                                                       Stinchcombe
Darling Nancy

That was a most moving letter about Boots. Oh dear I do hope he
doesn't settle down with that drab. All my friends seem to marry
into the Forbes–Quennell white slave market and it is the end of all
friendship. [. . .] Look at poor Randolph, peppered with Korean socialist shrapnel to get away from the tantrums of his tart.[1] Why can't
one's friends marry *nice* girls?

I go to London tomorrow to dispatch copies of *Helena*. One will
reach you soon. Don't puzzle your pretty head with it. It will be all
Greek – or worse still English – to you. But put it on a shelf & look
at its back now & then & think kindly of me.

I wish you had accepted the *Sunday Times* invitation to write the
caption for their picture. I don't much mind the papers saying I am
beastly, which is true, or that I write badly, which isn't. What enrages
me is wrong facts. They always are wrong in these knowing 'profiles'.
When they say I went to Cambridge or got the D.S.O. or was converted to Catholicism by the war, I eat the carpet.

It has been a disgusting summer – continuous rain since early June
and now nothing to look forward to but winter. I've had a succession
of guests to keep me agitated but not amused. The travel agents in
America are routing all their Irish tourists via Fishguard now telling
them to stop off a night at Stinkers on the way.

Well next week I take Laura to New York for a fortnight. I originally
planned the trip as a stimulant for her after childbirth but it is now I
who need it the more. It is the most wonderful health resort in the
world. I look to it to revivify me. In fact at the moment I am like a
patient lying comatose waiting for the doctor to come round with his
needle.

Osbert's last volume[2] is very heavy going. One good sentence:
'Although I was already an eminent author, it is a curious fact that I
experienced considerable difficulty at this time in getting anything
published'. He is already in New York being brought to life.

I hope to go to Jerusalem for Christmas; you can have no idea,
living as you do in lively theatrical circles when you come here, of the
awful flat dreariness of England under Welfare.

There was a lady here the other day who knows all about the New
York theatre. She saw your play in Edinburgh & thought it brilliant
but impossible to get past American censors – not because of dirty
language but of situation.

I opened my *Times* this morning to read a letter from Princess
Bibesco saying how splendid Sibyl [Colefax] was. When did she die?
I have read my paper daily cover to cover & seen nothing of it. I saw

practically nothing of her since she left Argyll House but I had a warm grateful place for her at heart.

Trim Oxford's wife[3] has become a great beauty, tell Honks. It will annoy her and it's true.

Come to think of it Henry Yorke married a nice girl but it doesn't save us from *Nothing*.

Love from
     Evelyn

[1] Randolph Churchill had been injured by a mortar shell while covering the Korean War for the *Daily Telegraph*.
[2] Osbert Sitwell, *Noble Essences*. His fifth and concluding volume of autobiography.
[3] Anne Palairet, married to Julian (Trim) Asquith, 2nd Earl of Oxford and Asquith, in 1947. Evelyn had described her in a letter to Diana Cooper as: 'A queer girl who looks up at you so that you always see white below the iris.' *Mr Wu & Mrs Stitch* ed. A. Cooper, p. 96.

30 September 1950   7 rue Monsieur, VII

Darling Evelyn

I call them the insect-women oh aren't they horrible & so mal-élevées. I mean Cyril brought Miss S to a v. small cocktail party I had & she sat & read a book! Mauvais genre they call it here. Then my brother in law Jackson has turned up with Mrs Bluefeet,[1] whom I haven't seen since we met her together, with Mrs Orwell in tow as a sort of dame de compagnie. All in corduroys & sandals. I *can't* bear them. Cyril said to me the trouble with you Nancy is one can't imagine you sitting on one's lap – have you ever sat on anybody's lap?

No I said, with some vehemence, nor have I ever allowed anybody to kiss me (almost true).

Sibyl's death was announced as 'Sibyl, mother of M[ichael] Colefax' – so somehow unsuitable.

I've been staying with my dear old Mme Costa de Beauregard in a house in which nothing has changed for 100 years. In the drawing room sit 4 old ladies, who have stayed there all of every summer since they were born & M. le Curé aged 87, who has been M. le Curé there since he was 27. Last all saints' day he asked Mme Costa, as he always does, for her list (people to pray for) & she gave him by mistake her private list, so he read out Louis XIV, Thérèse (old cook), Landru,[2] le duc d'Aumale, Marie-Ange (old gardener) etc etc. We asked her why Landru & she said she heard he had no family to pray for him so she always does every day. The house is like that in *Les Malheurs de Sophie*, extremely elegant in front & backing onto a basse-cour with vast manure heap covered with hens. The farmer, a handsome young man, has 18 children & to Mme Costa's sorrow none of them intend to take orders. But the youngest is only 4. The eldest daughter brought her fiancé to see Mme C. while I was there, a ravishing young man who had been in the Congo & SEEN PIGMIES. It is all like another world, the world you love but which would bore me, though I like to see it in progress. I fear it will end with her death (the daughter in law is an Englishwoman, a beauty, with service flat tastes) but at present everything is kept up as it should be, there is no feeling of decay.

This letter is meant to say bon-voyage & *do* come here later on. I'll protect you from the middle classes I promise.

Farouk has now got somebody called Honey child (her Xian name) & has given her a better jewel than he gave Miss S. Cyril went to see a flat here belonging to somebody I know, with a view to renting it. The concierge said 'you can't let it to him.' 'Why not?' 'Well he had a beard & high heeled shoes & looked like an assassin.'

So my friend won't. It's like the old Turk who saw Napoleon isn't it –[3]

    Best love
    NR

Don't know what you mean about England – champagne seemed to me to *pour*.

Thank you for *Helena*. I'll write when I've read it. Have you heard the name of Duff's novel *Operation Heartbreak*.[4]

[1] Janetta Kee was married to Derek Jackson 1951–6.
[2] The serial murderer.
[3] At the beginning of the century an old Russian who claimed to have seen Napoleon, on the march from Moscow, was asked what he looked like: 'He had a long white beard.'
[4] A fictional version of 'Operation Mincemeat', a wartime deception in which the corpse of a British soldier was crashed in an aircraft off the coast of Spain. He carried false documents which misled the Germans into believing that the Allied invasion of Sicily was an intended invasion of the Balkans.

[October 1950]   Piers Court
                                                    Stinchcombe
Darling Nancy
    I went to Colefax's Memorial Service. Well attended but only by the old. Everyone looked exactly like Rose Macaulay.[1] None of the young bothered to come except Liz & Raimund [von Hofmannsthal] who wore a carmine hat and yellow satin tie respectively.

    I had a busy London day despatching *Helena*s, going to confession, seeing the Woburn collection etc. & later dropped into White's to give a final basting to Quennell's goose (quite unnecessary, he is assured of 100% black-balling).[2] Who should I see there but Boots, woolly-headed wild-eyed, costumed as an American college boy. I said: 'I've been hearing about your spree.' He turned pale grey, eyes popped out, lips trembled, no sound. I thought he had not heard so I said much louder: 'I've heard about your SPREE.' Then in a sort of puppy yelp he cried: 'Most inaccurate I'm sure' & bolted out of the house.

Oh I do look forward to New York.

Don't try & read *Helena*.

Love
    E

I think [Fred] Warner kissed you once. Yes? No?

[1] Rose Macaulay (1881–1958). The novelist was thin and desiccated, and made few concessions to her appearance. She favoured 'a sort of shallow cloche hat with leaves around it', according to Patrick Leigh Fermor.
[2] Peter Quennell was elected without opposition.

9 October 1950   7 rue Monsieur, VII

Darling Evelyn

You've made it only too plain that you don't care 2 hoots what I think about *Helena* so this is merely to thank you for a handsome volume which (I don't mean the contents) made me gasp & stretch my eyes. Lady Honks was kept awake all night by it (contents).

So thank you very much.

Love from
    NR

I shall never be able to have a Turkish bath again.[1]

[1] The Empress Fausta is steamed to death in a Turkish bath in *Helena*.

9 November [1950]   Piers Court
                                                      Stinchcombe

Darling Nancy

Goose. Of course I value your opinion above all others about most things. But well no not about religion. Your verdict on Mauriac's article in the *Month* struck an icy stiletto into any hope I ever had that you could enjoy *Helena*. And I genuinely didn't want you to try because I knew it would be a bore to you. It was love that prompted me to ward you off it. Don't even open it or cut a page, I implore.

Six people think it the most beautiful book they ever read and I am first of the six. Otherwise they all say: 'What was the point?'

The Admiralty, the War Office, the Secret Service, the Foreign Office have all tried to suppress Cooper's book on 'Heartbreak'. But since it is being published in America the irreparable harm is done and they have grudgingly consented to let him keep his passport and his masonic apron.

Laura & I are greatly rejuvenated by our few weeks of luxury & make-believe in New York. It is a great health resort and so cosmopolitan that you can be happy & busy & never meet an American.

Do you remember a cold, awkward, ambitious, socialist protégé of Sibyl's called Gladwyn Jebb?[1] You should just see him now. He is the idol of American girlhood, the most sought-after television performer in the country. They can do something to the face with that apparatus. He looks like Sir Galahad. There are 'Jebb Circles' in every college. He gets 500 letters a day saying: 'Become an American, stand for President and we will vote for you'. They pursue him in the street & snip bits off his coat.

He has a stately home on Long Island where he entertains lavishly, lolling about like a Roman patrician and talking, I must say pretty dully, in a lisping fruity tone. And my word he is enjoying it.

Poor Osbert [Sitwell] is a tottering corpse. Edith is playing Lady Macbeth at the Museum of Modern Art on Nov 16th. Glenway Wescott as Banquo,[2] David Horner in a tartan dinner-jacket as MacDuff. Lady Ribblesdale[3] as the witches. Cheapest seats £5. I wish I could be there.

Sergeant Preston is as bald as an egg and very watery eyed. I suspect he drinks.

It is very much like being in Paris travelling in the *Ile de France*. Very slovenly, excellent cooking, hideous cheap decorations (Cunarders are hideous but very solid & expensive). The entire ship was manned by a great family of identical multuplets. Short, fat, bald chain-smokers – Captain, pursers, stewards, sailors all indistinguishable.

I hope my nest eggs arrive safely & remain safe.

It is exciting news that you are composing another novel.[4] You are clever to think of plots. Do take care of the grammar and don't introduce communist propaganda. Isn't it time you dedicated a work to me? Or are we estranged.

Much love from
    Evelyn

[1] Gladwyn Jebb (1900–96). Permanent Representative to the United Nations 1950–54. Ambassador to France 1954–60. Married Cynthia Noble in 1929. Created Baron Gladwyn in 1960.
[2] Glenway Wescott (1901–87). American poet and novelist, who in fact, took the part of Macbeth.
[3] Ava Willing (d.1958). Famous for her many lovers and outrageous remarks. Married to John Jacob Astor IV, then to 4th Baron Ribblesdale in 1920.
[4] Nancy had begun work on *The Blessing*.

10 November 1950   7 rue Monsieur, VII

Darling Evelyn

All right (I was in a bait). Well *of course* I loved *Helena* – you are a master of narrative & I read it solidly in a day how I do when I enjoy something. I particularly enjoyed the detective work in Jerusalem – of course the beginning – & of course the Roman part. After she left England it became a little foggy to me & some of the life went out of it until Rome. I think from the non-Catholic reader's point of view it's a pity you don't tell about the conversion & I think Constantius might have been a shade more of a person (I was going to say attractive). He is too much like Oliver Harvey – could Oliver Harvey have held down the Roman Empire for a record length of time?

Anyway it's completely absorbing & fascinating, every page. Stock are more than pleased with it & also with your translator – what made you choose her?

Next Wednesday I cut off telephone etc & begin. Yes I shall dedicate it to you if it's good enough. I am very nervous over it but once I've begun I expect it will seem easier. Since I started this letter I've been rung up 4 times – you see how one's poor brain isn't given a chance to bite on anything. Were it not for the Col I should retire to an orange grove to await the end (as my father always says).

I wrote about the eggs being all right. Letters to England have become very slow lately – I'll give this to my sister Woman[1] to post.

Don't you think *Operation Heartbreak* is the most awful name you ever heard? I call it Op: Sickmake – now you're *not* to repeat, Duff would kill me.

Col just back from Djibouti where his presence won an election for the Gaullists. He said 'we had a terrible list, headed by the Armenian in *Black Mischief*'. I haven't seen him yet & must now trot round all the neighbouring churches with candles for his safe return – I was in a fit of terror – aeroplanes.

You know Gladwyn Jebb is the love of my life – wonderful for me that he has made good. He is a very very nice person let me tell you. Duff loathes him so I rub in how famous he is with Duff's adored Americans. By the way do the Americans you meet start the chat with Tell me about yourself? I've had it twice lately.

Best love
     NR

Mrs Strong[2] used to say Gladwyn looks like a great cathedral – she was in love with him too.

---

[1] Hon. Pamela Mitford (1907–94). The least well-known Mitford sister. An expert on rural matters, especially rare breeds of poultry. Married to Derek Jackson, millionaire physicist and Grand National rider, 1936–51.

[2] Eugénie Sellers (1860–1943). An English classical archaeologist who lived in Rome. At the

beginning of the century she was obliged to lecture from behind a screen because her beauty
was so sublime that it distracted the students. Married the Orientalist Sandford Strong in 1892.

[postmarked 17 November 1950]   7 rue Monsieur, VII
[postcard]

Do write a line to Lady Honks – she is gravely unwell (not dangerously
ill) at 69 rue de Lille, Paris, 7ième.
    Col said to the Armenian 'do you remember Evelyn Waugh?' 'Yes,
a young writer, I went with him to Addis Ababa, awfully nice.' Coals
of fire?

10 December 1950   7 rue Monsieur, VII

Darling Evelyn
    I'm worried about my novel – I'm afraid it's dull. You see, no funny
props this time, no Uncle Matthew or Cedric, & I'm not sure I'm a
good enough writer to do without them. Still I must go droning on
& finish now, there are good things in it I believe & it's no duller than
many books one could name. I've done ½ the first draft, it has taken
me a month, so I guess the whole thing will be ready April or May
– I terribly wanted you to read the typescript (poor you but you did
say you would) but I guess from what Honks tells me that you (on a
racing camel) & your man Sykes (on a mule) will be gaping at the
Golden Gates round about then. Bother. But I also guess from the
evidence in my possession that you will pass this way?[1] Good.
    I saw Maurice who received so high an academic honour[2] that Col
was impressed. He made me laugh terribly with an imitation of Bootikins saying that Farouk is really Lorenzo de Medici. Some say Boots
is married to the Queen of the Seraglio – how can he face the shrieks?
    What did you think of *Op: Heartbreak*? Alone I say that it's very bad,
not one human soul agrees except my great new friend Prince Paul.[3]
    Oh dear, back to the dull book. When you are in the middle do
you sometimes ask yourself what novels are *for*? This is the best con-
structed of any of mine, a dreary virtue I must say.

    Love from
        NR

Oh! André Bay's book![4] Roger S[5] wants me to translate it what an
awful idea.
Col had a horrid motor accident & nearly lost an eye & was scalped.
All right now but it was *dreadful* at the time.

[1] Christopher Sykes and Evelyn were planning to pass through Paris on their way to the Near
East where they were collecting material for articles commissioned by *Life*.

[2] Maurice Bowra had been made Chevalier de la Légion d'Honneur for services to French literature.

[3] Prince Paul of Yugoslavia (1893–1976). Regent of his country, whose dealings with Hitler made him *persona non grata* in Britain.

[4] André Bay, *L'école des vacances* (1950). 'This is a book I recommend to anybody who is interested in the sick, hopeless despair, half physical weakness and half spiritual disgust, which holds so many French intellectuals in bondage.' NM, *Sunday Times*, 3 December 1950.

[5] Roger Senhouse (d.1970). Editor and bibliophile. As a young man, he was Lytton Strachey's last love. Co-founded the publishing company Secker & Warburg in 1936. Translated André Gide and Colette from the French.

[December 1950]

Darling Nancy

There is I believe no doubt that Boots has married the Sultan's Circassian slave.[1] The evidence is conclusive tho it is not known whether he gave her a ring. A Mrs [Edward] Hulton gave him a wedding breakfast. After the fifth course Boots had a seizure, fell off his chair frothing & gasping, was carried straight to a waiting van & whisked off to Tring where he spent the first fortnight of married life in a padded cell being starved and hosed and worse. He is now back in London enjoying a precarious tenancy of Sutro's flat in Curzon Street. Their total capital is £5 which Hulton gave him for tips at Tring and he kept, two sacks of sugar and a cottage in Kent which belongs to the sultana. Boots makes alternate proposals that she shall sell it & give him the money to go abroad with and that she shall build on a ball room. He writes daily to Lys begging to see her & saying how wretched he is, but she is adamant. This last titbit from Patrick Balfour who stayed here last week. The rest from my man Sykes and Mrs R. S. Churchill.

I long to read your novel & criticize tho what's the good you never take my advice. My dates are – leave London–Paris Jan 20th return probably via Paris about end of March. So if I can be any use, tell me. I don't think it would be advisable to risk your manuscript in the souks of Aleppo. I think you ought to devise *some* funny characters. You still have the delicious gift of seeing people as funny which I lost somewhere in the highlands of Scotland circa 1943.

Very sorry about Col. being scalped & blinded. Was it Gen. Moch?[2]

What are you plans for the next war? Do come here only please don't be patriotic again.

Sad about Duke of Devonshire.[3] They might have known it was madness to let him chop wood until the death duties were safe. To read the obituaries in *The Times* you would think that a composite character part Great Duke of Wellington, part Saintsbury, part Talleyrand, part Bron Lucas,[4] had left us, instead of that testy alcoholic we knew.

Randolph is in a bad way.

Now I will say happy happy Christmas. No presents for anyone this year on account of the handsome *Helena*s I gave quite lately. Do you think that will wash?

You spoiled all my efforts to cheer Honks by telling her you instigated them [. . .]

[incomplete]

[1] Barbara Skelton and Cyril Connolly were married in London on 5 October 1950.
[2] Jules Moch (1893–1985). Minister of the Interior responsible for breaking Communist-led strikes.
[3] The 10th Duke had died suddenly, at the age of 55.
[4] 8th Baron Lucas (1876–1916). A cousin of Laura Waugh who made a heroic flight over the German lines, from which he never returned.

15 December 1950   7 rue Monsieur, VII

Darling Evelyn

Honks has become a trouble maker of late – I've noticed it more than once. She said to me 'did you tell Evelyn I was ill?' 'Yes I think so –' this is now construed as having urged you to write to her. I am very cross. Anyway she was deeply pleased by your letter which lay on her bed 3 days running I noticed.

I am up again about the book & think it wonderful. When you say I never take your advice it's because you've only ever read them in proof when one can't alter – if you could endure the hell of typescript I promise to be obedient. I'm now in a worry over libel – filth marine[1] & Boots. Boots is called the Captain & he & all those girls (the Crew) run a highbrow theatre for plays written mostly by Indians. There is a description of a party after the 1st night of *Phèdre* in modern dress (Aricie is a dancing boy called Hara-See) which is I think not bad. The Crew, in mutinous mood, sit combing their hair over their faces while the Captain makes a pass at rich Ethel the bourgeoise heroine.

Anyway March will be just the thing, or if not ready then perhaps I could see you at Stinkers when it is.

The war. My inclination would be to stay here. To get on the roads with all the rastaquouères,[2] visiting Americans & collaborators would be a perfect nightmare & probably end in death anyway. But if I stay my only means of earning a livelihood would be by doing pro Russian propaganda & we know what happens to people who do that. The Col is staying. He says he can't incite others to resist & then run away himself. I would gladly join a maquis except I'd be such a nuisance to them a perfectly useless mouth to feed. The awful thing about me is all I'm good for is sitting up in bed writing what Cyril calls light novels like well grilled little cutlets (I don't grudge you your success any more than I would grudge the success of a restaurant which served well grilled little cutlets he said).

I've been reading *Helena* to Col & he loved it & I loved it more than before. Then he cheated & finished it on his own – I was very disappointed. He is better though still far from well.

Then will you both lunch with me 21st? How I long to see you.

I haven't got a present for Harriet or anybody else this year because no time for shopping. But I'll send her one via you in March. So long since I saw her I don't feel I know her tastes. Mrs Hammersley writes that she is off to a retreat where she expects to see Laura.

Best love, see you soon
   NR

---

[1] Nancy had painted a recognisable portrait of Louise de Vilmorin as the seductive mistress, Albertine Marel-Desboulles, in *The Blessing*.
[2] Flashy foreigners.

29 December 1950   7 rue Monsieur, VII

Darling Evelyn

I've written to your employee[1] to find out what form of collation I can offer & when. There is a dear fellow called Darsie Gillie,[2] who lives in a donnish room on the Ile St Louis & collects children's books & knows ALL about France (*Manchester Guardian*'s correspondent); he longs to see you, you were at school together. Perhaps that had better be in March. I think I know you'd love him.

Christmas cards are a nightmare to me, all understamped so I've never paid less than 1/- each. Like you, I have dozens from totally unknown people, in some cases bearing photographs of their totally unknown faces & those of their T.U. children to boot. But I forget people very soon so this means nothing & I can see from the fervid messages that once we have been very intimate.

Yes the Col agrees about *Helena* being a G W of A. He *has* murmured the word *Salammbô*[3] – I don't know if you mind that or not but I suppose it's inevitable & he is a great admirer of the work.

The whole Elwes family lunched here. I haven't seen Simon since his illness & was very sorry to find him so changed. The wicked Dominick is of course Prod in person, the other boys are ugly & deadly. Latest news of Prod is he went to Sicily & made the peasants dig channels for the lava as a result of which 3 extra villages were destroyed & he was obliged to flee by night. Are you shrieking?

Did you read Turnell, French novel?[4] It put me off writing my book for a week.

Fancy, an actress from the Comédie française is reading my book (*P of L*) on the wireless every evening. It began last night & they

introduced it, saying Mme Mitford est la plus Parisienne des Anglaises.
I *was* pleased.

> Fond love
> NR

[1] Christopher Sykes was making the practical arrangements for his and Evelyn's visit to the Holy Land.
[2] Darsie Gillie (1903–72). Nonconformist journalist on the *Morning Post* and briefly on *The Times* before joining the *Manchester Guardian* as Paris correspondent immediately after the war, a post he held for more than 20 years. He was educated at Rugby and Balliol.
[3] Gustave Flaubert's romantic novel (1862) set in ancient Carthage.
[4] Martin Turnell, *The Novel in France* (1950).

6 January [1951]   Piers Court
                                                    Stinchcombe
Dearest Nancy
   No I don't remember the old school chum you mention. If he is a
genuine Lancing boy he has a hot potato in the mouth. We all caught it
from imitation of a master called Roxburgh whom we greatly revered.
Driberg exemplifies it in a marked degree. Pretty little Ali Forbes
caught it at Stowe where Mr Roxburgh migrated. Anyway, genuine
or spurious, he would be a great pleasure to me. I haven't many
admirers left nowadays. Sykes tells me he has engaged a motor car in
which he proposes to drive me about Paris surveying the habits of the
people between the train from London & the train to Rome. Could
we not pick you up & take you to tea with this decent sounding fellow?
   I have felt so very feeble in recent weeks that at last I called in a
doctor who took my blood-pressure & pronounced it the lowest ever
recorded – in fact the pressure of a 6 months foetus. In an access of
sudden hope I said: 'Does that mean I shall die quite soon.' 'No. It
means you will live absolutely for ever in deeper & deeper melancholy.'
   The great news of the New Year is, of course, Maurice's elevation
to the Equestrian Order.[1] We are buying him a horse & spurs. As you
would expect he takes the subject with deadly seriousness. 'Many of
my pupils are now in the key positions. No doubt they wished to show
their loyalty. I prefer knighthood to the O.M.'
   It is really very odd as he has done nothing to deserve it except be
head of the worst College at Oxford and publish a few books no one
has ever read. My own explanation is that it was part of a secret treaty
made in Washington between Mr Attlee & Judge Frankfurter[2] but as
you don't know the American scene you won't see the point of that.
Speculation is rife. Other plausible explanations (1) His behaviour in
1926 at the General Strike (which gained Lindsay[3] of Balliol a peerage)
(2) His early tussles with Elizabeth Harman[4] (3) Parties for 3 a little
later with Betjeman & Mr Gaitskell[5] (4) a whipping by Lord Jowitt in
the Beefsteak lavatory.

Anyway he takes mockery in poor part.

Ann Rothermere, silly goose, has taken up the Concubine[6] and asked eight people to meet her at cocktails twenty two of whom came.

Did you hear about Philip Hardwicke[7] & Philip Dunne's opening meet? These two buffoons are Joint Masters of a pack of hounds[8] in the pansy country, insist on hunting the hounds themselves & quarrel of course furiously. The opening meet was at their best subscriber's house, they all sat about having drinks & wrangling who was going to hunt until P. Hardwicke claimed precedence from rank & decided to move off. No hound was in sight. Tremendous trumpetings & gallopings about, then sinister sounds from the farm quarters where they were at length found in the pig sty devouring a sow with all her litter.

Best love
Evelyn

[1] Maurice Bowra had been given a knighthood.
[2] Felix Frankfurter (1882–1965). Liberal judge of Supreme Court of the United States 1939–62, famous for his involvement in labour legislation, civil liberties and social welfare.
[3] A. D. Lindsay (1879–1952). Master of Balliol 1924–49. In 1926 he collected signatures to try to persuade the government to negotiate with strikers. Created life peer in 1945.
[4] Later Lady Longford. Bowra had proposed to her in 1929 and was turned down.
[5] Hugh Gaitskell (1906–63). Chancellor of the Exchequer 1950–51, leader of the Labour Party from 1955. 'He skilfully sought out some of the best-looking girls in the women's colleges and liked to dance with them, but he was equally at home in male society.' Maurice Bowra, *Memories* (Weidenfeld & Nicolson, 1966), p. 177.
[6] Barbara Connolly.
[7] 9th Earl of Hardwicke (1906–74).
[8] The Tedworth Hunt.

10 January 1951   7 rue Monsieur, VII

Darling Evelyn

I wrote to your employee for the time table of your visit – no reply. This doesn't seem right to me & one might ask what is he paid for?

I take it from your letter that you will arrive on Golden Arrow (about 5.30) & leave again at about 9? On Sunday 21st? This state drive planned by your chef de protocol seems to me doomed to failure. My calendar tells me the sun sets at 5.27 on that day – unless he has arranged for a torch light procession your admirers will hardly be able to see him whom they wish to salute, while the many noble monuments of this town will likewise be invisible to you.

May I suggest that you should come straight here & have a glass of wine with dear Mr Gillie (plum, just as you say) & perhaps the Col & Honks?

But I am in bad with Honks. Your friend Marie-Laure [de Noailles] is giving a ball, Fête de Village is the theme, & Honks wanted me to go as a tall ridiculous Englishwoman, with everything just wrong, in a group of other T.R. Englishwomen including Juliet [Duff]. Well I said it's what I spend my whole life avoiding & I *won't*. So I'm going with the village school as the school negress (not as ridiculous as it sounds. I shall be easily the youngest as I always am at parties here).

I've done the 1st draft of the book & have put it by for a week or 2 before starting to re write which is the part I enjoy. So I'm feeling tremendously cheerful. Am I allowed to say that 1950 was a heavenly year – well Holy, anyway.

The doctors always say that about low b.p. Mine is the lowest for my age anyone has ever had – & I faint in the morning continually & feel always tired & cold. But it shouldn't affect your spirits. Do you sleep with only one flat pillow like me? Anyway with any luck we shan't have strokes & lie for years at everybody's mercy like Mme de Chambrun whose husband *will* read her his latest essay in spite of two winks meaning no. 'My dear' said their old sister in law Dr Longworth de Chambrun the expert on Shakespeare, when telling me this 'he is boring her to death.'

I've just had the glittering news that I'm to pay taxes *here* & *not* in England. As they let writers off 40 p.c. for expenses before taking anything this seems like heaven to me.

Did you see *Time & Tide* with Betje's snakes & ladders?[1] I've been shrieking the whole morning over it.

I love Maurice being a Kt – didn't know about it, the Fr papers never said. Also, by living here, I've missed the full glory of the Stone[2] which must be bliss. Figaro says the English are forbidden to make jokes about it but that must be a bit of cattiness. I hear via Debo that the King is livid. To go back to Maurice I've never quite understood why he is a *Chevalier* of the Légion d'Honneur – he is evidently one of those people on whom honours settle by themselves. Anyway I'm all for it, I love old Maurice.

I must now go out shopping for the ball we are all in a state of ferment over it you can imagine – wonderful copy as I have just such a ball in my book.

Fondest love
    NR

Be a duck, re read the 1st page of this endless letter & tell me if you agree to its terms.

[1] A literary game devised by John Betjeman and illustrated by Osbert Lancaster. The aim was to get a book accepted among the '100 Best Books' exhibition at the Festival of Britain. Ladders included: 'Poem in school mag' and 'Meets Spender, Isherwood and Auden'; snakes included: 'Confuses Kafka with Kierkegaard'. *Time and Tide*, 2 December 1950.
[2] The Stone of Scone had been stolen by Scottish Nationalists from underneath the coronation chair in Westminster Abbey.

[January 1951]   [Rome]

Darling Nancy

What a lovely party you gave for Christopher & me. It was such a treat and stimulus to see you so elegant & surrounded by elegance. The only regret that I saw *you* so little. Also I had a horrible feeling that Miss Canavaggia[1] had been with you since four & would stay till ten. But it was a lovely party for us. Thank you, thank you.

Rome is lovely as always & our host & hostess John Russells[2] monuments of kindness. Christopher is being very pious but slightly inattentive in his humbler duties.

I will send you postcards from various interesting spots & shall pass through Paris I expect certainly in early March. I will telegraph from Athens or somewhere like that to tell you.

I have just been given a letter written by Honks on April 25th last year that wld have made all well between us. It came to Embassy at Rome a day or two after I left it. I gave a complete list of addresses to everyone from the Ambassador to the undergardener & no one ever thought of forwarding it. That is what our foreign service is like. It just happened that I dined there & they said 'Oh by the way there is a letter for you lying about somewhere.'

It was nice to see Colonel looking so well after his tribulations.

Love from
    Evelyn

[1] Maria Canavaggia translated *Black Mischief*, *A Handful of Dust* and *Helena* into French.
[2] John Russell (1914-84). Diplomat, first secretary at Rome 1951-3. Married Aliki Weiller in 1945. Knighted in 1965.

12 March 1951   7 rue Monsieur, VII

Darling Evelyn

The heroine's white satin egg reposes in safety with the confidante's white linen one.[1] I'm delighted that you may come with Laura what a treat for me if so. The Col, to whom I wired, rang you up 3 times at Travellers but no luck but I suppose you weren't there more than a day or so. I *was* disappointed to miss you.

My book is being typed. Shall I have an uncorrected copy sent straight to you? Only dearest dear no use telling me to put it in a drawer & re write it in a year's time. I haven't the force of character to do so though I will make any minor alterations you may be good enough to propose. You must remember the copy will anyhow require a good deal of correcting – I didn't have quite enough time for that with the MS & had to leave it as I can't bring myself to post them ever! I do so long to know what you think of it. I think the best so far, but of course one always does with the last effort.

I am so happy to be back it's like being in heaven. But I loved the I of W[2] & the extraordinary *Cranford* life there. The doctor & his wife, who are sweet, were raving about *Helena*. *I* always like to hear of that sort of public, I expect you rather despise it. The post master *himself* arrived with your telegram saying 'Mr Evelyn Waugh is in Paris' – Mrs Hammersley was so furious (at him having read it I suppose or because it was cheek?) but I roared. She took me to the local bridge club & I heard '& of course when in London I went to Nancy Mitford's naughty thing' – wasn't it lovely for me.

I got free specs from the health scheme in 3 days so was glad to see how well that works – blond tortoiseshell.

Oh I am happy to be back though!

Much love
NR

I'll have it sent unless you say no but oh dear I rather dread your comments, sure to be a douche of cold water.

[1] The nest-egg of royalties that Nancy held for Evelyn in Paris. Her reference is from Sheridan's *The Critic* where the heroine goes mad in white satin with flowers in her hair, while the confidante goes mad in white linen with straw in hers.
[2] Nancy had been staying with Violet Hammersley at Totland Bay on the Isle of Wight.

22 March 1951   7 rue Monsieur, VII

Darling Evelyn
You will receive *The Blessing* about Easter Tues: I should think. If you are really kind enough to make corrections I must have the copy here to correct mine with – it is the devil posting such things so I suggest that you'd better let Heywood do so unless you have some slave who does these things for you. The great thing is *not* to register, if one does the security have to read & photograph etc every page & then never send it on. I have experience of this. The best would be if somebody could bring it. When do you & Laura come? Flags are already (more flags) out.

L'Amour dans un climat froid is out & has had a long deeply serious criticism from Robert Kemp the best critic here. He says almost exactly all that you said & also that tout cela n'aboutit à rien,[1] but the words 'grand talent' do sugar the pill. Of course in French quite half the jokes are missed so it's rather wonderful if they like my writing at all. *P of L* has sold nearly 10 000.

Stock tell me that *Helena* will come out in Sept, they are in great despair over paper.

The Col is 50 & *minds*. I've never minded being any of the terrible ages that have overtaken me so don't quite understand, but I see he can hardly bear it, poor Col.

Harriet does sound sweet, but the backwardness of all modern children is rather alarming to me because I fear it means that they don't want to be able to read. I remember longing to so passionately because of escaping from my sad life & I know I was reading *Ivanhoe* on my 6th birthday because our present Nan came on that day & found me doing so. And it's one of the few books I still remember every word of.

Since I began this letter I've spoken to Col Georgia [Sitwell] Diana (Mosley) & Momo, so you do see why one *can't* work in Paris.

Best love
     NR

[1] This all adds up to nothing.

25 March [1951]   Piers Court
                                                            Stinchcombe
Dearest Nancy

The Blessing is admirable, deliciously funny, consistent & complete; by far the best of your writings; I do congratulate you with all my heart & thank you for the dedication.

The children's ball and the visit to Eton are particularly brilliant passages. I didn't at first see the point of the burglar incident but that became clear at the end. I confess I wished the child to be victorious and should have liked the happy end to be the father's imprisonment but I see that something softer was necessary for the book's consistency. The first act of betrayal, when the father comes to England to fetch the boy, is brilliantly executed. Nanny throughout is first class – never overdone. The whole sustained mood of levity is beyond praise.

Now for one or two criticisms. The Captain doesn't ring true to me. Ed Stanley & Boots don't mix. The harem is oriental and can only be maintained by flabby, dependent men. Not brisk men of action. The crew is wonderfully described. Could you not keep them just as they are but soften & fatten the Captain? And I think it is a pity to bring in *Little Lord Fauntleroy* in the oven. It is plain to the sharp reader that that is the plot. You might make it a little more obvious for the less sharp by making him suggest lace collar & velvet suit as the costume. But leave the actual name of the book to the last line of the chapter.

2) Dexter[1] is so richly funny as he stands that it seems a pity to make him a sham. Couldn't he be arrested for homosexuality or embezzlement of Marshall Aid?

3) Captain again. Should he not alienate Sigismond's affection by something more than a momentary fit of bad temper? The exposure of Hughie at Eton exposed a real awfulness in his character. Couldn't

you strike deeper into Ed Spain & make Sigismond detect a real
secondrateness?

4) The grammar is *much* better. 'Nobody' is singular. p. 328 l.45.

p 307 l.17. I don't like 'onto', 'on' or 'by'. Or expand 'entering . . .
found themselves on'.

p 178 l.8. omit 'in'.

Also somewhere early on, I can't find the place, you say *in propria
persona* that the baby looked 'terribly sweet'. That might be changed.
But these are niggling little complaints just put in to show I've read
every word with rapt attention.

The punctuation & misprints you will see for yourself. Several
French proper names have gone wrong in the typing. I will return the
MS. by ordinary post. It is not marked because there was nothing to
mark except what I have mentioned above. It is a most accomplished
work. But do please think a bit about Capt. & Dexter.

I notice that you have no idea of the privations of modern English
life. It shows how your friends love & fear you that they make a show
for your rare visits. In fact we are perishing with malnutrition &
boredom.

Oh by the way Bollinger even non-vintage is a good wine. I think
you should substitute Ayala or Lanson.

More congratulations. And more deep loving thanks for the dedication. I am immensely proud of it & of you.

Love
    Evelyn

[1] Hexter Dexter, the fatuous and self-important American in *The Blessing*.

28 March 1951   7 rue Monsieur, VII

Darling Evelyn

It was so faithful of you to telegraph I was on hot bricks. Thought
perhaps it is all a bit *dull* – I can see that Col does. But of course
Nanny & child mean o to him as a start. Hamish Hamilton takes your
view.

Fauntleroy. Of course, it began by being as you say, left to reader.
But Mrs Hammersley didn't twig *at all* so I thought I must underline.
Shall I put it back?

H.H. says the telephone conversation won't do – what do you think?
He says no child could. Col agrees.

Dexter simply cowardice, to save my bacon with the (after all very
friendly) Americans here, & Capt the same – I don't want to hurt old
Boots's feelings whom I love. He's really ½ Boots ½ Lehmann[1] more
than Ed.

Such a vile headache from correcting I must stop.

Fond love thank you thank you
    NR

P.S. Mauriac has received a telegram:
    'Pouvez faire la noce – l'enfer n'existe pas – prévenez Claudel
    A. Gide'[2]
Poor Claudel, 83, a bit late!!

[1] John Lehmann (1907–87). Writer, publisher and poet. Editor of the *London Magazine* 1951–61.
[2] 'You can live it up – hell does not exist – tell Claudel.' The joke was inspired by François Mauriac's obituary of Gide in which he wrote: 'If what we Christians believe is true, today Gide knows what we all will soon know. What does he know? What does he see?'

28 March 1951   7 rue Monsieur, VII

Darling Evelyn

I expect I wrote a very dull letter in answer to yours – I had a headache from correcting the many bad mistakes of the typescript (my fault, it's a terrible MS) & putting in countless corrections of the Col on tiny points to do with life here.

Now I've re read with yr letter in view. *Captain*. Except for appearance – & I can't decently give him 18 stone & a syphilitic (hereditary) nose – he is all you say – i.e. lazy & podgy & run to seed. Must he be physically fat as well? Sigi is *entirely* governed by self interest throughout, & the words which sealed the Capt's downfall were Run along to Nanny. In Hughie's case it was the terrible discomforts of Eton & nothing to do with Hughie himself which turned Sigi against him.

Dexter. Can't decide. Momo is reading it now & I'll see what she says. Col thinks he *should* go to Moscow. I rather love the jokes 'Dexter is worth 10 atom bombs' & so on. But I see what you mean.

Fauntleroy. They must leave some indication that they have deserted & not just gone out. I've taken out the sentences which baldly say it was the same plot, but I find the book in the oven not a bad device –??

I see on re reading that Jim Mucha & all that are a terrible crib on Scottie Wilson in *The Loved One* – do you mind? Hadn't occurred to me. Mrs Hammersley had hundreds of *New Writing* where I found them, it was quite unconscious. I think all my jokes come out of your books as they are the only ones I read.

Diana [Mosley], mother of 4 boys, thinks a little boy of 9 *could* imitate his mother's voice on the telephone – what do you say? It is Hamilton's only objection.

I'm *so happy* you like it. Col tells me it is slow – but he is a king tease & he tells others that it's wonderful.

When do you come? I do so long for you. I feel terribly unwell, I think it's only the cold, but it may be a decline. I've found such a lovely claret at my grocer I'm laying some in for when you're here. It's called Belgrave have you ever heard of it?

I find the words Brighton College have hurt the Col's feelings (he was there the dear darling) can you tell me the name of some equivalent school? Cranleigh?

Thank you *so* much for everything.

Love
    NR

Momo agrees with you about Dexter & I'm beginning to see you're right.

31 March [1951]   Piers Court
                                                       Stinchcombe
Darling Nancy

Now none of this. No complaints about headaches. Revision is just as important as any other part of writing and must be done con amore.

I don't think H. Hamilton is right about Sigismond's telephone technique. The child constantly varies in age from 5 to 25 and that is a fantasy which the intelligent reader will accept. (It is much odder that he should drive motor cars at high speed.) But I think it might be tactful to insinuate somewhere a reference to his powers of mimicry.

Dexter. Funk is a bad counsellor in art. The audacity always. But I understand your fears.

Capt. No, he won't do as he stands. That breezy, pushful fellow would have had no reluctance in embracing his heiress. Besides he is common and you aren't at your best dealing with common people. If you won't fatten & soften him because of your tenderness towards S. Boots (who I think since his marriage deserves no consideration) you should try him as languid & feeble – a sort of David-Cecil–Eddy-West. As he stands he won't wash. Only feeble men inspire that sort of Crew worship.

Fauntleroy. If people are so dull they must just lose a joke. Make Capt, when he is talking about the scenery, say 'Dress him in a velvet suit with a lace collar.' Even, if you must: 'I am sure I have seen a period drawing of something of the sort somewhere.'

You must work hard at this revision despite headaches.

Love
    E

1 April 1951   7 rue Monsieur, VII

Darling Evelyn

Just a word to say I've re written *Fauntleroy* & it's much better now.
But Hamilton said leave Dexter (to go to Moscow) & Col says it
strongly & Momo wavers but thinks on the whole perhaps better.
Hamilton also says if Capt gets any more like Bootikins we may find
ourselves had up for libel –

When you come remind me to tell you about Jonathan's 21 birthday
party it's a saga to end all sagas.

I didn't thank you enough for the trouble you have taken, I do so
now.

When do you come?

Love
  NR

2 April 1951   7 rue Monsieur, VII

Darling Evelyn

I *don't know why* you have this idea of the Captain. He is flabby to
the core. What about the guilty sun bath while the matinée is on, &
leaving everything to the Crew, who choose *and* produce the plays *and*
see to the financial side *and* run his house (he can't even get his own
breakfast when they go). He is described as a charming lazy intellectual
& doesn't seem to me to belie that in any way. His inability to make
love to Grace is another form of flabbiness. Why do you say breezy
& pushful? Truly I think you are wrong. The thing is I entirely agree
with you about what he ought to be like, but it seems to me he *is* like
it – ?

Debo could drive a car at 9, I well remember her doing so. Somebody had to work the clutch for her. I have re done *Fauntleroy* & it's
ever so much better – also the telephone conversation, which isn't
vital to the story. How awful about Sigi being 25, I had so congratulated
myself on his development between a backward 6 & a forward 9. Of
course French children are different – somebody once said to me a
French boy of 14 has a heavy moustache, 2 mistresses & a hoop!

Heywood writes that Boots' wife marks him for tidiness, lovingness
etc & if less than $^6/_{10}$ she turns him into Shepherd Market where he
spends the night. He says isn't it like the *Blue Angel* –!!

Please don't think I've taken no trouble over revising – there are
corrections on every page of the typescript & I had done the original
MS over & over again – I re-wrote the whole thing twice. People
always think I dash off my books with no real work, but it is not so,
I very honestly do my *best*. I've *pored* over the Capt ever since your

letter, but truly, except for his appearance, I don't see what you mean or that he is ever brisk or executive in the least.

Dexter is really taken from Hiss[1] & many of the things he says I copied straight word for word out of the trial. After all Dexter is born in America & is an American communist, not a Russian dressed up, which would be utterly false. As it is it seems to me to hold water.

I have to defend myself against the Col too. He says no father would leave his child up on that horse. I say the child is in *no* danger, since children have no fear of height, & it is far more amusing if he is there on his own. Col also doubtful about the heartless treatment of the children at the ball. But he admits (with guilty giggle) that Ch-Ed is to the life.

Dearest Evelyn now *please* don't be too governessy & say I take no trouble because it hurts my feelings.

Love from
    NR

Letters here are 4d now & understamped ones get delayed which is why I mention it, not only meanness –

[1] In January 1950, Alger Hiss had been found guilty of perjury in concealing his membership of the Communist Party.

8 April [1951]   Piers Court
                                                  Stinchcombe
Darling Nancy

Oh dear how awful about the stamps. My man didn't know. He does now. But what I must have cost you in the past. I *am* sorry. How odd the post office is. Why is it more expensive to write to Paris than San Francisco?

I am afraid I must have written far more sharply than I meant. It was your saying you had a headache from correcting & I feared you would think only of French accents & neglect the plot. Of course you are the final & only judge about that. And it's *excellent* as it stands. And it is just officiousness & bossiness that prompts half the suggestions. Writers are the worst advisers because they can't help thinking how they would have written it themselves. Constant readers are the thing. I met Pam Berry who was full of admiration but also full of keys to explain who everyone was, which I always find an infuriating sort of appreciation, don't you?

Mrs Friese-Greene is mad to read it and as you suggested sending it to Heywood Hill as one way of disposal I shall do that unless I get a cable saying Send it Paris at once. You should have seen the genuine schoolgirl delight on *every* face (even Corporal's) when I brought them the news that you had written a masterpiece. Cyril was less pleased.

'Yes,' he said, 'Yes. She keeps at it. I suppose she is constantly terrified by the thought of poverty in old age.' Goodness he is terrified and rightly so by poverty in middle age. He is in great troubles. Absolutely hates his wife whom he has taken to live at Sussex Place (telephone cut off for non payment & water too by the look of him) with Toynbee,[1] whom he absolutely hates because he has a steady job, and Toynbee's new wife – a juvenile American typist – and Mr Somebody[2] who is the broken hearted last husband of Blue Feet. Mr Hulton sent him first to Tring and then to the Scilly Islands & he is being sued by the Ministry of Health for not sticking stamps on his insurance card and he thinks he is being guided by Fate to a symbolic suicide. I said how d'you mean symbolic but he couldn't explain. Altogether in poor shape. Lys has been adopted by Alice Obolensky and given a suite at the St Regis (2nd best hotel in New York). That makes it much worse for him.

Everyone I met in London was in debt & despair & either much too fat or much too thin. Except I must say Pam [Berry] who is a sort of booster for paganism & Pam Churchill who is a very tasty morsel.

Poor Randolph is in hospital again with his little unhealed wound. No sign of June at the bedside. His legal & financial difficulties are huge. I must say I lead an awfully dull life here but when I see the alternative I am consoled.

Boots said: 'I am going to become a waiter at a fashionable restaurant so as to humiliate & reproach my friends for their ingratitude.' He saw a worried look, I suppose on my face & said: 'Ah, I see now I have touched even your cold heart.' So I said: 'Well no Cyril it isn't quite that. I was thinking of your finger-nails in the soup.'

Frank Pakenham asked me for the night to his new country home in the suburbs. He sent a great government car for me & I settled down to a comfortable drive when what should happen but I was deposited at Cannon Street Station to queue for a one class train.

Love from
E

[1] Philip Toynbee (1916–81). Novelist and critic. On the staff of the *Observer* from 1959. Married to Anne Powell 1939–50 and to Frances Smith in 1950.
[2] Robert Kee (1919–). Writer and broadcaster. Author of *The Impossible Shore* (1949), *Ireland: A History* (1981) and *The Laurel and the Ivy: The Story of Parnell* (1993). Married to Janetta (Blue Feet) Woolley 1948–50.

10 April 1951   7 rue Monsieur, VII

Darling Evelyn
    Oh do send your copy to Heywood – all the pros are falling over themselves for the only existing ones – Peters & Co I mean. I am

paralyzed about sending to America, can't do up parcels you see & don't want to send an uncorrected copy.

Does Cyril think we ought all to keep him? Why? I wouldn't mind actually, only if I send him a present he'll think it's to make up for the Captain so I can't very well – though, like Sheridan, 'how will he take it?' the answer would surely be 'in cash'.

I always feel so deeply sorry for writers who can't write, specially when they are as good as Boots. He's only too right, I am terrified of a penniless old age, but it's not that which drives me to the page, & money & writing are curiously divorced from each other in my mind. The money always feels like having won in a lottery when it comes.

Now the book has gone I have my worries, one of which is how not to go to various friends for the night. More & more I loathe to sleep out of my own bed, but the owners of country houses have only one idea which is to fill them with all the bores in Paris plus me. There, I'm being ungrateful.

Nobody knows about stamps here. All diaries of 1951 *and* the post office books of stamps say 3d & the rise got no publicity. At Christmas-card-time I used to pay about 5/- a day for little pictures of robins sent to reward me for inviting people to luncheon –! The really poor English here can talk of o else.

Yes I hate the people who apply a key to one's book. The fact is, the characters start (like S. African wines port-type–claret-type) by being Duff-type or Lulu-type, & then assume a life of their own in one's mind & it's a great bore when people begin to identify them. I *do so* wonder what the French will make of it. No English person has ever attempted such a thing since Henry James I suppose – & he is so much more American than English I always think. Maurice Baring[1] did it in Rome – as you know he is almost my favourite writer. (Oh how I shrieked, by the way, at blissful Sir Max's 'à la manière de' about him.[2]) I've sent it off to André Bay & await the verdict impatiently.

When do you come? It's piercingly cold here now, made for you. I do so wish you'd come for a good long visit sometime – I always feel really you would adore the French if you gave them a chance, but that you're in too much of a rush each time to see the point.

Have you read the new Koestler?[3] That's about Paris now – the characters live in bars & cheap hotels & talk endlessly about why they stopped being Communists. But it's pretty good & the first half is un-put-downable – et puis ça traine en longueur[4] in my opinion. Which this letter seems to be doing.

Best love – come soon.
      NR

P.S. Do you admit that when I came to live here you said I would never write another book that was any good? And that, on the contrary,

I have improved? By the way I really did work over the book you gave me, *King's English*.

[1] Hon. Maurice Baring (1874–1945). Prolific and successful novelist who wrote about Roman society in *Cat's Cradle* (1925) and *Comfortless Memory* (1928).
[2] Max Beerbohm wrote several parodies of Henry James, in particular 'A Mote in the Middle Distance' (1912) and 'The Guerdon' (1916).
[3] Arthur Koestler, *The Age of Longing* (1951).
[4] And then it drags on.

20 April 1951   7 rue Monsieur, VII

Darling Evelyn

Stock are sending you 2 books of the series in which they plan to include *Helena* (they say the translation is masterly). Now as you will see these books each have a preface by an eminent Frog writer, & they would like this for *Helena*. But I said (perhaps too officiously) hold on before you ask anybody & let me find out if Evelyn approves of the idea. It would of course be a first class Catholic writer or nobody. If you hate the idea they will abandon it, but as you know it is very usual here, & a help to a foreign book I believe. I don't know why they can't write to you themselves about it except that you have so put the fear of God into them that their nerveless fingers drop the pen when they begin a letter to you.

A letter from Stephen Tennant saying 'Do go & see General Eisenhower, Nancy. I hear he is such an interesting man & paints rather well.'

So *Helena* will come out in the autumn & they predict a success for her. French publishing is in a very tricky way just now as the books are more & more expensive & the public less & less rich.

Best love from
          Nancy

I've just received your postcard.[1] I went through every possibility before sinking into the I of Wight – but the reason for that was that really I get rather low if I have all my meals alone & also hotels in winter are truly sad.

I would like to be able to say Versailles. The town so beautiful, the walks in the Park which make you *love* Louis XIV & Le Notre, & the endless things to see in the Château itself. Then it would be so agreeable to have you near & see you once a week. BUT I have never yet had a good meal at Versailles. The Trianon Palace, where you would stay, is like a Ritz & has only adequate Ritz food, & I don't know of one good restaurant in the whole town.

Rambouillet horrible. Chantilly very possible – one or 2 *excellent* restaurants, lovely town, lovely museum. Diana is not a great respecter of work, but seems to be there less & less. You could swim in a sort of tepid Coca Cola in her garden.

Then there is the Loire district. I was very much recommended an hotel at Chambord by my darling Marie-Louise [Bousquet] who said all the things you ask for – i.e. little-town life going on, forest, masses of sight seeing to hand if you want it. But Touraine gets very hot & stuffy in the summer, I warn you.

Colonel says Vézelay, but he is not reliable about comfort. He says there are such wonderful churches & abbeys all around – & as it's in Burgundy I guess the food would be all right.

I know you don't like the heat so Aix must be ruled out. What about Nancy? I have a great friend nearby in one of the most beautiful châteaux of France who would put himself out I know. Food excellent, architecture smashing – I've never been there but feel I know all this. Have you a *Guide Michelin*? Otherwise I'll get one & look out the hotels for you.

I must say I incline to Chantilly. But if you come with Laura & motor could you not look round for 10 days or so – you might find something you liked tremendously, but it's as well to try out a place before deciding.

Fontainebleau is lovely too & there is a very good hotel I know, but has it been spoilt by Monty & Co?[2] Very likely. (Your friend Marie-Laure [de Noailles] has a wonderful house there, Mme de Pompadour's.)

I fear the million English we are promised for this summer will be a pest wherever you go – though as you live surrounded by 40 million of them you may not mind so much.

I have always found that one's romantic ideas about provincial hotels here get a rude shock whenever one stays in them. They are too often in some awful High Street not unlike a bit of Reading, hideous, gloomy, & food far from wonderful. I nearly went to the Pont de Gard where it seems there is a truly charming inn with one room which has a big balcony looking out at the Pont itself – but too hot for you I feel sure. The Bordeaux district I happen to hate, but many people like it, & the best restaurant in France is in Bordeaux as you know.

There – I've shot my bolt. Diana Coo might be more use to you, she is such a motor-er. They come back from film festival & Ed [Stanley]'s wedding tomorrow. I get more & more restless in her company owing to her vitriolic hatred of & lack of comprehension of the French. I despise people who live here to escape taxes & who hate the French – the Windsors are another case.

Best love – longing to see you.
   NR

[1] Evelyn had asked Nancy if she would recommend an hotel where he could work on his next novel, *Men at Arms* (1952).
[2] Field Marshal Viscount Montgomery of Alamein (1887–1976). The NATO Deputy Supreme Commander of the Allied Forces in Europe had his Headquarters at Fontainebleau.

8 May [1951]   Piers Court
                                                         Stinchcombe

Dearest Nancy

Thank you with all my heart for your most valuable letter of advice about my place of retreat. It was wonderfully kind of you to go to all that trouble. I have made no plans yet as the house has been full of family visitors & children on holiday and I have promised to insult some writers on the BBC[1] shortly and the Bishop is making a tour of this part of his diocese and I have to feed the greedy brute, but I think that before the end of the month Laura & I will bring our battered old motor car to Calais, drive as near Paris as she dares, come in by train, hoping to embrace you & collect egg unbroken by Prod then drive slowly to Monte Carlo & slowly back until I find a suitable place where she will leave me and return alone. I suppose you wouldn't care to join any of the tour?

My blood pressure is down again – 117. Not alarming but depressing. We keep killing sheep and I gorge fat mutton to keep strong.

Your great friend Spender has written a very shaming autobiography.[2] All the Americans over for the Festival of Britain are mad about your *Little Nut* [sic] and say what a vital theatre we have compared with Broadway.

Have you seen the list of '100 best modern authors' made for the Festival. The promoters have succeeded in giving maximum offence to all concerned & not concerned.

I am frightfully poor – right back to Canonbury Square[3] standards. You can't imagine what it costs to send a girl to school nowadays – more than a bride in our day. They have to take a whole bride's chest of sheets & towels & table napkins. And the maddening madening madenning??? thing is that I can't make any more because it all goes in tax if I try. I have just read an essay by Professor Day Lewis who says all artists in this age are frustrated & stultified because they have to work for profit. If only we could.

Harriet has gone to school and is driving all the nuns mad with her innocent prattle.

Oh I must tell you I went to the 100 Best Books with Bright Young Yorkes.[4] Mrs Yorke senior came all the way from Forthampton for the event and a horrible loutish son[5] who shakes hands with a clenched fist. Well it was a private view with a bar and Henry started handing us all glasses of sherry. 'That'll be twenty four bob' said the barmaid. It was just like Mr Pooter at the volunteers' ball.[6] Henry was so upset

he walked straight out to the Ritz Hotel opposite and bought & paid
for bottles & bottles of champagne.

He and Dig come here for Whitsun. *What* can I do to entertain
them?

> Best love
>   Evelyn

¹ In his broadcast, 'A Progressive Game', Evelyn criticised the books chosen for the Festival
of Britain exhibition (which included *Decline and Fall*) for being frivolous, irreligious and divorced
from real life.
² Stephen Spender, *World Within World* (1951).
³ The Islington flat where Evelyn lived with his first wife.
⁴ So-called because in about 1930 Evelyn was puzzling as to who all his 'Bright Young' friends
could be, and said: 'I suppose bright young Roy Harrod and the bright young Yorkes.'
⁵ Sebastian Yorke (1934–).
⁶ Charles Pooter suffered a similar humiliation at the East Acton Volunteer Ball in *The Diary
of a Nobody*.

11 May 1951   7 rue Monsieur, VII

Darling Evelyn

I would *love* to go with you as far as a day train could take me back,
it would be a terrific treat. Beautiful France in June is something I've
never seen. But all depends very much on the Col – he's engulfed in
his election (standing against Duclos, the Communist leader in the
reddest part of Paris) & depends on me for a little home life, or at
least I think he does. So perhaps we could leave it open. Anyway I'll
find out a good gastronomic itinerary for you. Honks is dying for you
to settle at Chantilly, I think she has written.

I was riveted by Spender. Funnier than anything even you have
written – I had to put it down & *scream* time & time again. Pink as I
may be (synthetic cochineal Diana calls it) I can't but see the hysterical
funniness of my fellow pinks.

Isn't it dreadful about the poverty. But need *girls* go to school – I
thought only boys, & that the girls could learn Greek from a local
priest & les soins de beauté from their mother. Perhaps this is a
romantic dream. I was dragged up with none of it, worse luck, hence
the grammar. It would be far cheaper – face cream costs less than gym
shoes you know, & a sprig of rosemary in rain water, the foundation of
a good complexion, nothing at all. (You ought to read *Gigi*.) You
would be richer if you lived here, but perhaps not happier – though
I don't know why not.

Diana M, just back from Ireland, tells of going to mass (Aly,¹ her
son, is very religious) in the R.C. church at Lismore. It was *crammed*
with people, all crying so that their tears splashed on the stone floor,
& sobbing out loud, & when she asked why they said 'It is Connolly
day.'

How horrid, 100 best authors, so invidious. Typical Festival idea – all right for you & Henry. How can one get the list, I long for it – I *love* H. being Pooter at the volunteers' ball.

Jonathan is engaged so we are all excited. Lovely Miss Wyndham.[2] Diana says he must marry at once, he'll never find such another beauty, & *so nice*.

Later. A letter from Mrs Hammersley 'If Stephen S had any guts, which he hasn't, he would kill Evelyn Waugh'. Why? Beastly review I guess.

Fondest love
NR

[1] Alexander Mosley (1938–2005). Publisher. The model for Basil in *Don't Tell Alfred* (1960).
[2] Ingrid Wyndham (1931–2010). Daughter of the painter Richard Wyndham. Married to Hon. Jonathan Guinness 1951–63 and to Paul Channon, son of Sir Henry (Chips) Channon, in 1963.

16 May [1951]   Piers Court
                                                     Stinchcombe
Dearest Nancy

All my heart goes out to the gallant Colonel in his lone struggle to salvage the French from themselves.

How very interesting about Jonathan. News to me. Which Miss Wyndham? Not I hope Dick's daughter. In any case she is bound to be a relation of H. Yorke's & that is not a thing to go into light-heartedly. He was here for a very long week-end. In London, where everyone is seedy, he did not appear notable. Here in the country he looked GHASTLY. Very long black dirty hair, one brown tooth, pallid puffy face, trembling hands, stone deaf, smoking continuously throughout meals, picking up books in the middle of conversation & falling into maniac giggles, drinking a lot of raw spirits, hating the country & everything good. If you mention Forthampton to him he shies with embarrassment as business people used to do if their businesses were mentioned.

Poor Dig very cowardly, quite belying her great moustaches, gentle, lost. She has picked up a whole proletarian argot which she employs with an exquisitely ladylike manner. I really think Henry will be locked up soon. Dig's brother is locked up already. It is a poor lookout for their wretched son.

I will soon send you a catalogue of 100 best books. I was to broadcast against them but the BBC think my comments in *very* bad taste ha ha.

By the way if you come to England don't wear your new spectacles. Word has got round how you obtained them. Popular fury rages. They would be torn off your nose & stamped into the carpet.

This is the review Mrs Hammersley thought offensive.[1]

Love
    E

Will start cabling as soon as I know plans for tour.

[1] A roundly dismissive attack on *World Within World*, in which Evelyn wrote: 'At his christening the fairy godparents showered on Mr Spender all the fashionable neuroses but they quite forgot the gift of literary skill … To see him fumbling with our rich and delicate language is to experience all the horror of seeing a Sèvres vase in the hands of a chimpanzee.' *Tablet*, 5 May 1951.

18 May 1951   7 rue Monsieur, VII

Darling Evelyn

Many thanks, I *did* enjoy it. Whomever rather worried even me,[1] though I only thought of course I must be wrong & how clever people like Mr S are who know these things. Did I tell you, when he came here after the war in the battledress of a journalist the frogs said 'Comme c'est bien de voir Spendair en soldat' & I said 'Oui, et pendant la guerre il était en pompier'[2] which had a great success. I felt rather awful afterwards because the pompiers were quite brave, but you see I was right. He seems never to have gone near a fire – once perhaps.

As for the other book,[3] I can't think how a firm like Constable could have published it – from what you say, I've not read it of course.

I've no time to read anything, the season here is in full swing & I'm having fun & enjoying it. (Stephen Tennant writes 'oh doomful question: *is fun, fun?*' answer *yes it is*, NR.)

My specs are lovely & I had the choice of 6 different rims so I chose blond tortoiseshell. I can't see why anybody should mind it must be pure jealousy. And they have a case (specs do I mean).

Yesterday I dedicated copies of my book in a big shop here called the Bon Marché. A loudspeaker announced the fact every 5 minutes. I can't say my arm *ached* with the effort, but I sold quite a good few & the whole thing was well worth it for the funniness. Customers kept asking me where they could buy braces & woollen vests & I made best buddies with a lot of floor walkers. You wouldn't have liked it, no good pretending.

My mother comes here 29th for a week so if you leave during that week I couldn't come, though I might meet you on the way back. Anyway, see you here which I long for & I'll have a cocktail mondain if you like, as I know you loathe the other sort.

Yes Dick Wyndham's daughter she is lovely, not unlike Diana.

Dig & Henry came here & I didn't see them in that livid light but my (health service) spectacles are pinker than yours. Col loved Henry who, very surprisingly to me, speaks excellent French.

I must go & dress for a grand dinner in aid of Chips. Are you gell-gell?

Fondest love
    NR

[1] In his review of Spender's autobiography, Evelyn had written: 'Only when he imputes his own illiteracy to others must the critic protest. He really should not represent Dr Edith Sitwell as saying: "The ghost brings extreme misfortune to whomever sees it." ' *Tablet*, 5 May 1951.
[2] 'How nice it is to see Spender dressed as a soldier' & I said 'Yes, and during the war he was dressed as a fireman.'
[3] Evelyn reviewed *Saints and Parachutes* by John Miller in the same article.

21 June 1951   7 rue Monsieur, VII
[postcard]

Lothario. From *The Fair Penitent*, N. Rowe 1674–1718. You were right.

My Dad enjoying himself, wolfing down beef as if he'd never seen food before. He goes out with a haversack & is the French person's idea of an English milord *all over* (the mad, as opposed to the cunning kind).

Don't know name of your pub.[1]

[1] Evelyn had taken Nancy's advice and was staying at a small hotel in Chantilly. Her card was sent c/o Lady Diana Cooper.

[June 1951]   [Hôtel du Château
                                                Chantilly
                                                Oise]
Darling Nancy

Many thanks for your p.c.

I am moving tomorrow to St Firmin. I am not at all sure it is a good thing. Tempers have been smooth as castor oil all this week. Duff & Diana pressing. No reasonable excuse for staying in hotel. Study cleared for me in attic with Diana's own fair hands. What else could I do? But there is bound to be a bust-up & then how can I move out again?

Now Farve's grande semaine is over I hope to see you. We seem as far separated as when I was at Stinkers. Couldn't you & Col come in his new parliamentary car?

Do you know I think Liz [von Hofmannsthal] is an awfully uninteresting girl?

I have written 12,000 words but none of them printable. Just a very rough draft. Time was I wrote 12,000 complete & polished in a week.

We went to dinner with Pattens. *Very* poor grub. Raimund made us 65 minutes late. They were rightly furious.

Last night I saw a circus of performing poultry (literally) while you no doubt were at Travellers Joy.

Love from
    Evelyn

28 June 1951   7 rue Monsieur, VII

Darling Evelyn

That all sounds rather sensible, & if you are working hard Satan won't be able to find so much mischief. I see you're having rather a struggle & feel for you. I'm now enjoying the fun of having one on the stocks. A telegram yesterday to say it has been taken by some society in America 'which means a packet for you'. Really – haven't they even noticed Dexter? Next time I shall speak out. Also 'Paramount seem interested'. Oh for dollars, against one's old age (just a little supplement to the 26/- a week would be nice). You've got 6 children to support *you* & are quite all right.

I go away on the 10th oh I long to sweat. Hope to see you before that – say the word & I'll take the little train & come panting down.

My father enjoyed himself – I never saw anything like the beef consumed. He described a restaurant we went to, to Peter de Polnay, & said 'then we dined in another & THERE WAS STEAK THERE TOO'.

I've found a most wonderful restaurant, what a pity you never come to Paris.

Best love, love to Lady Honks or is she in Oslo?
    NR

I look forward to a little light hearted badinage of course – just to remind me that I am English. Have received nothing but fulsome flattery since I last saw YOU.

Did you see that hen who lays to order? I envy you. Were there 1000 gynaecologists?

I hear Boots is upon us.

13 July [1951]   Piers Court
                                                    Stinchcombe

Darling Nancy

Peters will have told you of the final outcome of the Korda controversy.[1] It is a little better than we feared, is it not? He explained all the circumstances and I think he is not culpable. He has certainly been working feverishly in your interests during the past week.

Cooper got to the train drunk. It was a tolerable journey. Home seems very dank & dingy and shut in after the spacious views from St Firmin but it is a little more solid & much quieter. I came straight here so have no news. I hope you don't quite parboil your poor noodle in the sun at Hyères. It was very nice to see you so often in France.

Happy dollars
    E

[1] After some discussion over copyright, Nancy had sold the film rights for *The Blessing* to Alexander Korda for £7,500.

21 August 1951   St-Pierre du Château
                                               Hyères
                                               Var

Darling Evelyn

I gather that you sprang to the rescue of the poor *Blessing* with what the publishers call a quote. Thank you *very* much. Nobody can say that it has had a good reception but I believe it sells all right. How the English do hate the French – they either hate them or regard them as their own property & hate anybody else who tries to write about them. Never mind.

After 6 weeks of solid sweating I feel well – look young, it is very nice. The only sad thing is that I have to live in the cold North which makes me ill & wretched. The Col got one short week & came here, it did him good but he is very overdone. His maiden speech a signal success.

Marie-Laure is at a stone's throw from here. I love her, but not her court of American pederasts & French opium smokers. She has now got a friend of Cyril & Spender called, very suitably, M. Henri Hell.[1] Even she is sick of *him*. Very soon all this breaks up & they go to Venice for the BALL.[2] I have decided against, & go home on Monday.

I suppose you are plunged in your novel. I don't envy you. I think I shall never write another – only then what about my old age, Cyril would say.

Cecil B. seems to have had a hateful time with his play,[3] Peter de P's novel is an utter flop & all my correspondents are in the dumps – specially a Hungarian pen-pal who has been deported & says she can't get any nail varnish where she is.

Best love
    NR

Is it true the Sykeses have burnt down David Herbert's[4] house?
P.S. This will interest you. Tony's[5] servant (a charmer) is an ex sailor

called Sparks. We went to dine with Redé the Baron Redé[6] so different from the Baron Rede(sdale) whose lover Lopez has given him a yacht with 24 English sailors. 'All boys from Portsmouth' said Sparks. Tony asked him what the boys from Portsmouth thought of the set-up. 'Oh they know quite well that they are all *brown hats*.' It seems that brown hat is what sailors call buggers – why? Bruno Hat I say.

By the way we went over to Poor-Louis[7] – Duff had had a nose bleed so he & Diana had gone but John Julius & the girl[8] were there. I think nothing of this girl – she's not even very pretty & has a horrid mean little face.

[1] Henri Hell (1916–91). Pseudonym of José Lasry, a Franco-Venezuelan literary and art critic. Editor of the magazine *Fontaine* during the war. An intimate friend of Stephen Spender.
[2] Carlos (Charlie) de Beistegui's famous fancy-dress ball at the Palazzo Labia in Venice.
[3] *The Gainsborough Girls*, which Cecil Beaton took three years to write, had opened to leaden reviews at the Theatre Royal in Brighton.
[4] Hon. David Herbert (1908–95). Brother of 16th Earl of Pembroke. His cottage at Wilton, which was rented by Christopher Sykes, caught fire because of defective wiring.
[5] Nancy's host, Tony Gandarillas.
[6] Baron Alexis de Redé (1922–2004). Good-looking son of an Austrian banker.
[7] Evelyn's nickname for Paul-Louis Weiller (1893–1993), a rich and powerful industrialist whose villa, the Reine Jeanne, was near by. A close friend and benefactor of Diana Cooper.
[8] John Julius Cooper was engaged to Anne Clifford.

St Bartholomew's Day [24 August] 1951   Piers Court
                                                         Stinchcombe

Darling Nancy

Today is a glorious anniversary in the sad history of your adopted country. I hope you are keeping it with solemnity & splendour.

I ought to have written before but it has been a dull time for me – none of those events which make me think: 'I must write & tell Nancy that.' I have been at home all the time pegging away at my novel & associating with my children whose interests I do not share – chemical experiments, pony clubs, autograph collections. Mr Battersby[1] the Master of Chantilly came to stay. He is doing a panel for me. I quite liked him. An American Professor of Creative Writing also came. He wore a white dinner jacket with an artificial carnation in the button-hole. Now Laura is taking the three older children to Italy and I am having a series of male guests – Sykes, Pakenham, G. Greene etc. but the cook is on holiday & my man-servant, on whom I depend for my few comforts, has taken to his bed, so these guests will have poor entertainment.

I have had a lot of your reviews as they mostly seem to put my name in, and the press-cutting agent sends them to me (at 3d. a time). I am glad you don't take them seriously. Reviewers are lazy brutes & hate having to think. They want to say: 'Here is another Mitford, sparkling & irresponsible in her own inimitable way.' They can't bear to see a writer grow up. They have no influence at all. Everyone I know delights in *The Blessing* and I am constantly buoyed up with pride at the dedication.

Yes, it is true that the Sykeses have destroyed David Herbert's pretty house, which *The Times* newspaper described as 'an ornate bungalow'.

I did not attend Jonathan's wedding. It would have been very expensive in car hire and present so I took advantage of his failure to write to me, and kept away. But I wish the young people well.

I came back from France so corpulent that I could not button any of my clothes and as it would cost about £500 to get a new lot, I took a gruesome course of Dr Goller's diet so that in two weeks I shrank to the thickness of Eddy West. I am now swelling gently.

My poverty is very irksome. I notice I have mentioned it twice already. It is often in my mind. It is sad to have been poor all the time one was allowed to be rich, and now one is rich it is against the law. I am being sued for 3000 dollars which an American editor once gave me for a story I never wrote. There is no legal means of repaying him, as I willingly would, so I must go to prison soon. I shall write to Lady Mosley for advice about what to take.[2]

My novel is unreadable & endless. Nothing but tippling in officers' messes and drilling on barrack squares. No demon sex. No blood or thunder.

You should now write a shameless & complete autobiography.

All love
    Evelyn

Twenty years or so ago Sachie [Sitwell] gave Robert [Byron] & Tony Powell & Harold Acton & me and a few other friends free tickets for a revolting ballet called *Mercure*. Last week he wrote in the *Sunday Times* that he saved Diaghilev from ruin by introducing a claque chosen for their 'wild & fantastic appearance'. How I remember oiling my hair & knotting my little white tie for the occasion. And how I hated *Mercure*. I think we gave a few perfunctory claps out of politeness to our host.

Love to Col. He very kindly wrote to me about bare bosoms but I did a Jonathan & failed to answer. Please try & make him try to forgive me.

[1] Martin Battersby (1913–82). Painter and set designer. He had painted a series of *trompe l'oeil* panels for the Coopers at St Firmin.
[2] Sir Oswald and Lady Mosley were interned in Holloway Prison during the war.

29 August 1951   7 rue Monsieur, VII

Darling Evelyn

Our Mr Peters has just put on such an odd act. He telephoned this morning saying he was de passage & we arranged for him to come here at 3. As the clocks were striking I saw him come into the cour [courtyard] – I had a heavy vase of flowers in my hands, went into my bedroom, put it down fidgeted with the flowers a minute & went to open the door. No sign of Mr. P. It is now ¼ to 5. Do admit. He is rather a fantaisiste I believe, I've noticed it in him before. But it is terribly annoying as there are a hundred things I wanted to ask which seem too trivial or (specially) too rapacious to write. Money. I long for it. But huge sums appear on paper & none in the bank except the London bank which is no more good to me than – ha, at this point the telephone rings & a breathy female voice says in English that Mr Peters has had a puncture & will be along in ½ an hour. What *can* it all mean? More anon.

Well he came. Nothing was said as to why he was late & I didn't mention having seen him 2 hours before. VERY ODD.

Oh dear your poverty. It's like the little door in Alice – so much in life is like that. Even I rather suffer though I don't need money as you do. But people say – 'oh Book of Month in America, of course 5 years ago that *was* something but now it's very small beer.' By the way I wrote to my agent over there who is utterly ½ witted AND calls me Nancy though a complete stranger & said I must have your article on me[1] when it appears & she sent pages back saying of course she'd get it for me if she could but I must explain more about it etc. So I've given up. She also asks for my telephone number which is on *every* letter I have *ever* written to her –

A long letter from a Hungarian pen pal who has been deported saying it's not too bad, plenty to eat, but no nail varnish or hair dye but I can send them to her butler who goes out to see her every week.

Aren't other people's reviews a bore. I get many clippings of the books of Lady Somebody Something & even smaller fry who are said to be school of me. Perhaps I ought to refund you the threepences.

The Colonel is making his mark in the Chambre. But he complains bitterly of lack of air & lack of eloquence. Où sont les Lavals d'antan?

I met Miss Anita Loos[2] at luncheon. But they are all the same & she is not even well dressed. I then went & ordered the plainest little wool dress you ever saw from Dior £168. It's the last time. I humbly asked if they wouldn't take off the 8 but no they cried you are very *lucky*, all the prices are going up next week. They made me feel I'd been too clever for words. But after I felt guilty – all the poor people in the world & so on. It's terrible to love clothes as much as I do, & perfectly inexplicable because I'm not at all vain & Col who is the only person I care for doesn't know sack cloth from ashes.

I've got a small egg of yours in an old nest – did you know? I feel guilty as you might have wanted to boil it while here – only saw it after you'd gone.

Jonathan is a bad boy. I sent an expensive present & loving letter

– deep silence. I hope it means that he is happy. I thought John Julius
& his fiancée looked silly & I don't believe they sleep together either.
   Here comes the Deputy in his usual wild hurry.

   Much love
        NR

[1] Evelyn's profile of Nancy appeared in *The Book of the Month Club News*: 'Nancy received no education at all except in horsemanship and French. Liverish critics may sometimes detect traces of this defect in her work. But she wrote and read continually and has in the end achieved a patchy but bright culture and a way of writing so light and personal that it can almost be called a "style" . . . Nancy, who, having voted socialist and done her best to make England uninhabitable, broke from her chrysalis, took wing and settled lightly in the heart of Paris where we find her today.'
[2] Anita Loos (1893–1981). Author of *Gentlemen Prefer Blondes* (1925).

1 September 1951   Piers Court
                                                             Stinchcombe
Darling Nancy
   I can tell you something else rum about our Mr. Peters.
   Last night 10.15 telephone rang. Mr. Robert Henriques, a jewish
distant neighbour. He knows he isn't allowed to telephone to me so
I rate him roundly, spit on his gabardine etc. 'I'm very sorry but I
have Peters here. He wants to talk to you.' 'Well, Pete, what is it?'
'Can you come over here tomorrow?' 'No.' 'Well I'll come over & see
you some day later.' 'Are you staying long with Henriques?' 'No. Off
tomorrow.' 'Have you taken a house in the district?' 'No.' 'Then what
do you mean by saying you'll come over and see me?' 'I've been to
Paris to see Nancy.' 'Any trouble?' 'No, she sent her love.'
   What d'you mean small egg? I thought it was a whopper. Or have
I both ostrich and tit.
   Jonathan's mummy should beat Jonathan. Laura's brother Auberon
failed to thank for a book I gave him when he was at Ampleforth in
1936. I have never given him anything since.
   Sykes comes this afternoon preceded by a letter to say please need
he bring evening dress as Camilla burned his in the Herbert fire.
   'Book of Month Club promotion material' is what your barmy agent
should ask for.

   E

Beistegui Ball Day   7 rue Monsieur, VII
(leaves poor old St Bart cold)
[3 September 1951]

Oh Lord oh Lord when I got your letter I fell out of bed. Had utterly
forgotten ostrich or would *never* have left it in empty flat for 2 months.
Quite safe however. Whew! Yes there is a tit as well.

I'm in a fearful gloom. Don't become a French resident until Jan: (Prod told me November, I can't think why but I believed him). All the money I've earned will then be frozen for ever, just as if it didn't exist. Korda who was to pay me in francs probably can't. And I get no dollars until 60 days after the book comes out. So I may be obliged to spend the winter in England on account of no money here. Alice & the little door again with a vengeance.

Never mind, something will turn up & Korda still MAY.

If Henriques mayn't telephone I really ought not to write. *Don't answer.*

Mr Peters is very low in horse power isn't he? We sat in an uneasy silence for about half an hour after I had posed my questions & received these unsatisfactory answers.

I may go to England about the middle of this month as Col goes to Spain then (not for politics to buy clothes).

I hasten to post this in case you are worrying about ostrich.

Love
    NR

P.S. My publisher asked me if Henriques' novel would be good in French. I haven't read it. He's very puzzled by *Times Lit Sup* review of best fiction – 'what is *The Boat*? Who is A. Powell?'[1] etc.

I don't believe either Leslie[2] or Tony would do in French – quite.

I've sent for Gr Greene,[3] but feel sure it's too SAD for me. Is he distressed about Jouvet[4] – I am, very.

A very nice letter from Willie Maugham about *Blessing* – I was disproportionately pleased.[5]

Did you shriek at Raymond's article this *Sunday T* – about Mr Murry in his bath?[6] I can't help rather dying for the letters in a way.

I thought of writing down the bald facts of my life, not for publication but as a record. But they are so very odd really I wonder if people would believe. Do you think everybody's real life is quite different from what they manage to make it seem (they, assisted by parents & so on). Very likely. No dark secret, but everything different from the façade.

Oh dear I've again encroached on your time. Enclosed is to give you an idea of my *great* versatility.[7]

---

[1] Anthony Powell (1905–2000). Author described by the *Oxford Companion to English Literature* as occupying a territory 'contiguous with E. Waugh's, bounded at opposite extremes by N. Mitford and by Powell's Oxford contemporary and friend, Henry Green'. In 1951 he published *A Question of Upbringing*, the first in the twelve-volume sequence *A Dance to the Music of Time*.
[2] L. P. Hartley (1895–1972). Novelist whose books include *The Shrimp and the Anemone* (1944) and *The Boat* (1949).
[3] *The End of the Affair* (1951).
[4] Louis Jouvet, the great French actor and director, had died aged 64.
[5] 'I think it's far & away the best book you've written yet. It's not only consistently amusing,

but extremely shrewd. And it's very well written too, in just the style that kind of book needs.'
(W. Somerset Maugham to NM, 2 August 1951)
[6] In a review of *Katherine Mansfield's Letters to John Middleton Murry*, Raymond Mortimer revealed
that we learn 'how beautiful Mr Murry looked in his bath'. *Sunday Times*, 2 September 1951.
[7] Nancy enclosed an article in which she had unwisely ventured into Evelyn's preserve by
writing of a Catholic priest, the Abbé Bremond, that he was 'forced to leave the Jesuit order
for administering the last rites to an excommunicated priest, Father Tyrrell (uncle of the late
Lord Tyrrell, one-time Ambassador to France), a leader of the modernist school'. *Sunday Times*,
2 September 1951.

6 September [1951]   Piers Court
                                                               Stinchcombe

My dear Nancy,
    Bremond left the Jesuits by his own wish & with the consent of his
superiors some time before Tyrrell's death (who I don't think was uncle
of the ambassador). Tyrrell died in Miss Petre's house in Sussex, excommunicated. It is the duty of every priest to rush to the bedside of a dying
excommunicated man. Pollen was sent from Farm Street but found Tyrrell in a coma. There was also a Franciscan at the bedside who also had
been too late to find him conscious. Tyrrell never expressed a wish for
a priest or (as in *Brideshead*) made any sign of recognizing the priest's
presence. Bishop Amigo therefore could not allow him Catholic burial
(of course Catholic burial does not affect the destination of the soul). It
was then that Bremond appeared on the scene and in defiance of the
Bishop's orders conducted a service. It was not a question merely of his
praying for the soul but preaching a panegyric of the old heretic. For
this reason he (Bremond) was very properly excommunicated locally, as
far as the diocese of Southwark went.
    There is no reason why you should know all this, but if you don't
know, would it not be better to avoid the subject.
    Would it not be best always to avoid any reference to the Church
or to your Creator? Your intrusions into this strange world are always
fatuous.

    With love
        E

It is the telephone I forbid. All other modes of communication are
most welcome.
If you want to suck my eggs to keep your strength up until after the
frost, pray do so.

6 September 1951   7 rue Monsieur, VII

Don't start My dear Nancy I don't like it.
    I can't agree that I must be debarred from ever mentioning anything
to do with your creator. Try & remember that he also created me.

I admit however that facts should be verified before they are printed. I got mine from Bremond's godson,[1] it was very naughty & awful of him to mislead me & I shall scold. Tyrrell *was* the nephew, however, & Bremond says anybody could tell he was a diplomat by the ½ hearted way he swung the _____ (I don't know the word) at the funeral.

Very kind about the eggs but I can manage.

Mrs Hammersley your co-religionist liked my last article better than any I have done.

I don't defend my inaccuracies but it's your TONE that nettles me.

Love from
      Nancy

Thinking it over, I see how it arose. There must have been a confusion in my mind between last rites & funeral rites. Well really *they are* the last. So I think it was my mistake & not that of my informant after all – though leaving the Jesuits was his. Do you not revere the Abbé Bremond?

[1] Gaston Palewski.

7 September 1951   7 rue Monsieur, VII

Darling Evelyn

Your letter has been succeeded by a shower of two post cards from priests slightly I must say contradicting each other. Fr Martindale speaks of 'praying by his grave', Monseigneur Barton of 'preaching at his funeral'. Not exactly the same thing. The Monseigneur says the sanction applied was signing 'un acte d'adhésion sans réserve à l'encyclique Pascendi'[1] while you speak (as I understand it) of a partial excommunication by the Bishop of Southwark – which the Col says doesn't exist.

I am surprised by the illiterate *look* of these post cards – you would say an electrician, or seed merchant.

Now don't go on being cross & starchy.

Love from
      NR

I have written respectfully & grovelled.

[1] 'An act of unconditional adherence to the encyclical Pascendi.'

8 September [1951]   Piers Court
                                                     Stinchcombe
Darling Nancy

No contradictions. 'Praying at the grave' meant at the interment.
Funeral is a noncommittal word. There could of course be no requiem
mass. Accounts do differ slightly I think about what Bremond did &
said at that furtive ceremony.

'Partial excommunication' is not of course the theological term. I
meant a local excommunication applicable only in one diocese. If the
Col. thinks that doesn't exist, he must give up Couturier as his spiritual
director & get someone better instructed.

What is so awful is that you can't see the beastliness of your error.
It isn't just a matter of being caught out as we all are constantly in a
historical slip. It is this: you suggest the Church is so lacking in charity
that it would punish a priest for offering the last sacraments to an
excommunicated man whereas it is his absolute duty to do so. If you
think that, you know nothing of the nature of the Church. If you know
nothing of the nature of the Church you cannot understand any feature
of French History & that it is a sad state for a lady who sets herself
up as the mediating logos between France & England.

   Love
      E

I did not know the terms of Bremond's submission after his local
excommunication. No doubt Mgr. Barton is correct.
Martindale is very very old. He once wrote a fine fist. I've never seen
Mgr. Barton's.
The only seed merchant I know is Countess Palffy.[1] I suppose her
writing must in the nature of things be repellent. Electrician's type.
G. Greene is with me. Very sad & gentle.

[1] Louise de Vilmorin's family fortune came from plant seeds.

12 September 1951   7 rue Monsieur, VII

Darling Evelyn

I thought if excommunicated you were cut off from the Church &
all its consolations & that that was why people dread it so terribly.
Dying men don't always die – what happens if they receive the last
rites & then recover can they communicate again? Can you un excom-
municate yourself by repenting or recanting? I didn't know. It's lucky
you're on my side – the letter from Mr Coulsdon was milder than
one from you wld have been. Col sticks to his guns. He says Bremond
never really really left until this final to-do. Also Bremond's brother

at his death bed uncrossed his hands & put a Jesuit cross between them (or something, you probably know).

I read Gr Greene all yesterday. It is wonderful I don't at all agree with the critics who say that Bendrix was a horrible character. The only thing I couldn't swallow was that she could give up her lover like that, so brutally, without having something to put in his place. I know that subconsciously she had something but I don't feel that that's enough. Perhaps she was a little bit tired of him really – it is suggested that she may have been. What a sexy man he must be, Mr Greene.

Oh what a picture of terrible lives. Yet they are all quite rich in the book – Sarah's husband had more than £2000 a year which is more than I spend. And Bendrix wrote a novel every year lucky him yet he lived in a terrible bed-sitting room. And all that public house life, like poor people.

I lunched at the Embassy for Winston & sat next him. He talks like Sir Oswald Mosley – I was appalled. No wonder the Conservatives don't get in.[1]

Then all yesterday I had old Brian Howard on my hands. Pathetic. 'You don't know how difficult it is, my dear, to be an old cissy & keep your dignity.'

The French have told him he is persona non grata here (deadly secret don't repeat) & he wanted me to make the Col use influence. Took it rather badly when I refused. I must say I think it's too grossly unfair for words to pick on *him*. I sent him to see my lawyer but it won't be any good.

A letter from Jonathan, ending up 'And now I must thank Chips for his *Debrett*'. He sounds perfectly blissful.

Thank you for the *Month*[2] – I'll go on with this when I've read it.

Read it. Yes cattleyas & onions is perfect. Oh the horror the horror of people's lives thank goodness ONE has escaped. All that rain & public houses.

I enclose said post cards – don't want them back. Do agree about them being like tradespeople. Your fault is addressed to Col on whom I dropped them.

Best love
    NR

What a fascinating story it must be – is it written down? Would it be in the new Life of Hügel.[3] Would I understand enough to enjoy it (Hügel)?

---

[1] The Conservatives won the general election the following month and Sir Winston Churchill was returned to office as Prime Minister.
[2] The September issue carried Evelyn's review of Graham Greene's novel *The End of the Affair* in which he wrote: 'onions are made, perhaps in conscious allusion, to perform precisely the same function in the lovers' talk as "cattleyas" did for Swann and Odette.'
[3] Michael de la Bédoyère, *The Life of Baron von Hügel* (1951).

19 September [1951]

Darling Nancy

There is a first class French Catholic Encyclopaedia called I think the Apologetic Dictionary in numerous volumes. You must keep it at your bed side and consult it rather than poor wayward Col six times a day; it will save you from howlers. But I am afraid it can never make you *understand* anything supernatural. The fact that you can write of G. Greene's heroine that 'subconsciously she had something' is evidence of worse than defective education.

The habits of G. Greene's characters are *precisely* and in *every detail identical* with those of the Bright Young Yorkes.

G. Greene behaved well & dressed for dinner every night. Mrs Walston had never seen him in a dinner jacket before and was enchanted and will now make him wear one always. G. Greene spent his days patrolling the built up areas round Dursley noting the numbers of motor-cars. He takes omens from them.

Not that I would boast but – I put those words into B. Howard's mouth ten years ago in a book about him called *Put Out More Flags*.

Interesting slice of English life. Ever since marriage we have had a piano in the drawing-room which no one ever plays, and a man has come on a bicycle from Cheltenham to 'tune' it every quarter. Last time he came he said it had some internal complaint which it would cost £50 to cure. So I said, give me £50 and you can take it away, which he did. Result. Consternation. A hush over cottage and Hall, the cowman passes me with downcast eyes, the village women who come in sweep in tears. The furniture removers who carried it out treated it like a coffin. Apparently in the lower classes to sell one's piano is the last refuge of the destitute – an irrevocable step down from decency to squalor. Did you know?

Debo sent me an *insane* post card from Capri about the King. Is she really, frankly, a bit barmy?

I am scribbling away hard at my maximum opus. I think it is frightfully funny. A bad sign.

    Love
      E

26 September 1951   7 rue Monsieur, VII

Dearest Evelyn

I know you like news of the Bright Young Yorkes – pray turn to page 2 of the corporal's letter.[1] Does that lady-like Dig go to public houses I can hardly believe it.

My American publisher has surpassed himself. Wrote, through the agent, to say they haven't bothered to send me proofs & the book will be out next week. I know you think I don't care how many mistakes appear in my books but it's not so. I can't spell so am bad at correcting myself, but I breathe over dictionaries – it's not for want of trying. Rather a nice Dexter publisher came to see me yesterday called Cass Canfield. I note that since *The Blessing* the Americans I meet talk in short clipped sentences & look worried. Anyway Mr C C wants to do my next book, he is Harper's. I said I am utterly under the thumb of Mr Peters & he said you couldn't find a better thumb to be under.

I *long* for your book. I'm reading a French life of Buckingham[2] – the bliss of him – he wrote to James 'Dear Dad & Gossip'. And the *fits* & *screams* of laughter, just like ONE.

A Dexter of my acquaintance writes that he can't read T Powell or Henry Green but 'I am very keen on Christopher Sykes & *Helena*'.

Did you see an advert of *The Blessing* in *The Times* & next to it an account of a memorial service '. . . the Bishop of Norwich gave the Blessing'.

You *are* an old schoolmaster. I pass over your last letter in silence. I hear Lady Honks is upon you. Do tell.

Love
    NR

[1] Heywood Hill's letter has not survived.
[2] Philippe Erlanger, *George Villiers, duc de Buckingham: l'énigme du monde* (1951).

7 October 1951   7 rue Monsieur, VII

Darling Evelyn

I suppose being a novelist makes you so observant. If you want to know I tried to get to London for the funeral[1] but owing to a rush of returning BRITONS to BRITAIN there was only room on a 7 AM plane, which would have led to 2 funerals, so I gave up. Prod, in bed with a high temperature himself, never told me there was to be a service the next week. And indeed I call that a farce & so did he – the old lady being a complete pagan. I don't know why I bother to explain all this to you. I am the only person, except her own children, to be mentioned in her will however.

13 Oct

Don't know what happened to this letter. I'm staying with my darling Mme Costa de Beauregard (Mme de Valhubert) in the Seine et Marne, have been here on & off for a fortnight as Col is away doing the cantonal elections.

It is very like Bellandargues,[2] only alas M. le Curé has died & his successor, a handsome Dürer-like missionary, doesn't play bridge. The 3 other guests are old ladies who have all spent every summer here since they were one month old, photographs of their fathers & grand-mothers are all over the house. One wakes up with the sun shining through pink taffeta curtains & my room, in a tower, has sun all day. Mme Costa spends up to 8 hours a day in the chapel, the rest of the time she plays bridge & talks about Dior & déclassé duchesses – it's a very odd mixture. In the garden there's a summer house from which in 1914 one of the old ladies saw the Uhlans riding over the hill. They avoided the house however thinking it might be a trap.

My book is out in America with the more eulogistic of your so kind words on the dust cover. Hope Sergikins sees it.

Pam [Berry] was here (with me in Paris I mean). Goodness she is nice. Tomorrow I go home & Debo comes.

Love from
    NR

What a dull letter.

[1] Lady Rennell, Nancy's mother-in-law, had died on 20 September.
[2] Mme de Valhubert's château in *The Blessing*.

29 October [1951]   Piers Court
                                                     Stinchcombe

Darling Nancy

You know I think you are going to be the kind of person like Queen Victoria who effortlessly collects legacies. I can see the hoard grow, a cornelian brooch here, a nice sum of money there, chests of linen, a harp – most enviable.

I am cooling down after my popish heat. I think you were wrong about Madrid bookshops[1] unless the place has greatly changed since 1946. Then I found hundreds of Bumpuses all full of Gollancz Left Book Club publications.

It is a long time since I wrote. Honks [Cooper] and party came to luncheon. It was very difficult to get her in or out of the dining room. Physical force was needed in both operations. She won't be led only driven. She admired my moss on unweeded paths. 'You can't grow that in France.' I saw her again in London, full of delight at the politeness of the English lower classes. I went to London for the General Election – just like last time, same parties and same parties in H of C too. Cooper got veiners with a jewish hanger-on of Ann [Rothermere]'s called 'Freud'.[2] I have never seen him assault a jew before. Perhaps he took him for a Spaniard. He has very long black side-whiskers and a thin nose.

Poor Randolph. It was a very difficult seat and he didn't think he could get in. At the count he was so nervous he left the room and returned just as they were finishing. He asked the town-clerk, who

presided: 'How am I doing?' 'Thirty something thousand and something.' 'Isn't that rather good?' 'Oh yes you're quite safe. We've only
a few more to count and they can't affect the result.' Dazed with joy
he rushed out & told his committee. All embraced. Two minutes later
the town clerk padded out; 'Oh Mr Churchill I made such a silly
mistake. I gave you Mr Foot's figures.' He then had to be protected
from the mob by 40 policemen while he went to his train home.

Nothing he has ever done deserves such punishment.

Betjeman has the flu and has retired to the house of the Dowager
Duchess of Devonshire where he is waited on & washed by Lady
Elizabeth [Cavendish] while the high-church butler reads *The Unlucky
Family*[3] aloud to him. Meanwhile he has sold Penelope's house &
purchased a villa in the centre of Wantage – 'Oh the joy of being
back in real suburbia old boy' – and has left Penelope quite unaided
to make the move. He *is* Skimpole.

The rival Skimpole, Connolly, has fallen on hard times. He has
been hired by *Time* magazine to write a 'profile' of me which always
means a collection of damaging lies. He approached me obsequiously
with a series of fatuous psycho-analytical questions – did I suffer from
jealousy because my father loved him [*sic*] more than me? That sort
of rot. I said: 'On the day the article appears I shall horse whip you
on the steps of White's.' He turned green white yellow & grey and
then said: 'What will you pay me not to write it?'

Does the Col who spends so much thought on religious questions
know anything (a) of the number, if any, of apostasies among the
priests who have lately been going about disguised as 'workers' (b) of
a Dominican Père Perrin[4] who was at Marseilles most of the war and
the correspondent of a Great Fraud called Simone Weil?[5] Do please
ask and answer.

Are any of my eggs French? If so would you give them to Honks.
If they are all American and need my signature it must wait till I
come through.

Now that there is a tiny Conservative Majority the persecution of
the rich by the politicians will be greatly intensified so that they can
display class impartiality.

Love from
    Evelyn

[1] Nancy had written that Madrid bookshops were 'conspicuous by their absence'. *Sunday Times*,
14 October 1951.
[2] Lucian Freud (1922–). Artist grandson of Sigmund Freud. His work was represented in the
Festival of Britain exhibition 'Sixty Paintings for '51'.
[3] By Mrs Henry de la Pasture (1907). Evelyn discovered the children's book by chance in the
1950s and was delighted by it. Graham Greene admired it, and Auberon Waugh has described
it as 'One of the great classics of its genre to be put on the same shelf as *The Diary of a Nobody*,
The Young Visiters and *Cautionary Verses*'.
[4] Joseph-Marie Perrin, author of *Simone Weil telle que nous l'avons connue* (1952).

[5] Simone Weil (1909–43). Author and philosopher. Evelyn reviewed her selection of writings *Waiting on God* (1951) in the *Catholic Mother*, Christmas 1952. He was irritated by her attitude to the Church, doubted her 'ardent love for the proletariat' and mistrusted her 'zeal for self-sacrifice'.

31 October 1951   7 rue Monsieur, VII

Darling Evelyn

I thought I was supposed to keep off religious subjects. The Col is a different sort of R.C. from you. He loves the priests who go about helping the dear workmen & when I asked about the Pope's vision he said 'il se fiche du peuple'.[1] But I expect you will meet at the Golden Gate all the same. I'll ask about the friend of S. Weil. But I never see him now which makes me low in spirits. Not another woman so much as the last infirmity of N.M.'s.

I cannot imagine why you think I will receive legacies. I never have yet, at 46 (except a memento not money from Lady Rennell) & the various aunts who might have left me a pittance have noticed that I can earn my own living which is more than my other cousins can do, & will be more likely to choose them.

It's funny about Madrid bookshops. I was sensitive to bookshops when I went there, having just left one, & can remember thinking all the time what a dearth, & the Mosleys who go a lot & are very pro on acc/ of having a minister to take them round & special bull fights in their honour & banquets & so on say they hardly saw any. But other people agree with you. I'm afraid I shall get a My dear Nancy after my next article in which I speak of the revival of religious art in France & how RP Couturier hopes to get the 'triste salle de l'Assomption au Vatican' decorated by Picasso.

What to me is odd about Randolph is why he should think that anybody would ever vote for him? A man you wouldn't trust to post a letter for you – it makes no sense.

I often wonder what sort of world you would like to live in? Berlin under Hitler seems to come the nearest.

I shall give Lady Honks 20 eggs is that all right? That wipes out the tit. Do you know Debo's sad poem about a chaffinch whose nest has been destroyed 'too late to build too sad to sing'. She recites it with tears banging down her cheeks.

This letter is very disjointed – well Simon Harcourt Smith,[2] Mrs Aspinall Oglander,[3] the Frenchman who is translating Duke of Windsor's book[4] & Osbert Lancaster have telephoned during it.

Yes I don't like Freud. I knew him before he got into society & didn't like him then. Boots does though.

These profiles are a bore – except the one you did of me – because bound to break up friendships.

I will find out about R[évérend] P[ère] Perrin & let you know what
I hear.

Love
   NR

[1] 'He couldn't care less about the people.'
[2] Simon Harcourt-Smith; novelist and historical biographer.
[3] Florence Glynn; married to Brigadier-General Cecil Aspinall-Oglander in 1927. They were
friends and neighbours of Violet Hammersley on the Isle of Wight.
[4] *A King's Story* was translated by Georges Roditi and Marie-Madeleine Beauquesne.

3 November 1951   7 rue Monsieur, VII

Darling Evelyn
   You owe this treat to me being in bed with bronchitis. I asked Col
but he had never heard of the Père. He said S. Weil died in London
because she limited herself to the diet in occupied countries 'that is
to say the diet of Nina de Polignac, François Dupré . . .'[1] I'm afraid
the Col cannot be serious for very long.
   So then I asked a frog intellectual friend 'My dear *I* don't know I
haven't believed in God since my first communion.'
   'Don't you find it very dull?' I said.
   'You can't imagine how dull. I don't believe in love either. I fell in
love with you the first day I saw you – there at last I have embarrassed
you –'
   'But if you don't believe in it?'
   'Oh well with me it never lasts. It lasted 3 weeks which is practically
a record.'
   Oh I am glad not to be a frog intellectual.
   In my bed I've been reading the Duke's book have you? It brought
my childhood back to me *vividly* I suppose all English childhoods have
a common denominator. It (the book) is terribly good let me tell you
& whether he wrote it or Murphy a great deal of his very personal
charm & cleverness comes through.
   I am badgered & plagued by editors film companies & publishers,
I suppose you are too. *How* I wish they would write their own books
& leave ONE alone.
   I sent the eggs to Honks. Debo now talks of Woman Berry (we call
our sister Pam Woman). She, Debo, was here the other day. Meanwhile my sister Decca has been had up for being a Communist, out
on bail. She writes that for what she has done she can get 25 years.
Oh my poor mother. But from what we hear nothing much *will*
happen, as they don't mind open Communists in America nearly as
much as the hidden ones.
   Hamish [Erskine] is here, *very* poor & rather pathetic.

What mad letters American fans do write – mine are all judges. But I had a very fascinating one from the niece of Laetitia Hogg aged 5 whom I found in Père Lachaise & mentioned in *Blessing*. She (the niece) was astounded to come on her like that since her father, Laetitia's brother, always talked about her. Well she has such a touching little gravestone you can see she was a personality. 100 years ago she died. A great aunt of Quintin H.[2] evidently.

Love from
NR

Who is Anthony West?[3] I have just received a review of *Blessing* by him which fascinated me. It puts the American outlook on art & life in a nutshell. I have a feeling he is Rebecca West's son can this be true? What is the title of your novel?

[1] Two people who were rich enough to eat anything from a flourishing black market.
[2] Quintin Hogg (1907–2001). Politician and QC. MP for Oxford City 1938–50. Disclaimed his viscountcy in 1963; created life peer in 1970.
[3] Anthony West (1914–87). Illegitimate son of Rebecca West and H. G. Wells. His review compared Charles-Edouard de Valhubert, the philandering husband in Nancy's novel, with the adulterous duc de Guermantes in *A la Recherche*. 'Where Proust insists that it is an intolerable way to treat wives or mistresses, Miss Mitford tells us that it is divine for girls with common sense and nice manners to put up with such things.' *New Yorker*, 27 October 1951.

[November 1951]   Piers Court
[postcard]   Stinchcombe

If you praise the atheist temples at Vence & Assy it will be the end of a beautiful friendship. I went to a Picasso exhibition last week & looked hard and saw (a) that in youth he drew as well as a *Punch* artist of the period (b) that he has real comic talent & obviously enjoys making fools of his admirers (c) he has a distinct originality in a flibbity-gibbet way. He never repeats himself. Leaves that to his ghastly followers. Altogether a cleverer & more accomplished man than one could guess from reproductions. But as an artist of the fourth rank.

Please it is facts I want about Perrin. Is he still a supporter of Weil? Was he ever? His replies to her beastly letters aren't published in English or, I think, in French. Why did he withdraw his preface to the English edition of *Waiting on God*?

Also whether it is true that some of the priests who disguised themselves as workmen have apostasized. Of course I hope not, but it is being said here that several have. Even if Col is too busy to think of you or God, there must be someone who can answer.

L.I. of N. MIND *not* MINDS. V. vulgar error. Lovely lovely Cécile Howard is staying here. Now she comes from the French cultural bourgeoisie you once spoke of, and she is PERFECT so you were quite right.

E

5 November 1951   7 rue Monsieur, VII
[postcard]

All right you great bully I'll find out somehow. I haven't praised the
CHAPELS at Vence etc., not having seen them, I've just quoted the
RP Couturier who says it is a miracle that good modern artists should
want to work for God.[1]

My dear dear publisher H.H. came to Paris specially to beg me to
let him re publish *Wigs on Green* and *Xmas Pudding*.[2] He had read them
at Brit: Museum as they can't be got. Well I must say I was so touched
that I gave way, though I *know* unwisely.

[1] At the instigation of Père Couturier, the Dominican chapel at Vence had been decorated by
Henri Matisse.
[2] Nancy's third and second novels, published in 1935 and 1932 respectively.

[postmarked 7 November 1951]   Piers Court
[postcard]   Stinchcombe

You never take my advice. You love & trust H.H. But I urge you not
to republish juvenilia without rewriting. Or else somehow use them
in a treatise on the period quoting them as examples.

You are so *lazy*. But I am sorry for your great illness which no
doubt weakened your resistance to self interested flattery. Assy is more
disgusting than Vence.

Freud takes Princess Margaret to night clubs in saffron socks.

8 November 1951   7 rue Monsieur, VII

Darling Evelyn
Colonel says as follows: many priests who have had to resign on
account of having lost their faith have joined the ones who work in
the factories & this is a sort of comfort to them. Furthermore he says
the real priests who do so have in certain cases become communisant
(as they say here i.e. fellow travellers) because of the terrible misery
they see around them. He hasn't heard of any apostasy in the true
sense of the word.

(I think French people lose their faith more easily than others
because of their special character, but they *mind terribly*, like my poor
intellectual, because of it making life so dull.)

Col knows o of the Père Perrin, but I have put Miss Chetwynd[1] on
to it she knows lots of pasteurs who have become Trappists, you see
the sort of thing. She says she'll easily find out for you.

I'm in a great state about my early books. I think I told you Jamie
came over specially to ask me for them to be reprinted, which softened

me. Then I read them. Well *Wigs on the G.* which isn't too bad, I find, is a total impossibility. Too much has happened for jokes about Nazis to be regarded as funny or as anything but the worst of taste. After all, it was written in 1934, I really couldn't quite have foreseen all that came after. So that is out. *Xmas Pudding* is pathetic, badly written, facetious & *awful*. I can't conceive why he wants it & the fact that he does has shaken my faith in his judgement. The awful thing is that over a bottle of good wine at La Rue I said all right to both – but I can't let him do *Wigs* even if it is breaking a promise. If he does *Xmas P* I shall have to entirely rewrite it which will be as bad as doing a new book. Oh Misery I feel in a jam.

Honks has received the eggs but claims many more, only they need not be frog spawn.

I met a charming Mrs Boothby[2] & kept feeling she must be a relation of Laura but didn't like to ask.

A sad young man came to see me & said he invented the story of *The Blessing* & will I give him £500. I told him to go to Peters – thank you once more for Peters!

> With love
> NR

Is it true one of the Tory election cries was 'Dior dresses can be paid in London.'

[1] Elizabeth Chetwynd (d.1961). An English bluestocking who lived in Paris and reviewed for *The Times Literary Supplement*.
[2] Susan Asquith (1922–). Married Basil Boothby in 1946.

[November 1951]   Piers Court
                                                   Stinchcombe
Darling Nancy
   You could write a most amusing & interesting and popular work in this way: Describe yourself in 1951 taking up *Wigs on the Green* and rereading it for the first time since its publication. Print $\frac{2}{3}$ or half of the original text with constant interruptions from your 1951 self asking: 'Why did I say that?' or saying 'This still seems funny, why?' So in the easiest & most informal way possible you could write your reminiscences & the history of the deteriorating world and the improving authoress.

   It would be fun to write & huge fun to read. Do do it that way.

   You could produce a magnum opus with a minimum of labour and all the critics would acclaim it as a great 'DOCUMENT'.

   I haven't been elected Rector of Edinburgh. It was just a joke that didn't come off.[1] A really bitter failure has been the loss of 12 greatly over life size busts of the Caesars on eight foot, elaborate pedestals – circa 1800, that were in a house near here that was being sold up. I

asked the auctioneer what they would fetch. 'Ten bob each,' he said.
So I left a bid of £2 each & went away confident I should get them.
For days & nights I have been planning how to erect them, replanning
the whole garden for them. I would willingly have paid £10 each.
Now I hear that through laziness in not going to the sale some other
maniac has bought them. It is a crushing blow at a time when I need
a bit of fun.

    Love from
        Evelyn

[1] Evelyn was beaten by Sir Alexander Fleming and was more upset by his defeat than he was
willing to admit to Nancy.

25 November 1951   7 rue Monsieur, VII

Darling Evelyn
    I've been struggling with my article all the afternoon – must relax
(Oh I loathe work – do you think I'm rich enough now to stop?) I
went at luncheon time to see the books – can't get near them at any
other. Well you ought to come over you know – I've never seen such
an exhibition.[1] The catalogue in itself is a very good history of English
literature. I saw *Brideshead* & was impressed – so clean. My MSS have
telephone numbers etc scribbled all over them – I love the Col &
things like that.
    I never know what you feel about Mauriac – he is our daily pundit
here – thought enclosed might interest you.[2] Also the enclosed picture
of Shelley because do you admit it's the very image of Diana Spearman? Milton has a very syphilitic look I thought – well perhaps the
blindness –? Oh I lived in it, I mean the exhibition. I stayed for 2
hours & you know how tired I get. Really I can only lead $\frac{1}{4}$ of a life,
it is such a nuisance.
    I wish you'd come over as I've seen a rather large present I'd like
to give Harriet & don't think I can force any but a parent to take it
back. But next week I'm going to stay with Prod in Rome. Come for
Xmas I've got a lovely party on Xmas night – oh of course the kids,
& I suppose you put on a red dressing gown, knowing as I do the real
bonhomie behind that mask of iron. Come for New Year & I'll take
you to Violet [Trefusis] who has got a party. The exhibition only stops
on N.Y. day. I promise you ought to see it.
    I say my friend Lees-Milne has been excommunicated did you
know? I fear he will mind. The whole thing is too silly (I mean his
behaviour) & I blame Alvilde very much.[3]
    I've helped to organize a literary cocktail party the Windsors are
giving for his book when it comes out, next Monday.

I'll give one for *Helena* if you like, only you'd have to bare the gums a bit.

Pigeon Pie is better than the others. I've given it a brush up (I say, it's *full* of mirrors mantelpieces handbags etc don't tell my public or I'm done for). I must tell you it's very evocative of the phoney war & from that point of view rather fascinating. The heroine is Pam Berry to the life.

Why can't one write articles like letters – there must be nearly 400 words in this one oh the waste. But my next one won't be bad, Paul Léautaud[4] & ONU. They take me for ever, 8 hours a day for a month.

Jamie Hamilton asked me why you hate him. Is it known?

The frogs like *Blessing* better than the English do, & so do the Yanks. They dash at me & say I'm just too mad for words about Hector Dexter – no not mad that means X but whatever it is. Paramount are keeping in touch with me which means once a fortnight I have to go to the Ritz & see 5 or 6 Dexters who are very important & I ought to have heard of, & they all tell me how when they left the States all their friends sent *The Blessing* to them on the ship. Well, good for trade.

You realize why this letter is so long? *Anything* not to go back to the article. Well now I must for lack of space.

Love
NR

[1] An exhibition of 'Le Livre Anglais', with a catalogue by John Hayward, was being held at the Bibliothèque Nationale in Paris.

[2] Nancy enclosed an article by François Mauriac about the renewal of interest in religious art among contemporary painters. 'It is not the public that broke away from art, it is art that broke away from the public ... Modern art is based on references that are unverifiable for most people. Now, suddenly, painters have realised that a Christian population still exists.' 'La querelle de l'art sacré', *Figaro*, 21 November 1951.

[3] James Lees-Milne had not been officially excommunicated but by marrying Alvilde Chaplin, whose husband was still living, he was automatically excluded from partaking of the Sacraments.

[4] Paul Léautaud (1872–1956). Eccentric literary critic and diarist. In her article Nancy described a radio interview in which Léautaud declared that he loved cats and dogs above humans, that he had lived on nothing but cheese for eight years, and that he had never travelled farther than Calais.

[November 1951]   Piers Court
[postcard]   Stinchcombe

I think Mauriac is on the right lines but he has a subconscious snobbery (Frog sense) which prevents him telling the truth – that the painting of this century is not just a different species of the same genus as, say, Botticcelli (?) & Veronese. The cubists etc are just anti-painters. They are only bought by jews & lunatics.

What does 'pliés à une ascèse' mean?[1] Dictionary doesn't help. Mauriac's point seems to be largely to defend the sancta simplicitas which likes Burns & Oates statues.[2]

It is *not* known why I dislike Hamish Hamilton. I think perhaps myself being a publisher's son has something to do with it. I grew up with a respect for publishers & don't like to see people fall below my papa's standards. (Not goodness knows of *flair*. I mean of good behaviour.)

Besides I don't like people who are pushful without swagger.

Besides I shouldn't recognize the fellow if I saw him.

I wrote 4000 words yesterday.

Ed's first wife[3] came for a night to 'talk about Hazel Lavery'.[4] V. barmy.

I have been cruelly insulted by a Dominican.[5] I would like to burn them all alive.

I gave your name to a Mme de Lusignan saying *if* she already knew you she might question you about me; *not* introducing her if you don't know her.

[1] 'Peut-être parviendront-ils à le satisfaire, et je le souhaite ardemment, mais ce ne sera pas sans s'être eux-mêmes pliés à une ascèse.' 'Perhaps [the painters] will succeed in satisfying [the public], and I sincerely hope they will, but not without having submitted themselves to rigorous self-discipline.'
[2] Conventional religious figurines.
[3] Lady Victoria Audrey Chetwynd-Talbot (1910–94). Married to 6th Baron Stanley 1932–6 and to Gwyn Morris QC in 1945.
[4] Hazel Martyn (1887–1935). An American beauty who married the society portraitist Sir John Lavery in 1910. Evelyn had a brief affair with her in 1932.
[5] Fr Gerald Meath, in a review of Dorothy Sayers' *The Emperor Constantine*, had omitted 'Mr' before Evelyn's name. Evelyn chose to interpret this as an insult: 'To write of a man without his "Mr" or other prefix is to proclaim him, to the educated reader, as either a felon or a professional athlete – or, else, as dead.' *Tablet*, 17 November 1951.

1 December 1951   7 rue Monsieur, VII

Darling Evelyn

The answer as I understand it to your question about S. Weil is that in a Catholic country such a book had to be published with some sanction from the Church, but that in a heretic country no such sanction (or preface) was necessary.

A terrible article by Mauriac about death beds saying there is no such thing as a happy one because either you believe & are facing possible hell or you don't believe & it is le néant [nothingness]. I always feel that as everything in life is so heavenly probably death is too (I don't mean dying but actual death).

Of course (about the pictures) the French can't resist anything new, it's one of the attractive things about them. (Even old Mme Costa was painted by a Cubist in 1910, the funniest picture I ever saw.) But abstract art isn't new any more & the very young now love the old masters much more than the Impressionists & we shall see what we shall see. Couturier is not very young.

Pliés à une ascèse must mean enfolded or bent towards asceticism I suppose – does that not make sense?

You must read Sir F. Ponsonby *Three Reigns*.[1] There is a shriek on every page & the funniest description of the career of a bolter (horse not lady) I ever read.

Isn't it bliss about Lady Mary Grosvenor?[2] Colonel says I must write a book called Lady into Lord.

Next Thursday I go to Rome don't ask me why. But back (DV) for Xmas. Do write to me 167 via Giulia – oh but not if you're doing 4000 words a day. I wonder if I've ever done as much – I get such awful cramp after about 2.

I'm so thankful you've left Laffont. They say (on dit) that you & Graham Greene have been cheated out of thousands of pounds by them. Well I blame Mrs Bradley. I've already banked £800 from my 2 books which have only done very fairly well, partly because *LCC* was vilely translated. You've got one of the best translators here. Of course your name is a handicap & I never quite get over being asked 'aimez-vous Vogue?' by venerable littérateurs.

As you will see in the *S Times* if they don't cut my article, our publisher Stock got the prix Femina. Great excitement in the office.

Do you know John Russell? He is so nice. He has been staying with 2 American women & says that every evening at 6 they go to a psychiatrist for ½ an hour, an absolute routine. Can you beat it?

Best love
    NR

[1] Frederick Ponsonby, *Recollections of Three Reigns* (1951). An autobiography by the Private Secretary to Queen Victoria and Edward VII, and Equerry to George V.
[2] There was an unfounded rumour that the Duke of Westminster's daughter was turning into a man.

4 December 1951   7 rue Monsieur, VII

Darling Evelyn

He does keep on keeping on as my Nanny used to say. I expect you to agree with a good lot of this – but fancy having to have a Matisse to give you the goût de la vie every morning!! Even I find this a bit much.[1]

I sat next Monte[2] at luncheon – he'd spent the morning at Dior & quoted *The Blessing* extensively so of course I loved him. He said afterwards I wasn't at all what he had expected because SO NICE. So there.

I thought *he* read the Bible & hated women but clearly neither is true. He's terribly pretty did you know? And quite all there.

The Windsor party was bliss & thank heavens no jokes. (I had

enough of embarrassing times with royalties when married to Prod &
though funny afterwards it's torture while going on.)

Harriet's enormous present. Well I saw it from a bus & it was a
whole doll's dinner service, plates & knives & forks & 3 sorts of glasses
etc etc laid out in a huge box & it looked *fairy like*. But you know
when I saw it not from a bus it was all made in plastic & was truly
horrible, I couldn't give it. I'll find something in Rome & meanwhile
Dearest is to send a book.

I've got to go & dine with an Ambassador I accepted in the drunkenness of getting on so well with a F.M. & now I wish I could go to bed
& read Ponsonby. Better than Wodehouse, I advise it – a shriek on
every page.

Psse de Clèves now out in U.S. described in a review as a romantic
classical novel about a rich widow.

Write to Rome via Giulia 167.

Love
NR

I'm bored rather with Ldy M Gros: because IS IT TRUE? Nobody
can tell one that & if not, all quite dull in my view.

[1] In the continuing debate over sacred art, François Mauriac had written that a drawing by
Matisse in his bedroom helped to revive his 'appetite for life' each morning. 'Des couleurs et
des goûts', *Figaro*, 4 December 1951.
[2] Field Marshal Montgomery.

30 December 1951   7 rue Monsieur, VII

Darling Evelyn

I had a spiffing time in Rome they like my books there (old professors
sprang at me saying greater than Katherine Mansfield) & many parties
were given for me. I've written a facetious account of it all in the *S
Times*. (I've got a new pen from the dear Sutros & it can't spell at all
never mind.) What is heavenly for me abroad is that whereas at home
I am regarded as an inferior P. G. Wodehouse, foreigners take my
'work' (sic) seriously & speak of psychological insight etc & of course
this goes to my head like wine.

I have discovered to my fascination that beautiful Cécile H was
(what I call) a Chartreuse de Parme – I was once taken to Valmondois[1]
have you ever been there? It is the Broadway (Glos: Eng:) of France
– which perhaps tells you nothing. But I hear that *she* really is all you
say & it's not only your old eyes glazed with love that see her thus.

My new sister in law Rosie [Rodd] is jolly nice, pretty & everything.
How could she have married that miserable worm of a Taffy? Did
you see her when you were in Rome?

Dear old Prod leads a funny life of sleeping all day. He wouldn't come to the parties because he said they were given by Neo Fascists, but as I don't live there I thought unnecessary to take a line. Anyway the Wops were our enemies, it's not the same situation as here. Poor things they are in a mess all right, I never saw anything like the misery. I suppose it has always been the same, in Italy, as regards food, but now there is the housing shortage too.

Is D'Arcy[2] a friend of yours? He *was* faithful – on the doorstep every morning at 11 to take me shopping & sight seeing, & I went to see his harem of 1000 boys, very fascinating.

The Mallets very civil, I dined there, but Victor whom I used to dance with is an old gentleman now – I had a shock & so no doubt did he. The horror of the new Embassy!

I had an Xmas party here of 18 it was very nice but rather too much undergrowth. Next year I must prune more carefully. How was yours? [. . .]

Happy N.Y., love
    NR

Bebino Salina[3] whom you may know has an aunt who at 45 became a man rather nice because it shows it can happen in the upper classes.

[1] Cécile Howard's family, the Geoffroy-Dechaumes, lived at Valmondois in the Val d'Oise.
[2] Sir D'Arcy Godolphin Osborne (1884–1964). Envoy Extraordinary and Minister Plenipotentiary to the Holy See 1936–47. He was Governor of the Borgo di Ragazzi, the 'boys' suburb' where a school for homeless orphans was set up by priests after the war.
[3] An Italian playboy.

[December 1951]   Piers Court
[postcard]   Stinchcombe

I wrote to you at Rodd palace. Did the letter get stolen by communists? It had all my brief news & boundless good wishes for darling darling 1952. I consider it most unhealthy & rather alarming that all your recent letters have been full of transformations of sex. I don't believe it will do you any permanent good in the world of letters if you become Lord Redesdale. I suppose it is because you want to get in the Academy & wear that pretty uniform.

I don't quite know what you mean by *Chartreuse de Parme* applied to Cécile who is pregnant again (still Mondi).

You must get your hands on *Life* Magazine's *History of Western Culture* a thing of horror unexampled since E. West's history of G. Sutherland.

E

I did not find Mrs Taffy a lady.

5 January 1952   7 rue Monsieur, VII

Darling Evelyn

How deeply boring, your letter never came. But probably will be forwarded when the Taffys return from winter sports. People aren't ladies any more (didn't you know that) in England. Here there is the great dividing line of *bien* – Rosie is not *bien* I admit, but I thought her beautiful nice & funny which is quite a lot.

Chartreuse de Parme. I have to say it in order to remember Geoffroy-Dechaume that's all.

There's a great row (open letters) going on between Mauriac & Cocteau[1] – the same old Gide–Claudel row on more spiteful lines 'Tu dis que les pierres ne parleront pas – une pierre a parlé: Toi.' 'Je t'accuse d'inculture'[2] (the worst thing a Frenchman can say to another).

Of course old Mauriac wins really but not in such a steam rollerish way as Claudel did over Gide. One rather nasty touch was when he said to Cocteau 'do remember you are now 66 & very soon you will have to meet your God'. Poor Cocteau (like me) sees himself as an eternal 28 & won't care for this at all.

I only ask the '50s to be as heavenly as the '40s – for me. I suppose you will blow up. But everybody must see the world out of his own little window & *I* enjoyed every moment of the 1940s. What is so nice & *so* unexpected about life is the way it improves as it goes along. I think you should impress this fact on your children because I think young people have an awful feeling that life is slipping past them & they must do something – catch something – they don't quite know what, whereas they've only got to wait & it *all comes*.

I've got a nice present for Hattie & the next traveller can take it. Thank her for her very well written letter.

You won't make a quick dash over here to see your MS in the Galerie Mazarine? I believe you would be fascinated by the exhibition – which has been prolonged another fortnight such a huge success is it.

I'm dreadfully bored by the lone captain[3] are you?

Fondest love, Happy N.Y.
        Nancy

No foreigner, not even I if I were Lord R, can get into *the* Academy. Don't cite [Charles] Morgan, he is a member of one of the 5 Académies housed in the Institut de France but *not* the Académie française.

---

[1] Jean Cocteau (1889–1963). His play *Bacchus* opened at the Théâtre Marigny on 20 December. François Mauriac walked out of the performance in disgust and wrote a letter to the *Figaro* accusing Cocteau of blasphemy. Cocteau replied by attacking Mauriac for being, among other things, frivolous, uneducated and a bad Christian.

[2] 'You say that stones will not speak – a stone has spoken: You.' 'I accuse you of being uncultured.'

[3] Captain Kurt Carlsen, master of an American freighter, had spent six days alone aboard his crippled ship before being taken in tow by a British tug.

8 January 1952 (the sweet thing)   Piers Court
                                                            Stinchcombe

Darling Nancy,

I liked your Roman letter[1] very much. I expect you are now reading many protests giving you the precise dimensions of St Peter's and St Giles's. I thought it a good joke. Pope & vicar less funny because it has no sort of relation with the truth. I mean he doesn't drop in for a game of croquet and apart from his spiritual status he is the only monarch in the world now who keeps a proper court. Mlle Canavaggia, the old lady you were so kind to, sent me some reviews of *Hélène*. To my simple mind they seemed rather praising but of course I don't know the nuances so they might have been full of irony. Also, of course, I don't know the importance of the reviewers – they may have been Desmond MacCarthies or the idiot whose name I forget who insults us both in the *Evening Standard*.

I have written to *S. Times* not about your Rome but about a Mr Wiggin who despises all books that 'fail to influence behaviour'. You would be all right with Wiggin. Think of the efforts we all make now not to say 'note paper'.

You have already given a very nice present to Hattie. Didn't you know? She is dotty. Sad, but one must expect 1 in 6 to be – much more by the latest statistics. Her report said: 'a most imaginative child. Unhappily her imagination is filled with grim images.'

I have finished that novel[2] – slogging, inelegant, boring – and what little point it has will only be revealed in the fourth volume at least four years hence. Still there were some dunderheads who didn't appreciate *Helena*. Perhaps they will like it.

I am afraid you are right when you say that there are no ladies & gentlemen now. It was a most important distinction basic to English health & happiness. You see we are the most elaborately stratified people in the world but no one, unless he makes it his special hobby, knows a thing about the strata except those immediately above & below his own. Everyone was convinced that there was a great impassable line between 'gentlemen' and 'the lower classes' and everyone drew that line immediately below his own feet. 'You're no lady' was the traditional battle cry between two drunken charwomen scratching out each other's eyes in a pub.

There are two graves in Stinchcombe church of a father & son, early & middle 16th century, one saying 'Jos. Hinks, Yeoman' and the other 'Jos. Hinks, Gent'. So there must once have been a technical distinction, as between officers and NCOs in the army. Both Hinkses

owned the same small property. Can it have been the grant of a coat
of arms. In the nineteenth century there was a universal common
accent for all the educated. Also a moral code attached which the
18th century knew nothing of, and in the 19th century the high aristocracy seldom observed. The great thing was that *everyone* thought himself
a gentleman and closely allied with Dukes, and everyone below him
contemptible. So there was a stable, contented society. It never
occurred to me to think I wasn't a gentleman until Lady Burghclere[3]
pointed it out. I have a friend called Michael Trappes-Lomax[4] who
treats me with genial equality but, in fact, regards no one as a gentleman who hasn't 32 quarterings. I think it was the American marriages
in the 90s and the lady shopkeepers in the 20s who made all the
trouble. It is a fascinating subject. A book on it would be a best seller
as it is still the first concern of 80% of the reading public. I think I
may write it.

Mrs Taffy was pure Billa [Harrod] to me.

There was a competition in *John o'London's Weekly* to name the most
odious books in the language. We were both in the short list.

How I agree about the horrors of the Embassy at Rome. But wasn't
'Reeking' too strong.[5]

You ought to have mentioned the Embassy (Legation?) at The
Hague among the good ones. It is Alba's old palace. Splendid. Especially necessary to mention it *now* because the Office of Works want to
move.

I can't get on with D'Arcy Osborne. Goodness *he's* a gentleman
and a half.

I *must* get abroad at Easter. How many eggs have I?

Love from
     Evelyn

---

[1] 'Rome is Only a Village', *Sunday Times*, 6 January 1952. 'Rome is a capital city only in name;
in fact and at heart it is a village, with its one post office, one railway station and life centred
round the vicarage.'
[2] *Men at Arms.*
[3] The mother of Evelyn's first wife.
[4] Michael Trappes-Lomax (1900–72). Rouge Dragon Pursuivant of Arms 1946–51, Somerset
Herald 1951–67.
[5] In her article on Rome, Nancy had written: 'After the war we saw fit to install our Ambassador
and his enormous staff in the former German embassy with its frightful architecture, inconvenient situation and what are now called unpleasant associations, in other words still-reeking
torture chambers.'

10 January 1952   7 rue Monsieur, VII

Darling Evelyn

Gentleman here means crook. 'Gentleman's agreement' (pronounced in French) = two crooks making some black market deal in

a bar & gentleman tout court is a burglar dressed like a bourgeois. 'Un gentleman s'est évadé en dérobant pour 8 millions de bijoux.'[1]

ONE is always surprised when taken as belonging to a lower strata of society than ONE supposed. E.G. I was surprised at being lumped together with Theodora Benson[2] & Betty Askwith[3] as 'members of the titled middle classes' though on reflexion I saw that this was fair enough. When I was a child my French gov: used to say that we were toute petite noblesse, which I remember annoyed me *terribly*!!

Isn't it funny about jokes & whom they tickle. Raymond sent a telegram saying 'Vicarage best joke ever made'. I only said centred round the vicarage & goodness it is – why all the families that count are descended from vicars come to think of it.

You have got about 1400 eggs I counted 3 or 4 times but it's like a bird, I can't count over 10 my attention wanders. Anyhow well over 1000. Why not come to Florence for Easter – I shall be there, very possibly Colonel too, at Violet's.[4] Then Harold [Acton] could be in waiting, Osbert not far off etc etc. Do think of it.

I adore D'Arcy he is a real character for a novel. He came every day at 11 to take me sight seeing – he is analphabet[5] you know. Picking up Ranke's *Hist of the Popes* he said 'this looks rather good – is it just out?' In the Farnesina he said 'these frescoes are by some quite well known artist' (Raphael). He is in love with the Queen & the Pope & has tinted photographs of them all over his flat. Somehow one expects him to be enormously cultivated & all this is a never-failing surprise.

Robert Kemp & Gérard Bauer are two reviewers of great standing; the long review in *Fig: Lit:* can but do good. I'll find out soon from literary friends what the general impression is, meanwhile all the shops are stocking it I see.

I dined last night with Ed Stanley & wife[6] of whom I take a very poor view. She is *not* a lady, or very nice or very pretty. Here comes a journalist to interview me.

Love
    NR

I've always noticed that royal people think everybody else is the same, the Dow Lady Airlie & the cook, all equal.

---

[1] 'Gentleman' on its own means a burglar dressed like a bourgeois. 'A gentleman escaped after stealing 8 million francs' worth of jewellery.'
[2] Hon. Theodora Benson (1906–68). Author of light novels including *Salad Days* (1929), *Concert Pitch* (1934) and *The Man from the Tunnel* (1950).
[3] Hon. Betty Askwith (1909–94), daughter of 1st Lord Charnwood. Novelist, and biographer of Lady Dilke (1969) and the Strachey and Benson families (1971). Married to Keith Miller Jones in 1950.
[4] Violet Trefusis had inherited the Villa dell'Ombrellino from her parents.
[5] Illiterate.
[6] Thérèse Husson, Lord Stanley's third wife.

14 January   Piers Court
Sweet 1952 never been kissed   Stinchcombe

Darling Nancy

So I have been doing sums for weeks & find I am hopelessly ruined
(financially *not* morally). So I have come to a Great Decision to Change
my Life entirely. I am sacking all the servants (five does seem a lot to look
after Laura & me in a house the size of a boot) and becoming Bohemian. I
shall never wear a clean collar again or subscribe to Royal Lifeboat
Fund and I shall steal people's books & sell them & cadge drinks in
the Savage Club by pretending to know you. It is no good trying to
live decently in modern England. I make £ 10,000 a year, which
used to be thought quite a lot, I live like a mouse in shabby-genteel
circumstances, I keep no women or horses or yachts, yet I am bank-
rupt, simply by the politicians buying votes with my money.

The trouble is getting servants to go. There is no shortage of them
now because no one can afford them. And they cannot become harlots
because apparently men don't pay women now, they just rape them
& take *their* money. But go they shall, if I have to burn the house
down.

The sentence in your last letter about royalty seeing the Airlies &
the cooks as equal in rank occurs in the novel I have just sent to be
printed. I only mention this in case you accuse me of cribbing later.
Goodness that novel is dull and what is worse all falling to bits. But
I was going mad trying to set it right so off I sent it.

I don't at all like Florence. Must I come *there*?

Did I ask you to ask Col (if he was ever in an army) what is the
French for 'Halt. Who goes there?' 'Stand or I fire.' 'Take two paces
forward & be recognized.' Also do the black French soldiers of Senegal
use French for such conversations or some sort of coon talk.

I have read the papers & learned that the Gaullists are collaborating
with the Communists. Is this your influence or just a newspaper lie.

I don't think you quite appreciate the great Importance of my
Discovery about Gentlemen. It explains all our national greatness
1815–1914 – that everyone felt his natural allies to be those above him
(and in his eyes equal) in Social Scale. Perhaps everyone has known
this fact for years.

All love
        E

I sent three exquisite original early Victorian drawings, joined by
exquisite contemporary calligraphy to Clarissa[1] whom I love next to
Cécile. She thought it was a Christmas card and promptly burned it.
Can you at all explain this? You know I call Honks 'Baby'? Embarrassing but true. Anyway I got a mad letter the other day of the kind one

gets most days. No interest. High brow madness typewritten in English.
The odd thing was that the address was 'Chez Baby' 16 Rue de Condé,
Paris VI. It began 'Dear E.W.' and was signed 'Mary O'Connor'. Is
Chez Baby a night club. But one doesn't take a typewriter to a night
club – or does one now? I thought it very rum.

[1] Clarissa Churchill (1920–). Niece of Winston Churchill. Married in 1952 to Anthony Eden
(created Earl of Avon in 1961), Prime Minister 1955–7.

16 January 1952   7 rue Monsieur, VII

Darling Evelyn
    Life without servants is not worth living – better cut down in any
other way. I can't understand why you don't come & live here. If
Laura wants to farm France is the richest agricultural country in the
world. Your children would become bilingual which is always an
advantage & *you* would have all the comfort & luxury that you like.
You don't really care for the English, except about 3 friends who
would visit you here – in fact I think you positively loathe them. The
day one sets foot in France, you can take it from me, PURE happiness
begins. You never heard me say heavenly 1928 or lament the end of
1935 did you? Of course I know it's partly that dear dear Colonel, but
I don't see him all the time by any means & every minute of every
day here is bliss & when I wake up in the morning I feel as excited
as if it were my birthday.
    I'll find out about your words of command & finish this later.
    'Halte – qui vive?'
    'Arrêtez – ou je tire'
    'Avancez (sous commandement)'
    'Deux pas en avant pour identification' No – he's not sure will ask.
The Senegalese will say the same in petit nègre – i.e. putting I instead
of E & U. 'Ti vint missi'. 'Pour examen d'identité ou pour inspection,
deux pas en avant.'[1]
    He's going to ask [General] Koenig for sure but thinks this is all
right but nearly 30 years since St Cyr is long. Anyway it isn't utterly
wrong, I mean wouldn't shock. Most of our military expressions came
straight from the French anyway.
    I've been awful about writing. Last week I dined out every night,
but it tired me too much & I never even managed to read the *NS &
N*, so this week I've refused everything. On Fri I went to the Rothschilds
who took me out hunting (only in a motor) & I can think of 0 but
how many best sellers before I can have a house near a forest & a
horse. Elie de R[2] says oh nonsense I will mount you, & so on, but to
me that would be too much anxiety. I never saw such beautiful horses
in my life. Think of the fun, you gallop hard in the heavenly woods

all day & no frightening jumps. Made for an old lady like me. The woods are so huge that you can ride from Chantilly to Belgium without leaving them.

Yesterday 200 American ladies gave a luncheon for me & I was introduced as one of the famous daughters of Dr Redesdale. Must write & tell the Dr.

How I die for your book (not very original of me).

By the way I loved your *ST* letter about etiquette & pornography[3] but screamed aloud at the lady who wondered if you had read the Bible.

Oh the hunting, I burn with desire. I've described it in *S. Times* so won't bore you with it here. Come & live here, we will find houses adjacent & share a groom.

I saw my homme d'affaires just now & said I've made £10 000 this year. He clicked his tongue & said it was simply terrible & will *all* go in tax so I said really how much & he said well in principle you would pay nearly 3000, but of course I can get you off some of that, but you'll pay well over 2 I'm afraid. So you see. (French Popkin.) Isn't it almost your duty to come?

Really this letter is too long like a schoolgirl's. So goodbye.

Love
    NR

Re-read your letter.
Can't explain chez Baby. Honks is however in a very odd frame of mind at present.
No the Gaullists are not collaborating with the Communists though as both are in opposition they sometimes find themselves in the same lobby. (The English don't & don't try to, understand Fr politics.)

---

[1] 'Halte-là! Qui vive?' were the only French words of command used by Evelyn in *Men at Arms*.
[2] Baron Elie de Rothschild (1917–2007). 'Elie to me, as I always tell him, is like First Soldier in a Shakespeare play, he rattles noisily on, makes a very loud pointless speech & rattles off again.' (NM to Lady Pamela Berry, 16 June 1952.) He was married by proxy to the learned Liliane Fould-Springer while in prison camp in 1942.
[3] In his reply to Maurice Wiggin's contention that writers were only important in so far as they influenced behaviour, Evelyn had written: 'I can only think of two classes of writing (both of which I eschew) calculated to do so – books of etiquette and of pornography.' *Sunday Times*, 13 January 1952.

27 January 1952   Piers Court
                                                   Stinchcombe
Darling Nancy

I have long recognized your euphoria as a pathological condition as morbid as Honks's melancholy. You each choose minor exterior conditions to explain your states – oddly enough the same one – France.

You have made great friends with a Pole who has introduced you to a number of other Poles. You have found some Jews for yourself, such as your hunting friends and the lady[1] who gave me caviare & pretended to like painting, filling her drawing-room with fine works of art and all the time secretly sipping Picasso in her bed-room. You are the kindest possible hospitaller to your distressed fellow countryman. And you spend long hours with the Harveys talking socialism. This is not the France of Louis IX or Joan of Arc or Bossuet or the Curé d'Ars. All the great Frenchmen & women would repudiate it. Still less is it the real modern France that fills the world with its self pity.

Your delicate nostrils detected the smell of blood in poor Victor & Peggy [Mallet]'s awful house. I retch at the smell of blood all over France – the blood of the hundred thousand massacred in the épuration. What's more I see the guilt of that unexpiated horror in the eyes of all Frenchmen from the hall porter at the Travellers to Père Couturier.

Of course the French have numerous skills and once had the very purest taste. I am told their music-hall songs are very witty.

Anyway your 'France' is pure fantasy. It may afford you some pleasure but it is transferable.

I have had more mad letters from Paris in different hands. Very rum. Not by Frenchmen but in pure idiomatic English & American. And stark mad.

I get two a week usually from England or USA. Paris is quite a new centre. The letters are not the least personal. I mean they don't accuse me of imaginary injuries or anything like that. They are just drivel which might be addressed to anyone.

I should like details of Honks's rumness. She has seemed desperately unhappy in all her letters lately. She is in London now but I can't go up to see her on account of rheumatism. Is she turning into a man, too? Her crustiness is highly masculine.

Snow & thaw here. Beastly.

Thank you & Col *very much* indeed for military information of great value.

The wines on the list look tempting but the friendly merchant (another non-French member of your circle I note) doesn't seem to know about rates of exchange. I think I must make some purchases in Paris when I come over. His English prices are not lower than Peter Thursby's,[2] and he is a friend too.

If you had heard a lecture by an English francophile socialist on the wireless in praise of Corbusier's fiasco at Marseille, I think even you would have been sick. Or did you write it for him?

Lots of love
        E

[1] Marie-Laure de Noailles.
[2] A wine merchant, married to Poppy Baring.

29 January 1952   7 rue Monsieur, VII

'Philip I am getting cross'

Really you might as well say you see the guilt of St Bart's Eve in their eyes or the guilt of the killers of the Smithfield martyrs in the eyes of the porter at White's. Really what rubbish. Is England the England of Shakespeare? Is Germany that of Goethe? (I must say Spain *is* that of Philip II – you might go & live there.)

You are not very accurate in all your statements. Marie-Laure is ¼ Jewish – her grandmother Mme de Chevigné was the original Mme de Guermantes (Duchesse). On ne peut être plus gratin.[1] Do I feel a note of anti semitism creeping into your thought? Is this not something rather new?

I'm going to write about modern architects who don't seem to think twice before dumping some monstrosity in front of a masterpiece. The sky scraper which now obscures Amiens cathedral from the surrounding plain, the new entrance to St Peter's, the Faculté de Médecine here. I shall say that architects must be more thick skinned than writers – what writer, for any money at all, would write a sonnet & have it bound up with Shakespeare's, or add a scene to *Hamlet*?

Can you think of any other examples of modern architecture ruining a beautiful town?

The joke is these sky scrapers are quite uninhabitable. Of course they are a Communist ideal, too easy to control people who are all shut up in one huge box.

My furniture has arrived from London, for 2 days I unpacked & it was like getting hundreds of presents. It looks *so* nice here. A few of my father's things he gave me, including a lot of prints. The van man picked up one of Disraeli & said 'Who is this?' 'One of Queen Victoria's ministers' I said. 'Comment, Disraeli?' Can you see an English removals man saying 'This *must* be M. Thiers'?

Fancy the wine being so expensive, what a swiz. Here it is far cheaper than at the ordinary wine merchant. Do you ever buy a barrel & have it bottled? I think I must do that when I am properly installed. The house smells of grapes for days after.

Best love
     NR

[1] One can't be more upper-crust.

10 February [1952]   Piers Court
                                                               Stinchcombe

Darling Nancy

I have been wretchedly low spirited, plagued by a sort of rheumatism and common cold. I can't get rid of my servants. Three went last week, one is back already saying I *must* employ her because her mother won't let her go to a factory and she *must* stay in the district because she is in love. I say: 'I can't afford you.' She says: 'I'll come without wages.' I say: 'It isn't your wages only it's the expense of keeping you which is much more.' But she is back with her trunk shovelling down butter & cream and American hampers. Meanwhile two village women who occasionally 'obliged' have permanently ensconced themselves at much higher wages, so my economy campaign has done no good.

While I lay in bed in agony I had to break an engagement in London with Honks – not even an engagement to take her out; merely to meet her at the house of some friends of hers for dinner. Do I get a letter of tender sympathy? Not at all. A scolding saying: 'Never do it again – plan & fail. *I* am too old & easily bruised' (my italics). There is egocentric mania there.

Do your foreign set know that our King is dead? Mr Churchill made a dreadful speech on the TSF.[1] Triteness only enlivened by gross blunders. His worst remark was in commending the late King's patriotism. 'During the war I made a point of keeping him fully informed. He understood all I said wonderfully. I even disclosed to him military secrets.' His most inept historical parallel: comparing our present Queen with Elizabeth Tudor: 'Neither grew up in the expectation of the crown.' Elizabeth Tudor had been formally bastardized & declared ineligible by Henry VIII and all three estates of the realm. She survived alive because of the high Christian principles of Mary Tudor, when in any other royal family, she would have been executed. She was jockeyed into place by a gang of party bosses and executed the rightful heir Mary Stuart. All the newspapers are full of glorification of Elizabeth Tudor, the vilest of her sex.

I suppose George VI's reign will go into history as the most disastrous my unhappy country has known since Matilda and Stephen. One interesting point stands out. The King died at the moment when Princess Elizabeth first put on a pair of 'slacks' – within a matter of minutes anyway. The Duke of Windsor lost his throne by his beret much more than by his adultery.

It would be too late for your article I'm afraid for me to add anything to your list of modern buildings spoiling old. The new Bodleian Library you will surely have mentioned. Most of the real dwarfing – such as St James's Street – where two lovely houses Brooks's Club and Boodles are quite ruined was not I think the work of proud architects but simply of shop-keepers who never gave any thought to the matter.

There is Soane's elegant obelisk at Reading but that is too minor a
work of art for anyone except Betjeman to make a great fuss.

It was decent of you to say the frog-jews like *Helena*. I bet they
don't. But thank you for saying so. Yes, I am afraid I must admit to
a shade of anti-jew feeling. Not anti-semite. I rather like Arabs. It
dates from my visit to Israel this time last year. It was there I realized
that all jews were not like John Sutro and Lord Rosebery.

I live so much out of the world that it was a great surprise to me
to read in *The Times* that Lord Rothermere had been given a decree
nisi against Ann. He must already have filed the suit at the time they
gave their Christmas party; I suppose he has found a new girl? I always
found him a bore. It is a great thing for Ann, whom I love, to be rid
of him & to have the chance of being made an honest woman.[2] I
suppose that Christmas party will be remembered as the last private
party ever given in a London private house.

Connolly has written this morning about the North Downs thrusting
out to sea like a bunched fist. I believe he will soon emerge as a
regional poet with ballades about the nutbrown ale of Kent. But his
Irish name & Fenian features will haunt him to his death.

> Love from
> Evelyn

[1] *Télégraphie sans fil* – the wireless.
[2] According to the laws of the Church, Ann Fleming's marriage to Lord Rothermere, a divorced
man, was invalid. As the widow of Lord O'Neill, she was now free to marry the novelist Ian
Fleming.

12 February 1952   7 rue Monsieur, VII

Darling Evelyn

I'm very sorry about your ill health. Have you a good dr whom
you trust? I think the winter in Northern Europe is very trying to
(what fashion papers call) the over forties. I keep well by staying in
my little warm box of a room, temp: over 80, seldom going out &
never staying away.

But were it not for Col I'd go & live in the South all the winter.

They have been very nice here about the King & there are signs
of mourning wherever you look – many private houses & all public
buildings have flags at ½ mast or Union Jacks covered with crêpe.
Let the cynics say what they like, we are loved in France since the
war.

Yes hard to imagine 2 Elizabeths more different than that plump
little girl & the skinny red-headed harridan.

You mustn't be against European Jews – I'm sure Palestine is too
awful – but you might as well be against the English because of
America now do admit.

There is such a wonderful exhibition here of the paintings of Philippe de Champaigne. That is the France you love (though he was a Belgian). Many relics, too, of the Port Royal. I almost think you ought to come specially to see it.

I'd forgotten the New Bodleian – perfect example, thank you. Still at least it's not a sky scraper.

I've got the *Ency: Britannica* sent by Dearest – 11th edition. I read it all day. The values are very odd. All the people ONE loves, like Pompadour, Buckingham, Charles II are treated with great severity. Charm evidently didn't count, in 1911, nor did love of art, as a virtue.

Letters from Mme de Maintenon's confessor to his Bishop have come to light. Mme de M aged 78 complains that it exhausts her terribly to make love every night with Louis XIV aged 74. But the priests were implacable – she was his wife & it was her duty. Really those Bourbons! (His grandson the King of Spain killed 3 wives – Louis XV nearly killed Mme de Pompadour & I'm told the sons of Alfonso XIII are just the same.) Won't do for the *Sunday Times* I fear.

Lady Honks lay in bed, ill, in rue de Lille, & I had a nice long chat one morning until Poor Louis [Weiller] arrived. I hadn't seen her since before Xmas. She seemed quite as usual, though people say she has been so sad.

Don't understand the Rothermere divorce. Surely he must have connived at her adultery for years? The divorce laws must have altered since my young days. I'm afraid Ann will only go & get another lover – she is one of those who don't like husbands.

I told Col about 'you have made great friends with a Pole who has introduced you to a lot of other Poles' & all he said was 'I rather like Evelyn'.

Come soon for a little visit ça vous changera les idées.

Love
    NR

[postmarked 22 February 1952]   Piers Court
[postcard]   Stinchcombe

I think I may come to Paris Sat. March 1st for a day or two. Will Port Royal Exhibition still be on. Will you be free at all? My plan is to go south to try & cure pains & melancholy & stay longer in Paris when cured & able to enjoy it. Pains *very* bad today.

Love
    E

25 February 1952   7 rue Monsieur, VII

Darling Evelyn

How lovely. You must let me know for sure & I'll go birds nesting.
I will keep the week-end – I always do now anyway as Col has his
only quiet moments then. Momo [Marriott] is here & I suggest she
might have us all to dinner on Sat (I can't here because of Marie who
spends Sat: evening in some mysterious way of scrubbing which I
never like to interrupt).

Yes P de C has only just begun.

Where shall you go in the South? I hope you won't find it depressing
– Ld & Ldy Beveridge[1] who came to see me on their way back said
it's nothing but old ill people. What *are* these pains – should you not
see a doctor here on your way? I think it sounds very worrying.

I had such a week – 4 lots of total strangers came to see me (they
call it fitting me in) including Beveridges. Well I didn't mind them
because he is a saint. Then a terribly nice lower class gorilla called
Douglas Glass[2] & wife ('me & the wife are here we could fit you in – ')
in red trousers & long gold ear-rings. After the first shock I really
loved them. He is a photographer it seems. Then a pair of *literal brutes*
called Sir Lionel & Lady Smith Gordon[3] who looked, in the peerage,
plutôt bien & wrote rather nicely, & sat telling me in loud upper class
voices how well they knew the royal family & SMELT. Perhaps I
could learn to read character by handwriting it would be a great help.

Oh how nice it will be to be fitted in by you after all this. Try not
to torture me, no badinage I beg.

  Fondest love, I am very excited. Laura too?
  NR

[1] 1st Baron Beveridge (1879–1963). Economist and social scientist, author of the Beveridge
Report which laid the foundations of the Welfare State. Married to Janet Philip in 1942.
[2] Douglas Glass (1901–78). New-Zealand-born artist who was chief official photographer to
UNRRA in Germany after the war; his work on the *Sunday Times* 'Portrait Gallery', 1949–
61, established him as a portrait photographer. Married Audrey Richardson in 1941.
[3] Sir Lionel Eldred Pottinger Smith-Gordon (1889–1976). Industrialist. Married to Eileen
Adams-Connor in 1933.

Ash Wednesday 27 February [1952]   Piers Court
                                                    Stinchcombe
Darling Nancy

Badinage? What could be more sharply calculated to drive me to
fury than the description of Ld Beveridge as a Saint?

Honks has struck by telephone. She won't let us lunch together on
Sunday. You know what she is these days. I can't defy her without
wounding her, so I consented to our both lunching at Chantilly on

Sunday. Probably the last thing you want. I felt awful about it but Saint Beveridge makes it a little better.

I come with no plans & no jagger. I will take advice from all. I thought of Palermo or Seville rather than Monte Carlo. Could Momo be induced to drive me on a tour of Vence, Assy and Marseille to see the new Corbusier–Couturier architecture. I think I ought to see it.

I can't make out from your letter whether Smith Gordon smelled or said the royal family smelled. Or whether they told you how well *they* (Smith Gordons) smelt.

I know that ape. It photographed me.

Well it seems I must sleep at Chantilly Sunday night anyway.

I will telephone to you from Travellers on arrival.

Looking forward to trip greatly.

Pains come & go. Gone today. They are rheumatic not cancer.

Lady Audrey Morris (Ed's wife) says she was cured of such pains by a spa in France.

I have hired a governess called Miss MALE. If we put that in a book people would say how far fetched.

Love
    E

It is true after all (re Honks) about tyranny imposed by sensitiveness.

[April 1952]   Piers Court
                                                         Stinchcombe
Darling Nancy

Your presents gave much keener joy than this letter suggests. Holy Communion has transformed your god-daughter and she is in a very likeable state.

I have come back to bills & chills.

Thank you so very much for letting me fit you in. It was a pleasure to see your Pole recovered from his melancholy but I am sorry he did not let me lend him sporting clothes for Ireland.

Mr Peters tells me Sir Alex. Korda is going to film *The Blessing* after all so perhaps that will bring you to England for a bit in the summer. I do hope so.

Please give my love to Glorious Debo.[1]

Just had a letter from a group of American school girls asking me the Secret of Happiness. *Me.* I wrote back sharply that they were not *meant* to be happy but if they thought they were, you were the one to consult.

Corporal Hill loyally displays *Pigeon Pie*. I suppose you will go to H. Hamilton's Ball.

It is *much* cheaper writing to you in Ireland than in France. Cheaper

for you to write back too. So please tell me the news of Lismore. Does
Charlie's[2] ghost stalk there still?

> Love
>   E

[1] Nancy was staying with the Devonshires at Lismore Castle in Co. Waterford.
[2] Lord Charles Cavendish (1905–44). Second son of the 9th Duke of Devonshire. He and his
wife Adèle, sister of Fred Astaire, were given the house as a wedding present in 1932. Lord
Charles died there in 1944.

12 April 1952   Lismore Castle
                                                      Co Waterford
                                                      Eire

Dearest Evelyn

That's awful news about Korda. But I can't go to London. Perhaps
they'll do it in France. Anyway I'm quite useless at working on films
as they need quick wits & mine are slow.

Have you ever been to Ireland? It's very pretty. But nothing one
didn't know before so not very easy for an article. I can't think of one
original thing to say.

How *can* people live in the country? I always wonder that after 24
hours of it.

One does feel terribly well, there's that to be said – a sort of decar-
bonization from municipal water & so on, but oh the slow the dragging
the sustained boredom. 'Better than that' (over the time of day) begins
at once for me, whereas in Paris it's always hours ahead of what one
hopes.

Don't be so beastly about *Pigeon Pie*, it's very funny, all the parts
about Pam Berry are at least. The sales manager at H.H. says he
could sell 10,000 copies of each of my old books, but he admits I'm
quite right not to allow it.

Did you read *Hugh Walpole*?[1] I'd looked forward to it as a terrific
treat – can't get on with it. Tried skipping, tried the index, tried
everything, no good I can't. I believe the English buy books entirely
on dullness or perhaps I'm in a bad mood, run down like a clock, it
may be that because now I'm trying *Youthful Q Vic*[2] & can't do that
either.

I still don't know if Col can come & don't quite know what to hope,
I fear he might find it dull. It's the dragging hours, isn't it? How do
you manage when you're not working?

Next Sat I go to Birr[3] & then home on 24th after 2 nights with
sister Pam. I look forward to seeing Birr.

Debo is glorious but eaten by guests & Andrew I find *very* charming.
So are the 2 children – simply perfect really.

The party has now poured in so goodbye.

Love from
   NR

[1] A biography by Rupert Hart-Davis (1952).
[2] Dormer Creston, *The Youthful Queen Victoria: A Discursive Narrative* (1952).
[3] Birr Castle in Co. Offaly, seat of the Earls of Rosse.

26 April 1952   7 rue Monsieur, VII

Darling Evelyn
   Total to me is the mystery why you don't live in Ireland. I should
have thought the round peg would have happily dropped into that
round hole years ago. Never have I seen a country so much made for
somebody as *it* is for *you*. The terrible silly politeness of lower classes
so miserable that they long for any sort of menial task at £1 a week,
the emptiness, the uncompromising Roman Catholicness, the pretty
houses of the date you like best, the agricultural country for Laura,
the neighbours all lowbrow & armigerous & all 100 miles away, the
cold wetness, the small income tax, really I could go on for ever. (*So*
cross about my article,[1] they cut out every joke – they generally do I
must admit but this time I thought they went too far. Having wired
to me 'masterly performance' & thus raised my hopes. Never mind.)
   Do explain, at length. I remember you went to look at a Castle, so
what happened? Perhaps you saw an elemental & fled incontinent?
But any priest can fix an elemental, surely.
   I enjoyed it really & it certainly did me good. But those islands
have a lowering effect on my spirits which quite alarms me because
what would happen if I had to go back & live in them? Gaston I had
to put off, it was too disappointing he'd actually taken his ticket. But
when he could get away Debo was house full, & full of rather dull old
aunts etc, & none of the other visits fitted for dates. But I see he would
enjoy it & next year he must come.
   My flat is painted & I'm buying furniture like mad – it looks so
pretty I long for you to see it. The heaven of being back, summer is
here too.
   The bright young Yorkes are at Lismore. Debo has never seen
them, she invited their *son* who it seems is a genius, an all round
masterpiece of nature, but he couldn't go & she got them instead. I've
seen very varied reviews of *Doting*,[2] have sent for it – bet I shall enjoy
it.

   Much love – write –
      N

[1] 'Over to Ireland', *Sunday Times*, 27 April 1952. 'The Irish, whose qualities of mind and heart

were so cruelly misused for centuries, are now applying all their energy to becoming a nation. They have made up a language and are busy trying to learn it, without much success, judging by the fact that they still have to print an English crib under all notices and forms which are written out in Irish.'
2 By Henry Green (1952).

Labour Day [1 May] 1952   White's
Up the Workers of the World
down with la vie de château

Darling Nancy,
   Among the countless blessings I thank God for, my failure to find a house in Ireland comes first. Unless one is mad on fox hunting there is nothing to draw one. The houses, except for half a dozen famous ones, are very shoddy in building and they none of them have servants' bedrooms because at the time they were built Irish servants slept on the kitchen floor. The peasants are malevolent. All their smiles are false as Hell. Their priests are very suitable for them but not for foreigners. No coal at all. Awful incompetence everywhere. No native capable of doing the simplest job properly. No schools for children. Above all the certainty that once one pulls up roots & lives abroad there is no particular reason for living anywhere. Why not Jamaica? Why not Sicily? Why not California? On the move like a jew all one's life.
   I have been in London ten days – long empty days & nights. Saw little Pam [Berry] a bit & the bright young Flemings and Mrs Freeze-Greene & Osbert & Sutro & his monkey and witty worm friends here. Home tomorrow gladly. [. . .]
   Doting is pitiable but I don't at all rejoice. There are not enough writers for one not to mind one going to seed and there are too many contemporaries in decay.
   I dined tonight with Roy Campbell[1] (*Dark Horse*) a great boastful simple sweet natured savage. I feel quite dizzy from his talking to me.
   Kind Mr M Berry[2] will send me to Africa for the children's next holidays.
   Poor Maimie [Vsevolode] is broke.
   All the talk here is of poverty & disease.
   B. Y. Yorke's son cannot shake hands. He offers a closed fist.
   I am writing a little essay in abuse of Père Couturier.
   Tony Powell's new book[3] is said to be excellent.
   Boots has dropped writing his psycho-analysis of me.[4]
   Henry Bath's health gives grave anxiety.
   Met E. Marsh in the Duveen Gallery of the Tate gazing despondently at a new acquisition made of barbed wire & cork. He said: 'I have just realized that I am no longer quite contemporary.'

Mrs Fleming *very* pregnant. It is hoped that Mrs Fleming senior[5] will shortly marry money.

Love
    E

[1] Roy Campbell (1901–57). South-African-born poet who came to England in 1918. In 1951 he published his second volume of autobiography *Light on a Dark Horse*.
[2] Hon. Michael Berry (1911–2001). Chairman and editor of the *Daily Telegraph*. Created Baron Hartwell in 1968. Married Lady Pamela Smith in 1936.
[3] Anthony Powell, *A Buyer's Market*.
[4] Connolly received his $1,000 fee from *Time*, but the profile was never published.
[5] Ian Fleming's mother, then in her sixties, was engaged to the octogenarian Marquess of Winchester.

10 May [1952]   Piers Court
                                                        Stinchcombe

Darling Nancy

Please I want your advice. My eldest daughter Teresa, fourteen, good, brave, sensible, unattractive, quite clever has reached a stage in her education when I think she should have six months in France. *Not* at a convent. She has had too much of convents since she was six, but in a virtuous family from which she could attend a day school – convent maybe. She knows no French & would be lost in a school at first. She ought to spend a month or so on French alone, with cooking & French arts of living. Can you suggest what is best & how to set about arranging it? She does not need 'finishing' – just beginning. The ideal thing wld be to find a family who would accept payment in pounds, perhaps for their own child's schooling here. Or Laura & I would take in a frog girl in exchange. I suppose I *could* arrange payment in francs but it would not be easy. She is a very troublesome little girl.

More about Ireland. You have no conception of their mole-like malice. Detraction is their passion. You should have heard the wireless programme commemorating the centenary of George Moore's[1] birth. They had been at work on it for years collecting reports from everyone who had ever known him from the groom at Moore Park to Dublin literary colleagues. One after another the cracked old Irish voices took up the tale for nearly two hours, each demolishing bit by bit every corner of his reputation. That was Ireland all right.

I have been in London quite a lot. Pam [Berry] is very nettled because I said the upper classes had all left London. 'Why there's me & Dot [Head] and . . . and Dot and me.' So she asked me to a party to launch me in London Society & there were she & Dot & Honks (not exactly a London figure) & Sir Laurence[2] & Lady Olivier (the dead spit of Lady Rosse)[3] and Mr Thomas,[4] First Lord of the Admiralty, and a most unarmigerous dancer named Ashton[5] and we went to a ghastly

American play – no attempt to translate it into English & then we went back to Dot's and that was London Society. But Pam has a very good cook. Other meals I had in London made me sick – literally.

How very cleverly Dot paints suddenly.

Oh I forgot to say that J. J. Cooper obliged with a few songs.

Page proofs of my fiasco have come, so full of misprints that my eyes dazzle. Things like 'is' for 'it' on every line. In the old days printers did that sort of thing for you – did they not?

I read your play about the sex-change.[6] I expect it is full of *doubles entendres* that I missed.

You are taking Col on a cultural tour of England. Yes? No?

Please please advise about Teresa's education.

Love
    E

[1] George Moore (1852–1933). Anglo-Irish writer born at Moore Hall in Co. Mayo. Helped to set up the Irish National Theatre and wrote about Dublin life in a fictionalised trilogy of memoirs, *Hail and Farewell* (1911–14).
[2] Laurence Olivier (1907–89). The actor and his wife, the actress Vivien Leigh, had just returned from a triumphant run in New York where they played the title roles on alternate nights in Shakespeare's *Antony and Cleopatra* and Shaw's *Caesar and Cleopatra*.
[3] Anne Messel (1902–92). Married to Ronald Armstrong-Jones 1925–34 and to 6th Earl of Rosse in 1935.
[4] J. P. L. Thomas (1903–60). First Lord of the Admiralty 1951–6. Created Viscount Cilcennin in 1955.
[5] Frederick Ashton (1904–88). Principal choreographer to the Royal Ballet 1935–70. Knighted in 1962.
[6] Nancy had written a short play for a charity revue. Other contributors included Violet Trefusis, André Roussin, Henri Sauguet and Arturo Lopez.

13 May 1952   7 rue Monsieur, VII

Darling Evelyn

About Teresa I don't know *what* to suggest. People are always asking me this though generally for older girls, but I never can help, I'm so much not in that world. All I can say is should I hear or think of such a thing I'll tell you. What about Mrs Howard – might she not help?

I'm engulfed in – not work exactly – but sort of work & the Paris season, & feel *frantic and overdone*. Too many English, telephone all all the morning so that I can't get out of bed, all wanting money – three borrowers yesterday & trying to cope with my sketch, my *S. Times* article *and* a cocktail party of 150 which I give next week for *Blessing* in French. It's too much. I ought to live in the country at this time of year, but then Col? Oh isn't it all difficult.

I suppose the Irish really suffer, & always will suffer, from a powerful inferiority feeling which makes them hate their few great men because they always go to England as quick as they can get there. It's just like those silly Italians. Not content with their beautiful country & great artistic prestige they want to rule the world. I've just finished *Ciano '37–'38*[1] – there's a shriek on every page. Poor old Musso bellowing like a bull because a deputation of Italian workers relieved themselves on the staircase of the Munich Brown House! Comme je les comprends.[2]

I was very much surprised by Mr Angus Wilson's remarks about me in the *Observer*.[3] Did you see them? I thought he would despise me much more than that, though Raymond [Mortimer], who is here in spiky mood, tries to persuade me that it was meant to be horrible.

A message from Hamish Ham that *Pigeon Pie* has sold 10 000. What madness. Rather sad when you think what it would have meant to me when it first appeared & I was penniless.

I'm sorry for this dull letter & being so useless about T, but I promise to think about her.

Love
    N

Getting clothes too – such rubbish when all one ever needs in summer is a fur lined mackintosh.
Yes I heard about you barracking at that play I'm sure you were quite right.

[1] *Ciano's Diary 1937–38* (1952) by Mussolini's foreign minister, Count Galeazzo Ciano, with an introduction by Malcolm Muggeridge.
[2] How I understand them.
[3] In a review of the reprint of *Pigeon Pie* (1940), Angus Wilson wrote: 'At a time when good English novelists are carefully effacing their personalities, when narrative has almost been engulfed in sensibility, Miss Mitford writes really interesting stories in a fascinating personal tone.' *Observer*, 11 May 1952.

29 May 1952   7 rue Monsieur, VII

Darling Evelyn
    I know this is not what you asked for, but the Colonel has a young girl, child of a friend 'très convenable et recommandable à tout égard' who wants to go to England to learn English 'comme bonne d'enfant ou gouvernante'.[1] I merely mention it. I do think about Teresa as well but so far haven't heard of anything, people always say why not a convent, which is what you don't want.

A letter from Stuart Gilbert, old highbrow who has always lived here & who translated James Joyce (!) saying he classes *The Blessing* with the works of his favourite living novelist (you) '& before him Norman Douglas'[2] & speaks of my 'understanding of French mentality so different from what the Bloomsbury intellectuals imagine it to be'. If you knew him you would see why I am so pleased – also he says it's very well translated.

Have you seen *Billy Budd*?[3] I have. It lasts from 9 p.m. to 1 A.M. The story is fascinating & the officers' mess is simply luncheon at Chantilly, they all sit round singing *Don't like* the French, the damned Mounseers. But it's rather long & I 'dined' first with an English chum who merely gave me mousetrap cheese sandwiches & honestly I thought I would expire with hunger. The English are wonderful the way they can manage on no food, aren't they?

I say, do English people never say Mrs & Miss any more? I was enraged at being rung up by a Lady Meyer,[4] young wife of the 4th secretary here who said 'Is that Nancy Mitford?' You know I never take umbrage – well I took it. I've only seen her once I may add.

Bootikins won't speak to me, because of the Captain. What can I do to make it up? Has this ever happened to you? I *mind*. Everybody complains of his wife. She dined with a friend of mine, who had made great efforts both of food & company, & asked if she might eat her dinner alone on a sofa. If you see Boots do try & pacify him for me – I love him.

I thought of going home for my publisher's ball but now the time approaches I feel I can't. English trains are so dirty & then it tires me.

My vendeuse from Dior just back from Buckingham Pal. It seems the frozen tears have already turned to dimpling grins. Nobody can bear to mourn nowadays can they?

They've sold 10 000 of *Pigeon Pie* did I tell you? What can it mean? Did you see an article in *Observer* saying what a stern moralist I am – I roared.

I've just been reading a book by M. de Pange[5] which is made for you. He is a legitimist & a Catholic & even would like to see the Emperor of China back on his throne. When the Gestapo put him in prison he sat reading Pascal & reflecting on his own enormous superiority to the barbarians.

This letter is patchy I know but what can I do? The telephone peals away like a mad alarm clock the whole morning.

If you go to Africa do call in here it is on the way.

Love
    N

Dined with a lot of earnest & im*pour*tant Americans last night & they played a game asking each person 'what does "the stone of insult" mean to you?' One said the stone where village women wash their clothes, another the stone dividing two tribes & so on. I said a very small diamond offered for ONE's virtue. They said how interesting & symbolical & what a light this game casts on people's inner souls, & they rather implied that my inner soul hadn't shown up too well.

[1] Highly suitable and commendable in every respect who wants to go to England to learn English as a nanny or governess.'
[2] Norman Douglas (1868–1952). Expatriate writer whose books include *Siren Land* (1911), *Fountains in the Sand* (1912) and *South Wind* (1917).
[3] The opera by Benjamin Britten.
[4] Barbadee Knight; married to Sir Anthony Meyer, diplomat and politician, in 1941.
[5] Jean de Pange, *Mes Prisons* (1952). An account of his imprisonment during the Second World War.

Whit Sunday [1 June] 1952   Piers Court
                                                            Stinchcombe

Darling Nancy

I hope your poor noodle has not been battered out of shape by the police. I have thought of you often during the last few days and pictured you charging at the head of the communists.[1]

It is very nice of Col to offer me a young girl. Is the offer reciprocal or do his convenable chums merely want to get rid of their daughter & go on a spree? If they would take Teresa in as an exchange – it is worth thinking about.

I am greatly interested to learn that you know Stuart Gilbert whose work I treasure as a classic example of ingenuity run mad. Have you read his exposition of *Ulysses*?[2] A laugh (not wholly derisive either) on every page.

It is a very terrible truth that modern English – not that I suppose a Lady Meyer to be English – *do* tend to omit proper prefixes when addressing the notorious. I am not troubled on the telephone because I don't use the device, but I often get letters from strangers beginning 'Dear Evelyn Waugh'. Perhaps there is some excuse in your case since 'Mitford' is a nom de guerre. One would have written, I suppose 'Dear Saki'; 'Mr Saki' would be absurd. What I most resent is the omission of 'Mr' when other prefixes are retained: 'Sir Maurice Bowra, Dr Edith Sitwell, Lord David Cecil, Brigadier Maclean and Waugh'. My father taught me that the omission of a prefix meant that the man referred to was either a professional cricketer, a convicted felon or else dead.

I am quite sure Boots would never be offended by anything you wrote about him, least of all the portrait as 'the Captain' which is so flattering as to be barely recognizable. I am sure that any coldness he shows springs from his natural shame of his consort – a disgusting person in every way.

H Buchanan has been here for three days on a professional visit, cataloguing my books. He worked hard & well but in his hours of relaxation was embarrassingly boastful.

I keep seeing Carol Reed[3] (Pempie's husband) who seems to be ready to employ me on a film. What he needs is simply someone to talk to about it. Not very exhilarating work, but he promises good wages.

I have written to Miss Canavaggia in the hope of her finding a home for Teresa. She should be in touch with middle class intellectuals, & I hope, keeps clear of the Paris riots.

Advance copies of my sad little book ought to be ready in a few weeks. I will send you one from my loyal loving heart, but be warned: don't try to read it. If *Pigeon Pie* sells 10,000, it ought to sell 9,000. The great thing is that there is simply no competition these days.

Did you see English newspapers making a scandal of Cadogan Cooper's Academy picture with the entrancing title: *Jealous husband, disguised as a priest, hears his own wife's confession.* I wanted to buy it, wrote to him asking the price, got the answer 700 guineas.[4] I could get a Boucher for that.

'Stone of Insult' to me is the Epstein *Lazarus* just erected in New College Chapel.

You could go to your publisher's ball in a French aeroplane. People are saying he is a Jew and had his nose punched by a boxer instead of cut off by a plastic surgeon. What a pity he did not marry Boots's conk instead of poor Boots.

    Love
       E

[1] One person had died and 230 people were injured in Communist demonstrations in Paris against the American General Ridgway.
[2] *James Joyce's Ulysses: A Study* (1930).
[3] Carol Reed (1906–76). One of Britain's leading cinema directors whose films include *The Way Ahead* (1944), *The Third Man* (1949) and *Oliver!* (1968). Married the actress Penelope (Pempie) Dudley Ward in 1948. Knighted in 1952.
[4] The artist presented the picture as a gift to Evelyn.

3 June 1952   7 rue Monsieur, VII

Darling Evelyn

No, Col's girl is more or less working class & wanted to learn English in lieu of wages. Nurse or nursery gov: It might suit somebody for the summer hols though I know it's not what you want. Canavaggia is just the one to ask – though that class do live in desperate discomfort except as regards food, but perhaps a little girl wouldn't notice.

Lady Meyer is English all right she looks like a pug & I am told persecutes the Queen when at home, one lady in waiting's full time work keeping her out of the Palace. Sir Anthony is a handsome Jew, but quite English & not bad really.

Mary Gore-Campbell-Mayall[1] if you know who I mean has come here with nice husband en poste. I can see they will be a pleasure in my life. You must know her, Robin Campbell was a friend of yours I remember.

Yes Boots has made speeches to French friends of mine about the beastliness of *The Blessing*. It seems he saw himself as one surrounded by the most beautiful & desirable women of our generation & minded what I said about the Crew. But he told Spender that he really loves me & in 2 or 3 years time will be able to see me again. No good asking *you* to pour oil as your cruse is dry, but John Russell might.

Prod looked in yesterday. He has bought a yacht & lives on it & is transformed. Clean, handsome, tidy, sober & punctual. A sort of Carlsen. Isn't it too splendid.

I've never read a word Stuart Gilbert has written but I quite see it would be as you say. He is a *dear* & you must meet him next time. He has married what I take to have been his cook (French) & I love her too.

I wonder if you read *Julietta*?[2] I'm reading Daudet's *Sapho*[3] it is terribly good & so exactly like life here to this day. I suppose England has changed much more than any other European country in the last 50 years how do you account for it? More under the influence of America I suppose because of sharing a language.

Novels about London written in the 80s (& the subtitle of *Sapho* is *moeurs Parisiennes*) are like something in Mme Tussaud to us, whereas all the descriptions in this book, of the streets, the staircases, the rooms the restaurants are of the same town we live in now. The sentiments are a bit old fashioned because female courtesans are a thing of the past everywhere, male ones having taken their place. That's an idea, one might re-write *Sapho* up to date, *his* past slowly unfolding its hideous secrets & *his* age suddenly revealed (37).

Oh dear I can't because of Marie, who reads my books & is my censor.

Col saw the *Tatler* the other day – he says it is refreshingly free from any homosexual influence. Perhaps I ought to take it in.

What are your summer plans? I stay here until Aug 15 & then go to Hyères & Florence, to try & get warm.

Love from
      Nancy

Whatever does Handy boast of?

[1] Hon. Mary Ormsby-Gore (1914–92). Married 1936–46 to Robin Campbell and in 1947 to Lees Mayall, first secretary in Paris 1952–4. He was knighted in 1972.
[2] Louise de Vilmorin, *Julietta* (1951). A novel.
[3] Alphonse Daudet, *Sapho* (1884). The study of a young artist's disastrous affair with a model.

16 June 1952   7 rue Monsieur, VII

Darling Evelyn

I talked to an old trout younger than me I expect with girl of 12
about Teresa & she said the difficulty would be lessons as no day
school would take a child who couldn't speak French. Then she said
do beg him to consider the convent school at Morfontaine, a beautiful
château (she said) & absolute perfection in every way.

I mention it because she & another lady were so insistent, & because
I think it will be difficult to find the family you are looking for. If you
did think of it I would get you further particulars.

I long for your book. I'm reading Tony [Powell]'s but the sad thing
is I seem to be going blind – can't read all day as I used to & even
writing an article gives me a headache. I told this to a French critic
who said it's a very good thing for a novelist not to be able to read –
yes but what about the hours of boredom? I shall start going to balls
again – in fact I now see why it is middle aged people who like balls
so much.

One Fr paper said *Blessing* was un roman d'une élégance rare, so I
was pleased.

About Tony – I don't think his novels have enough story, in every
other way they are perfection. I do think Catholic writers have that
advantage, the story is always there to hand, will he won't he will he
won't he will he save his soul? Now don't be cross.

Peter de Polnay's travel book[1] is very amusing, I laughed out loud
several times. Good print too, so I read it all yesterday. I hope *Men
at Arms* has good print. You see I've given up going to balls in order
to read more & it is very disappointing to find I can't. Spectacles by
the way are no help. I got a pair from your health service in the I of
Wight & they give me a *far* worse headache than none, though I have
recourse to them when desperate i.e. when reading your letters.

A friend of mine came over from England for one of the balls &
said to his dinner partner 'who is that over there who looks so nice?'

'There is nobody nice here' was the reply.

Fond love do write
        N

[1] *An Unfinished Journey to South-Western France and Auvergne* (1952).

18 July 1952   7 rue Monsieur, VII

Darling Evelyn

What do you do with all the people who want interviews, with fan
letters & with fans in the flesh? Just a barrage of nos? I fear I am too
weak-minded, & then Marie cannot tell a lie – & then I live in a glass

house so they see me through the window. I think this is a bad time of year, the fans are all on the move. It is making me very bad tempered. Do you answer their letters? But then *I'm* not *you*, & for some reason they all think, from my books, that I am very NICE. I should ask E. M. Delafield or Angela Thirkell[1] for advice, not you.

Then National Book League, Cambridge Union & Eton Literary Society – what [do] you do about them when they invite you? When I say I live here they write again saying choose your own date. Never mind, but it's a bore & all takes time. You are so lucky to like Americans my hatred grows every day – anyway I never answer *their* letters.

Why not come & pay us a visit next week? Harold [Acton] arrives 26th & John [Sutro] will be here, & it's so nice & empty, the town I mean, except for your dear dear Americans drinking iced coffee & cream with their beefsteak.

I'm supposed to be translating *Chéri* for the stage (Binki [Beaumont]). Don't believe it will come to much, but it got me an hour with Colette whom I admire more than anybody – any woman at least – so it has been worth while. She sees nobody, now. I felt very shy. She admired my clothes so that was nice.

Dominick Elwes came to see me – it all took me back to my early married life – the looks, the get-rich-quick line of talk. Only whereas old Prod is good at heart I feel this boy is really bad. I took very much against him. He calls Simon [Elwes] old Frankenstein which I did think terribly funny. I do love the way *we* are now the enemy just as our aunts & uncles & (above all) parents used to be to us. I skilfully parried the question of an advance which loomed throughout the interview.

Got a gushing letter thanking for my 'hospitality' (a glass of Dubonnet if that) & promising to come again very soon. He doesn't know how thoroughly inoculated I am! Though Frankenstein *is* really worth a fiver or so.

The French like *The Blessing* & it sells. But they say I am *too* wicked about them – I only wish they could have seen my English reviews.

The *Sunday Times* say I must broaden my horizon I think they are really dying for social gossip – in which case they must go elsewhere. I am greatly teased because I can't think what I shall write about if exhibitions etc are debarred.

I'm glad you're in love, such an agreeable state, while it lasts. But I suppose the christening will give the coup de grâce.

Momo's niece is engaged to my 2nd cousin[2] so we are now relations. Rather nice.

Do come, I've got lots of jokes too long to write.

Fondest love from
    N

Are you good at film work? I envy you if so.
Col dies for you.

27 July [1952]   Piers Court
                                                  Stinchcombe

Dearest Nancy

   I am not greatly troubled by fans nowadays. Less than one a day
on the average. No sour grapes when I say they were an infernal
nuisance. I divide them into

   (a) Humble expressions of admiration. To these a post-card saying:
'I am delighted to learn that you enjoyed my book. E.W.'

   (b) Impudent criticism. No answer.

   (c) Bores who wish to tell me about themselves. Post-card saying:
'Thank you for interesting letter. E.W.'

   (d) Technical criticism. eg. One has made a character go to Salisbury from Paddington. Post-card: 'Many thanks for your valuable
suggestion. E.W.'

   (e) Humble aspirations of would-be writers. If attractive a letter of
discouragement. If unattractive a post-card.

   (f) Requests from University Clubs for a lecture. Printed refusal.

   (g) Requests from Catholic Clubs for lecture. Acceptance.

   (h) American students of 'Creative Writing' who are writing theses
about one & want one, virtually, to write their theses for them. Printed
refusal.

   (i) Tourists who invite themselves to one's house. Printed refusal.

   (j) Manuscript sent for advice. Return without comment.

   I also have some post-cards with my photograph on them which I
send to nuns.

   In case of very impudent letters from married women I write to
the husband warning him that his wife is attempting to enter into
correspondence with strange men.

   Oh and of course

   (k) Autograph collectors: no answer.

   (l) Indians & Germans asking for free copies of one's books: no
answer.

   (m) Very rich Americans: polite letter. They are capable of buying
100 copies for Christmas presents.

   I think that more or less covers the field.

   Love
      E

All purposes.

> **PIERS COURT,**
> **STINCHCOMBE,**
> **DURSLEY,**
> **GLOS.**

Mr. Evelyn Waugh greatly regrets
that he cannot do what you so
kindly suggest.

PIERS COURT, Nr. DURSLEY.

———

Mr. Evelyn Waugh is abroad and his letters
are not being forwarded. He will deal with
them on his return.

Useful for people who want to visit one.

29 July 1952   7 rue Monsieur, VII

Darling Evelyn

You are heavenly. *Bref*, however, I note that you do answer, even
if only with insults. I was rather hoping you would say you don't
bother to.

How do you know if Americans are rich? I suppose you assume
they all are. I *never* answer their letters & I rather hate accepting their
dollars though I force myself to swallow that bitter pill.

A man today writes that he has written a satire will I get it published
in France. Another begins 'my excuse for writing you (sic) is that I
am remote from civilization'. I sent that to Debo whose favourite song
is called civilization & runs Bingo bango bongo I'm so happy in the
Congo. It is said to remind her of Ali Khan.[1]

I give a cocktail party for Harold tomorrow. You did *embarrass* him
in Sicily,[2] I knew you had.

If you are angelically sending me your book, & if it will be posted
after 5th Aug: could I ask for it to go to Château St Pierre, Hyères,
Var, where I shall be until Sept:. I do die for it & John Russell says
it is imminent.

Your card about abroad has given me an idea. I will get a photograph of a house (any house) made into postcards & say I am down
here working – so sorry I shall miss you. Yes but then people always
say if you are away may I stay in your flat? Or in the case of Dominick
Elwes just come & do so, with a friend.

What about your eyes? Mine are failing.

Much love do keep in touch as Honks always says.

                N

[1] Prince Aly Khan (1911–60).
[2] 'My trip with Evelyn was not a success, since I was recovering from 'flu at the time ... My
brain was half-addled, no match for so critical a companion. Our genial, garrulous Italians,
moreover, seem to exasperate him. He becomes a pukka Victorian Englishman, apt to snap
at all and sundry.' (Harold Acton to NM, 9 April 1959)

31 July [1952]   Piers Court
                                                     Stinchcombe

Darling Nancy

Who please is Blaise Cendrars?[1]

Also will you ask Col whether Fr Leopold Bruckberger[2] is a genuine
hero or no. I have been reading his journals and am puzzled.

My work for Carol Reed is over. The story got more infantile & at
the same time more incomprehensible every day.[3]

I went to dinner with [Cecil] Beaton. Greatly surprised by invitation
& suspicious of the cause – I supposed Miss Case of New York must

be the object of the party. But no, there was no object, Beaton was just entertaining his friends & very nice friends they were & very fine the entertainment.

Another little party at the Heads. Dot is preparing to be the Evita Peron of the English military despotism. Antrim, Norwich & Randolph & Head shouted the ceiling down, telling the same stories, full of foul words, over & over again. These people treat stories like songs. They like them to be old & familiar & repetitive. Each in turn told the same anecdote, each louder than the last.

My Battersby trompe l'oeil is up and looks well. What do you think of it?

Children, their cousins, their friends, are all upon me. I am going [on] a tour of the British armies in Germany at Head's suggestion.

After being very hot it is cold again so all the flies from the garden are now in the house.

You will not guess what the big reliquary contains in Battersby's picture. It is Campion's rope. I have re-read my forthcoming book – *awfully* bad. But as I have remarked before there is no competition.

Jim Wedderburn has revived the Viscountcy of Dudhope (if we had invented that name customers would complain) so Diana goes down one more place.[4]

Love
E

I met poor Frankenstein Monster[5] in London. He is very very barmy and it ill becomes his mad son to mock him.

Frankenstein believes that he is under private instructions from the late King to solve the Ulster problem by having Princess Margaret declared Queen of an independent and united Ireland.

'I have got to go & see de Valera about it next month'.

'Got' is the operative word.

F. sits in White's and whenever a Duke passes he points his stick and says: 'I shall require *you* shortly' (for a picture of the Knights of the Garter). But he is radiantly happy & pretty & that's more than can be said for me.

Maimie & Vsevolode follow the old, almost abeyant custom, of residing together without speaking. Difficult without servants.

[1] Blaise Cendrars (1887–1961). Swiss-born poet, novelist and adventurer.
[2] Raymond Leopold Bruckberger; provocative Dominican priest whose journals, *One Sky to Share*, were published in English in 1952.
[3] Evelyn had been working on the script of a spy story: 'The Man Who Was'. The film was never made.
[4] Duff Cooper's induction into the House of Lords as Viscount Norwich meant that Lady Diana descended from the precedence accorded to a duke's daughter to that of a viscountess. The revival of the senior viscountcy of Dudhope lowered her by a further notch.
[5] Simon Elwes.

20 August 1952   St-Pierre du Château
                                                  Hyères

Dearest Evelyn

The pen is an improvement – but I can nearly always read your
writing you know. Years of practice.

I was surprised about Clarissa.[1] The French papers too, who say why
then did poor King Ed have to abdicate? (Because she was a common
American I suppose.) *They* refer to Anthony as le dauphin du parti con-
servateur – is he so failed? Who is in the ascendant? Anyhow they both
look very happy & you know how much I like happiness.

How much is your plot? I terribly need one. I'm translating *Chéri* –
the play not the book, but don't see much future for it, but it amuses me.

Here we are obsessed by the fate of Sire Jacques Drumont, an
English millionaire who has been murdered with his wife & small child
while camping out.[2] Though all are very sorry for Sire Jacques, & Lady
Ann his wife, it is rather hoped that this will cure English millionaires of
their mania for camping, they are a bore & start forest fires everywhere.

Don't be so snooty about *Helena*. You as an ex publisher must know
that 6000 is good for a translation, even at home where circulations
are larger, much, than here. Do try & be nicer, even only a little. Oh!
Harold's stories about you!! The map of Ararat – I must say I *shrieked*.[3]

I am hot & happy & stoking up for the winter. But there are certain
worries ahead when I get home again which rather weigh on my
spirits. Perhaps they will dissolve (only housing & finance, nothing
serious). In Oct I shall go to London for a family & Momo wedding,
I can't resist it. Too funny to think of my great grandfather & Otto
Kahn being joint ancestors, somehow. Perhaps a few, much needed,
brains will percolate into the family.

I was amused to see how Raymond cracked up the 'new' Proust
novel – it has generally been pronounced unreadable here & people
are furious with Mme Mante-Proust for publishing it.[4] She is insatiable
for money or never would have. How people do scribble away in the
grave, have you ever noticed? Nothing like death for one's output.

Such an amusing journey down but I shall *Sunday Times* it I think
– I drove with my Anglophile friend the Princesse de Chimay[5] & we
spent 3 nights on the way, her contribution being Noailles & Bourbon,
mine 2 English pederasts in Provence.[6] However they have 20 important Picassos & she was impressed. How different from an Englishwoman of that sort (county) who wouldn't know a Picasso from a
Léger or even notice either.

I LONG for *Men at Arms* you have whetted my appetite with all
this girlish diffidence.

Fond love
     N

There is a wonderful play in Paris about Carmelites[7] – even Col didn't drop off. I wonder, if one told you the story beforehand, whether you wouldn't enjoy it. It's by Bernanos.

[1] Evelyn's letter about Clarissa Churchill, who had recently married Anthony Eden, has not survived. (See EW to NM, 29 September 1952, p. 291) Clarissa had been brought up a Catholic, Eden was divorced, and they were married in a registry office. Evelyn wrote to Ann Fleming: 'Clarissa's apostasy has upset me more than anything that has happened since Kick [Hartington]'s death. I can't write about it, or think of anything else.' *Letters of Evelyn Waugh*, p. 380.
[2] Sir Jack Drummond, a biochemist, and his wife and daughter had been murdered by a local farmer.
[3] 'We must have appeared like that film duo Laurel and Hardy . . . I was forever trying to smooth the feathers [Evelyn] had ruffled, but I suspected he had ruffled them rather mischievously, to watch my reactions . . . The British consul at Palermo, rather a dodderer . . . was treated very curtly. "I've got something that would interest you – a map of Mount Ararat." "Why should I be interested?" Evelyn bridled, "has the ark been found there?" ' (Harold Acton to NM, 9 April 1952)
[4] Marcel Proust's niece had given permission for the publication of *Jean Santeuil*, an unfinished and discarded novel begun before *A la Recherche*. Raymond Mortimer reviewed it favourably in the *Sunday Times*, 17 August 1952.
[5] Jacqueline Hennessy; married in 1923 Prince Jean de Caraman-Chimay. She was a cousin of Annabel Hennessy, daughter of 2nd Baron Windlesham.
[6] Douglas Cooper (1911–84), art historian and critic, and John Richardson (1924–), biographer of Picasso, shared the Château de Castille near Uzès which they had transformed into a private museum of Cubist painting.
[7] Georges Bernanos, *Le Dialogue des Carmélites* (1949). The story of the nuns of Compiègne martyred during the Revolution.

25 August [1952]

Dearest Nancy

A propos of your comment on the French grief when people die:[1] I have just heard from Mlle Canavaggia that her father has succumbed to a long & painful illness at the age of 91. The 'shock' was so great that she fell down in the street injuring her head.

Of course we know all about *Dialogue des Carmélites* here & long for its appearance in London tho' I fear we can't raise a team to compare with Annie Nore, Balachova and Dol.[2]

I have lately been faced with one of the crises of middle life. The bootmaker I have gone to for 30 years has gone out of business. So after much consultation & cogitation I have taken up with a Cambridge man & went last week to be measured. I found Cambridge a delightful little town. I visited Mrs Walston (G. Greene's chum) where she lives in inelegant profusion with Mr Walston. She came with me to the scandalized bootmaker & ordered a pair of boots of the kind horses used to wear for shaving lawns – (How can you not like shawn lawns?) – quite circular 'to wear in Ireland'. Do not psychoanalysts attach great importance to boots? What does this aberration mean?

My plot is this. A man (you might prefer to make him a woman) with a rather unusual name like Gregory Peck. A slightly distinguished

but absolutely unknown man such as say the librarian at the House
of Lords or permanent head of the Colonial Office – the sort of man
who has never had his name in a newspaper except to announce his
marriage. One day his wife says: 'How funny, dear, there is a new
film actor with your name.' The actor becomes an international hero.
At first the man is mildly ragged by his friends & colleagues. Then
his life becomes a nightmare. He books rooms for his annual holiday
at Scarborough and finds the whole town turned out to greet him,
the hotel furious when they find he is not the actor etc. etc. His name
comes up for a knighthood and is crossed off because it would look
ridiculous etc. Then his wife becomes fan of the actor and he finds
her affections vicariously alienated. First ¾ of book is his utter ruin.
Last ¼ his revenge. I think he ought to become equally notorious for
drugs, communism, unnatural vices etc. so that he consummates the
complete ruin of his namesake. They might meet in the end, both
down and out, both with their names changed, & become friends
without ever knowing one another. Any use?

   The late J. Drummond was a poor dietary expert, no millionaire.
He slept out because he couldn't afford an hotel.

   IMPORTANT PICASSOS indeed. Talk about my becoming
nicer! You couldn't write an obscene phrase like that except to offend.

   Love
      E

¹ 'The French hate death, the English rather welcome it for their friends and relations . . . The
French passionately mourn and miss their friends and would like to keep them on earth at
the price of almost any suffering.' *Sunday Times*, 17 August 1952.
² Cast members of the French production of *Le Dialogue des Carmélites*.

26 August 1952   St-Pierre du Château
                                            Hyères
Darling Evelyn
   I *love* the plot, but it's more for you than for me. I'm not good with
inoffensive Civil Servants. Do you remember when Robert was in
America he met a young film actor who thought Robert Byron such
a thrilling name & immediately took it? We must assume that he was
killed in the war I suppose. (Did I tell you, talking of names, that I
received a long fan letter ending up 'by the way are you THE Nancy
Mitford?' What could it mean?) But handled, as they say, by you it
would be glorious & I *beg* you to get on with it.

   Harold [Acton] went to the *Carmélites* & did a *wonderful* imitation of
them marching to the scaffold. They were canonized, as you probably
know, in order to tease the 3rd republic for turning out the nuns.
What fascinated me was that one of them was called Mlle Brard, the
very odd name of my concierge. I think it's a play which acts itself &

could hardly not be good – I wonder who is producing it – & translating, such wonderful language. Not I hope Xopher Fry.[1]

Poor Mlle Canavaggia – oh yes they mind terribly, even those who believe in another life, no nonsense about far the best & one must never even hint at it. I must say I've never felt it with beloveds, myself. I keep telling Tony [Gandarillas] that it's our duty to our friends to be murdered – think how much more we should have enjoyed Sire Jacques if we had known him, even slightly. My fans would love it. But Tony isn't very keen on the idea & refuses to walk on the hill by moonlight. Now la chasse has begun bullets whistle and whine ceaselessly – what they shoot, unless grasshoppers, is a mystery to me. Oh well I did see a hoopoe the other day & very pretty it was, but wild – you'd have to be a goodish shot. (Oh dear I'm Ararating now, a form of meridional toll-gating.)

I've just read a life of Louis XIII. Did you know the courtiers got him into bed with his wife (they'd been married 23 years) by a sort of trick, & sent word to all the Paris convents to pray like mad & the result was Louis XIV. She'd had several miscarriages, but years before, which in a way makes it stranger.

Do forgive this long & rambling letter, anybody can see I've got no work to do can't they. Nothing to read either is there anything you've enjoyed? I've sent for A. Wilson.[2]

Love from
     N

I admit about important Picassos – like you I sometimes *can't* resist. I slightly admit about teasing the 3rd republic, though it was told me by a French theologian of great seriousness (not the Col. The Col is expected here in a day or 2 & I'll go on about Bruckbugger. Oh *why* did you want to know about Cendrars, by the way?)

---

[1] Christopher Fry (1907–2005). Actor and dramatist. He translated several plays by Jean Anouilh, but not *Le Dialogue des Carmélites*.
[2] Angus Wilson, *Hemlock and After* (1952). Evelyn admired the novel, describing it as 'a singularly rich, compact and intricate artefact . . . whatever its defects, it is a thing to rejoice over.' *Month*, October 1952.

[postmarked 25 September 1952]   7 rue Monsieur, VII
[postcard]

I've just returned from Venice to find nearly 3 weeks post & Aug: Hare's book[1] which they want me to review AND *Men at Arms* for which thank you so much. I don't dare begin it until I've done all these duties or I know it will engulf me for a day. In Venice the *one* copy was being torn from hand to hand – aren't booksellers idiots really not to cash in on holiday places more. I travelled home with

an antiquarian bookseller & wife who knew all about Heywood &
when I said my name they said won't the girls be thrilled! They'd
been to Jugo S. & say there's a wonderful shop in Zagreb.

[1] Augustus Hare, *The Years With Mother* (1952), edited by Malcolm Barnes.

27 September 1952   7 rue Monsieur, VII

Darling Evelyn
  Goodness it's good. Apart from the shrieks (loudest of all when
Corporal Hill shot himself) the things I thought *génial* were the relationship of the father with the other people in the hotel & the way in
which you take yourself off in the act of administering snubs. I *love* de
Souza, & of course the Brigadier. Neither the wife nor the sister seem
real to me but I can't say why. You see women through a glass darkly
don't you.
  I love the way English Roman Catholics are exactly as snobbish as
middle European princes, I never knew it was so, but it has the ring
of truth when you tell about it. Was it wise to kill off Apthorpe?
  I only saw Connolly's review[1] well really I suppose, considering the
box & also your dédicace[2] with which all Venice rang, it could have
been worse. I really don't feel impelled to read the great master work
about a fish.[3]
  I shall be in London 14th-24th Oct – any hope of seeing you?
  I did love Venice. If *Hut* succeeds in N.Y. I intend to take a flat
there & a gondolier next summer & do it all slap up. But it is a big
IF – in my view it will run for 2 nights.[4]
  I've just paid income tax here for the first time. On a sum over
£2000 they take, including super tax, just under ⅓. Seems reasonable
compared with ours doesn't it. But of course the indirect taxes are far
larger than at home. Income tax is 18% super tax up to 40% but you
are let off ⅓ of everything tax free if you are in the category of artist.
  I've seen nobody but Momo – have been doing a Venetian article
& Aug: Hare & answering millions of letters. But last night I permitted
myself to read you.

      Much love & thank you for sending it
         N

You never told me why you wanted to know about Cendrars – I read
some short stories by him when I was away – not bad.
Isn't Cyril a shriek 'I pleaded that we might keep Hong Kong'. *Fancy*
him being intended for the F.O. too.[5]

[1] A lukewarm critique: '... for the first time I found myself bored by the central section of a
Waugh novel ... One raises the silver loving cup expecting champagne and receives a wallop
of ale.' *Sunday Times*, 7 September 1952.

² Evelyn had inscribed his copy: 'To Cyril, who kept the home fires burning', a double-edged allusion to Connolly's brief wartime career as a fire-watcher and as editor of *Horizon*.
³ Ernest Hemingway's *The Old Man and the Sea* was reviewed by Connolly in the same article.
⁴ The play opened on Broadway in October and ran for 29 performances. It was later released as an MGM film starring David Niven, Stewart Granger and Ava Gardner.
⁵ Cyril Connolly had described a luncheon in 1950 at which Donald Maclean argued that Britain should give up all colonial possessions in the Far East. 'I pleaded that we should be allowed to keep Hong Kong and Malaya for their dollar earning capacities,' wrote Connolly, and continued that he too had been intended for the diplomatic service and 'had always regarded it since with some of the wistfulness which he [Maclean] felt for literature'. *Sunday Times*, 28 September 1952.

Michaelmas [29 September] 1952   Royal Crescent Hotel
                                                               Brighton
Darling Nancy

Laura's annual jaunt. A come-down from previous jaunts in *Queen Mary* & Plaza Hotel, New York. But very salubrious.

I was asked to dinner to meet you by the Cambridge Union & refused not for lack of longing to see you, but from the belief we can arrange a happier rendez-vous when/if you come.

Two things. 1) I believe you keep my letters. A month or so ago I wrote a nasty one about Clarissa. Will you be very kind & burn it? 2) I believe Ann is in Paris. How is she? Her letters are very sad. She never mentions her son.¹ Is it all right?

Leave *Men at Arms* until you have read the whole of the national library. I sent it with full preliminary warnings.

Laura & I went to visit the old Belloc² yesterday by elaborate pre-arrangement with children and grand children. I have known him quite well for nearly 20 years. It was slightly disconcerting to be greeted with a deep bow & the words: 'It is a great pleasure to make your acquaintance, sir.'

He was greatly annoyed because 'Nancy' (Astor)³ had not asked his wife, dead this 30 years, to a party 33 years ago. 'Poor woman she has not grasped the European decencies.'

He wore black broad cloth garnished with garbage, enormous labourers' boots and an open collar. I in rather smart & conventional tweeds. He squinted at me for some time & said: 'We all wear exactly the same clothes nowadays.'

But he had a noble look still like an ancient fisherman in a French film.

All love
    E

When you have time to write please tell me any *English* gossip you hear.

If you see Dominick Elwes please rub in that he never thanked me for a £10 birthday present & make it your excuse for withholding benefactions. That will learn him.

[1] Caspar Fleming (1952–75) was born on 12 August.
[2] Hilaire Belloc (1870–1953). The writer was in declining health and died ten months after Evelyn's visit.
[3] Nancy Langhorne (1879–1964). American-born wife of 2nd Viscount Astor. The first woman to sit in the House of Commons.

30 September 1952   7 rue Monsieur, VII

Darling Evelyn

What a very rum request. I *specially treasure* your nasty letters, posterity will love them so. However just as you say.

Ann is here & I go to see her tomorrow. She's in bed, not well. I think when ladies not absolutely young have babies they often feel sad afterwards, it is physical & passing.

I suppose you won't be at the N[ational] B[ook] L[eague] dinner for me either, nor at Hamish Hamilton's? *Where will you be?*

I've no English gossip except that the Coops are going to emigrate back again to the old land. What a pair of fidgets they are.

I'm frightened of Dominick Elwes. I see him as one of those youths who murder old ladies (me). He met an old pal of mine the Marquis de Lasteyrie & talked a great deal about his darling aunt & then said 'I want to go to Venice do you know anybody there?' to which Lasteyrie, who saw through him like a glass, replied 'Is not Venice itself enough without knowing people?'

Belloc old sounds exactly in every respect like you now.

I'm worried about the expense of living in Paris – it's clearly beyond my means. Prices have leapt up again since I was away.

At Fulco's[1] house party in Sicily a Miss Roosevelt (one of his guests) was found in bed with a peasant. When asked why she replied 'well all the others are pansies.' Quite true, but rather incontinent of her wasn't it? General Eisenhower[2] has turned into pure knock about hasn't he I am greatly enjoying it all – heavenly when the platform collapsed & very nice when he lost his place in his speech.

I've got some long funny snobbish middle European stories for you but when shall I see you?

Fond love
  N

I wrote about *Men at Arms* to Stinkers.

[1] Fulco Santostefano della Cerda, Duke of Verdura (1898–1978). Sicilian-born socialite jeweller who set up a business in New York in 1939.
[2] General Eisenhower was running for President and was elected later in the year.

3 October 1952   7 rue Monsieur, VII

Darling Evelyn

I could dine with you on 14th but I am always worried after a journey but I think I'll fly which is less worrying. On 15th I lunch with Pam [Berry] couldn't you barge in? It was to be a tête à tête but *I've* no secrets that you haven't wormed out years ago & I don't expect *she* has.

I thought Peters was much younger than me. What is his secret – we must find out. It can't be healthy living so must be Bogo, Ritzoderm or something like that. Do tactfully ask.[1]

I went to the *Carmélites* again & loved it more than ever. Alas I see in *Times Lit: Sup:* that it has been very badly translated,[2] just as I feared.

I've had long talks with Ann – very cheerful, loves her baby, but *not* very well.

Let me know if you would like me, worried, on 14th. I would love it. I've got a *lovely* dress for dinner.

My American publisher is here he is called Klapper. The horror of having to see such people –!

   Best love
     N

I see you are now modelling yourself on Crouchback – it won't be the same. Col has just rung up 'Evelyn's book is very dull but *very* fascinating'. What can he mean? He missed the whole point of thunder box though by not realizing what it was.

[1] A. D. Peters had recently had a 60th birthday.
[2] By Michael Legat as *Fearless Heart* (1952).

8 October 1952   7 rue Monsieur, VII

Darling Evelyn

Nouvelles Littéraires are of no importance whatever – I only wish they were as they constantly devote words of eulogy to my oeuvre. It is a huge weekly paper looking like the *Daily Telegraph* & just about as dull.

I saw [André] Bay, very much excited by *Men at Arms*. But it seems Mlle Canavaggia doesn't feel she can do it so now there is the all-important question of a translator. I know you don't care, but *I do*.

I'm lunching with Peters 16th couldn't you kill 2 birds by coming too? That evening somebody you've never heard of, called Hamish Hamilton, gives a dinner for me so I shall have to rest before that. But you might come to Debo's at about 5 if free? 4 Chesterfield St. Or see you chez Corporal Hill (the late) at about 12?

Thanks for the 11 cents, I am delighted & dashing off to the post office to change them.

I die to see you, it seems an age.

Little Hut hit a record last week – you must admit!

Eddy West has written telling me to bring him 6 bottles of Cortizone – they cost £50 in PRECIOUS francs – it's exactly like asking me to give him £50 because what can *I* do with *pounds*? Oh dear one's friends. I've written explaining the agony & saying that if you tell me I *must*, I will. Of course he will tell me! 'Invalids are so selfish' E.S-W.

Oh I am excited to see you – try & be nice to me if you can – be like Crouchback would. By the way I want a long talk with you about Mrs Crouchback. I can see what you're up to – she's going to fall in love with him again. Well it's not possible & I'm telling you so. Women may be unaccountable but they never fall in love twice with the same person, it's a definite rule. That look of desire he thought he saw when the telephone bell rang was a figment of Crouchback's imagination I promise you.*

Do you think the *Sunday Times* would send me to Moscow to do the fashions, interior decoration, current plays & so on?

I do so long to go.

Best love be nice
    N

* Re reading in cold morning light I see that this is most presumptuous of me & I apologise but all the same I leave it.

23 October 1952   4 Chesterfield Street
                                          London, W1

Darling Evelyn

[. . .] Well *never* have I enjoyed anything so much as Cambridge,[1] it was one long shriek. The boys are heaven, real faces (you know what I mean) well dressed, very polite (Mrs Rodd, no nonsense about Mitford) & very giggly. We shrieked from the moment I arrived. There were 3 Indians come to bring greetings from the students of India – I am sorry to say they added to the shrieking. I think you're mad not to go, but of course you *are* mad. And the beauty – that perhaps you know. The boys said 'what shall we be – foreign office?' 'Oh *no*,' I said. 'BBC?' 'Oh *no*.' 'Well you have been the greatest influence in our formative years, do tell us what to *be*.' But I couldn't.

As for last night (NBL) I lapped it up like a saucer of cream. 150 tweeded readers saying things like 'Oh Miss Mitford you look like a beautiful French actress'. Well you do *see*. In the end I got so over excited that I made a little speech. I could really have taken part in the Union debate I mean I wouldn't have been worse than some of the speakers. With everybody so friendly it's not difficult. Fancy the

NBL ladies all cried at the end of Linda they said – one for ½ an hour.

Of course you are accustomed to all this adulation but after my quiet little life in Paris it seems intoxicating to me.

Yes I was sad not to see you more. You were dreadful at dinner, insulting my friends no doubt you have forgotten. But come over for the *Carmélites* – read the bad English translation – or I'll tell you the story I know it by heart now. Give notice, because it is packed.

I said to one of the Indians 'how sensible of you to come by boat, I'm sure it's the best way but of course nobody does now.' 'There were 600 people on my boat.' I must go I'm so busy.

Love
    N

They were red Indians i.e. Communists. My Mr Sampson said 'I always think Communism would be the best thing for India' & they were *not at all* pleased.

[1] Nancy had dined at the Cambridge Union and later spoke in London at the National Book League.

27 October 1952   7 rue Monsieur, VII

Darling Evelyn

I never understand publishers' statements – I have tried with this one but truly can't. But if something is wrong would Mrs Bradley not know about it?

The Burberry flat was like a fortune teller's & I got very nervous but Bertrand Russell[1] did appear after a longish wait & fascinated me. He is so exactly like members of my family long since dead, inflection of voice & so on. Very much puzzled by the modern world I thought. I'm sure that when he was a socialist all those years ago he thought that cottagers would be better off *in their cottages* but hadn't envisaged Crittall windows & ice-cream. (Do you notice that nobody speaks of ices any more, always ice-cream.) He said to me 'are you happy?' 'Perfectly happy from morning to night.' 'Good gracious you're the first person I've ever heard say that.'

Oh dear why are people so sad, I wish I knew.

Come soon.

Love
    N

[1] Nancy was a distant cousin of the philosopher.

2 December 1952   7 rue Monsieur, VII

Darling Evelyn

I hear you agree with me about Lady Derby's intense cowardice in not coming to the help of her unfortunate servants. Stabbing in the back, with a stainless steel knife, might not have been very practicable but she could easily have strangled him.[1]

I'm working hard – life of Pompadour.[2] I'm enjoying it terribly, the reading, haven't put pen to paper yet. It will be my *Campion*.[3] Meanwhile I see what you suffer when my books come out – all my press cuttings are eaten up by Mrs H-Smith's *Fever of Love*.

Silly old Stock. When you sent me the statement I thought the sums were wrong – then they rang up in a fever to tell me that ass of a Bay had made a mistake between actual *sales* & *books on sale*. As Jacques Brousse,[4] who reads for them (& loathes them) said to me they are perfectly maddening but one can't say they are dishonest.

I'm now in a great state about the novel of my friend Gary[5] which I think, & so would you, perfectly wonderful, & which has been received here in deep silence. The fact is, so queer is the literary life here, that a book launched in the absence of the author hardly can succeed. Gary is a diplomat, en poste in New York. It (the novel) will be published by M. Joseph but then what will the translation be like?

I'm going to Redesdale for Xmas, feeling like Captain Scott (it's on Hadrian's Wall) but I shan't touch London I fly to Manchester, met by Debo. They are moving into Chatsworth, did you know? Are you coming over to escape from your kids at all?

Col is vice-president of the Chambre – did I tell you? He arrives with drums & outriders, greeted by the General on duty & enjoys it.

Much love from
        N

I couldn't get Tito guest of Shame[6] anywhere, I *did* so long for it.

---

[1] Lady Derby was in no state to help anyone: she was the first to be shot and badly wounded by a crazed footman and lay in a pool of blood while her butler and under-butler were murdered.
[2] *Madame de Pompadour* (1954).
[3] Evelyn's biography *Edmund Campion: Jesuit and Martyr* (1935).
[4] Jacques Brousse translated *Madame de Pompadour* into French.
[5] Romain Gary, *Les Couleurs du jour* (1952), appeared in English as *The Colours of the Day* (1953), translated by S. Becker, and was a great success.
[6] Marshal Tito had been invited to Britain by Anthony Eden, Secretary of State for Foreign Affairs. Evelyn wrote an article attacking the visit ('Our Guest of Dishonour', *Sunday Express*, 30 November 1952) which he followed up with letters of protest to the *Spectator*, the *New Statesman* and *The Times*.

Part IV
1953–1956

EXCEPT FOR *The Pursuit of Love*, which was completed in three months, Nancy had always found the writing of her novels an effort. She was an intensely autobiographical novelist who, as Evelyn pointed out, had used up all her plots in this one book. By turning to historical biographies, she solved the problem of a story line and in the process revealed a talent as an accomplished historian. It was a measure of her success that she took her novel-reading public with her and won the respect of several specialists for *Madame de Pompadour*, *Voltaire in Love* and *The Sun King*.

The 'U' and 'Non-U' (upper- and non-upper-class) furore sparked off by Nancy's article entitled 'The English Aristocracy' took even her by surprise. It was commissioned by Stephen Spender, editor of *Encounter*, as part of a proposed series on European nobility. Nancy immediately saw the potential for a mighty tease and set out to poke fun at aristocrats. Using an imaginary Lord Fortinbras as a typical specimen, she mocked the aristocrats' attitude to work ('the purpose of the aristocrat is most emphatically not to work for money'), and to wealth ('there is nothing so rare as for the scion of a noble house to make a fortune by his own efforts'); she teased them for opening their houses to the public ('the lowest peasant of the Danube would stick at letting strangers into his house for 2s. 6d.') and for being philistines ('the English nobleman ... seems to have lost all aesthetic sense'). While preparing the article, Nancy was sent a learned paper by Professor Alan Ross on upper-class linguistic usage which delighted her. With Ross's permission, she incorporated extracts into her *Encounter* essay, including his concept of 'U' and 'Non-U'. It was her popularisation of this material that led to an overnight obsession with the words 'writing-paper', 'chimney-piece' and 'looking-glass', as opposed to 'notepaper', 'mantelpiece' and 'mirror'. Evelyn weighed in on the controversy with an 'Open Letter' to Nancy, also published in *Encounter*. He used it as an opportunity to inveigh against some of his usual

bugbears, such as the angry-young-man school of literature and to air
his own, idiosyncratic views about class. He also had a go at Nancy
herself, pointing out that she was twelve when her father succeeded
to the peerage, and that if her uncle had not been killed in the war,
she would have been brought up 'in a ranch in Canada or a sheep-run
in New Zealand'. He ended by accusing her of being a rabid Socialist
and of inciting class war.

Evelyn's dyspeptic response to Nancy's article may have been influenced by his deteriorating health. He was very overweight, suffered
from sciatica and rheumatism, and was tormented by insomnia. To
relieve these distressing symptoms, he took strong doses of bromide
and chloral, washed down with *crème de menthe*. When this poisonous
cocktail produced delusions, he decided on a sea journey to restore
his health. It was on this voyage to Ceylon in 1954 that he experienced
the temporary mental derangement described in his novel *The Ordeal
of Gilbert Pinfold*.

As soon as he stopped taking the drugs, Evelyn's symptoms disappeared but a hilarious incident in June 1955 showed that persecution
mania had not entirely relinquished its hold. He received an unexpected visit at Piers Court from Lord Noel-Buxton and Nancy Spain, a
reporter on the *Daily Express*, that left him feeling 'tremulous with
rage'. He roared at the intruders, dismissing them 'in terms intelligible
even to them', and was furious when Spain recounted her version of
the events in the *Daily Express* a few days later. He wrote a fierce and
very funny reply in the *Spectator*, ending: 'In Lord Noel-Buxton we see
the lord predatory. He appears to think that his barony gives him the
right to a seat at the dinner-table in any private house in the kingdom.'
This was Evelyn at his most malignantly comic, but he felt that the
intrusion had violated his privacy. The neighbouring town of Dursley
was also fast encroaching and in July he put Piers Court up for sale.

8 February 1953   7 rue Monsieur, VII

Darling Evelyn

Are you keeping up your Tito-tease from Goa or are you back?[1]

I am working as never before. You can't think what writing a life like *Pomp* drags one into because luckily for you Helena's friends didn't all write mémoires in 6, 8 & 10 volumes. But it's not as awful as a novel all the same – & I should enjoy it if my eyes weren't so uncertain (one day perfect & the next blind). I'm having a day off. *Picture Post* rang up & offered much gold for an article on Marie Besnard our poisoner.[2] So I downed tools & spent a horrible day in newspaper offices mugging up the case, & another horrible day writing it up & telephoning the result to London which took ¾ hour & exhausted me. After which I took to my bed with waves of nausea. How can any human, let alone any woman, be strong enough to be a journalist? 'Please punctuate' the secretary kept saying as I read – what a bully just like you.

I dined with a war time companion of yours called Robert de Lesseps.[3] He rather loves you.

Colonel went over to London to be televisioned. He received a letter from an English bumble which I swear is genuine & not a leg pull 'Oh Monsieur what a conquest you have made, how I longed to kiss your face, as I believe they do in France, or even for a *closer embrace*'.

I'm so tortured by Fr books having no index ever – you can imagine how it trebles the work. Then I sent for G M Young's *Ld Macaulay* (because I'm sure M spoke in no flattering terms of Pomp) & wanted to verify. No index. Is this not unusual in an English book? It all adds to my eye trouble. I can't run down a page as I used to, looking for a name.

Much love do write
    N

P.S. I saw the Goa ceremonies on a film. They looked wonderful. *Punch* wanted my Paris letter but I decided to stick to the old *Sunday Times* do you think I was right?

[1] Evelyn had visited the Portuguese dependency for an article on the celebrations to mark the 400th anniversary of the death of St Francis Xavier.
[2] 'The Mystery of the Missing Arsenic', 7 February 1952.
[3] Robert de Lesseps (1915–81). Grandson of Ferdinand de Lesseps. Married to Beatrice-Marie Duggan in 1945.

10 February [1953]   Piers Court
                                                            Stinchcombe

Darling Nancy

Yes, home from India some time now. Goa was heaven. I wrote a few words about it for your great new friends, *Picture Post*, but what with the black Portuguese telegraphist & Mr Hulton's sub editor, they got sadly buggered. Now I have written a most instructive article which no one will print.[1]

I should like to see *Punch* restored to splendour but I am sure you are right to stay with the *Sunday Times*. I think it is a first principle to stay with editors and publishers – and shops and restaurants too – until they are beastly to one. Then to sweep out without remonstrating. Needless to say I don't observe this precept myself but live among brawls.

Don't have anything to do with Ian Fleming's Queen Anne Press. They are dreadful people to deal with. I don't suppose you ever got a Christmas book[2] from them from me, did you? I carefully inscribed two dozen copies & addressed the labels. Only ten acknowledgements. So I thought well people are like that nowadays until I met a chum or two & asked & learned they were mostly lost or astray. But the misprints are so many & glaring that I am quite glad. And the wood engravings by a protégé of Betjeman's[3] dull as be damned.

Your last article on Paris had an awful howler. 'Each' used in the plural.[4] You really must take care now you are doing a work of scholarship. But I was delighted to read that Col has grown a beard. No wonder the Director of the Wallace Collection wished to kiss him elsewhere than on the face.

I have had a lovely fortnight making illustrations for a bright young short story.[5] I think in your country they call the work 'collages'? I mean cutting out bits of prints & sticking them together & drawing on them with black & white & changing all the expressions as Lord Berners used to do.[6] When I am paralysed I shall do nothing else.

I have gone stone deaf in one ear which makes all social intercourse impossible. I am stupefied in the presence of more than two people. Still perfectly all right tête à tête.

Surely 'vivant' means 'debauchee'? Could you not legitimately call Falstaff a 'bon vivant'?[7]

After Goa I made a swift tour of the temples of South India. Fascinating & exhilarating. All the lovely sculpture that looks so odd in museums suddenly looking appropriate. The Indians are much more servile than most foreigners. I can only bear intimacy really & after that formality or servility. The horrible thing is familiarity.

At the railway stations the notice 'Gentlemen's Waiting Room' has, since the Mountbatten retreat, had 'Gentle' painted out and 'Upper Class' substituted.

The famous filthy sculpture of South India is all the invention of poor blind Aldous Huxley.

The Tito tease is the greatest fun to the participants. We are uniformly victorious. No one else bothers about it, of course, but it is all cabled to him I believe, and Mr Eden is said to fret in his bed.

I have had terrible letters from an earnest papist saying how can I praise your books when you make your hero make a sacrilegious communion. Do I praise your books?

My daughter, Margaret,[8] at school in the centre of the storm havoc, wrote: 'There was such a wind the other night that a tree was blown down near the chapel.'

All love
     Evelyn

[1] 'Goa: Home of a Saint' was published in the *Month* and *Esquire*, December 1953.
[2] *The Holy Places* (1952), a long essay that was the fruit of Evelyn's 1951 visit to the Christian shrines of the Middle East in 1951.
[3] Reynolds Stone (1909–79). Typographer and engraver who cut the letters in the stone memorials for Duff Cooper, Winston Churchill and T. S. Eliot. In 1954 he designed a letter-heading for Evelyn.
[4] 'As soon as each saw how the other felt they started clapping ostentatiously across me at each other.' 'In Paris', *Sunday Times*, 1 February 1953.
[5] *Love Among the Ruins: A Romance of the New Future* (1953), a grisly short story illustrated with engravings by Canova, carefully amended by Evelyn.
[6] Gerald Berners was adept at touching up photographs of celebrities in such a way as to make them grotesque. 'One of his masterpieces was a photograph of George V with a group of army officers; his uniform could be opened to show a naked female body, a bearded lady.' Diana Mosley, *Loved Ones* (Sidgwick & Jackson, 1985), p. 102.
[7] In her *Sunday Times* article, Nancy had written that English was full of French words that meant nothing in France, giving as examples: *bon viveur, objet de vertu, savoir faire* and *blancmange*.
[8] Margaret Waugh (1942–86). Evelyn's second, and favourite, daughter. She married Giles Fitz-Herbert in 1962 and died when she was hit by a car crossing Chalk Farm Road in north London.

13 February 1953   7 rue Monsieur, VII
Darling Evelyn
    No *Holy Places* – I thought perhaps I wasn't Holy enough & was greatly teased that Pam apparently *was*. I'm tired. *Parlement* – I don't understand it – French history books don't tell. Delightful neighbours at dinner when you ask say that they can do the 7 wonders, the labours of Hercules, the 9 muses, anything you like except explain the constitution of the Parlement. Then I do try not to be too anti clerical because of the cruel words I shall get from you; but it is up hill work. Oh! Unigenitus! Never mind, Benedict XIV was a *dear*, I can't say enough for him. (He's the one Col has in his salon.)
    How tiring it is, to write. One forgets. I do so try with grammar (I must look for each) but you see with me it's by ear. I can't understand the rules. My brain is a very uncertain instrument & I must only hope for a better one next time.
    Today I signed the lease of this flat. The custom is to give the landlord £500 for each room when you buy a lease – my landlord refused one penny. I feel so overcome, I don't know what I can do in return. Perhaps leave some money to his children. Haven't I been lucky, falling in with such a good & charming man?
    I must go to bed. This was really in case you still thought me ungrateful for *H.P.*

Love
  N

16 February [1953]   Piers Court
                                                      Stinchcombe
Dearest Nancy

I used to know about Parlements. They were courts of law, not
legislative assemblies. About a dozen of them I think with areas of
jurisdiction depending on ancient feudal fiefs. The Parlement of Paris
covered well over half France. Under the parlements were a multi-
plicity of manorial & provincial courts. There was no Court of Appeal
against the Parlement but the King could & often did remove tricky
cases for trial by the Council. The parlements managed the police &
as a result certain trade regulations. They claimed the right to register
(and thus to veto by refusing to register) the King's decrees.

I think you will find all this & much more to your purpose plainly
set out in the *Cambridge Modern History* Vol. 'French Revolution'.

If you are going to touch Jansenism at all you must get it right and
the only way to get it right is by study of Ronnie Knox's *Enthusiasm*.[1]
An absolutely essential book for you anyhow (skip first 100 pages). Tho'
mostly dealing with L. XIV reign, you'll never grasp the ecclesiastical
position of XV without it.

I presume you know Tocqueville's *Ancien Régime*? Doesn't that give
all about Parlements? I thought it did.

Of course by 1789 no one had any idea what the constitution had
been & wanted a new one anyhow.

    Love
      E

Don't answer. I know it's hell writing letters when engaged on literary
work.

[1] A history of religious fanaticism published in 1950 and dedicated to Evelyn.

19 February 1953   7 rue Monsieur, VII
Darling Evelyn

You *are* faithful & clever. I'm sending for all those books – & Ste
Beuve's *Port-Royal* has been republished here. I've always known I
must read that. The *Ency: Britannica* which I've got, is a help in a small
way & I do more or less grasp the functions of the parlements but not
how they are constituted. They seem to represent the King rather
than the people. Nobody here knows, it *is so ODD*. Colonel hastens
to change the subject – I asked my lawyer who *fled*.

Are you busy? If not, one word of advice. Who am I writing for?
Hamish Ham wants me to do it as a novel & that I won't (can't really).
But I feel it's no good doing it as though for, say you & G M Young[1]
because though you may read it in order to be able to tease for the

next 20 years, G M Young won't bother to read it at all. As for my public such as it is they won't give a damn for parlements or Jansenism.

The question really is how much politics should one put in? She was intimately concerned with them for about 5 years only, the beginning of the 7 years war. Wars are simple, even that one, compared with the internal stuff. I wish you wld just put on a P.C. the name of a typical reader – he whom I should be out to entertain without irritating. Oh it's no good asking you, you are such a tease & anyhow it will be the same in the end. One does what one can in life. As you were.

You wld hardly believe that anybody who had after all spent one year in a convent could know so little about the R.C. religion as Mme de P. She was incapable of grasping what it was all about, though so clever in many other ways.

I would love to see you – are you coming over at all?

Best love & THANKS
              N

So many things I want to ask as I plod along. References: a bibliography at the end? *Not* footnotes I think.

[1] G. M. Young (1883–1959). Historian; author of *Gibbon* (1932), *Victorian England* (1936) and *The Government of Britain* (1941).

[February 1953]   Piers Court
                                                   Stinchcombe
Darling Nancy
   On no account a novel. A popular life like Strachey's *Queen Victoria*, to be enjoyed by Honks [Cooper] & Pam Berry. Plenty of period prettiness. Write for the sort of reader who knows Louis XV furniture when she sees it but thinks Louis XV was son of XIV and had his head cut off. There is no limit to the amount of knowledge *you* must have. The question is how much to impart. Aldous Huxley fails in this matter of taste, particularly in *Devils of Loudun*, he can't resist giving irrelevant information. But I am sure your artistic taste won't fail you.
   I write from memory, but I think it is fair to say Mme de Pompadour's influence in politics was disastrous. The defeats of 1759 were her defeats. But I daresay historians have changed their views since I stopped studying.
   As far as I remember, the *Parlements* were King's Courts like our royal courts temp. Henry II, designed to break the power of the feudal courts. By Louis XV time I think the feudal courts had not much more power than English J.P.s. *All authority IN THEORY emanated from the throne*, but the parlements soon became practically hereditary themselves. The noblesse de robe (from whom incidentally most of

the best Jansenists came) were a group of wealthy & learned families who shared out the legal appointments among themselves. But Tocqueville will tell you all this, I am sure.

Strachey, in *Q.V.*, knew all the politics of the reign inside out and just drew on his knowledge here and there when it was necessary for his portrait. It is like the knowledge of anatomy that is necessary for drawing a clothed figure – but I suppose with your views of art you won't admit that it is necessary.

I imagine Mme de P. as Phyllis de Janzé.[1] Phyllis did too I think.

Love
    E

---

[1] Phyllis Boyd (1894–1943). Intelligent and beautiful *femme fatale* who had studied art at the Slade with Dora Carrington. Married Vicomte Henri de Janzé in 1922.

24 February 1953   7 rue Monsieur, VII

Darling Evelyn

Thank you very very much. I did read Taine before starting, but had to give it back, & at that time, knowing so little, much must have gone over my head. Tocqueville is clearly the boy. What you say has clarified my ideas, & as for needing to *know* oneself, curiosity pushed one to that I find.

I wanted to ride my anti feminist hobby horse & say that Mme de P though prettier & better educated was quite as hopeless as the female deputies today. But I'm not sure. The modern view is that *all* came from the King & that she acted as a private secretary to that intensely shy & inarticulate man. But the policy was his (renversement des alliances etc).

The defeats of '59 were the direct result of Closter Seven which was Richelieu's fault & Richelieu was her enemy of always. After that, lack of good generals which takes us back to the system. (Nobody not noble could have a high command.) Oh how one *longs* & *longs* for Maurice de Saxe.[1]

I'm fed up with French historians – no index & never a date. It must be child's play to write books on the Brownings or Carlyles compared with this. Still I am carried on by the jokes which are truly heavenly.

I saw Pomp more as Daisy Fellowes, but now you mention it she must have had something of Phyllis. Always at home in her comfortable pretty room like that. But did Phyllis fall in love (except Hubert[2] I know she was with him). Pomp literally worshipped the King, he was God to her, & never from the age of 9 thought of anybody else. Very cold, physically, which makes it perhaps understandable, her great faithfulness, no physical temptations.

I went to the Chambre the other day. There is an earnest Communist lady called Rose Guérin, a deadly bore, & when she gets up to speak the deputies begin to hum a tune the words of which are 'Ne parle pas Rose, je t'en supplie'.[3] How *can* women be so idiotic as to go butting in to male assemblies?

Have you followed the case of the Finaly children[4] it is intensely fascinating & nobody here talks of anything else.

Much love & thank you again
   N

I suppose we belong to the last generation which will be able to understand the mentality of a man like Louis XV. He was not so different from – say – my father or Eddie Devonshire, in outlook & prejudices, but the type will soon have died out I imagine.
Oh you mean Quebec '59? I think she *can't* be blamed for that, it was due to the decay of the navy since before her time. She gave a million of her own money for the defence of Canada.

[1] Comte de Saxe (1696–1750). Created Marshal of France in 1746, he led the French army during a period of victories.
[2] Hubert Duggan (1904–43). Stepson of Lord Curzon. Conservative MP 1931–43. Evelyn intervened at his deathbed to have the last rites brought to him, an episode that inspired the death scene of Lord Marchmain in *Brideshead Revisited*.
[3] 'Don't speak, Rose, I beg of you.'
[4] Robert and Gerald Finaly were two French orphans whose parents died in Nazi concentration camps. They were brought up in a Roman Catholic children's home until an aunt in Israel applied for them to live with her. The head of the home refused, the children were hidden, and their aunt was eventually awarded custody after a two-year legal battle.

14 March 1953   7 rue Monsieur, VII

Darling Evelyn
   I hesitate to bother you again, but you are so kind perhaps you won't mind. But if you are busy Tito teasing[1] don't answer. I've read *Enthusiasm* & it is a *great help*. But as you know Catholicism is a closed book to me. I don't intend to say very much about Jansenism because it is an immense subject & doesn't really affect my story. But am I right in thinking that it is a sect & not a heresy? Or is it a sect with certain heretical doctrines? Can such a thing be? Can sects exist at all in yr Church? as set forth in the Bull Unigenitus? Fr Knox is terribly against, isn't he – I feel rather sad at his mocking so much because to me it is associated with charming images P de Champaigne, Pascal & so on. But I see that St Médard[2] is rather a joke. 'Défense à Dieu de faire des miracles dans ce lieu'[3] he doesn't put in, but so funny. I loved the nun who got fearful giggles. I haven't read the whole thing because I've so much reading & my eyes aren't behaving very well, but when I've done *Pomp* I greatly look forward to Mme Guyon.[4]

I suppose you are sharpening a stiletto for Tito as I see he has got
a bullet proof motor. Or shall you invite him to White's & give him
a poisoned cocktail?

At Versailles they went into mourning for enemy princes when they
died, even in the middle of the war, but not for the Grand Turk
because he was 'infidel'.

I do hope you will like the book & not be too cruel about it – *I*
think, now, that it will be good. I understand the Parlements now.
Barbier is the boy – Tocqueville not much good but I don't believe I
got the right book.

I'm off to Versailles on 7 Ap: to write it. Then I shall get to know
the Palace thoroughly wh is an intensely important factor. My flat is
to be done up at the same time. I'm *excited* to begin writing, you know
the feeling.

        Much love
            N

---

[1] Since his article in the *Daily Express* the previous November, Evelyn had kept up a steady
campaign against the Yugoslav leader's visit to Britain.
[2] In 1728 the tomb at St-Médard of the Jansenist priest François de Pâris became a popular
place of pilgrimage for mad religious convulsionaries.
[3] 'God is forbidden to perform miracles here.'
[4] Jeanne-Marie Guyon (1648–1717). French mystic who promulgated the doctrine of Quietism.

14 March [1953]   Piers Court
                                                        Stinchcombe
Darling Nancy

The Tito tease has turned out a great tease for me. All my time &
energies in the last month seem to have been spent on it – genuine
public spirit fatally combined with the itch to have the last word. Last
week I went all the way to Glasgow to address 4000 or less Irish
Catholics. The Duke of Norfolk has been prodded into action to
present a remonstrance. Everyone, whether pro or anti Tito, is sick-
ened by this first excursion of Clarissa into public life. The London
police say they can't protect him unless his residence is kept secret,
his engagements not announced, a bullet-proof car provided for him;
even then they fear assassination. Apart from the Duke of Norfolk
and whatever gunmen the Russians send, there are 5000 Yugoslav
refugees in the country, all with scores to settle. So what with one
thing and another Clarissa is unpopular and has announced that with
brilliant originality she will paint the interior of Stafford House (now
called 'Lancaster'. Why?) 'broken white', in a desperate bid to regain
the confidence of the party.

The Glasgow visit was very exhausting. I suppose I am a very bad
guest. I always complain loudly if I am not offered enough to drink.

In Glasgow their one aim seemed to be to intoxicate me. Great goblets of neat whisky thrust into one's hand every ten minutes. And I resented that too.

I am becoming a Russian Imperialist, in reaction to the politicians. What is wrong is not Russia but Communism. Our policy is to bribe all the small states to remain communist but quarrel with Russia. If they are going to be communist it's much better Russia should rule them. Great Empires never seek war; all their energies are taken up in administration. Our troubles now come from Clemenceau destroying the Austro-Hungarian Empire. The one certain way to start Third War is to establish half a dozen independent atheist police states, full of fatuous nationalism & power hunger.

Did I tell you that Robin Campbell has abandoned painting & now composes music?

I went to see the apotheosis of Art-nonsense – the International Competition for a statue of an Unknown Political Prisoner.[1] Were the prize winners illustrated in your press? Scottie Wilson is a Velázquez beside them.

Randolph has become an angelic character – hugely fat & jolly. I am sure it was that periodic banting which destroyed his charm. He has a wonderful new idea for a book – English Country Houses. 'Which, Randolph?' 'Well I thought Longleat, Chatsworth, Blenheim etc' 'But haven't they been done rather fully? And what do you know of architecture, genealogy or decoration?' 'Oh, it's going to be a *popular* book.'[2] Bless him.

Love to Mme Mme de Pompadour
　　　Evelyn

Simon Elwes sent out an invitation 'RSVP The Private Secretary' Cheek?

---

[1] The prize was won by Reginald Butler for a sculpture described by *The Times* as 'an iron cage on a stick'.
[2] Randolph Churchill, *Fifteen Famous English Homes* (1954).

19 March 1953　　　　　　　　　　　　　　7 rue Monsieur, VII

Darling Evelyn

Thank you *so* much. I did wish that Fr (or Mgr) Knox had told us what happened, exactly, after Benedict XIV had more or less cancelled the bull in an encyclical letter. As far as I can see from contemporary memoirs there were a few more demonstrations & even convulsions & then the whole thing died down for ever. Which is odd considering there were still a million Jansenists including most of the rich bourgeois. Louis XV seems to have handled the whole thing with great skill. I

wonder if I ought to deal with the expulsion of the Jesuits? It was put
down to Pomp:, quite wrongly, but didn't happen until after her death.
The whole transaction is unbelievably dull, I've a good mind to skip
it.

I'd never heard of Reg & his cage until you told me & then that
very evening there was a killing article in the *Monde* about a man
breaking it up in front of an 'apathetic crowd of Londoners'. £4000
– what *does* it all mean? I did love Reg saying he thought he wld be
able to make it as good as new. Thank *heavens* it was insured.

I do hope you'll come before a hundred years, my flat is beginning
to look lovely & will be a dream *I* think. I've got a dark green Aubusson
which makes an enormous difference & the garden is being done by
hundreds of dear little Arabs.

Such a to do with my US publisher because Peters, rather unwisely
perhaps, gave him notice without realizing that he's still got one more
book coming to him. I fear he will ruin poor *Pomp* now out of spite.

I opened an American mag at my dentist's and saw a picture of 'a
monolithic pond-side library' don't you think we might sell Stonehenge
(for dollars) to make monolithic revolving book cases?

   Much love & thank you
         N

I looked everywhere for Laura at the agricultural show, it was lovely.
Oh your ink is so pale.[1] *Poor* posterity.

[1] Evelyn's letters of this period were written in blue ink on blue writing paper.

[March 1953]   Piers Court
                                                    Stinchcombe
Darling

I am very sorry indeed to hear of your American difficulty. The
same thing happened to me – they just printed a few copies of *Handful
of Dust*, sent out none for review, and let it flop – but at that time I
didn't sell any copies in America anyway. But in your position this
could be disastrous. I am sure Peters is doing all he can to rectify his
mistake, but it is a very grave mistake indeed.

It has been a lovely week for Art lovers – first Reg's Folly and then
Picasso's eikon of Stalin.[1]

Jesuits It all depends whether you are treating Pomp purely as a
figure of before the deluge or as a symbol of the coming disasters.
The expulsion of the Jesuits at the height of their theological triumphs
over Jansenism and Quietism, was the first great victory of the Free
Masons who were to bedevil Europe & the Americas for 150 years or
more. You'll have to go into Masonry seriously I think. No good asking

Norwich. He won't blab even when tight. As *Pomp* is your magnum opus would it not be worth while pausing & interpolating a hasty novel to finish your contract with your American publisher?

You could even hire a ghost to produce something unpublishable. That would liberate you.

Tito's visit has been an undisguised fiasco. It has really been a very happy week.

Reg's statue has been taken up in Parliament. His defender – Sir Leslie Plummer,[2] the man who cost us £80,000,000 in ground nuts, who you would have thought would have changed his name and gone to Tasmania.

One can get posterity ink – quite black. The trouble is you have to wash your fountain pen every two days. Would it help your poor failing eyes.

I am quite deaf now. Such a comfort.

I hope you will publish a £3.3 edition of *Pomp* with fine illustrations. Those, incidentally, are the hot cakes today.

Honks is starving at Tring. I expect you knew. We have just killed a sheep and gorge.

I long to see your parterre. I may be going to Honks at the end of April. But you'll be at Versailles?

Love
E

[1] Picasso had drawn a portrait of Stalin, who died on 7 March, for a special issue of *Les Lettres Françaises*. His depiction of the Soviet leader provoked a furious outcry among French Communists.

[2] Leslie Plummer (1901–63). Labour MP for Deptford from 1951. As chairman of the Overseas Food Corporation 1947–50, he was responsible for the disastrous attempt to grow groundnuts in East Africa. In a House of Commons debate, he defended the proposal that Reg Butler's statue should be rebuilt the size of Nelson's Column on the cliffs of Dover. Knighted in 1949.

24 March 1953   7 rue Monsieur, VII

Darling Evelyn

It's all right really about America because they've got to give me 5000 dollars advance which I imagine is all I'm likely to make anyway as Americans can't read. My biggest sales are always at home – *Blessing* though book of the month, only made 18,000 dollars.

Also I hate them so much now that I ALMOST (I don't say quite) don't care to touch their beastly money. Did I tell you about the one who, looking at the Institut de France[1] said 'I wonder they don't pull down all this junk & put up ap*our*tment buildings here.' They'll blow us all up before they've finished, they & the Germans their great friends you'll see. I don't care, but I'm sorry for Harriet. How *can* you like them?

Nobody whose father was one could take free masons seriously. Waffling off to Oxford with his apron, I can see it now. Your letter has really decided me to leave the Jesuits alone, since I have no stand-point from which to write about them. If my book *has* a message or meaning it is to proclaim the value of pleasure. Here (at Versailles) were 1000 people living but for pleasure & enjoying every single minute of it. As for the deluge, that is another story, & has been done, often enough.

If you go to Honks in April you might perhaps come over & see me? It's the sort of thing Honks doesn't mind doing.

Momo says Tito's visit was a huge success but Col agrees with you that it was perfectly meaningless. I see all the critics agree about Reg, even *NS & N*. It is such rubbish to say good art takes years before it can be understood – look at Cimabue (?) whose pictures were carried in triumph through Florence. Everybody here acclaims Picasso – it is those boring old impressionists, who weren't understood at first, who make people like Reg possible. *Isn't* it queer that the Communists repudiate Picasso who is certainly their trump card in France. It's a thing I cannot ever understand – no wonder their papers don't sell any more.

I've got *Cambridge History*, a great help – & Carlyle *Fred the G*: he describes Pomp as 'high rouged, unfortunate female whom it is not proper to speak of without necessity'. I note there's not a word about Fred's buggery, except terrible wailing after battles (by Carlyle) over the dead blond young men.

Hard to believe he was my Uncle Tommy's[2] godfather & Uncle T going very strong – he seems further off by aeons than Pomp does. Can't put him down, can one?

Best love
    N

---

[1] The fine seventeenth-century building by Louis le Vau that houses the Académie française.
[2] Hon. Bertram Thomas Carlyle Ogilvy Freeman Mitford (1880–1962). Succeeded Nancy's father as 3rd Baron Redesdale in 1958. The historian Thomas Carlyle became his namesake's godfather in the year before he died, aged 86.

31 March 1953   7 rue Monsieur VII

Darling Evelyn

I have now read 29 long books dealing with the years 1740–64, some serious & some frivolous, some by contemporaries & some by reputable modern historians, some by Catholics & some not. But I have never seen the word free mason mentioned (except with regard to the Comte de St Germain who, it is said, was either a free mason or a member of the Intelligence Service). As free masonry is not a bee in my bonnet I really don't see the point of dragging it in. I should have to learn about it, & as it is never spoken of, apparently, in books, *you* would have to come over & teach me & you would find me dreadfully slow, it would take months of your time. Then I should have to re-write what I have already done, from this angle. Evil in high places is a very attractive idea, I admit, if you believe in evil. I don't think I do. I think poor human beings go bumbling along trying their best from day to day without a very clear idea of what they want. A few Germans have a clear idea & commit dreadful crimes trying to achieve it, but even they don't start off by being evil.

In the story I am writing I don't find that anybody can be dignified with the title of evil. The worst character is Richelieu who was a plain straightforward traitor & a great illustration of the fact that traitors, once convicted, shld be eliminated, if not from life itself anyhow from public life. But his 4 wives & all his mistresses & all his men friends simply loved him, he must have been rather nice!

I'm so pleased to think I may be seeing you, you'll find me very boring company because I can think of nothing but THEM, & it will be even worse when I'm shut up with THEM at Versailles.

Best love
    N

I'm sorry this letter lay about & got dirty.
A French expert on 18th cent came to see me yesterday & was rather fascinating about free masons. He believes in them. *He* says the Jacobites brought them here – very odd, I thought they were R.C.s (the Jacobites). I must look them up in the *Ency: Brit*.
Honks will bring you over to Versailles when you come.

28 May 1953   Pension Maintenon
                                             rue du Peintre Lebrun
                                             Versailles S & O

Darling Evelyn
   Thank you for number 44.[1] I love it, I've just finished it. Almost too disgusting but I know now not to read your gift books while dining. I think Colonel will enjoy it very much. Who is Johnny McDougall?

I went to Chantilly yesterday – Duff is blooming but Diana looks awfully ill & strained & (only for your ears) got really drunk I thought at dinner. I think she is worried out of her mind oh dear what can one do. And yet she's going to England – how contradictory people are & how does one understand the working of their brains?

Nearly finished my beardless[2] book. I'm wondering whether to re write it. Oh I have tried hard this time & I've sent for the book on punctuation. At present you can't see for ;s they are like a flock of starlings over it. I copied out a chapter for Peter Q's mag:[3] & it was greatly improved thereby. So perhaps the whole book had better be done – might as well make a job of it I suppose.

They wanted me to go to America with *The Little Hut* but I said I was a Communist before the war & that made it quite all right not to go. Wasn't it a brainwave, Prod thought of it.

I'm sorry to write on ½ a wedding invitation but I forgot to bring down any writing paper this time.

The Americans here have got a tube called Kwikwip out of which they squeeze whipped cream on to their fruit. It makes a disgusting noise. Ugh.

Love
N

[1] No. 44 of a limited edition of *Love Among the Ruins* which was dedicated to Evelyn's publisher, Jack McDougall.
[2] As the result of a botched sterilisation, Clara, the young ballet dancer in *Love Among the Ruins*, grows a 'long, silken, corn-gold' beard. A second operation to remove the beard reduces her face to 'something quite inhuman, a tight, slippery mask, salmon pink'.
[3] 'Madame de Pompadour's Theatre' appeared in *History Today*, August 1953.

30 May [1953]   Piers Court
                                   Stinchcombe

Darling Nancy

I don't believe I have written to you since our day at Versailles. I did enjoy that. It began my recuperation which was nearly completed by a day in bed overlooking the garden quad at the Ritz. Then the Norwiches returned & I have not been quite well since. Norwich was clearly heading for a breakdown. Poor Diana was morbidly restless and irascible. It is very odd her coming here for the Coronation. All the letters I get from London are written in despair. I spent a day there to sign the copies of my silly little story & took a cab down the main streets to see the decorations. They were abominable. The politicians have contrived to be both common & feeble in a unique degree.

Dear dotty Debo tells me you are making her learn to read. Is that kind?[1]

I read long articles about French politics. Pray tell me why I never see Col's name mentioned? I think he is pulling your leg when he tells you that he is a leading politician.

Even here the coronation has its horrors. I am giving a garden party to the Dursley Dramatic Society whose president I have been for 15 years without ever meeting one of them. The Stinchcombe Silver band will play throughout the afternoon. My fear is that they will think '5.30–7.30' means they are expected to stay two hours.

There is not a single flower in the garden & the lawn-mower has developed engine trouble. I have asked the Vicar too. Oh God. Also I have all my daughters (& various friends of theirs whose parents live in Africa) on my hands again. We have killed a sheep & will eat roast mutton at every meal. I have Susan Mary [Patten] coming, which is nice for us – Gloucester Cathedral, Stanway, Stratford-on-Avon. I think you *should* go to New York. All I hate about it – the hot rooms, geniality etc., you would enjoy.

I always knew you were a Communist. I do wish McCarthy[2] would start his good work here on the Mountbattens and Day-Lewis. Poor Frank Pakenham's book[3] is falling flat. They can't get anyone to review it because everyone loves him too much. I do hope your diagnosis of Diana is correct. I feared real barminess.

I wish you had said you liked the illustrations of *Love Among the Ruins*. Perhaps you didn't.

I visited the Jungman sisters. Their condition of destitution & privation, though serious, has been greatly exaggerated. Very pretty little cottage, clean & sweet smelling, two sorts of jam (Tiptree) hot scones, plum cake, China tea, lilies-of-the-valley.

J. McDougall is an Oxford chum who is now head of Chapman & Hall. The dedication is a little joke on account of his now occupying my late father's chair. 'Nostri' may have foxed you. In that sense it means 'in our days'.[4]

H. Buchanan has been most disloyal about *Love Among the Ruins*. McCarthy will get him soon if he doesn't watch out.

Love

E

[1] Nancy pretended that her youngest sister had the mental age of a nine-year-old and had never learned to read.
[2] Senator Joseph McCarthy's anti-Communist campaign had America in its grip.
[3] *Born to Believe*, an autobiography.
[4] The dedication of *Love Among the Ruins* runs:
  'Johanni McDougall
  Amico qui nostri sedet in
  loco parentis'

7 July 1953   7 rue Monsieur, VII

Darling Evelyn

I think I owe you a letter – I've been dreadfully busy packing up the Marquise [de Pompadour] & being lady in waiting (or agent) to Debo who came here for a Fri–Tues of intensive work. The Marquise is being typed by a young Abbé – John Russell calls him that, & now I can't see him as anything else, though he is really an ill & poor young American. When they are ill & poor – so rare – they can be rather nice, I've noticed. There aren't enough Abbés in the modern world – at the time of the Marquise everybody had one sitting about being agreeable.

I have to spend all August in England, rewriting *Hut* for North America, sheer waste of time in my view. But Marie's holiday always spells death, & I might as well eke out the month in London as anywhere else, I suppose.

Debo arrived agog for pleasure. Colonel took her to the Grand Prix in the President's box for which I took the credit. I rang up Momo & said 'bet you haven't done as well as *that* for Nin [Ryan]' – a slight pause & then 'Nin is not a Duchess'.

The Colonel's precedence (as Vice Pres:) is 6th in France – far above Dukes & Academicians, & he *loves* it, in a giggly way. Altogether I've been rather a wonderful agent lately. Christopher [Sykes] sent me a Mr Kurtz who is writing a book about Marshal Ney[1] – I got Napoleon Murat for him, & he has got a Ney relation to fork out a lot of stuff hitherto unpublished. Mr Kurtz was impressed & so was I!

A Dr Cobban,[2] of London University, is going to read my book & take out the bloomers. He is the greatest living expert on 18th Cent: France it seems. I had such struggles with the Parlements that I thought it wiser. Do you agree with me that a preface, appendices & so on are a mere bore? I thought a bibliography & really good index would be enough? *I* rather like people's dates in footnotes when first mentioned, but I know it's not the fashion.

Your torturing of Susan Mary[3] is all over Paris – poor little thing looks more like a Nazi victim than ever.

Shall I see you in Aug:? Brought up by Lord Redesdale I have no fear of mental anguish & can hold my ground in any country house, however rude (in the sense of rude forefathers).

As for sights, & nights at Stratford, I wouldn't be standing for any of that. I once went there for the Bard's birthday, quite enough for me. But I rather die for *you*, to sharpen my wits.

Eddie Gathorne-Hardy[4] is here. He has become a Grand Old Man of pederasty; I like it when people develop along their own lines, what is depressing is when, like Brian H[oward], they are still girls together aged 50.

I arrive, to stay a night or 2 with Momo, about the 24th & then I think I shall rent Heywood Hill's little house for August. Anyway, shop will know my movements.

Love from
    N

---

[1] Harold Kurtz, *The Trial of Marshal Ney: His Last Years and Death* (1957).
[2] Alfred Cobban (1901–68). Author of *A History of Modern France* (3 vols., 1962–5).

[3] Susan Mary Patten was in England for the coronation celebrations and spent a night at Piers Court. At dinner, where only the family were present, Laura wore a ball dress and tiara, Evelyn white tie and decorations, and the children their Sunday best. After the meal, Evelyn called on Mrs Patten to make a speech describing the ceremony at Westminster Abbey. 'I shall never know what the point of all this was . . .' Susan Mary Alsop, *To Marietta from Paris* (Weidenfeld & Nicolson, 1976), p. 225.
[4] Hon. Edward Gathorne-Hardy (1901–78). Authority on 18th-century antiquarian books and a keen amateur botanist. The intemperance of his Oxford days led Evelyn to use the name Martin Gaythorne-Brodie in the first impression of *Decline and Fall* for the character of Miles Malpractice.

8 July [1953]   Piers Court
                                                          Stinchcombe

Darling Nancy

You do not understand the meaning of the word 'eke'. It means to make something last longer by adding something else to it. eg. eke out butter with margarine. When you write: 'I might as well eke out the month in London as anywhere else', you commit a gross vulgarism. But I am glad you are coming to England to polish up your English. You may fall into poor Harold's pit of having no language.[1] Of course we will meet. You would be very welcome here if you can bear a host of children. I have no summer plans, have been in a lethargy, no work done & publisher fretting. Soon I must concentrate if I still can.

Susan Mary was a tough & appreciative little guest on whom I spent great trouble & money. She enjoyed herself no end.

I do congratulate you on having finished your work. Mine is all before me.[2]

Old Driberg came here last Sunday, very fat & sinister & gave me a repulsive book he has written in praise of himself named (believe it or not) *The Best of Both Worlds*. Much worse than Pakenham's.

Patrick Balfour gave a party last week – real old Bohemia & everywhere I moved I found rakes & wantons of the 20s gravely discussing child welfare & education.

I am sorry but not surprised to learn that your campaign to teach Debo to read has come to nothing. I am engaged on the same task with my daughter Margaret. They should be caught young.

I forget, are you obsessed by Ruskin as I am? There is a beautiful little book of his last (unpublished hitherto) love letters,[3] just out.

You should safeguard your investments with Cpl Hill by forbidding his assistant from advising customers *not* to buy books. He is doing this with my last novelette. Great cheek and bad business.

Love from
     Evelyn

[1] Harold Acton was brought up in Florence speaking Italian and English. Despite being educated at Eton and Christ Church, he neither lost his Italian accent entirely nor acquired a perfect ear for written English.

[2] Work on *Officers and Gentlemen* (1955) was progressing slowly.
[3] *The Gulf of Years: Love Letters from John Ruskin to Kathleen Olander* edited by Rayner Unwin. Evelyn reviewed it for the *Spectator*.

17 July 1953   7 rue Monsieur, VII

Darling Evelyn

H Hamilton came over to fetch the Marquise & took her to his hotel yesterday afternoon, to read before dinner. I was to meet him at dinner & nearly *died* on the way, thinking he might say he was sure some other publisher would like it & so on. However, radiant smiles & (verbal) caresses, so the dear girl will see the light of day. Oh the comfort 'tis to me.

John [Sutro], who is here, says he will take me down to see you in his motor. Would that smile on you? I shall have to find out what *work* I'm supposed to do, I seem to be getting a lot of social engagements. I must try & get my eyes fixed up – can't read at all now. Also do you think there would exist in London a teacher of punctuation? I did so try, with this book, but from what Jamie says ('can't get on very fast, I'm too busy putting in commmas') I can see I've not succeeded – & as for paragraphs –!! I did buy a book on the subject but it fogged me worse than ever. I would like to become a good writer, & it should be possible because I see I have the exact temperament required, as well as some talent. Not enough intellect, no education & no technique. C'est embêtant.[1]

The Coopers asked Rosamond Lehmann to stay for 10 days & left, themselves, after 3. I don't know if they sent her the poisoned jug as well. It's quite a technique they've got, isn't it,[2] a lowering treatment. She was very weepy about it. Then they made her, as a sop to their own consciences no doubt, ring up a French person she hardly knows & suggest herself for a few days. She didn't want to a bit, but Diana forced her. The lady was delighted & just as R was ringing off she said '& what is so specially wonderful, I've got Lucian Freud here' whom R *detests*. Do admit it's funny! But not for poor Rosamond, whom, for the first time, in her adversity, I rather liked. Oh do look at those commas – they came quite naturally.

I had a nice chat with a Prof Ross.[3] He is off to North Norway where he expects to find some Danish dialect hitherto lost. He wanted to see me about note paper & so on. He has written a paper about all that for some Finnish university – I told him he should publish it in London, under the title of Are you a Hon? He would make his fortune. He blenched.

Much love I do long for you
      N

[1] It's a bore.

[2] Evelyn had quarrelled with Duff Cooper during a visit to Chantilly. The precise cause of the row was not recorded but Duff Cooper accused Evelyn of 'sponging' and offered to teach him how to hold his wine. (See *Mr Wu & Mrs Stitch* ed. A. Cooper, p. 180). On his return to England, Evelyn, who was beginning to suffer from the hallucinatory symptoms described in *The Ordeal of Gilbert Pinfold* (1957), spread the story that Duff Cooper had attempted to poison him.

[3] Alan S. C. Ross (1907–80). Philologist. Professor of Linguistics, University of Birmingham, 1951–74. Originator of the terms 'U' and 'Non-U'. In an article in the Finnish philological journal, *Neuphilologische Mitteilungen*, he drew on *The Pursuit of Love* as a source of upper-class speech.

19 August [1953]   Piers Court
                                                        Stinchcombe

Darling Nancy

Very many thanks for the tantalizing glimpse of the Magnum Opus. Think no more of the criticisms of the Photographer Royal.[1]

Your punctuation is greatly improved but now a little heavy and occasionally illogical. e.g. 'During this time, 122 performances, in all, were given of sixty-one different plays, operas and ballets.'

1) No comma is permissible after 'time'. You should use it if you said 'During this time, five years.' But in your sentence there is no sort of parenthesis or change of construction.

2) ', in all,' with or without commas is clumsy. You could say 'Many performances, 122 in all, were given.' You could say 'a total of 122 performances was given'. If you love the 'in all' it will be happier comma-less.

3) Why write '122' and 'sixty-one'? You can change numerals for words when there is a great disparity. eg. 'The two men walked 3406 miles', not 'the 2 men'.

I have begun a drastic cure for obesity which takes the pleasure from life, except for happy moments such as I enjoyed reading your extract.

The day after I saw you I met Randolph whom I had been treating with great kindness in the affaire Norwich, taking the blame on myself & saying 'If after nearly 30 years acquaintance I am ass enough to write anything to him which I don't want repeated, I deserve all I get'.[2]

He met *me* with reproaches saying 'I really think you have the most unreasonable attitude to Duff'. That was too much. It will be at least a year before I can speak to him again.

I don't think I made my point quite clear about that business. I did not say: 'I can't tolerate Cooper' but 'I only tolerate Cooper for his wife'. And a great deal of exacting toleration I have had to do. But I have never been a friend of his, done anything with him alone, barely had a drink with him at White's. Therefore I did not want to stay in a house party of total strangers with him alone. I explained this (too vigorously) to Randolph because he was whining that the party had been 'arranged for me'.

I seem to have overheard many family rows when host has said to hostess 'Well he's your guest not mine'.

Dear Coote was here last night, a benign influence, not greatly cast down by the loss of her uncle.[3]

I foresee that if your play is a success in New York you will visit them & love them there. Great heat in all rooms & gross direct compliments.

All love
    Evelyn

[1] Cecil Beaton, who illustrated the cover of *Madame de Pompadour*, had been discouraging about the book.
[2] Randolph Churchill had asked Evelyn to stay for a weekend when Duff Cooper had also been invited. Evelyn refused the invitation, saying: 'It is not only fear of infection that makes me ask you to excuse me. I find him so impolite that I really can't sit at table with him.' When pressed, he continued: 'Cooper I have never tolerated except for his enchanting wife.' *Letters of Evelyn Waugh*, p. 406. Churchill showed Evelyn's letter to Duff Cooper.
[3] 2nd Duke of Westminster had died on 19 July, aged 74.

22 August 1953   10 Warwick Avenue[1]
                                            London W2

Darling Evelyn

I'm so glad you liked the extract & thank you for the remarks about punctuation which I shall study.

Raymond most kindly read the MS. He says the book is extremely unorthodox & reads as if 'an enchantingly clever woman were telling the story over the telephone', that many people will dislike it extremely but that as far as he is concerned I have got away with murder. He says perhaps I should have left out wars & Jansenism which read as they might if written by Fragonard.

I was rather taken aback – I had seen the book as Miss Mitford's sober & scholarly work – but then I saw him & he had obviously enjoyed it though he says the whole enterprise is questionable & many will find it very shocking. He says don't re write, it won't be any better if I do, but he has made a lot of suggestions (in the text) & I'll take it back to Paris & work on them.

A D Peters read it. He thinks many of the anecdotes should come out but Raymond says not. I can't take everybody's advice anyhow. I think it must be very uneven in the writing, & I must look at that again. I've told H.H. to wait another month.

The history expert Dr Cobban was forced to admit that he had enjoyed it, & made surprisingly few observations.

So –

I think Randolph is *too* disgusting. Whatever one may think of your letter, & I think you went too far really, it was quite indefensible to show it. In France that is the *one* rule, never make trouble. Nobody would ever speak to him again if he lived there. People who do that sort of thing undermine all civilized intercourse & make society impossible. But I have never liked Randolph since the evening when he hectored the Colonel at the top of his voice in a restaurant. He exemplifies a sort of brutal island rudeness which is one [of] the things I have fled from, & which you never never meet with in France.

The play, after glittering rehearsals with Peter Brook & me saying never has it been so good, has not come up to our expectations. Unfortunately an enormous, enthusiastic audience at Brighton is spoiling the actors dreadfully. I don't think for a single moment that it will do in New York & I'm thankful not to be going.

I return to Paris on Friday & only live for that – I feel quite different with the ticket in my bag. Everybody here so kind & I've enjoyed it all in a way but I don't feel very well & I long very much for the Colonel.

Back to Brighton this afternoon. I shall be in London Monday & Tuesday, Brighton Wednesday – it is all rather tiring.

> Much love
>   Nancy

[1] Nancy was staying in Heywood Hill's house while attending rehearsals of *The Little Hut* before it went to America.

23 August [1953]   Piers Court
                                                     Stinchcombe

Darling

Has John Sutro gone really mad? Did you read his letter in Saturday's *Times* newspaper.[1]

My cure for obesity (plain starvation) is very effective and very lowering. My family have all left me on account of my low spirits, ostensibly so that I can work, but the pen falls from my fingers.

How clever Raymond is.

As you say, you can't take everyone's advice and I wouldn't dare give mine on a subject so far from my knowledge. But I think you should consider the effect that Dr Kinsey's report on the loose morals of his countrywomen[2] (don't pretend you have not heard of it) may have. I shouldn't be surprised to see a great anti-smut in England & America. Probably I am wrong but I seem to scent it. It wld be an awful nuisance for you to have your book banned. It is all rot to say that it promotes sales. You would lose heavily in money and honour (most undeservedly I am sure. Nothing 'offensive' in extract).

I don't think Peters's literary advice valuable. He is [a] good negotiator but no better critic than C. Beaton.

The 'one rule in France, never make trouble', seems not to be closely observed at the moment. I hear it is very difficult to reach Paris because of the troubles. Don't trust too much in that ticket in your bag. You will long for your easy journeys on the Brighton Belle.

I have written a comic letter to *The Times* newspaper about John Sutro but I am afraid they will detect its falsity.

Love to any friends you see.

I am already so thin as to [be] unrecognizable & none of my clothes fit.

    Much love
       Evelyn

[1] John Sutro and Graham Greene had written to inform readers that they were forming an 'Anglo-Texan Society for establishing cultural and social links between this country and the State of Texas' (22 August 1953). Years later, Graham Greene admitted that the idea was a joke: 'conceived in a mood of tipsy frivolity with John Sutro after a pint or two of Black Velvet in the Edinburgh to London Express', after they had picked up two 'delightful' Texan girls. *Daily Telegraph Magazine*, 22 November 1974.
[2] Dr A. C. Kinsey's *Sexual Behaviour in the Human Female* had just been published.

24 August 1953   10 Warwick Avenue, W.2.

Darling Evelyn

I think you will have to forgive Handysides. Great splashing tears fill his eyes whenever he thinks of you – he LOVES you, you see & it isn't to be thrown away, real love. I think what he did much less bad than Randolph's behaviour especially as he has always boosted your books more than anybody, always refers to you as the Master & so on. Look at the sales figures at H. Hill's for yr books. I admit it was very tiresome of him, & exceeding his – I can't think of the word, I am so tired.

Oh how I long to leave this exhausting town & go home. Only 3 more days.

Do forgive Handy oh do it quite worries me.

    Love from
      Nancy

25 Aug
P.S. Got your letter this morning. Oh I never saw John Sutro's letter – what was it? How annoying – I take in *The Times* here too but must say I hardly ever do look at the letters. They all seem utterly pointless to me.

Don't know what you mean about smut. Are my books ever the least improper? You know they're not. (*Little Hut* is, I grant you.)

If you get thin you will feel tired & feel the cold as I do. It is a great mistake I should say.

I see your side has bought beautiful Highcliffe[1] I am so delighted to think the garden & so on will now be looked after properly.

Handy says Kinsey is a fake. Oh do forgive Handy.

Would you say it is a bit hypocritical of the English the way they blame the French so much for not paying taxes & yet devote every waking hour themselves to paying as little as they can? Alan Lennox-Boyd was describing with a wealth of detail how Lord Iveagh[2] has got out of paying a single penny by living 5 years longer than he should. And yet by the way they go on when they speak of the French you would think they all eagerly ask if they couldn't be allowed to pay a little more than they owe.

I wouldn't find it very inspiring to be governed by Lennox-Boyd, myself.

[1] Highcliffe Castle in Hampshire had belonged to Peter Rodd's aunt, Violet Stuart Wortley.
[2] The 2nd Earl of Iveagh (1874–1967) had transferred his huge wealth into trusts which avoided taxation; on his death, through his longevity, only £178,113 was paid in duty.

15 September 1953   St-Pierre du Château
                                                     Hyères

Darling Evelyn

I really think that, next to starting a book, the worst thing in the world is finishing one – having finished it I mean. I have lost the poor Marquise, as the Dauphine said when she died (we she said really) & I miss her fearfully, my constant companion for nearly a year. Also I feel doubtful about her reception – the photographer royal may be very representative of MY PUBLIC, whatever that means. However as I don't need money for the moment I shall be very contented if a few, such as yourself, approve of her.

I came away from England with a deep contempt for the theatre public – & a resolution never to work for it again as long as I live. Any finer points there may be in the play pass entirely unobserved – the name of Dr Kinsey is introduced & they laugh for 5 minutes. Peter Brook, one of the cleverest people I have ever met, has been entirely corrupted in the 3 years since I first did the play with him. Well, I suppose it is the same public that reads one's books & if so all I can say is to hell with it. A great eye-opener to me. But at least with a book you don't have to sit listening to their asinine guffaws.

I did think London too awful. I suppose no town can ever have changed so much in 7 short years. If I had to live in England again I think I would go to the Isle of Wight – at least it smells good.

Here I am en plein dans la pourriture.[1] My dear old host cooks up his drugs in the kitchen, Marie-Laure de Noailles next door has a Spanish lover[2] who knocks her about & sleeps with her butler, & in the local pub Jean Hugo & Frosca Munster,[3] both over 60, are having an illicit honeymoon. The joke is they all spend their time trying to keep these facts from *me*. I am supposed to be very prim, a sort of English governess who must not on any account be shocked. But I do nothing but sleep – all night, 12 hours & most of the day. I was quite done in when I arrived.

What a bore, your quarrel with Duff. Now you'll never come to Paris again.

Much love
    N

[1] Surrounded by decadence.
[2] Oscar Dominguez (1907–57). Spanish Surrealist painter.
[3] Frosca Munster (d.1963). Russian-born friend of Christian Bérard and Jean Cocteau.

17 September 1953   Piers Court
                                                     Stinchcombe
Darling Nancy

What a strange girl you are. Your magnum opus finished and you are not elated? Would to God mine were. No need of money? My children starve & my clothes fall in rags about me. You should be dancing in the streets not sprawling in the sun. The sun is the great enemy of the human race. In civilized times everyone hid from it. O yes, I know, you will tell me that Louis XIV lay naked on the roof of Versailles surrounded by naked cardinals & duchesses and I shan't believe you.

I can't think what you mean by my 'quarrel with Duff'. I am on terms of tender intimacy with him.

What do you know of Belgium? I am thinking of taking Laura there for her harvest-home treat. Am I right in thinking that the Belgians are still well disposed to the English? There are few places where an Englishman can now set foot without being stoned. It is true that the Belgians behaved disgracefully to their King. Apart from that I know nothing against them. They have some fine pictures have they not?

I am reading an enormous life of Dickens, by an American professor of course,[1] which gives details of every chop he ever ate & every speech at every public banquet. Did you know that he was a perfectly awful man?

School holidays have been agonising but are at last bit by bit coming to an end.

I am *much* thinner than when you last saw me. Really rather pretty.

Love
    E

[1] Edgar Johnson, *Charles Dickens* (1953). Evelyn wrote of it: 'This work ... can only be of interest to a patient and devoted reader ... An enormous amount of facts have certainly been accumulated, many of them ... of absolute unimportance.' *Spectator*, 2 October 1953.

25 September 1953   St-Pierre du Château
                                            Hyères

Darling Evelyn

I have been to Belgium. Very ugly, very nasty people, wonderful food, wonderful pictures. You might enjoy it, as the whole human race seems uniformly nasty to you.

No, Louis XIV & the cardinals never went near the sun, but died of gangrene in the *most unlucky* parts of their bodies (at least he did & so did Cardinal Dubois). So you can take your choice. I never do sprawl in it now, I remember too well when I was young seeing old ladies of 48 with their skins, mahogany, one mass of well oiled cracks. I made a resolution that never would I get like that & nor I have. But it does me good to run about the mountains here & bathe & have bright sunlight filtering through my clothes. If you could see me you would understand. I go home on Monday.

A usually reliable source informs me that your quarrel with Duff has taken a *new* & *nasty* turn. Operation Mincemeat seems rather a come down – pity they didn't call it Sickmake all the same.[1]

Are you fascinated by the great Culme-Seymour Jackson scandal?[2] I can't remember if we've talked about it.

How much money a year do you need to live on? It interests me to know. I can do on £200 a month, & I've saved up enough to bring me £100, then the *Sunday Times* is £30. So if I could save up a little more I should be home. But oh *The Hut* is shut, & that lovely steady hot water bottle of £300 a month has been taken out of my bed. I feel very chilly. I'm sure it won't succeed in America. What of John's play[3] – have you seen it?

F-M the Viscount M[ontgomery]. of A., K.G. has asked me to luncheon. I'm very curious to see the set up. When I met him I thought he was *bliss* do you know him? So pretty.

Much love
    N

3 Aunts & Stephen Tennant arrive in Paris next week, do admit.

[1] Following *Operation Heartbreak*, Duff Cooper had written his memoirs, *Old Men Forget* (1953).
[2] Derek Jackson eloped with his wife's half-sister, Angela Culme-Seymour; they lived together for three years but were never married.
[3] John Sutro had invested in a production of *The Devil's General* by the German playwright Carl Zückmayer.

[October 1953]   [Brussels]
[postcard]

Your public, darling?[1]

    E.

[1] Evelyn's postcard was of a painting by Antoine Wiertz, 'The Romantic Reader', showing a
large naked woman lying languidly on a bed reading a novel.

19 October 1953   7 rue Monsieur, VII

Darling Evelyn

    Charmerende og vittig som Oscar Wilde, funklende som Evelyn
Waugh.[1] These magic words occur on *L in a C Climate* in Danish.
Written by a member of *your* public darling I suppose. (*Our* public
really.) How was the trip? You were evidently preoccupied with ART.

    Well I had my luncheon with Monty. He is terribly like my Dad –
watch in hand when I arrived (the first, luckily) only drinks water, has
to have the 9 o'clock news & be in bed by 10, washes his own shirts,
rice pudding his favourite food. All my books by his bed & when he
gets to a daring passage he washes it down with Deuteronomy. But
oh the glamour! He sat me next him although there were a French
marquise & an English peeress at the bout de la table. I do hope I
did well – not absolutely sure though. He took me to see an awful
little English garden with maples turning red, & I was obliged to say
that I couldn't look – too ugly. He *was* surprised. His ADC told me
he said to a French general 'I know what you're like – I've read *The
Blessing*' & the Frog replied 'Yes well *I've* read *Love in a C.C.*'

    What thick rich paper Danes print their books on don't they.

    What are you up to? Settling down for the winter? Oh how I dread it.

    What is happening in the French church, I can't make out. Do be
a duck & send me the address of the *Tablet*, I want to take it in (& I
am not fishing to be given a subscription). Or do you advise the other
one more. Does the English church ever make a stand against Rome?
Is the French church doing so now? What do you feel about the
prêtres ouvriers [worker priests]?

    Monty says his French ADC cheats over taxes & then goes to
Church as if it wasn't a sin to do so. He also says he (the ADC) thinks
the poor will be in a sort of servants' hall in heaven. Well so do you.

    I'm finishing *Enthusiasm*, it is lovely.

    Monty loves Tito & is all for him. Do you love Monty – did you
ever go over the top with him? That's what I should enjoy. La Gloire.

    Momo has been here – she is very pro German which I think, for
a Jewess, is low.

    Much love
        N

What can funklende be? It sounds most improper.

[1] 'As charming and witty as Oscar Wilde, as sparkling as Evelyn Waugh.'

22 October 1953   Piers Court
                                                         Stinchcombe

Darling Nancy,

I find Lord Montgomery's courtship very odd & rather nasty. I have always heard the worst accounts of him, I suppose that his charm for you is the contempt of the Americans. We thought him a whipper snapper who did down good Lord Alexander[1] by sucking up to journalists & politicians. There must be some secret & disgusting reason for his washing his own shirts. How, pray, did you come to see his bedside?

God alone (literally) knows what is happening in the French Church. The Dominicans all seem mad bad & dangerous to know. All this devotion to Miss [Simone] Weil. As far as I can make out there are two quite different kinds of prêtre ouvrier. There are simple missionaries who sometimes go native and contemplatives who find the conveyer belt conducive to prayer. *Tablet* address is 128 Sloane Street. Subscription 42/- at home or abroad. There is usually at least one readable article a week. The literary part is bad because no publishers send them books to review. It is not a sin to cheat over taxes in most modern states. Don't worry your head about the theology of this. Just take it from the theologians. It is not true that any Catholic thinks the poor go to a servants' hall in heaven. Read Bossuet's great sermon on the Eminent Dignity of the Poor. Also Gospels. Dives & Lazarus. It shows the sort of pipsqueak Ld Montgomery is that he puts these ideas into your poor puzzled nut. I wish Senator McCarthy would grill Lord Montgomery and expose his communism.

Belgium was very restful for Laura after harvest & holidays and very expensive for me. Much worse than France. Cheapest wine £1 a bottle in restaurants. The natives talk a queer gibberish but look *good*. I don't mean pretty, but virtuous. Brussels was full of undesirable Britons such as Gaitskell and Hugh Fraser.[2] There was a man called Peter Ustinov[3] who was *very* funny – like John Sutro at his old best. Magnificent pictures everywhere. We spent most of the time in Antwerp. Excellent cooking. Half a dozen splendid churches all oddly enough in the quartier toléré.[4] I have never seen a quarter like it in Europe. The girls are exposed in shop windows and leap about like monkeys to attract attention. And all the good middle-class families troop to church through these streets with their eyes downcast.

Wiertz was rather a disappointment. I had heard so much about him but his painting isn't good enough. Better in photographs. Younger

Breughel stupendously good. Oh how bored one gets with Temptations of St Anthony with devils blowing trumpets from their behinds.

Have you heard of the lady who writes under the name Edith de Born[5] – An austrian-hungarian-jewess I suspect – married to a French banker called Bisch? She writes in English quite beautifully. *Daughter of the House* etc. We stayed with her in a fine house in their Park Lane in Brussels. I thought Bisch was Belgian until the last day and dropped brick after brick. No possible way out & back from a gaffe as big as that. Telling him patronizingly how well the Congo was run compared with Algeria – that sort of brick.

What has happened to Prod? I never hear of him now.

Poor Sir John Gielgud[6] has had trouble with the police. Is a reception being arranged in Paris for Lord Montagu?[7]

Cooper's memoirs in *Sunday Times* are all an enemy could ask. But I am his friend now so I weep for him.[8]

Now I put on my woollen underclothes & settle in for the winter to finish second vol of war novel.

If you listen to BBC *New Reading* on 25th you will hear a bit cribbed from *Highland Fling*.[9]

Do you *dread* the publication of *Pompadour*?

Reviewers won't let you change subjects except T. S. Eliot whose subjects were so obscure. But no one pays attention to reviewers now – which is rather a bad thing really.

> Much love
>   E

[1] Field Marshal Alexander (1891–1969). Commander-in-Chief in North Africa, when Montgomery, who was in command of the 8th Army, became a national hero.
[2] Hon. Hugh Fraser (1918–84). Conservative MP. Married to Hon. (later Lady) Antonia Pakenham 1956–77. Knighted in 1980.
[3] Peter Ustinov (1921–2004). Actor. Knighted in 1990.
[4] Red-light district.
[5] Edith de Born; Austrian-born author whose books include *Daughter of the House* (1953), *The Imperfect Marriage* (1954) and *The Flat in Paris* (1960). Married to Jacques Bisch.
[6] John Gielgud (1904–2000). The actor had been fined £10 for 'persistent importuning'.
[7] 3rd Baron Montagu (1926–). He had been charged and imprisoned for indecent assault.
[8] After an exchange of mollifying letters, Evelyn had made up his quarrel with Duff Cooper.
[9] A description of the Isle of Mugg in *Officers and Gentlemen*.

30 October 1953   7 rue Monsieur, VII

Darling Evelyn

Many thanks for your letter & address of *Tablet* (how odd, somehow, Sloane St).

I've been most exceedingly busy doing nothing – not a moment to

myself & yet seeing nobody. I don't quite understand it. Now I've
cleared the decks for the proofs of *Pomp* & here they aren't, very
tiresome. Yes I *utterly dread* her appearance & keep holding up poor
H Hamilton on various excuses. For one thing I now believe it (the
book) to be very bad & badly written. I am more at sea than ever
about punctuation. I think I had better give up writing altogether, it
is too difficult for me. One faint ray of encouragement is that Peter
Q has taken another chapter for *History Today*.

I am surprised at what you say about Monty. I had always supposed
that Alexander was an amiable nincompoop, like Eisenhower. The
courtship however was of short duration – I did myself in by saying
that English gardens are so hideous I can't look at them.

Why is FOG now called Smog? I am getting out of touch I fear.
When we were little we used to enjoy a good pea souper.

I say have you read *The Go-Between*?[1] Lovely stuff. Yes Operation
Embarrassment is very hard to laugh off. (It reads much better in
French by the way.[2])

Prod lives on a small yacht, usually tied up at Golfe Juan. He is a
perfectly happy human being & the idol of the local population there.
He looks exactly like some ancient pirate – bone thin, pitch black,
white hair & beard & dressed in literal rags. He wears steel rimmed
spectacles. He has a villainous Spaniard who does the chores – when,
on one occasion this fellow displeased Prod he ran up a signal 'Mutiny
on board'. However nobody in the modern world, except Prod, can
read these signals any more so nobody came to the rescue. Last time
he went to England he was shown that list of dutiable goods at the
customs. He asked for paper & pencil & wrote down everything that
is on it: 'perfume handbags ladies underwear etc etc'. It took ages &
they had to keep the train. Then they asked him to open his suitcase
& it was empty. So they said they would have him up, but Prod said
'you can't have me up for declaring what I haven't got, only for not
declaring what I have got'. Do say he's lovely. If you want a bit more
Basil Seal you would be well repaid for a visit to Golfe Juan. I might
come with you. Just at the moment I am on cool terms with the old
boy because a form which he must sign in 2 places so that I can
recover about £3000 in tax rebate, has just come back after *18 months*
signed in *one place*. It's almost too much to bear. He has had it since
April 1952. In a covering letter he states that he is off to Italy, no
address, & will I pay a bill for him at the Travellers. No, I won't.
Mutiny in the rue Monsieur.

That's Prod – as you asked.

I've been staying with my holy friend Mme Costa de Beauregard.
She is now 85. She spends always 8 & sometimes 10 hours a day on
her knees in a totally unheated chapel. Her maid goes & leads her
out at meal times otherwise I think she would never move. After dinner

she keeps up a flow of wickedly malicious conversation until 1 AM. I shall miss her dreadfully when she dies.

> Much love
>   N

Have you read the P G Wodehouse letters?[3] He never seems to stay in one place more than a week. Not a joke in the whole lot – as far as I've read.

[1] By L. P. Hartley (1953).
[2] Duff Cooper's autobiography appeared in French as *Au-delà de l'oubli* (1960).
[3] *Performing Flea: A Self-Portrait in Letters* (1953).

10 December 1953   7 rue Monsieur, VII

Darling Evelyn
    I have received – perhaps at your orders? – *Campion* in French. Though horrible to look at it seems very well translated – indeed I re read the death of Elizabeth with *pleasure*.
    I must say I was shocked at the [André] Maurois preface, however we don't feel the same about collaborators I know. Maurois is a particularly horrible human being. Probably you have never met him.
    When I was in London I made up my quarrel with Cyril. He was at a dinner party, sitting across the table from me – never said hullo, looked freezing, & I was desperate for an opening. Bobbie Helpmann,[1] next to me, said 'Do you know who I miss most in the world? Constant.'[2] I could see that Cyril was listening, & I said to him 'Do you know who *I* miss most in the world? You.' And he melted. Wasn't it lucky – I don't know how I would have started otherwise. So after dinner we chatted for hours about all the people I lived with while doing *Pomp* – he knows more than I do about them so this was a great pleasure. Oh how I love clever people. Great is my relief – I really minded about Cyril. I've sent him some Mouton Rothschild, to seal the reconciliation.[3]
    I enjoyed London this time, much more than usual. Everybody very nice to me. I enjoyed the glory of being asked to Winston's party & finally loved the party itself, but went through slight agonies of terror before it as I had nobody to go with. However at 6.30 Jim Thomas rang up & said I could dine with him, after which all was plain sailing. (Talk about sailing, I was very much shocked to see that the weather vane in the Admiralty board room was quite inaccurate.)
    Oh Evelyn, you haven't got a compte rendu of your interview on the wireless?[4] I hear it was masterly in the extreme, & am furious at having missed it. I must take in the *Radio Times* I think.
    Is it true that Christopher is in a difficult mood? People said so, &

I must say he wasn't very nice to me. I don't think his book[5] has been praised nearly enough in the papers.

I now long feverishly for the appearance of *Pomp* – not until March, however.

Much love
  N

[1] Robert Helpmann (1909–86). Australian-born dancer, actor and choreographer. Knighted in 1968.
[2] Constant Lambert (1905–51). Composer and critic.
[3] Nancy's accompanying note read: 'An impermanent record of an impermanent breach, with love from Nancy, in the wrong & ashamed of herself.'
[4] An interview with Evelyn on *Frankly Speaking* was broadcast on 16 November.
[5] Christopher Sykes, *A Song of a Shirt* (1953), a novel set in Cairo during the war.

11 December [1953]   Piers Court
                                                             Stinchcombe
Darling Nancy

Did I send you last Christmas a little book of mine called *The Holy Places*. I inscribed them all on the eve of leaving for India & half didn't arrive & half I suppose I forgot to address and anyway it was a mass of horrible misprints. Anyway a new and greatly improved edition de luxe is out this Christmas. If I didn't send it last year I should like to send it now.

I am afraid I had no hand in sending you the frog *Campion*. It was a great surprise to me when it arrived yesterday morning. I thought Maurois was a dead Jew who wrote about Shelley.[1] 'Collaboration' of course means nothing in my country. The greatest non-collaborator I ever met was that publisher with the woollen scarf. I saw an epitome of the fall of France in his helpless selfishness when his motor-car broke in the Bois de Boulogne.

I did not realise that your breach with Boots had ever been serious. He is a darling. I regret his misalliance with Conk daily. He sent me *Golden Horizon* – a selection from his magazine. 'Golden?' I wrote to him. 'Grey, pink, yellow. Not Golden.' It is striking, reading the selection, how poor the contributions were. It was fun monthly as it appeared though there was always a nasty accent – RAF – pansy – which broke through. I suppose from Spender and Watson. It is too absurd to look back to it as the Golden Age.

Christopher is a mystery. I haven't seen him for more than a year though I have made repeated loving attempts to meet him. Always rebuffed or chucked at the last moment. I fear something is amiss. I daresay connected with that son whom he adores[2] & the shadow of Daniel.[3] But I am more alarmed still by Randolph who I fear will be in a strait-jacket quite soon.

My broadcast was pretty dull. They tried to make a fool of me &
I don't believe they entirely succeeded.

I am stuck in my book from sheer boredom. I know what to write
but just can't make the effort to write it.

Best news of the week is that Trevor Roper, the demon don, has
written an article[4] with four historical errors in the first three lines.

Curious case of 'Experiment with Time'. I sat next to Maurice
[Bowra] at dinner. He (and I) praised the Ashmolean. He raised subject
of Arthur Hughes's *Return from Sea*. He said: 'I hear there is a version
of it with a second figure, a sister's, sitting by the boy's side.' Self:
'That's the only version I know. Isn't that the one in the Ashmolean?'
'No, no, old boy. Do find out for me where the other is.' I looked it
up in my library. Sure enough, Ashmolean version contains sister. I
investigate further and learn that when first exhibited the picture
contained only boy. It failed to sell so Hughes painted in sister to add
pathos. No living human eye, except Sir Maurice, has seen the original
version. It may be prevision of what will happen when Sir K. Clark[5]
gets to work with his vitriol & wire brush removing what he calls
'over-painting'.

See how *I* praise Sykes.[6]

Love
    E

[1] André Maurois, *Ariel* (1923). A life of Percy Bysshe Shelley.
[2] Mark Sykes (1937–). Married to Helen Homewood 1962–5 and to Valerie Goad in 1968.
[3] Daniel Sykes (1917–67). Christopher Sykes's younger brother. An interior decorator, he had
been a registered heroin addict during the war.
[4] A study of Sir Thomas More and the English lay recusants in the *New Statesman*, 5 December
1953. The article ended: 'Come unto us, say the Roman clergy, come into the Church, says
Mr Evelyn Waugh (for in the intellectual emptiness of modern English Catholicism only the
snob-appeal is left) . . . and join the old English recusants in their armigerous tombs.' Evelyn
wrote to attack the article and a heated correspondence ensued. (See *Letters of Evelyn Waugh*,
pp. 642–7)
[5] Kenneth Clark (1903–83). Art historian. Director of the National Gallery 1934–45 and
surveyor of the King's Pictures 1934–44. Created life peer in 1969.
[6] Evelyn enclosed his review of *A Song of a Shirt* in which he praised the novel's originality and
humour. *Time and Tide*, 12 December 1953.

15 December 1953   7 rue Monsieur, VII

Darling Evelyn

No I never received *The Holy Places*, I would love to have it.

Yes you did Christopher proud. I wonder if it sells, I do hope so,
it would set him up to have a success & he does deserve it. I fear that
people's children are not always the joy to them that childless people
imagine – well, Margaret is a joy to you.

I dined last night with the Ismays[1] – did you know him in your
military days? He is a *dear*, I really love him. There were 14 foreign

secretaries, I got Eden & van Zeeland,[2] both very chatty. Eden looks very well – Clarissa was there, beautiful, & I lunch with her today.

Lord Ismay, whom I got in a corner after dinner, has been to Laeken & 'had it out' with the young King[3] about his father's behaviour in the war – very fascinating, I'll tell you sometime. The boy, who sounds a misery, didn't make any remark at all. But then Leopold[4] appeared in an Old Etonian tie, most friendly! I am always fascinated by accounts of Laeken, it is certainly one of the oddest set-ups in Europe to-day.

Somebody said to Raymond M 'I hear you took a lot of slang out of Nancy's book.' 'Not really. I suggested that she might not say *Louis XV was perfect heaven* 3 times on one page.'

I read Duff's book yesterday. Not enough meat, is there. But Aug: Hervey,[5] which I read the day before, is lovely stuff, & so well edited. He describes Pompadour as 'a rock of diamonds'. Wasn't she lucky!

Much love & happy Xmas – my present will be *Pomp* when she appears.

Nancy

I must own that I have very much come round to your view of André Bay. He is hopeless – *but* he is ill.

[1] General Lord Ismay (1887–1965). Chief of Staff to Churchill 1940–46. Secretary-General of NATO 1952–7. Married Laura Clegg in 1921.
[2] Paul van Zeeland (1893–1973). Belgian Minister for Foreign Affairs 1949–54.
[3] King Baudouin of the Belgians (1930–93). Succeeded to the throne in 1950.
[4] King Leopold III (1901–1983). Surrendered his country to the Germans in 1940; abdicated in 1950. In 1941 he made a morganatic marriage to Liliane Baëls, created Princesse de Réthy, with whom he lived at the royal palace of Laeken.
[5] *3rd Earl of Bristol – Journal 1746–59* (1953), edited by D. Erskine.

29 December 1953   7 rue Monsieur, VII

Darling Evelyn

Thank you very much indeed for the lovely book – so pretty, so rare, & so very interesting. I love it & read it with fascination & quite long, now, to go to the Holy Land – as much as I ever long to leave here, that is.

Pomp is Book of the Month (England) for March. I am pleased, because C. V. Wedgwood[1] is on the jury it seems, so she must think it *honorable*.

I've had a long & affectionate letter from Boots, so evidently that quarrel is over, thank goodness. Also one from Christopher who comes here next week & says he will come & see me. I worry about my friends sometimes, it comes from not being among them. Happy as I am here, & much as I love all my new friends, the old ones are irreplaceable.

I'm off to see if I can possibly afford a red lacquer chest of drawers which I spied in a shop on Xmas Day. Such a beauty.

Much love from
Nancy

I sent a card to Harriet but there is a postal strike here so she may not receive it. This goes with Mark [Ogilvie-Grant].

[1] C. V. Wedgwood (1910–97). Historian whose books include *The Thirty Years War* (1938), *Richelieu and the French Monarchy* (1949) and *The Trial of Charles I* (1964). Made DBE in 1968.

5 March 1954   Piers Court
                                                         Stinchcombe

Darling Nancy

Pompadour arrived yesterday morning & I have spent two days of enchantment in reading it. Thank you so very much for such a lovely present. It is very seldom that I have been so sorry to come to the end of a book.

I think you have managed your vast mass of material brilliantly. Never a dull page & never a page that is not unmistakably your own. The quotations all fit into the narrative most naturally & you bring a real sense of intimacy with the complicated scene. I am sure you need have no fears about its success. It is very clever of your Mr Hamish [Hamilton] to produce it so well at so modest a price. Beaton's drawings always give me goose flesh but the wrapper is easily disposed of. Everything else admirable.

It is very long since I wrote to you. I have been suffering from a sharp but brief attack of insanity. My alienist thinks that it was due to excess of drugs not to any constitution defect.[1] But it was alarming at the time. It caught me in solitude on board ship going to Ceylon. A disastrous expedition.

So Père Couturier has joined Norwich in purgatory.[2] Which do you miss the more? Again, deepest thanks & deepest congratulations on Poisson.[3]

Love
E

[1] Evelyn had been gradually poisoning himself with a daily cocktail of bromide, chloral and alcohol. He suffered a period of aural hallucinations and madness that inspired *The Ordeal of Gilbert Pinfold*.
[2] Duff Cooper had died on New Year's Day, Père Couturier on 8 February.
[3] The Marquise de Pompadour was born Jeanne-Antoinette Poisson.

8 March 1954   7 rue Monsieur, VII

Darling Evelyn

Such praise from *you* brought tears to my eyes (or are you still a
little bit mad – it's rather frighteningly unlike you. No, the bit about
Couturier & Norwich reassures me).

Yes I noted a long silence – I imagined you were doing your novel,
& didn't like to interrupt. Then I saw Mr Peters, who terrifies me
more than any living man, & he told me you had gone to Ceylon.
You *are* eccentric, Evelyn.

Did you love Cyril's review of *Pomp*:[1] I literally screamed with laughter, in the street where I bought the paper. It is a masterpiece, & he
gets his own back for *The Blessing* without any hard knocks, or harder
than I can take, which is so clever. Harold's[2] I thought crusty & unfair.
They both, greatly to my surprise, still cling to the 19th century view
of Louis XV, which has been abandoned by the historians here as
well as by such as Dr Cobban. In fact *he* says if Louis XV had lived
another 10 years there would have been no revolution. Meanwhile the
Daily Sketch, voicing the view that here is the Book of the Year, says:
'*Criticism of the Book*. It says too little about Pom-Pom's fabulous hair-dos
& breathtaking clothes.'

Have you heard of the Abbé Pierre?[3] They say he is the only man
in Europe rich enough to keep Pam Churchill.[4]

Do write soon again, & say how you are. Is the book finished?
Peters says it's wonderfully good.

I've been in the South of France with Daisy Fellowes – quite alone
with her for a fortnight, in a luxury I didn't know existed still in the
world. Very enjoyable indeed & saved me from the cold weather.

Poor Honks Cooper, I have very lowering accounts of her from
Rome.

Prod appeared, with a fiancée.[5] But doesn't want to be divorced –
& Francis[6] came to beg me not to divorce him. The fiancée is one of
those pathetic tramps who seem such a feature of the modern world
– daughter of London School of Economics don. (The don is ONE's
age, it gave me quite a shock.) Do admit. Oh I would like to see you
it seems an age.

Love
    N

[1] 'Love at Versailles', *Sunday Times*, 7 March 1954.
[2] Harold Nicolson wrote that *Madame de Pompadour* would be enjoyed by the educated and
uneducated alike, but that it was 'not history'. *Observer*, 7 March 1954.
[3] L'Abbé Pierre (1912–2007). Pseudonym of Henri de Grouès, a Jesuit priest who in 1949 set up
the Association Emmaüs to help the poor.
[4] Hon. Pamela Digby (1920–97). Daughter-in-law of Winston Churchill who was married to
the film producer Leland Hayward 1960–71 and to W. Averell Harriman 1971–86. After her
divorce from Randolph Churchill in 1946, she was notorius for her liaisons with Aly Khan,

Gianni Agnelli and Elie de Rothschild. Appointed American Ambassador to France in 1993.
[5] Peter Rodd never remarried.
[6] 2nd Baron Rennell (1895–1978). Peter Rodd's elder brother. Married Hon. Mary Smith in 1928.

2 May 1954   7 rue Monsieur, VII

Darling Evelyn

What are your news (as Col always says) it seems an age since I heard from you.

Mine are that I'm going to Moscow at the end of this month, to stay with the Hayters (ambassador).[1] At least I am if I get a visa – they've had my passport for an age. Iris Hayter says they are reading my books, good luck to them, but one of the secretaries here says all depends on Burgess.[2] To tell the truth I shan't cry if I don't get it. The idea is very nice, the Hayters write of the Opera the Ballet & a big ball on 10th June, & of course I see myself floating in the arms of Vronsky. But I fear that the cold reality will be back to Hector Dexter – I'm quite sure Moscow is indistinguishable from New York. The fact is, East or West, I loathe journeys.

I am surrounded by charming Woodleys, I think even crusty you would like them & to them you are as God. I can see that they regard me as the Marie Corelli of the age, though they are far too polite to say so. Partly Hamish Hamilton's fault for splashing 70 000 all over everything – such a bore in every way. ONE knows it means 35 000 – everybody else thinks one is a millionaire.

My crazy friend Prof Ross has written a pamphlet, 'extrait du bulletin de la Société Néo Philologique de Helsinki' printed in Finland but written in English, called 'Linguistic Class Indicators in Present Day English'. It is full of sentences like 'the ideal U-address (U = upper class) is P – Q – R where P is a placename, Q a describer & R the name of a county … But today few gentlemen can maintain this standard & they often live in houses with non-U names such as Fairmead or El Nido.' What *will* the Finns think? Prof Ross is himself U & has hardly said a thing which I disagree with. *P of L* is one of the sources I'm happy to say.

My eye falls on 'I may mention that people sometimes sign themselves with the surname only; this usage is very non-U' (I should think so indeed). 'Pleased to meet you.' This is a very frequent non-U response to the greeting how do you do?

Home: non-U. They've a lovely home / U: They've a very nice house.

I keep thinking of the Finns. Isn't the academic world queer!

The Professor has just been to Norway on philological business – to pay for his trip he took a photographer to illustrate some articles.

When he got back he said to me 'The man is a physical coward.'
'How did you know?' 'I noticed it when we were climbing up a cliff.'

He is an oddity. He worked out a system for winning at roulette,
went off to Enghien casino with it & hasn't been heard of since.
However I think he's safely back at Birmingham at which university
he professes.

Do write – best love
N

[1] William Hayter (1906–95). Ambassador to USSR 1953–7, Warden of New College, Oxford,
1958–76. Married to Iris Grey in 1938. Knighted in 1953.
[2] Guy Burgess had fled to the USSR in 1951 after being unmasked as a spy.

5 May 1954   Piers Court
                                                       Stinchcombe
Darling Nancy

My news are the great news that all my children have at last disappeared to their various places of education. My unhealthy affection
for my second daughter has waned. I now dislike them all equally. Of
children as of procreation – the pleasure momentary, the posture
ridiculous, the expense damnable.

It is sad to read that La Rue is shut. My newspaper this morning
says you could eat eight courses there for 2,500 francs. I did not find
it so on my last visit.

Your mad chum's reference to U-address = P.Q.R. must be a tease
of Osbert [Sitwell] who has had to change his NOTE paper from
'Renishaw Hall, Derbyshire' to 'R. H., Renishaw, Nr Sheffield'. U
speech is fast disappearing. An officer in the Blues was lately heard
to order: 'Two beers', in the anteroom at Windsor.

I look forward to the film of *Pompadour* with her & Louis going hand
in hand to the guillotine.

I don't think you will find Moscow at all like New York. You will at
any rate be safe from the impertinences of the natives. No telephones,
invitations, philosophic speculation by taxi drivers and lift-men, inter-
viewers, autograph collectors etc. which make New York hideous. You
are being invited there simply to cheer up the isolation of the diplomats
& to tell them the gossip of the Free ha ha World.

What news of Honks? I hear the Sunday galas are in full swing
again.

You know that poor Maureen's daughter[1] made a runaway match
with a terrible Yid? Well this T.Y. has painted a portrait of Ann
Fleming with a tiara all askew, obviously a memory of his mother in
law. It is a very careful, detailed, neat picture not like some I could
mention & that makes the tiara funnier.

So I had a very happy day in London with Cyril Boots. (It is so unfair they have taken to calling a dreary politician 'Smarty Boots'.[2]) He was in the uttermost abyss of melancholy. His Animal[3] has been sacked from the Zoo & sent home to Oak Cottage in disgrace. Not for the usual offence. She chewed her tail. Mrs Boots refuses to cook for him. He bought a silver knife, fork & spoon in a leather case to send to Lys [Lubbock]. Poignant. We went from shop to shop where Boots examined silk shirts & antique silver & complained bitterly that he could not afford to buy all he saw. I asked him why he always wears such horrible clothes and he said it was to spite Molly MacCarthy who ruined his life 30 years ago by telling an admiral he (C.B.) was a bugger.[4] 'I *had* a bowler hat,' he said, 'and an umbrella, and a top hat. I resolved never to use them again.' Later we were joined by Mrs Boots who had been changing her clothes in the loo at the Ritz. Suddenly Cyril could only talk classical Greek.

Have you heard about the 'Edwardians'? They are gangs of proletarian louts who dress like Beaton with braided trousers & velvet collars & murder one another in 'Youth Centres'. Poor Cecil is always being stopped now by the police and searched for knuckle-dusters.[5]

I hope you won't travel alone to Moscow. Since I lost my reason on the way to Ceylon I have a resolve never to move without an escort.

I saw Simon Elwes a lot at Downside at Easter. He lectured me on the importance of the artist representing the Zeitgeist. Hard words coming from him. Poor Christopher has Lady Russell[6] quartered on him for life.

All love
    E

[1] Lady Caroline Blackwood (1931–96). Author of *Great Granny Webster* (1977), *The Fate of Mary Rose* (1981) and *The Last of the Duchess* (1995). Married to the painter Lucian Freud 1953–7, to the composer Israel Citkovitz in 1958 and to the poet Robert Lowell 1972–7.
[2] David Eccles (1904–99). Conservative MP for Chippenham Division of Wiltshire. Created Viscount Eccles in 1964.
[3] A coati.
[4] Connolly had once confided in Molly MacCarthy that he found women 'unnecessary' and had 'no use for them'. She took this to mean he was homosexual and when Connolly fell in love with her niece, Horatia, daughter of Admiral Sir William Fisher, Molly told her sister that Connolly was 'upside-down'. (See Clive Fisher, *Cyril Connolly*, Macmillan, 1995, p. 83)
[5] 'Cecil himself joked in speeches that a teddy boy had approached him and said: "The job's on tonight with razors." ' Hugo Vickers, *Cecil Beaton* (Weidenfeld & Nicolson, 1985), p. 372.
[6] Christopher Sykes's mother-in-law; she died in 1968.

[postmarked 16 May 1954]   [Moscow]
[postcard]

Oh I do wish you were here. The art gallery is acres & acres of every
picture tells a story – & *such* stories! Ending up with what my father
wld describe as a gloomy old bitch – Robert [Byron]'s favourite picture
(eikon). I goggle all day with fascination.

Next week 3 days in Leningrad & then home.

Love
    N

When did you last see your father?[1]

[1] Nancy's postcard was of a Russian narrative painting in the genre of *And When Did You Last
See Your Father?* by William Frederick Yeames (1878).

18 June 1954   Piers Court
                                                            Stinchcombe
Darling Nancy
    I do hope that you are going to publish an essay telling us all about
your experiences in Russia. Or are your lips sealed by your obligations
to the Ambassador? If so, please write for me and posterity in a long
full letter.
    Our news is that Lord Camrose has kicked the bucket. Pam is in
floods of crocodile tears. There is much speculation about who will
control the *Daily Telegraph*, who will live at Hackwood, which Berries
will at once divorce, which will bring into the open unsuitable wives
and husbands hitherto kept in cellars & garrets. Lord C's last act was
to give Pam the house he had taken for Randolph. Randolph has
been peremptorily evicted & Pam is tearing out fine Queen Anne
woodwork. Randolph is buying a palace in the outskirts of Bath.[1] It
comprises one really magnificent ball-room which cannot be suitably
furnished for less than £10,000, one very fine secondary ball-room,
which might be done for £5,000 and two attic bed-rooms which lack
room for a pot. There is a noble terraced garden leading directly to
a public cemetery.
    Cecil Beaton has produced a curiously incompetent book.[2] You will
be surprised to learn that you and I and Harold Acton & Oliver
Messel came down from Oxford together & thenceforward lived in
close intimacy with Loelia Ponsonby[3] for whom we provided dance-
bands, cabarets and practical-joke Art Exhibitions. You may also be
surprised to learn that the great leaders of fashion were Alice Obolensky, Phyllis de Janzé, Diana Vreeland[4] and Cecil's Aunt Effi[5] (a new
character). There are gross historical misstatements on every page. I
was asked to review it. It shows how I have softened since my lunacy,

that I have refused. Ten years ago I should have romped into it.

Will you be coming to England at all? Perhaps from Fionn O'Neill's[6] ball? I like to go to one party a year and shall go to that. Do come. It will be all old fogies.

I long to write to *The Times* newspaper, which is full of laments for the dispersal of the Chatsworth treasure, to tell of Debo's aspirations with the india-rubber.[7] But I don't. Soft again you see.

Much love from
    Evelyn

[1] The sale did not go through and later in the year Randolph Churchill bought Stour House at East Bergholt in Suffolk.
[2] *The Glass of Fashion* (1954).
[3] Hon. Loelia Ponsonby (1902–93). Married to 2nd Duke of Westminster 1930–47 and to Sir Martin Lindsay in 1969.
[4] Diana Dalziell (1903–89). High priestess of American fashion: fashion editor of *Harper's Bazaar* 1937–62, editor-in-chief of *Vogue* 1962–71. Married to T. Reed Vreeland.
[5] Jessie Sisson (1863–1950). Cecil Beaton's maternal aunt. Married Don Pedro Suarez, Bolivian Envoy Extraordinary, in 1890.
[6] Hon. Fionn O'Neill (1936–). Ann Fleming's daughter by her first husband. Married to John Morgan 1961–75.
[7] Nancy used to pretend that her sister's fingers itched to rub out old master drawings at Chatsworth. The Devonshires were having to sell important works of art in order to settle death duties.

20 June 1954   7 rue Monsieur, VII

Darling Evelyn

Oh Russia *was* fascinating. So much more beautiful than I'd expected for one thing. I was 11 days in Moscow & 3 days quite alone in Leningrad (Hotel Astoria). I wonder if you got my postcard.

I can't write about it for publication. William [Hayter] would rather not & I feel I couldn't anyhow – the Russians were so nice to me & it would be a poor return to mock at them. Many American women do this, & exhibit their pathetic clothes in smart New York shops, I don't think it is decent human behaviour. But I am writing every detail for chums & will send.

I must tell you – I asked to see Soviet writers. But I was told that on 29th of May they had all gone to the country, to write. But I saw a lady from the State publishing house. I said to her 'how many copies would a best-selling novel sell?' She replied 150 million. 'Goodness' I said 'I can't wait to come & live here.' She said as they often do, it is a stock phrase 'This has its good side & its bad.' 'Well I can't see what the bad side can be for the writer. What is the name of the novel which has sold 150 millions?' 'Well there is The Testing of the Steel – &, of course, Cement.' By this time I was distinctly giggly. They are just like Americans just as I knew they would be. The *Pravda*, reviewing a novel while I was there (one gets the *Pravda* in English, it is a joy) said: 'The Seasons is well written & well observed. This is quite so. But this novel does not summon to anything nor struggle with anything –' just what the Americans always say about ONE's books. *Pomp* by the way *very* badly received there – they say it seems to have been written by Daisy Ashford.[1]

We are all very much pleased about the new government, though I wish Col could have had a job. But he could only accept War or Foreign Affairs & Koenig was the obvious choice for war. Better than a minor ministry remain as he is – just Vice President.

How fascinating about Cecil's book. I was invited to a Foyle luncheon for it. No I shan't come to England – I've had enough of hideous clothes & uneatable food to last me for many a moon, in Russia.

I feel rather worried about your great new goodness, I hope it's all right.

I didn't know about Chatsworth. I must say I can't feel as desperately sorry for D & A as I would if they cared for the objects.

Oh my happy life. It came over me in waves, when I was away, how lucky I am, & when I woke up & realized I was back in my own bed an enormous smile spread over my face. But I'm more than glad I went. I brought buckets of caviar & asked all the greediest people I know. They sat in a holy circle & never spoke to me once, except to say, in loud asides, that the others were making pigs of themselves.

I'm trying to find out what it would cost to get my essay on Russia printed – if too much (I am utterly ruined) I will send you the typescript first, before it is in ribbons.

Fond love
    N

[1] Daisy Ashford (1881–1972). Child author of the inimitable *The Young Visiters* (1919).

18 July 1954   7 rue Monsieur, VII

Darling Evelyn

Since Bonny-boots is dead
That so divinely
Could foot it & toot it
(Oh he did it finely)
Say, lusty lads, who now shall
bonny-boot it?

I found this in a book of English madrigals – are you shrieking? I did love Bonny-boots's article today in the *S. Times* & the photograph of the Sergeant's bald patch.[1] Oh the bliss of our friends. I hear that you say Cecil's book is the fruit of sexual excess.

I'm working on a play[2] which we must hope will be another *Little Hut* – somebody else's play of course I'm incapable of writing one.

Walter Monckton[3] sent a message *via* Momo that if I print my Russian journal some unscrupulous journalist will publish it. Isn't it strange. I thought one would have been protected from that by some nice law. As nearly all my acquaintances are unscrupulous I have decided not to print it.[4] Heywood has got a typewritten copy which you are welcome to read if you can be bothered. It's rather dull, to tell you the truth, but accurate.

I thought your letter in *The Times*[5] was perfectly excellent, just what I always think. The *rubbish*.

Are you all right? And happy?

I'm staying here for the present. The Col's mother is dying, & he minds passionately, & I don't like to leave him in empty Paris. But I love Paris at this time of year so it's no sacrifice.

Much love
      N

I *screamed* at the idea of you being better dressed than the Col. But even you are better dressed than most Russians.

[1] Cyril Connolly had written a travel diary of his Mediterranean holiday: 'At twenty we travel to discover ourselves, at thirty for love, at forty out of greed and curiosity, at fifty for a revelation.' The article was illustrated with a photograph showing the back of Stuart Preston's head. *Sunday Times*, 18 July 1954.
[2] Gilbert Miller, the American impresario, had asked Nancy to help translate *L'Heure éblouissante* by Anna Boracci.
[3] Walter Monckton (1891–1965). Minister of Labour and National Service 1951–5, Minister of Defence 1955–6. Created 1st Viscount Monckton in 1957. Married the Countess of Carlisle (Biddy) in 1947.
[4] Nancy's account of her visit was eventually published in *The Water Beetle* (1962).
[5] 'Painter and Patron: Responsibilities to One Another.' *The Times*, 17 July 1954.

20 July [1954]   Piers Court
                                                    Stinchcombe
Darling Nancy,

Look here, I mean to say, dammit, what do you mean you 'screamed' at the 'idea' of my being better dressed than Col. I grant him all other superiorities but as far as clothes go, he is to me as Mary Dunn is to you. You must see that.

An annoyance. There is a negligible politician called I think D. Eccles. The English have begun to call him 'Boots'. Spoils our joke.

Did I tell you that Pam has ordained that 'broken pediments are no longer fashionable' and is known everywhere as 'Lady Palmyra'.

I am so glad you approved of my wail in *The Times* newspaper. It cannot be said too often or too loud that all Art is the art of pleasing.

The Letters of Nancy Mitford and Evelyn Waugh 341

In my unhappy country today literally thousands of louts go at the public expense to 'Art Schools' where they are taught to release their Ids and Libidos & Egos and other foreign matters & then they expect to be supported at the public cost for the rest of their lives.

O dear Honks. I went to a ball the other night – Ann Fleming's at Loelia [Ponsonby]'s Surrey villa. I like to go to one a year – well I'm not asked to many more. I agreed to go with Honks. We were to dine at the villa. I said, Let me hire a nice car & we will dress in London & drive down & drive back and sleep in comfort at our respective rooms. No, not at all. We must stay with Dot & Antony [Head], who live about as far from Loelia as the Hyde Park Hotel. All right let us go in the early afternoon & see Dot in comfort. No not at all. Kept waiting in poor Little Lady Norwich's modest flat for hours & hours. Arrived at Dot's 6.30. I say we must leave at 7.30. You don't understand. In England people are punctual. Besides Ann wants to get dining room cleared for supper and ball begins 9.30 etc etc. No. Honks won't leave till 8.30 (asked for 8). We arrive at 9.15. Everyone half way through dinner. Honks meanwhile has decided she will return to London that night. 'We can't both chuck. It's too rude. You must stay with Dot.' Then the linkman says very civilly Please please don't leave your motor just here in front of the door. Honks forgets she has all her luggage in it & leaves it & of course later loses it. Then Dot telephones she has gone to bed & won't go to ball & will send taxi 100 miles for me. I return 4 am alone. Jolly sad. One nice thing. Antony was stuck in London. I had room with door 'communicating' with Dot. Old butler locked door & took away key.

Ball was louche & gay.

I saw Debo & Andrew – not there. Debo with ribbon-bound whip – very erotic. I keep hearing such sad things about her and when I meet her I am blinded by her pure innocence.

My book[1] grows steadily and is OK. I have Boots as a Corporal of Horse in the Blues, composing Palinurus during the battle of Crete.

Yes Boots's article was blissikins. You see, granted Art = art of pleasing ('Id quod visum placet' Aquinas) those who are not pleased *ever* are simply inartistic. The hyper fastidious become philistines.

Monckton is deeply implicated with CP through Mountbattens. O for that good clever Senator McCarthy to clear them all up. Of course you can easily protect your copyright by giving copies to British Museum etc. & selling one to a chum. But Monckton has to protect Russian prestige. And the Dean of Canterbury has a stranglehold on Biddy.

All love
E

P.S. I have been asked to a ludicrous Congress in Geneva in September

but I have never been there and have nothing else to do & they pay
my expenses so I have said yes.

[1] *Officers and Gentlemen.*

26 July 1954   7 rue Monsieur, VII

Darling Evelyn

This ruthless selfishness & utter lack of sensibility make it impossible
for me to see Lady Honks any more, deeply as I have loved her. Here
she is surrounded by a little band of bores & crooks mostly Anglo
Saxon, who hedge her in – Chantilly is always filled with them & no
hope of seeing her alone. I've given up – also I don't think she likes
me very much now. She played a cruel trick on poor old Leslie Hartley
the other day, which I think will put him off going abroad for ever –
& all because she wanted to avoid a tête à tête with Alan Pryce-Jones.[1]

Well I read your words about Mary Dunn to the Col – secure in
the knowledge that he is the Idol of Savile Row he laughed as much
as I did. Poor Col, his mother is dying – he minds dreadfully.

A letter from Ld Kemsley saying is there anywhere in the world he
can send me at his expense to write for the paper. Doesn't it seem a
waste. The only place I would rather like to see is the South Pole, &
I'm too cissy for that – I mean it would only be *interesting* if one went
on foot, like Scott.

I keep reading about Pam Berry & a new character called *Sybil*
Connolly[2] being the Queens of Fashion. But Pam is in my eyes what
Col is in yours – the dangling rose & gypsy trend are very far from
my idea of elegance. How mysterious it all is – why no. 11 Downing
St?[3]

Really Evelyn the *Tablet*. I read: 'A pilgrimage to Beaulieu' – dated
from The House in the Wood. I do think it is rather bold of them! I
am getting very fond of the *Tablet* by the way.

The art of pleasing. Yes I agree – perhaps you should add all but
the very greatest art?

Can a Tory be a Communist? My mother sent me an article from
The Scotsman by a woman who was in Russia exactly when I was. She
begins by saying 'I am a true blue Tory' & then enunciates a tissue
of lies: 'I never saw any slums'. (The whole place is a slum.) And so
on. All very suspect & *why did she get a visa?* Silly old *Scotsman*.

Come here on yr way to Geneva *do*, I need you.

Love
    N

Raymond's article yesterday seemed to run with the hare & hunt with
the hounds.[4]

[1] Alan Pryce-Jones (1908–2000). Man of letters. Editor of *The Times Literary Supplement* 1948–59.
[2] A Dublin dressmaker.
[3] As President of the Incorporated Society of London Fashion Designers, Lady Pamela Berry had persuaded the Chancellor of the Exchequer, R. A. Butler, to lend his official Downing Street residence for a party for overseas fashion buyers.
[4] Raymond Mortimer's review of a study of modern poetry, *The Broken Cistern* by Bonamy Dobrée, could be interpreted as trying to please both academic specialists and the general reader.

10 August 1954   7 rue Monsieur, VII

Darling Evelyn

Just to say I'm off on a yacht,[1] leaving no address for some time. I asked John [Sutro] to send you my Russian piece, as I've decided not to have it printed. Either keep it, very kindly, for the present, or send it to Heywood if it clutters you up.

I think I shall have to go to England in Oct: so see you then I hope. Oh I long for the book. Bonnyboots & wifie came to breakfast & I told him he was in it as a soldier. 'A frightful coward, I expect' he said gloomily. Oh how deep is my love for him – she was looking too beautiful, & they were both very nice to me. He had had a typical passage with *S Times*. He wrote saying he could do a German article if they sent some money. They wired 'money difficult – please wire article at once'. So he didn't!

I look forward to Ed's book.[2] The central character is Prod, by name, & Ed has made him sign a paper that he won't sue for libel. What would all us pen pushers do without Prod!

Momo has been here. Somebody said to her 'Derek Hill[3] lost all his money in Turkey' (meaning pocket picked) to which the child of her father cried: 'Don't tell me he bought Turkish bonds – how mad.' She has been very very tiresome, but I love her.

Must pack.

Love
N

[1] The *Sister Anne*, belonging to Daisy Fellowes.
[2] Edward Stanley, *Sea Peace* (1954). A chapter on Peter Rodd described him as 'a devil, a hoodoo, a poltergeist: a compound of Doctor Strabismus, because he thinks he knows everything, and Tsetse fly because he will give you sleeping sickness because he is such a bore, and a Double Cross which all his friends must bear'.
[3] Derek Hill (1916–2000). Portrait and landscape painter.

7 September 1954   St-Pierre du Château
                                                   Hyères

Darling Evelyn

I've got back from my mystery cruise (with Daisy Fellowes, to the Balearic Islands). It has had one or two results. I have made friends for life of a Spanish grandee, in whose company Daisy chucked me off the boat at a moment's notice.[1] (Not what you think – he is in love with a Turk of the male sex) & I have taken a wild fancy for boating.

This is more than unfortunate – even were I Daphne du Maurier[2] I doubt if I could make enough to keep a yacht. Owing to Daisy's ill-considered action my grandee & I were a week together on the island of Majorca before we could get transport to Barcelona. It was very agreeable since Palma is a most beautiful city, with acres of 17th century palaces, all well known to my friend. But oh your fellow countrymen. They swarmed everywhere, in the vilest of tempers all having run out of money & unable (like us) to get off the island. They besieged the young lady at Cook's, who replies to every question 'I'm afraid I haven't got a clue' (overheard while changing money I didn't bother her). Then their habits! I promise you they made messes on the floor of the loo in my hotel, like dogs.

By the way the Turk is for your ears alone, as I think the poor darling *minds* having these tastes, & as I have become deeply fond of him I don't want to hurt him in any way.

Here nobody talks of anything but the démarches of Graham Greene (Colette).[3] Were you surprised? Do you think he knew what a deeply vicious life she had led – her stepson, the long affair with Marguerite Moreno & so on? Not that that makes any difference I know to the legal side. Little as I understand these matters I was amazed at his letter I must say – & so was Col.

I'm doing another play – adapting – in the hopes of a little money. It's so nice the way it comes in every month, from a play, instead of in huge indigestible lumps half of which go in taxes & the other half one loses on the Stock Exchange.

I'm glad you liked my piece on Russia. (I long now to go to Tashkent & Samarkand. Have you read Koestler?[4]) Half the pleasure to me was being with really clever people like the Hayters. Most of the people I stay with are quite uneducated, & it made a very pleasant change. You would love them.

I shall be here another week or 10 days – then Paris. London in November.

Much love
   N

Do write.

---

[1] Nancy and Don Alfonso Falcò, Prince Pio, were put ashore because Daisy Fellowes's lover, Lord Sherwood, had arrived and she wished to be alone with him on her boat.
[2] Daphne du Maurier (1907–89). The best-selling author of *Rebecca* (1938) and *My Cousin Rachel* (1951).
[3] Greene had written an open letter to the Cardinal Archbishop of Paris in the *Figaro Littéraire* (14 August 1954) attacking him for refusing to allow any religious ceremony at Colette's funeral.
[4] *The Invisible Writings* (1954). A second volume of autobiography.

15 September [1954]   [Piers Court
                                                       Stinchcombe]
Darling Nancy

I have just returned home from a week in London where – need I
tell you? – ill-informed reports of your Balearic adventures are rife.

I spent almost all the week sitting in White's with decrepit old
cronies drinking too hard but it was a necessary relief from the endless
school holidays. Now Downside has gone back and I have only my
affectionate younger daughters at home so I can creep into convalescence.

Fond farewells with the Laycocks just off to Malta. One dinner at
Ann Fleming's where she had asked a great booby called Darwin[1]
whom we mocked – otherwise just Ed and Harry Stavordale and Ran
[Antrim] & Randolph & Ali Mackintosh[2] & Jack McDougall. I get no
feminine company these days since poor Clarissa's awful misalliance
and I miss it.

Sir Maurice Bowra has transferred his patronage from Pam to Ann.
'Mrs Fleming is aristocratic & corrupt. Lady Pamela is neither.'

You will have read Ed on Prod no doubt. Not very good.

I long for you in November. I am sure you would not be comfortable
here. I will come to London to see you.

It is not the English who make messes on the floor. It is their dogs.
It is not always easy to distinguish I know but you must remember
their habits from the days of your youth.

Graham Greene's letter was fatuous and impertinent. He was tipsy
when he wrote it at luncheon with some frogs & left it to them to
translate and despatch. He is dead to shame in these matters. You
will go to his play in Paris?[3]

       All love
          E

[1] Robin Darwin (1910–74). Painter. Principal of the Royal College of Art 1948–67, Rector
and Vice-Provost 1967–71. 'Evelyn Waugh ruined my chances of becoming part-time ancient
student at the Kensington College of Art. He came to dinner the same night as Robin Darwin
and attacked Robin for several hours, referring to him as Gilbert Harding and generally being
insulting. I barely know Robin and he appeared quite defenceless and rather humourless –
finally he fled into the street sobbing "why does he hate me so?" ' *The Letters of Ann Fleming*
edited by Mark Amory (Collins, 1985), p. 145.
[2] Alastair Mackintosh (1889–1968). Aide-de-camp to Lord Leopold Mountbatten during the
First World War; equerry to Princess Beatrice in 1920. Married Constance Talmadge in 1926
and Lola Emery in 1927.
[3] *The Living Room* (1953).

5 October 1954   7 rue Monsieur, VII

Darling Evelyn

I think Dear Princess.[1] If you were writing in French it would be
Princesse only – but Princess without the dear looks odd.* Did you

go to their Cotswold house, Ste Preuve?[2] They are the most English French people I know, but their food isn't.

I did so hope you would have been coming here on your way back, for the GG first night. Faithful John [Sutro] is here for it. (John Marriott? No.)

Debo is here, staying with Jungle Jim.[3] I wrote & said I wished she could find a pale face to stay with for a change. Debo has got the most disastrous taste in people, I must say – but I must also say that when one tells her so she takes it in good part.

I've no news. I would have loved to see you, but must come over I think before Xmas.

Fond love
     N

* On the envelope you put Princesse Jean de CC – no Madame.

[1] Evelyn had been a guest of Princess de Caraman-Chimay at the celebrations to mark the restoration of Rheims cathedral.
[2] Château de St Preuve north of Paris.
[3] Prince Aly Khan.

19 October 1954   Piers Court
                                                      Stinchcombe
Darling Nancy

Very many thanks for your instructions about addressing Mme de CC. I wish you would issue a little edict about the correct treatment of foreign nobility by English correspondents. I don't think such a thing exists. It is sadly needed.

The jaunt to Reims was enjoyable though it rained all the time and the frog photographers blasphemously interrupted the dedication of the window with continuous blinding flashes. I wish all press photographers could be painfully executed. They not only make every public event unseemly but produce such deplorable records. The best feature of the Cathedral ceremonies was Lord Sempill who appeared in a kilt in attendance on the Archbishop. 'Sa soeur est devenue son frère'[1] I was able to tell neighbouring frogs but they thought this a commonplace in my country. The frogs were *not* very generous hosts – Mercier instead of Krug, no coffee but Odette Pol Roger was jolly. The Pommery caves really are a spectacle. Have I written all this already? Graham Greene prefers spirits to wine and was not happy. As we started he saw the name [Alan] Pryce-Jones (a harmless gentle Welsh journalist) on the list and said: 'I can't go. I won't meet Pryce-Jones. He's too negative.' Well he came. That evening we all went to bed at about midnight – Lord Long haranguing the night porter – 'Don't tell me *all* brothels are closed. I'll wake them up' – Next morning we met again at ten Graham looking ghastly. 'I didn't get to bed till after four.' 'What were you doing?' 'Drinking marc.' 'Who with?' 'Pryce-Jones.' I hear that his play has had a great success in Paris.

There is an impertinent, incompetent parody of you in *Punch*.[2] Do you want to see it? I find I don't at all care what any paper writes about me any more. No pleasure from praise, no pain from blame. Boredom either way. Pleasure in praise went first – anaesthesia to blame is newish.

My brother Alec[3] is really becoming very eccentric. He is spending the winter – where do you think? – in Copenhagen. His reason – it is 'so convenient for London'. I go to Jamaica in the New Year. No hope I suppose of luring you there too? I stay believe it or not at 'The Great House, Roaring River'.

Poor Debo got blown up by a publicity seeking wop painter.[4] Serve her right. She is too naughty.

We have all been most anxious about you and the Dides case.[5] First the Moscow re-education to renew connexions with Spanish refugees, then the mystery cruise, the illicit landing with the Spaniard. You are fortunate to live in the only country where treason is O.K. I saw Lord Sherwood[6] in Brighton. He was tight as an oyster about the mystery cruise.

Laura is greatly revived by her stay at Brighton. Harriet and children's holidays had reduced her to the verge of melancholy.

Boots writes a lot about Hazlitt's unhappy love life. I think he sees himself as H now, not as Rochester.

Sykes has fallen victim to the charms of Spender and is a ruined man.

My mother-in-law is deeply aggrieved because a frog newspaper has announced (without a shadow of truth) that my father-in-law committed suicide and she is told that frog papers never apologise.

My salutations to the Polish Beau Brummel.

E

[1] 'His sister has become his brother.' There was an unfounded rumour that Lord Sempill's sister had become a man.
[2] 'The Pursuit of Fame' by Julian Maclaren-Ross, *Punch*, 13 October 1954.
[3] Alec Waugh (1898–1981). Novelist and travel writer.
[4] While the Duchess of Devonshire was being painted by Pietro Annigoni, the stove in his studio exploded.
[5] A French Secret Service shenanigan involving Chief Inspector Jean Dides, head of the anti-Communist police squad.
[6] Sir Hugh Seely (1898–1970). Daisy Fellowes's lover, known as H.L. (Hated Lover). Liberal MP 1923–4 and 1935–41. Created 1st Baron Sherwood in 1941.

21 October 1954   7 rue Monsieur, VII

Darling Evelyn

Will you please tell your m in law that Frog newspapers are
OBLIGED to print denial of an error in the same column & same
type as the error. Her solicitor should write at once, in English, to
the editor & demand this. I have twice had to avail myself of this
law.

I don't know why you say the only country where treason is OK.
I never shall forget the song & dance you made when a few traitors
were shot here after the war.

Oh do be more explicit about Debo. Annigoni is a ghastly painter
but I've always heard he's a very nice man.

I was invited to the window opening at Reims oh what a pity –
had I known you'd be there! I imagined hundreds of strange journalists.

Yes Graham Greene's play has had the best possible reception –
viz violent disagreement. It will run for months. I wonder if I could
bear it – I can't bear sad things at all now.

I've been with my darling old friend at Fontaines les Nonnes & that
is sad. She has lost her son of about my age & the English daughter
in law is behaving exactly like a French person in an English novel –
with frivolity, heartlessness & in a positively *evil* way about the will.

Mme Costa is leaving beautiful Fontaines to be a nunnery again
as it was until the revolution, since the young Mme C says it is
damp dreary & difficult to run – she only dreams of a chintzy mews-
flat in Paris. She is perhaps the only person in the world whom
I hate.

Pam Berry is here – affectionate & jolly, in her nicest mood. I love
her all right. Oh do send the *Punch* parody. Yes I'm like you, blasée
about the newspapers. Thank goodness, since many writers suffer I
believe. I'm really too happy to be upset by that sort of thing, perhaps
that is the explanation.

Pam Churchill is after the Polish Beau Brummel. He is puzzled,
but not displeased.

Do you know a Pole called Chapski? He's a friend of your brother
in law & such a dear & so brilliant in a Polish way.

I've been reading Giles Romilly's book about prison,[1] it is very
funny in parts & altogether rather enjoyable.

As I've nothing to write I read a book every day, it comes very
expensive. What can I write? I've never known such a paucity of ideas.
Beau Brummel says 'a book about a fascinating French politician' –
'all right Colonel, but what's the plot?'

Do you really think I'm a Communist? It shows a surprising ignorance of human nature – surprising I mean in such a successful novelist
as yourself. Or do you see me as half-witted? In that case why have

Nancy's letter asking for advice on *Madame de Pompadour*

Below right: Cecil Beaton's cover for *Madame de Pompadour*. EW to NM: 'Beaton's drawings always give me goose flesh but the wrapper is easily disposed of' (5 March 1954)

Below: David Herbert, Nancy and Prince Pio of Savoy, stranded in Majorca after being thrown off Daisy Fellowes's yacht, August 1954

Raymond Mortimer, 1953.
EW to NM: '. . . your chum
who looks like a Maltese
pimp . . .' (19 May 1950)

Graham Greene, 1953.
NM to EW: 'What a sexy
man he must be, Mr
Greene' (12 September
1951)

Above: Lady Pamela Berry. EW to NM: 'Did I tell you that Pam has ordained that "broken pediments are no longer fashionable" and is known everywhere as "Lady Palmyra"' (20 July 1954)

Above right: Clarissa Churchill, shortly before her marriage to Anthony Eden. EW to NM: 'I believe you keep my letters. A month or so ago I wrote a nasty one about Clarissa. Will you be very kind & burn it?' (29 September 1952)

Ann Fleming. NM to EW: 'I'm afraid Ann will only go & get another lover – she is one of those who don't like husbands' (12 February 1952)

Evelyn, photographed for the *Sunday Times*. EW to NM: 'I wish you had accepted the *Sunday Times* invitation to write the caption for their picture. I don't much mind the papers saying I am beastly, which is true, or that I write badly, which isn't. What enrages me is wrong facts' (27 September 1950)

A postcard from Nancy about *Men at Arms*, September 1952

I've just returned from Venice to find nearly
3 weeks post & Aug: Hare's book which they
want me to review and *Men at Arms*
for which thank you so much. I don't dare
begin it until I've done all these duties
or I know it will engulf me for a day. In
Venice the one copy was being torn from
hand to hand — aren't booksellers idiots
really not to cash in on holiday places
more. I travelled home with an antiquarian bookseller & wife who knew all
about Heywood & when I said my name they
said won't the girls be thrilled! They'd been to [...]

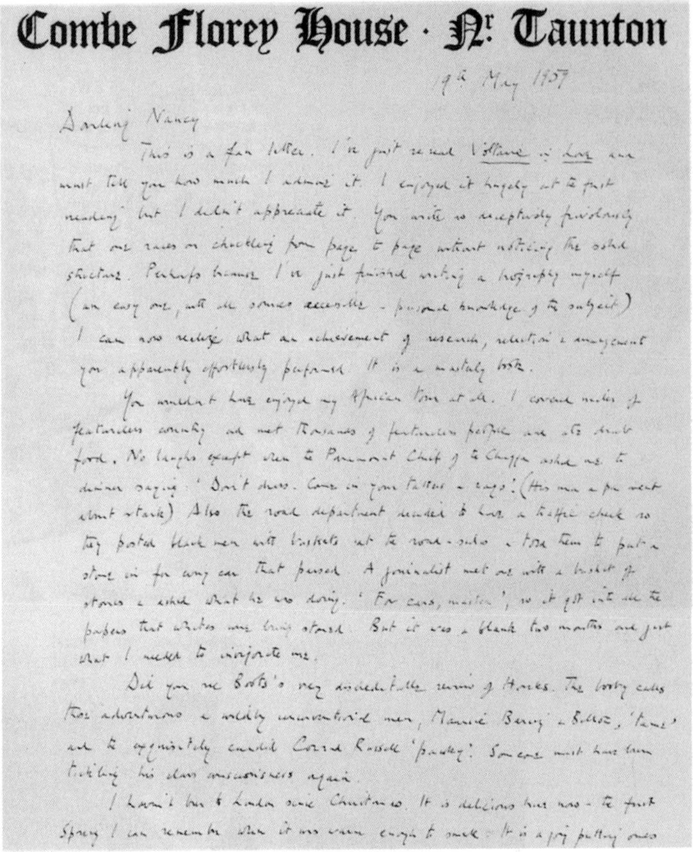

Combe Florey House · Nr. Taunton

19th May 1957

Darling Nancy

This is a fan letter. I've just re-read *Voltaire in Love* and must tell you how much I admire it. I enjoyed it hugely at the first reading but I didn't appreciate it. You write so deceptively frivolously that one races on chuckling from page to page without noticing the solid structure. Perhaps because I've just finished writing a biography myself (an easy one, with all sources accessible – personal knowledge of the subject) I can now realize what an achievement of research, selection & arrangement you apparently effortlessly performed. It is a masterly book.

You wouldn't have enjoyed my African tour at all. I covered miles of featureless country and met thousands of featureless people and ate dull food. No laughs except when the Paramount Chief of the Chagga asked me to dinner saying: 'Don't dress. Come in your tattoos & rags.' (His men & he went about stark) Also the road department decided to have a traffic check so they posted black men with baskets at the road-sides & told them to put a stone in for every car that passed. A journalist met one with a basket of stones & asked what he was doing. 'For cars, master', so it got into all the papers that whites were being stoned. But it was a blank two months and just what I needed to invigorate me.

Did you see Bob's very discreditable review of Horners. The booby calls those adventurous & wildly unconventional men, Maurice Baring & Belloc, 'tame' and the exquisitely civilized Conrad Russell 'pawky'. Someone must have been tickling his dear [illegible] again.

I haven't been to London since Christmas. It is delicious here now – the first Spring I can remember when it was warm enough to smell. It is a joy putting ones

Evelyn's fan letter about *Voltaire in Love*

Combe Florey. EW to NM: 'It has possibilities of beautification. If only I were a pansy without family cares I could make it a jewel' (14 October 1956)

Jessica Mitford, 1960. NM to EW:
'My sister Decca has written her
memoirs & got a huge advance from
Gollancz. I said to Honks "never
mind darling probably she doesn't
speak of us." "If she's got a huge
advance it means that she DOES"'
(22 May 1959)

Nancy (*right*) and
Diana Mosley on the
island of Inchkenneth
during their mother's
last illness, May 1963

Nancy (*right*) and Jessica Mitford at rue Monsieur, 1962

NM to EW: 'As I know you notice writing paper I hereby show you my new effort – the Mitford moldiwarp – Raymond says undermining like mad no doubt' (10 January 1966)

Paris   4 March 66

Much love – do keep in touch Nancy

Dearest Evelyn

Thanks very much for your letter. I've asked Gy Gy to luncheon – he can but say no & then I won't tease him again. There are so few agreeable English people here now – Embassy zero, journalists, ex: Darsie Gillie, the same; they are all true horrors & loathe the French as common English people always have. One long bleat about plumbers doesn't make for interesting conversation!

Evelyn being interviewed by
John Freeman on the *Face to Face*
programme, 1960. EW to NM:
'Last week I was driven by
poverty to the humiliating
experience of appearing on the
television. The man who asked
the questions simply couldn't
believe I had had a happy
childhood. "Surely you suffered
from the lack of a sister?"'
(21 June 1960)

One of Evelyn's last letters to
Nancy

you liked me for 26 years? Or perhaps you don't know what Communism is? Yes, that must be it. I advise you to go to Russia & see for
yourself. Game & set.

 Much love
  N

Your mother in law's man of affairs must say to the Fr editor that his
client demands a denial, to be printed, according to French law, in
the same column as the original statement.

[1] *The Privileged Nightmare* (1954), his experiences as a prisoner of war in Colditz.

23 October 1954   Piers Court
                    Stinchcombe
Darling Nancy
 Very many thanks for the information about French law. I will pass
it on to my mother-in-law who says she was told of the hopelessness
of her case by the 'Embassy'. She does not specify which of the
numerous officials sought thus to embitter Franco-British relations.
 More instruction please. What is the force of 'Cher Ami' as the start
of a letter? Is it more or less intimate than the use of a Christian
name? Are the following expressions colloquial frog:– 'Comme vous
êtes complètement film star aujourd'hui.' 'Je crois bien' (I bet) 'que vous
n'avez pas trouvé cela en Egypte.' 'Quel drôle de panier' (What an amusing shopping basket). 'Enfin, madame, c'est génial.' (Well that's brilliant
of you). Spoken by a smart Levantine woman – not high Parisian.[1]
 Here is the *Punch* parody. No good really.
 I do not think communists half-witted – merely very very wicked.
The fact that you approve the communist organised massacres after
the 'Liberation' is plain evidence of party direction, if not membership.
I have in my possession a photograph of you with Driberg in the days
of the popular front. I am not sending it to McCarthy because I love
you. All your lovely dollars will stop flowing if the truth comes out.
 It is indeed hard to think of novel plots for novels. You see nothing
that happens to one after the age of 40 makes any impression. My
life ceased with the war. When I have squeezed the last thousand
words out of that period I shall have to cast back to my still unravished
boyhood.
 If you had come to Reims the frogs would not have let us meet.
They took elaborate precautions to keep chums apart at table. I haven't
drunk a glass of champagne since I left, owing to the surfeit of inferior
vintages.
 The English papers have stopped reporting the Dides case. What
is the truth of it?

A letter from a lady who is writing a thesis on me. What 'training college' did I go to before taking up 'the career of teaching'? What is a 'thunder box'?

I couldn't enjoy *The Living Room* in English. Graham says the French production is worse. He has become a member of White's. I wonder whether he will suffer the customary transmogrification into Philip Hardwicke. I saw Philip at an exhibition of modern painting the other day, standing in the centre of the room & buying pictures by pointing at them with his umbrella. 'Send that round – and that – and that – and that.'

What do correct French catholics think of the Index? I was asked the other day & couldn't answer. My impression is that those who are scrupulous at all are very scrupulous. Right?

I long for your visit to London. Don't spend every minute with Pam. I hope to have finished my work in progress and to be in a jolly leisurely mood by mid November.

Fondest love
    E

[1] Phrases required by Evelyn for a conversation between Julia Stitch and the two Egyptian millionairesses in *Officers and Gentlemen*.

27 October 1954   7 rue Monsieur, VII

Darling Evelyn

Your pretty paper – I riposte with my last sheet of nice paper. I get lazy about ordering it & oh how it melts away.

The French sentences are all right except the film star one which should be Ce que vous avez l'air *star* aujourd'hui – or – mon cher, vous êtes d'un *star*.

Cher ami is less than a Christian name. The Col, always so cautious, writes to me Chère Amie & signs respectueusement. Very occasionally it is Ma chère Nancy & respectueusement et affectueusement, & he always signs Connaught Hotel, an old established joke.[1]

The Index. I must ask Mme Costa, who is truly pious (the curé told a fellow guest there that he wondered if so much praying didn't sometimes ennuie le bon Dieu[2]). I've been down there several heavenly days lately, my favourite place, I think, on earth. I've a sort of feeling that the Index is regarded as being intended for uneducated people & children, but I'll ask her. Col says the clergy advise people what to read & what films they should see.

I'm a little bit worried about your mother in law – it has occurred to me that this rule may not apply when the person in question is dead. But it is so grave to accuse somebody of suicide that any decent paper will surely contradict. Let me know what happens – Col knows many editors & could probably help – which paper is it?

I could easily have a photograph of *you* with Driberg if I ever kept photographs. You know quite well you love the old boy.

The Dides case is simply a head-on collision between the Russian & American secret services who for years seem to have been selling each other secrets. Merely une affaire de policiers, no decent people involved except poor M. Mons who was bamboozled entirely. Very enjoyable – it goes happily on.

Thanks for *Punch* – I thought it funny in parts.

You can't imagine how wonderful Gen: de Gaulle's book[3] is – such beautiful language & noble sentiments. I wish you would read it.

Much love
N

P.S. Col *furious* because Edmond Barrachin[4] has been pronounced the best dressed man in the Chambre. It is too bad. What a pity you are not a député.

I think 'c'est amusant, votre panier' is perhaps more lively than quel drôle de panier. It depends exactly what you mean. Quel drôle de p. is really what an extraordinary basket – & not very complimentary. 'Enfin Mme c'est génial' would have to be the end of a speech – enfin betokens a kind of summing up. If it's an exclamation on its own, you should put 'Ça, c'est génial'.

A little bit difficult without the context.

[1] One evening during the war, a receptionist at the hotel had prevented Nancy from accompanying Palewski up to his bedroom.
[2] Bore the Almighty.
[3] *L'Appel 1940–42* (1954), the first in a three-volume autobiography *Mémoires de guerre*.
[4] Edmond Barrachin (1900–75). Deputy for the Hauts de Seine. Married to Mabel Forest-Bischoffsheim in 1923.

14 November 1954   7 rue Monsieur, VII

Darling Evelyn

I wish, in return for telling you how to address foreign nobles, you would tell me how to decant wine. Nobody here does, unless they want to give vin ordinaire & pretend it is a bit better, but ever since reading about Lord Cardigan I've had a horror of *black bottles* on the table.[1] All I really want to know is how long before the meal one is supposed to do it – does the wine chambrer in the bottle or in the decanter? Don't hurry to reply as I know you're busy. Oh and does one decant white wine or only red?

What is *Lady Margot*? I see it on my Italian publisher's list. What's Daphne's book like? A sort of real life *Vile Bodies* I suppose. I'll read it at Debo's where I go for Xmas – I then go to Ed West etc for N

Year & then London for a week or so where I hope very much to see you.

Pomp comes out here tomorrow – such a pretty book, I'm delighted with it. I've been giving a series of luncheons for the critics, which have rather blocked my private life but have been great fun I must say.

You can't imagine how wonderful Gen de Gaulle's book is, I believe even you will think so (if it is decently translated). The critics here say that no homme d'état [statesman] has been able to write like that since Chateaubriand.

I asked about the Index. The answer was there are very few books on the Index, but the faithful pay great attention to the list of books plays & films posted up in the Churches. But I'm sure in my own mind that there are very few French people, however pious, who would not read a book, because it was on the index, if they wanted to. Of course they would keep it away from servants & children, though. What about you? Would you think it wrong?*

Pomp has been banned in Eire. When I asked why I was told because of the title.

Fond love
N

* For instance, Gide is on the Index – would you expect Claudel not to have read Gide?

[1] At a regimental dinner in 1840, Lord Cardigan arrested and imprisoned one of his officers for ordering a bottle of un-decanted Moselle. Cardigan had mistaken the wine for porter, which he forbade at the mess table and which, like Moselle, came in a black bottle.

16 November 1954   Piers Court
                                                   Stinchcombe

Darling Nancy

Very many thanks for your kind help with my frog dialogue. The book is done at last, posted off to the printer and not to be seen again until June. You will be able to sympathise with my sense of elation. It is short and funny & completes the story I began in *Men at Arms* which threatened to drag out to the grave.

Poor Prod is plainly awfully barmy. The only disquieting feature is that he can, I believe, sue as a pauper at the public expense, lose his case & leave Ed and me to pay our lawyers.[1] It may be necessary to have him certified. Do you mind particularly?

Lady Birkenhead[2] was here on Sunday full of the delights of Rue Monsieur. Have you been seeing Auberon Herbert, do I gather? How did you find him.

Daphne has written her memoirs.[3] Contrary to what one would have expected they are marred by discretion and good taste. The childhood part is admirable. The adult part is rather as though Lord Montgomery were to write his life and omit to mention that he ever served in the army.

When oh when do you come to London. Please let me know in good time.

All love
    Evelyn

[1] Peter Rodd had taken offence at Lord Stanley's portrait of him in *Sea Peace*. In his review of the book Evelyn wrote: 'The man to whom a chapter has been devoted, is dubbed "Prod". Others have tried to write the portrait of this singular character. None, perhaps, has fully succeeded ... "Prod" has an element of genius which Lord Stanley quite misses in casting him in a P. G. Wodehouse part and in crediting him with a desire to please which is most unfamiliar.' *Time and Tide*, 28 August 1954.
[2] Hon. Sheila Berry (1913–92). Writer. Married 2nd Earl of Birkenhead in 1935.
[3] Daphne Fielding, *Mercury Presides* (1954).

20 November 1954   7 rue Monsieur, VII

Darling Evelyn

Yes our letters crossed. Many thanks about decanting – my fine Georgian decanters are the wrong shape, what a bore.

Oh dear Prod. He wrote a sort of wild letter saying he was quite broke but intended to sue you & Ed. As I hadn't heard of Ed's book, then, I thought it was something to do with *Black Mischief*. I wrote back vehemently saying that I consider it the lowest known way of making money & why can't he work like everybody else. Then, about a week ago, I saw Adelaide [Lubbock] who told about Ed's book, which does sound too beastly (I think Ed is utterly despicable now). Anyway Ad said that Prod was deeply wounded by it. Oh poor Prod. Serves him right for having such a friend, I suppose, but even so better keep quiet. I suppose you & Peter [Quennell] reviewed it – I can't imagine how all this has escaped me. While I was in Russia I expect.

No doubt Prod is a little bit mad, but that's no reason to mock him & be unkind. I thought that was understood even by savages. (I'm working myself up now – after all I haven't seen any of the passages in question – but Ad who is quite sane says that Edward has been most *terribly unkind*.)

What can be done to stop him from suing? What can be done for Prod anyhow? If one gives him money it is scattered to the four winds. I suppose the best would be to find somebody in Italy who would dole it out to him every week – or even pay the tradesmen. Sometimes I believe he is literally hungry.

Has he got a case against Edward do you think? I suppose the good Edwin Rutherford, our excellent solicitor, must know about all this.

Is there a great hurry or would it do if I went to see Edwin early in Jan?

I must say I don't specially mind him going for Edward, but he must leave you & Peter alone.

Did I tell you about Brian How[ard]'s visit? He looks literally the most saintly figure imaginable – Abbé Pierre isn't in it, for looks. I think those sad old drunks like him & Prod often do become rather saintly. How strange. Like in your book –

Well, let me know what happens won't you.

Much love
  N

22 November [1954]   Piers Court
                      Stinchcombe

Darling

You wrote to me in August: 'I look forward to Ed's book. The central character is Prod, by name, & Ed has made him sign a paper that he won't sue for libel. What would all of us pen pushers do without Prod?' so it isn't any good your thinking you will escape the Prod libel actions for that is all I said about the poor old boy in my review.

Mrs Lubbock or someone must take him under the wing.

Ed's account of Prod was certainly nasty but I thought 'if the old boy doesn't mind, who else need?'

Of course if it is all an invention of Ed's that Prod gave him an *imprimatur*, we are all in the soup. It will be a great nuisance. No money for Prod or honour for anyone. You and your family!

I sent an American acquaintance three pages of typescript & asked 'is the american slang authentic?' Weeks passed. Now I have back 50 pages on Embassy paper giving the opinions of three public relations officers.

Love
  E

24 November 1954   7 rue Monsieur, VII

Darling Evelyn

I see I've got softening of the brain. I must have been on my mystery cruise when the book came out as I've never seen a single word about it – or the book itself – & Prod's letter utterly mystified me as I told you. He must be mad to give Ed such permission. I wonder who told me about it in Aug – Ed himself, I guess, I remember dining with him & the Mayalls, & a Frenchman in the restaurant said afterwards that it was shameful to be so drunk (as Ed) when with ladies.

I don't think I mind Prod suing Ed who is really vile, but he must leave you & Peter alone. I think I can fix it. I'll tell him that I'll give you his letter saying he needs money & so is going to sue you. (In fact I can't, as I've lost it). Tell me any new developments, won't you.

Oh my poor eyes. I go to a LADY every morning, who is supposed to teach me how to see. I rather believe in her.

Had a gruelling time with a young man from *Match* who is going to do 1500 words & 2 pages on me. It was like being psychoanalysed. I gave him what you wrote once in an American paper. He said what is your Father like? and I said exactly like Dominici.[1] He was surprised.

Much love
      Nancy

Very amusing book on Worth.[2] There was an American in Paris then called Mrs Moulton[3] – *literal* Susan Mary [Patten].
How I hope I shall never be tried in a court of justice – I seem to get moonier every day.

[1] Gustave Dominici, the man accused of murdering Sir Jack Drummond and his family.
[2] Edith Saunders, *The Age of Worth: Couturier to Empress Eugénie* (1954).
[3] Formerly Lillie Greenough of Cambridge, Massachusetts, wife of an American millionaire, Charles Moulton.

16 December 1954   7 rue Monsieur, VII

Darling Evelyn
    How I shrieked at your review of that poor man's book![1] Ever since I can remember he has brought out some nice book every year & the reviewers have said so charming & people have given each other copies in the certitude of pleasing, & now all of a sudden a dreadful avalanche obliterates the poor fellow – for ever, I should think.

I went to London for one night, only to see my dad. Expensive & tiring. All he said was 'it's a perfect nuisance – as soon as I arrive in London everybody wants to *see* me – I wish they'd *leave me alone*'.

My mother asked me to tea at 5 & went off to a cinema at 5.30 – she hasn't seen me for a year.

My dad pulled out a handkerchief & an enormous spanner came out of his pocket with it. I said I suppose you've got a ball of string on you & he said no I always use elastic bands now, & pulled out about 50 thick ones from another pocket. Wouldn't an assassin be surprised – as a matter of fact he always carries a lot of money too.

I'll be in London the week of Jan 3rd any hope of seeing you? My only engagement is dinner on Jan 4th. I'm going for N Year to Eddy West, longing for it.

I saw Bonny Boots footing & tooting it among the 18 cent: pictures
– he looks rather thin & sad – oh dear the pictures are lovely, have
you seen them?

I read Daphne [Fielding]'s book but I was rather disappointed. The
fact is things like follow my leader in Selfridges need to be dished up
by you – recounted in their native baldness they don't seem very
funny.

Stephen Tennant is here, looking for an engagement 'to strip off
mink & ermine in front of a jet curtain – Monsieur Vénus – I am
followed everywhere, Nancy, for my beauty.' 'I need the money
because I have spent all my capital on statues & balustrades, they all
blew down in the gales, but they look rather pretty, lying in the grass.'
He really *is* off his old head.

I'm supposed to go, with Col, to Debo for Xmas but it depends on
politics & weather. But anyway I'll come over after.

> Much love
> Nancy

The history critic of *La Croix* has just been to see me – oh he is made
for you & now I shall be able to find out the answers to all questions.
He's writing an enormous Histoire de la Chrétienté en Angleterre.[2]
An old DEAR (& loves *Pomp*).

[1] Evelyn had reviewed *The Victorian Home* (1954) by Ralph Dutton (later Lord Sherborne). 'A
book which cannot be wholeheartedly commended to any class of reader ... The illustrations
... are very poorly reproduced. The text is trite and patronizing ... the only readers likely
to derive enjoyment from it are those who indulge in the badger-digging of literary blood
sports, the exposure of error.' *Sunday Times*, 28 November 1954.
[2] André D. Tolédano, *Histoire de l'Angleterre Chrétienne* (1955).

18 December 1954   Piers Court
                                                    Stinchcombe
Dearest Nancy

A happy Christmas, wherever you may be.

How about January 7th for us to meet? I will come up for luncheon
– Ritz Hotel 1.15 – if that suits you. We might go again to the pictures
at Burlington House.[1] I was dazed by delight at my first visit. Fragonard
in full splendour for the first time in my experience, a fine Tiepolo, a
delicious Oudry still life. You must tell me more of this painter. I think
Poor Pam had a deplorable Pug by him. Otherwise I know nothing.

Allan Ramsay was a revelation too.

Did I tell you that David Cecil, having pretended to be at work for
15 years on a life of Lord Melbourne, dashed it off suddenly in emu-
lation indeed in exact stylistic imitation of *Pompadour* & that the Americans bought an edition thinking 'Lord M.' meant Lord Montagu?

I have had a grave week as my mother has just died, aged 84. You say the English always say 'Happy release' at a death. It was really so in her case. Not that she was in pain, but bitterly weary and irked at her dependent state. She was found by her maid dead in her arm chair. So for her it was happy, but it fills me with regret for a lifetime of failure in affection & attention. And of course there has been a lot of uncongenial work with relations & lawyers.

Children come flooding in by every train. It is rather exhilarating to see their simple excitement & curiosity about every Christmas card. 'Look, papa, the Hyde Park Hotel has sent a coloured picture of its new cocktail bar.'

When I reviewed that Victorian book I took the writer to be a bumptious young puppy. I hear he is an aged and wealthy pansy. What astounds me is the standard of reviewing. The book was a congeries of platitude & misstatement produced like a prep-school examination paper on 'jellygraph'. I keep opening papers which say 'Mr Dutton's scholarly & penetrating work – impeccable taste – sumptuous production' etc.

I went to Oxford & visited my first homosexual love, Richard Pares,[2] a don at All Souls. At 50 he is quite paralysed except his mind & voice and awaiting deterioration and death – more dignified than John Hayward,[3] no lolling tongue, but more helpless. A wife and four daughters, no private fortune. He would have been Master of Balliol if he had not been struck down. No Christian faith to support him. A very harrowing visit.

Debo's face in the *Daily Mail* this morning from the wop painter whose work gives me the creeps.

Until 7th.

Much love
     Evelyn

How disgusting about the frogs all getting drunk. Is it a lie put about by the CocoColo makers?

[1] An exhibition of 'European Masters of the Eighteenth Century' at the Royal Academy included *Fête de Saint Cloud* by Fragonard and *Banquet of Cleopatra* by Tiepolo.
[2] Richard Pares (1902–58). A history scholar who was at Oxford with Evelyn. Professor of History at Edinburgh University 1945–54. Married Janet Powicke in 1937. He suffered from creeping paralysis.
[3] John Hayward (1905–65). Critic, editor, bibliographer and bibliophile who developed muscular dystrophy in his youth.

21 December 1954   7 rue Monsieur, VII

Darling Evelyn
     I am very sorry to hear about your mother – death is always a horrid shock I think. But I allow it to be for the best when somebody is 84 & not happy.

The 7 Jan: Ritz Hotel 1.15 – I long for it. Oh aren't the Burlington House pictures heavenly – I didn't have nearly long enough because I met so many friends – Cyril – H. Hamilton & many from here, dealers, Rothschilds etc as well as various old lords tottering among their ancestors. Oudry is adored here, unknown at home except, I suppose, for his direction of the Beauvais manufacture of tapestry.

Yes reviewers always miss the point don't they. But then they never *read* the books – as a writer one is well aware of that! But I loved *Ld M*. What do you mean about copying my style – I don't quite like it considering everybody says what awful English he writes for an English teacher.

There was a talk about women writers on the wireless here last night & the talker said all these women are too busy writing themselves to read books, & no man is going to read a book by a woman, so the result is nobody reads books any more.

I thought Raymond's remarks about Our Queen yesterday were asking for the accolade.[1] When he says Stuart madness he is on shaky ground – what about George III William IV & the lamented Windsor? The lamented W sent me his book to sign yesterday because I've been too lazy to struggle up to Neuilly & do it – which made me feel a pig. All news on 7th I die for it. If you wish to put me off, tell Bookshop golden boys & girls.

Love
   N

My new Catholic friend said 'You have kept the throne, which I envy you, but we have kept our old religion.' Very true.

[1] In a review of *Queen Anne's Son* by Hester Chapman, Raymond Mortimer had written that the death of the Duke of Gloucester, aged eleven, 'must appear a happy event. Had he survived and produced heirs, perhaps with their full share of Stuart folly, the head of the State today might be some seedy President instead of a beloved Queen.' *Sunday Times*, 19 December 1954.

19 May 1955   7 rue Monsieur, VII

Darling Evelyn

If the Card Collector[1] can do with cards which have been written on 'pour mémoire' I can get her hundreds of them, they rain upon me.

Would you point out that the Rose Cottage[2] specimen is intensely rare – possibly unique – & surely ranks with the penny black if not with a first folio Shakespeare.

I'm off to Greece on the 31st May. I don't care for the season here, since I never go to balls, & I love to be here in July & August when one can cross the road in peace. So that is my plan (I have to go somewhere for a month on account of Marie's holiday). Come too.

You know how people can't read – only writers know to what extent they can't – well 10 people now have said to me I see you have started again in the *Sunday Times* under the name of Ginette. It is intensely irritating – & nothing to be done that I can see. The real Ginette is a horror. I've done an article[3] on the Marie Antoinette exhibition *Sunday T.* however, which you may enjoy. Also I long for your comments on my article about the Aristocracy[4] – it will be in the *Encounter* of July I believe. What about *O & G*? Should you be going to send me one, & should it be out in June, do send to Hôtel de Grande Bretagne, Athens.

What of the election? I've greatly enjoyed accounts of the television appearances – how can they all be so bad when it's their trade?

My fire screen, which I bought for £50, takes up half a page of the MA catalogue & is said to be worth at least £800. Not a bad investment was it – I'm delighted.

A dull letter – no news.

Love from
Nancy

Anne Hill's mother had a ghastly operation for cancer. Her sister wrote 'I hear you have been seedy' to which she replied 'just a little attack of cancer – quite all right now'. Do admit the wonderful English understatement.

[1] Margaret Waugh had started a postcard collection.
[2] The house at Strand-on-the-Green where Nancy lived when she was first married.
[3] 'A Queen of France', *Sunday Times*, 22 May 1955.
[4] 'The English Aristocracy', *Encounter*, September 1955.

21 May 1955   Piers Court
                                                                   Stinchcombe
Dearest Nancy

Very many thanks for the cards. I have told the child to thank you. If she does so properly – she can't spell any better than her papa, I mean from the heart – do please send her 'pour mémoires'.

You are wise & fortunate to go to Greece – lovely at this season. Bad food & wine and bugs in the prettiest places. Why do you not also press on to Beirut where you wld find French food and speech, lovely castles and temples in the hills?

Laura is excited about the Election as her brother is standing for a hopeless seat in Co Durham[1] and she and all her family have been up there having a high old time. Eden will get in and nothing will be better or worse for it. I think Socialism was a thing like Prohibition in America.

I don't know your screen. Well that's my fault for not going to visit you but it was a bit difficult from Chantilly, with no motor car of my own if you see what I mean. What is MA catalogue – Marie Antoinette? Modern Art? A little thing by Léger perhaps?

I will try to get hold of *Encounter* for July.

O & G won't be out till end of June. Better send it to Rue Monsieur?

Good books for you to read on your voyage: Chapman's *Dreyfus Case*, Powell's *Acceptance World*, Newby's *Picnic at Sakkara*.[2]

O I suddenly see in your letter that you have written on Marie Antoinette Exhibition so of course *that* is MA catalogue. Silly of me.

No one sane could suppose you wrote so movingly of France's debt to Noël Coward.

Journalists keep insulting me. I thought I was proof against hurt but I do find cumulatively they set up an itch. Particularly as *all* their facts are always wrong, but if one wrote to correct them people just think 'Pompous ass'.

Love
E

---

[1] Auberon Herbert stood as a Conservative for Sunderland North and lost by 2,836 votes.
[2] Guy Chapman, *The Dreyfus Trial*; Anthony Powell, *The Acceptance World*; P. H. Newby, *The Picnic at Sakkara*; all published in 1955.

---

14 July 1955   7 rue Monsieur, VII

Darling Evelyn

Howstupidyouare why not my sort of book? Of course the moment it arrived I downed tools & read & read all day. I felt furious with Smarty for his review[1] (which I knew to be all wrong by instinct) at the time, far more furious now. What does he mean by slow? What does he want? Then they all crack up a book called *Going to the Wars*[2] so much that I bought it – embarrassingly bad I thought & *so* tiresome. That's slow if you like. I call slow when you can't get interested in any of the characters or remember a single one when you finally put the book down.

I'm glad to say Mr John Raymond,[3] a very nice new friend I believe you'd like, entirely agreed with me yesterday, & *he* was outraged because in the *NS & N* (for which he works) you were lumped in for review with other novelists.

So heavenly here, wonderful weather & my flat so pretty after the houses of rich Greeks. But oh I did enjoy myself. To begin with I love that enormous heat, it makes me feel really well & lively (we had 113 one day, generally between 90 & 100).

I went to Crete – goodness how they love us there. The housemaid in the hotel kissed me when I said I was English, & everybody treated me like a sort of saint or heroine.

I met Paddy's Cretan Runner,[4] quite by chance in a bus. He was clasping his book! So touching. Of course not a bit surprised to hear I'd been staying with Paddy & had read the book, he would have been amazed if I hadn't.

Knossos is a dreadful fraud – did you not make a little détour to see it? (As Sir A Evans has entirely rebuilt it in steel & concrete it would have made excellent shelters by the way.) Of the works of man in Greece Mycenae impressed me the most, but there are few of them.

I enclose some cards for Miss M & please thank her for the thank you letter & say that will cover the future as well as the past. But I expect she has given up by now, knowing what children are.

I'll send you the lords.

Much love & deep admiration
　　Nancy

[1] Cyril Connolly had written: 'The general effect in *Officers and Gentlemen* is of a series of amiable cartoons in which the characters become easily distinguishable but seldom real, comedians in a series of humorous sketches, actors who have studied their parts but not read the play.' *Sunday Times*, 3 July 1955.
[2] By John Verney (1955). Second World War memoirs by a Yeomanry officer, described by Raymond Mortimer as 'a work of art' and 'a tale of adventure most vividly told'. *Sunday Times*, 24 April 1955.
[3] John Raymond (1923–77). Literary critic and author.
[4] Patrick Leigh Fermor had translated *The Cretan Runner: His Story of the German Occupation* (1955) by George Psychoundakis, a wartime runner in the Cretan Resistance.

15 July 1955   7 rue Monsieur, VII

Darling Evelyn

Of course I *shrieked*.[1] I know Miss Nancy Spain.[2] She was born at Redesdale & her grandmother was old Mrs Spain whose garden was the pride of the Redewater valley. She's a funny rough creature (Nancy) but I rather like her & I think she's very fond of me. Not your type. As for the Lord,[3] it proves all I say in my article. (Pam [Berry] I believe has wheedled a proof out of Stephen, do make her pass it on.) Lords will do *anything* except an honest day's work is my cry, but do read it. (Only I've just added a lovely bit about upper class usage, so perhaps don't read it until it comes out.)

Oh *do* send Miss Spain's piece[4] I'll faithfully return it. I'm laughing so much I can hardly hold my pen.

Why did Lady Honks throw away the letter about the poor dead young man? Goodness you do hit her off. When I *think* of poor old Enid Jones's effort –![5]

Fond love
　　N

[1] Evelyn had sent Nancy his article 'Awake my Soul! It is a Lord', which gave his version of an unwelcome visit from Nancy Spain and Lord Noel-Buxton. They had been dismissed by Evelyn with 'Go away, go away! You read the notice, didn't you? No admittance on business!' 'I'm not on business,' replied Lord Noel-Buxton, 'I'm a member of the House of Lords.'
[2] Nancy Spain (1917–64). Novelist, broadcaster, journalist on the *Daily Express* and *News of the World* who died in a light-aircraft crash on her way to cover the Grand National. Her obituary in *The Times* recorded that 'trousers were her almost invariable costume'.
[3] Rufus Alexander, 2nd Baron Noel-Buxton (1917–80). BBC producer 1946–8; on the staff of *Farmer's Weekly* 1950–52.
[4] 'My Pilgrimage to See Mr Waugh', *Daily Express*, 23 June 1955.
[5] Ruby Maclean, in Enid Bagnold's novel *The Loved and Envied* (1951), was a less successful portrait of Diana Cooper than Evelyn's portrayal of her as Julia Stitch.

16 July 1955   7 rue Monsieur, VII

Rough draft (don't return) of letter to *Spectator*[1] NR

Sir

    Mr Carlisle says that 'Mr Evelyn Waugh's article in your issue of July 8th is the worst example of bad manners to be granted space in your columns since the Sitwell correspondence'. I don't remember whether the Sitwell correspondence was on the same subject, but I would like to say here & now that it is no wonder if elderly writers become bad tempered. Dogs which are constantly baited turn savage, & writers are supposed to be more highly-strung than dogs.

    I am not a quarter as famous as Mr Waugh, but nobody would believe the extent to which I am teased & tortured by strangers. I personally have no complaint against journalists who, in my experience, always ask for an appointment & are quite ready to take no for an answer. It is the unemployed bore who drives one mad. He telephones, he writes, he even surges into my flat, through the french windows, unannounced.

    It so happens that my nerves are rather strong, but in the end they will probably give way & then another example of ill manners may find itself, Sir, in your post bag.

Yours faithfully
    Nancy Mitford

[1] Nancy's letter was published, with a few minor amendments, in the *Spectator*, 22 July 1955.

18 July 1955   Piers Court
                                                  Stinchcombe

Darling Nancy

    I hope you and Col danced about the streets like mad things on 14th to celebrate the liberation of M. de Sade.

    I am surprised & delighted that you managed to get through *Officers*

& *Gentlemen*. Mrs Stitch threw away Guy's letter because she thought it contained the incriminating War Diary of Hookforce in Crete. War Diaries had to be sent to C.H.Q. Records by Intelligence Officers.

Here is Miss Spain's article. Please return. I gather you see the *Spectator* so you will have read Lord Noel-Buxton's infamous attempt to put the blame on the woman. Only a socialist and a quaker could be quite so caddish. I know nothing of either of the pilgrims except for that one incident. I don't think Miss Spain can be very nice, whatever her grandmother's horticultural gifts, as I have had a mountainous mail from people as different as Edith Sitwell and Violet Bonham Carter,[1] telling me of sufferings at her hand in the past. Nor do I think Mr Raymond can be very nice. I have read some very common articles by him. Are you getting into the wrong set?

I look forward to seeing the final draft of your letter in the *Spectator*. I don't think journalists are any better than tourists. The difference is that there are lots of idle tourists in Paris and none in Stinchcombe while the journalists are fairly respectable people like Mr Giles.[2] In England there are beastly journalists who can only get into print if they are offensive. I don't take any Beaverbrook papers but I gather they specialize in beastliness. The *Spectator* has been running a very effective campaign against them. Mr Gilmour[3] seems a high minded young man. He has a *very* attractive wife.

I find about journalists that even when one has been hospitable to them and quite liked them & thought they quite liked one, they invariably put some awful statement into one's mouth. Politicians have to face the risk because they live on popular votes, but for novelists it would not affect the sale of a single copy if we were never mentioned in the Beaverbrook press. The editors know this and it riles them.

It is so long since I wrote that I forget what I last told you. Did I say that Desmond Guinness came here with a wife[4] like Tilly Losch who has learned English solely from your books? An enjoyable couple.

Knossos is a wonderful fake is it not? I particularly relished the 'reconstructions' of the frescoes. A whole school of design contrived out of bits of plaster the size of a thumb nail.

It has been so hot that I haven't been to London at all & missed Debo's water gala which I gather was highly enjoyed by all.

Did I say you should read *Picnic at Sakkara* by a Mr Newby. Awfully funny. Not so Mr Wain[5] whom everyone cracks up. I have a theory which I shall develop into a thesis, that the trouble with all young writers is that they read English Literature in the Schools so have taken against it. Good writers & critics read for pleasure & relaxation from Latin & History.

On Saturday I saw *Murder in the Cathedral*[6] at Gloucester. I went not
expecting to like it much & was deeply moved.

Lady Jones got Honks right in the cemetery.

Love

E

[1] Violet Asquith (1887–1969). Daughter of the Liberal Prime Minister H. H. Asquith and
herself a Liberal spokesman and orator. Married to Maurice Bonham Carter in 1915.
[2] Frank Giles (1919–). Author and journalist. Paris correspondent of *The Times* 1953–60.
Foreign editor of the *Sunday Times* 1961–77, director of *Times Newspapers* 1981–5. Married to
Lady Katherine (Kitty) Sackville in 1946.
[3] Ian Gilmour (1926–2007). Editor of the *Spectator* 1954–9. Subsequently Conservative MP and
Minister. Created life peer in 1992. Married Lady Caroline Montagu-Douglas-Scott in 1951.
[4] Princess Marie-Gabrielle (Mariga) von Urach of Württemberg (1932–89). Married to Nancy's
nephew Desmond 1954–81.
[5] John Wain (1925–94). One of the 'angry young men' of the 1950s whose novel *Living in the
Present* had just been published.
[6] By. T. S. Eliot (1935).

19 July 1955   7 rue Monsieur, VII

Darling Evelyn

I think she's a great deal nicer about you than Lord? Masefield,
who appears frankly gaga (as no doubt he is).[1] No I don't see the
Spectator but a friend telephoned to tell me that Ld N-B had written
saying that he is a timid, civilized fellow, fond of Roman fords, so of
course I rushed to the Invalides & got a copy. There was a tired
sweating mob of English, fighting their way to the S of France, who
looked amazed at my shrieks as I read. Terrible rubbish – the shrinking
sensitive chap he describes himself as would have waited in the motor.
So would anybody conversant with upper class usage. Perhaps my
letter is too much about me & not obviously enough a crack at him,
but I thought the unemployed bore would tease. I've been dying to
say all this for ages. Can't truthfully say I've suffered from journalists.
The English ones won't do me because of *S Times* & journalists can't
write about each other. Of course I get Swedes & things, but can't
read their digs so that's all right.

The son in law of Ldy V B Carter came just now – called Grimond.[2]
I met him at the Opera, very nice indeed. I read your letter to him
& he said if Miss Spain is up against you & me & Edith & Ldy V she
could hardly have picked a tougher quartet. (Well she's not really up
against me.) He said he's been here a week & hasn't met the mistress
of a single French politician. Hard cheese.

Knossos – the reconstructions – more shrieks. A whole bull fight
out of what *might* be the end of a bull's tail. And don't you love the
way it's all art nouveau? And all those pots like they used to make on
the stage at *Chu Chin Chow*?[3]

Very rude of you to speak like this about socialists when you know I'm one. I think it's the Roman fords that are his undoing what *are* Roman fords anyway?

Yes I'd forgotten Honks in the cemetery it was perfect.

Mr John Raymond is nice & clever & likes me so of course I like him.

Do come over, I need you.

Love from
    Nancy

I loved Laura sighing deeply.[4]

[1] Nancy Spain and Lord Noel-Buxton had visited John Masefield before calling at Piers Court. When asked whether Evelyn was 'a nice man', the Poet Laureate had replied: 'I met him once ... or was it his father? Yes, I think I knew the father better.' *Daily Express*, 23 June 1955.
[2] Jo Grimond (1913–93). Leader of the Liberal Party 1956–67. Married Hon. Laura Bonham-Carter in 1938. Created life peer in 1983.
[3] By Oscar Asche (1931).
[4] 'I rang the bell. Mrs Waugh, a beautiful woman in a twin set and slacks, came immediately, sighed deeply and leaned against the door jamb.' *Daily Express*, 23 June 1955.

23 July 1955   Piers Court
                                                    Stinchcombe
Dearest Nancy,

In the last two days two separate parties from Paris have passed through Stinchcombe. One told me and the other confirmed the terrible story of your social ostracism.[1] If I had known, I would not have made untimely jibes about your frequenting the wrong set. I *am* sorry for my heavy footedness. You must be lonely & chill sitting with Mr Raymond & Miss Spain.

Of course I was as shocked as any frog by your attack on Marie Antoinette but since we once had an estrangement after Mosley's Albert Hall Meeting, I had resolved never to let your subversive opinions influence my love.

Some of my informants say you may be readmitted to the fringes of Society. Others that you will have to change your name & go to Dakar. Well it is warm there and you will like that.

Love from
    Evelyn

[1] Nancy had upset many of her French friends by writing that Marie Antoinette was one of the most irritating characters in history and had deserved a traitor's death. 'She was frivolous without being funny, extravagant without being elegant, her stupidity was monumental: she was one of those people who cannot put a foot right.' *Sunday Times*, 22 May 1955.

25 July 1955   7 rue Monsieur, VII

Darling Evelyn

I do live but for you. Well the ostracism all occurred when I was away. Gaston says Anglo French relations haven't been so bad since Fashoda. (I don't really know what all the fuss is about as I am on *their side* for cutting off the head of an Austrian spy. Why do we dance on 14th July then?) However now I'm back they can't resist me, & empty though Paris is I don't have many meals alone with Miss Spain.

But the great new joke is I've been offered (& eagerly accepted) £1000 a month to do dialogue for a Marie Antoinette film.[1]

Poor old paddler,[2] I'd rather be me than him. Darling Rufus indeed. Did you like my article on Greece?[3] Sadly cut. I wonder where I could place the rest of my interesting witty reflections on that country.[4]

Did we have a quarrel over the Mosley meeting – I'd quite forgotten. I remember Prod looked very pretty in a black shirt. But we were young & high spirited then & didn't know about Buchenwald.

I must say I agree with you that the war was at its most enjoyable when we were against two of the fiends. I daresay that happy time will come again – rather nice if the super brutes from America weighed in too. Then we *could* go down with flags flying.

Do tell who your Paris visitors have been oh *do*. You've soaked my appetite.

    Love from
        Nancy

Very fond of that editress's letter, the one who overheard darling Rufus.[5]

[1] *Marie Antoinette* (1956), directed by Jean Delannoy, starring Michèle Morgan and Richard Todd.
[2] In the continuing row over the inopportune visit by Nancy Spain and Lord Noel-Buxton, Evelyn had described the latter's investigations into Roman fords as 'sensitive scholarship and intrepid paddling'. *Spectator*, 22 July 1955.
[3] 'Wicked Thoughts in Greece', *Sunday Times*, 24 July 1955.
[4] In her collected essays, Nancy reinstated a paragraph criticising the 'unspeakable' American reconstruction work at Knossos and Stoa. She described the Agora Museum 'as though the French had allowed Frank Lloyd Wright to build his idea of a Petit Trianon at the bottom of the *tapis vert* at Versailles'. *The Water Beetle* (Hamish Hamilton, 1962), p. 97.
[5] Joan Werner Laurie, editor of *She* magazine, had written to confirm that she was in the room when Nancy Spain read her *Express* article over the telephone to Lord Noel-Buxton. *Spectator*, 22 July 1955.

2 August 1955   7 rue Monsieur, VII

Darling Evelyn

You must have been pleased at the note of high lunacy on which Ld N-Buxton concluded the correspondence. May all your enemies perish thus – darling Rufus is evidently a candidate for the bin.

I was going to the Riviera this week but am now rather sadly obliged to stay here as Peters has picked up a very remunerative piece of work for me. I'm to write the English dialogue for a film on M-Antoinette (quite funny when you think of the fuss). As I haven't earned a penny yet this year I feel I must accept, & much as I long to go back to the heat am bound to say that Paris is heavenly at present.

Everybody has gone – at least, 2 millions have – except le bon géant, as a paper described the Col.

My learned friend Mrs Arthur[1] places *Os & Gs* among the great novels of the world – she held forth for half an hour on its merits. If you knew the extent of her knowledge learning & taste you would be gratified. (Normally her mind is engaged upon Mme Guyon & the Abbé Bremond.)

Poor widowed Smartyboots[2] – rather sad, isn't it, when he so loves to be the one that chucks.

Who wrote the *Observer* portrait?[3] Randolph's ghost? I thought it very very good.

Much love
Nancy

P.S. Decca arrives with her children end of the month. I'm half delighted & half terrified. Seventeen years –
What are the Stinchcombe's plans for welcoming F. M. Bulganin?[4]

[1] Esther Murphy (1895–1962). American intellectual. Married 1929–33 to John Strachey, MP and journalist, and to Chester Alan Arthur, great-nephew of the US President Chester Arthur.
[2] Cyril Connolly's wife Barbara had left him for the publisher George Weidenfeld.
[3] The unsigned profile described Evelyn as 'a man of great if rather tigerish charm' and ended: 'Embittered romantic, over-deliberate squire and recluse, popular comedian, catholic father of a family, Evelyn Waugh is one of the oddest figures of our time.' *Observer*, 31 July 1955.
[4] The Soviet Premier made a ten-day visit to Britain the following year.

5 August 1955   Grand Hotel
                                                   Folkestone

Dearest Nancy
Mrs Arthur sounds splendid. I hope she exercises wide influence.
I met another traveller from Paris. I said: 'I hear Mrs Rodd is entirely ostracized.' 'Oh not at all. I saw her with' – and then a string of names. But all those names were jewish american or English. Dur parmesan. Mrs Arthur, despite her brilliant literary acumen, doesn't sound like the Faubourg. Well perhaps Hollywood will bring some comfort. Lots of the people there have taken very august names. 'Guermantes' in every studio cafeteria speaking with strong Danubian accents.
I have come to live here for a bit, everything nice except the cooking and the customers. I see Ann [Fleming] and Bettine Davison[1] – Noël

Coward and I don't do any work which was the object of my coming.

Yesterday I went to London to stand godfather to Edith Sitwell who has submitted to the Pope of Rome. She looked fine – like a 16th century infanta and spoke her renunciation of heresy in silver bell like tones. Afterwards a gargantuan feast at her Sesame Club. I had heard gruesome accounts of that place but she gave us a rich blow-out. Very odd company none of whom I had seen before, only one I had heard of – the actor Alec Guinness,[2] very shy & bald. He is turning papist too, so there is something to balance the loss of Miss Clifford[3] who is marrying a man with no legs & two wives. Think of *choosing* to be named Atalanta Fairey! No sense of propriety. Ed Stanley has written a first rate essay on Belloc as preface to the *Cruise of the Nona.*[4] Ann says he is impotent and greatly depressed about it.

The Connolly affaire is still hidden in deepest cloud. He seems to have sold the ticket for Greece which John sent him & to be lurking in St Tropez with or without (no one knows) his concubine & her jew.

Honks has had a tooth out and gone to starve with Loelia [Ponsonby]. The tooth drawing was sudden. Ann telephoned to Loelia to say she would be arriving in a weakened state and would need some nourishing broth. Loelia replied: 'I have sent my cook on a holiday. I made it quite clear that there would be *no* meals.'

I keep sending notes to the chef 'Don't put cornflour in the sauce' etc. Now he comes up and glowers at me in his white hat from behind a screen in the dining room.

I am sorry you thought the *Observer* 'profile' good. I found it grossly impertinent.

How impatient I am with the rot in the papers about science. Really, to spend millions of pounds of public money in letting off invisible fireworks! A football 200 miles away, travelling at 18,000 miles an hour. They are howling mad.[5]

Love
Evelyn

---

[1] Bettine Russell (1905–94). Married Hon. Patrick Davison (later Baron Broughshane) in 1929.
[2] Alec Guinness (1914–2000). The actor was received into the Roman Catholic Church in 1956 Knighted in 1959.
[3] Atalanta Clifford (1932–). Married to Richard Fairey 1955–60.
[4] By Hilaire Belloc (1925), reissued in 1955.
[5] The USA and USSR had announced that they would attempt launching of earth satellites in 1957.

1 September 1955   Piers Court
                                                   Stinchcombe

Dearest Nancy

Thank you very much for sending me *Encounter*. I read your essay with keen relish. I wish it had been much longer.

The exposition of Fortinbras is first class; also all your rebuke to upper class for their capitulations. I think you are less sound on the economic position of the rich. You say there are a few great houses still kept in style, but their owners once kept half a dozen houses apiece going full blast. It is simply that a few families were so awfully rich that a reduction of 90% in their position still leaves them fairly imposing. And even they are not escaping tax, they are spending capital and despair of their heirs having anything eg. the Duke of Beaufort.

I am sure you have worked earnestly at your facts but are you correct in saying that 382 peers have coat-armour *in the male line* from pre-Tudor times? Surely not. I should have thought fewer than 100 and of them half Scottish who did not regularize heraldry (or legitimacy) until late. I am no genealogist but almost every august family I can think of had a female succession at least once & surname & arms granted to an outsider.

I wish in your Upper-class Usage you had touched on a point that has long intrigued me. Almost everyone I know has some personal antipathy which they condemn as middle class quite irrationally. My mother-in-law believes it middle-class to decant claret. Lord Beauchamp thought it m.c. not to decant champagne (into jugs). Your 'note-paper' is another example. I always say 'luncheon' but you will find 'lunch' used in every generation for the last 80 years [by] unimpeachable sources. There are very illiterate people like Perry Brownlow who regard all correct grammar as a middle-class affectation. Ronnie Knox blanches if one says 'docile' with a long o. I correct my children if they say 'bike' for 'bicycle'. I think everyone has certain fixed ideas that have no relation to observed usage. The curious thing is that, as you say, an upper class voice is always unmistakable though it may have every deviation of accent and vocabulary. Compare for instance the late Lords Westmorland, Salisbury, Curzon. A phonetician would find no point of resemblance in their speech.

Herbaceous borders came in as an economy. The first drawing in of horns when potting & bedding-out became too expensive.

Oh I have forgotten your poor eyes. I should have written large as I do to Honks.

Must not Miss Maxwell's cruise be hell?[1]

I have committed an inexcusable solecism in the *Spectator* 'Anadyomene' for 'Anadyomenos'.[2] What can be more ignominious than to

use a rather recondite word and to use it wrong? I am hiding my
head in shame – a bourgeois quality, you tell me.

> All love
>   Evelyn

¹ Elsa Maxwell (1883–1963). Party organiser and *New York Post* columnist. She had organised
a tour of the Mediterranean aboard Stavros Niarchos's yacht *Eros*.
² In the title of his review of *The Cruise of the Nona* (26 August 1955). Evelyn corrected the slip
in the next issue of the *Spectator*.

2 September 1955   7 rue Monsieur, VII

Darling Evelyn
    Even I can't resist a disloyal shriek at the enclosed – like failed BA
isn't it? Anyhow it will do for the collection – or has she switched to
gold fish by now. I know what children's collections are.
    Of course what you say – every family inventing its own taboos –
is true. I hadn't thought of it, do wish I had.
    My eyes – they simply get tired, but I can read your writing, &
even the telephone book, when they are rested, in the morning. Later
in the day they hurt frightfully & then give out.
    I got the figures in my essay from the college of heralds so I think
& hope they are correct. I wasn't surprised about the 382 direct male
line etc because it's the case with my own family & I thought must
be fairly usual.
    When the Colonel read the piece he merely said 'Who is this Scrope?
He must be a bore.'
    About the money I expect you're right, but they all seem to me to be
rolling. Won't Smarty be cross about artists etc being so rich – I put it
in to tease him. I told you about him being Pavlov's dog didn't I?
    My Communist sister has arrived in England with husband child
& child's repellent friend. The child has been told that Andrew [Devon-
shire] makes his money by selling slaves. When Debo heard she said
'but if we had any slaves we wouldn't *sell* them for anything.' They'll
be turning up here soon, I'm only fairly excited – how I loathe Americans. Vive Salk!¹
    Back to the male liners – you see that counts many families like my
own who were obscure squires for hundreds of years & then became
rich & were ennobled – Brasseys, Haigs are cases in point. Rodds I
think too.
    I'm loving my film life. All the people are so nice, the text which
I'm translating is simply perfect, & I'm left in peace to work here. It
should be a wonderful film I think. My Hollywood refusal,² which
they know about, has given me prestige, & I am treated like some
precious object, on no account to be shaken or dropped.

One of them said he lives in Hall Road so I said 'then you must know John Sutro' & he does, but not as a neighbour. I still see John as the young squire of Hall Road!

With love
    Nancy

I see the *D[aily] T[elegraph]* says we love lords. Is it as simple as that? Not sure.

[1] Jonas E. Salk (1915–95). Inventor of the polio vaccine. The first large-scale vaccination programme in America had shown that the Salk virus was not completely safe and had caused many cases of paralytic polio.
[2] The previous year, Nancy had turned down a lucrative offer from MGM to work on the film script of Daphne du Maurier's novel *Mary Anne*.

11 October 1955   40A Hill Street
                                                   Berkeley Square
                                                   London, W1

Darling Evelyn
    Yes, I trust you.[1] The fact is, with me, my love of shrieking is greater than my amour propre. My skin is thick. And, great protection, I never can take myself very seriously as a femme de lettres. So I suffer less than most people – most writers I mean. It is very lucky.
    I'm in a poor way (health). No voice at all, I don't think I can ever cross the Channel again, it's too *bad for me* (Eddy [Sackville-West]).
    I would love Stinkers, but it seems to shorten my other visits too much. Mrs Hammersley is on her last legs & I promised to be there a week, & I rather want a little time at Debo's whom I so rarely see. Give my love to Laura & Hatty & please let me come next time I come over – if ever.
    Enclosed is a letter from the Prof [Ross] which I don't want back. Isn't he lovely & dotty. Lindisfarne –
    I think an open letter is a very good idea.
    Fancy I heard the gun battle & Mollie [Buchanan] *saw* it lucky her, that is she saw the man with the smoking gun in his hand. I saw the blood being tarred over.[2]
    Oh I do feel ill.

Much love
    Nancy

[1] Evelyn was weighing in on the 'U' and 'Non-U' controversy with 'An Open Letter to the Honble Mrs PETER RODD (NANCY MITFORD) on A VERY SERIOUS SUBJECT', published in *Encounter*, December 1955.
[2] A police chase of jewel thieves in Charles Street, Mayfair, had ended in a shoot-out in which two policemen were injured.

17 October 1955   Wilmington
                                                   Totland Bay

Darling Evelyn

I've had this letter,[1] which I don't want back. I've told him that I
think your article is less concerned with U stuff than with attacking
your poor old friend, & therefore not likely to interfere with Peter
F[leming]'s. He, as far as I know, is quite amiably inclined towards
me. Do let's all stamp on bye bye, bye the bye. I'd no idea people
said it, I mean des gens de connaissance, but have had some horrid
shocks this time in England.

It must be called the U Book, don't you think?

I go to Debo on Wednesday. I fell very ill after I saw you – no
voice at all & felt as if I might die. The sea air has cured me, but it
took days. [. . .]

What is the Midget up to? My belief is they were married when he
went to Clarence House for 2 hours.[2]

      Fondest love
          N

Have you seen a photograph of Townsend's mother? Very non-U I
thought.

[1] From Hamish Hamilton suggesting that Nancy's article 'The English Aristocracy' and Evelyn's
Open Letter should be published in a book, together with contributions from Peter Fleming
('Strix'), John Betjeman, Professor Ross and Christopher Sykes.
[2] Princess Margaret announced on 1 November 1955 her decision not to marry Peter Townsend.

19 October [1955]   Piers Court
                                                   Stinchcombe
                                                   Nr Dursley
                                                   Glos.

Dearest Nancy

Thank you for sending Hamilton's letter. I can't deal direct with a
man who, not knowing me at all, refers to me by my Christian name,
but I will send *you* a proof of my letter when I get one. At present
only a manuscript exists which I have sent to the *Encounter*. It is about
4,000 words long. Except that I expose you as a hallucinated communist agent there is nothing in it to hurt. I deal with heraldry, genealogy,
precedence, conception of 'gentleman', the finances of the aristocracy
and such important topics. Very little about verbal usage. That was
a minor issue in your article and I think it very morbid of your readers
to attach such importance to it. Professor Ross did not seem to me to
do much except borrow from Uncle Matthew and the old Society for
Pure English Tracts and to invent the expression 'non-U' which I

regard as vulgar in the extreme – like VD for venereal disease and PC for postcard. 'U Book' would be a dreadful title.

This is writing paper or letter paper. Single sheets are note paper. Pray note 'Glos' on the engraving (and always write the departments of France in full in future. No 'S et O'.)

All love
    Evelyn

21 October 1955   Edensor House
                                              Bakewell
                                              Derbyshire
Dearest Evelyn

Here's my answer, more or less (I've polished it up & also instead of *I agree with* most of what you say, have put *I am not prepared to argue with*). After all, once we get into the realms of right & wrong side of blankets ALL is speculation. Game & set over Fortinbras's reason for only 2 as you may admit.[1]

What title do you suggest? Do say, to the Mau-Mau H.Q.[2] whither I return on Monday for a few days.

I've made friends with the Priestleys.[3] *She* a beauty & *he* a duck. Lovely food.

I've NEVER in my LIFE put S & O or A.M.[4] on letters – what an awful idea. As bad as U – quite.

Fond love
    N

[1] In his Open Letter, Evelyn had disagreed with Nancy's contention that aristocratic families have only two offspring: 'Surely they have more children? Impotence and sodomy are socially O.K. but birth control is flagrantly middle-class.'
[2] Momo Marriott's house in Hill Street.
[3] J. B. Priestley (1894–1984). Novelist, dramatist and critic. Married in 1953 to the writer and archaeologist Jacquetta Hawkes.
[4] Short for 'Seine et Oise' and 'Alpes Maritimes'. Nancy regularly used these abbreviations in her correspondence (cf. her letter to Evelyn, 18 August 1946).

21 October 1955   Piers Court
                                              Stinchcombe
Darling Nancy

The editor of the *Encounter* has mistakenly sent me a letter written to Mr Weidenfeld.[1] He says: 'I have looked through our correspondence and I find that we have not promised the aristocracy series to anyone else. So you have first call – though, as I say, it is going to be many months before the series is anything like complete ... When we have the other articles in, we can then write to authors and tell them of our plans.'

It is a strange underworld you have led me into.

I have instructed Peters to make it plain that the *Encounter* have only first serial rights and are not empowered to make any arrangements about book publication. Perhaps you will do the same & also warn your friend Hamilton of these subversive jewish plots. Or is Hamilton also a Jew? I have heard it suggested.

Love
   E

[1] George Weidenfeld (1919–). Publisher. Created life peer in 1976.

21 October [1955]   Piers Court
                                                       Nr Dursley
                                                       Gloucestershire
Darling

Look. I have found some old note-paper with Glos. in full.

You will now have found my letter exposing the Kristol[1]–Weidenfeld plot. I thought it great impudence of Kristol to think he can arrange our publishing for us.

I think the book should have a pompous name 'An Enquiry into the identifiable characteristics of the English Aristocracy' or 'The Patrician Anatomy'. Something like that.[2]

Your letter of reply is not very honest about your red sympathies, is it? You call the *New Statesman* your 'Mag' and rejoice in every noxious word. Of course everyone will think that it is The Party which restrained you from publishing your Moscow travel-diary. Are you sure it is a good plan to print a reply? If there is anything in my article you think impolite, say and of course I will change it. I think you miss the point about putative parentage. I merely meant pedigrees were not infallible in attributing character, eg. noses. There are only about four shapes of nose. People say 'look there is the Fortinbras nose.' Rot, really.

I grieve deeply to learn that you like Priestley, but I am happy to say that your other new literary friend John Raymond has written well about Belloc in 'the Mag'.

Fond love
   Evelyn

I say do you think it proper when writing to me in public to refer to Spender as Stephen? I should never call him that. 'The Editor' or 'Stephen Spender' or Messrs Spender & Kristol. No?

[1] Irving Kristol (1920–2009). American author, co-founder and co-editor of *Encounter* 1953–8.
[2] *Noblesse Oblige: An Enquiry Into the Identifiable Characteristics of the English Aristocracy* (1956) was the title eventually chosen.

25 October 1955   40A Hill Street, WI

Darling Evelyn

How I have been shrieking! The PLOT – gunpowder – treason – PAPISTS getting their own medicine.

Listen love. I think you are quite right that I ought not to answer, but then you MUST modify your statement that I'm a communist agent.

It doesn't matter here where everybody knows it's a joke, but in Paris where I live these things are taken seriously. We are a bit too near les voisins [neighbours] – & no tank trap. See?

So, as you have said you'll do as I ask, I've withdrawn the reply, but you must also change your piece. You know I'm not a Communist Evelyn, now *don't* you *don't* you? So it's not quite fair to say it, in cold print.

You know why I loathe Americans & that it's because they *are* communists really in their way.

Think of me as a *Christian*.*

Love from
    N

* early, if you like.

All Souls [2 November] 1955   Piers Court
                                                     Stinchcombe

Dearest Nancy

I have cut out all reference to communism & attributed your class-war battle cry to your admiration for Lloyd George.

I haven't changed the 'Hon' bit because after all it was you who made the Hon joke public property, even if you didn't originate it. It will always be linked with your name, not with the Duchess or the Communist.

Is that satisfactory?

Fond love
    Evelyn

4 November 1955   7 rue Monsieur, VII

Darling Evelyn

Yes that's perfect. I know you can't tell the difference between Lloyd George & Stalin, but other people can.

I'm trying to write a paper on Saint Simon[1] – it's exceedingly difficult. So far I've merely plunged once more into the *Mémoires* which must, I suppose, be one of the great books of this world. I'd really forgotten how stunningly good they are.

Blissful to be back again. I enjoyed my visit, but physically it's too much for me, a visit to London – I think I'll never cross the channel again. Perhaps I'll take to a shawl.

John Raymond, whom I told of your approbation says: 'the Elder's approval has given a great lift to the spirits.'

I had sister Decca here for nearly a week. She is the same as ever, though Debo doesn't think so, & we had a very happy time. Diana Cooper came one day & when she had gone Decca said how beautiful Lady Corde Cooper is, Corde having been her name for our sister Diana!! Are you shrieking?

Much love
      N

My mother says the shape of this envelope is very non-U.
I *do* appreciate the Gloucestershire paper.

[1] 'The Great Little Duke', *New Statesman*, 3 December 1955.

19 November 1955   7 rue Monsieur, VII

Darling Evelyn

Are you alive? I have been buried for 3 weeks in an article on Saint-Simon, the most difficult thing I've ever done I think, & very brave to take it on! I hope it's more or less all right – I've got in one two nice teases anyway, & got my own back on Harold N[icolson] for saying that my *Pomp* was not history.

It all arose because I wrote to John Raymond & told him what you said about his Belloc article. Of course he trod on air 'the Elder's approval has given a great lift to the spirits' & immediately asked me for an article! (*N.S. & N.*)

I do love you being the Elder, & the fact that all those young men would give pages from Raymond or Cyril for one line from you, you old crusty-pots.

Madame de Pange, descended from a lady in waiting of M[arie]-A[ntoinette], also beheaded, has asked me to her son's wedding.

M. de Mun, whose name speaks for itself, told me that the culte for M-A is something quite new. I think I am forgiven but I shall have to watch my step.

I had Decca here for a week – unchanged and so sweet. Also her Romilly daughter[1] who is a beauty. I very much hope she'll send her here in a year or 2 to learn French & then I must find her a nice French husband (receipt for happiness).

I go a great deal to see them turning the film of which I did the

English dialogue. It will be one of the very best historical films – & *so* pretty to look at. It's like a Turkish bath or a railway journey, being in the studio. Nobody can get at one – such bliss.

With love from
    Nancy

[1] Constancia Romilly (1941–).

21 November 1955   Piers Court
                                              Stinchcombe
                                              Nr Dursley
                                              Glos.

Darling Nancy
    Pray note 'Glos' above.
    By the way here is a point. I knew a woman who could not bear to say 'W.C.' for the London postal district because of its indelicate associations and always said 'West Central'. Thus the wheel of gentility turned full cycle into aristocratic eschewal of abbreviations.
    Also I knew a woman who said 'Edgar Allan Po-ee'.
    Talk of indelicacy. Boots's conc, no chick, has decided she wants a baby and all the doctors in Kent are making excavations to clear the way for this happy event.[1] Boots displays the debris they remove. But conc will not reveal whom she has designated as father.
    Your Mr Raymond got sharply rebuked by a typical *New Statesman* reader for his exercise on Belloc. I shall look out eagerly for your St Simon article. Are you not now rather glad you decided not to repudiate the *New Statesman*?
    I think my anti U article will fall flat because it needs to be read line by line with yours. I have heard no more of the Jewish plot for publication.
    I went to London for a night last week. You know I really can't bear Randolph any more. He makes White's uninhabitable & has become just like Lord Portarlington sitting there all day & buttonholing. He also constantly insults Clarissa in print, which comes very ill from him who with Cooper was the chief architect of her misalliance. I went to Momo's to – oh look here's another bit of pre *Encounter* paper turned up[2] – to Momo's to meet Clare Luce. She asked Randolph too who immediately began hectoring her about American policy in Italy. Well no one is better equipped than Clare to deal with hostile reporters and the whole luncheon instead of being a happy reunion of old friends became a press conference with Clare giving long, detailed, entirely satisfactory, patient, and utterly boring answers to his cross-examination.
    I went to the Stanley Spencer[3] exhibition with Honks but she

couldn't see the point of it, so that was spoiled. So the only good part of my chilly expedition was the gruesome account of conc's womb.

Have you any plans for February? I must go somewhere warm, not necessarily torrid, if possible free of Americans. Impossible to find.

I presume your Saint Simon is the socialist count not the courtier duke.

Debo has taken to writing to me.

Fond love
    Evelyn

[1] Barbara Connolly was in hospital for an operation to remove fibroids.
[2] The writing-paper heading had 'Gloucestershire' printed in full.
[3] Stanley Spencer (1891–1959). A retrospective of his work was being held at the Tate Gallery.

23 November 1955   7 rue Monsieur, VII

Darling Evelyn
    Even Winston always puts in the Spencer to avoid W.C. I always think it's rather common of him – his American blood no doubt. But even I wouldn't care for the initials of an old neighbour of ours V.D.

I wrote to Decca & said I'm doing Saint Simon – mine, not yours, but she won't see the joke I fear. She's certainly never heard of the Duke.

Can one find anywhere warm in Europe in Feb? I don't believe it. I would love to go away then, but don't know that I ought to as I've earned no money this year, except for the film, & I'm trying to economise. When I have got £100 000 I shall stop worrying but for that I must write some more books. If I could be sure to die at 3 score years & 10 I've really got enough to last me but nowadays everybody seems to live to 100.

Jeanne Stourton[1] has just telephoned – very disappointing, I can't see her as I'm all the time in the film studios. Do tell her I was sad if you see her.

Randolph, to me, is simply a typical Englishman, one of the reasons why I live here. I do value politeness more & more. Mrs Luce sounds hell, how can you like her?

Don't you think Scottish & Briton for Scotchman & Englishman are very non-U? I'm going to say so. I'm slightly adding to my piece.

I toy with the idea of going to live at Versailles. Paris is so full of motors now one can't go for a walk because impossible to cross the roads.

Love from
    N

I've put a footnote to cheers, saying 'see P. 40 *Men at Arms*[2] but Mr Crouchback was a saint & we can't all be so wonderful'.
Has Jeanne Stourton written books? She talked in a confraternal way I thought – felt I ought to know.
Is she married? Who to?
I mean to whom.

[1] Jeanne Stourton (1913–87). Married to 6th Baron Camoys in 1938.
[2] ' "Here's how," said the major.
"Here's how," said the mousy wife.
"Here's how," said Mr Crouchback with complete serenity.
But Guy could only manage an embarrassed grunt.'
    Men at Arms (Chapman & Hall, 1952), p. 40.

24 December 1955   7 rue Monsieur, VII

Darling Evelyn
    Wrong as usual. My Christmas present to myself is a Baskerville Bible (you wouldn't be allowed it of course, poor you) brought over by the Sutros. Scene at the customs: 'Et ce paquet, Monsieur?' 'Il s'agit, Monsieur, de la Sainte Bible.' 'Bon – bon – allez-y.'[1]
    Your *Encounter* funnier than I'd remembered, I loved it. I'm deeply involved with a Mr de Marris who sends me volumes by registered post every day to prove that *he* fought at Hastings & wants to be added to Malet & Co. But my anonymous mentor, while aware of his claim won't allow it. Yesterday another registered packet saying he's going to write & complain to YOU. He evidently thinks I bow to all your decisions in life. Well, I do, really.
    Here are some cards for the collector – I daresay she has stopped by now, however. Don't let her write – I'm getting very tired of Our Queen's face. The turkey man, giving Marie the 2 she had ordered, had marked them La Reine Elizabeth. He said he couldn't remember my name. I've got a dinner of 18, Boxing Day, a very odd mixture of old Counts & Princesses, young *NS & N* chaps 4 in number, the history master at Radley whom they are bringing, Sutros, Daisy Fellowes, Gulbenkian's daughter[2] recently cut off with only 30 million pounds, etc. I'm rather nervous, such an odd mixture. Said that before – it's the procession which is distracting me. As always on Christmas Eve in Paris there is a literal procession of men delivering presents – already this afternoon I've had orchids carnations roses, 2 scarves a pencil marrons glacés, sweets a bag a bottle of scent & a book. French chaps may not be very good at politics but they are a whizz at Christmas presents.
    Marie got out her best apron this morning, in preparation & ever since the procession began has been half disapproving & half pleased 'C'est pour une fortune –!'[3] She's awfully like a Nanny.

I saw Brian How[ard]. Rich, but not long for this world I guess. He has left all to Sam.[4] What a lot of lower-class buggers are going to be the millionaires of the future. I suppose they'll all marry & have 8 children like you say Lords do.

Happy Christmas – lucky 1956.

Love
   N

Am I allowed to say blissful 1955? Probably not, owing to floods in America or train accidents at home.

P.S. U-talk. I'm adding as non-U Scottish & (specially) British for U-*Scotch* & *English*? Don't you agree? When did that vile Scottish begin? Before I wrote *H. Fling* because I remember Thornton Butterworth changed all my Scotch into it & in those days one put up with such things. Since, when I have complained to Jamie he says it's not worth it for the thousands of letters we should get. However he has consented this time. In *Pomp* I got by with one Scotch, to my delight.

[1] 'And this parcel, sir?' 'It contains the Holy Bible.' 'All right, all right, go on through then!'
[2] Rita Gulbenkian; married to her father's secretary Kvork Essayan.
[3] 'It's a fortune's worth!'
[4] Brian Howard's companion of his declining years. 'Sam' died in 1958 and Howard committed suicide three weeks later.

29 December [1955]   Piers Court
                                                Stinchcombe
Darling Nancy

My poor spastic Hatty is not able to express herself. I can assure you that the copy of *Uncle Tom's Cabin* which Handy sent her at your order, caused deep joy. Also the cards you sent Margaret. Thank you thank you.

I don't suppose you see *Punch*. I enclose an example of the banal by-products of your communist tract.[1] We have scotched the jewish plot, but we must watch out for 'Hamish Hamilton' who may wish to adulterate our contributions with trash of this kind.

Scotch, Scottish, Scots – you really must look up the history of these terms in the Oxford dictionary (incidentally scholars like Ronnie Knox think it barbarous to speak of that work other than as 'Murray's').

'Britain' can only be used of these islands in Roman times. 'Great Britain' or 'the United Kingdom' in modern age. 'British' is the only possible adjective in certain rare cases. You can't say 'Great British' or 'United-Kingdomly'.

But have a care you do not step outside the limits of polite conversation into those of the King's English. That is the study of a life time and it is too late for you to start. The charm of your writing depends on your refusal to recognize a distinction between girlish chatter & literary language. You will be lost if you fall into pedantry. Stick to pillow cases v. pillow slips.

Have you seen Eric Siepmann's autobiography?[2] I roared. He thinks Col. is a jew. Is *he*? I mean Siepmann.

Fond love
Evelyn

[1] Paul Dehn, 'A Woman of a Certain Class', a mocking article on 'U' and 'Non-U'. *Punch*, 28 December 1955.
[2] *Confessions of a Nihilist* (1955).

2 January 1956   7 rue Monsieur, VII

Darling Evelyn

Faithful of you to send the *Punch* which indeed I hadn't seen. But I *screamed* with laughter – didn't you? I should have thought it would enhance our anthology?

I don't care what you say about Scottish & British. The fact is they are non-U, & when I was a child nobody thought of saying them.

Yes I greatly enjoyed 'old Siep's' book, though he might have been nicer about Prod to whom he was God. Is he a Jew? I shouldn't think so. (The Colonel, by the way, is a Roman Catholic like you, the Pope & Mrs Clare Luce.)

I say old Willie has capped it, in the *Sunday Times*. Can't quite see why if the young men in the book are what he says. I've never understood about this Amis.[1] Would I enjoy it? No.

I did have a lovely Christmas party – 14 to dinner including 4 young English intellectuals (*N.S. & N*) who livened the whole thing up tremendously. We played charades & I wish you could have seen Violet Trefusis (Cleopatra) being carried in a carpet to the bed of Anthony (John Sutro).

I've reviewed Mrs Ham's book[2] for *NS & N*. Do I write so badly? Oh dear & you don't know how I try. Not as badly as Mr Steegmuller[3] I hope. I've been greatly discouraged by the reviews that book has received – shows that there's no point in taking trouble as everything counts the same to English critics.

Oh dear – what can ONE write now? I need another best seller & then shall be able to live on my income (I've saved up £40 000, are you impressed?)

Much love, Happy New Year, from
Nancy

I was afraid you would say *Uncle Tom* is a Communist tract. I had a very well-expressed letter from Hatty.

[1] *Lucky Jim* (1955) by Kingsley Amis had been chosen by Somerset Maugham as one of his 'Books of the Year'. 'Mr Kingsley Amis is so talented, his observation is so keen, that you cannot fail to be convinced that the young men he so brilliantly describes truly represent the class with which his novel is concerned . . . They have no manners, and are woefully unable to deal with any social predicament. Their idea of celebration is to go to a public house and drink six beers. They are mean, malicious and envious . . . They are scum.' *Sunday Times*, 25 December 1955.
[2] *Letters from Madame de Sévigné*, selected and translated by Violet Hammersley (1956).
[3] Francis Steegmuller, author of *La Grande Mademoiselle* (1955).

[January 1956]   Piers Court
[postcard]   Stinchcombe

Col can't be a Roman Catholic. He didn't know what O.P. meant after a clergyman's name.

I thought the *Punch* article awful. I trust you, who know H. Hamilton, to protect us against such intrusions.

Do you regard J. Sutro as a young intellectual? I know you think his wife the best dressed woman.

I have been in debt always since 1922. It is clever of you to have saved.

E

3 January 1956   Piers Court
                                                   Stinchcombe
Darling Nancy

It was loyal and sweet of you to commend poor old Crouchback to the readers of the *Sunday Times*.

You must be very much gratified at the success of the Party in the frog elections.

Isn't it odd of Osbert Sitwell to accept a CBE? A C.H. would have been more suitable.

O black and putrid 1956.

E

Some Television woman has just telephoned to say will I perform *with you* in London. I presume it is a bluff when she says you will be there? Anyway I don't the least want to do it but would do so as an act of unselfish love to you if for any reason you want it done.

8 January 1956   7 rue Monsieur, VII

Well the Colonel may not know about OP (I thought it meant out of print) but if he had been willing to vote against the Church schools he would be in Parliament now. His *second de liste*, who ratted on them

2 days before the election campaign began, got in. I daresay you & the Pope would have stood as firm, but *would Mrs Clare Luce?*

What is OP? You have whetted our curiosity now. Does one have to know it to get into heaven? Marie, who plods off to Church at 7 in this nasty dark weather, doesn't know – will she go to Hell? I don't worry a bit, for either of them. As M-Antoinette said, when she refused to see a (republican) priest 'God in his mercy will be my support.' (The actress, until I stopped her, said 'God in his mercy has my support.')

I've been reading Bagehot, *The Eng: Cons:*, it is lovely stuff. Some ass in some paper went for me over sensible men of ample means. I thought it came out of Bagehot which I can't have read since I was 16 or so – got hold of a copy & sure enough. I was pleased that my memory, usually so poor, should have played up for once.

A little affection – not much love
   N

11 January [1956]   Piers Court
                                                         Stinchcombe
Dearest Nancy

I am sorry to learn that Col. has lost his seat but I am glad that it should be in such a good cause. Where will he wear his beautiful dark suit now, unless at mass on Sundays? My brother-in-law has been turned down at Taunton for his Faith.

O.P. = Ordinis predicatorum = of the Order of Preachers = the correct address of a Dominican friar. Col revealed his ignorance in the case of Couturier.

I notice Carlyle wrote 'Scotchmen'. It was neither upper nor lower class, simply a period use. Of course Scotchmen nowadays make a thing of it – part of the regional revival we find so tiresome.

You must try & love me again.

I have collected a great deal of interesting information about fish-knives for inclusion in your book. Please insist that there is no note thanking Kristol & Co for 'permission' to reprint. Their permission is not required and we caught them trying to sell what was not their property to another Jew. Remember?

Saw Honks at Mells last Sunday – in high spirits. I played Scrabble much against my will with Ronnie Knox & much to my surprise won all the time. He kept the score. Every hand it was 50 to me, 12 to him. At the end, totting up, he said with feigned surprise 'You seem to have beaten me.' 'I had all the luck.' 'Yes, you are 7 ahead.' Don't tell Col. It may shake his faith.

Teresa, my eldest daughter, is coming out in London this summer. Expense ghastly. How can I save £40,000?

Graham Greene recommended a pornographic book[1] in the *Sunday Times*. I mean the sort of book you go to jug for.

Robin Campbell's dreadful son has been trying to make love to my Margaret.

I am glad you have not heard of Mr Kingsley Amis. *Not* a worthy man.

Love
    E

[1] Vladimir Nabokov, *Lolita* (1955).

---

18 January 1956   7 rue Monsieur, VII

Darling Evelyn

Enclosed which I don't want back, answers you. It's true he said, but too late, don't put an exact figure, say about a third.[1] I've had an awful time with Mr de Marris as you may gather – have been longing to put the old boy in & have at last melted Unicorn's stony heart. Hope not too late.

Debo, hearing that Col is looking for work asks if he'd like to go there as under keeper – £6.10 & a suit. He doesn't need a suit as you know (it's *lovely* the Gloucestershire – Glos. – one) but jumps at the job because, he says, he has read *Lady Chatterley*.[2]

Rather jealous about Villiers blood because I so adore Steenie.[3] But my old cousin B. Russell said 'our brains come from the same source.' He *has* Villiers blood but didn't mean that.

I read your letter to the Col. You *couldn't* shake his faith.

I've just lunched chez Jebb with Monty. He loves me. He's off to stay with your friend Tito – then the Pope – then Franco. I said Franco will give you a bull fight like he did my brother in law Sir Oswald. Monty didn't quite like it – 'of course mind you I'm not going in an official capacity'.

I had a very funny letter from a Canadian *admiratrice* saying that she, & everybody in her village, are outraged by your letter to me in *Encounter* & wanted me to know it. Though interlarded, she says, with loving expressions, it has a nasty sneering tone & your disclosures (my grand-father's 1902 peerage I suppose) at the end are most indelicate. I shrieked.

Have you seen Osbert's illustrations?[4] I long for them.

I'm going to Roquebrune 13th Feb, in case you'll be sunning in those parts at all? It's partly to escape Marie-Laure [de Noailles]'s party which couldn't cost less (for a dress) than £100. Not worth it if like me you can't keep awake. But I suppose you're saving up for your own ball.

Much love
    Nancy

[1] Nancy enclosed a letter, that has not survived, from Sir Iain Moncreiffe of that Ilk (1919–85), a leading expert on heraldry and genealogy, Unicorn Pursuivant of Arms, which supported her claim that the families of 382 peers had borne arms in the direct male line since before 1485.
[2] D. H. Lawrence's novel, not published in Britain until 1960, had long been available in foreign editions.
[3] Nickname given to George Villiers, 1st Duke of Buckingham, by James I.
[4] Osbert Lancaster illustrated *Noblesse Oblige*.

9 March 1956   7 rue Monsieur, VII

Darling Evelyn

[. . .] I hope you've been asked to the lecture at the Wop embassy on: U and Non-U nell'italiano parlato. My Dutch translator writes to say that no one there talks of anything else, and shall he call the Hons' cupboard the Cave of the Nobles? Do you love Osbert's pictures? What a feast it's going to be for those reviewers who loathe ONE.

As I've begun a book[1] (dull) any excuse not to get on is eagerly snatched & I've been buried in *My Dear Duchess*.[2] It's very badly edited. For instance, 'Viscountess V' is Lady Sydney (Vss Viper). The editor puts Lady Valentia. Poor Lady Waldegrave is identified for *no reason at all* with one 'Maria' whose real name ½ an hour at the L[ondon] Library would easily reveal.

The letters are no more amusing than the Stanley ones & if I were C & Hall I'd reprint those, or a boiling down of the 2 vols.

Mrs Woodham Smith[3] gave a lecture (first class) yesterday. She is small & waspish & looks 100, I *greatly* took to her. Reminiscent of Diana Spearman. A lady. She has a husband who sees to the business side. I'm trying to find out if Colette's widower would like to marry me – he's a whizz at that, business I mean, just what I need.

I'm giving a huge party for Heywood. It seems the British Council is flooded with telephone calls from intellectuals saying oo ees Aywood Eel? I'm sure they think he's a sort of Godot.[4] He comes over the same day as the Q Mother – rather nice if they got into each other's skins like *Vice Versa*.[5]

Mrs Woodham Smith gave an awful account of England 'everybody moving into smaller houses' & throwing away their family archives. What has come over them all?

Do write, it's an age.

Love from
    Nancy

At that moment in comes a German friend of mine – 'come to say good-bye, tomorrow I go into La Trappe.' Rather terrific –!

[1] *Voltaire in Love* (1957).
[2] *My Dear Duchess: Social and Political Letters to the Duchess of Manchester 1858–69* edited by A. L. Kennedy (1956).

[3] Cecil FitzGerald (1896–1977). Biographer and historian whose books include *Florence Nightingale* (1950) and *The Reason Why* (1953). Married George Woodham-Smith in 1928.
[4] Samuel Beckett's influential play was first staged in England in 1955.
[5] F. Anstey, *Vice Versa or A Lesson to Fathers* (1882). A novel in which a father and his schoolboy son change places.

12 March 1956   Piers Court
                                                     Stinchcombe
Darling,

[. . .] The English are convalescent from their U fever. I think H. Hamilton's little venture will fall flat. I haven't seen O. Lancaster's illustrations. I don't think very highly of his talents in general.

Diane [Abdy] has been unconscious for 10 days. Her son Valentine is probably lame for life. All this the result of a motor accident. One is in hospital in Bristol, the other in Truro. Poor Bertie flits distractedly between the two beds.

In another accident Moggy's[1] second son (his first injured his throat so badly that he wears a leather collar & whispers) has hurt himself less badly; his companion dead.

I saw Colette's 'husband' at Monte Carlo. He is quite pretty. Greek I think.

I hope you are keeping your savings in dollars. Francs and pounds are said by those that possess them to be very shaky.

Has Col obtained light, dignified and remunerative work? They require a French master at my son's preparatory school in Somerset. Shall I put in a word for him? He might have to take a new name to convince parents he is not Polish.

Have you seen Claud Cockburn's very dishonest book?[2] My cousin alas.

I went to *Waiting for Godot* but I went with Daphne so we got there rather tight for the second act only. Couldn't make head or tail of it.

The *Sunday Times* say you are writing a Kinsey report on the sex life of Voltaire. I look forward eagerly to it.

I blush to confess I greatly enjoyed the American life or rather death of Lady Mendl.[3]

I hope to keep Low Week at Chantilly. That is the week after Easter Week in case you don't know.

When you ask of the English 'what has come over them all?' you are like Queen M. Antoinette. There has been a revolution here. Your sans culottes have triumphed. You must try & grasp this fact.

Lady Pam has a grand new word, 'dedicated'. She can only read dedicated writers. You and I are not dedicated.

Re La Trappe. Glad you know some Christians. Pity it had to be a Hun.

Fondest love
    Evelyn

[1] Hon. Imogen Grenfell (1905–69). Married 6th Viscount Gage in 1931. Their second son Henry was 21 years old.
[2] *In Time of Trouble* (1956), a first volume of autobiography.
[3] Ludwig Bemelmans, *To the One I Love the Best* (1955), an account of his friendship with Elsie de Wolfe, the American actress and interior decorator married to Sir Charles Mendl.

19 March 1956   7 rue Monsieur, VII

Darling Evelyn

Do read this. I think it one of the very best novels[1] I ever read & I believe you will too. Mrs Bedford is here a great deal – I haven't seen her since reading her book but I don't doubt it is partly autobiographical.

Keenly waiting for Low Week.

Love
     N

Mrs B can't get it published in America because 'there is no interest in Germany before 1914'!!!!

I've just spoken to a great friend of Mrs B – it seems the book is largely autobiographical the uncle actually died of ill treatment – etc etc. Will tell when I see you.

[1] Sybille Bedford, *A Legacy* (1956).

22 March 1956   Piers Court
                                                          Stinchcombe

Dearest Nancy

I am hugely grateful to you for sending me *A Legacy*. I read it straight through with intense pleasure. For the first half – up to the marriage of Jules & Mélanie – I was in full agreement 'one of the best novels I ever read' as you say. After that I found a slight falling off, as though the writer had suddenly taken a stiff dose of Henry James, particularly in the long talks between Sarah & Caroline. Also I think it was clumsy to have any of the narrative in the first person. The daughter relates things she cannot possibly ever have known as though she were an eye witness. But these are small blemishes. What a brilliant plot! How grim the military school incident! How intensely funny the Jewish household & Gottlieb and the monkeys and the christenings! Clara is a failure half the time, I think. The writer doesn't know much about Catholicism. 'Is it not insisting on error, this making images of what is itself illusion' could only be said by a sort of bogus theosophist (p. 188) and (p. 354) 'It is presumption even to talk of being saved' by a despairing Calvinist. The English is slightly odd in places. 'Merz's' is always written instead of 'Merzes' as the plural of Merz.

I wondered for a time who this brilliant 'Mrs Bedford' could be. A cosmopolitan military man, plainly, with a knowledge of parliamentary government and popular journalism, a dislike for Prussians, a liking for Jews, a belief that everyone speaks French in the home . . . Then, of course, it came to me. Good old Col. He *has* employed his retirement well. Do give him my genuine homage.

Best love
    Evelyn

25 March 1956   7 rue Monsieur, VII

Darling Evelyn
    Colonel Bedford is delighted with your praise – I've never heard such a shriek. Like us he greatly admires the book, & like you cared for it less after the arrival of Caroline. He says he is a conservative character & had got used to Mélanie.
    I am much less critical & all seemed perfect to me, I do hope those idiotic critics will do their bit. I think, to be fair, that terribly as they over praise 2nd class books, they do pounce with relief on good stuff when they see it. I spoke of *A Legacy* to John Raymond who is here & he said at once that he had heard of it from a colleague on *NS & N* who is going to praise it highly.
    The real Mrs Bedford is a small, fair, intensely shy woman, about 40 I suppose, half German. There is something very *sweet* about her, but never would you suspect talent & when a mutual friend sent me the book I dreaded having to read enough to be able to comment. You know! Of course I was immobilised for days.
    I've just telephoned to John Raymond who said 'it's only a quarter past you know' & then said 'oh I'm sorry, I thought you were somebody I'm going to Church with –' Is he a co religionist of yours? I do like him so much, & so would you.
    Well I live for Low Week. If my telephone is cut off (I must begin to work) please send a word. I need you.

Love
  N

[March 1956]   Piers Court
                                                     Stinchcombe
Darling Nancy
    I have written a tiny warm notice of Col's classic for the *Spectator*.[1]
    I come in the aeroplane they call the Epicure on April 10th and go straight to Chantilly. Do you visit there? I may, if Honks encourages

it, bring my 13 year old daughter[2] who is in need of refinement. Will you be able to tear away from Voltaire's sex life to accompany us sight-seeing?

Your chum N. Spain has very conveniently libelled me[3] and I hope for a great sum of tax-free damages.

Interesting about Mr Raymond going to church. I thought I had detected a healthy note in some of his recent utterances.

Do you see *Spectator* or shall I send a copy?

My eldest daughter is coming out and there is horrible talk of balls & such fripperies. Will you come to her ball at the beginning of July – in a tent in Kensington shared with Angela Antrim and Rose Baring. Well, no, of course not but if you're in London then come to dinner & just look in. July 5.

All they speak of in London is Randolph's bad behaviour – not very new.

Love
    E

[1] Evelyn criticised the technical shortcomings of *A Legacy* but welcomed it as 'a book of entirely delicious quality' (*Spectator*, 13 April 1956). Sybille Bedford was 'madly pleased by Faithful Evelyn' and wrote to Nancy: 'As usual, he writes like an angel. Practically every line reconciles one to spending the rest of one's writing life tossed in the fiction bins.'
[2] Margaret.
[3] Nancy Spain, book critic for the *Daily Express*, had said in an article that the sale of Evelyn's books were dwarfed by those of his brother Alec. Evelyn had provoked the attack by saying that reviews in the Beaverbrook press had no influence on sales.

30 March 1956   7 rue Monsieur, VII

Darling Evelyn

You are a faithful old thing to do that. I got my dear Mrs Arthur onto a sofa & forced her to tell all about Mrs B. The fact is it is all autobiographical except the plot – the uncle was murdered at that charming establishment. The daughter of Mélanie lives here, I know her quite well. The Merzes are Herz, the great friends in the past of such as Goethe, who paid for the translation of Shakespeare etc. Mrs B. herself, as in the book, was brought up until 12 by Jules who then died. Flighty but literate English mother & Mrs B uncertain whose child she really is.

I can get the *Spectator* very easily.

I saw Lady Honks & cadged an invitation for Low Week. Any excuse to down tools is good enough for me! But I die for *you*.

I hear James Pope-Hennessy[1] is now Sir Oswald's right-hand woman. How somehow sinister – do you think he composes the Death List?

You are lucky to be libelled. One can't be here 'Elle écrit des romans faciles et mêne une vie qui l'est tout autant' is keenly sold by Heywood

& Handy who, I hear, *press* it upon the customers (Dumaine).[2]

What did dear Nancy say? She telephoned the other day & said something about being in trouble with you, but I thought it was old Roman fordery again.

No dearest I can't go to a ball even for you. Ce n'est plus de mon âge[3] & I've no wish to make a guy of myself.

So Low Week – Col will long to see you.

Fond love
    N

[1] James Pope-Hennessy (1916–74). Author of literary biographies and of *Queen Mary* (1959). His boyfriend, Len Adams, was a supporter of Sir Oswald Mosley.
[2] Jacques Dumaine, head of protocol at the French Foreign Office, had written in his diaries, *Quai d'Orsay 1945–51*, that Nancy 'writes fanciful novels and leads an equally frivolous life'.
[3] I'm no longer of an age.

24 April 1956   Piers Court
                                          Stinchcombe

Dearest Nancy

The Book of Shame[1] has arrived with Lancaster's crude & careless sketches. I saw the artist on my way through London, got up as a popinjay and looking supremely ridiculous.

Thank you very much for asking Margaret & me to your whisky party. One of the ladies made advances to her but since it was a lady this did not put undesirable thoughts into her head. I thought the man you called 'Beachcomber'[2] extremely sinister.

Someone named Davenport[3] has written me a long letter about 'Mrs Bedford' whom he claims to know. He accuses her of unnatural vice & says she wrote an unpublishable treatise on Brian Howard.

Was it chez Col that I saw some very pretty silver gilt tea-spoons? Are they English by Edward Fennel circa 1820? If so would he like me to give him a pair of sugar-tongs which match? I found them in a shop. Vine pattern. We thought it jolly decent of Col to ask us to his nest and would like to show our love & gratitude. But perhaps I have confused his spoons with someone else's whom we visited in Paris.

It is nice to be in a country where communists are so rare that people turn out to stare at them. And the porters do not play cards in the National Railways.

Susan Mary [Patten] gave a delightful dinner party and Meg & Mrs Pol Roger acted to us.

O the shame of the Book of Shame.

Love
    Evelyn

[1] *Noblesse Oblige.*
[2] Sanford Shanley; highly cultivated American for whom Nancy made an exception and whom she regarded as a friend.
[3] John Davenport (d.1966). Literary critic for the *Observer* and the *Spectator*.

26 April 1956   7 rue Monsieur, VII

Darling Evelyn

How you do carry on about the Book of Shame. It (the book) is very funny indeed.

You'll turn that poor child into a Kitty Giles who, if anybody speaks politely to her, thinks they are making advances & ripostes with I love my husband. I thought Margaret had a nice little Victorian look – Beachcomber whom I've just been to *Bérénice* with (matinée for kids, nobody over 8 except ONE) thought her very pretty so look out.

The Colonel loves presents more than anybody I know, both giving & receiving. He *would* be pleased – yes he has silver gilt spoons c 1820 didn't know they were English. How observant you are. I shan't tell him, it must be a surprise.

How odd about Mr Davenport. He was the other person who gave *A Legacy* a good review. I'd give a lot to read the treatise on Brian.

A man from *Picture Post* came about the B of Shame. He said he had done you & you'd been most exceedingly amiable, which of course was nice for him only bad for trade. Fact is the public looks upon you now as the Rev: Brontë & is fearfully disappointed if you don't rush at journalists with a poker. I liked this chap.

I suppose you'll be taking part in the Cambridge Union's debate – This House wishes to be U (or non-U, I forget). Nancy Spain is speaking. Of course all the odium of the B of S will fall upon me & you'll all cash in. I didn't know they were going to say edited by, nor did I edit it, nor even see it in proof (except my piece). Rather naughty I think. Never mind.

I've taken a room at Torcello from 24 May, to work. Chucked it here working I mean, it simply gets on my nerves to try.

Oh dear, you do hate the human race. It can't be quite right.

Love from
    Nancy

3 May 1956   7 rue Monsieur, VII

Darling Evelyn

He'll be *so* pleased you can't imagine. I wonder whether Malcolm Bullock would bring them, he comes for Whit – such a small smuggle. Could be arranged via Heywood & Hill & Handy & Sydes. I think if the tongs were left with them they would surely find a friendly pocket. I'll write & explain shall I, and write to Sir Malcolm.

Do you receive Shame letters? I do. One said Bert & Reggie (see my essay) are non-U names. Another that he the writer is descended from A the Great's sister! & thanks me for my splendid work on behalf of his class. Furious Scotch ones, whom I refer to Ld MACaulay.

Did you shriek at my Mr Raymond's review of Winston's book. *Gallipoli*[1] is a masterpiece have you read it? (You would have made a masterpiece of it, too. Different.)

Torcello is said to be utterly deserted, best food in Europe. Can *both* be true? I've got a great desire for silence, heat & hard work. Hemingway wrote a book there. I leave on the 24th.

If Malcolm says he *will* perhaps better have the tongs sent to his club – Turf? – as the shop is capable of losing things.

Much love
     N

[1] By Alan Moorehead (1956).

Whitlow Week [May] 1956   Chez M. Cipriani
                                                Torcello
                                                Venice
Darling Evelyn

Your piece in the *S Times*[1] – how I shrieked. How it makes me die for your Mémoires. Do let's have them soon.

I am in great comfort here & working well. But sometimes I feel rather sorry for Napoleon & Makarios – I haven't even got an honest English knight to tease. That belfry Ruskin describes the view from is permanently locked up. *Cloches, cloches, divers reproches*, begin at 6 AM & go on intermittently all day. Just now they were reproaching like mad so I dashed to the belfry – as locked as ever. Is this not rather sinister?

The only other people in the hotel are a pair of lovers. They look at me with deep distrust – & have all meals in their room. Last night they entertained a mystery guest who came in a motor boat & rushed upstairs & thereafter one heard bottles clanking in ice. Rather jolly, as Debo would say.

Debo is in love with Daphne's husband.[2] I think we shall soon be regretting the reign of Good King Aly if you ask me.

The beauty of what I see from my balcony is really indescribable.

Between 2 boats there is a flood of Americans dangling deaf-aids & asking each other where they live in America. What difference can it make? The word duodenal recurs. I mingle with them, hating. But today I ran into François Valéry[3] who had come to see the Black Madonna, which makes it a day of note.

With great difficulty I've settled to my book & now I see the way clear. But it has been a struggle.

Do write.

Love from
N

I'm still enjoying the U jokes – but only, I am assured, because at a distance. I loved Prof Ross's letter[4] in *S. Times*. But we shall get quite a nice lot of lovely money it seems?

---

[1] 'Lesson of the Master', a description of Evelyn's two encounters with Max Beerbohm. *Sunday Times*, 27 May 1956.

[2] Alexander (Xan) Fielding (1918–91). Adventurous and romantic wartime secret agent. Author of *Hide and Seek* (1954), an account of his time with the Cretan Resistance, and *One Man and His Time* (1990). Married to Daphne, Marchioness of Bath, 1953–78, and to Agnes (Magouche) Phillips.

[3] François Valéry (1916–96). Son of the poet Paul Valéry. Diplomat who so loved Paris that he managed never to be posted abroad.

[4] Alan S. C. Ross had written to complain that several reviews of *Noblesse Oblige* had described a Finnish journal as an odd place to publish his article on 'U' and 'Non-U'. 'Sentences such as: "... published in, of all places, Finland ..." may well hurt the feelings in that country.' *Sunday Times*, 27 May 1956.

---

7 June [1956]   Piers Court
                                                        Stinchcombe
Darling Nancy

O the horrors of U. In this morning's *Times* the entire Burmese cabinet have adopted this damnable prefix.

It is clever of you to be able to work. My life is greatly disturbed by Teresa's London début and Laura's waiting attendance on her. Also by people coming to see the house, which I have put up for sale. But I look forward greatly to finding a new one if I sell this. Castle preferred, 50 rooms 50 acres a water fall £5000. It should not be difficult to find.

I can't blame Debo for falling in love with Mr Xan. I am a little in love with him myself. But it will make her very unpopular if she robs Daphne.

I say do you in your large literary circle know of a Maurice Baring, male or female? Have Honks & I ever spoken to you of Maria Pasqua, the grandmother of a Downside monk[1] who in the 1860s was the most popular child model (Trilby not mannequin) in Paris and was purchased from her father by an eccentric English Countess of Noailles, married to an aged, dull Norfolk squireen, a cousin of [Duff] Cooper's? It is a most moving story of Beauty in captivity, very sad & full of authentic, bizarre detail. Not a plot for you or me, but it could be made a great work of art by someone. Who? All the documents are available & the daughter's (monk's mother) not quite good enough attempt at writing them up. If you think of anyone, do tell me.

Your Mr Raymond has been behaving oddly, trying to pick up my 17 year old niece[2] in London and telephoning to her from a neighbouring public house. He also wrote improperly of John Evelyn. Is he a friend of Mr Beachcomber? I bet he is.

Tony Powell has accepted a CBE. No sour grapes but I think it very WRONG that politicians should treat writers as second grade civil servants. Osbert Sitwell opened the breach by accepting this degrading decoration. I trust you will stand out for CH or Dame.

I went to stay in the lowlands of Scotland – *very* beautiful. They talked of U there. I stopped on the road home with socialist jews at Cambridge. U again. There was a song, do you remember, 'And you know darn well that it's U again.'

Laura and Teresa are here for a few days playing a kind of patience with debutantes' names fitting them into dinner parties for balls.

Love
    Evelyn

[1] Father Aelred Watkin; he was Auberon Waugh's housemaster.
[2] Annie Grant (d.1984). Married in 1958 to Sir Ian Fraser, chairman of Rolls-Royce 1971–80.

11 June 1956   Torcello

Darling Evelyn

Can you get over them going *on* with U? I mean really we've had enough – even I have & you know how one loves one's own jokes. As we are on the subject the best was: I'm dancing with tears in my eyes 'cos the girl in my arms isn't U.

Well I'm rather cross with John Raymond – he seems to love & admire that odious crook Harcourt Smith.[1] But I don't see that he can be blamed for courting your niece? At least it's not your nephew & that in itself is rather rare.

If Lady Honks has told me about this peasant girl once she has 16 times. *Enough*. Harcourt Smith might do it, why not?[2]

Beachcomber is turning up here next week & told a mutual friend you said he was a killer & instead of shrieking the friend said 'well don't tell *him*, you will drive him right off his rocker if you do. You know what Americans ARE.' The fact is he's a gentle creature but like all of them rather insane.

The bliss of this place is beyond words. On a wet day, like today, there are arcades round the 2 churches for one's walk. The churches themselves you know from Ruskin. Then the island is like the work of every Impressionist painter rolled into one & painting in heaven.

The hotel is like staying in a millionaire's house with the host away. I'm the only person here they make their money at luncheon & tea (when one is working – & by lunching early one escapes the crowd). Then by 6 p.m. the island is empty & at dinner time there are 5 excellent waiters waiting on ONE. Only *you're* not to come here because you'd be unkind to Gastone the head waiter who is a *dear*. And you'd find some obscure detail to complain about – I know you.

Don't you *mind* leaving the little house where you've lived so long?

Fancy Tony getting a medal. No certainly I wouldn't accept Dame nothing could be more non-U. I wouldn't accept anything from those ravening murderers not that I'm likely to have the chance.[3]

Best love
Nancy

I shall *long* to hear about the ball.

[1] Simon Harcourt-Smith wrote a life of Lucrezia Borgia, *The Marriage at Ferrara* (1953), in which he heavily plagiarised an Italian biography, *Lucrezia Borgia* (1939) by Maria Bellonci.
[2] Dom Aelred's sister, Magdalen Goffin, eventually wrote the life of Maria Pasqua, published in 1979.
[3] Nancy accepted a CBE in 1972.

8 August 1956   St-Pierre du Château
                                                     Hyères
Darling Evelyn

Yes one or 2 people at Monte Carlo told me this but as I can't do X words & never see *The Times* it left me rather cold.[1] Would you say it's more impressive than being in a *N. Statesman* competition? No surely not.

My interesting news (interesting to me) is that Besterman[2] the great Voltaire expert is on my side & will read my MS. He will also give me a room to myself at Les Délices & help me in every way. If only my eyes were all right I should feel certain of doing something really good, but I am dreadfully handicapped by them & sometimes they seize up altogether. You can't think how maddening it is. Mrs Bedford has the same thing & suffers dreadfully too, but for a novel it is less deadly than for what I'm doing.

Girls of 18 are always unbearable – Meg will be just the same. It's an unhappy time & you must try & remember that you are a Christian.

Did you know that my dear Mme Louise (daughter of Louis XV) is probably going to be canonized? That's Monte Carlo gossip too.

I go home tomorrow week, to lovely empty hot Paris. I long for it after such months away. Cocteau says they show my room at Torcello before the church or anything – surely better than X word?

If I can find it I will enclose an article (don't want it back) which rather bears out what I say about rich lords.

Somebody sent me a cutting from America saying that I turned down 5000 dollars a week so *must* be a Communist.

This letter is all about me – I apologize.

Love from
    N

What is your definition of Barbary? Outside the range of Randolph's voice?
P.S. Oh is it true that at your ball a lot of *real* tarts got in through the garden & took away all the girls' partners including Leslie Hartley?

[1] The clue for 'first class' in the *Times* crossword on 2 August read: 'Mitfordian notion of accommodation in a U-boat?'
[2] Theodore Besterman (1904–76). Editor of Voltaire's collected letters.

12 October 1956   7 rue Monsieur, VII

Darling Evelyn

I've just seen H*arold*.[1] He reproached me for liking rude people, I said but you like Evelyn & he was forced to admit he does. He was lovely & I only wish I'd had tablets by me to write down every word. Poor Hamish Hamilton was there, just back from Africa with hundreds of photographs of lions, Harold perfectly politely, but ruthlessly, refused to allow him to show them. H.H. says Xopher [Sykes] is sending his son to Oxford on the proceeds of the Book of Shame. I suppose your ball came out of the same pouch – I however need more than £500 to keep off starvation which now looms. The question is, & the Colonel always asks it before my books come out, will the general public like *Voltaire*?

I love him more & more – terribly like you except he could hardly be described as a Roman Catholic *too*. Well I don't know – he died shriven. Are you excited about St Thomas? I am *very*.

I saw Peters. I think he hates me so why does he always telephone when he comes here? Very strange.

I'm in the country mostly, with my darling Mme Costa. She prays all day & I work & we meet at meals, it is perfect. I'm going there now for a fortnight as Collikins is off to Russia & Paris is so dull without him.

End of Nov I must go to London. I was going to Bolshoi but chucked, I can't bear downing tools at present – you know.

I hear your daughter Teresa is beautiful & fascinating how lucky for you.

Do write – I get letters with only a day's delay & it is a treat with my breakfast. No newspapers or wireless.

    Much love
      Nancy

[1] Harold Acton stressed the second syllable of his name in a continental fashion.

14 October [1956]   Piers Court
                                                     Stinchcombe
Darling Nancy

It was very nice to see your handwriting once more. When you last wrote you said you had lost your sight and that correspondence was a great hindrance to your life of scholarship, so I refrained from gushing.

I am interested in your statement that Voltaire was shriven. Has this now been proved? As you know there has been endless controversy on the subject for two centuries. About a year ago there was a correspondence in a popish journal – I think the *Tablet* – & I was left with the impression that the priest was called without his consent and only performed his office after V. was comatose. It will be most cheering if you have new evidence to the contrary. I have always supposed him the vilest of men. It will be lovely to see him in the role of Col.

Mr Peters loves you. Mr Acton does not like me. I am not rude.

My daughter Teresa is squat, pasty-faced, slatternly with a most disagreeable voice – but it is true that she talks quite brightly. She has cost me the best part of £1500 in the last year & afforded no corresponding pleasure. Margaret remains the star of my existence. I took her to stay at Lady Pam's ornamental villa but she was not in good form as I had struck her the evening before so she sulked all the week-end.

Since you see no newspapers I will tell you that Randolph got £5000 damages last week from the *People* for calling him a 'hack'. Very encouraging for litigants.

I have had rather a hellish summer dashing about in the rain to look at houses and always being disappointed or, when I found a beauty, learning from the survey that it was due to collapse any day. I have at last settled on one 7 miles NW of Taunton in very pretty truly rural surroundings.[1] It has possibilities of beautification. If only I were a pansy without family cares I could make it a jewel. As it is the eight of us & two servants settle in in December with 2 loos and 2 baths and no heating. For six weeks, from October 31st, Laura & I will be homeless with furniture in store. I am ½ way through an interesting case history of insanity.[2] Disturbing. I think there may be an avid public for a book on barminess. Did you know that 1 in every 35 in England go into the bin and that 41% of all hospital beds are occupied by what are dubbed 'psychiatric' cases.

Robin Campbell came here last night. Absolutely horrible, with the prevalent underdog snarl at every successful man & woman.

Love
E

[1] Evelyn spent the last decade of his life at Combe Florey House, now lived in by his son Auberon.
[2] *The Ordeal of Gilbert Pinfold*.

[October 1956]   Piers Court
                                                  Stinchcombe

Darling

  Could you be very kind & translate for me into idiomatic U French
a few lines of dialogue for something I am writing.

  (Middle aged fashionable women talking)
'He is always trying to get into my house. He's asked several of
his friends to bring him. Of course I say No.'
'Do you know any of his friends? I thought he only knew the
most dreadful people. No one in London knows him.'
'It's always possible to take in a few people for a short time in a
foreign country. Most people in Paris have seen through him
now.'[1]

———

  Would it be an awful bore to translate that for me?
  Did I tell you that Boots, since he got his legacy from P. Watson,[2]
spends all his time gambling with great success on the Stock Exchange.

      Much love
        Evelyn

[1] For a conversation between Mrs Cockson and Mrs Benson in *The Ordeal of Gilbert Pinfold*.
[2] Peter Watson left Cyril Connolly £1,000.

19 October 1956   Fontaines-les-Nonnes
                                             par Puisieux
                                             for a few more days

Darling Evelyn

  In such a case how can one tell what really happened? If however
intention counts at all we can be sure he [Voltaire] intended to die
within the rules. He minded passionately about Xian burial & one of
the greatest fusses of his whole life was made because Adrienne Lec-
ouvreur was refused it. At Cirey he built the chapel next door to his
bedroom so that he could hear the Mass when he was ill. He loved
God, I promise you.
  You know how good you are at thinking of titles for books oh could
I wheedle you into thinking of one for me now? What it should be is
Voltaire's love affair, but without that tiresome rhyme. The theme of
the book is the behaviour of this oddest of human beings during a
long love affair (a very testing relationship). Besterman has suggested
Love & Genius but I don't quite like that & Heywood says for goodness
sake call it what it is. Colonel Voltaire perhaps – really no they aren't
very much alike & even I can't make them. As for Emily heaven
preserve ONE from being like her. (It's all right, heaven has.)

Our hostess, at luncheon, suddenly asked Where did William the Conqueror die? Old M. de Rohan-Chabot aged 90 came out of his dream & said 'Et qu'est ce qu'il faut étudier pour le dîner?'[1]

I enclose your phrases which present no difficulty as one so constantly hears those very words!!

Tomorrow the Bishop of Meaux comes to luncheon always a tremendous occasion.

Much love
    N

[1] 'And what should we study for dinner?'

23 October [1956]   Piers Court
                                                         Stinchcombe
Dearest Nancy

Thank you very much indeed for the French translations. I wish I could make a suggestion for your title but I don't know nearly enough about the subject. Is there not perhaps some luminous key-phrase used by Voltaire himself. How about 'Sense & Sentiment', 'Brain & Heart', 'The credulous sceptic', 'Voltaire in Love', 'Emily's thorny bed'?

How wonderful for you to salute the successor of Bossuet. I have to write to Rue Monsieur as I haven't got the address of your retreat.

This is the Last Day in the Old Home. Tomorrow the furniture vans arrive. I am elated & exhilarated. Poor Laura mopes.

My psychopathic treatise is not quite finished.

All next year I shall spend in the Court of Queen's Bench suing Lord Beaverbrook.[1] Randolph has opened a golden road of tax free progress. Professional litigant seems to me a happy calling for my last years.

Couldn't understand Decca's jokes in *Observer*.[2] It seemed to me it was just political jargon of all parties – not particularly radical.

Beaton slipped a disc carrying Garbo's jewel case.

Love
    E

[1] For a review in the *Daily Express* of Rebecca West's *The Meaning of Treason* which had endorsed the view that Evelyn's writing encouraged 'a climate of treason'.
[2] A glossary of left-wing terms ('L' and 'Non-L'), selected from Jessica Mitford's booklet *Lifeitselfmanship, or How to Become a Precisely-Because Man*. Examples included: '*L*: The correctness of that policy will be tested in life itself, *Non-L*: Time will tell whether that plan was O.K.' and '*L*: Projecting an incorrect perspective, *Non-L*: Suggesting a bum plan.' *Observer*, 14 October 1956.

9 November 1956   7 rue Monsieur, VII

Darling Evelyn

The Col says I'm to write & tell you he thinks of you every morning at breakfast when his sugar-tongs appear.

Nobody loves presents as much as he does – a very nice trait I always think.

It's rather like writing to a disembodied spirit though because where to send? The quiet London club no doubt. Did I tell you about my Dutch translator who was taken to a quiet London club where 25 English poets read aloud their poetry? What a scene! He adored it.

I'm here for a few days – back to Fontaines next week.

1st Dec I go to England – London for a few days & then the 'lads' (Raymond Eddy & Co)[1] & Leslie H[artley] & Gerry Wellington[2] & Debo for Xmas.

Then back here to *write* the book – I've got nearly all the stuff for it.

There's a Mitford omnibus, I've been reading *Pursuit of Love* all the morning, I say it's good. Colonel says it would be sad stuff without Fabrice, however.

Any hope of seeing you early in Dec?

Much love
    N

[1] Raymond Mortimer and Edward Sackville-West shared a house at Long Crichel in Dorset.
[2] Gerald Wellesley (1885–1972). Succeeded as 7th Duke of Wellington in 1943.

13 November [1956]   Pixton Park
                                             Dulverton

Dearest Nancy

It is tantalising to think of you in England and our being sundered. I can't ask you to Combe Florey, much as I long to show it to you, as it will be quite uninhabitable for many months. If you are going to stay at Bath with Leslie Hartley you might perhaps drive over to see us (50 miles) or from the buggery house at Crichel (also 50) but it's a long drive in the winter & you couldn't possibly bear to stay a night in the present condition of the house.

I may be at Hyde Park Hotel for the night of 10th. Would Debo have me for a couple of nights after Christmas while you are there? Andrew [Devonshire] is said to be pro Egyptian. I suppose Col. Nasser is a free-mason.

We are leading a very disturbed life though not nearly as disturbed as we shall be when we start living at C.F. My mother-in-law lives in a turmoil of public & private benevolence. She has given me a room to work in but the flow of guests of all ages races & classes makes me highly nervous and my book doesn't prosper. How are your poor old eyes? I am not so much deaf as baffled by noise.

No news of Honks. Did she return to Chantilly? Last heard of in Geneva. Everyone except me is greatly overexcited about the Suez Canal. I caught cold visiting girls' school, which is just as well as my flow of cigars from New York has suddenly ceased. Sanctions? and I can't smoke anyway with a cold.

Miss Rebecca West has gone mad & thinks I am responsible for making her bastard disloyal. One way & another I have a lot of truck with lawyers at the moment.

This house is full of fine furniture falling to pieces. My daughter Teresa is said to have established herself as a wit at Oxford. Bills for her ball still come in. Never again.

Did I tell you? I was sent the proof of a first novel by an unknown lady.[1] The theme (very well done) proves to be the hallucinations of a Roman Catholic novelist. Just what I'm writing myself. Jolly disconcerting.

Love
    Evelyn

[1] Muriel Spark, *The Comforters* (1957).

17 November 1956   Fontaines-les-Nonnes
                                    par Puisieux
Darling Evelyn

I'm beginning to wonder about coming. I know the English when they are in an economizing mood – any excuse to make one travel in a 3rd class corridor on a 1st class ticket & to take away the electric bar from one's bedroom. I'm going to see what CUTS are announced before I budge.

Seen from here they seem to be too busy squabbling among themselves about Suez to have noticed what is happening in Hungary. But I think also they hate any form of rebellion & always really think people should obey whoever is strongly in power.

Here Hungary is a passion – I've never seen the French so united about anything. There have been giant demonstrations money is pouring in & the organization of l'Aide à la Hongrie is beyond praise. They remember all they went through in the occupation, secret police, collaborators, deportations to the east, torture chambers – all is the same, except that the French had a good hope of being rescued & the Hungarians had none.

Andrew is wildly anti Nasser & Debo wants to write up Astors Go Home on the house of the hitherto adored Jakie.[1] I can't mind much one way or the other & have *greatly* enjoyed the fury of the Americans here. Of course it was wrong not right of Sir A [Eden], but one can't always do right. I hope he likes the results, that's all.

If I come over I think I shall be in London on the 10th we might meet before dinner. If I go to Debo I'll ask her to ask you, but it may not be possible as their house seems to get smaller & smaller & *I've* got to sleep out. She says they are going to move into Chatsworth after the baby.[2]

  Much love
     Nancy

[1] Hon. John Jacob Astor (1918-2000). Anti-Suez Conservative MP for Sutton Division of Plymouth 1951-9. Knighted in 1978.
[2] The Devonshires' youngest child, Sophia, was born in March 1957. The family moved back to Chatsworth in November 1959.

31 December 1956   7 rue Monsieur, VII
2 January 1957

Darling Evelyn

Did Miss Harriet write that long, informative & well-composed letter of her own accord or was it the result of torture? I am greatly impressed by it, but I rather hate the idea that her whole Christmas may have been ruined by 'have you written to Mrs Rodd, Harriet?'

I note that she has no French – nor, it seems has the Berry girl in spite of Pam's French room & all.

I've written the first page of my book & feel better. Isn't starting difficult! So I went out & bought a dress I couldn't afford & have now downed tools until after les fêtes.

It was very nice to see you but I was rather shocked by your great intimacy with those dull actors & wished we had been you & me & Pam. I admit that the actors are both *very pretty* but prefer to see them on the boards. Conversation in England *has* become dull hasn't it? Either pounding rudeness like that of Randolph Ed (& yourself when fully sane) or else a sort of under water quality. I only mean in company. Has it always been so? I think the way they flog that old dead horse Suez is almost unbelievably dull. I seem to remember that it was the same when I was a child over free trade & protection (always comes back to *trade*, with les Anglais).

So, have a happy new year. I was sorry to see the end of 1956, which I greatly enjoyed.

  Love from
     Nancy

Part V

1957–1961

NANCY AND Evelyn wrote perhaps half a dozen letters to each other in 1957, of which five have survived. Over the next ten years they exchanged some one hundred and twenty letters, a fraction of their previous output. There are several reasons why they ceased to be such regular correspondents.

With the move from Piers Court to Combe Florey House at the end of 1956, Evelyn became even more reclusive; people and parties no longer interested him, he rarely visited London and had no gossip with which to entertain Nancy. He felt increasingly listless and melancholic, and easily succumbed to paranoia. On 28 October, his fifty-third birthday, he gave up keeping a diary. When he took it up again four years later, it was no longer to record his days but simply to make sporadic notes of whatever passed through his head. At the end of 1956, he had advertised in *The Times* for an ear trumpet, a clear message to the world that he was now an Old Man.

Although Evelyn felt that his life had become ineffably tedious, it was none the less a productive period for work: he wrote a biography of the theologian Monsignor Ronald Knox and a travel book, as well as the last volume of his war trilogy. All around him, he could see the collapse of the civilised values he held dear. In an article entitled 'I See Nothing but Boredom . . . Everywhere', he deplored the prosperity that was creating a 'classless society' but which left him poorer than before. He predicted the loss of all national character, an ironing-out of differences in speech and dress that would lead to drab uniformity. To escape this dismal vision, he sought solace in his faith; religion became his main concern. Nancy was excluded from this obsession, as were most of his non-Catholic friends.

Nancy, who usually restarted the correspondence when it began to flag, spent the first half of 1957 struggling to write *Voltaire in Love*. The research had been particularly laborious as she was suffering from severe headaches and aching eyes. Reading or writing for more than a few hours a day was impossible and she began to worry about losing her sight. The problem was solved the following year by a new pair of spectacles, but meanwhile she wrote fewer letters to all her friends. In July 1957, she received the devastating news that the Colonel had been named Ambassador to Rome. He had requested the post as a personal favour from de Gaulle, in order to escape Paris where his love life had become particularly complicated: he was deeply involved with a married woman who was a near neighbour of Nancy. The prospect of Paris without the Colonel was unbearable; Nancy hid her pain and despair from her friends but Palewski's five-year absence left her desolate. It was harder to keep up the brave front that Evelyn so admired and her letters to him became shorter, less frequent and lost some of their sparkle.

Shrove Tuesday [5 March] 1957   Combe Florey House
                                            Combe Florey
                                            Nr Taunton
Darling Nancy,

I saw Debo last week. I feel it my duty to tell you that she is spreading a very damaging story about you: that you have allowed yourself to be photographed by the Television.[1] Of course I don't believe it, nor does anyone who knows & loves you, but I think you should scotch this slander before it spreads to people who might do so. It would entirely destroy your reputation as U governess.

Col. sent me such a pretty drawing at Christmas. What was it?

I had an exhilarating expedition into the law courts[2] and came out two thousand pounds (tax-free) to the good. But there were anxious moments. At the end of the first day I would have settled for a fiver. A disgusting looking man called Russell[3] from the *Sunday Times*, not the pretty [John] Russell I met with you, gave evidence against me. The judge was a buffoon who invited the jury to laugh me out of court. But I had taken the precaution of telling the Dursley parish priest that he should have 10% of the damages. His prayers were answered in dramatic, Old Testament style. A series of Egyptian plagues fell on Sir Hartley Shawcross[4] from the moment he took up the case, culminating in a well-nigh fatal motor accident to his mother-in-law at the very moment when he had me under cross-examination & was making me feel rather an ass. He had to chuck the case & leave it to an understrapper, whose heart was in the court next door where a Bolivian millionaire was suing Lord Kemsley for saying he buggered his wife (the Bolivian's wife, not Lady Kemsley). I had a fine solid jury who were out to fine the *Express* for their impertinence to the Royal Family, quite irrespective of any rights and wrongs. They were not at all amused by the judge. All the £300 a day barristers rocked with laughter at his sallies. They glowered. That was not what they paid a judge for, they thought.

So Father Collins got £200 and a lot of chaps in White's got pop. But there has been some retribution. I was all set for Monte Carlo when an appeal came to take Ronnie Knox, who has had a cancer operation, to the sea side. He couldn't face the journey to Monte Carlo. He wouldn't even accept Brighton. Torquay it has to be. So I am off there tomorrow for three weeks. I love and revere Ronnie but –

Write to me there at the Imperial Hotel putting my mind at rest about this terrible Television scandal.

Did you know Sir Oswald Mosley had mumps? And that Debo doesn't at all like jokes about it. She has a Dutch follower & looks very large & pretty.

    Love
        Evelyn

[1] Nancy was interviewed by John Ellison for the BBC programme *At Home*.
[2] Evelyn had won his case, heard before Mr Justice Stable, brought against the *Daily Express* for publishing Nancy Spain's article.
[3] Leonard Russell (1906–74). Founder and editor of *The Saturday Book* 1941–51; influential literary editor of *Sunday Times* 1945–54. Married to the film critic Dilys Powell in 1943.
[4] Hartley Shawcross (1902–2003). Attorney-General 1945–51. Chairman of the Bar Council 1952–7. Knighted in 1945, created life peer in 1959. His junior was Helenus Milmo.

22 May [1957]   Hôtel de Paris[1]
                                                   Monte-Carlo

My Dear Nancy

Many American ladies are dismayed by some utterances of yours (on the Television I suppose) in criticism of their country.

Do you realize that the USA are entirely the creation of the accursed race, the French? They it was who sent a band of atheists and free-masons to subvert the loyal & pampered English colonists. They armed the rabble against our brave soldiers. They built the capitol at Washington, the Statue of Liberty in New York and the dreadful United Nations Headquarters. They introduced republican institutions, alcoholism, avarice, immodesty and all the dire features of that stricken land.

Oh the pleasure of leaving France with its disgusting liberties, equalities & fraternities and stepping into this fortress of monarchy & christianity, where the natives are civil and handsome and happy, without the black guilt of the épuration, the Drummond massacre, the existentialists, the worker-priests, the Algerian atrocities and all the multiform horrors of the Gaul. I do not suppose there is a single Picasso in the principality.

   Yours affec.
       E. Waugh

[1] Evelyn's second action against the *Daily Express*, for its review of *The Meaning of Treason*, was settled out of court. He received £3,000 damages, plus costs, and took Laura to Monte Carlo to celebrate.

21 July 1957   7 rue Monsieur, VII

Darling Evelyn

Oh pretty *Pinfold* – you are faithful. I've just got back from a month in Venice & found him. The shrieks! Of course I downed tools (proofs) & read it in one gulp – lovely *stuff*. I'm glad to see those silly critics have understood for once. I read Driberg on the beach. My Italian friends are all getting it as a reward for nurturing me. I do wonder how much they will understand. The box, the bruise & the niceties of Margaret's conversation & bedding-out may be lost on them I fear. My favourite chapter was when Pinfold turned into James Bond.

Colonel very much pleased with his new job.[1]

So back to my proofs. I wish I knew if the book is any good – at this stage how can one tell?

Much love
    Nancy

[1] Palewski had been appointed Ambassador to Rome.

24 October [1957]   Combe Florey House
                                           Nr Taunton
Darling Nancy

I feel great guilt about yesterday. I was so dazed & worn with travel that I didn't show the welcome or the gratitude I felt. I resolve in future always to sleep in London before going out to luncheon.

I have read a third of *Voltaire* with keen pleasure. The characters are as alien to me and as vivid as those of *Lucky Jim*. You have a unique gift of making your reader feel physically in the presence of your characters. What horrors they were! The book should correct two popular heresies 1) Cinema-born, that only beautiful people enjoy fucking 2) Spender-born, that the arts flourish best in a liberal society.

I am only waiting to finish this letter & throw myself back into *Voltaire*.

Laura is delighted at the prospect of your winter visit to us. Come whenever you can for as long as you can bear it.

I feel I was grumpy too about Debo and her wife.[1] It is affection for her that makes me censorious.

Pam has very kindly asked me to dine with her and you on Monday. Alas my feeble frame simply cannot support another journey.

Fond love
    Evelyn

[1] Lady Katherine Fitzmaurice (1912–95). Married Viscount Mersey in 1933. Her nickname derived from an involved family joke which started when a man repeatedly referred to his wife as 'Kitty my wife' in one breath. As Lady Mersey's name was Kitty, she too became known as 'Kitty my wife' which was eventually shortened to 'wife'.

28 October 1957   40A Hill Street, W1
Darling Evelyn

Thank you so much for your 2 letters. It was good of you to come all this long way & I appreciate it as your American friends would say, beastly gushers.

Your questions.[1] I suppose a very regular woman would be rather sure at 3 weeks – me for instance. I always knew after about a fortnight & always miscarried at about 5 weeks – but no doubt what it was. I think du Châtelet had considerable doubts by the time the baby was born & Mme de Créquy says he would not have recognized it had it lived – but she is unreliable & hated Em so I didn't quote Père Menou. Voltaire, in his mémoires I think, says all that about him. I imagine Stanislas was really impotent & had to have a maîtresse en titre & Père Menou personally loathed Boufflers. He probably thought Em would lead a virtuous life at the Court, conducting her studies. Little did he know her. Very glad you like it on the whole – don't you think Voltaire is Smarty boots in person? After 2 or 3 very unfavourable notices the Sunday papers are in favour, thank goodness.

I long for the visit & sometime you will tell me whether to come before or after Debo where I go for Christmas.

    Much love
        Nancy

[1] Evelyn's letter with queries about *Voltaire in Love* has not survived.

9 January 1958   7 rue Monsieur, VII

Darling Evelyn
    Many thanks for Spainery. The charming Tristram Powell[1] was reading the *D.E.* & I said to him 'you know Mr Waugh is Miss Spain's keenest fan' to which he replied 'well he's got a good goggle today' & handed me the paper. Yes, indeed.[2]

My visits were lovely, would I had the pen of a Mme de Graffigny. The only sad thing, Charley and Violet were both in bed with Asiatic. Oh how my spirits rose, though, at the sight of the Mansart roofs & the smell of tobacco-laden drains this afternoon.

Andrew's sister[3] had a motor accident & he & Betj[eman] hung at her bedside. The doctor asked Betj for an autograph which the old fellow gave whereupon the Dr let out a cry like a wounded bull 'but *you're not* the Duke of Devonshire?' Admit.

A boast. Sir Lewis Namier[4] said to me 'only a specialist like myself can realize what a lot you know about the 18th century.' Do be impressed.

I saw Mells (outside). Oh the charm.

    Much love
        Nancy

[1] Tristram Powell (1940–). Film director; son of Anthony Powell.
[2] An interview by Nancy Spain with an American beatnik poet in which he described 'a strange English week-end' with Raymond Mortimer, Lady Juliet Duff and Edward Sackville-West.

The latter 'was up half the night, beard and all, sincere tweeds and all, talking'. *Daily Express*, 4 January 1958.
³ Lady Elizabeth Cavendish.
⁴ Sir Lewis Namier (1888–1960). Historian whose works include *England in the Age of the American Revolution* (1930) and *Personalities and Powers* (1955).

24 January 1958[1]   [Combe Florey House
                                                    Nr Taunton]

Have you seen that old Brian Howard has kicked the bucket? You will mourn him more than I (or, perhaps, than me). I must admit he dazzled me rather 25 years ago but, though I hadn't set eyes on him for 15 years or more, I went rather in terror of him in late years. I was always afraid that he would suddenly rush at me in some public place and hit me and there would be painful publicity 'Middle aged novelist assaulted in West End hotel'.

[Alan] Pryce-Jones wrote an obituary in *The Times*. All he could say was that poor Brian showed great promise in impersonating Bruno Hat. It was Tom, anyway, who sat in the wheel-chair as I remember it.

I am just off to Rhodesia[2] so there's no need to spend all those francs in answering. I have insured my life for £50,000 for the two days of the journey (only costs a tenner) I couldn't possibly earn that sum however hard I worked in the few years of activity left to me (not with taxes) so it will be *much* the best thing for my poor children if the aeroplane blows up. In fact the only chance they have of a liberal education. But I suppose I ought not to pray for it on account of the other passengers who may not have been so foresighted.

I'll write from Rhodesia. The snow here (and the chance of fifty thou for the little ones) reconciles me to the journey but I am sure it is a hideous and dull country. Not at all like lovely Abyssinia.

I see that the French clergy have taken to murdering their mistresses now – and you say they are such an example to us.

¹ The original of this letter has disappeared. It was seen by Christopher Sykes when he wrote his biography of Evelyn and these extracts are quoted in *Evelyn Waugh*, pp. 394–5.
² To research his life of Ronald Knox.

21 March 1958   Combe Florey House
                                                Nr Taunton
Dearest Nancy

    We were all so sad to read of your father's death.[1] I know well how fond you all were of him and what a break with your past his death will make. It must be some consolation to know how fond he was of you and how much you were able to make up for Tom and Bobo. He had the life and death he would have wished, I think. I didn't know him and when I saw him years ago he thought me a 'sewer' so it isn't easy to say more than that you have my love & sympathy in your loss.

I got back from Rhodesia a fortnight ago. It is an exceedingly dreary land but there were enough chums to make it an amusing month. Do you know that if white Americans go there they are listed as 'Europeans'; blacks are 'Foreign natives'.

Simon Dalhousie[2] was very jolly and Daphne Acton[3] a saint. I have returned to hear ugly stories of Pam befriending Mr Muggeridge.[4]

My eldest son became a Cornet of Horse today and is off to Cyprus to torture school girls.

Still immersed in *Knox*. I keep mislaying all the documents. I have got to the age when I need a secretary.

Best love
　　Evelyn

[1] Lord Redesdale had died on 17 March, four days after his 80th birthday.
[2] 16th Earl of Dalhousie (1914–99). Governor-General of the Federation of Rhodesia and Nyasaland 1957–63.
[3] Hon. Daphne Strutt (1911–2003). Married to 3rd Baron Acton in 1931. She had been a close friend of Ronald Knox and was an important source for Evelyn's biography. She and her husband settled in Rhodesia after the war.
[4] Malcolm Muggeridge (1903–90). Evelyn and the journalist had never been on good terms and had recently crossed swords at a Foyle's luncheon for the publication of *The Ordeal of Gilbert Pinfold*. Muggeridge's affair with Lady Pamela Berry began in 1953 and lasted for ten years.

26 March 1958　　　　　　　　　　　　　　　　40A Hill Street, W1

Dearest Evelyn

Many thanks for your kind letter. It is sad, but the odd, violent, attractive man he used to be had already gone except for an occasional flash. He was so weak & so very deaf.

Three funeral services. The Protestant sort so very much more upsetting than yours, with the sad words & the hymns one has known from a child. I'd rather have the R.C. mass which flows over you like a great force of nature – the cremation however not as horrible as I had imagined & made better by a Canon with a real, not parsonic voice reading the prayers.

I go to I of W tomorrow – home on Tuesday.

Love from
　　Nancy

P.S. My sister Pam rather saved my bacon at Rochester by suddenly whispering: 'Isn't it nice that the *whole* of the Foreign Legion has come' (British).

25 June 1958   7 rue Monsieur, VII

Darling Evelyn

I see that Auberon has been wounded[1] what a terrible worry for you. I'm really writing to tell you that Uncle Matthew had a lung shot away in S. Africa – was 4 days in a bullock wagon – the wound swarming with maggots – however he lived to be 80 & only died of boredom in the end. So don't be too anxious about Auberon's future health. My father could hunt & shoot all day, though he couldn't run. He had 2 years of trenches in the 1914 war.

I'm just off to Venice for my hol, for the whole of July. (Hotel Cipriani.)

    Love & sympathy from
      Nancy

Voltaire always used to speak of St John's winter – here it is again –

[1] Auberon Waugh had accidentally shot himself with a machine-gun.

11 July 1958[1]   Munich

Thanks awfully for your letter about Bron. It was a very anxious three weeks and painful for Laura who had to spend them under armed guard in the great heat, which she hates. But now he is back in England with good hopes of recovery. It is Harry [Stavordale] who has been struck down. You saw? His only surviving son murdered.[2] Tragedy doesn't seem appropriate to him & Nell. There is no conceivable human mitigation of their suffering.

[1] The original of this letter has disappeared. The extract printed here is from Sykes, *Evelyn Waugh*, p. 397.
[2] Hon. Stephen Fox-Strangways had been killed on emergency operations in Cyprus.

19 November 1958   7 rue Monsieur, VII

Dearest Evelyn

Not me (*S.S.*).[1] I haven't sent any, so great is my meanness I suppose! Really because I don't count it as my work but as belonging to wonderful Miss Norton. You will never know how amazing I think her translation. She is the greatest living bore, next to Besterman. [. . .]

What I did send was a little thing for Harriet's stocking. I sent it to White's because in the shop I forgot the word Taunton & their *Who's Who* only gave Stinkers.

I always feel like that in London, fuddled. (No acknowledgement I beg.)

Thank you, my eyes I think are cured by this wonderful Mr Trevor-Roper[2] not Za-Za's[3] husband, his brother. I have for the first time specs that don't hurt. *Wonderful.*

How fascinating about the devil. But you know the Bourbons had an idea that all descendants of St Louis were sure to go to heaven which is why (one's always told) they didn't mind taking a few risks. Of course no prédicateurs [preachers] were so terrific as those of Louis XIV so perhaps they inspired doubt of this comforting theory. I can't believe in black magic – do you really? It all seems like play acting to me – bogey bogey in the dark & so on.

I would love to go to India with you, but we should quarrel. Besides Marie becomes sad here without me & I've been away such a lot this year. It would be too expensive to take her, rich as one is, & she is too old & timid.

Oh how I love Boots being le grand dauphin.

I never see *The European*.[4] I think cantankerous writing is a bad habit which must be guarded against. Have you read the book of the year I mean *Kitchener*?[5] I simply lived in it, funnier than Monty[6] whom I am greatly enjoying now.

I suppose you hate Monty – well I LOVE him, more & more. I do wonder if you knew him in the war?

Your cousin Mr Cockburn is in bad. He says (last book)[7] that Col Passy murdered a man. Passy, they say, can't get less than £25 000. Don't you find it very odd that (a) he should write it & (b) that the printers should print it? Babyish.

It is heavenly to be able to read for a long time on end & I now see how handicapped I was when doing *Voltaire*. Now I'll read a lot of books & then perhaps write a novel.

I wish I could see you & have a good chat. Didn't like to disturb you while I was over as you weren't apparently in circulation & I hoped you were working. I long for the book.

Well, the Channel is between us which seems a pity. I know you don't care to come here.

Much love
    Nancy

---

[1] *Saint-Simon at Versailles* by Lucy Norton had been sent to Evelyn by the publishers. Nancy wrote the preface.
[2] Patrick Trevor-Roper (1916–2004). Ophthalmic specialist. Author of *The World Through Blunted Sight: An Inquiry into the Effects of Disordered Vision on Character and Art* (1971).
[3] Lady Alexandra Haig (1907–97). Daughter of Earl Haig. Married to Rear Admiral Clarence Howard-Johnston 1941–54 and to Hugh Trevor-Roper, later Lord Dacre of Glanton, in 1954.
[4] A monthly political and cultural magazine published by the Mosleys 1953–9.
[5] Philip Magnus, *Kitchener: Portrait of an Imperialist* (1958).
[6] Field Marshal Viscount Montgomery, *Memoirs* (1958).
[7] Claud Cockburn, *Crossing the Line* (1958), a second volume of autobiography.

24 November 1958   White's

Dearest Nancy

It was addressed to me & I could not resist opening Harriet's Christmas present. What a lucky child she is to have a godmother who is both so kind and clever at finding pretty things. She will have a treat when she re-opens it next month.

I shall keep Christmas in London. I have long wanted to & this year I have the honourable excuse of visiting my son in hospital.

I am so glad about your eyes. They must be full of tears today at the humiliation of the frog socialists.[1]

I thought Claud Cockburn's accusation of murder injudicious. Journalists are always so cocksure about secret information. But I wouldn't advise your chum to sue him – he has no money at all. I have never heard of his publisher & I suppose he is penniless too. So your chum could be left with costs to pay.

Pray do not speak of Lord Monty.

I wonder why you think we should quarrel in India. You wouldn't like the grub and you can't get a drink. It is [a] big price to pay for seeing obscene sculptures.

Read *Memento Mori* by Muriel Spark.

Now I know *St Simon* wasn't a present from you I shall pass it on at Christmas.

    Love
        Evelyn

[1] In the first round of parliamentary elections the Socialists had gained only 15 per cent of the votes.

19 May 1959   Combe Florey House
                                                   Nr Taunton

Darling Nancy

This is a fan letter. I've just re read *Voltaire in Love* and must tell you how much I admire it. I enjoyed it hugely at the first reading but I didn't appreciate it. You write so deceptively frivolously that one races on chuckling from page to page without noticing the solid structure. Perhaps because I've just finished writing a biography myself (an easy one, with all sources accessible – personal knowledge of the subject) I can now realize what an achievement of research, selection & arrangement you apparently effortlessly performed. It is a masterly book.

You wouldn't have enjoyed my African tour[1] at all. I covered miles of featureless country and met thousands of featureless people and ate drab food. No laughs except when the Paramount Chief of the Chagga asked me to dinner saying: 'Don't dress. Come in your tatters & rags.'

(His ma & pa went about stark.) Also the road department decided to have a traffic check so they posted black men with baskets at the road-sides & told them to put a stone in for every car that passed. A journalist met one with a basket of stones & asked what he was doing. 'For cars, master', so it got into all the papers that whites were being stoned. But it was a blank two months and just what I needed to invigorate me.

Did you see Boots's very discreditable review of Honks?[2] The booby calls those adventurous & wildly unconventional men, Maurice Baring & Belloc, 'tame' and the exquisitely candid Conrad Russell 'pawky'. Someone must have been tickling his class consciousness again.

I haven't been to London since Christmas. It is delicious here now – the first Spring I can remember when it was warm enough to smell. It is a joy putting one's head out of the window at dawn (before the second swig of paraldehyde) and snuffing.

Is this a chestnut? The Turkish Ambassador said of *Lolita* (an indecent book that is enjoying a vogue in America) 'I don't like reading about such things. I prefer to see them.'

Did you ever know Ronald Graham?[3] Margaret is growing just like him. Can it be the bottle?

But I am wandering from the point, which is to say Hurrah for *Voltaire in Love*. What's next?

Love
    Evelyn

Andrew Devonshire in his cups called me a sponger. It rankles.

[1] Evelyn had accepted £2,000 and a free cruise to write a travel book advertising the Union Castle Line. The result was *A Tourist in Africa* (1960).
[2] In his review of *The Light of Common Day* by Diana Cooper, Cyril Connolly had described this second volume of autobiography as 'gossip-writing', albeit by the 'queen of gossip-writers'. *Sunday Times*, 17 May 1959.
[3] Sir Ronald Graham (1870–1949). Florid Ambassador to Holland 1919–21 and to Italy 1921–33.

22 May 1959   7 rue Monsieur, VII

Darling Evelyn

Oh how I love praise. My feelings were rather hurt by the critics, most of whom downed it completely (*Times*, *T.L.S.*, *Manchester G*, *Punch* which was savage – well all of those were) or else said it was quite amusing. Smarty-boots & John Davenport liked it. However the public is faithful & it will be a penguin. My French translator speaks as you do & that is very satisfactory because a translator really knows a book.

What next indeed! I can think of nothing but a house I'm trying to buy. You know how, to write a book one must think of it in trains

& at concerts & specially in motor cars – well I can think of nothing but this house.

I long for *Knox*, it will be such an amusing – interesting I mean – companion to Diana's mémoires. Such a good thing they appear like that simultaneously.

I've just been in Burgundy. It is the countryside of one's childhood; empty, marvellously cultivated, dusty white roads, huge rivers, forests & villages unchanged since the time of the crusades. Happy good looking healthy people. I often wish one had 9 lives, if so I would spend one of them in Burgundy. Of course the weather does add – has there ever been such a spring! I have to wake myself up even here in Paris for the dawn chorus which has everything but a nightingale.

The nourritures terrestres[1] are working at full bat for me at the moment. (Do you remember 'blissful 1952'?)

My sister Decca has written her memoirs[2] & got a huge advance from Gollancz. I said to Honks [Mosley] 'never mind darling probably she doesn't speak of us.' 'If she's got a huge advance it means that she DOES.'

Andrew must be mad – I sometimes think he is. Goodness knows you are more sponged *on* than anybody.

I must flee – I'm writing two dull articles against time.

Love
   N

I haven't thanked enough for your letter which *delighted* me. Didn't you think *Lolita* an excellent novel? I *did* love it.

[1] Earthly fare.
[2] *Hons and Rebels* (1960).

29 June 1959   Combe Florey House
                                      Nr Taunton

Darling Nancy

Is it persecution mania or was your interview in the *Daily Express*[1] deliberately aimed at me, to make me gobble like a turkey with baffled rage? That was certainly the effect. I had to loosen my collar & lie in a darkened room for an hour after reading it.

Where is your new house? Burgundy or still in Paris? It is very invigorating, I found, to move in middle age – also crippling in expense.

Will anyone kind be in Paris in August? I suppose not, but I suppose some diplomats have to sit it out. Susan Mary? I have lost her new address. The reason I ask is that my convalescent son has today gone off to France, beginning at the sea side near St Raphael. Contrary to my advice he is determined to go to Paris in August. Do I know any Americans or English who might be there? [Frank] Gileses? I have told him no one, but I suppose Giles has to do his work there, no?

I hoped by now to have sent you a copy of my *Knox* but the socialists have made a strike against the literary world.

Boots bought smut from Corporal Hill. They have had trouble before with smut buyers who refuse to pay because they know the Corporal daren't sue. I said Boots was much more frightened of the police than they were, and I am right. Boots has coughed up.

Deka's(?) Dekka's(?) Decka's autobiography will just be socialist propaganda. No spicy bits about you & Honks, I bet.

Honks Cooper gave a buggers' ball in London. I went & who should I find queening it there but Antony Head. When I tell people they say: well, of course, he always used to make plaster casts of vegetables.

She had a great crush at Hatchard's bookshop when she sat there to sign copies. Devonshire took six but none of her buggers turned up.

No, I didn't think *Lolita* any good except as smut. As that it was highly exciting to me.

Tell me about your new house and your summer (any chance of your coming here) and your winter. Jan & Feb loom up. We shouldn't quarrel you know if we were together. Where will you be.

Love from
    Evelyn

<hr>

[1] Nancy had been interviewed by John Cruesmann on 'Morals, Money and Men'. She ended on a characteristically provocative note: 'I often think that the worst part of being in a Russian camp or an American prison would be one's companions, good, kind, serious – and long-winded.' (29 June 1959)

6 July 1959   S Vio 373
                        Fondamenta Zorzi
                        Venice

Darling Evelyn

I see what you mean about the interview (got £200 for it) but you must have liked the French not divorcing, Monty being lovely & the bit about American prisons? Pam seems shirty but I suppose that's part of her work. I think you'll like an essay on tourists to appear in *Encounter*.[1]

It seemed to me *Lolita* did what the reviewers always say about Mme Bisch – 'she does exactly what she sets out to do'. A wonderfully meaningless phrase when applied to her but fits Nabokov like a glove.

I've just read *A House in Vienna*[2] & may be gel-gel but couldn't quite see the point. A bit jokeless – no?

Well I shall be in Paris in August, but am I kind? And what could I do for him do you think? I'm very willing. Everything is shut then, it's just a very pretty empty town with no motor cars. I hope to be beginning a book then.

My house is at Versailles, a great beauty or at least a tiny pocket beauty. You might pray for me to get it. It belongs to 4 people – 3 want to sell it to me & the 4th doesn't but may have to. I've wanted it for 6 years – it was built by Pomp's homme d'affaires as a pied à terre at Versailles when he came to see her. He was Colin & it is called La Colette.

Are you loving *Q. Mary*? 'The Kaiser thought she had been hypnotized'[3] oh how I shrieked!

In Jan & Feb I suppose I shall be deep in my book. No we wouldn't quarrel but your standard of living is too high for me.

This is a nice little comfortable flat I've taken, if ever you wanted such a thing they let it the whole time. Here until beginning of Aug:

Much love
    Nancy

About the interview, you may have noticed that certain phrases meant nothing at all. This is because Ld B[eaverbrook] thinks that sounds more lifelike.

[1] 'The Tourist' was reprinted in *The Water Beetle* (1962).
[2] By Edith de Born (1959).
[3] When the young unmarried Duchess Marie of Mecklenburg-Strelitz was discovered to be pregnant, the German Emperor fancied that the footman responsible for her condition must have 'hypnotised' her. James Pope-Hennessy, *Queen Mary* (1959).

5 August 1959   S. Vio 373
                                                                  Venice

Darling Evelyn

[. . .] I go home today week, so if there's aught I can do for your boy I am at his disposal. I must begin a book – that means solid headache for a year & I dread it.

In Sept I go to my old Mme Costa who has invited me for 4 or 5 months – I may stay quite a long time if I find I can work there.

I've loved being here, as usual. I live in a little world, all seeing each other all day, in 6 weeks I haven't had one meal alone. But now the Italians are packing up & letting their houses to the onrushing sewers & in another week all fun will have fled. One regrets leaving the less. Already a fearful Mrs Sigrist has appeared with French chef & 2 black slaves. Some friends of Momo's called Reitzman[1] too – she went to the same charm school as S. Mary (old charm school tie) & he is a literal Heck Dexter. The Emir of Nigeria very pretty, specially his Prime Minister huge & pitch & dressed in vast folds of pale blue taffeta. Had tea with them – hard to know which way to turn for chat

as Debo always says of Windsor Castle. 'What do you think of the
news?' 'Our secretaries read the news & tell it to us later.' 'Shall I tell
you now? Eisenhower is going to Moscow.' Total lack of response. I
am glad one doesn't have to talk to blacks very much – or to Mrs
Sigrist or the Reitzmans for that matter.

  Much love
    Nancy

¹ Charles Wrightsman (1896–1986). Texas oil millionaire and art collector. Married to Jayne
Larkin.

22 October 1959   Fontaines-les-Nonnes
                                                   par Puisieux
                                                   (home on Monday)

Darling Evelyn
  I am not an unbaptized child of 2; I can read; in fact I have read
Mgr Knox's *Enthusiasm*.
  I am now *glued* to your book fighting off Mrs Hammersley's
onslaughts. She is bored with Miss Howard & covets *Knox*.
  My mother will like it. I said to Honks [Mosley] 'Muv doesn't really
care for *Voltaire* I'm afraid.' 'No, but she *only* enjoys books about
Victorian clergymen.'
  I once met the Mgr, with you at Ann's. You must have been burying
somebody – I remember you were dressed as Ernest, black edged
handkerchief & all.
  Did you enjoy *Prof*?¹ I screamed with laughter for two whole days,
sitting under an oak tree in this beautiful country I love so much. I
was transported back to dotty old England, misty & queer, to the
Oxford of one's youth.
  I'm trying to write a novel.² Not easy to organise the requisite
solitude.

  Fond love from
    Nancy

¹ Roy Harrod, *The Prof: A Personal Memoir of Lord Cherwell* (1959).
² *Don't Tell Alfred*.

26 October 1959   Combe Florey House
                                                   Nr Taunton

Dearest Nancy
  I should have written before to thank you for sending me your
article on Tourists and to tell you how greatly I enjoyed it.
  I am greatly interested to learn that you were baptised. I thought
that the Mosaic law was fully enforced by your father. You will find

your meeting with Ronald recorded in the book if you get so far.

I am told that you announced to the press that the hero of your new book was [Sir Oliver] Harvey the socialist ambassador. Surely you cannot have been so imprudent? It will lay you open to libel actions – not so much from him as from his understrappers, valet, chauffeur etc. But I do admire your capacity to write a novel. I am half drowning in the surf of a wretched little travel diary about Africa.

Dotty old France, misty & queer, must be very enjoyable now with cabinet ministers shooting one another just like the Levant.

I lunched at Melbury yesterday – the only great house that keeps its doors shut to the tourists. Harry & Nell [Ilchester] have been in it only a year and have re arranged everything and found unknown treasures and hung the walls with silk and made it a brilliant spectacle. And no heir. The ghost of their murdered son tramped everywhere.

Does Honks send you *Action*?[1] The number after the general election was very funny.

I was [in] Oxford last week. Maurice roared. I think he is obsessed by the prospect of retirement and wants to fall dead of a seizure at his own table.

Boots is to become a father by a new conk.[2] A chilling thought.

Love from
  Evelyn

[1] Sir Oswald Mosley's broadsheet.
[2] Cyril Connolly married Deirdre Craven in 1959; their daughter Cressida was born the following year.

13 January 1960   Combe Florey House
                                                    Nr Taunton

Darling Nancy

How very bitter to miss you.

Of course I should not dream of using the telephone. I long to see you but I fear I shall not be stopping in Paris.

I hope you are cleaning Corporal Hill's Augean stable.

Laura & I shall be in Venice at Baur Grunwald 22nd Jan – 28th. It is her first visit. I have forgotten my way about. We don't aspire to enter high Venetian society but if there is a sort of Leslie Hartley still who doesn't mind acting as cicerone, it would be very kind if you'd ask him to call (not on telephone) or if there is a distressed gentlewoman who does this professionally I would gladly engage her.

How are your poor eyes? Someone told me they were giving trouble again – I hope falsely.

Goodness the boredom of the Eden memoirs.

I long for your new novel. Powell has written one called, I hear, 'The Pagoda of the Amber Moon'.[1]

I hear Chatsworth is kept at an American temperature. Well, you will like that.

Laura & I go to Homburg for a night – my fault. I thought it would be fun to see where Monte Carlo started. Now I realize it will be an uncomfortable journey and very cold & nothing left.

I saw Boots for a moment but didn't ask about his baby – I mean literally baby, not conk.

   Love from
      Evelyn

Is Honks painting *all* the swastikas?

[1] Anthony Powell, *Casanova's Chinese Restaurant* (1960). Evelyn gave the novel a moderately favourable review in the *Spectator*, 24 June 1960.

24 March 1960   Combe Florey House
                                                 Nr Taunton

Dearest Nancy

How very nice to see your writing again and how bitter to have to say that I don't see any hope of our meeting in London. Does your English tour include a visit to Crichel? You would there be half way here. Can't we coax you to adventure as far as this? London is a dreadful place full of demonstrating students. No friends left there. I hope the reason for your visit is the delivery of your new novel to your funny looking publisher. I look forward to it and to Tony Powell's 'Pagoda of the Amber Moon' (I think it is called) as the only readable books of the year.

I had a very enjoyable little winter tour, first with Laura then with my daughter Margaret. I have had to pay for it by writing some very uncongenial articles for the *Daily Mail*. Venice in January was damp & cold but empty & silent and mysterious. I had never been there in mists before. Monte Carlo was delicious – no Americans within hearing. Homburg was hell but we stayed only one night. A great mistake. I saw a lot of Mark [Ogilvie-Grant] in Athens. He is going to Delphi to greet Debo. He broke the news of the Armstrong-Jones fiasco[1] with great glee.

Colonel Gaston's affection is gratifying & inexplicable. He has grown much prettier but is very restless in his fine house.[2] The footmen literally run behind him as he darts from one saloon to another. He eats his food too fast. It is very good and deserves lingering attention. I think he has the death-wish strongly.

I saw Mrs Taffy Rodd acting ludicrously badly in a film.

If you have a minute to spare in Chelsea do call on Maimie [Vsvelode] who is lonely and sad working at a shop called Sloane Gallery, 277 Kings Road.

I was very sorry indeed to hear that the sale of your Versailles house has fallen through. I hope this will induce you to return & live in England.

I am told Chatsworth is kept at stupefying heat. You must like that.

Everybody who has read my life of Ronald Knox has written to point out horrible mistakes & misprints.

The Oxford Chancellorship[3] was a great conflict of loyalty – hatred of socialists against hatred of Trevor-Roper. Anyway I am not a MA and couldn't vote.

Since you saw this house the porch has come down and a balustraded perron gone up – much improved.

My family are well but inordinately expensive.

Much love
    Evelyn

Is *Hons & Rebels* any good?

[1] Princess Margaret's engagement to Antony Armstrong-Jones had been announced earlier in the month.
[2] Evelyn had visited Palewski at the Palais Farnese, the French Embassy in Rome.
[3] Harold Macmillan, backed by Hugh Trevor-Roper, was standing against Sir Oliver Franks.

26 March 1960   7 rue Monsieur, VII

Darling Evelyn

Oh dear we never see each other. I went yesterday to a Mass for Mrs [Eugénie] Strong at St Roch. She was born 25 M. 1860, christened & married there – I thought of all the dead people & also how sad it is not to see more of the people one loves when alive. (I must make a list of dead people for such occasions – Mme Costa has one, headed by Landru 'pauvre homme il n'a pas de famille à prier pour lui'.[1])

I can't come & stay as I would have loved because the Death-wisher[2] comes in Easter week & I must be in London the whole of my 4 day visit to see my mother.

Hons & Rebels is awfully funny. It is a dishonest book, full of lies, & my sisters MIND. She is a cold-hearted creature & always has been – one of those women who only care for husband & children.

The book can't be done for this year. My eyes are very bad & 500 words a day of re-writing is all I can manage. I'm afraid this may make the book jerky, I simply can't read chunks of it at a time. I'm writing it 3 times instead of twice as I used to. Have finished 2nd draft this week.

Chatsworth was even too hot for me – I must say I was there in muggy weather. It is a wet heat, so as not to spoil the objects of art. The water is green in one's bath which is very pretty, but now the cook's teeth have gone green & she has given notice. Nothing perfect, as my grandmother used to say.

Funny that you tour the whole of Yurrup & don't come here – never mind.

Love from
     Nancy

Oh the letters about mistakes & misprints of course I get thousands. *Some* very useful one must say. People love to show off, don't they!

[1] Landru, the mass murderer. 'Poor man, he has no family to pray for him.'
[2] Gaston Palewski.

18 May 1960   Combe Florey House
                                         Nr Taunton

Dearest Nancy

I bought a copy of Decca's book & read it with keen attention. I can well understand that it is wounding and I was able to detect numerous errors of fact, but it has filled me with curiosity. Someone told me you reviewed it. Is this true? If so where can I find your review? What surprised me was that she not only gives a nasty impression of the people against whom she has conceived grievances, but about those she presumably loves. I don't think I ever met Esmond Romilly. Certainly I didn't know him at all. She makes him quite detestable. What did he do in the Canadian Air Force? She describes him as sub-humanly incompetent with every sort of mechanism. What became of her second child by him? It must be grown up.[1] Is it simply an American like all the rest of them? Did Decca write all the book herself? It seems by two hands, half fresh & funny if false and half trite & stodgy – the first page of the last chapter, for instance; can she have written that? Is she not now married to a sort of jewish don. Can he have put in the sticky bits. All that cheating & stealing & lying combined with sermons on socialism seems very odd. Do you think it true that the captain of the English ship, intent on abducting her, gave his word not to? Didn't she come to Europe last year? Did you see her?

Margaret now works in London canonising 40 martyrs at £10 a week.[2] No London season for her. Can't afford it and Teresa collected the most awful friends at great expense. She is very happy canonising. I went up to London to entertain her. I shall never go to that city again. I can't eat anything they cook there. Had to live on caviar at £1 a teaspoonful. She made me go to a play about Lawrence of Arabia. All the actors except Sir Alec Guinness were comic buggers & the plot was all buggery – as far as I can gather false to history. We went to the Soane Museum which is still very empty & pleasant.

Poor Maimie came to dine with us. She could only talk of the hardships
& humiliations of her life which are indeed gruesome. We also had
the Jesuit[3] who is Margaret's employer. It was not a happy combi-
nation. She told him she always read the psalms for the day which I
am sure is an illusion derived from memories of the schoolroom at
Madresfield. The poor Jesuit thought his leg was being pulled.

Our asparagus is abundant & delicious – far better than anything
you can get in France. I wish you were here to eat it.

Is Decca still a communist? Jolly uncomfortable for her in U.S.A.
I should have thought. She doesn't seem to have done anything to
help the 'Loyalists' in Spain. Just sponged on them.

You see her book has upset & puzzled me a great deal. I barely
knew her. Odd that it should. You see you made her so amusing &
sweet in your novels it is very disconcerting.

I am toiling away at third volume of war novel.[4] There have been
no good new books except an unfinished posthumous one by a Sicilian
duke[5] – not Fulco [Verdura]. Tony Powell's forthcoming volume of
his polylogy is a disappointment, but I don't think you admire him
anyway, do you?

There are no English left in London.

Is it true Momo is very ill?

Do write & tell me your news and explain Decca more fully.

Love from
Evelyn

[1] The Romillys' daughter Constancia was nineteen; their first child died of pneumonia aged
four months.
[2] Margaret was working as assistant to Father Caraman who had been appointed Vice-
Postulator of the Cause of the English and Welsh Martyrs.
[3] Father Philip Caraman; editor of the *Month* 1948–63.
[4] *Unconditional Surrender* (1961).
[5] Giuseppe di Lampedusa, *The Leopard* (1960).

24 May 1960   Lismore Castle
                                                   Co Waterford
                                                   Eire

Darling Evelyn

No I didn't review it. When I wrote to her I said I thought there
was a chill wind & she was rather hurt. We are on the best of terms
& always have been. What I feel is this. In some respects she has seen
the family, quite without knowing it herself, through the eyes of my
books – that is, if she hadn't read them hers would have been different.
She is absolutely unperceptive of my uncles & aunts, Nanny, Dr
Cheatle[1] & the characters whom I didn't describe & who all could
have been brought to life but simply were not. I haven't said this to

anybody but you as it sounds so conceited. Esmond was the most horrible human being I have ever met. I did say in my letter to her 'you have presented him as the original Teddy-boy' but none of the reviewers made that point.

Clever of you to see the two voices. I am quite certain much of it was written by Treuhaft who is a sharp little lawyer & who certainly made her write it in the first place. The words cash in are never off his lips. (I quite like him but *oh* Americans.) The Romilly daughter is (was, 2 years ago) a stunning beauty.

I've just written the last words of my book. It's not good. I am truly very much handicapped now by my eyes being so poorly – can't read it over & over as I used & therefore I fear it reads jerkily.

I've been here the whole month & go home on Friday. Most of the time with Eddy West about 13 miles from here.[2] I'm stunned by the beauty, emptiness & *pure* pre-new-world atmosphere of Ireland – can't imagine why you don't live here. Some v. nice neighbours, too. Marvellous butchers, one had forgotten what meat can taste like.

I think that's all. Debo has carried off your letter – she *terribly* hates & minds the book.

> Much love
> Nancy

I think they are secret Communists now – call themselves Liberals. But when in Paris their bedroom is always knee deep in *l'Humanité*[3] I note.

[1] The Mitford family general practitioner.
[2] Edward Sackville-West had bought Cooleville House, Co. Tipperary, in 1956.
[3] Organ of the French Communist Party. The Treuhafts resigned from the Communist Party in 1958.

18 June 1960   7 rue Monsieur, VII

Darling Evelyn

Do I pander to this sewer?[1] I have said I will answer questions *if you agree*. I've also told him to read Tony P[owell], Honks etc etc, but I suppose he must have done that.

I've finished *Don't Tell Alfred* oh what a relief. It seems awful twaddle to me, now, but Gladwyn [Jebb] who has read it thinks it's all right. How difficult it is to say what one wants to. I find writing becomes far more difficult, not less.

Debo's Emma is here – a most fascinating creature – very clever & serious & high spirited – takes in everything. She says she's the only one of her contemporaries who hasn't written a book – Lucy Beckett, her great friend aged 16, has written three. Your boy the only one who is actually published (not out yet is it?).[2] What a mercy if he can be a writer as he would hardly be strong enough for office life I imagine.

I go to Venice 4 July – I long for it, it's my yearly treat.

I saw Honks Cooper – I expect you know she's going to live in the red light district like I used to.[3]

Much love, tell your thoughts re Linck Jr
    Nancy

[1] Charles E. Linck, Jr., an American student preparing a thesis on Evelyn, had written to enquire where he could obtain certain 'facts', which he needed 'very earnestly'.
[2] Auberon Waugh, *The Foxglove Saga* (1960). A novel which Evelyn described as 'bizarre' and 'very funny'.
[3] Lady Diana Cooper was moving to Warwick Avenue in Little Venice.

21 June 1960   Combe Florey House
                                                  Nr Taunton
Darling Nancy

What good news that you have finished your novel both for your avid public & yourself. I long to read it. Printers are so lazy nowadays that there is a huge period of gestation.

I am very sorry you should have been bothered by Chas E. Linck, Jr. I have no memory of him. I always throw away letters from Americans unread. I am sure no one will publish his book & that it is simply a ruse to make himself a bore.

I did not find Debo's Emma at all forthcoming when I once met her but I hear good accounts of her on all sides. Mark Grant tried to have her devoured by wolves on Mount Parnassus.[1]

Last week I was driven by poverty to the humiliating experience of appearing on the television.[2] The man who asked the questions simply couldn't believe I had had a happy childhood. 'Surely you suffered from the lack of a sister?'

My daughter Margaret publishes a book today *Forty Martyrs* – a work of research for the Jesuits. First printing 100,000. More than I have ever had or I daresay you either.

Debo was seen hopping in a London street with Freud holding up a foot calling the attention of passers-by to her new shoes.

I saw a sickeningly silly play about people turning into Rhinoceros.[3]

I rather long to go to the London Library sale[4] but shan't. I think the prices will cause much jealousy among our confrères & consoeurs.

What a rum time to go to Venice. You will find it full of trippers.

Love from
    Evelyn

[1] Mark Ogilvie-Grant had managed to lose a group of people on Mount Parnassus, including Emma Cavendish, her father and brother. Their ship left without them and to this day passengers on Hellenic cruises are warned not to be late.

[2] Evelyn was interviewed by John Freeman for the *Face to Face* series.
[3] Eugene Ionesco, *Rhinoceros* (1959).
[4] At a fund-raising sale in aid of the London Library, the manuscript of Evelyn's *Scott-King's Modern Europe* fetched £160. The manuscript of *A Passage to India* by E. M. Forster raised £6,500, and T. S. Eliot's transcription of *The Waste Land* went for £2,800.

6 October 1960   Fontaines-les-Nonnes
                                                  par Puisieux

Darling Evelyn

I say Mr Linck's book about you is going to be lovely stuff. Today's queries: Was Freddy Furneaux-Smith (sic) Sebastian? Why didn't you (me) & Diana Cooper become Roman Catholics? Did you & Evelyn (sic) & Lord Berners & Anthony Powell plan the humour & wit of your novels in a certain way? Did Tony Last go abroad to read Dickens because he couldn't envisage life with Diana Cooper?

We (why the royal?) have been encouraged to visit Garsington & Julian Vinogradoff[1] which ought to be great for us – all those places where the bright young set used to have fun! It must have been wonderful.

Don't you die for it. I am being rather splendid in egging him on discreetly – no actual lies but I can't bear to spoil the trend, as you must realize.

I'm coming over for my book, unless there's a railway strike, on the 27th Oct: – then away for a long week end. Any hope of you being in London the week after? *Do* review the book – I'd rather have a few knocks from you than honey from another (or perhaps it will be knocks all round). Or indeed perhaps I am flattering myself & it won't be reviewed at all. Ole Nole (Coward) has a novel[2] coming out the same day & what I really foresee is that we shall be lumped together as two old has-beens, dead as dust. Bother.

Mme Costa said yesterday, about 'Fabiola', 'Il paraît que, point de vue naissance, ce n'est guère plus brillant qu'Armstrong, mais M. le Curé a des renseignements très satisfaisants sur son âme.'[3] Oh good! Mrs Hammersley who is here says England has become dreadful & her doctor has given up & now keeps a sort of factory of chickens who live in the dark & are called broilers. What does it all mean?

    Much love
    Nancy

[1] Garsington Manor had been the Oxfordshire home of Philip and Lady Ottoline Morrell, and a favourite meeting place for the Bloomsbury group. Igor Vinogradoff married their daughter, Julian.
[2] Noël Coward, *Pomp and Circumstance* (1960)
[3] King Baudouin of the Belgians was engaged to Doña Fabiola de Mora y Aragòn. 'Apparently, insofar as birth is concerned, she's no more of a catch than Armstrong, but M. le Curé has some very satisfactory information regarding her soul.'

10 October 1960   Combe Florey House
                                                   Nr Taunton

Darling Nancy

I long to read your new book & should very much like to review it. The difficulty is that, I have no doubt, every other reviewer wants that treat & I am not a regular reviewer. I am asking the *Spectator* for it but I fear it will have gone out already. Have no fears of its reception. Everyone is agog & loyal Handy has been whetting appetites.

I did not send you a copy of my African pot-boiler because I am ashamed of it & have sent it to no honoured friends.

We must meet when you come to England. It would be lovely if you would come here but it is too much to ask, I am sure, of what the Americans call your 'tight schedule'. I could come to London if you have an evening or a luncheon free. I have no engagements ever. Just tell me when you can fit me in.

I have read Honks's third vol.[1] Jolly good, though of course all the praise of cad Cooper makes painful reading.

I refuse all communication with Mr Linck but I see that it is irresistible to pull his leg.

My anxiety is boundless for your safety in the imminent frog civil war.[2]

I heard from a friend in New York that Momo is at death's door. I expect you knew. John inconsolable, living in the hospital beside her & seeing no one. Henry Lamb[3] died yesterday after a long period of senility. Boots caught Botulism in Sardinia. I thought it always fatal but beefy Boots has survived. I read with revulsion of your junketings with Miss Spain.

I must say I like the idea of you & Tony Powell & Gerald Berners and me planning the wit & humour of our novels together. Paper games, do you think? I never knew Victor Cunard. I fear his death must be a sad loss to you.

Longing to see you.

Love
    Evelyn

[1] Diana Cooper, *Trumpets from the Steep* (1960).
[2] A mass demonstration in Paris for negotiated peace in Algeria had been called for later in the month. It was violently broken up by the police and many people were injured.
[3] Henry Lamb (1883–1960). Painter best known for his portrait of Lytton Strachey (1913). He painted a memorable portrait of Evelyn in 1930. Married Lady Pansy Pakenham in 1928.

12 October 1960   Fontaines-les-Nonnes
                                                   par Puisieux

Darling Evelyn

I'd love to come & stay – that's what I was hinting at. The thing is I can't suggest a date because I'm already in a muddle between

Debo & Gerry Wellington. When that's cleared up I could come (*if* you don't mind middle of week?*) after one or the other, whichever is easiest for getting to you *from*. Is there a magic train from Reading or possibly one from Chesterfield? Time will show. (There may, I am told, be a General Strike & if so I shall stay here – don't want to be caught in the Old Land with no hope of escape.)

How I pray you'll do *Alfred* – you are kind to try. Heywood says Diana's book is splendid but I could hardly bear what came out in *Sunday Times*. Anyhow she has a huge public & will sell. What I've been living in is Lesley Blanch *Sabres of Paradise*, such a fascinating story of a man almost exactly like my father (physically too). The only trouble is the writing which sometimes becomes unbearably awful. What a pity Paddy [Leigh Fermor] can't get hold of such an interesting subject instead of wasting his excellent language on Greek peasants.

The story of Momo is heartrending. Five weeks ago her secretary said it will be over in a few days. She is in tortures. The whole thing is a lesson never to get in the power of doctors – but for them she would have died 6 months ago at least. They drove her mad with the treatment & have kept her hanging on, half drugged & in pain, all the summer. John says how can one believe in God? I admit the naïveté, but all the same it does seem hard that Momo, who really never hurt a fly, should suffer like that.

Yes, Victor's death is perhaps the greatest blow I have ever had – outside my family. I loved Robert [Byron] more but saw much much less of him.

You must be pleased & proud by the way about your son's book. Faithful Handy told me your exchange of letters.

As soon as I know exactly what I'm up to I'll write again.

Love
    Nancy

26 October 1960   4 Chesterfield Street
                                              London W1

Darling Evelyn

Could you have me Thurs: 10th – Sat 12th Nov:? I go to Stratfield Saye that day, so if you could find me a train for Reading all would fit in splendidly.

There is a rumour that you like my book. *Daily M.* critic came to see me he says the children are all wrong oh bother. He evidently had not seen ONE joke.

Momo's funeral looms on Monday oh the sadness.

Much love
    Nancy

I didn't send you the book as I guess you've got a copy?

27 October [1960]   Combe Florey House
                                                    Nr Taunton

Darling Nancy

Yes, your communist manifesto, *Alfred*, is your best novel. I have
reviewed it for a funny little paper[1] run by Evelyn Gardner's niece
and a beaver whose name escapes me – Rosse? Rose?[2] He calls me
'Evelyn'. I hope they send you their December number in which my
homage will appear.

The golden dates of your visit are inscribed. You should leave
Taunton (if you must) at 4.15 on Saturday 12th Nov. arriving Reading
at 6.23. You do not say where you are coming from. If from Chatsworth the train is 12.3 at *Sheffield* (like Ed) arriving here at 5.19. Unless
Andrew has feudal rights to stop it where he will, it does not, apparently, stop at Chesterfield in the winter.

There has been no mention in my paper of Momo's death. That
is the loss of living in the country. I ought to go to her funeral. When?
Where? Could you bear to telegraph?

If you are coming from Chatsworth, would you like to bring Debo
with you? Would she care to come? If so, I will write & invite. There
are a large number of pheasants taking refuge from my neighbours
but as we have no dog they run away & hide when Bron goes out
with his gun. Otherwise the 'entertainment' would be pure chat.

You said earlier that Alfred was elected Warden.[3] Your students
remember such things.

    Much love
        Evelyn

[1] The *London Magazine*, December 1960. Evelyn wrote: 'It is a socialist tract, the most explicit
that Miss Mitford has yet offered us. She has never dissembled her subversive opinions but
until now she has preferred to work in the class-war as what used, in her youth, to be called
a "fifth columnist".'
[2] Alan Ross (1922–2001). Editor of the *London Magazine* since 1961. Married to Evelyn Gardner's
niece, Jennifer Fry, 1949–85.
[3] In *The Pursuit of Love*, Alfred Wincham is elected Warden of St Peter's College, Oxford; in
Don't Tell Alfred he is back in the chair of Pastoral Theology.

29 October 1960   Chatsworth
                                                    Bakewell
                                                    Derbyshire

Darling Evelyn

I'm *so sorry* to be such a fidget – I wondered if Wed 16 or Thurs 17
Nov: would be the same to you? A tablet to my father is to be unveiled
on the 9th & my various relations round Swinbrook would like me, I

think, to stay for more than just that night. If the week after doesn't do for you & 10th is all right don't bother & I'll come. Cld you tell me to 4 Chesterfield St. It's complicated fitting things in during a short stay.

Book v. badly received. Luckily I foresaw that this would happen sooner or later & I think I've saved up enough to live on.

Love
    N

30 October 1960   Chatsworth
                                                             Bakewell

Andrew has just come with your letter. Oh dear I feel I'm being a trouble, with change of plans not quite my fault. Dreadful about Alfred being a Warden it comes from my fan in Monte Carlo being dead, he always knew these things & was going to help me & he died when *Alf* was hardly begun. (He knew everybody's age. I once asked him what Fanny's surname was & he said 'Logan, same as Uncle Matthew's butler, a fact which has always puzzled me.')

Your *kind* words about the book very well received after some awful reviews. Sunday papers are better however.

Debo is off to shoot with her adored Colonel Stirling,[1] it's the Colonel now all day.

I go back to Chesterfield St now.

    Much love
        Nancy

Hope you got my telegram. When I left London they were planning to have no chaps in aid of keeping Randolph off.[2] I hope this hasn't all changed since. Anyway it will be too hateful – better skipped.

[1] William Stirling (1911–83). Lieutenant-Colonel of the 2nd SAS regiment 1943–5.
[2] From Momo Marriott's funeral.

1 November 1960   4 Chesterfield Street, W1

Darling Evelyn
    I come I come (10th). I must see you. I'll get a train at Cheltenham that's easy. On the Sat: I must get myself to Reading. I *apologize* for boring you with changes of plan. One of the horrors of coming here is trying to fit everything in – now I've got a sore throat & feel miserable.

    Momo's funeral was poignant about 6 ex beauties all with Rolls Royces & black fur hats.

I've rarely been so depressed in my life as I am today.

Love from
    Nancy

Jean (parlourmaid) is dosing me with Beecham's powders. I feel like a horse.

New Year's Eve 1960   7 rue Monsieur, VII

Darling Evelyn
    Many thanks for sending the review & many thanks *indeed* for writing it. It's really the only good one I've had & now Handy has stabbed me in the back by conjuring up a vision of a Belgian-type mob baying outside the shop for its 15/-. I can see the time has come to chuck it & I spend my days & little remaining eyesight counting out my money. If only one got an honest 5% as of yore I would be more or less all right. I think I'd better start by having all my teeth out as it costs £25 here to have one stopped.
    Meanwhile I've bought a Longhi, a perhaps Pellegrini from Mrs Frank, a Lemoine sketch for a ceiling & another small picture & my leeveeng (French for salon) is transformed.
    Thank Hatty for her letter. The scarf seems to have been more of a success than the evening bag of yester year.
    Did you read an article about Hydra in which the writer said he had expected to find you & me & the Duke (sic) of Winchester? What could he have meant? Not a word about Paddy-whack[1] whom one might expect to find it was very odd.
    The sweep is here. For some reason this utterly disrupts a French household – I don't remember what happens at home but it can't be so awful or I would. Marie slightly mourns the day when little boys from Savoy were sent up the chimney in person – but then, like you, she is a reactionary.

    Much love, happy 1961
        Nancy

London Mag: still hasn't come & one can't get it here so I might never have read your kind words if you had not sent them.
P.S. Smashing review in *Weak Blad* (Dutch mag which is always on my side).
Did you read *Sowing*?[2] Masterly. Koestler's new book[3] is screamingly funny. There's a dreadful one I'm now reading by a witless American about Sir Max.[4] One feels for him, his last years poisoned by this interfering sewer.

[1] Patrick Leigh Fermor.

[2] By Leonard Woolf (1960), the first in his five-volume autobiography.
[3] Arthur Koestler, *The Lotus and the Robot* (1960), a critical examination of Zen and yoga.
[4] S. N. Behrman, *Conversation with Max* (1960), based on interviews with Max Beerbohm conducted in his old age.

4 January 1961   Combe Florey House
                                           Nr Taunton

Darling Nancy

No, no, no. You must not think of giving up the novel. As I said in all sincerity *Alfred* positively clamours for a sequel. Handy has all the concealed malice of the underdog. Don't believe a word he says. Reviewers are a paltry lot.

It has been a bad year for the old jumpers – Elizabeth Bowen, John Betjeman, Leslie Hartley down & out of the race; Tony & you still in the saddle thank goodness, though Tony is sitting unsteady with his arms round the horse's neck & irons flying. You must collect yourself for the next fence. Graham Greene is going to have a heavy fall. I have just read his newest book[1] about lepers *not* what Americans call 'inspirational'.

I have just been editing a little life of La Veuve Clicquot-Ponsardin[2] – very interesting. I had always vaguely supposed her a woman of the Second Empire. Did you realise she was born 12 years before the Revolution & widowed in year of Trafalgar (Austerlitz to you), the daughter of a Jacobin deputy, ancestress of three dukes? Wine was at first a minor concern; her husband liked trotting round on a horse so he paid more attention to his vines than the banking & cloth-weaving which were the source of a very modest fortune. But I expect you knew all this.

I have not yet had my teeth out. The day cannot, I suppose, be far off. You can get them drawn free here but not replaced. I don't much care for Uncle Matthew 'dentures'. I believe one can rub one's gums with a preparation which hardens them well enough to chew most things. Anyway I like soft food & prefer pâtés & mousses to hunks of meat.

What do you suppose 'nouvelle vague' VAGUE means? According to my dictionary either 'vague news' or 'new waste-land'. Idiot English reviewers are always using it.

I bet you can't say 'Lovely, lovely 1960'.

All love
    Evelyn

[1] *A Burnt-Out Case* (1961).
[2] Jacqueline de Caraman-Chimay, *The Life and Times of Madame Veuve-Clicquot-Ponsardin* (1961). Evelyn contributed a preface.

7 January 1961   7 rue Monsieur, VII

Darling Evelyn

Vague (feminine) means a wave. But I see also in Larousse: *Fig: et poét*: Objets qui se succèdent sans cesse.[1] Wasteland seems quite as good, but I think that wld be *un* vague.

I *loathed* 1960 & the death of Victor is something I shall never get over. I don't know if I can go to Venice without him, but if not, what to do during Marie's holiday? I feel so well at Venice, & then I've got many friends there. But it seems to me I should be in floods all the time, from arriving at the station & him not there to meet me, onwards. Oh, *alas*!

I know about La Veuve because my friend Jacqueline de Chimay wrote a book — perhaps the very one you are editing?

I've been sent an American book on the Necklace affair.[2] The writer says she spent 4 years here working on it — in 100 000 words she tells what Harold Nicolson does in 3 pages,[3] no more & no less. No new information, though I believe the jewellers have a mass of interesting stuff so that, until they allow that to be seen, it's sheer waste of time to write anything at all. Poor Yanks, always so inept. They really do seem to be subsiding at last, however.

Mr James Murray,[4] 1st sec: here, was sent for by the ambassador & told he is to be chef de mission. 'The only trouble is I haven't got a large enough map of Africa to show you where.' It then transpired he is accredited to the pigmies, 800 miles from the nearest white man. (Typical of the times as our gov: used to say.) 'Mr Sylvester will help you to open the office.' Alas Mr Sylvester is a giant — there is now a horrid rumour that the pigmies, on learning about democracy, one man one vote, quickly castrated all the giants. Poor Mr Murray, being Scotch, isn't a bubble of fun, but even he lets out an occasional hollow laugh when recounting these things.

What to read? The book about Sir Max was rather funny, not as meant to be by the author though. One could just imagine poor Sir Max's face when he heard this ghastly American had turned up again!

I enjoyed Harold N, but it's not truly good. I loved *Sowing*. I'm now reading Monckton Milnes[5] & liking it quietly (old book by Pope Hennessy). My eyes not good at all.

Much love
        N

[1] *Figurative and poetical*: Incessantly self-renewing form.
[2] Frances Mossiker, *The Queen's Necklace* (1961).
[3] *The Age of Reason* (1960).
[4] James Murray (1919–2007). First secretary in Paris 1957–61, Ambassador to Rwanda and Burundi 1962–3. Knighted in 1978.
[5] A biography of Richard Monckton Milnes, 1st Baron Houghton (1809–85), by James Pope-Hennessy (2 vols., 1949, 1952).

17 January 1961   Fontaines-les-Nonnes
                                             par Puisieux

Darling Evelyn

Yes one has to make one's own decisions. First of all though, *never* Mme La Princesse unless the person is royal. Non-royal Princes get their titles from Savoy or the Empire it is not a French title. Also never Mme la Comtesse (except on envelopes), it wld be like saying Her Grace the Duchess, old fashioned, no longer the usage.

As one writes for the English eye I put the Comtesse with a capital C. A comtesse is not comparable to an Eng: countess – she may be infinitely less (the wife of the great great grandson of the second son of a count, marquis or duke) or infinitely more, like the Comtesse de Paris. What I do in books as in life is to introduce the character as the Comtesse de X & refer to her afterwards as Mme de X. In the case of a duchesse I refer to her as the duchess (in English). It seems to run more smoothly. You still say Mme la Duchesse when speaking to one but only servants say Mme la Comtesse. Only the King says Comtesse.

The head of a family is Comte de X; all the rest are Comte Jean de X, the same with princely families (though the head is generally a duke). Jacqueline is Psse Jean de CC (La Psse on an envelope).

Wouldn't Kingsley Amis enjoy this letter.

Love from
    N

Example of my own method:

All eyes now turned to the door through which the Duchesse de Dreux-Brézé slowly advanced on the arm of M. Furet. This duchess, whose private life was, to say the least of it, tumultuous & whose piety was only equalled by her immeasurable greed, was one of the greatest beauties of our own or any other age . . .

There was a low murmur from the dowagers' bench when the Marquise de Q took the floor with her husband's cousin, Comte Jean de Q. A little while later, at the supper table, I heard Mme de Q asking, in her small reedy voice, for a glass of ginger pop. There seemed to be no available footman (I learnt afterwards that those who were not already lying, drunk & insensible, on the back stairs, had rushed to the hall in the hopes of handing his coat to the Swedish ambassador, well known to every lacquey in Paris for his ridiculous habit of dealing out colossal tips), so M. de Q got up & went himself to the sideboard. As soon as his place became vacant it was occupied by the Marquis de Q who addressed himself to his wife. Although what he said was inaudible everybody knew that he was supplicating her, for the sake of their sixteen children, to respect her own position in society. Trembling with rage Mme de Q rose to her feet & told M.

Furet that she would be requiring her carriage at once. The unfortunate host, seeing that this ball which had cost the aspirations of a
lifetime as well as etc. etc.

My pen seems to have run away with me.

7 June 1961   7 rue Monsieur, VII

Darling Evelyn

If you're not busy (& if you are, *when* you're not) will you explain
something to me?

You know *death* – (my brother Tom aged 3 said once Grandfather,
you know *adultery* –)

Well, one dies, is buried & rises again & is judged. What happens
then between death & the end of the world? Are we what the French
call en liberté provisoire? Do we sleep? But I'm always hearing people
say he's in a better place *now* or he knows *now* this that or the other.
Do elucidate. I asked Mme Costa but she is too deaf, I couldn't get
through what I meant; she merely said she prays for me, not, I thought,
very hopefully. My dear Bishop of Meaux I was so fond of has died.
M. le Curé hates me, I wouldn't ask him anything. One or two friends
(Catholic) were quite as much puzzled as I am, when I put it to them,
& said they wld be glad to know what I find out on the subject.

I've been in Ireland & enjoyed it in a quiet way, as I always do. At
the end of this month I go to Venice, back here in Aug:

Death again. It seems there is in Rome a saintly child who died,
recovered, & when asked what it had been like said perfectly heavenly
so they let him die again. Well that's not sleep, but at the same time
he can't have had the court martial so how can it have been heavenly?
[. . .] If we go to heaven first, then have the resurrection of the body
(like finding your motor after a party) & then have the court martial
& then go to hell that seems awfully disappointing?

Oh DO TELL

Love
    N

9 June 1961   Combe Florey House
                                                Nr Taunton

Darling Nancy

At the moment of death each individual soul is judged and sent to
its appropriate place – the saints straight to heaven, unrepentant sinners to Hell, most (one hopes) to Purgatory where in extreme discomfort but confident hope we shall be prepared for the presence of

God. Our bodies remain on earth & decay. Only Our Lord's & Our Lady's bodies were assumed into a different order of existence. All this is quite straightforward. It is called 'the Particular Judgment'. You will remember that Our Lord said to the penitent thief '*This day* thou shalt be with me in paradise.' It has never been suggested that his body did not follow the normal course of mortality.

The Last or General Judgment is something quite different & very mysterious. It is the end of the world and of time. It may happen at any moment now or in the remote future. The Christians of the first century seem to have expected it momentarily. At the Last Judgment those still living will be judged there & then. There is no appeal for us who have died earlier from our particular sentences. The change will be our reunion with our bodies. What comprises these bodies no one claims to know. They will be individual, recognizable and free from the defects of our present bodies. In 13th century it was generally held that these bodies would have full physical existence – position, weight etc. Modern theologians think these terms poetic & metaphorical. No one pretends to understand the mechanics of the change. The essential principle is that we are *not*, as most orientals believe, spiritual beings temporarily encumbered with a body which we gladly shed & then lose our personalities in some all embracing soul. God had to become man & take a body to show us this. The body is not simply a source of sensation, temptation, pain & decrepitude. It is us.

Besides heaven, hell & purgatory there is generally believed (though not dogmatically defined) limbo where the unbaptised noble savages go. They never enjoy the beatific vision. Neither do they suffer the pains of hell.

It is generally believed that children under 7 are incapable of mortal sin. The Curé d'Ars said of a child of 5 'It's lucky she died when she did. She will have a long time in purgatory. Had she lived she would have been damned. She was far gone in sin.'

Bossuet's death was indeed a sad loss to the Church. I am surprised you have only lately heard of it.

I am a having grievous time with weddings. A daughter last week, a son at the end of the month.[1] Most fatiguing and costly.

Love from
     Evelyn

If you are gravely concerned about the problem of the reunion of soul & body I will look up a sermon of Ronald's which makes as much sense of it as reason can.

[1] Teresa was married to John D'Arms on 1 June, and Auberon to Lady Teresa Onslow on 1 July.

12 June 1961   7 rue Monsieur, VII

Darling Evelyn

Thanks awfully. I quite understand & also I see it wasn't so foolish not understanding because there is a confusion between the two judgements. As for the body being us, of course one knows the truth of that – I must say I hadn't realized it was a Christian doctrine. I thought on the contrary that the body was supposed to be mortified & kept under in every possible way, even dirty, so that the soul could blossom. If it is really us, then we should look after it accordingly – no?

I hope you are pleased with the marriage of your brilliant boy & also I hope she has got a little money?

I met a charming Colonel who is the godfather of Harriet. I said to Raymond Mortimer who was there, on discovering this link, are we not called Gossips? And he said yes & you never can marry. How too sad. But he has a very pretty wife already.

I wish there was something to read – when will your book be finished? This is a reflection, not a question as I see you *are* very busy. I've got nothing to read & no ideas about what to write, a more satisfactory occupation since I get through the books I read so very quickly.

Thank you again for your long & fascinating exposé.

    Love
        Nancy

19 June 1961   Combe Florey House
                                                Nr Taunton
Darling Nancy

No, you haven't got it quite right. The body is an essential part of us. That doesn't mean we must pamper it. St Paul says 'bring it into subjection' like schooling a horse. There are two contrasting heresies – Boots who thinks his beautiful body is made to be crammed with rich food and covered with kisses and Lady Astor[1] who thinks her body is an illusion. Good people (not I) whack themselves with chains & wear hair shirts, just to remind themselves forcibly that they are not all soul.

If the Col you speak of is Col Bill Stirling & he remembers he is Hatty's godfather, remind him he has not yet sent her a christening present still less any tokens of affection at Christmas. He was a rich man when I asked him to stand sponsor. Now I fear he has ruined himself at cards. He was a very indulgent commander to me at one stage of the war.

Can't advise anything to read – I am fortunate in having such a bad memory that I can read the same detective story every six weeks and still wonder who the murderer will be.

Bron's young lady is pretty and has a little money. Alas she is one of the most tiresome kinds of protestant – she can't see the difference between her Church & the Pope's and has to be restrained from making sacrilegious communions in foreign churches.

Try *Pauvre et Saint* (Editions du Seuil) by D. Pézeril. That will show how good people look after the bod.

Honor Guinness[2] was received in the Church. It is rumoured that Eric Dudley[3] is under instruction.

Oh dear I have to go to London today. Horrible place in the summer.

Love
    E

[1] Nancy Astor converted to Christian Science in 1914 and had all the intolerance that goes with religious fanaticism.
[2] Lady Honor Guinness (1909–76). Married to Chips Channon 1933–45 and to Frantisek Vaclav Svejdar in 1946.
[3] 3rd Earl of Dudley (1894–1969). Married as his third wife in 1961 Grace Kolin, former wife of Prince Stanislas Radziwill.

21 June 1961   7 rue Monsieur, VII

That's funny because I asked Col Bill Stirling what he gave as a Xening present (remembering that Laura said at the time mine was the nicest & knowing how rich he is, I was curious) & he said he couldn't quite remember, as if he couldn't remember whether 100 or 1000 pounds or perhaps 10 000.

I've been reading Boots on *Promise*[1] & told Debo *she must* (the Eton part). She doesn't care for books without pictures but luckily there is a very very pretty one on the cover – Boots himself looking as you once said like a miners' leader & unlike real life.

I've been tidying for the summer hols what a lot of your letters I've got, I must ask Randolph how much he will give me for them. But my summer plans seem to be collapsing & very likely I shall end up in the Temperance Hotel Isle of Wight.

The Wrightsmans are here – do you know them? Old Chourlee is the 7th richest man & about the 4th nastiest but I love him he makes me *scream* with laughter. Yesterday he announced sadly that the Ritz is an under developed area. It seems he bought a picture in London & paid for & now gets neither it *nor his money back* which the Duke of Leeds has pocketed.[2] I said I do love it when the Br–ish turn cunning. He looked at me sadly but speechlessly. He's always rather sad. Weighs himself twice a day (body again).

Love
    N

¹ *Enemies of Promise* had been republished as a Penguin Modern Classic with a new preface by Cyril Connolly.
² Charles Wrightsman had bought the portrait of the Duke of Wellington by Goya; he was refused permission to take it out of the country and eventually sold it to the National Gallery for the price he had given for it.

20 October 1961   7 rue Monsieur, VII

Evelyn your book!¹ Surely one of your very best, oh how I love it. I've blinded myself for a week by reading for far too long but how could one stop? I wish you could have heard my screams when the Serge² appeared at your father's funeral. (Colonel always says but will the general public . . . ? But in fact the general public *does*.) But you are horrid about that good old Serge & I'm afraid he'll *mind*. So naughty making him talk American. Wrightsman (Goya) nearly died when the *D. Ex* reported him as having said: oh Gee why it's painted on board. I was much nicer about Susan-Mary³ – admit.

Of course your politics are nefarious, but writers aren't meant to understand them – somebody asked me to sign a manifesto the other day & I replied Nobody asked Marie Corelli what she thought about Agadir. But the reviewers won't like your attitude at all.

The abortion part is so good – her really not wanting one I mean. It must be exactly like that.

Oh you clever thing.

I must go to London to see Mama in November but think I can't embark on country visits as I've been away from here too much this year. You might be about, perhaps? Anyway I'll tell the date when I know it.

   Fond love & congrats
      Nancy

¹ *Unconditional Surrender.*
² Evelyn caricatured Stuart Preston as Lieutenant Padfield ('Loot').
³ Susan Mary Patten contributed to aspects of Mildred Jungfleisch (pronounced 'Youngfleesh') in Nancy's novels.

[postmarked 24 October 1961]   Combe Florey House
[postcard]   Nr Taunton

THANK YOU FOR KIND ENCOURAGEMENT
HAVE SENT GASTON COPY
CAN'T THINK WHAT YOU MEAN ABOUT 'SERGEANT'
I SHALL BE IN LONDON SATURDAY NOVEMBER 25TH SAILING
NEXT DAY

   Love

22 October 1961   7 rue Monsieur, VII

Darling Evelyn

I've finished it. I didn't think you brought out the *amusingness* of the buzz bombs – but then I realized that if they were going to kill poor Virginia you couldn't very well. But in fact people one knew were never killed in raids – I mean no human being of any sort that I knew was, except Myrtle.[1] So there is an unreality about this death which you would be the first to point out in the work of another.

Still I'm glad about the happy ending. I expect they'll like Trimmer's kid far better than their own.

Nabokov[2] came to see me, not *Lolita*, his cousin the musician. He wants me to ask you if you'd allow him to make a short opera of *Pinfold*. He's a most attractive amusing man whom I think you would like – I really feel sure you wld though difficult to know with you. He seems to have some fascinating ideas about *Pinfold*. If you would consider it, he'd no doubt go to England & talk it over.

You got one thing wrong. Spruciboots never dived from a flying bomb – he dived off to the country for the duration of them. You probably weren't in London & so don't remember the extraordinary behaviour of many of our friends. But old Ruby sat them out.

    Love from
        Nancy

I've never despised the English bourgeoisie so much as during the air raids – they were lamentable – they used to come into the shop, buy large armfuls of books & bugger.

[1] Myrtle Farquharson (1897–1941). She was killed in a London air raid. Married to Robin d'Erlanger in 1925.
[2] Nicholas Nabokov (1903–78). Composer and musicologist.

[October 1961]   Combe Florey House
                                                Nr Taunton

Darling Nancy

You killed a heroine in child-birth. That is a very rare occurrence. Several chaps I knew were bombed in the chapel at Wellington Barracks.

Only Box-Bender thought the ending happy.

Nabokov may make an opera of *Pinfold* if I may sing in it & design the scenery.

I was in London for V2s and agree they were not at all alarming, but I passed through during V1s and got the impression people were nervous. Wasn't it then the lower orders jeered at Sir Winston? I certainly heard two upper class ladies discussing whether they ought to pray for V1s not to fall on them.

I made bourgeois Box Bender and Elderbury bugger – if by that term you mean decamp.

Love from
 Evelyn

And especial love to your poor eyes. Have you no one to read to you? In England everyone would. The French are such selfish hogs. Think how we all read to Peter Beatty.

25 October 1961   7 rue Monsieur, VII

Darling Evelyn

I'm writing to tell you the following story, recounted by Desmond Guinness. 'We met a very pretty girl in Dublin & asked her to stay – in the end she stayed a week & then we took her to Dublin where we met the old mother –'

Well who d'you think the old mother was? It took some time to work it out & then it was Baby Jungman. Oh how Diana & I did scream – I said I must tell Evelyn.[1]

Good & very understanding review in the *D.T.*

You needn't write to me in Braille by the way, but my eyes are a perfect bore because I can't read after dinner & the time before going to bed seems endless & I hate dining out more & more. Since television the wireless here, which used to be fascinating, has become much less good. The English wireless is nought but the other Nancy [Spain] & fond as I am of her one doesn't want her, showing off, every night.

Are you going to America to note the shelters?

How can a good man like you tell such lies? (Serge)

Do you mean that Nabokov may perhaps make the opera? I'm sure you can sing in it.

Love
 N

How odd the controversy over R. Macaulay.[2] I had a furious letter from Rebecca [West] about it. Didn't read the extracts but it seems wicked of the cousin.

[1] Teresa Cuthbertson's daughter, Penelope, married Desmond Guinness in 1985.
[2] A literary storm had blown up around the posthumous publication of Rose Macaulay's *Letters to a Friend 1950–52* (1961), edited by her cousin Constance Babington-Smith. The confessional letters were addressed to Father John Hamilton Johnson, an English priest who lived in America, and recorded Macaulay's affair with an ex-Catholic priest and married man.

Part VI
1962–1966

WHEN HER mother died in May 1963, Nancy wrote to the Colonel: 'I have a feeling nothing really *nice* will ever happen again in my life, things will just go from bad to worse, leading to old age & death.' In spite of these gloomy predictions, the next five years of Nancy's life were not without happiness. Palewski returned from Rome in 1962 to take up an appointment as Minister for Atomic Energy; his social and official engagements kept him as busy as ever, but at least Nancy could talk to him on the telephone and see him whenever he would spare the time. She embarked on a life of Louis XIV at Versailles, a book that was a pleasure to write and with which she felt completely satisfied when it was finished. Published as *The Sun King*, it was another best-seller and ensured that she was comfortably off for the rest of her life.

With the publication of his autobiography, *A Little Learning* (1964), Evelyn bowed out of the world. Physically enfeebled by years of neglecting his health, he was emotionally broken by despair. The marriage of his favourite daughter Margaret to Giles FitzHerbert in 1962 left him feeling bereft and betrayed. The Second Vatican Council, with its emphasis on ecumenism and the vernacular, seemed to open the gates to the kind of liberal religiosity which he despised, threatening to deliver him to the anarchical forces from which he had fled when he embraced Catholicism. Nancy's attempts to rouse him from his torpor met with small success.

7 March 1962   Combe Florey House
                                          Nr Taunton

Dearest Nancy

Have you been plastiquée? As a notorious socialist you must be in great danger.[1] They missed Graham Greene by inches and he is much less forthright in his subversive utterances. Do come to England where it is safe.

I have been away for months taking my daughter Margaret in my footsteps in British Guiana. We missed the riots there by several days – also those in Caracas. We also just missed two domestic murders. All very disappointing for Meg. Golly the food was horrible in the Caribbean. Oh the joy of getting on board a French ship. We joined her midway in a cruise which included H. Nicolson & Vita, Sillitoe[2] the policeman not the proletarian novelist and a new Jewish chum named Sir Philip Sebag-Montefiore-Magnus-Allcroft.[3] There were also a lot of frogs on board who never stopped shaking hands with one another. H. Nicolson is quite senile. He awoke for a few minutes a day to tell very old English stories in French. Lady N. was accompanied by a lady who kept saying: 'Where's Vita? I *must* get at her hair.' There were also Letty Cotterell in a poor way – diabetic, cataracted eyes & a bit alcoholic – terrible shakes before her third gin – and a lot of noisy elderly English women who talked all the voyage of what tips they should give at the end. But the cooking was splendid. The frogs seem able to unfreeze frozen food so that it still has a taste – fruit & cheese always au point, delicious bread, plenty of caviare. The ship is named *Antilles*, should you ever think of taking a cruise.

Do you remember Patrick Buchan-Hepburn?[4] He is a lord now & lives in unexampled splendour in Trinidad. There is a portrait of him in every room.

I climbed precipices in Guiana & did not die.

Saw Daphne [Fielding] in Lisbon. It is all rot about her leaving. A story put about by Diana who now wants to collect everyone in the smoke of Paddington Station.

Have you read Isherwood's new publication?[5] Awfully clever & amusing. No change at all since his Berlin days. He makes himself out to be very young & rather nasty. Perhaps he is.

A propos of buggery – what about J. Sparrow's exposure of *Lady Chatterley*.[6] It was all new to me tho everyone else says he knew about it all along.

Same subject. Poor Boots can't show his face in White's. Apparently Cecil Beaton was interviewed on the television and the fellow said, 'But have you no *men* friends, Mr Beaton.' 'Yes. One. Cyril Connolly.'

Daphne tells me Debo is now installed in White House Washington.[7] You can't approve of that much. Worse than Freud.

Did you ever know an old spinster called Rose Macaulay? It appears she was no spinster but had a lover (hallucination?) and she wrote a lot of disagreeable letters to a protestant clergyman in America. The publishers said did I mind references to myself in them. There were all kinds of strictures on 'Evelyn'. I didn't know her, so I said, yes I minded. I met her at Mrs Fleming's once & thought her sharp but ladylike. Not at all the kind of person to gush to a parson.

I expect you will recognize characters in Isherwood's book. I couldn't.

Is it normal for frogs to shake hands so much or have they picked it up from the Americans? All the sailors, even, shook hands whenever they passed one another on deck.

Love from
Evelyn

[1] Terrorist bombing in Paris over the Algerian crisis was at its height.
[2] Percy Sillitoe (1888–1962). Director-General of MI5 1946–53. Knighted in 1942.
[3] Sir Philip Magnus-Allcroft (1906–88). Author, as Philip Magnus, of *Sir Walter Raleigh* (1951), *Gladstone* (1954) and *King Edward VII* (1964).
[4] Created Baron Hailes (1901–74) in 1957. Governor-General of the West Indies 1957–62. Evelyn had stayed with Lord Hailes during his Caribbean tour.
[5] Christopher Isherwood, *Down There on a Visit* (1962).
[6] John Sparrow (1906–92). Warden of All Souls College, Oxford, 1952–77. From evidence in the text, he demonstrated that Mellors sodomised Lady Chatterley and that D. H. Lawrence advocated the practice. *Encounter*, February 1962.
[7] The Duke and Duchess of Devonshire were staying with the Hon. David Ormsby-Gore (later Lord Harlech), British Ambassador in Washington.

10 March 1962   7 rue Monsieur, VII

Darling Evelyn

Very glad you have stopped reading Dickens to Meg in the jungle & returned safely. I've just got back from Rome where I've been (Farnese) for a few days – very nice because hardly any social life at all – just one dinner of 26 & one large luncheon party.

Yes the French do shake hands. The other day I saw 2 buses in a traffic jam & the drivers leant out & shook hands. Funniest of all are the children arriving at the infant school near here & all shaking hands with each other. In the Chambre the deputies all do it once a day but if they have already seen each other in the morning & are busy it seems they dash past each other shouting re for re-bonjour. They are a polite & formal race, the French.

Diana Mosley saw Cecil being televisioned & saying how much he hates you. I was asked to go in for this programme – no fear. It's the only sad thing about living here that one doesn't see these glories.

Yes wasn't it too strange about Rose Macaulay. I read the letters which seemed rather dull & showed, as you say, a person one hadn't suspected. Can she really have had a lover? On aura tout vu.[1]

A boring question. Did Hatty ever receive my Xmas present? It was a night dress from Harrods. It's not that I want to be thanked but I don't want her to think I was unfaithful. Do tactfully enquire.

Debo & the White House. I must tell you all the tales, they are *too funny*. He can't be worse than Freud can he?

Must go back to the *Master of Ballantrae*[2] which Col lent me for the journey & which I can't put down.

Fond love – I come over for a few days to see my mother, about 20th I guess, might you be in London?

N

[1] Now we'll have seen everything.
[2] By Robert Louis Stevenson (1889).

13 March [1962]   Combe Florey House
                                          Nr Taunton

Dearest Nancy

Laura says yes Hatty got your very kind Christmas present and was delighted with it. It was very WRONG of her not to write.

By the way Colonel Gaston Farnese never thanked me for sending him my last book.

It would be a great treat to see you in London even in Lent. Are you dining anywhere e.g. Ann Fleming, where I could intrude? Or have you a free luncheon? Where will you stay?

I wonder where the frogs picked up this nasty habit of handshaking. I suspect democracy citoyen francmaçon all that.

Love
        E

[postmarked 16 March 1962]   [7 rue Monsieur, VII]
[postcard]

They picked it up from *us* dear boy – Marie Antoinette used to speak of le shakehand à l'Anglaise.

I'll be in London next week but all rather fidgety as only 3 nights to see my mother. Don't know where I stay even. Bother it. But if you're there anyway I must see you.

25 March 1962   7 rue Monsieur, VII

Darling Evelyn

We should have enjoyed ourselves more without Violet [Powell]. Do you think Tony suffers. If so he is wonderfully good & loyal. I couldn't stand it I'm afraid. There were such a lot of things I wanted to say oh bother.

I'm preparing (Hamilton's idea but I'm all for it) a book of essays, already published, mostly. There is one that hasn't been, on our old Nanny & the account of going to Russia I wrote in 1954. Others I am cheering up a bit. Hamilton implored me not to tell you because he thinks you will stop me. I hope to disarm the critics by calling it *The Water Beetle*.

Colonel is here. He wrote about *Uncon: Sur:* at the time what can have happened. He is completely truthful so we must believe he did write. As I can never really read his writing I didn't see he had said this in my letter. It would have been unlike him not to – specially as he loved the book.

Debo is sad that you have become her enemy – why have you? She says he used to try on my hats for me.

Roger Hinks[1] has got a Swedish phrase book (quite a recent one) & one of the phrases is Can nobody row me over this lake before sunset? The torso of a young girl in a museum is described as maid's trunk. Sort of jokes I do love.

You won't come over? No, there's no more Chantilly, I do see. Oh dear – well I'll see you in October I hope. It was *so good* of you to come up. You don't look very well, pray take care of yourself.

> Much love
> Nancy

What is Hatty's job? I don't seem to have been consulted how too strange.

[1] Roger Hinks (1903–63). Art historian who worked at the British Council.

27 March 1962   Combe Florey House
                                                Nr Taunton
Darling Nancy

I must agree – Pam's party was a disappointment. Not her fault or yours. Partly mine – I had come to London too late or too early. Either one should have a bath & change or rush straight from the station. I had sat 6 hours in White's drinking too much – indeed I was tight. Also I had had a shock there. I can't remember if I told you. I was sitting in the hall at 7 pm being no trouble to anyone, when a man I know by sight but not by name – older than I, the same build, better dressed, commoner – came up & said: 'Why are you alone?' 'Because no one wants to speak to me.' 'I can tell you exactly why. Because you sit there on your arse looking like a stuck pig.'

That, added to a letter from Clarissa to Ann [Fleming] saying that

the Haileses in Trinidad, whom I thought I charmed, found me a
frightful bore, and Debo's idea that I am a counter-hon have worked
to produce strong Pinfold feelings of persecution.

Why, I wonder, does H. Hamilton suppose I shall not rejoice in
your essays? – Pinfold himself. C. Sykes lunched with me the day after
Pam's fiasco. He has got involved in the idea you first mentioned to
me, that I should sing in an operatic version of *Lolita*. Rum.

I got back in time to receive a socialist – Lord Walston – who was
conducting an agitation in Taunton. Without his wife he is very jolly.

Cambridge, to purge the shame of Snow–Leavis,[1] are giving Graham Greene a doctorate. Jolly good. When [Ivy] Compton-Burnett
was proposed for a doctorate at Oxford, the council merely asked:
'What has she given to the building fund?'

Poor Hatty is not fit for employment. The Jesuits in their charity
have taken her into Farm Street & allow her to make cocoa for the
secretaries. She is 'coming out' in a very modest way. Laura's mother
is giving a ball for her at Pixton. I presume you would hate to come?

I think Tony Powell suffers frightfully from all human contact. Violet
is no more painful to him than you and I. There is an affinity between
him & Henry Yorke which, no doubt, the Cambridge School of Literature will eventually investigate.

I am reading *Middlemarch* for the first time, with enjoyment.

Perhaps I might come to Paris for the week-end of Hatty's ball
here.

I say, *Michelin* guide have, I see, introduced a sign marking restaurants where there is no wireless. I suggested this in a letter to *The
Times* five or six years ago. Do you think it conceivable that they paid
attention? I should be proud and dePinfolded if I thought I had started
this great reform.

Love from
    Evelyn

I hope your vaccination has not 'taken'. I have Meg vaccinated on
her thigh not her arm.

[1] The critic F. R. Leavis had violently attacked the work of C. P. Snow in the Richmond
Lecture at Downing College, Cambridge.

29 March 1962   7 rue Monsieur, VII

Darling Evelyn

It's only in Blighty such horrid things occur. Can you imagine at
the Jockey Club such a scene? Je vous dirai, Monsieur, pourquoi
personne ne vous adresse la parole – c'est que vous avez l'air,
Monsieur, d'un cochon égorgé. It would certainly mean (if it happened

but I don't think it *could*) ou pour cent mille francs de fleurs ou la carte de visite,[1] as I once heard Princesse Sixte say about somebody who had gate crashed a dance. Then what makes Ann *tell* you that some fiend of an expatriate (can't read the name) finds you a bore? The very last thing anybody could reproach you with. Here such dewdrops are never passed on – the passer-on would soon find herself isolated. The English must have a deep sense of insecurity to behave like this. I despise them & am far too thin skinned to live among them.

I think Debo has cause to be offended judging by the things I've heard you say (which I did not pass on but others have). But you were a bit gris [tipsy] – another Island custom *unknown* here among the upper classes.

When is Hatty's ball? Do come. I shall be here the whole of April until 27th – Ireland in May & here again in June.

No my vaccination hasn't taken yet. I really believe my good doctor cheated a bit – he didn't like doing it as I nearly died, when a baby, of it.

There has been an almighty fuss here about wirelesses in restaurants & a public opinion poll registered 77% against. The owners say A the tourists & B the staff want them. Interesting about *Michelin* I expect they got the idea from your letter.

I've been reading the *Master of Ballantrae* which is very rum. One has to skip the Master's travels. Rather nice when they all go to New York & say he has driven us to live among savages.

Middlemarch is such a putting off name I find.

Oh do sing in *Pinfold*. Anyway do meet Nabokov I'll eat my hat if you don't love *him*.

> Come
> N

I was done on the arm so as to be able to have a bath. How did Margaret manage?

[1] Either 100,000 francs' worth of flowers or a challenge to a duel.

[April 1962]   Combe Florey House
                                                         Nr Taunton
Darling Nancy

My writing again. How you will groan. It comes from our frustrated meeting. No need to answer. But I must explain about boring the Haileses because it has been what young people call 'traumatic'. Hailes was a pretty young politician you may have known as Patrick Buchan-Hepburn. I knew him slightly years ago. He is now Governor General of the now defunct Federation of the West Indies. I had never met

his wife but took a liking to her, and they were jolly hospitable to Meg
& me. The crucial point is that I was confident they both enjoyed my
visit. It made a lovely change, I thought, from most of their official
visitors. When I briefly returned to Trinidad they sent ADCs to drag
me back. I talked loud & long & they laughed like anything. Now I
find I bored them. Well of course everyone is a bore to someone. One
recognizes that. But it is a ghastly thing if one loses the consciousness
of being a bore. You do see it means I can never go out again.

Same in a lesser degree with Debo but I knew I was being a bore
there because she turned on the television at dinner. It is not knowing
that is fatal. 'Your best friends will not tell you' like those American
advertisements.

Don't please strain your poor eyes & waste your valuable time in
answering.

Love
    E

I have written an article to say it is absolutely unforgivable to arrive
at dinner drunk.[1]
Middlemarch wasn't any good really.

[1] A review of *The Pan Book of Etiquette* in the *Daily Mail*, 12 April 1962.

10 April 1962   7 rue Monsieur, VII

Darling Evelyn

Do try & get it into your head that whatever else you may be you
are *not a bore*. I think you are wasted on people like Buchan-Hepburn
with whom one would sooner have been seen dead than dancing, in my
recollection of old ballroom days. Funny of you to eschew civilization as
you do. Voltaire used to say one has to choose between countries
where you sweat & countries where you think. Life is short & it is
better to stay in the latter. Specially YOU who don't even like sweating. Another thing. This news about you boring the bores seems to
come from Clarissa, with whom you are not on good terms? Not quite
convincing.

Isherwood. Well I agree with every word in that long letter to *TLS*[1]
this week. I'm not sure I'll ever be able to speak to another pederast.
(But oh the brilliance of the beginning. Later the blanketing dullness
of America descends.)

I've written a long description of Captain Scott's last months for
my book. (It made me cry twice.) I do wonder *why* I have! The book
I call *The Water Beetle*, hoping to disarm.

I'm going to Ireland 27th Ap for 3 weeks. Perhaps I've told you this already. Will be here for the whole of June. Come. What are your plans?

Rain rain GO TO SPAIN. It pours, all & every day.

Much love
    N

[1] A letter from J. W. Quinton criticised a review of Christopher Isherwood's novel *Down There on a Visit* for failing to draw attention to the book's 'amoral sentiments': 'it is fashionable for critics to attack Waugh for the special brand of socio-religious exclusiveness that is apt to falsify his scale of values in this way, while Mr Isherwood's far more questionable (and more easily imitated) standards are apparently accepted with admiration.' *Times Literary Supplement*, 6 April 1962.

[postmarked 15 April 1962]   Combe Florey House
[postcard]   Nr Taunton

P.S. I have had a letter from Gaston – not very easy to read but *very* kind about the book I sent him. However one sentence stands clear 'Rome s'ennuie de vous'. So you see it is not persecution mania nor the malice of Lady A[von] but plain truth that I am a bore.

    E

[postmarked 17 April 1962]   7 rue Monsieur, VII
[postcard]

It means Rome bores herself without you. SILLY, do learn French instead of brooding over Buchan Hepburn. Colonel is in the new Govt so that is heavenly he was boring himself at Rome now the house is finished. You are clever to read his writing I can't but perhaps he took pains with it – I go to Ireland 27th.

4 July [1962]   Combe Florey House
                                               Nr Taunton
Dearest Nancy

I was titillated by your publisher's appeal for identification of the water beetle rhyme.[1] I had never heard and when you said you were to call your collected pensées *Water Beetle* I did not see the point. Now all is plain. An excellent, disarming title making everything easy for reviewers. How I look forward to the book. I hope you have expunged all the profanity that sometimes taints your occasional papers.

I think you find an unwholesome pleasure in observing the decay of English decorum. How about this. Ten days ago Pam Berry asked me to stay for the night. I found her in an ugly mood railing against all her social superiors. To stop the flow of vilification I led her to

politics, said I thought U Thant an enemy and added: 'The government must be pretty hard up to get people to meet him. They even
asked Laura & me.' Next Sunday's *Telegraph* had the enclosed paragraph in a column to which Pam admittedly contributes, suggesting
that I claim a (non-existent) intimacy with the Prime Minister – repeat-
ing the stale & embarrassing impertinence of Muggeridge of three
years ago. In our youth there was much talk of 'sneak guests'; 'sneak
hostesses' are something quite new. At least the poor hungry young
gossip-writers needed the guinea they got for abusing hospitality. Pam
does it out of pure malice. I got a pained letter from Macmillan's
secretary. Pam joins Randolph among the legion of the damned.

My summer has been much disturbed by Harriet's 'coming out'.
My mother in law who never gave a ball for Laura or her sister
decided she must give a ball for Harriet, here in Somerset. Our lives
have been made hideous plotting house-parties. All the young scrupu-
lously and often superfluously write to thank for parties. They can't
bring themselves to answer invitations. My mother in law insisted on
matriarchal style. No caterers. All our kitchens have been filled with
veal bones stewing to make aspic; all our poultry were slaughtered.
Unlike Uncle Matthew's aged peers, our 'young men' were all 30 year
old alcoholics. It was from this ball that I imprudently fled to Pam.

After Pam I went to Penelope Betjeman. Now there is a jewel for
you. Mad as a hatter and overflowing with pure kindness. All the time
I was with her she never said one disagreeable word about anyone.
A most cleansing experience after Pam's unending gush of denigration,
detraction and calumny.

Hatty is pretty from the crown of her head to her collar-bone –
hideous below and half baked in mind. But she seems to be enjoying
her season. Do you go to Venice this summer. Diana has been lent a
little house & has engaged a pansy attendant but isn't looking forward
to it. Do cherish her. She is not happy.

Am I getting crotchety, or is Pam's behaviour blackguardly?

Reading the Wilde letters.[2] The saddest thing is his euphoria in the
first few days after leaving prison, all turning to dust immediately. The
reviewers complain that there are too many pleas for money, but the
poor beast was penniless.

I toil away at autobiography.[3] What a dull life I seem to have had.

Love from
    Evelyn

[1] From Hilaire Belloc's *A Moral Alphabet*. The verse for the letter 'W' runs:

The WATERBEETLE here shall teach
A sermon far beyond your reach;
He flabbergasts the Human Race
By gliding on the water's face
With ease, celerity, and grace;

But if he ever stopped to think
Of how he did it, he would sink.

[2] *The Letters of Oscar Wilde* edited by Rupert Hart-Davis (1962).
[3] *A Little Learning* (1964).

10 July 1962   23 Dorsoduro
                                          Venice
                                          Here until Aug then Paris
Darling Evelyn

I must tell you that I don't love Pam as I used to. She is spoilt &
I think it's Michael's fault, also I suppose the newspaper world is
completely corrupting – anyway her faults are getting worse & she
doesn't mellow. I think what she did to you is unpardonable.[1] (Droll
idea, to invite you with that man-eater I must say.)

Well hundreds of water beetles appeared – some accompanied by
other poems saying Nancy of course never got beyond the letter U,
what a lot of spare time people seem to have. But I can't use it.
Flabbergasts the human race by gliding on the water's face with *ease
celerity and grace*. Won't do – what a bore.

I expect Diana will come after I've left. Imagine she'll hate being
here – even I find it too full of ghosts. I see Victor [Cunard] getting
off every steamer (I used to sit & wait for him on the steps of the
Salute every morning to go to the Lido) & I miss him so much I
almost wonder if I wasn't in love with him. It's the jokes of course.
The receipt for being missed is to live in a small society of which one
is the life & soul & not to die too old. I love my Italian friends but
there are many jokes they wouldn't see. For instance I heard 'there
are 4 Amurrican worships in Venice' & was vaguely imagining people
like Cass Canfield & wondering who when I realized it was WAR ships.
Nobody to tell it to.

I didn't feel I could face Wilde. I greatly enjoyed a book called
Crash 1929,[2] which depicts American worships in full discomfiture, also
Aug: 1914.[3] Short of a book I bought the *Code of the Woosters*[4] & have
been shrieking but the selection of Penguins is deplorable, in all the
shops they are the same: *The Day of the Triffids*[5] what can that be &
Ldy C[hatterle]y, in literal hundreds. Someone has blundered. None of
yours or mine, I can always fall back on either at a pinch.

The boys on the beach all have tiny wirelesses tucked away with
their private parts so that hands are free to fondle. These little objects
give out an indescribable din. Isn't science wonderful, really the world
is becoming so vile that one won't mind dying half as much as somebody like Mazarin did.

Much love
    N

Sister Diana is writing her mémoires,[6] they are dazzling and screamingly funny.

[1] The real culprit in the matter was Auberon Waugh who had tipped off Kenneth Rose of the
Sunday Telegraph about the Prime Minister's invitation to his parents.
[2] J. K. Galbraith, *The Great Crash, 1929* (1955).
[3] Barbara Tuchman, *August 1914* (1962).
[4] P. G. Wodehouse, *The Code of the Woosters* (1938).
[5] John Wyndham, *The Day of the Triffids* (1951).
[6] Diana Mosley, *A Life of Contrasts* (1977).

18 July 1962   23 Dorsoduro
                                                Venice

Darling Genial
    Would you put My little victim? May I trouble you to turn your
active mind to double U or is that too much? I find it almost irresistible.
For the rest I have arrived at: She aggravates the human race by
gliding on the water's face putting people in their place.
    I sent you a PC yesterday in full flush of gratitude but you'll probably
get this first.
    Dined with the C in C Med[1] on his warship last night. He is a
Holland-Martin so of course red hair. It was a corner of a foreign
field etc. Uneatable food & the women were sent to the loo after
dinner. A funny moment at the toasts. The Admiral: Pres of the
Italian Republic – Pres of the French Republic – Pres of the American
Republic – At this point the Prefetto said, with an excess of zeal, Her
Majesty Queen Eliz of England which the Admiral drily interrupted,
The Queen. How inarticulate the English are! I sat next the Captain
& tried to get him going on Capt: Scott, but though he knew all about
the expedition & was at school with the nephew of Oates he couldn't
say anything to fascinate me. The Italian Admiral was obviously a
dear. He had taken his submarine into Tobruk, which he thought was
Italian – the English, who thought it was an Eng: sub: rushed on
board & began to unload it, suddenly all realized, there was a battle,
the Ad lost an eye but got his ship away. What a story.

    With many more thanks for your so kind consideration & love from
        Nancy

[1] Vice-Admiral Sir Deric Holland-Martin (1907–77). Commander-in-Chief of Allied Forces in
the Mediterranean 1961–4.

21 July [1962]   Combe Florey House
                                                Nr Taunton

Darling Nancy
    Your letter has come before your post-card so I don't quite under-
stand your reference to double U. Is it your suggestion to name the

book 'Double U' or 'W'. The latter would be striking & memorable, if a little puzzling at first glance.

The rhyme: if you want it to be a parody of Belloc, your version won't quite do. He was a strict grammarian. 'Aggravate', as meaning 'annoy' is pure nursery & peasant language.

You can't have 'place' (singular) after 'their' (plural) unless you are using 'people' collectively e.g. 'the people'. You could say 'putting plebeians in their place', as tho there was one place only for the lot of them – outer darkness.

Someone always responds to the Loyal Toast. In some messes the president says: 'Mr Vice, the Queen' and the Vice-president says: 'The Queen, God bless her.' Sometimes it is 'Gentlemen I give you our Colonel-in-Chief, the Queen' and then everyone before drinking grunts 'the Queen'. There are many variations but always someone says 'the Queen' in response.

Middle aged men often want to go to the loo after dinner. I bet the Prefetto was bursting. Of course he couldn't leave the ladies at the table.

The Navy are renowned as 'the Silent Service'.

I am *greatly* impressed at your being asked to dinner by C in C Med. Much grander than those frogs you frequent in Paris.

Love from
Evelyn

23 July 1962   23 Dorsoduro
                                               Venice
Darling Evelyn

Thanks very much. I'm sorry about aggravate – but in a way I *am* a Nanny & a Peasant. Can't one really say oh don't aggravate me? (Haven't got *Ox Dic* here.)

I've been reading Maugham *Writer's Notebook*[1] my goodness the poverty there. I see now why people are so down on him but with the stories I think he manages to cover up marvellously. When one reads the *W's N* the mask is off. I also read some essays of his & to my amusement he too has done Aug: Hare[2] – whom he knew. Mine is much shorter & it's funny how we have chosen quite different features to describe, on the whole. The book called *Aug: 1914* fascinated me & so did the *Blue Nile*.[3] Then I read Boswell & wondered why one ever bothers with modern books at all!!

I'm off on Friday & about time too. Nearly all my friends who live here go on the 1st & Diana Cooper arrives with a crowd of sewers on the 3rd. Susan Mary is the first swallow to be seen (in the distance). That nosy lady called Mrs Wyndham,[4] like John the Baptist, has been sent on to count Honks's spoons & forks.

I gave my annual dinner party at the Grand Hotel. To my despair
the nice head waiter has gone & is replaced by an idiot who, when I
said what about the menu, would only reply slice of fish slice of chicken.
I worried very much, but in the end the slices were quite eatable &
the bill *half* what it was last year so the old adorable waiter must have
been the king of robbers.

Do you know the David Somersets?[5] I always see them here, they
have become part of the landscape. He is I think the best looking man
I ever saw & one of the funniest – irresistible, in fact. I guess he's
nicer here than at home.

> Much love & *thanks* for kind assistance
>   N

[1] W. Somerset Maugham, *A Writer's Notebook* (1949): extracts from the many volumes of notes
he had kept since the age of 18.
[2] Nancy had written an article on Augustus Hare for *Horizon* in 1942 which was reprinted in
The Water Beetle.
[3] Alan Moorehead, *The Blue Nile* (1962).
[4] Violet Leverson (d.1979). Known as 'Auntie Nose'. Married to Guy Wyndham in 1923. Author
of *The Sphinx and her Circle: A Biographical Sketch of Ada Leverson* (1963).
[5] David Somerset (1928–). Succeeded as 11th Duke of Beaufort in 1984. Married Lady Caroline
Thynne in 1950.

[July 1962]   Combe Florey House
[postcard]   Nr Taunton

Why not adapt it, saying 'after Belloc', to:
     'Titillates the human race (or British race)
     'By gliding on the water's face
     'Assigning each to each his place'?
or 'Incorrigibly out of place'?
or 'Contemptuous of power and grace'?
or 'A bit of arsenic and old lace'?
or 'Superior to time's dull pace'?
     Or something like that which you can easily better.

E

[received 22 August 1962]   Combe Florey House
                                                 Nr Taunton
Dearest Nancy,
     I am excited to read that next Sunday we shall have a sample of
your reminiscences.[1] A very nice change from Cyril's grand tour which
fizzled out in Sicily – I daresay through bad editing. The *Sunday Times*
is ruining itself with Lord Snowdon's blindingly ugly & banal coloured
supplement.

Aggravate – of course *you* can use it to mean what nanny meant, but Belloc would not have done so and if it is meant as an adaptation of him it rings false. Never mind. I am just a retired school-master. Fewer than a thousand readers will notice and of them most will be pleased because it will give them a momentary sense of superiority.

I write to give you news more important to me than to you. You remember my daughter Margaret to whom you showed such kindness in Paris? Well, she has fallen head over heels in love and I can't find it in my heart to forbid consummation. 'Young love satisfied' was what Belloc put beside 'broad lands to leave' as the desiderata of a happy life. There are no broad lands to leave. He is a penniless Irish stock-broker's clerk named FitzHerbert of good family but rather caddish & raffish appearance. 27 years old and has not done a hand's turn – his stock-broker's clerkship began on the day of his engagement. A Catholic of not very pious disposition, father killed honourably in the war, a brother I haven't been allowed to see, who I suspect is a skeleton in cupboard (as is mine, and also Laura's for that matter). She had a number of suitors of the kind an old fashioned father would have preferred, but she must have FitzHerbert, & so she shall. She wants children & that is a thing I can't decently provide for her. I expect that in ten years time she will be back on my doorstep with a brood.

Bloggs Baldwin says he never met you. Rum. He came here the other day & my son, James, said: 'At last I have met a P.G. Wodehouse character in the flesh.'

I am told that this Common Market will make good French wine prohibitively expensive here. As you know we can buy it in London much cheaper than in Paris. The cellar, whose poverty you remarked, is being rapidly filled in panic.

Love from
    Evelyn

[1] 'Mothering the Mitfords', a portrait of Laura Dicks, the Mitfords' nanny, appeared in the *Sunday Times*, 26 August 1962, and was reprinted in *The Water Beetle*.

22 August 1962   7 rue Monsieur, VII

Dearest Evelyn

So do I congratulate you? Anyway, love to Margaret. A (modest) gift will follow in due course. The psychiatrists say that a great many chaps take a turn for the better at *age 30*. (You know that advert which says £4000 at *age 56* – I waited a whole year in vain, it's all a horrid hoax.)

My sister Decca is here. You may know she is writing a book called

The American Way of Death, which is a factual *Loved One*. (She saw Mr Joyboy who said: I never read the book but somebody told me Mr Waugh said I was very sincere.) Well, can you tell her, did you have reviews in the undertakers' mags? If so, sort of what did they say? She takes them all in & they are a treat, like the *Tatler*, to her. She says *Oh good* when they arrive.

Oh dear, my mother is displeased with what I shall say about her in the *S Times*.[1] Nothing to be done as the book is being printed. It comes from seeing one's own life & all one's relations as a tremendous joke which one expects them to share. Bother.

Aggravate. Please see *Ox: Dict*: Though of course you are sure to be more right than it.

A good idea to buy wine as it is certain to go up here in price I believe.

I'm going to Madagascar with Raymond Mortimer. I've never been out of Europe unlike what you say about our generation & think it's time I did. Decca's m. in law says what's Madagascar got that American hasn't? Answer of course no Americans.

I liked your essay on Guinea very much.[2] Smarty v. disappointing. Have you seen the film wh: is called here *Divorce à l'Italienne*?[3] It's the best ever, I go every day – made for you. Puts one off living in beautiful palaces in Sicily & even puts one off living in a hot climate. *Oh* it's funny. Will remind you of when you embarrassed Harold. How I would like to go with you to it.

That's all. If you have any answer to her query Decca is here until Tuesday next 28th.

Love
Nancy

Gollancz won't do her book, too disgusting. Her American agent resigned on seeing it & the publisher refused it. But new publishers are giving twice the money so that's all right.

---

[1] Nancy wrote that her mother lived 'in a dream world of her own'. She described how one day Unity rushed to tell her that Decca was standing on the roof ready to commit suicide; Lady Redesdale is said to have replied: 'Oh, poor duck, I hope she won't do anything so terrible,' and calmly returned to what she was doing.
[2] 'Eldorado Revisited', *Sunday Times*, 12 August 1962.
[3] *Divorce Italian Style* (1961), a comedy directed by Pietro Germi, starring Marcello Mastroianni.

[received 28 August 1962]   Combe Florey House
                                                          Nr Taunton

Darling Nancy,
    The *Oxford Dictionary* was not planned like the French to exclude misuses of words and establish what is correct. Its readers hunt for

misuses & proudly display them. Your 'aggravate' is 7th of the mean-pings & the authorities are negligible except when it's used conver-sationally in fiction by people of low education. Fowler: 'Aggravate, aggravation – The use of these in the sense *annoy, vex, annoyance, vexation* should be left to the uneducated. It is for the most part a feminine or childish colloquialism, but intrudes occasionally into the newspapers.'

Warn Decca before she goes all out in mocking the Americans that almost all the features of their funerals that strike us as gruesome can be traced to papal, royal & noble rites of the last five centuries. What is unique & deplorable would probably not strike her – the theological vacuum, the assumption that the purpose of a funeral service is to console the bereaved not to pray for the soul of the dead.

Years ago, I vaguely remember, there was a vogue for yankee undertakers' journals among Gerald Berners, G. Wellesley, Malcolm Bullock & Co. A fellow socialist of hers called Cedric Belfrage wrote a book[1] about undertakers in U.S.A. Not very good.

When her book is published I shall get all her press cuttings – bother.

You may congratulate me on my great beauty of character in surren-dering my daughter to FitzGiles – not on the acquisition of him as a son-in-law. On no account send a present.

I look forward to a time when wedding celebrations will be outré as funeral celebrations now are.

Dr Eaton of Forest Lawn (the 'Dreamer' not 'Joyboy') wrote to me about a year ago asking me to sign a document disclaiming any inten-tion of mocking him. Of course I refused and have heard no more. But I think Decca should take advice from lawyers before publishing. Please tell her I did not believe her story that an English naval officer attempted to shanghai her from Spain giving his word of honour for her safe return.[2]

Love from
    Evelyn

---

[1] *Abide with Me* (1950).
[2] In *Hons and Rebels*, Jessica described how, after her elopement to Spain, the captain of a destroyer attempted to lure her back to England with promises of roast chicken and chocolate cake.

29 August 1962   7 rue Monsieur, VII

Darling Evelyn

   Decca has just gone so I've sent her your letter which will fascinate her no doubt. I miss them both – Bob is a very nice person & clever. They are rather provincial but that rubs off visibly & if they lived here they would be a pleasure to us all. *How* I wish they could.

I see you were right (I knew it really) about aggravate. I must say the *O.D.* *is* rather a trap – I always thought it consecrated a word or usage, even if it says colloquial. Here they only admitted bistro last year & many a word is clamouring to get in.

Decca's book. Her American & English publishers rejected it but Simon & Schuster & Hutchinson have taken it. I must say her own favourite chapter which she gave me to read is too disgusting, I couldn't stomach it, but from what she has told me much of the rest must be fascinating & funny. Bob *is* a lawyer so he must know what you can publish I suppose. It will be amusing to see how it is received. Apparently all the doctors are for it & most of the clergymen.

I rushed out to get some more wine on reading your letter – it has already gone up in a frightening way – for £40 I got a tiny little heap in one corner of the cellar. I shan't give good wine to people who don't really like it any more.

Love
   N

3 September 1962   7 rue Monsieur, VII

Darling Evelyn
   Can't resist sending this to make you laugh.[1] I believe it's rather true about that Captain – I remember great plotting between him & Prod more than me, at old Milly Sutherland's villa. Aggravate – oh dear.[2]

I go to my sister Pam about 20th Sept. I seem to remember that Bristol, where I think I can fly from here, is a small train journey from you. Would you like to have me for a night? But I fear that if you are working it would be a disturbance & I even hesitate to write. If you don't answer I shall entirely see why. Pam lives between Cheltenham & Gloucester, for meeting purposes.

I wish you would come here & see this town now it is cleaned. A daily happiness for the citizens.

Love from
   Nancy

[1] Jessica Treuhaft's letter has not survived.
[2] Nancy braved Evelyn's disapproval and adapted the third line of Belloc's verse to: 'She aggravates the human race.'

[September 1962]   Combe Florey House
                                                    Nr Taunton

Darling Nancy

Thanks awfully for Decca's delicious letter. I don't doubt that Prod
conspired to kidnap her. What I don't believe is that an English naval
officer gave her his word of honour for safe conduct. Surely you who
have dined with C.-in-C. Med must see it is impossible? An American
communist, of course, wouldn't think it at all odd.

Please, please come & visit us when you are in England. As you
say Bristol to Taunton is no great distance. We can send a motor if
you tell us your time of arrival. And there are easy trains from Taunton
Cheltenham & Gloucester. I must warn you – school boys' holidays
still on & Laura cooking. But you plainly relish the decay of amenities
in the land of your origin. So do come. You can write a water-beetle
contrast between the standard of living of an English novelist and a
French grandee.

Have you considered the danger of R. Mortimer dying on your
hands in Madagascar? Better take one of Decca's morticians in your
suite.

Here's the catalogue of my wine-merchant[1] – the best. How do
prices compare with Paris? I have an idea that, just as whisky is cheaper
in Ascension Island than Scotland, so we get the finest wine cheaper
than you do.

    Longing to see you
         E

[1] Berry Bros. & Rudd.

11 September 1962   7 rue Monsieur, VII

Darling Evelyn

Berry is a name of my childhood. Uncle Matthew used to say that
as he loathed wine himself he trusted Berry to see that what he gave
his guests was up to the mark. Well, on the list as it happens there is
a wine (Lynch Bages 1955) which I've got. I paid 4.50 francs for it,
about 6/6 & Berry charges 17/- so it's as I thought, much cheaper
here. Tom Mosley always takes over wine, in bottles, when he goes
to London & says it pays him even with the duty. His Irish driver
Jerry,[1] however, has words of consolation for *you*. He read in the *Cork
Examiner* that the English are now making their own wine & 'have got
de Gaulle worried'. (I wish it was his only worry.)

About my visit. If World War III doesn't break out I come over on
24th to go to Pam but (if you liked) could go a day or two sooner
& see you UNLESS Raymond wants to come here & talk about

Madagascar. I'm waiting to hear from him. If so I might go to you
after Pam where I'll be about a week I think. Are all dates much the
same to you, or decidedly *not?* If so we might even wait until I'm in
England to settle. The trouble is everyone is scattered – Pam abroad
– Raymond about to go & so on I'm having difficulty in co-ordinating.
Don't answer this, wait for my next in which I'll try to be more explicit.
Colonel & I wanted to go to C-worth 6th Oct but now Debo may be
in Uganda. How fidgety everybody is!*

   Love
      N

Decca's chapter on cremation is called 'The Joy of Cooking' (title of
U.S. Mrs Beeton).
* All this is too dull don't read it.

¹ Jerry Lehane went to work for Sir Oswald Mosley in 1956.

13 September 1962   7 rue Monsieur, VII
Darling Evelyn
   Alas my clever scheme for going to you is knocked on the head by
my mother's sudden change of dates & the fact that Debo is whisking
us off to Chatsworth. I'm so disappointed though probably much
better for you on account of work.
   Do you like Gerry Wellingtonia? 'I was talking to the curator of
the Military Museum & remarked what a curious custom is the presen-
tation of enormous pieces of plate to regiments. Oh he said this isn't
plate it's silver. I suppose he thinks the late Duke of Portland's magnificent folio *The Plate at Welbeck* refers to electro from Mappin's.' How
Victor [Cunard] would have loved that.
   I'm weakening on Madagascar. It takes 6 weeks there & back &
costs £1000. As I'm perfectly happy here this seems utter madness.

   Much love
      Nancy

[postmarked 3 October 1962]   Combe Florey House
[postcard]   Nr Taunton

10 October [1962]   Combe Florey House
                                               Nr Taunton
Darling Nancy

How very nice to have your collected essays. I read them all when
they came out. They seem fresher & brighter than ever on re-reading.
Have you not done some polishing? I wish they had not those coarse
drawings[1] – most unsuitable to your elegance & stuck into the wrong
places by your publisher – but it is a lovely book to have. Thanks
awfully for giving it to me.

I was driven to London by a young people's house-party here and
heard the sad news of your mother's accident. I am very sad for you
all. Being in London I found myself swept up into Ian Fleming's film
jamboree. The film – *Dr No* – was absolutely awful – fatuous & tedious,
not even erotic. None of the characters had any character at all so
that it was impossible to remember them from one scene to the next.
Ann's party was very bizarre – Andrew & Debo, Mr and Mrs Maudling
(Chancellor of the Exchequer), the old Diabolic Doctor [Somerset]
Maugham & Clarissa [Avon], Mr Thomson (newspaper magnate)
Diana & me and the American Ambassador[2] & his wife (she
enchanting).

There was also an underworld of 90 who were not allowed caviar.
Poor Boots found himself thus graded & minded awfully.

Mrs Bruce the American said you liked her. I am not surprised.

I am writing a little review of *Water Beetle* for *Sunday Telegraph*. I hope I say the right thing. I delight in the book.

Meg has Maltese fever. She is setting up house in a lightless, oak panelled billiard room in Westbourne Terrace. She was deeply moved by your kindness in sending her a present. Her fever prevents her from writing at the moment.

Best love
      E

[1] By Osbert Lancaster.
[2] David Bruce (1898–1977). Ambassador to France 1949–52 and to United Kingdom 1961–9. Married Evangeline Bell in 1945.

10 October 1962   7 rue Monsieur, VII

Dearest Evelyn

Oh I am delighted that you will review it. Well (illustrations) I thought the cover very funny & nice & also the mad butler. I spoke about them being in the wrong place, most annoying & even more so the fact I am only to receive 12% because Osbert must have 2½%. I always weakly leave these things to Hamilton, presuming he knows his work.

I simply love Evangeline but she is a funny one as you may find out. I will enlarge when I see you.

Thanks awfully, my mother is much better. It was a shock to see her face entirely black & swollen & she was so feeble, but she has made a remarkable recovery. All the same I have put off my journey outside Europe for another time.

You hadn't read all the essays. Scott, Ireland (except for 3 sentences) & Russia are Virgin Soil. I rewrote them all, & added a bit here & there.

When do we see your mémoires?

I'm off to Fontaines on Friday. I simply long for it.

Love
      Nancy

[postmarked 24 October 1962]   Combe Florey House
[postcard]   Nr Taunton

This is obviously a useful tip,[1] but I don't fully understand the method. How do the lines fuse? Does he cut the pages down the middle & stick them together? We must learn to fold in before we fold up.

[1] Evelyn had enclosed a newspaper cutting which described the American novelist William Burroughs' 'fold-in' technique: 'He typed a page of text, folded it vertically in the centre and then laid it alongside another page similarly folded so that the lines of the different pages fused ... The method, he said, enabled him to lead the reader forwards, backwards across time tracks, and it helped him to discover new images.'

24 October 1962   Fontaines-les-Nonnes
                                                         par Puisieux

Darling Evelyn

You are a brute. Well I've got a Left & Right with Miss Laski[1] & you, very sad not to be praised by Fellow Socialists. Oh how I *screamed* at your review though.[2]

Raymond had a go at the proofs & passed the Syntax – he also let two misprinted dates go by so perhaps he didn't take as much trouble as he said he had. (Don't tell him.)

Mrs Hammersley said yesterday Dreadful things we are seeing. I said yes, orange trees, roses & René coming out to announce a delicious luncheon. The talk here is all of the *concile*,[3] rather above my poor bird brain.

Oates did commit suicide – what else? They all meant to, & had the pills handy, but in the end decided against. If Cherry-Garrard[4] had been more of a chap he would have rescued them, but nobody has ever said so. He had every *logical* excuse for not trying – the dogs were sick, so were the men, the weather was awful & he had been ordered not to go beyond a certain dump. All the same, Scott or Amundsen would have tried, no doubt. (I must explain that he went out before Atkinson & came back again, for the above reasons.)

Mme Costa told the Curé yesterday that it's rather sad that the most good person she has ever known (*me*) isn't in the least religious. The Curé who has never liked me shrugged his shoulders to the skies. But Mme Costa, like *me* & *Monty*, & *somebody else we know* loves to tease. How I wish you knew her. She *so much* reminds me of my old Dad.

Much love & many thanks for flaying me alive, poor little unpretentious *Water Beetle*.

    N

[1] Marghanita Laski reviewing *The Water Beetle* wrote: 'Despite some illustrations on nice grey paper by Mr Osbert Lancaster, this collection of mostly reprinted trivia hardly adds up to more than a non-book.' *Observer*, 21 October 1962.
[2] In his generally affectionate review, Evelyn classed Nancy as a writer 'who can write but cannot think'. He described her as 'entirely oblivious of all moral and spiritual judgements', exposed her inconsistencies and teased her for calling Stalin a 'dear old soul'. But he ended: 'When most of our writers have sunk, she will still be gliding on the water's face.' *Sunday Telegraph*, 21 October 1962.
[3] The Second Vatican Council.
[4] Apsley Cherry-Garrard, author of *The Worst Journey in the World: Antarctic 1910–13* (1922).

27 October [1962]   Combe Florey House
                                               Combe Florey
                                               Nr Taunton

Darling Nancy

'Flayed' indeed! I anointed your carapace with spikenard. There
were no mistakes of syntax in *Beetle*. I was enumerating your general
excellencies & defects. It was what a publisher calls a 'good selling
notice'. Not so Comrade Laski's.

If you had had a Christian upbringing you would know that suicide
is very wicked. Scott & Co. may have been tempted to this sin but
they resisted. Oates just went for a walk in the snow. There was a
very high probability that he would not come back but that is not the
same as taking poison or shooting oneself the nature of which acts is
lethal. There is nothing lethal in the nature of going for a walk any
more, say, than in swimming among sharks or crocodiles. By the way,
was his body found? I have always thought Scott may have eaten him
as the Italians ate Amundsen.

The Council is of the highest importance. As in 1869–70 the French
& Germans are full of mischief but, as then, the truth of God will
prevail. The spirit of that wicked Père Couturier still lives on in France
& must be destroyed. I hope your hostess and her Curé agree.

The redundant Combe Florey[1] is for the benefit of motorists not
postmen. It tells them to look for an outlying hamlet not for a town
house. New York is a huge state extending to the Canadian border.

My daughter, Margaret, was married in a tea gown of her great-
grandmother's out of the acting cupboard, used in countless charades,
and looked very pretty. High lace collar. All male guests (except one)
looked absolutely horrible. They had hired tail coats but neglected to
provide themselves with starched collars.

Daphne Weymouth has suddenly become a very old woman with
long white hair.

The wedding was a ghastly expense. I wish I were richer.

Did I tell you how poor Boots got on the wrong table at Mrs
Fleming's party & was given no caviar & was still in tears the next
day? Boots is up to something rather fishy in collecting letters, I think
for sale in America. Be wary. There is a nice nest egg for us all in
our senility in our correspondence. American Universities are buying
them at extravagant prices.

My daughter saw a book on furniture in which a circular pedestal
table was described as a 'loo table'. 'What big lavatories they must
have had.'

Fondest love
        E

[1] On Evelyn's new writing paper.

All Saints' Day [1 November] 1962   Fontaines-les-Nonnes
                                                  par Puisieux
Darling Evelyn

We must think of Robert [Byron] & Tom [Mitford] today – those
are the ones I miss the most. It will be nice to see them again, rather
soon now.

I'm told Randolph gives 5/- for one of your postcards & for letters,
S.G. as they say in French restaurants (selon grandeur) [according to
size]. I must have a gold mine though I pity the person who goes
through my papers as I throw letters hugger mugger into a drawer.

Oh this house! The latest drama is that the little boy installed a
microphone in the drawing room – found out because one of the old
ladies heard Mme Costa & the Curé deeply talking in an attic at
midnight. She went to investigate – of course it was naughty Jean
playing a record. Now he makes *allusions désagréables à table* to all the
nasty things they have said to each other about him. Not me, luckily.
Partly out of contrariness & partly because I always feel on the side
of the young & partly I must confess because I spied the mike attached
to a standard lamp (but only the last day of its existence) I have always
stood up for him. Now he's off to do his service militaire poor child.
Everybody very cross with me for shrieking about the microphone &
Mrs Hook, Mrs Hammersley's English maid, said I must be showing
off.

The Bishop of Monaco was here – fresh from the *concile*. He is a
brute in human form – Mrs H minded me meeting him (putting off
one's conversion she thought) but I weigh the *dear* late Bishop of Meaux
against him, much heavier. There's a life of Père Couturier do you
want it? A new Abbé comes today to say Mass. What are Abbés called
in England? Perhaps you don't have them.

Of course I was *delighted* with the spikenard – only teasing.

Much love
     N

P.S. What you say about Daphne. We are all *old* now – I realized this
for the first time at Pam Chichester's mass. Maimie – Joyce Britton
Jones – Romie – it was a most painful eye-opener.

28 November 1962   7 rue Monsieur, VII

Darling Evelyn

Just in case you are going to London during the next few days I
shall be (from tomorrow for a week) at Hotel Adria, 88 Queen's Gate.
Only a fleeting visit before the Xmas rush to see my mother.

Esther Arthur my funny old friend you met once here fell dead on

Friday to the usual Anglo Saxon chorus of *far* the best. Thinking she
has no relations here & few friends really – not everybody's cup of
tea – I went to order some flowers. The shopkeeper said in that
threatening & uncompromising way to which the French shopper is
accustomed 'le premier prix pour les couronnes: *10,000 francs.*'[1] I swallowed this bitter pill & forked out (£7). But at the cemetery quelle
horrible surprise! My wreath was the kind of thing a trades union
sends to the Pres: of the Republic. It took two men to carry it. All the
old lesbians looked absolutely astounded & I was treated like the widow
by the undertakers.

Oh dear I shall miss her.

I hear that when Jamie gave a dinner for Mrs W. Smith & *The
Great Hunger*,[2] Harold [Acton] said in ringing tones: Pray God I don't
have to sit next Old Fraudey.

Do you love *Pale Fire*?[3] Oh how I screamed with laughter. Largely
written in Harold Acton's voice, I thought.

Do you know the Bon Marché (sort of Whiteley's) has got four *real
English guardsmen in uniform* as a publicity stunt? Don't you think it's
shameful?? Imagine what they must be up to after closing time.

    Much love
       N

[1] 'The cheapest wreath is *10,000 francs.*'
[2] Cecil Woodham-Smith, *The Great Hunger* (1962).
[3] By Vladimir Nabokov (1962).

[December 1962]   Combe Florey House
                                             Nr Taunton

Darling Nancy

Oh dear alas no I can't be in London now. Damn.

I suppose you will go to the Cooper Memorial celebrations. Monty![1]

I enjoyed *Pale Fire* awfully & thought the poem no parody or pastiche
but a jolly good composition in its own right. *Much* better than *Lolita*.
But a show-off. Too clever by half. But a pleasure.

Now Madagascar's off where will you be Jan–Feb? I have no plans,
don't particularly want sun, just change. India? Must see it quick
before the Chinks take over.

Can it be true that ladies of fashion now wear tweed skirts at night?

Was Miss Arthur the American journalist who made advances to
my daughter, Margaret? I greatly enjoyed funeral story. Don't know
'Frauders'.

    Much love
       Evelyn

[1] Field Marshal Viscount Montgomery presented the Duff Cooper Memorial Prize to Michael Howard for *The Franco-Prussian War*.

Sunday, 3? [2] December 1962   Adria Hotel
                                                88 Queen's Gate
                                                London SW7

Darling Evelyn

I don't know how you can be so disloyal to the Man who Led you to Victory. Anyway he asked Lady Honks to ask *me* to the prize day do be jealous.

If you want a sunless change why not come & dig in at Paris for Feb? You could imbibe some food & drink & *civilisation française* & oh how I should laugh – in fact copy for a book most likely, just what I need. It would be rather expensive because your standards are so high but nothing compared to a journey. Madagascar would have cost more than £1000 I reckoned.

I liked your chapter on your father[1] very much – what a charming face he has got.

No the journalist was Janet Flanner[2] the Pope of Paris Lesbians. Esther was a large sandy person like a bedroom cupboard packed full of information, much of it useless, all of it accurate. I was truly very fond of her. I think she was very unhappy & she whacked the bottle like merry hell as *my* father would have said.

Cyril's book on the Pavillons[3] is quite wild. Don't quote me, however. Hardly one of the houses illustrated in it is a pavillon; nearly all are hôtels particuliers or châteaux. All very pretty however. He wrote & asked to dedicate it to me & then didn't – no explanation. What can this mean?

I went to see Lady Honks's house. When I took 12 Blom they gave me £100 with it – *she paid* £8000. Times have changed.

You owe this delightful letter to the S. Ken Museum I mean V & A being shut. I got up early to spend an hour there. Now I'm waiting for Heywood to take me to Richmond. If you cleaned all those Victorian buildings they would become very pretty as you will note during your two months at Paris.

Tell your thoughts.

Love
    N

[1] An extract from Evelyn's autobiography, *A Little Learning*, had appeared in the morning's *Sunday Telegraph*.
[2] Janet Flanner (1892–1978). Author, under the name 'Genêt', of the famous 'Letter from Paris' which appeared regularly in the *New Yorker* 1925–75.
[3] Cyril Connolly, *Les Pavillons* (1962).

23 December 1962   7 rue Monsieur, VII

Darling Evelyn
   Happy Christmas.
   I'm *so wondering* what you will make of Sybille Bedford's new novel
called (v. bad title I think) *A Favourite of the Gods*. It has been tremendously advertised by the Lesbian World here as better than *A Legacy*
which it is certainly *not*. There are of course excellent things & one
reads on, but to me there is a certain naïveté, underlying a sophisticated
story, which pulls one up from time to time & then the characters are of
wood. Wooden figures after Henry James. The strange thing is that this
tough little person & ferocious Lesbian, always dressed as a motor racer,
should choose to write about an age of elegance, beautiful Princess,
unfaithful (but fond at heart) Prince & so on. A sort of *Golden Bowl* upside-
down. Oh do say what you think, I'm so curious to know. Make Collins
send it if they haven't already. The beginning – the first quarter – is
excellent & one thinks it is the prelude to an unfolding which doesn't
happen – in fact the flower dies in the bud. Hardly one joke.
   What about Nassau? I think the *rudeness is so disgusting*.[1] How I loathe
Americans more & more.
   I enjoyed myself in England by dint of only going to London in a
thick fog. I was 10 days at C-[hats]worth – two monster shooting
parties of 14 people all old friends of long ago, white where they used
to be black & much less fierce. Friendly in fact. Your adorer General
Laycock was there with a v. governessy wife I thought, well she was
a governess so that's in order.
   Arriving at Orly I ran into Cecil [Beaton] & Raymond off to Madagascar & was *so* glad not to be going. It is delightful here – a million
people have left Paris & the result is one can move about by day &
sleep by night. Marie & I are alone in this courtyard. The Sutros &
Harold will partake of my turkey.

   Much love – bonne fête
      Nancy

---

[1] General de Gaulle had not been invited to attend a meeting in Nassau between President
Kennedy and Harold Macmillan at which Britain agreed to buy the American-made Polaris
missiles.

Childermas (a feast dear to parents)   Combe Florey House
[28 December] 1962   Nr Taunton

Darling Nancy
   Too late to wish you a Happy Christmas. Instead I wish you all
good things in the new year – prosperity, vigour, hosts of loving &
faithful friends, new adventures & discoveries of every kind.

I was sorry to read of your uncle's death.[1] I hope it is not a painful bereavement & that you will not be obliged to travel through the ice to the funeral.

Ice or no ice you are well out of the journey to Madagascar. Think of Beaton snapshotting all the nigger boys.

Nothing against Lady Laycock please. You speak of the woman I love.

I was bitterly disappointed by Miss Bedford's new book. Lovely first chapter – then it went to pieces. Why the switch from first person to third? I can only suppose it is the first of a number of volumes. If so she ought to have waited and brought them out together. Quite pointless as it stands &, what is more, full of solecisms & anachronisms. I pointed out a few hundred of the more glaring ones to Mark Bonham Carter & advised him to withdraw & correct it, but he hasn't answered. Umbrage perhaps.

I had to spend Christmas in London. Young FitzHerbert my son-in-law was struck ill & whisked off to what looked to me like an alcoholics' ward so I had an expensive time cheering Meg with caviar. Then came the snow. I got home to find the drive impassable to wheeled vehicles.

When FitzHerbert was first taken ill Honks & I dined with Meg. 'Where's Giles?' 'He's lying down. He doesn't feel very well.' 'What's the matter?' 'I haven't bothered to call a doctor. I expect it's "two-day flu".' 'Has he got a temperature?' 'Yes, 104.6°. You always have a high temperature with "two-day flu".' On the fourth day he turned yellow like a chrysanthemum. The doctor diagnosed a severe sort of jaundice. So I had to return to London. His hospital is near Kensal Green[2] – very convenient if he takes a turn for the worse.

Don't you think you might hire me as a professional model – comic Englishman in Paris. You could charge my keep against income tax.

I have the idea of going to Menton for a few weeks work. Is that a suitable place? It always looks most inviting. Someone told me of an hotel called Westminster which has a library of pre 1914 English novels. Do you know anything of it? I can't afford a grand hotel this year after all these weddings.

We spend the evenings reading Shakespeare aloud. All our editions have different versions.

I have been writing to various men who were at school with me asking whether they object to revelations of their delinquencies. I think it may have caused a seasonable chill in some reformed breasts. There is a pompous ass called Hot-lunch Molson[3] whom I don't suppose you ever met. I have a full diary of his iniquities in 1921–2. Perhaps he will fly the country.

Love from
    Evelyn

[1] 3rd Lord Redesdale.
[2] A cemetery in north London.
[3] Hugh Molson (1903–91). Unionist MP 1931–61. Created life peer in 1961. 'I asked "Lord" Hot-lunch Molson if I might say he was tight at Lancing on Ascension Day 1921. He replied that he did not mind but that the revelation would cause great grief in the High Peak Division of Derbyshire.' *Letters of Evelyn Waugh*, pp. 586–7.

2 January 1963   7 rue Monsieur, VII

Darling Evelyn

I've just spoken to the Lesbian who makes the most sense in the Paris colony. She says Sybille gave her the typescript &, appalled by it, she made a few anodyne suggestions mostly concerning matters of fact but they were very badly received indeed. Then S got a telegram from her American publisher saying a really great book & so on after which there was no question of any changes. My Lesbian says she needs a really clever publisher & that there is such a man at Collins but he doesn't deal with her – Bonham Carter too busy with other things. But she didn't need a clever editor for *A Legacy* and I simply think she is one of the many who can write *one* novel – like Mme de La Fayette. Interesting to see what press she gets.

I *loved* my uncle but he was very ill, hated it & couldn't have recovered; he had sold his flock of sheep, great prize winners, & lost all interest in life. A darling if ever there was one, funny like my father without his rampageousness. Now my uncle Jack[1] who always wanted to be a lord is on his death bed. No station master will ever see him to his seat & the only person who will say milord to him is an ancient maid-of-all-work. It's almost too sad. My aunts most angelically forbade me to go to the funeral – indeed I doubt whether I should have got there; there will be another almost at once.

Menton I love. I know it very well. The best hotel I believe (I've never stayed in one but at Cap Martin & Roquebrune with friends) is d'Angleterre. Henry May[2] the great enemy of Willie Maugham lived there for years. But you know the food is deplorable now on the Riviera. Why don't you go to some *real* place? I could easily find out where there is a good hotel in a small town not on the coast. It would be so much more amusing & you could get some pre 1914 novels from the London Library.

Already postcards of pretty man-eating niggers or should I say cannibals have begun to arrive from the dear ones. I'm *too thankful* to be au coin de mon feu![3]

Happy New Year

Love
    N

They say the English papers are too frightened of the dealers to print Picasso's statement (that for 40 years he has been making fun of the public). True? If so I will enlarge – it's v. interesting.[4]

[1] Hon. John Mitford (1885–1963). He died on 31 December, having been 4th Baron Redesdale for just over a year.
[2] Henry May; American who was the model for the pretentious Elliott Templeton in *The Razor's Edge* by Somerset Maugham.
[3] By my fireside.
[4] This was an imaginary confession concocted by the Futurist Giovanni Papini and published in a book of spoof interviews, *Il Libro Nero* (1951). The Russians had arranged for this 'confession' to resurface in a Yugoslav magazine in order to get back at the French Communist Party.

7 January 1963   Combe Florey House
                                                Nr Taunton

Dearest Nancy

Yes, the grub has always been beastly south of Lyon except in old fashioned international places like Hotel de Paris Monte Carlo & a little place I know in Nice called something like Normandie (why?). I know what you mean about Menton not being real. Does one want a *real* place – wireless & terrorists – to work in? I thought Feb in Menton might be all aged English spinsters still. But I'm open to suggestions. What do you suggest? Heat not required (or indeed procurable) but the chance of an afternoon stroll. Sitting-room essential & the proper respect due to a superior race. I am told Westminster Hotel Menton is run by an aged Swiss widow who doesn't know about the decline of England (brought about by your horrible friends Montgomery & Attlee & Churchill). Menton at least looks Italian not frog.

I have seen nothing in English papers (or American) about Picasso's recantation. You may be sure that they are not frightened of dealers, who have no influence here. I don't think there are a dozen pictures by the old impostor in the whole country. American & French Jews bagged the lot. His exhibition here after the war at the Tate – 1946? – was an obvious practical joke. I wrote to *The Times* to say so. But he began his absurdity before – a nauseating picture of prostitutes in Avignon. When that clever man Munnings[1] said P. was a fraud Boots wrote to *The Times* 'in the name of English culture' to apologise. I suppose the communists have made him blow the gaff at last. I should *very much* like to see the text of his recantation. Why don't you write it up for the English papers. He is not at all respected here but we are always pleased to see charlatans exposed. How jolly funny for that Jewish lady who gave me caviar and showed us lovely paintings & had a Picasso hidden in her bed-room. What name? Something grand like Rochefoucauld or Breteuil?

Thaw impends. I don't suppose you remember this house. The back is a glass covered yard. About ten tons of snow will soon fall from the roof onto this glass & under it is a hogshead of Burgundy awaiting bottling.

That clever little nigger Naipaul[2] has won *another* literary prize. Oh for a black face.

Ann Fleming's drunk sister[3] has died 'a great relief. Much the best thing etc?' Poor Ann is cut up.

> Love from
> Evelyn

[1] Sir Alfred Munnings (1878–1959). Sporting painter, president of the Royal Academy 1944–9.
[2] V. S. Naipaul (1932–). The novelist had just been awarded the 1963 Hawthornden Prize; his previous awards included the John Llewellyn Rhys Memorial Prize (1958) and the Somerset Maugham Award (1961). Evelyn admired his 'exquisite mastery of the English language which should put to shame his British contemporaries'. *Month*, November 1962. Knighted in 1990.
[3] Mary-Rose Charteris (1919–62). Married to Roderic Thesiger 1940–46 and to Nigel Grey in 1949.

10 January 1963   7 rue Monsieur, VII

Darling Evelyn

Two suggestions would be Hôtel des Cloches à Beaune, near Dijon (excellent food & wonderful wine) or the Sextus at Aix en Provence. These are the Colonel's choice. But I daresay Menton *would* be rather good for your purpose; it has a reassuring Brighton-like aspect. When working one doesn't want to be plunged into a new world in fact probably better not. Also it has the merit (Menton) of having been chosen by you & therefore nobody will be blamed if it turns out to be horrid.

Well a statement by Picasso was read out on France III, the serious programme here, in which he said that the public nowadays knows o about art & as soon as he realized this, in the 20s, he decided to amass an enormous fortune. He feels ashamed of himself now, but there it is. The more he despised the public the more it grovelled. But *he* does know what painting is & he thinks it time to say so. The great painters are Giotto (so funny, somehow, shades of Ruskin) Rembrandt – I think Rubens – & Goya (which I find an odd choice. The Goya exhibition here put me off him). So after hearing this – it went on for a quarter of an hour, fascinating, I expected the papers to be full of it. Not one word. It seems they fear the whole art market would collapse if it came out. But I bet it wouldn't. Look at the Chrysler affair. They would only say Picasso had gone mad etc.

Marie-Laure [de Noailles] is ¼ Jewish & the rest of her very grand indeed, she descends from Petrarch & the Marquis de Sade. And she gave you caviar I don't think you are very grateful.

About Ann's sister, one is sadder when pathetic people die who have had wretched lives. I minded far more about Bobo than about Tom though of course I miss her less. I still miss him terribly & always shall I suppose.

Much love from
Nancy

[postmarked 11 January 1963]   Combe Florey House
[postcard]   Nr Taunton

Dame Cecil Beaton, whom you described as going to Madagascar, has reappeared in London saying that he went to photograph lions in Tanganyika with Duchess Ashley-Cooper.[1] Very rum.

E

High praise of Dame Bogus Bedford in this morning's *Times*.

[1] Lady Lettice Ashley-Cooper (1911–90). She had accompanied Cecil Beaton and Raymond Mortimer on safari in Kenya and then to Madagascar.

15 January 1963   Combe Florey House
                                                Nr Taunton
Darling Nancy
   Thank you very much for the names of the hotels which I shall remember when I am next on a jaunt. I think for my purpose the Anglo Swiss atmosphere of Hotel Westminster, Menton, sounds most propitious. Monte Carlo is being ravaged by that disgusting motor race. I inadvertently arrived there once before in race week & it was hellish. So a week today Laura & I go to Menton. I don't suppose it will be much warmer – snow at M.C. yesterday – but Laura needs a change & holiday from household responsibilities.
   I *loved* the lady who gave me caviar though she looked 100% Levantine. What was funny was finding the evidence of her secret vice. I am fascinated by the story of Picasso's confession. Did you hear it yourself? These things often get misreported – in fact wireless hallucination is quite common. I remember in the war people used to doze over their sets & then believe they had heard of the most extraordinary victories & defeats. Have the frogs anything like the *Listener* which publishes the text of important utterances? I should awfully like to read the old rogue's actual words. I can't conceive why something like *Time* magazine has not jumped at it. Was he being interviewed & caught out or making a prepared statement?
   Trains aren't what they were before the war so I shall fly to Nice which means, alas, that I can't drop in on you in Paris.

Mrs Bedford's book is getting high praise everywhere. Reviewers are too young to know when detail is authentic or spurious thirty years back.

The frost here has been very severe. Drive impassable. Very few taps or lavatories working. Deluges impending when there is a thaw.

I will send you a post card from Menton.

I have an uncle dying – a senile clergyman. I can't say I mind at all except that I may have to take in his twin sister here for her last years which would be a grave inconvenience. I very seldom mind people's deaths. I long for my own.

My two sons have been models of good behaviour this holidays. One has given up smoking and both are sober most evenings. No evidence of demon sex.

Goodness, a cataract of water has suddenly begun to flow outside my window. I must investigate.

Love from
    Evelyn

20 January 1963   7 rue Monsieur, VII

Darling Evelyn

I didn't know Laura was going too. In that case Menton is *far the best* as there are various potterings to occupy her morning. Give her my love. If you don't like Westminster move to Hôtel des Anglais – two old inhabitants of M mourned when I said Westminster. Don't forget you can take a box at the cinema like an old fashioned pew – very comfortable. How I wish Henry May was still alive. Shall you see old Willie [Maugham]? Rumour has it that Heywood has adopted Handy.[1]

About Picasso. I didn't invent it because everybody's talking about it although, like a ghost, nobody actually heard it except me. But as you say one listens in a very idle way. I turned on after the beginning & was of course entranced but didn't immediately make notes because I thought to read it in all the papers. No it wasn't his own voice. The emission is a very serious one, always a commentary on some feature of current affairs, on the Fr equivalent of the 3rd programme.

I've asked Gaston to find out from his friends on French wireless. The speaker seemed to be quoting from a statement 'then he went on to say etc' & the whole thing lasted about 15 minutes. I had begun to think I must have dreamt it until I was told that it has been very much talked about.

I don't think wireless features here are reprinted – the whole thing is more haphazard than at home but *much* livelier.

Do you *completely* trust A. D. Peters?

Love from
    Nancy

[1] Somerset Maugham had recently adopted his secretary, Alan Searle.

25 January 1963   Hôtel Royal Westminster
                                         Menton A.M.

Darling Nancy

When you ask do I completely trust Mr Peters, do you refer to his honesty or his wisdom? I am sure he never embezzles our money. I have known him once or twice be injudicious but much more often he has proved himself astute.

I don't think there is any Hotel des Anglais here. There is a Grande Bretagne, a Londres, a Balmoral, a Victoria; there is even a café named 'The Can-I-help-you English Snacks' but I have seen nothing of Hotel des Anglais. There is a very good Angleterre in Copenhagen. Perhaps you are thinking of that. Perhaps it is a hallucination like the Picasso recantation. Do not be worried about hallucinations. I had them very severely ten years ago. No recurrence.

This is a very polite, dowdy hotel full of lame English & athletic Italians carrying tennis rackets & dog whips. The only Frenchman wears a red stud in his button hole & leads a cat on a yellow cord. The natives of Menton are all very old & carry armfuls of mimosa. Grub of course beastly but a modest casino where we win 50 francs daily before·dinner & that pays for our dinner.

Laura has gone for a week to Naples leaving me to work ha ha. Brilliant sunshine. No new building this side of Monte Carlo. Cannes has become like the Great West Road.

I hate to speak well of an innovation but the London–Nice aeroplane is *much* more comfortable than the old blue train.

I got tipsy in London passing through and enjoyed it very much kissing lots of young girls. I don't think they enjoyed it much.

There are 2000 popular English novels here all pre 1914.

Love from
    Evelyn

[postmarked 27 January 1963]   [7 rue Monsieur, VII]
[postcard]

Oh how *tiresome* you are.

Never mind, I won't interrupt your work with any more delusions illusions or allusions. I just send this lovely P.C. which you don't deserve.[1]

Love
  N

[1] A postcard of a mournful 1930s lady, surmounting a mawkish poem entitled 'God Bring You Home Again'.

2 February [1963]   Hôtel Royal Westminster
                                      Menton

Darling Nancy,

'Damn,' you will say, or in your cosmopolitan way: 'Merde. *His* writing again. The man who bored the Haileses out of Trinidad.'

But it's all right. This doesn't need an answer. I write from the extremity of loneliness which will be relieved by the time you get this by Laura's return. I have spoken to no one since she went to Naples.

I was never much of a one for parlez-vousing, as you know, but 30 years ago I could often catch on to what the frogs said and even make a few intelligible noises myself. Now I might be among Chinese. Words fail me more & more. I find it with English too – a shrinking vocabulary.

[. . .] Did you know that the frog priests who have taken to trousers call them their 'clergymans'?

This is a *very* nice hotel but I am dying of boredom and infertility. I went to the cinema & understood what you meant by 'sitting in a box like an old pew'. I read it as 'jew' & was puzzled. I couldn't understand a word of the film, named *Ophelia.*[1] The heroine was hideous.

My treat today is to visit the Salle des Mariages in the town hall decorated by Cocteau.

One can never get a chair in the casino. I like to sit down & play away for hours for minimum stakes. I hate having to shout to the croupiers over rows of old women.

DON'T ANSWER

Lots of love
  E

[1] By Claude Chabrol (1962), starring the beautiful French actress Juliette Mayniel.

4 February 1963   7 rue Monsieur, VII

Darling Evelyn

[. . .] I hasten to write as a friend just back from Portugal has just told me the Fieldings are in the S of France. He didn't know where. Have you any means of finding out? It seems to me they would be a boon to you at present. But I suppose Laura won't be eternally at Naples.

I was sent a book called *Coronet Among the Weeds*[1] written by a girl called Bingham (whom I can't find in the peerage). I nearly cried at its badness & jokelessness & now see that it is a masterpiece hailed by all & Miss Foyle says it is *the* publishing event of the year. On the other hand Nicholas Lawford's book[2] is perfection so no doubt that will be duly downed by all the critics. Oh so good & funny & genial.

Can't think of anything to amuse you. I sit in my igloo, so hot that the Col does the Death of Chatterton when he comes, & daren't put a nose out of doors. I'm reviewing a book about Voltaire with no index for the *N Y Times* which I thought had packed up. Nobody will read it but it gives me the pleasure of being forced to have a go at V's letters. They are like a visit to the Louvre – you go in thinking to look at one picture & you are still there at closing time.

Excuse dulth.

Love
     N

I had meant to tell *you* about *en clergyman* – how I screamed. It, the dress I mean, was brought in here by Teilhard de Chardin.[3] Now the Arch B of Paris has forbidden Church music do you understand why? Oh & my tomb. I've left £4000 for a tomb with angels & things. People are *AMAZED* & clergymen have told Debo that angels aren't allowed. Again I ask why? Surely it's an ancient instinct to want a pretty tomb? And one has always seen angels.

[1] A first novel by Hon. Charlotte Bingham (1942–), daughter of 7th Baron Clanmorris. In 1964 she married the playwright Terence O'Brady with whom she collaborated on many successful television series, including *Upstairs Downstairs*.
[2] *Bound for Diplomacy* (1963).
[3] Pierre Teilhard de Chardin (1881–1955). Palaeontologist, geologist and unorthodox theologian who developed an evolutionary interpretation of mankind in *The Phenomenon of Man* (1955).

9 February 1963   Combe Florey House
                                              Nr Taunton

Darling

Your tomb. You can get a slap up angel for £4000 – do you really mean that sum or was it a slip of the pen for N.F.? But where will you set it up? Protestant parsons are tigers in this one matter in which they retain authority. Lately a poor widow put 'for ever in my thoughts' on her husband's grave & was made to remove it. The Church of England does not believe in angels any more. I presume you want to be planted at Swinbrook.[1] Unless the parson there is exceptionally venal & snobbish you haven't a chance of an angel. Also the French customs are very strict about exporting corpses. Your best plan would be to die in Genoa – very comfortable hotel called, I think, Columbus – where every licence is given to sculpture. Or you could buy a plot at Brookwood – near the foot guards but not really very nice.

I am engaged at the moment in trying to get permission to build a 12 bedder vault here. Bishop of Bath & Wells not forthcoming at all. Perhaps Mrs Hamish Hamilton could get you into a Jewish cemetery – they believe in angels. So do Mohamedans but they aren't allowed to make statues of them.

There is a very nice cemetery at Menton full of the English who were sent there to die of consumption. I cheered up a lot there after Laura joined me. There was a lovely bus full of Lolitas which collected them from school at 11.30 and eventually went, shedding them alas, to Monte Carlo.

My life here is embittered by the presence of a senile aunt. She described a friend as 'rather poorly with cancer'. The Pope is said to be in that condition too. I have just written his obituary for the Yanks.

I saw Peters in London. He shone with simple honesty. But there is some delay in getting money from America. I wonder if his Yank agent is as honourable as he.

Love
    E

[1] Nancy was buried in the churchyard of St Mary in Swinbrook, Oxfordshire, near the house where she had lived as a child.

15 March 1963   Chatsworth
                                                      Bakewell

Darling Evelyn

Oh poor you & your poor aunt – I do feel sorry for all. Think if ONE ends up in that situation. Poorly with cancer – my char in the war once said she had a little touch of the change.

Oh the cemetery at Menton. I remember once crying out: Jim – Jim here's a hon. Montpellier has one, that much older – they went there to die in the 18th century.

It's too stupid if one can't have a tomb. Everybody else has got one covered with angels (look at Maréchal de Saxe) who are thinly disguised cupids at that. I leave it to Debo, she'll manage.[1]

I go now to the Hayters, Sister Pam & home again.

I said to Debo it would amuse me to meet the Portlands[2] who are the great friends of my great friend at Venice Alphy Clary.[3] So she rang up one evening & asked them to lunch the next day & they came. They are quite old & live 25 miles away – they had only been here once before & Debo has never seen the inside of their house. When they said goodbye (having seen every inch even the loos) they said we nearly died of terror when we realized it was your sister Nancy. Debo shoots with the Duke & is on sort of jolly masculine terms with him. She once said how much money have you got to which he replied nine – big ones.

So I go & catch my train.

Much love
Nancy

P.S. A skin doctor from South Africa writes to ask if I've ever known a member of the upper classes with skin disease because he never has. Well, what about it? Oh yes & what are your views on *my dear*. I think it is a class distinction – one writes My dear Bishop even if one hardly knows him & dear Mabel (housemaid) even if one's greatest love. Debo spits on this notion however & always writes Dear Bishop. Tell your thoughts.

I found the Fieldings for you – too late.

[1] Nancy's grave is marked by a simple stone carved with the Mitford family emblem, a mole.
[2] 7th Duke of Portland (1893–1977). Married to Hon. Ivy Gordon-Lennox in 1915.
[3] Alfons, Prince Clary-Aldringen (1887–1978). Author of an autobiography *A European Past* (1977).

[postmarked 16 March 1963]   Combe Florey House
[postcard]   Nr Taunton

Upper class skin disease. Job (Bible) leaps to the mind also Basil Dufferin, Eddy West and my mother-in-law (psoriasis – very disagreeable). Was there not a leper King of Bohemia? or am I dreaming? Diana Cavendish certainly. Oh there are hundreds.

Church of England would let you have an angel if it looked like Epstein's *Rima*; not if it looked like a Bernini.

E

24 May 1963   Combe Florey House
                                              Nr Taunton

Darling Nancy

I was in London yesterday & heard from Mrs Friese Green the news of your mother's illness and of your sad vigil on Mull. She told me you wanted letters. It is a long time since I wrote, but my life is so dull that there is little to tell.

I have been made a new-fangled thing called a 'Companion of
Literature', the invention of Freddy Birkenhead, no emoluments, no
adornments, no precedence, no duties – average age 78. I am by far
the youngest. They live scattered between Cap Ferrat, California &
Hong Kong so I don't think I shall enjoy much companionship. But
I thought it would be stuck up & unfriendly to Freddy if I refused. I
have to go to a banquet which I dread.

Prince Richard of Gloucester is being sent to stay with Harold
Acton to broaden his (H.R.H.'s) mind. Harold was examined by the
Duke and pronounced most suitable.

Daphne has finished her treatise on Rosa.[1] It is jolly good but I
think full of inaccuracies. My friend B. Bennett (Hyde Park Hotel) has
bought the Cavendish & proposes to rebuild it & retain the name.
Daphne mentions you as an habituée. Surely not true?

My daughter Margaret attends a 'Pre-natal clinic' in Paddington
where she is the only patient who is both white & married & is treated
as a rare bird.

Your lunatic cousin Randolph has set up as proof corrector.

Mrs Fleming has spent £5000 on a gorilla by Nolan;[2] I £200 on a
touching scene by Arthur Hughes – *The Convent Boat* portraying grim
nuns rowing a novice away from her mourning family. Mr Fleming
is very jealous of the Duchess of Argyll who has been paid £60,000
for pornography. The Duke is getting about 40 thou.[3] Peters refused
to handle her affairs. I spent most of yesterday with him & am convinced of his high honesty and devotion to our interests.

Birds fall dead all round us poisoned by farmers. Our asparagus,
usually our one good crop, has failed – a few stunted purple stumps.

Harold Acton has also written a novel[4] – did I tell you? Very odd &
funny. He has forgotten the English language – a warning to all
expatriates.

Do they talk Gaelic on Mull? I couldn't understand John Betjeman's
last Celtic joke book.[5]

Darling Nancy, I haven't said a word of sympathy about your
mother's illness, but I feel it keenly.

Love from
    Evelyn

[1] Daphne Fielding, *The Duchess of Jermyn Street: The Life and Good Times of Rosa Lewis of the Cavendish Hotel* (1964). Evelyn contributed a preface.
[2] Sydney Nolan (1917–92). The Australian painter was exhibiting at Marlborough Fine Art where his painting of a gorilla was sold to Ann Fleming for £1,200. Knighted in 1981.
[3] Following a scandalous divorce, the Duchess of Argyll had been paid £55,000 by the *Sunday Pictorial* for her indiscreet memoirs. She brought a case against the Duke, preventing him from publishing four out of a projected six articles in the *People* containing intimate details of their married life. He was expelled from White's for publishing the first two.
[4] *Old Lamps for New* (1963).
[5] *Some Immortal Hours. A Rhapsody of the Celtic Twilight wrought in word and water colour by Deirdre O'Betjeman* (1962).

29 May 1963   4 Chesterfield Street, W1

Darling Evelyn

Your letter arrived at a very good moment for me, just as we were
leaving the island,[1] & cheered me up considerably during our journey
South of 12 hours.

We took my mother over the water to Mull on a marvellous evening,
8 pm, with the bagpipes wailing away, it was very beautiful. All the
men of the neighbourhood came, all talking Gaelic to each other (since
you ask).

During a great storm, when we were cut off for 2 days from Mull,
at the start of her illness, an intrepid neighbour called Ogilvie-Forbes
rowed over in a sort of rubber ball, moved quietly into the bothy &
never left us again. He is a co religionist of yours. Well he held a
service over her coffin which was too perfect in every way & greatly
appreciated by us & by the dear fellows who did all the things one
has to.

It seemed all *real*, not like when one dies at the London Clinic. Also
the good Scotch doctor didn't insist on cruel things to keep her alive
a few more days – the nurses said in a hospital it would have been
very different.

We are all pretty tired. The funeral is tomorrow.

Much love & thank-you dearest Evelyn
     Nancy

And for 2nd kind letter which has just arrived.

[1] Lady Redesdale died on 25 May, soon after her 83rd birthday. She had been living since
the war on Inchkenneth, an island off the west coast of Scotland.

28 September 1963   7 rue Monsieur, VII

Darling Evelyn

It's an age since I heard of you – then John showed me your railway
letter[1] & I thought I must make a sign of life.

Have you seen Decca's book? It is the *Loved One* blown up into a
huge balloon – very funny & ghastly. It makes a great fuss in America
& not bad sales, 60,000 in print, which is a good thing as they are
not well off. But more fuss than sales I think as often happens with
that sort of book. I wondered if perhaps you would review it but I
think it's upon us now, in England. Gollancz wouldn't do it so Hutchinson has.

Emma has been here with her husband[2] they seem about 14 –
adorable – perfectly happy. They caught a lot of butterflies in the S
of France which wildly flap about on a piece of cork. 'Quite dead
Aunt Natch, it's only nerves.' Whether my nerves or the butterflies' I

wasn't quite sure – mine were shattered. I said it will be a case of Have you anything to declare? Butterflies. But they weren't with it (as they wld say).

Gaston came to Chatsworth after the wedding & we went over to see Osbert. Oh *dear* – two shades in a ghostly house. It was tragic. Debo said cheerfully as we drove away: 'last time we see the dear old place under that management I bet.' If Reresby[3] takes it on I salute him – I never saw such ingrained gloom. However a little white paint does wonders with a house no doubt.

I had a very nice summer – Venice & Greece where Mark [Ogilvie-Grant] took me to Euboea & Samos. At Euboea we stayed with a Bart called Sir Aymer Maxwell[4] whose brother writes books about otters. In the next house Paddy & Joan [Leigh Fermor]. Sir A has got a yacht & we went for many delightful expeditions. But an Austrian lady writer having just been eaten by a shark rather spoilt the bathing for this L.W. (She was a poetess so serve her right.)

Cyril, wife & child have been here, in sunny mood. I gave him that portrait of him by Jean de Gaigneron & he was awfully pleased – I told him you said it was like a miners' leader.

Any hope of you here? John took me to a restaurant where the food was so delicious that I thoroughly over ate, as I seldom do – it made me wish you were there. I go next week to Fontaines for about three weeks I suppose off & on.

Love
    Nancy

P.S. Having left Athens with Dr Ward[5] in a coma I longed to know what had happened – no newspapers on Samos. So I made Mark go to the police station where there is a wireless & enquire. 'Dr Ward is dead. You have lost a fine man.'

---

[1] Evelyn had been in correspondence with John Sutro over the 40th anniversary celebrations of the Oxford University Railway Club.
[2] Lady Emma Cavendish married Hon. Toby Tennant on 3 September 1963.
[3] Reresby Sitwell (1927–2009). Succeeded his father, Sir Sacheverell, in 1988 and lived at Renishaw Hall, the family seat in Derbyshire.
[4] Sir Aymer Maxwell (1911–87). Brother of Gavin Maxwell, the author of *Ring of Bright Water* (1960).
[5] Stephen Ward, one of the men at the centre of the Profumo scandal, had taken a drug overdose.

4 October 1963   Combe Florey House
                                                          Nr Taunton
Darling Nancy
    How interesting that you should remember: 'Have you anything to declare?' 'Butterflies.' It is the one passage that has stuck in my mind

from my adolescent admiration of Firbank. Indeed I cribbed it in *Vile Bodies* 'Anything to declare? Wings?'

Your letter reached me at Forest Mere Hydro – Boots's beauty parlour – where I am spending a fortnight. Health, not vanity. I had grown too ponderous to move. Also I found in the last year that I could no longer get tight (a condition I enjoy) however much I drank. After 4 days of total fast I have lost 10 lbs & been promoted to carrot juice (disgusting). I hope when I leave to get tipsy on a glass of wine. I have not yet experienced the euphoria which all the habitués claim to enjoy on the fourth day.

I did review Decca's treatise.[1] Of course it was all stale eggs to me. Ever since I wrote that book kind, unknown correspondents have kept me supplied with bizarre press-cuttings on the subject. But I admire Decca's industry (or was it her husband's?) and loyally commended it.

As I don't drive a motor I am dependent on Jack McDougall who lives some way off, for treats. Yesterday he took me to the Watts Gallery,[2] near Godalming. Do you know *The First Oyster, B.C.*? As funny as painting as I ever saw. Tomorrow he promises to take me to see Winchester.

Can you tell me whether John Sutro & Diana Mosley are chums again? Was he one of the luncheon party which assembled at Gunter's when she came out of prison?

I never leave home between Easter & Michaelmas. I have made no winter plans for a long journey but I expect that Laura & I will go to Menton for February.

Osbert tried to enliven Renishaw by painting the oak panelling all colours of the rainbow. A great mistake. It ought to be like the Dedlocks' seat.[3]

I went to a literary banquet in London. Your friend Spender wore the wrong clothes, had his CBE hanging down to his waist like an eye-glass & lit his cigar before the loyal toast. He caused great offence to his confrères. He then forgot to take away the certificate of honour which he had received on behalf of Aldous Huxley. The banquet was a foible of Freddy Birkenhead's.

Glad Emma is happy. It won't last. Tennant marriages never do.[4]

Did I tell you that my daughter, Margaret, attends a pre-natal clinic in Paddington where she is the only patient who is both white & married?

This is a wretched letter. My hand trembles from fasting & my mind runs slow. I will write again when my strength is renewed.

Love
    E

---

[1] Evelyn reviewed *The American Way of Death* in the *Sunday Times*, 29 September 1963. 'Miss

Mitford and her husband, Mr Treuhaft, have together produced what is (as far as I know) the
first full study of the economics and anthropology of North American burial customs. It is easy
to guess the nature of their collaboration; here is little Decca, teasing on the telephone, there
is solid Bob at his desk doing his sums. The result is a book to enchant those ignorant of the
subject.'
[2] The former house of George Frederick Watts (1817–1904), a painter in the grand, often
ludicrous, style of 'High Art'.
[3] Chesney Wold, Sir Leicester Dedlock's ancient Lincolnshire seat in Dickens' *Bleak House*.
[4] This one has.

7 October 1963   7 rue Monsieur, VII

Darling Evelyn
    I rang up Diana & said is it true you had a coming out party at
Gunter's? Quite true, YOU gave it. She can't remember if Sutro was
there but thinks he must have been. (Really the state of *my* memory
is such that I might never have lived at all.) She is on the best of terms
with Sutro now – was there ever a coldness? Oh I suppose while they
were actually baiting there must have been.
    Yes I saw your review the day after I wrote – didn't realize the
book was coming so soon. My mother thought that book *and Hons &
Rebels* were largely written by Barb – they did a lot of the work when
staying with her in Scotland. It seems the publishers prefer the name
Mitford to Treuhaft can't think why!! I greatly enjoyed your joke
about nobody being allowed to make money except writers.
    Don't starve to death I should miss you. I've been reading about
le radeau de *La Méduse*[1] – they began eating each other after four days
which seems very uncontrolled when you think of Tring & about 30
of them seem to have eaten about 60 in a week or two. They can't have
done anything else. Somebody shld have told them about enjoying a
glass of wine more after a fast.
    I'm off to Fontaines for my yearly treat – very gloomy weather still
that won't affect the company & the grub.

    Love
        N

[1] The shipwreck of a frigate that caused a huge political scandal in 1816. Due to the incompetence of the captain, most of the passengers perished; of the 147 survivors who crowded on to
a small raft [radeau] with no food or water, 15 survived 13 days before they reached dry land.

26 October 1963   Fontaines-les-Nonnes
                                                    par Puisieux

Darling Evelyn
    Thank you very much for your lovely book.[1] I read it again &
again of course couldn't stop until the end. But it gives rise to certain
reflections. I'm afraid that, in literature at any rate, middle aged people

become dull. Take *War & Peace*. As soon as all those charming, funny, touching adorable Rostovs are married, settled in life, they are so different & so stodgy that we are quite glad when the book comes to an end. I find the same with you – except that with you one longs for it to go on – I'm not sure but I see the difficulties. I loved the two young ones, the little one saw of them. Now Evelyn seriously, do you think being brother & sister would really have stopped them marrying? I call this rather naïf. Lord & Lady Dunmore, my father's great friends, were brother & sister so one always heard. They had a very happy marriage, I don't believe young people today would care a fig & NOR WOULD BASIL SEAL – but the trouble is Prod has turned into you & this falsifies everything. It is a great mistake in fact because never the twain could meet & it's wrong to try & make them. I do agree that naughty people are often reformed when they become rich but I don't believe however rich *Seal* was that he would have become that sort of good citizen, or broken his daughter's heart over such a silly quibble. Or was he meant to be jealous? If so we are in deep water indeed. Perhaps it's all too short – I don't know, but I'm not convinced. Were you, really?

Abbé Girard, the nicest of the priests who came here, asked for *Voltaire Amoureux*. I said to Mme Costa what should I put as a dédicace? She said perhaps nothing – I'm afraid if you do it will be very compromising for him after his death; you are (in English) such a beautiful young (sic) lady, it's not as if you were Mme de Pange! In the end she made me put avec mes sentiments respectueux. I shall be interested to know what he makes of it.

Decca is lecturing all over America on dead bodies. It now appears that Bob has got a sort of self-service firm so they stand to make millions apart from the royalties. It wanted thinking of as Gladys my maid used to say.

Love – *thanks*.
    N

[1] *Basil Seal Rides Again* (1963). Evelyn's last work of fiction.

29 October 1963   Combe Florey House
                                             Nr Taunton
Dearest Nancy
    Your odious letter was on my breakfast table on the morning of my 60th birthday. Ah, at least one old friend has written to congratulate me on reaching the age when I am exempt from jury service and can no longer decently be expected to carry anything. Not at all. A sharp reminder that my powers are fading and that I am a bore.
    All you say, I refute. The story is too short, not too long. It would

have made a novel. Old people are more interesting than young. One of the particular points of interest is to observe how after 50 they revert to the habits, mannerisms and opinions of their parents, however wild they were in youth. I see it on all sides as well as in myself. B. Seal had highly conventional parents. His change & recovery of his youth are the theme of the story.

I hope it is clear that the claim to have fathered Albright was totally false – a device to save his daughter whom he loves to excess from marrying a beatnik.

Your family, if reports at the time were true, were peculiarly tolerant of incest. It is a taboo deeply rooted in the most heathen. I do not think that morals have declined much since the age when Byron was driven from the country. As for that girl's heart, it will mend quickly. Of course Basil was fiercely jealous. That should be apparent.

The only fault I admit to is the misspelling of Clicquot.

We have just returned from a visit to Ann Fleming's edifice.[1] She has spent as much as the government have on the reconstruction of Downing Street, pulled down a large commodious house & put up a cottage – only access to the only 'living-room' is through the dining room. Only one narrow staircase. Only one fireplace. It stands in a narrow strip of marsh surrounded by woods where the shooting rights are kept by the vendor, and some acres of flat farm land also belonging to him & ripe for development as a housing estate. The one room is quite large and she has bought the furniture for a London flat. Hundreds of lorries & bulldozers have been at work all the summer excavating the swamp and importing soil. Ian is facing prosecution for plagiarism and may be not ruined but seriously inconvenienced.[2] He looks & speaks as though he may drop dead any minute. His medical advisers confirm the apprehension.

The few bedrooms are tiny cubicles with paper thin walls through which every cough & snore is audible.

My own house, though better than Ann's, is invaded by son, daughter-in-law, granddaughter and a swarthy monoglot nannie, second generation Spanish communist refugee to south of France.

Love from
    Evelyn

[1] Sevenhampton Place, near Faringdon.
[2] A writ had been issued against Ian Fleming by Kevin McClory and Jack Whittingham alleging breach of copyright over *Thunderball*. McClory was awarded all literary and film rights in the screenplay, and all film rights in the novel.

All Souls' Day [2 November] 1963   Fontaines-les-Nonnes
                                                    par Puisieux

Darling Evelyn

I love you passionately & copy you slavishly as you very well know
& certainly didn't mean to be odious – I did write in a hurry but
surely I must have said that I read *Seal* all in a gulp at the second
reading which (for me) is *tout dire*.[1] All the same no good pretending
he wasn't the father, what about the star sapphire eyes & proud &
furious mouth? As for incest, what about all this ear-nibbling? Oh
come! Surely I didn't say it was too long? That would be silly indeed.

Dreadful about Ann's house, & everybody agrees with you, because
think of the beauties she might have saved from the National Trust,
at that price.

L P Hartley is coming to lecture on the novelist's responsibility –
can he have noticed that Mrs Beecher-Stowe is the architect of all our
troubles? We had *La Case de l'Oncle Tom* on the T.V. oh dear it made
one die for a few slaves. But how *expensive* they were – I hadn't realized.

A friend writes from Jersey that Grandey[2] has got an advertisement in
the local paper: Lord Jersey will shoot anybody who trespasses on his land.

Debo writes that Andrew may give up being a Duke & call himself
Ld Cavendish. 'Herbal (the boy)[3] doesn't care for this wheeze (credit)'.
The said Herbal who is Bertie Wooster riding again, is coming to
Paris next term to learn bridge.

Deep love – live another 60 years please – from your devoted
disciple.
        NR

Rather glad to think I shan't have you on the jury if I commit a crime.
Home on Tuesday.
You *couldn't* say that my ma in law was conventional! Also when you state
that middle aged people become their parents you are merely agreeing
with me that they become bores. What you mean is they are like what
their parents were in middle age viz duller than in youth. Q E D.

[1] Says it all.
[2] 9th Earl of Jersey (1910–98).
[3] Marquess of Hartington (1944–).

Christmas Day, 1963   7 rue Monsieur, VII

Darling Evelyn

Happy Christmas – how's everything?
May I ask you two questions?
I'm *doing* Louis XIV at Versailles.[1]
Now when the Dauphine, Marie-Adélaïde, was dying she asked her

Jesuit confessor to send her some other priest. He understood that she
wanted a non-Jesuit. But why? Surely as she knew she was dying she
only had to confess, repent & be absolved, whatever she had done? I
can understand one might want a less strict confessor for every day
but on a death bed why?

Then, have you ever been interested in Mme Guyon?

If so do you take the view, as I do, of Mgr Knox or that of Abbé
Bremond? She must have been you'd think completely maddening
but many people loved her, including level headed Mme de Maintenon, who had her worldly side.

Are you off to Menton? Have you finished your book? I've only
just begun mine but so far I'm enjoying it & my eyes have taken a
turn for the better – very unexpected. I thought they would get steadily
worse until death.

    Much love from
        Nancy

Don't answer if you're busy Mr E.W. regrets he is unable to do as
you so kindly suggest.

¹ *The Sun King* (1966).

30 December 1963   Combe Florey House
                                              Nr Taunton

Dearest Nancy

    Thank you very much for your pretty Christmas-card.

    I am delighted to learn that your poor old eyes have taken a turn
for the better. May they progress.

    I don't know much about the Dauphine Marie-Adélaïde. I should
guess that her conscience was not heavily burdened with mortal sins.
A likely explanation of her choice of confessor might be this: the Jesuit
casuists of her period had a reputation (partly deserved) for laxity
particularly in their treatment of the great. I think perhaps her normal
confessor had told her not to fuss & that she was all right & that when
the time came to settle her final accounts she felt the need of someone
stricter, not as you suggest less strict. But this is a pure guess.

    Nor am I an authority on Mme Guyon. I think she was no saint,
a booby & lacking in true sincerity & humility. She was treated with
undue harshness through becoming involved in high intrigues of which
she was personally innocent. Fénelon, if I remember correctly, was a
half-hearted supporter. You can't fault Bossuet. And certainly the kind
of revelation she claimed was prevalent in contemporary France, and
took in others some very rum forms. But I am sure she was ill-treated.
If you want expert but not completely orthodox advice on her, try

my brother-in-law Alick Dru (DRU) Bickham Manor, Timberscombe, Somerset.

Laura & I go to Menton for the beginning of February – not, alas, stopping in Paris.

I do hope someone assassinates the Duke of Edinburgh next year.

Love from
    Evelyn

Mme Guyon was slippery – as Ronald Knox makes plain.

2 January 1964   7 rue Monsieur, VII

Darling Evelyn

What you say about the Dauphine is *too interesting* & surely true. The strange thing to me was that when she asked for the parish priest (&, when he couldn't be found, for any priest) her confessor didn't seem to have minded but just set about getting somebody. Now I understand.

I think she may have had a lover but her children were undoubtedly the husband's. But she was distressed about something, at the end. She was a strange creature – adored by all. Oh dear, life is very short & unsatisfactory isn't it.

I've had a good deal of fun reviewing an American life of Mme de Sévigné by a PhD *characteriologist* (her idea not mine) called Mrs Allentuch.[1] She attributes the most sinister reasons to things like going for a walk. What an idea for an American to pick on Mme de S – she has read 179 volumes about her not counting hundreds of articles. She could have saved her breath to blow her porridge – you never saw such rubbish.

I do congratulate you on the birth of the top best seller of the 80s.[2]

Please tell Miss Harriet she will receive a gift when somebody goes to England. Oh I always forget, these girls don't hang about at home playing patience & wishing the Prince of Wales would suddenly appear, like we used to, so you probably never see Miss Harriet. Don't bother.

Excuse this untidy letter, I know you don't like it, but I'm so busy.

Did you get the Col's Xmas card? That is his ministry.[3] The little summer house in the foreground is now the base, with five others, for those statues of towns in the Pl de la Concorde. (Strasbourg & Nancy were draped with crêpe from '71–1918.) That's all!

Love
    N

Thank you very much indeed for answering. Guyon was badly treated in a way, being so much taken up & then dropped, but not cruelly treated, I think. Don't care for Fénelon.

Did you know Harold A[cton] has inherited 6 million dollars?

[1] Harriet Allentuch, *Madame de Sévigné: Portrait in Letters* (1963).
[2] Auberon and Teresa Waugh had just had a son, Alexander. In 1995 he published *Classical Music: A New Way of Listening*.
[3] Palewski was Minister for Scientific and Atomic Research 1962–5.

30 July 1964   23 Dorsoduro
                                                    Venice

Darling Evelyn

It's an age since we wrote – I'm working hard & so I suppose are you. Taking the opportunity of a break to send a little news. I'm carefully not reading your book in *S T*[1] though couldn't resist John [Sutro] & Robert [Byron], both *génial*, but I see by what I have read you are strictly keeping to truth so you will be a boon to the future historian, who can tell with half an eye who keeps to it & who does not. On the whole the *bores do*, so you will be a double boon & great rarity. Well done.

I'm writing a book about Louis XIV but not a life, aspects of his reign which amuse me. Oh I've told you this already when we spoke of Bossuet. Now I've read all his sermons & also many of Bourdaloue's & at last I see why the Victorians were so fond of reading sermons. (Freud I suppose now takes that public.)

I went to Istanbul to stay with a friend (Paris neighbour) called Ostrorog – an adorable, melancholy, erudite man whose mother was sort of Turkish & who lives in a pink wooden palace at Kandilli – next village to Scutari. He showed me Constantinople from top to toe – have you been there? It's amazingly unspoilt & the Bosphorus almost completely so. There is a charming society, built on French civilization – one goes everywhere by boat – the Turks seem more gentle, sweet & refined than any Greeks or Italians (though of course WE KNOW that there is another side). I've seldom enjoyed a visit so much. Now I'm here until Monday when I go home to work.

Debo's boy has moved in, harboured by my angelic hostess – he is a *great* pleasure to me. Don't bother to answer as you are still busy I expect.

Much love
    N

[1] Extracts from *A Little Learning* were serialised in the *Sunday Times* before publication.

6 August 1964   Combe Florey House
                                                Nr Taunton

Dearest Nancy,

Jolly decent of you to write. No, I am not at all busy – just senile. Since we last met (when?) I have become an old man, not diseased but enfeebled. I read my letters & work at *The Times* cross-word & never set foot out of doors. I was mildly ill in Menton in February & so spoiled Laura's hols. I am making up for it by taking her to Spain in October. I don't like the food & can't speak the lingo & don't much look forward to it, especially as I must write an article at the end.

In a few weeks you will receive a copy of my interminable autobiography. I look forward to your studies of Louis XIV. I lately read Sir Winston's *Marlborough*. How he alienates all sympathy. I found myself on every page praying 'Oh God, do defeat the Grand Alliance.'

Living as I do, seeing no one & reading only *The Times* newspaper I am quite bewildered by Bob Boothby's case. £40,000 paid out of court when they had not mentioned his name.[1] If one is incapacitated for life by the negligence of a motorist one is lucky to get £4,000. Perhaps in Constantinople you missed it all. One curious point – the unnamed peer was said to have gone to an 'all-male' party of licentious clergymen at Brighton. Now in November last John Sutro & I organized a party to Brighton to celebrate the 40th anniversary of the foundation of the Oxford Railway Club. Bob was there. Clerical dress was not worn but I remember thinking how very clerical most of our voices sounded – impotent grandfathers to a man. Can that have been the origin of the rumour?

Seldom a week passes but I read of a contemporary acquaintance falling downstairs, usually fatally.

    Best love
        E

[1] The *Sunday Mirror* had alleged that an unnamed peer was being investigated by Scotland Yard for his homosexual relationship with a gangster. The German magazine *Stern* identified Lord Boothby as the peer and Ronnie Kray as the thug. Lord Boothby denied the allegations in a letter to *The Times* and five days later the *Mirror* offered him £40,000 compensation plus costs.

12 September 1964   Fontaines-les-Nonnes
                                                par Puisieux

Darling Evelyn

It's so good of you to send me your book thank you very much. I'm going to read it on the 28th & will then write properly. The thing is I'm writing mine & in constant pain from eyes so that it would be no enjoyment to read it now. On 28th I go to Paris for a week to entertain Debo (*come*) & then I shall be longing for something to read.

It's so funny the way you are practically married to Decca now.
When she was here she received a telegram from *Life* or *Time* offering
her 1000 (or a million) dollars to review *A Little Learning* but was going
to refuse as she was off to Hollywood to do I forget what about the
filming of *The Loved One*. I greatly enjoyed her visit she is such a darling
– I forced her to buy some expensive clothes, you can't *think* how rich
she is! When she heard the price her eyes became gooseberries but I
made her & then of course she looked so pretty. She had 17 people
to stay on my mother's island including Ph Toynbee who seems to be
a re-incarnation of old Baz [Murray]. Goodness the tales!

I'm rather discouraged over my book. Hamilton says it won't sell
because of one by Cronin[1] (so *bad* but of course the public is not to
know that) so it has got to be one of those picture books which
Americans like. I shall make more money but of course nobody will
read it. (But it will eventually be a Penguin, the only thing which made
me accept.) £3, so nobody whose opinion one cares for will even buy
it. I cling to Voltaire's statement that books of value always find their
own level – I don't say it is one but if it isn't, it doesn't matter if it
sinks.

Heavenly here as always. From my bed at this moment I see the
shepherd grazing his 300 sheep in the park. He has golden hair, a
real crook, a little flute with which he controls his incredibly clever
dog, a blue blouse (his mantle blue) & a transistor which is slung over
his shoulder. He comes from near Calais & must have been one of
those *skeleton* children all eyes I saw from the train in 1945. They all
seem to have grown up into a wonderful generation, I suppose the
famine was fairly short.

Much love – good luck with your book –
Nancy

[1] Vincent Cronin, *Louis XIV* (1964).

20 October 1964   Fontaines-les-Nonnes
                                             par Puisieux

Darling Evelyn

Of course I loved your book – such a picture of one's youth – all
the visual part of it so brilliant – & the characterization of chums. I
didn't know 'old Baz' [Murray] had been a friend of yours how odd
that I didn't. He has got a saintly daughter you would love called Ann
& a beauty called Venetia not saintly at all.

When I first grew up, if there was an evening with nothing on I
used to get onto the top of a bus & drive through the suburbs – I
always thought they would be the place to live in (any of them in
those days) with their pretty little houses buried in lilac & often a

paddock or stables like the real country. I hated the real country (boredom) but always longed for fresh air & trees.

Too heavenly here as usual, perfect for work, esp as Mme Costa has given up bridge as a sacrifice to get her 20 yr old grandson back onto the straight & narrow.

My book has come to a pause & I'm off to Paris for 10 days.

We had the Bishop of Monaco (just the 3 of us) he took off his X & ring & thumped Chopin waltzes on the piano with many a wrong note. He says the Pope is longing to get rid of the Bishops. Mme Costa evidently disapproves of the Council – she won't hear about it, saying they bake the bread & I must eat it but I don't want to look on.

Have you read *Les Mots*?[1] I think you would love it. I too read *Marlborough* – there's something not quite right isn't there, but it's useful for the clear exposé of the battles. My book is going to have hundreds of pictures, 40 in colour. I put up a good deal of resistance at first but have come round to the idea. To begin with it's so good to be able to show everybody's face – then the mode of life becomes more clear in the mind – finally one can have as many maps & genealogies as one wants. It will be a Penguin after a year or 2. Mr Rainbird[2] what a sinister name, who is assembling it *claims*, as the *Daily Telegraph* wld say (I write to them once a week about their awful use of claim, to no avail of course) well he claims that he got orders for 100,000 copies at Frankfurt book fair wh, at 3 gns, seems more than promising.[3] Peters is all for it.

Decca went to Forest Lawn & they seem to have told her yes this rich English lord was here & when his wife died & she was buried here & he got the bill he was so furious he wrote *The Loved One*.

Voilà.

Much love
Nancy

[1] By Jean-Paul Sartre (1964). An autobiographical essay about childhood.
[2] George Rainbird (1905–86). Publisher who invented the coffee-table book.
[3] *The Sun King* was published to enthusiastic reviews and sold 25,000 copies within two years. General de Gaulle admired the book and recommended that his Cabinet read it.

10 February 1965   7 rue Monsieur, VII

Darling Evelyn

An age since we wrote. My book has gone to be typed and I've come up to breathe. It was a great effort but I think & hope the best I can do. I always think that is all one can ask of oneself & when the critics begin their song and dance that really is the answer.

I'm sure you never got the long letter I finally wrote (ages ago now)

about your book which I so adored. I saw Abbé Jung, to my horror, gather up the letter & put it in the pocket of his soutane. He has never been known to post anything though he always goes off laden with letters. Perhaps when he gets into what they call here *clergyman* viz an ill-fitting grey suit & round collar, the letters will have more of a chance but so far he is holding out. The village curé to my sorrow got himself a *clergyman* the first day he could & looks too horrid.

I dined with Randolph on his way to Morocco he told all the lovely tales about the D of Norfolk at the funeral[1] but his chief topic as always was you.

Did you know (but I'm sure you did) 'la plus perdue de toutes les journées est celle où l'on n'a pas ri'[2] was said by Chamfort – I came across it the other day.

Is there anything to read? Not having opened a new book for a year I thought to have a feast. I sent for *The Siege of Vienna*[3] it's too deadly dull (how can it be!) & as far as what I know goes, inaccurate.

I'm reading *The Beauties of the Bosphorus* by Miss Pardoe[4] which is complete perfection. 'Vain were the expostulations of the worthy old Effendi ... when did an Englishman ever yield to such arguments?' That's the stuff. I expect you know it.

Colonel is wading through the complete works of Thackeray which he asked for for Xmas. I thought they would be given away, but not by Handysides. I suppose Col thinks he will get on better with Mr Jenkins[5] if he knows all about Col Newcome.

How's your health? I would love to see you but can't get away for some time as next I'm going to work on a film (funny) about cannibals.

Much love
Nancy

[1] Sir Winston Churchill's state funeral took place on 30 January.
[2] 'The most wasted of all days is that on which one has not laughed.' Chamfort's maxim was engraved on the sundial at Madresfield Court.
[3] By John Stoye (1964).
[4] Published in 1838.
[5] Roy Jenkins (1920–). Minister for Aviation 1964–5, hence Palewski's *vis-à-vis* in Britain. Created life peer in 1987.

Shrove Tuesday [2 March] 1965   Combe Florey House
                                                 Nr Taunton

Dearest Nancy

Yes indeed I got your kind letter about my book and was & am most grateful for it. Please forgive my long delay in answering. I have been very idle lately. I do congratulate you on having finished your book. I am under contract for three & have not set pen to paper. I am not diseased but enfeebled. Tomorrow I have most of my teeth out. It is suggested new snappers might stimulate my waning appetite. Honks [Cooper] is convinced I am moribund. On the very rare occasions when I go out now I find that everyone over 55 is watching everyone else of the same age for evidence of decay. And what a lot of deaths there have been in the last 12 months. I can count a dozen in my own small circle – most of them slightly my juniors. It would be inconvenient for Laura if I kicked the bucket – otherwise no apprehensions.

The innovations in the Church are deeply distressing to me. I can't understand plays or films nowadays.

Oh what a whine this is. No doubt my spirits will improve when I am toothless.

Yours ever affec.
E

[postmarked 4 March 1965]   [7 rue Monsieur, VII]
[postcard]

I worry about your snappers & fear it is all *horrid*. Do come & live here, a panacea for everything. Oh the reforms. I had a dreadful quarrel with the Curé who loves them & ended by saying I see you are a Jansenist he was deeply offended. *Not for me to speak* I know. I hear you may do a book for Rainbird he is so nice to work for, I urge you to.

Love
N

29 May 1965   Combe Florey House
                                           Nr Taunton
Dearest Nancy,

You praised Mr Rainbird highly. He came here and I thought him a dull dog and a great snob.

What do you know of a Mrs Lancaster who gives you as reference in soliciting help in writing a treatise on Brian Howard?[1] I can't believe he will be [the] subject of many biographies. It would be a pity if some hack who didn't know him or see his point, should take him in hand. Is she American? What age? Except you & Nancy Cunard there are few women who knew him.

It has been a year of deaths beginning with Alfred Duggan,[2] then Baby Jungman's boy,[3] then Harry [Ilchester]; the other day Phil Dunne. There has not been a fortnight without a funeral. Ian Fleming is being posthumously canonized by the intelligentsia. Very rum.

Honks tells everyone I am dying. I don't think it's true. But I suffer in dignity & pleasure from my new snappers and I do no work.

Love,
        Evelyn

[1] *Brian Howard: Portrait of a Failure* (1968), edited by Marie-Jacqueline Lancaster, sister of Loretta Hugo.
[2] Alfred Duggan (1903–64). Brother of Hubert. After a reckless and drunken youth, he returned to Catholicism and, with Evelyn's encouragement, became the author of successful historical novels and biographies.
[3] Richard Cuthbertson had been killed in a motorcycle accident, aged 24.

2 June 1965   7 rue Monsieur, VII

Dearest Evelyn

I don't know either of them. I only said I like working for Rainbird because he has produced wonderful Mrs Law[1] who has been the greatest possible help (such as reading the proofs & finding hundreds of solecisms & also finding a Professor to look at my MS) & who is a genius at getting pictures, placing them exactly right & so on.

As for Brian's biographer I don't know why she says she knows me. She wrote out of the blue. Like you I think it's most sad if Brian is messed up as it almost seems certain he will be but what can one do? I feel for poor Emerald [Cunard] too as Daphne [Fielding] hardly knew her, wasn't the kind of person she liked & certainly isn't up to it. But there you are. We didn't think of doing them ourselves & can't, I suppose, complain when somebody else takes on the job.

The only *woman* who went to bed – if you can call it bed I seem to remember it was on the floor of Mrs Ernest Guinness's drawing-room – with Brian was Romie [Hope-Vere]. It was her boast for many a long year.

I've been longing for news of you, didn't like to bother. Randolph's book,[2] though screamingly funny in parts, was pretty poor I thought. I supposed the reviewers had been up to their catty tricks but for once they were quite right about it.

I've been writing the dialogue for a film with two lovely very funny very young frogs. Huge sums of money from M.G.M. & I've seldom enjoyed myself more. It will never be made though. When I tell you that it's about an ex Eng: colony & that it ends with the American Vice-President being eaten by the (adorable) blacks, you will see how unlikely. M.G.M. must be mad – they've already spent £50,000 on it!

Fancy Rainbird being a snob! I imagined a humble little fellow, illiterate, who has a genius for selling books. That's the idea Peters gave me of him. One must never meet these people, that's what it is. I'm in a good position, here.

I go to Mark & then Venice for July & shall be here August &
might go to Harold in Sept with the Sutros. Why don't you?

Much love
Nancy

I've utterly mislaid your letter but I think I've answered everything.

[1] Joy Law; editorial director of Rainbird, who did the picture research for *The Sun King* and
Frederick the Great (1970).
[2] Randolph Churchill, *Twenty-One Years* (1965), an autobiography.

3 September 1965   7 rue Monsieur, VII

Darling Evelyn
    I'd love to know how you are – it's an age since you wrote.
    I've been in Venice & Greece & came back to *hear* the *P of Love*.
One Slade[1] has made a musical comedy of it – I've written the dialogue
& I really believe it may do.
    Last night I dined with Robert Morley & his sweet fat daughter &
several young Englishmen with hair the usual length & no lace or
jewels. (Debo gives an awful account of the get up of one's friends'
children & one sees the sewers everywhere here & in Venice so I was
agreeably surprised.) One I greatly took to, called Frith[2] (*Derby Day*).
He writes poetry & earns his living by teaching at a school in Wales.
Robert said Frith knows all about wine so he'll choose. The child
breathed o'er the wine list & finally came up with Château Lafite 53.
I let out a scream you naughty boy it will cost £100 but Robert (who
is such a dear) said let him be, he knows.
    Old Robert has been in Hollywood for the *Loved One*.[3] When he
arrived he got a message to go to the costumier. Why? I've got my
clothes. It's for that scene when you're in drag. (Do you know this
word? It means a man dressed as a woman.) Oh no darling – if there's
any question of that I go home. But it's our best scene – you, in drag,
pillion on a motor bike. NO.
    He says the film is so revolting people *are sick* on seeing it. That's
the influence of Decca's book I guess.
    I asked him if the Redl play (Osborne)[4] is really so indecent. Well
darling there are two scenes of men in bed together. Honestly, the
Old Land! (I had a letter from an old French count saying I love your
books & above all I love thinking of how the proper English must
blush as they read them. Shrieks!)
    I know all about the Redl case from Prince Clary who, as a young
Lieut in the Austrian army at the time, knew Redl quite well, but
from what I hear of the play Osborne had missed all the tricks. Also,
Clary, who may be naïf though, says there cld never have been a drag
ball at that time.

I think I'll go & stay with Harold later this month. Do tell your news, if not a bore.

Love
    Nancy

[1] Julian Slade (1930–2006). Author and composer of *Salad Days* (1954). His adaptation of *The Pursuit of Love* received a cool reception when it opened in Bristol in May 1967 and never transferred to London.
[2] Nigel Frith; author of *The Lover's Annual: A Story in Verse* (1965).
[3] Directed by Tony Richardson with a screenplay by Terry Southern and Christopher Isherwood (1965). Robert Morley played the part of Sir Ambrose Abercrombie.
[4] John Osborne, *A Patriot for Me* (1965). The play about Colonel Redl, a homosexual officer in the Austro-Hungarian army, was refused a licence by the Lord Chamberlain and was first staged privately for the English Stage Society.

5 September 1965   Combe Florey House
                                                Nr Taunton

Darling Nancy

It was *very* nice to hear from you. I have not written because the last 10 months have been ineffably dreary – my only excursions to dentist and funerals and my house perpetually full of grandchildren.

I read in a paper that you had gone into the musical comedy world. I hope it is rewarding. I find I can't follow the plot of any plays or films nowadays, whether it is my decay or theirs I don't know. The girls all seem hideous and the men common. Diana Honks says I am dying of drugs. Don't believe it, but my loss of teeth has deprived me of all pleasure in food.

No one in this house wears unsuitable clothes but, like you, I hear alarming accounts from more fashionable resorts. [. . .]

The film of *Loved One* is a great annoyance to me – one of the few occasions when Peters has let me down. He sold it years ago to a mad Mexican for a paltry sum with the assurance that it would never be produced but that Alec Guinness and I might have an agreeable jaunt together in Mexico. The next thing I heard was that an American company had bought the rights from the Mexican and were producing an elaborate travesty. No redress.

I've never heard of Redl play. Shows how I am out of the swim.

The buggering up of the Church is a deep sorrow to me and to all I know. We write letters to the paper. A fat lot of good that does.

I enjoyed Hemingway's Parisian memoirs;[1] did you?

Laura finds consolation in horticulture. I am a dreary companion for her these days.

Oh the hell of people who write theses. I get them from two sides – Ronnie Knox's works & my own.

La Pietra is grand but very uncomfortable. Have you stayed there before? Better stick to the hotel and see Harold [Acton] when convenient.

I remember men dressed as women – Beaton, Byron etc – at parties in 1927 but they did not call it 'drag'. What an odd name. Dragging the skirts?

I pray that your poor eyes are clearer.

With much love
    E

¹ *A Moveable Feast* (1965).

10 September 1965   7 rue Monsieur, VII

Darling Evelyn

You mustn't bother about a film. As Voltaire said of critics, it is the insect of a single week. *The Blessing* I know was murdered – I never saw it & now it is forgotten. But a book goes on for ever.

Mr Slade came with the *P of Love*. The songs very pretty – the dialogue terrible. I tremblingly asked if I might re-write it – he allowed me to, then was kind enough or clever enough to say that it was far better – as indeed it was! Funny how few people can write dialogue – I shall never in future sell any rights without stipulating that I must do it myself.

I feel for you over the Church. Even I *mind terribly* the thought of immemorial beauty being cast away in a few months. How lucky I am to believe in God without any religious instincts or needs. I hate this Pope – to hell with the Pope is a sentiment with which I cordially concur.

Do you know, my eyes are cured. I've no idea why – I thought they would get worse and worse, & now they are as good as when I was young & I can read all night if I want to. What a strange machine the body is! Oh dear how hateful, not tasting food – but I think it's a temporary condition?

I'm so sorry you are low in spirits. Why don't you come here to have a change? Of course *I* always think one can't be very low in Paris but that depends on liking the French & I'm not sure you *do*! (Do you remember Père Couturier?)

I expect I shall like La Pietra – I always like grand houses. People find the Malcontenta depressing but I think to wake up there in the morning is a positive happiness. I'm off to Harold, on Sunday.

Much love & to Laura
    Nancy

10 January 1966　　　　　　　　　　　　　　　　　　　Paris

Darling Evelyn

As I know you notice writing paper I hereby show you my new effort – the Mitford moldiwarp[1] – Raymond says undermining like mad no doubt.

Also Happy New Year to all, & I'd like to know how you are.

Back to the paper – my old pen pal Sir Hugh Jackson[2] (who once wrote 'my sister in law has been in Paris – she always puts up at Crillon's'[3]) has a lovely handmade sort which I intend to copy. This is rather too much like blotting paper. Sir Hugh has got – lucky him – the prettiest writing I ever saw except oddly enough that of my father. Does it depend on teaching would you say or is it all part of ONE? Prod's is very nice.

I lunched with Mr Fisher,[4] sales-manager of the mysterious Rainbird, who is here trying to force my Louis XIV on reluctant French publishers. (What a change from the old days when all that was left to luck. I bet every penny of royalties will be scrutinised too.) Well Mr Fisher says your book on the Crusades is nearly finished – how I long for it. Runciman[5] is a bit dry for me but it's a fascinating subject. I wonder what you make of Philippe-Auguste; he was a real oddity. At Bouvines he fell off his horse, couldn't ride for nuts, & lay for ½ an hour while the Germans prodded & banged away at his armour, until he was rescued with hardly a bruise. Voltaire wrote a very funny account of it – saying you didn't have to be very brave if you were a knight. Guillaume des Barres, one of his *compagnons*, is buried at Fontaines & rarely a day goes by without his name being mentioned so that he always seems like a fellow guest. If I've told you this already you must forgive. Old Age.

We are cushioned in deep snow here, very pretty.

Much love
　　Nancy

Des Barres was told his wife had died – brought back a beautiful Moor – found wife in the pink & lived with both, like sisters, in great contentment. V. holy man.

[1] Nancy's new writing paper was embossed with a golden mole, the Mitford emblem.
[2] Sir Hugh Jackson (1881–1979). An amateur historian with whom Nancy began to correspond in 1955. They wrote regularly to each other until her death but never met.
[3] The Crillon, on Place de la Concorde, one of Paris's most luxurious and expensive hotels.
[4] Edmund Fisher (1939–95). Publisher who worked at Rainbird 1962–9.
[5] Steven Runciman, *A History of the Crusades* (3 vols., 1951–4).

25 January 1966   Combe Florey House
                                                   Nr Taunton

Dearest Nancy

I was aghast to read of your nephew's (Taffy's boy's)[1] death and
have heard no explanation of it. He was given a Requiem Mass so I
presume he had lost his reason. I met him sometimes at Downside.

I admire your new NOTE paper.

Rainbird is indeed a man of mystery. He seems to be an agent for
literary agents and publishers. I have written none of the book I
promised him. An excellent popular history of the crusades was written
just before his death by Alfred Duggan.[2]

Graham Greene has set up as a Parisian. No doubt you knew. His
handwriting is quite illegible.

Handwriting – a lot depends on health. I have trembling hands
nowadays. Not drink – I have lost the art of eating.

   Best love
      E

[1] Saul Rodd (1933–66). Gustaf and Yvonne Rodd's eldest son had committed suicide.
[2] *Count Bohemond* (1964). Evelyn contributed a preface.

[postmarked 1 February 1966]   [7 rue Monsieur, VII]
[postcard]

I ran into Dominick Elwes in the street & he said: they drove poor
Saul mad (he said with a wealth of feeling) by *finding him jobs*. Of course
one quite sees that would drive D. mad. I didn't know Saul – never
saw him, but was really appalled – what a ghastly thing.

Mr Rainbird *is* a funny old codger – gave me a v. good luncheon.
Haven't seen Gr: Greene he probably dreads compatriots.

   N

28 February 1966   Combe Florey House
                                                   Nr Taunton

Dearest Nancy,

It is a long time since I wrote to you; so long that I do not know
when. If I repeat myself, pray forgive me.

Graham Greene's address is 130 Boulevard Malesherbes Paris 17. I
cannot tell you if he is alone there. I suspect not. But he is more social
than his books would give one to think.

The attack on Diana[1] was (to me) terribly shocking. Not the loss of
her fur coat & whatever else the ruffians took but the loss of dignity.
I think it is coming home to her. She has been deserted by servants

& that Iris[2] (whom I have never liked or trusted). When Lord Noel-
Buxton and your friend Miss Spain intruded in my house I put it on
the market next day because I felt it was polluted. That was a mere
impertinence, not a physical outrage. There should be a Praetorian
Guard of Pansies (we know from the war how brave they are) to keep
a standing 24 [hour] picquet on all these widows like Ann.

My health is slightly better. I keep getting the news that I am dying
& drug soaked. Not true. But I am very idle because taxation in my
country removes what the newspapers call 'incentives'.

Your dud goddaughter Harriet spends her days in the College of
Arms and her evenings as cloak-room attendant in an expensive restaurant but she still costs me a great deal. My finances are embarrassed
by a trust fund invented years ago by Peters which now appears to
be invalid.

I have escaped from my Rainbird contract (clever Peters) and shall
now slog away at autobiography. M. Bowra's autobiography[3] will be
a great disappointment to people like Lady Pamela who read only for
malicious gossip. It is really very soft & dull. He said you and I had
sexual connexions. I explained to him that it was not so & he expunged
the offending passage.

Love

E

[1] Lady Diana Cooper had been tied up and her house burgled.
[2] Iris Tree (1897–1968). Poet, writer and childhood friend of Diana Cooper who had been
staying with her at the time of the burglary.
[3] Maurice Bowra, *Memories 1898–1939* (1966).

4 March 1966   [7 rue Monsieur, VII]

Dearest Evelyn

Thanks very much for your letter. I've asked Gr Gr to luncheon –
he can but say no & then I won't tease him again. There are so few
agreeable English people here now – Embassy zero, journalists, ex:
Darsie Gillie, the same; they are all true horrors & loathe the French
as common English people always have. One long beef about plumbers
doesn't make for interesting conversation!

I went to see Andrew [Devonshire] installed as Chancellor of
Manch: Univ: It was grandeurs et misères all right. Would you like
to hear the menu of the Banquet? Attended by learned men from all
over Europe – I sat between a frog & a wop of great charm & gravity
(glad to have me as they didn't speak English); the menu: tinned
grapefruit, broiler & the greenest of peas, tinned grapefruit. No water,
one died of thirst owing to air conditioning, viz no air, & had to slake
it with very sweet white wine in thimbles.

Then I took a train & left the sheltering wing of Debo. Never again. Did you know that porters are forbidden to carry luggage? 'There are three of them in the porters' room but if the inspector saw them carrying luggage . . .' (he would castrate them I suppose). Don't you wish we could live in a writers' room & be forbidden to write?

I'm sorry about the Crusades but what I die for are your mémoires. Interesting about Maurice's.

My book comes out 1st Oct. I've rather lost interest & have forgotten where I picked up my facts so shall be very easy game for the Miss Mitford is wrong again school of criticism. My plagiarist (you may have seen, Hamilton brought a case)[1] wrote to the judge to say he got my book out of the free library. That was the part I minded most!

Diana – wasn't it hateful. I'm afraid it may have upset her more than it seemed to have. She telephoned when I was away & Marie said her voice was quite changed & she was greatly distressed not to find me here.

A lovely letter from Gerry Wellington saying that, with the disappearance of Bromo the sheets, weighed down with a paper weight engraved at the Pontifical Mosaic Factory with the family arms, are replaced even in gentlemen's houses by the Roll. I've mislaid it or would send.

Much love – do keep in touch
Nancy

[1] Nancy's publishers brought a case against Ian McInnes, author of *Painter, King and Pompadour – François Boucher at the Court of Louis XV*, for plagiarising *Madame de Pompadour*.

Evelyn died of a heart attack on Easter Day, 10 April 1966. Nancy wrote to his widow: 'Oh Laura I am so miserable. I loved Evelyn I really think the best of all my friends, & then such an old friend, such a part of my life . . . For him, one can only say he did hate the modern world, which does not become more liveable every day.'

The end of Evelyn's suffering marked the beginning of Nancy's. In 1969, after months of pain, she was operated on for a malignant liver tumour. The cancer spread to her spine but remained undiagnosed for four long years. Nancy spent the end of her life in excruciating pain, interspersed with brief periods of remission, which she endured with characteristic courage and lack of self-pity. She consulted doctors in England and France, submitted to innumerable tests and underwent a further major operation before Hodgkin's disease was correctly diagnosed. Nancy's physical suffering was compounded by a devastating emotional blow: in March 1969, Palewski married Violette de Talleyrand-Périgord with whom he had been in love for many years. Nancy tried to disguise her misery by dismissing Violette as a 'non-person', and the marriage as one of mere convenience. Although Palewski remained a friend, it was the final mortification. She died on 30 June 1973.

Biographical Notes

BERRY, Lady Pamela (1914–82). Spirited, shrewd and mischievous younger daughter of 1st Earl of Birkenhead. Her wedding in 1936 to Michael Berry, son of 1st Viscount Camrose, was a high point of the social season. After the war she exercised her talent for lavish entertaining and her love of gossip by hosting one of the most sought-after tables in London. Her friendship with Nancy and Evelyn was meteoric. In 1949 Nancy described her as 'blissful Pam Berry', and over a period of six years they exchanged hundreds of letters and met regularly. By 1954, when Michael Berry succeeded his father as editor-in-chief of the *Daily Telegraph*, their friendship had withered and their correspondence had dried up. A sharp letter from Nancy to the *Telegraph* in January 1955, making fun of Lady Pamela's forays into the fashion world, marked the end of their intimacy. Evelyn admired Lady Pamela greatly at first but by 1955 was writing to Maurice Bowra, 'Lady Pamela has faded from my life like a little pat of melting butter.'

CONNOLLY, Cyril (1903–74), (Smartyboots, Boots, Bootikins, Bonny Boots). One of the most promising of Evelyn's Oxford contemporaries whose gifts as a critic were to prove greater than his creative talent. After the failure of his only novel *The Rock Pool* (1936), he retrieved his reputation with a book of biographical essays, *Enemies of Promise* (1938). In 1939, with Stephen Spender, he founded the literary magazine *Horizon* which he continued to edit throughout the war. From 1951 he was an influential literary critic on the *Sunday Times*. He was married to Jean Bakewell 1930–45, to Barbara Skelton 1950–56 and to Deirdre Craven in 1959. Connolly regarded Nancy with disapproval tempered with affection. She enjoyed his wit and cleverness and was genuinely upset when her portrait of him as the self-indulgent Ed Spain in *The Blessing* caused a rift in their friendship. Evelyn caricatured him more unkindly as Everard Spruce, founder of *Survival*, in *Unconditional Surrender*. His uneasy relationship with Connolly, which combined rivalry, derision and fondness, drove him to tease and mock him whenever the occasion arose.

COOPER, Lady Diana (1892–1986), (Honks). Evelyn fell romantically in love with the greatest beauty of her generation in the early 1930s. They were never lovers but their friendship survived his rudeness, her self-absorption, and their frequent quarrels. They corresponded frequently and she appears as Mrs Stitch in *Scoop* and *Sword of Honour*. Nancy saw a great deal of Lady Diana after the war, when the British Embassy was the meeting-place for the Parisian *beau monde*. Lady Leone, the troublesome former Ambassadress who takes up residence in the gatehouse of the Embassy in *Don't Tell Alfred* (1960), is an unmistakable portrait of Lady Diana. Married to Alfred Duff Cooper in 1919.

MITFORD, Deborah (1920–), (Debo). Nancy's youngest sister married Lord Andrew Cavendish, younger son of 10th Duke of Devonshire, in 1941. He succeeded to the title in 1950. Evelyn was attracted to her and wanted to be a close friend. Although Deborah looked up to Evelyn, she had neither the time nor the inclination to cultivate a deep friendship with him, and hurt his feelings without meaning to. Nancy nicknamed her sister 'Nine', which was what she pretended her mental age to be, and maintained that she had never read a book. But her condescension towards Deborah's intellectual and artistic skills developed into admiration as she undertook the enormous task of restoring Chatsworth to its former splendour. Her respect for her sister would have increased had she lived to see her become a regular columnist, lecturer and the author of several books. The Duchess may have had Nancy's teasing in mind when she chose as the opening lines of *The House: A Portrait of Chatsworth* Thomas Hobbes's words: 'Reading is a pernicious habit. It destroys all originality of sentiment.'

MITFORD, Diana (1910–2003), (Honks). Married to Bryan Guinness 1929–34 and to Sir Oswald Mosley, leader of the British Union of Fascists, in 1936. Her deep friendship with Evelyn lasted just a year when, after the break-up of his first marriage, he took refuge with her and Bryan. They lost touch when Diana's son Jonathan was born in 1930. When Diana wrote thirty-six years later to ask Evelyn why they had stopped seeing each other, he replied: 'Pure jealousy . . . I was infatuated with you. Not of course that I aspired to your bed but I wanted you to myself as especial confidante and comrade.' Diana devoted a chapter to Evelyn in *Loved Ones*, a book of pen portraits. Nancy's relationship with the most beautiful of her sisters was complicated. She was closest to Diana in interests and they shared many friends, but she was jealous of Diana's children and happy marriage. When Sir Oswald was arrested in 1940, Nancy denounced Diana to the authorities as 'an extremely dangerous person'. 'Not very sisterly behaviour,' she admitted, 'but in such times I think it's one's duty.' Nine days later Diana was arrested under Regulation 18B and spent the next three and a half years in Holloway Prison. Despite Nancy's disloyalty, the sisters became close after the war, especially after the Mosleys' move to France in 1951.

PALEWSKI, Gaston (1901–84), (Fabrice, Colonel, Col). A shrewd and loyal politician, he descended from a Polish family that settled in France in the eighteenth century. He began his career as a protégé of Paul Reynaud, and was one of the first to rally to General de Gaulle in London in 1940, becoming both his closest confidant and his political adviser throughout the war. He was appointed head of de Gaulle's *cabinet* in 1942 and held the post until the General's resignation in 1946. Thereafter he played an active role in the Rassemblement du Peuple Français where his major concerns were the fight against Communism and the construction of a united Europe. A passion for intrigue and a certain dilettantism prevented him from reaching the top-ranking posts he coveted. He was elected a Deputy in 1951 and held the post of president of the Conseil Constitutionnel 1965–74. His time as Ambassador to Rome 1957–62 was perhaps the happiest period of his life. A celebrated womaniser, he made a late marriage to Violette de Talleyrand-Périgord, Duchess of Sagan, in 1969.

RODD, Peter (1904–68), (Prod). Handsome, arrogant and irredeemably unreliable son of 1st Baron Rennell, he was said to have proposed to Nancy as a joke. They married in 1933. He drank heavily, was unfaithful to Nancy from the outset and squandered her earnings. By the beginning of the war, their marriage was effectively over. When Nancy settled in Paris, Peter made occasional, unwelcome and often embarrassing appearances. His mother left him a small income on which he managed to subsist after the war, living on a boat in the Mediterranean, then in a flat in Rome, and lastly in Malta. Nancy and he were finally divorced in 1957. Evelyn had known Peter at Oxford and loathed him. He drew on his character for the roguish Basil Seal in his novels.

WAUGH, Laura (1916–73). Granddaughter of the Earl of Carnarvon and a cousin of Evelyn's first wife. Her pretty, delicate looks led Nancy to describe her as 'an exquisite piece of Dresden china, so fragile that one felt she must snap in two'. She was studying in London at the Royal Academy of Dramatic Art when she first met Evelyn, but was happiest living in the country. After their marriage in 1937, she turned her back on social life to devote herself to her herd of cows and, in a more detached manner, to her children. Her intelligence and strength of character were a match for Evelyn's, and her ability to retreat into a world of her own provided a refuge from his difficult temper and bouts of melancholy.

WAUGH children. Despite his express dislike of other people's children, and a cultivated indifference to his own, Evelyn produced a family of seven, one of whom lived only a day. The surviving members consisted of Teresa (1938–), Auberon (1939–2001), Margaret (1942–86), Harriet (1944–), James (1946–) and Septimus (1950–). Three of his children followed Evelyn into literary careers: Auberon became a distinguished columnist, contributor to *Private Eye* and editor of the *Literary Review*; Margaret wrote *The Man Who Was Greenmantle*, a biography of her maternal grandfather; and Harriet, Nancy's goddaughter, became a well-regarded novelist and reviewer.

Index

Waugh's Bright Young Things

'Funny, very funny, laugh-out-loud funny' David Lodge

Decline and Fall

Sent down from Oxford in outrageous circumstances, Paul Pennyfeather is oddly unsurprised to find himself qualifying for the position of schoolmaster at Llanabba Castle, where his colleagues are an assortment of misfits, rascals and fools. Then Sports Day arrives, and with it the delectable Margot Beste-Chetwynde.

Vile Bodies

The Bright Young Things of 1920s Mayfair exercise their inventive minds and vile bodies in every kind of capricious escapade, whether it is promiscuity, dancing, cocktail parties or sports cars. A vivid assortment of characters, among them the struggling writer Adam Fenwick-Symes and the aristocratic Nina Blount, hunt furiously for ever greater sensations, until darkness is revealed beneath the glitter.

Brideshead Revisited

Charles Ryder, a lonely student at Oxford, is captivated by the decadent Sebastian Flyte. Invited to Brideshead, Sebastian's magnificent family home, Charles becomes infatuated with its eccentric, artistic inhabitants the March-mains and the life of privilege they inhabit – in particular, with Sebastian's remote sister, Julia. Gradually, though, he comes to recognize his spiritual and social distance from them.

Waugh's Black Comedies

'Our time's finest satirist' Gore Vidal

A Handful of Dust

Bored and restless after seven years of marriage, beautiful Lady Brenda Last drifts into an affair with the shallow socialite John Beaver, and forsakes her husband Tony and his Gothic pile Hetton Abbey for the glamorous Belgravia set. But both Tony and Brenda are propelled towards utterly different fates than they had imagined.

Black Mischief

When Oxford-educated Emperor Seth succeeds to the throne of the African state of Azania, his subjects are unruly, and corruption, double-dealing and bloodshed are rife. With the aid of the Minister of Modernization, Basil Seal, Seth plans to introduce his people to the civilized ways of the West – but will it be as simple as that?

Scoop

Lord Copper, newspaper magnate and proprietor of the *Daily Beast*, prides himself on his intuitive flair for spotting ace reporters. Acting on a dinner-party tip from Mrs Algernon Stitch he feels convinced that he has hit on just the chap to cover a promising little war in the African Republic of Ishmaelia, in a brilliantly irreverent satire of Fleet Street.

Put Out More Flags

Upper-class scoundrel Basil Seal, mad, bad and dangerous to know, creates havoc wherever he goes. And when Neville Chamberlain declares war on Germany, it seems the perfect opportunity for more action and adventure. But, with Europe frozen in the 'phoney war', when will Basil's chance to be a hero finally arrive?

Waugh's Later Novels

'A writer of genius' Kingsley Amis

The Loved One

Following the death of a friend, poet and pets' mortician Dennis Barlow finds himself entering into the artificial Hollywood paradise of the Whispering Glades Memorial Park, where death is packaged American-style. There, Dennis encounters Aimée, the naïve Californian corpse beautician, and Mr Joyboy, the master of the embalmer's art, in a dark and savage satire.

Helena

The Empress Helena, mother of Constantine the Great, made the historic pilgrimage to Palestine, found pieces of wood from the true Cross, and built churches at Bethlehem and Olivet. The conflicting forces of the age, and the corruption, treachery, and madness of Imperial Rome combine to give Evelyn Waugh the theme for one of his most arresting novels.

The Ordeal of Gilbert Pinfold

Gilbert Pinfold is a successful novelist of mature years, afflicted by insomnia and moments of paranoia and memory-loss. He decides to solve his problems by going on a cruise to the tropics, but instead of a cure, the journey on board the *Caliban* spells disaster. Tormented by taunting voices in his cabin, Gilbert is brought to the very brink of insanity.

Waugh on War

'Arguably the best British prose fiction to come out of the Second World War' Will Self, *Independent*

Men at Arms

Guy Crouchback, determined to get into the war, takes a commission in the Royal Corps of Halberdiers. His spirits high, he sees all the trimmings but none of the action. And his first campaign, an abortive affair on the West African coastline, ends with an escapade which seriously blots his Halberdier copybook.

Officers and Gentlemen

Guy is now attached to a Commando unit undergoing training on the Hebridean Isle of Mugg, where the whisky flows freely and HM forces have to show proper respect for the omnipotent Laird. But the high comedy of Mugg is followed by the bitterness of Crete – and the chaos and indignity of a total withdrawal or surrender.

Unconditional Surrender

Guy Crouchback has lost his Halberdier idealism. A desk job in London gives him the chance of reconciliation with his former wife. Then, in Yugoslavia, as a liaison officer with the Partisans, he finally becomes aware of the futility of a war he once saw in terms of honour.

Men at Arms, Officers and Gentlemen and *Unconditional Surrender* were also extensively revised by Waugh and published as the one-volume *Sword of Honour*.

'One of the masterpieces of the twentieth century' John Banville

Waugh Abroad

Labels

Waugh chose the name *Labels* for his first travel book because, he said, the places he visited were already 'fully labelled' in people's minds. From Europe to North Africa, as he cruises around the Mediterranean his pen cuts through the local colour to give an entertaining portrait of the Englishman abroad.

Remote People

Perhaps the funniest travel book ever written, *Remote People* begins with a vivid account of the coronation of Emperor Ras Tafari – Haile Selassie I, King of Kings – covered by Waugh in 1930 for *The Times*, and continues with subsequent travels throughout Africa.

Ninety-Two Days

In this entertaining chronicle of a South American journey, Waugh describes the isolated cattle country of Guiana, populated by a collection of visionaries, rogues and ranchers, and records his nightmarish experiences travelling on foot, by horse and by boat through the jungle into Brazil.

When the Going Was Good

Between 1929 and 1935 Waugh travelled widely and produced some of his finest writing. In this collection he writes about a train trip from Djibouti to Abyssinia; his travels in Aden, Zanzibar, Kenya and the Congo; coping with unbearable heat and being plagued by mosquitoes.

Waugh in Abyssinia

In 1935 Italy declared war on Abyssinia and Waugh was sent to Addis Ababa to cover the conflict. His acerbic account filled with descriptions of the often bizarre life of a war correspondent, rubbing shoulders with Arab spies, pyjama-wearing radicals and less-than-honest officials.

Waugh Beyond the Novels

'The supreme writer of English prose in the twentieth century'
Clive James

The Complete Short Stories

In this collection of short stories composed between 1910 and 1962, Evelyn Waugh's juvenilia are brought together with later pieces, some of which became the inspirations for his novels. These witty and immaculately crafted stories display the finest writing of a master of satire and comic twists.

Work Suspended and Other Stories

From 'Work Suspended', which depicts the struggles of Plant, a writer of detective fiction, to 'Basil Seal Rides Again', in which the hero of *Black Mischief* defeats the children of the Sixties, these stories satirize the British social milieu of the twentieth century. The volume also includes the fragment 'Charles Ryder's Schooldays'.

A Little Learning: An Autobiography

Drawn largely from his early diaries, *A Little Learning* recalls Evelyn Waugh's idyllic childhood in Hampstead, his subsequent years at school, which were mostly unpleasant, with nihilism and bullying rife, his Oxford days and his time as a prep school master in North Wales.

A Little Order: Selected Journalism

Whether celebrating Hogarth or savaging Hollywood, mocking modern manners or defending traditional English architecture, expressing his loathing of Marxism or his love of P. G. Wodehouse, Evelyn Waugh's journalism is sparkling, sometimes vitriolic and always full of good sense.

The Letters of Nancy Mitford and Evelyn Waugh

Nancy Mitford and Evelyn Waugh matched wits in more than five hundred letters over twenty-two years. Dissecting their friends and criticizing each other's books in a barrage of hilarious repartee, this correspondence provides a colourful glimpse into the literary and social circles of their times.

The World of Waugh

'I am devoted to him. I love him. I admire him. I cherish him. I respect, revere and esteem him as highly as I do any English-language novelist of the twentieth century. I re-read him almost constantly' Stephen Fry

'A comic genius' *The Times*

'He wrote like an angel ... A fallen one' *Irish Times*

Fiction

Decline and Fall
Vile Bodies
Brideshead Revisited
A Handful of Dust
Black Mischief
Scoop
Put Out More Flags
The Loved One
Helena
The Ordeal of Gilbert Pinfold
The Sword of Honour Trilogy
The Complete Short Stories
Work Suspended and Other Stories

Non-Fiction

Labels
Remote People
Ninety-Two Days
Waugh in Abyssinia
When the Going Was Good
A Little Learning: An Autobiography
A Little Order: Selected Journalism
The Letters of Nancy Mitford and Evelyn Waugh

'Words should be an intense pleasure' Evelyn Waugh

Nabokov beyond the novels

Collected Stories

In these sixty-five stories of magic and melancholy, Nabokov displays an astonishing range of inventiveness. A man at his desk is interrupted by the appearance of a woodland elf in his room; a barber shaves the face of a man who once tortured him; a shy dreamer makes a deal with the Devil. The *Collected Stories* are perfect displays of dazzling sleight of hand, fantastical fairy tales, intellectual games and enchanting glimpses into lives of ambiguity and loss.

Collected Poems

Vladimir Nabokov is acknowledged as one of the greatest prose stylists of the twentieth century, but his first love was poetry. This landmark new collection brings together the best of Nabokov's verse, including an extensive number of pieces that have never appeared in English before, newly translated from the Russian by his son Dmitri Nabokov. Filled with charm, irony and exuberance, these verses are masterpieces of style and precision.

Coming in April 2010

Letters to Vera

A brand new landmark collection of Nabokov's charming, moving letters to his wife, muse, editor, translator and selfless companion Vera, none of which have never appeared in print before.

Coming in April 2011

www.penguinclassics.com

Contemporary ... Provocative ... Outrageous ...
Prophetic ... Groundbreaking ... Funny ... Disturbing ...
Different ... Moving ... Revolutionary ... Inspiring ...
Subversive ... Life-changing ...

What makes a modern classic?

At Penguin Classics our mission has always been to make the best
books ever written available to everyone. And that also means
constantly redefining and refreshing exactly what makes a 'classic'.
That's where Modern Classics come in. Since 1961 they have been an
organic, ever-growing and ever-evolving list of books from the last
hundred (or so) years that we believe will continue to be read over and
over again.

They could be books that have inspired political dissent, such as
Animal Farm. Some, like *Lolita* or *A Clockwork Orange*, may have
caused shock and outrage. Many have led to great films, from *In Cold
Blood* to *One Flew Over the Cuckoo's Nest*. They have broken down
barriers – whether social, sexual, or, in the case of *Ulysses*, the
boundaries of language itself. And they might – like *Goldfinger* or
Scoop – just be pure classic escapism. Whatever the reason, Penguin
Modern Classics continue to inspire, entertain and enlighten millions
of readers everywhere.

'No publisher has had more influence on reading habits than Penguin'
Independent

'Penguins provided a crash course in world literature'
Guardian

The best books ever written

PENGUIN (🐧) CLASSICS

SINCE 1946

Find out more at www.penguinclassics.com